PENGUIN CLASSICS

THE DIVINE COMEDY 2: PURGATORIO

DANTE ALIGHIERI was born in Florence in 1265 into a family from the lower ranks of the nobility. He may have studied at the university of Bologna. When he was about twenty, he married Gemma Donati, by whom he had four children. He first met Bice Portinari, whom he called Beatrice, in 1274, and when she died in 1290 he sought consolation by writing the *Vita nuova* and by studying philosophy and theology. During this time he also became involved in the conflict between the Guelf and Ghibelline factions in Florence; he became a prominent White Guelf and, when the Black Guelfs came to power in 1302, Dante was, during his absence from the city, condemned to exile. He took refuge initially in Verona but eventually, having wandered from place to place, he settled in Ravenna. While there he completed the *Commedia*, which he began in about 1307. Dante died in Ravenna in 1321.

ROBIN KIRKPATRICK graduated from Merton College, Oxford. He has taught courses on Dante's *Commedia* in Hong Kong, Dublin and – for more than twenty-five years – at the university of Cambridge, where he is Fellow of Robinson College and Professor of Italian and English Literatures. His books include *Dante's Paradiso and the Limitations of Modern Criticism* (1987), *Dante's Inferno: Difficulty and Dead Poetry* (1987) and, in the Cambridge Landmarks of World Literature series, *Dante: The Divine Comedy* (2004). His own published poetry includes *Prologue and Palinodes* (1997), and currently he is working on a long poem (in five acts) entitled *Paradise Rag*.

DANTE ALIGHIERI

The Divine Comedy 2: Purgatorio

Translated and edited by
ROBIN KIRKPATRICK

PENGUIN BOOKS

PENGUIN CLASSICS

Published by the Penguin Group
Penguin Books Ltd, 80 Strand, London WC2R ORL, England
Penguin Group (USA) Inc., 375 Hudson Street, New York, New York 10014, USA
Penguin Group (Canada), 90 Eglinton Avenue East, Suite 700, Toronto, Ontario, Canada M4P 2Y3
(a division of Pearson Penguin Canada Inc.)
Penguin Ireland, 25 St Stephen's Green, Dublin 2, Ireland
(a division of Penguin Books Ltd)
Penguin Group (Australia), 250 Camberwell Road, Camberwell, Victoria 3124, Australia
(a division of Pearson Australia Group Pty Ltd)
Penguin Books India Pvt Ltd, 11 Community Centre, Panchsheel Park, New Delhi – 110 017, India
Penguin Group (NZ), 67 Apollo Drive, Rosedale, North Shore 0632, New Zealand
(a division of Pearson New Zealand Ltd)
Penguin Books (South Africa) (Pty) Ltd, 24 Sturdee Avenue, Rosebank, Johannesburg 2196, South Africa

Penguin Books Ltd, Registered Offices: 80 Strand, London WC2R ORL, England

www.penguin.com

This translation first published in Penguin Classics 2007

3

Translation copyright © Robin Kirkpatrick, 2007
The text of the *Commedia* is reprinted from *La Commedia secondo l'antica vulgata*,
edited by Giorgio Petrocchi, Edizione Nazionale delle Opere di Dante Alighieri a cura della
Società Dantesca, copyright © 1994 by Casa Editrice Le Lettere – Firenze

The moral right of the editor has been asserted

Set in 10.25/12.25 pt PostScript Adobe Sabon
Typeset by Rowland Phototypesetting Ltd, Bury St Edmunds, Suffolk
Printed in England by Clays Ltd, St Ives plc

ISBN: 978-0-140-44896-2

Contents

Commedia Cantica 2: *Purgatorio*

Acknowledgements

Thanks of many kinds are due. To those, especially Vittorio Montemaggi and Matthew Treherne, who continue to offer welcome advice on matters ranging from rhythm to theology. To those who have given, in their great authority, both encouragement and criticism, Pat Boyde, Zyg Baranski, Píero Boitaní, Matthew Reynolds, David Wallace and the early readers of the original proposal. To Hilary Laurie for painstaking and perceptive attention to the details of the text as it was prepared for the press, and to Sally Holloway, who makes the process of copy-editing a pleasure.

The *Purgatorio* is thought by most of its readers to be the subtlest, liveliest and most beautiful *cantica* of the *Commedia*. It is therefore entirely appropriate that I should dedicate this translation, with love and gratitude, to Anna and Laura.

Chronology

1224 Saint Francis receives the stigmata

1250 Death of Emperor Frederick II

1260 Defeat of the Guelfs at the battle of Montaperti, leading to seven years of Ghibelline domination in Florence

1265 Dante born, probably 25 May

1266 Defeat of Imperial army by the Guelfs and the French under Charles d'Anjou at the battle of Benevento

1267 Birth of Giotto; restoration of Guelf rule in Florence under the protection of Charles d'Anjou

1274 Deaths of Thomas Aquinas and Bonaventure

1282 The influence of the guilds starts to grow in Florence

1283 Dante begins his association with the poet Guido Cavalcanti

1289 Dante fights at the battle of Campaldino; Florence, having defeated Arezzo and Ghibelline factions at Campaldino, begins to extend its supremacy over Tuscany

1290 Death of Bice (Beatrice) Portinari

1292 Dante compiles the *Vita nuova*

1293 *Ordinamenti di Giustizia* promulgated in Florence

1294 Election and abdication of Pope Celestine V; election of Pope Boniface VIII

1295 Dante enrols in a guild

1296 For five years, Dante is actively involved in the political life of the Florence commune; *Rime Petrose* probably composed

1300 Dante elected to the office of prior; fictional date of the *Commedia*

1301 Crisis and *coup d'état* in Florence; Charles de Valois enters the city; return of Corso Donati; defeat of the White Guelfs by the Black Guelfs

1302 In his absence, Dante formally exiled and sentenced to death by the Black Guelphs

1303 Dante seeks refuge for the first time in Verona; death of Pope Boniface VIII

1304 Dante probably engaged until 1307 on the *Convivio* and the *De Vulgari Eloquentia*; birth of Petrarch

1305 Pope Clement V detained in Avignon

1307 Possible date for when Dante started the *Commedia*; accession of Edward II to English throne

1308 Henry VII of Luxembourg elected Holy Roman Emperor in Rome

1310 Dante writes his epistle to Henry: '*Ecce nunc tempus acceptabile*'; Henry enters Italy

1312 Possible (though much debated) date for when Dante started *De Monarchia*; Henry crowned Holy Roman Emperor

1313 Emperor Henry VII dies; Boccaccio born

1314 Dante begins living for six years in Verona, under the protection of Can Grande della Scala

1318 Dante in Ravenna: in close contact with Guido Novello da Polenta

1320 Dante in Latin verse correspondence with the humanist Giovanni del Virgilio; lectures at university of Verona: *Questio de Aqua et Terra*

1321 Dante dies in Ravenna, 13 September

Editor's Note

Dante called his poem a 'comedy'. Only in the sixteenth century was the now-familiar adjective 'divine' attached to Dante's original title by readers impressed by the ambition of the work who were eager to enhance its reputation. For similar reasons, this adjective has been kept on the cover of the present translation. However, there are good reasons, discussed in the introduction to the *Inferno*, for retaining Dante's less showy designation and, beyond the title page, it is this title that has been preserved.

The *Commedia* is a single poem of one hundred cantos, subdivided into three parts, the *Inferno*, the *Purgatorio* and the *Paradiso*, each part constituting a *cantica*. The present translation, however, will appear in three separate volumes. The *Inferno* was published in 2006 and the *Paradiso* is in preparation at the press.

Each volume contains an introduction specific to the *cantica* represented within it. Volume 1, *Inferno*, however, contains a general introduction to the *Commedia* as a whole.

Commentaries and notes have been edited according to standard practice. However, the text of the translation – in an attempt to respond to the density and variety of Dante's poetic practice – frequently employs non-standard forms of punctuation and capitalization.

Introduction

PURGATORY

'Here, too, dead poetry will rise again': these words, at line 7 of first canto of the *Purgatorio*, announce a new phase in the evolving narrative of the *Commedia*, and suggest that, in Dante Alighieri's mind, the second *cantica* is more than merely a sequel to the *Inferno*. It is, rather, a rebirth, a resurrection. Indeed, the first canto of the *Purgatorio* is punctuated by references to new beginnings: at line 18, as dawn rises, the scene in Purgatory begins 'afresh' to bring delight to Dante's eyes; at line 136 a reed plucked from the shores of the mountain is immediately 'reborn' as another shoot takes its place. Dante's arrival in Purgatory also marks a return to the point in his journey where the poet thinks he should have been all along. Towards the conclusion of *Purgatorio* I (at lines 119–20) the poet speaks of returning only now to the road he should be taking 'as though, returning to a path we'd lost, our steps, until we came to that, were vain'.

From the vantage point of the second *cantica*, the *Inferno* and the journey described in it were nothing but a detour and a waste of time. In *Inferno* I, Dante had set his set his sights on a sunlit hill which promised him salvation from the dark wood. His journey had taken him far from that hill, into the very depths of the pit of Hell. Yet, as early as *Inferno* 14, Dante had begun to anticipate the plan that he had conceived for the second phase of his travels. He speaks there of the rivers of Hell (line 116) but also alludes to the river of Lethe (lines 131–2), in which he will be purified on the summit of Mount Purgatory.

Now, as the second *cantica* begins, the constrictions of Hell and the ice that had beset its lower circles disappear: the shores of Mount Purgatory are slowly revealed to view as the sun comes up, and the waves around the island lap tremulously in the light of dawn. The reader's attention is drawn at every point to effects not only of regeneration but also of motion, process and pleasure. The verse of the canto itself responds to this new perception, speaking of how poetry will hoist its sail and 'race now over better waves' in the notably light and liquid rhythms of the opening *terzina*.

To many modern ears, the word 'purgatory' speaks hardly less than 'hell' of sin and suffering. Yet nothing could be further from Dante's understanding. At every point, the *Purgatorio* emphasizes the redemption of human nature and reveals the possibilities in human beings that are eclipsed and eroded by sin. This is already evident from the account given in *Inferno* 34: 121–32 of how Mount Purgatory came to exist, when Satan, falling from Heaven, pierced the globe of the earth and extruded the land mass of the mountain into the southern hemisphere. God then went on to place the Garden of Eden on its peak, thus ensuring that Satan's fall, though a catastrophe, would serve a providential purpose in providing a habitat for Adam and Eve. The *Purgatorio* now confirms and extends the implications of this initial sketch. Even when the first inhabitants of Eden themselves succumbed to Satan, the garden was to remain as a token of the happiness that human beings at first experienced, and now, by entering Purgatory, may come to experience once again.

The second *cantica* divides into three broad movements. The sequence from canto 1 to canto 9 describes an area, usually known as the Ante-Purgatory, on the foothills of the mountain which lies outside the confines of Purgatory itself and is subject to temporal and meteorological conditions exactly comparable (at least in its lower regions) to those of any other area of the earth's surface. Beyond this region, the mountain is less familiar, being divided, as described in cantos 10–26, into seven terraces, each with its own distinct topography, where Dante

imagines the various forms of penance by which their in-
habitants progressively expiate each of the seven capital vices
(the so-called 'deadly sins') of which they have been guilty
in their earthly existences. The last seven cantos of the
cantica are devoted to the Garden of Eden, or Earthly Para-
dise, located on the summit of the mount, where, for the first
time since her death, Dante encounters Beatrice, under whose
instigation in *Inferno* 2 his journey through the other world
began.

Where the *Paradiso* offers an account of a Heavenly Paradise,
the immediate point of arrival of Dante's purgatorial journey
is, emphatically, an Earthly Paradise which, in the extended
conclusion to the work, from canto 28 to canto 33, is described
in richly sensuous terms. The stars that Dante sees in *Purgatorio*
1: 23–4 are the stars that shone on the day of Creation, and
the only human beings that, till now, have seen these stars are
Adam and Eve. From this point on, the purpose of purgation
is to recover humanity's lost innocence. But for Dante this does
not involve, initially, any desire to transcend or diminish the
human experience. On the contrary, the second *cantica* is con-
cerned above all with the ways in which we may restore, by our
own choices and intentions, the innocent brilliance of percep-
tion and sensuous experience that the human race, in the
persons of Adam and Eve, was originally created to enjoy.
To that extent, the *Purgatorio* is Dante's '*recherche du temps
perdu*', and also expresses, first and last, his unfailing confi-
dence in the moral capabilities of human nature.

A similar understanding derives from the opening phase of
the *cantica*. The penitents whom Dante encounters in this
region have all in some way wasted their time on earth: by
deferring due repentance for their sins; by failing to repair
an order of excommunication; or by neglecting their political
duties. These penitents suffer no pain as long they remain in
the Ante-Purgatory. They do, however, experience frustration
at being constrained to wait on the outskirts of Purgatory
proper, and this frustration itself is an indication of the value
that time possesses for Dante. To waste time on earth is to
ignore the opportunities that we have in our temporal lives to

discover the purpose of our existence and to give practical expression to this purpose. Conversely, waiting in the Ante-Purgatory, while it painfully denies the opportunity for any active pursuit of our best intentions, is also a positive resource in which the soul is given time to mature (as does Belacqua in canto 4, lines 98–139), and the senses, too, begin to sharpen in their response to temporal phenomena – the warmth of the sun, the play of shadows, the peculiar luminosity (in canto 8) of flower colours as dusk begins to gather (in Dante's Purgatory, even night-time has its purpose). The travellers spend three nights on the mountain. In canto 6, they are deprived at night of the power to move. But in this enforced period of waiting, their physical senses yield to the power of imagination and dreams. And each of the three dreams that Dante experiences contributes a new insight in his penitential quest.

It is only in the central cantos of the *cantica* – cantos 10–26 – that penance directly involves suffering. Yet even here the *Purgatorio* is concerned more with recovery and regeneration than with pain. Dante's Purgatory is emphatically not a place of trial or examination. All the souls who are admitted here will eventually arrive in Paradise. Penance, therefore, must be seen as a form of training for a full participation in and enjoyment of the ultimate truth of existence.

In this light, it is significant that Dante abandons the broadly classical categories of sin that he developed in the *Inferno* and here for the first time looks at sin in terms of the famous seven capital vices of the Christian tradition: pride, envy, gluttony, lust, anger, greed and sloth. This departure in itself reflects a new confidence in redemption. For to speak of pride or gluttony or lust from a Christian perspective is to acknowledge that all sins are redeemable, and, under the disciplines of confession and repentance, subject to appropriate remedies.

Christianity would have no meaning unless, through grace, it envisaged the forgiveness of sins. At the same time, the penitents of cantos 10–26 are seen as very conscious, even heroic, participants in their own salvation, ready and able to tolerate centuries of painful endeavour on each of the seven terraces in pursuit of their ultimate goal. Punishment here is wholly different from that displayed in the *Inferno*. There, pain was imposed on uncomprehending victims whose unrepented sins had deprived them of any understanding of what human life could truly be. In the course of their penance, the protagonists in *Purgatorio* painfully but purposefully, through self-knowledge and effort, recover the reality of their own existences. They actively choose to be where they are, and indeed it is they themselves – not some divine adjudicator – who decide when their penance has been sufficient. (See *Purgatorio* 21: 58–60.) It is for this reason that, at canto 23, line 72, one of the penitents declares that the pains he suffers should properly be described as 'solace', or exquisite pleasure. 'Delight' returns to Dante's eyes in *Purgatorio* 1. Pure pleasure is the condition of the Earthly Paradise. And any attempt at the recovery of the human self, in the fullness of its being, is also an expression of delight in existence. Notably, all the spirits of the penitents, at every stage of their purgation, possess bodies – ghost bodies (as is explained in *Purgatorio* 3 and 25) but bodies none the less, capable of experiencing the physical joys as well as the physical pains of Purgatory.

No precedent exists for the view that Dante takes of Purgatory, and few subsequent thinkers or poets have explored the implications of his vision. (Only Seamus Heaney, perhaps, in *Station Island* (1984) comes close, identifying Purgatory, in its geographical location, as an island in Loch Derg, Ireland.) As Jacques Le Goff has shown in his great study *The Birth of Purgatory* (first published in French in 1981), the formal doctrine of Purgatory had, in Dante's time, only recently begun to be defined in theological terms. In the visual arts there was no representation of Purgatory to match the many extremely vicious depictions of Hell that crowded the walls of late medieval churches. If anything, Purgatory was simply envisaged as a subdivision of a subterranean Hell, differing only from that in being a temporary rather than an eternal state. Thus, as late as 1370 – fifty years after Dante's death – Saint Bridget of Sweden (*c.* 1303–73) wrote in vivid terms of the sufferings a soul, newly dead, who had been guilty in life of lies and pride:

Then it seemed to me that a band was bound around his head so fast, so painfully that the forehead and the noddle came together. The eyes were hanging down the cheeks, the ears were as if they'd been burnt by fire, the brains burst out of his nostrils and ear-holes, the tongue hung out and the teeth clashed together . . . the shoulders were broken and hung down his sides and the bones were drawn out as it had been a thread.

> Quoted in Eamon Duffy, *The Stripping of the Altars*
> (New Haven and London, 1992), p. 339

The differences between Saint Bridget's conception of Purgatory and Dante's are immediately visible. Penance, for Bridget, is reduced to passive suffering. The human being, far from being sensitive to delight in its sensuous as well as its ethical aspect, is perceived in all its anatomical fragility as an object of disgust. The God who imposes this penance could reasonably be regarded as a viciously destructive tyrant, and certainly not as the creator of Adam, Eve and the Garden of Eden.

For some readers of the *Commedia*, Saint Bridget's vision will undoubtedly recall the worst excesses of Dante's own *Inferno*, especially, perhaps, its moral scheme, which emphasizes the vindictive tit-for-tat of the *contrapasso*, in which God devises a punishment to fit the crime. It may be argued that the *contrapasso* is not as central or as unquestionable a feature of the *Inferno* as some critics have made out. (See introduction to the *Inferno*, pp. lxxx–lxxxi.) In any event, it is clear that in the *Purgatorio* – returning to the 'lost path' at the end of the canto (line 118) – Dante sets out to develop an ethical vision which not only outstrips his medieval contemporaries' but also, in its humanity, variety and understanding of God's creative purposes, goes far beyond even his understanding of Hell.

Consider the differences between Dante's view of Purgatory and Saint Thomas Aquinas's (*c.* 1225–74) view as summarized by his followers in the supplement Appendix (1.2, 2.2) to his *Summa Theologiae* III (*c.* 1265–74). For Thomas, Purgatory is the realm in which, through extended penance, a sinner may expiate the residual effects of those venial sins which had not been confessed before his death, and where the prayers of the

Church on earth can shorten the term of penance allotted to such a sinner. Dante is not deaf to the implications of this view. He has a particularly strong sense of how Purgatory can be seen as a prayer community in which the living and the dead co-operate in the salvation of individual sinners. But Thomas still locates Purgatory as an underground region, close to Hell, where the one mode of penance is 'transitory fire', which acts specifically to cleanse the dregs and dross of sin. The guiding metaphor for penitence here is that of purging away impurities.

Dante's emphasis could hardly be more different. For him, penance, far from being simply fire, is as varied as are the sins that gave rise to it, ranging (even leaving aside the subtleties of the Ante-Purgatory and the Earthly Paradise) from physical labour, to blindness, to submersion in noxious fumes, to head-long speed, to prostration, to ritual processions round sacred objects. Such variety is, of course, a product of Dante's endless inventiveness as poet and narrator. However, it also betokens a vividly analytical interest in the causes and consequences both of sin itself and also of the human appetite for virtue. In the *Purgatorio*, as in the *Inferno*, Dante interests himself in the psychological motives that lead individuals to sin and, conversely, incline them to rediscover human worth in all its diversity. (See especially the commentaries to *Purgatorio* 13 and 14.) So, too, he concerned himself with the social consequences of vice and virtue, often looking back to the violence and confusion of his contemporary political world which engendered sin, but, equally, looking forward to the ways in which the virtues, properly practised, can encourage justice and the return of a Golden Age. (See especially commentary to *Purgatorio* 20.) Then again, here as throughout the *Commedia*, Dante's intense imagination frequently produces a redefinition of issues that, in other hands, would have become oversimplified or inert. For instance, Aquinas's 'transitory fire' of purgation appears in the *cantica*, but only once, and only, specifically, as the part of the penance of the lustful on the last terrace of the mountain (described in *Purgatorio* 26). The suggestion must be that fire – and even lust itself – is one of the 'warm-hearted sins' (to quote Dorothy L. Sayers). These sins are the last and hardest to be eradicated. But because the desire for good has been instilled in us by God, the temperaments that generate such sins are also those which bring us closest to the love of God. The lustful stand on the very threshold of the pleasures that are enjoyed in the Garden of Eden.

This also points, however, to the fundamental difference between Aquinas and Dante, and to conclusions that could hardly have been anticipated on the evidence of the *Inferno*. Aquinas's metaphor of 'purgation' is only tangentially applicable to the processes of penance that Dante depicts. In the *Purgatorio* Dante's concern is not with purging (or even with that transcendence of and detachment from sin that *Inferno* showed to be necessary) but with the sharpening of ethical purpose. Thus when, in the last line of *Purgatorio* 26, he finally concludes his treatment of the capital vices, he speaks of the last of all sinners hiding himself 'in the fire that sharpens them' (*'nel foco che li affina'*.) *'Affina'* here could plausibly be translated as 'refines', but the Italian word is also constructed here out of an *'a'* ('to' or 'towards') and a *'fine'* – an 'end' or 'goal'. In other words, purgation does not burn away but recuperates the best of human intentions and capabilities and refocuses them on that 'end' (which is also an origin) which resides in the fulfilment of human possibilities.

In this perspective, penance ceases to be a matter of chastisement or submission to a rule and becomes more a matter of productive work. The aim of purgation is similarly not only to help the sinner conform to a divine rule but also to recover and display the excellence of which he had always been capable. Thus one of the major features of the central cantos of the *Purgatorio* is the invention-within-an-invention of what critics now call the 'whips and bridles' which punctuate the treatment of each of the capital vices. These are the *exempla* – drawn from both scriptural and classical sources, and treated with great elliptical virtuosity in Dante's verse – which illustrate the nature of a sin and its corresponding virtue. Envy, for instance, is illustrated in *Purgatorio* 14: 133–5 by the thundering words of Cain, who had killed his brother out of envy and now knows that all men are entitled to slay him. But already, at canto 13, lines 28–30, generosity (the opposite of envy) is depicted in the words of the Virgin Mary at the Marriage of Cana, 'Look! They have no wine', which prompt Jesus miraculously to turn water into wine of unimaginable quality and undrinkable quantity. Note that here, as in every case, the 'whip' exemplifying virtue precedes the 'bridle' exemplifying vice. The memory of sin may act as a necessary restraint on human presumption, even in the pursuit of virtue. Yet the real stimulus to action is the attraction and *excellence* of virtue. The systematic reference, in each episode, to the Beatitudes – enunciated by Christ in the Sermon on the Mount – confirms that the purpose of Purgatory, with all its paradoxes, is to liberate otherwise untold possibilities in human nature: 'Blessed are the pure in heart: for they shall see God' (Matthew 5: 8).

To speak of virtue as 'excellence' is to identify a further feature of Dante's new ethical vision. Everything he records in the *Inferno* would have disposed us to believe that human nature was irredeemably corrupt and in need, above all, of iron-handed regulation. Rules certainly matter to Dante – or did in the first *cantica* of the *Commedia*. Now, though, in the *Purgatorio*, ethical principle ceases to be a form of control and becomes instead (as it did for Aristotle and, recently, for neo-Aristotelians such as Alistair McIntyre and Martha Nussbaum) an encouragement to the 'flourishing' of our natures in the full spectrum of their powers. It quickly becomes apparent that emotions here are no less valuable than philosophies, dreams as important as formal argument, and imagination as important as intellect. Yet none of this (on the Aristotelian model) points merely to egotistical self-realization. 'Excellence', rather, is a contribution to the communal enjoyment of existence, displaying to others the extent of what can be achieved, and inviting them to collaborate in pursuit of that achievement. One of the most notable differences between the *Purgatorio* and the *Inferno* is a change of, so to speak, camera angle, which draws attention to groups rather than individuals. The self-congratulatory monologues that characterized the great episodes of the first *cantica* are now replaced by choruses and conversations which, while always attentive to the particular qualities of the speaker, attribute value to the mutual ambitions of a developing community. It is in this sense that penance for Dante may be seen as a form of work. The proud, for instance, in cantos 10–12, may labour heroically in their penance under the weight of great boulders. But this is not, so to speak, a work-*out*, to be regarded with pride as a way to spiritual muscle. As with the building of medieval cathedrals, when stones were man-handled for miles across rough terrain, this activity is intended to build a communal architecture of ethical relationships: the penitents are themselves first seen in this sequence as if, bent beneath their burdens, they are themselves part of the structure of a building, as gargoyles and corbel stones are. (See *Purgatorio* 10: 130–39.)

Though in the *Purgatorio* Dante advances far beyond a vision of Hell, he also recovers and develops a profound strain of Christian humanism, which goes back, in Dante's case, to his celebration of Beatrice's human excellence in his early work of poetry and prose, the *Vita nuova* (c. 1293). It is highly significant that the final episode of the *Purgatorio* should be dominated by Beatrice's presence. Despite the evidence of Hell, it is Beatrice, throughout the *Commedia*, who sustains Dante's confidence in human nature. This is, in part, to say that in Beatrice Dante sees revealed the perfection of nature that God intends all human beings to enjoy. The full implications of such perfection are displayed, through Beatrice, in the *Paradiso*. But the confidence which Beatrice inspires in the virtues and faculties with which human beings are, specifically, endowed manifests itself throughout the *Commedia*. And the *Purgatorio* in particular depicts what the search to recover such perfection must involve.

One indication of this is that second *cantica* returns to that love of science – or, in medieval terms, the wisdom of God as displayed in the created universe – that impelled Dante's thinking in his other early work, the *Convivio* (c. 1294–1307) and which has its place also in the *Paradiso*. This is particularly evident when, in exploring the passing of time in cantos 4 and 9 of the *Purgatorio*, Dante produces great astronomical (and mythical) designations of time. Time is worth celebrating, along with space, as one of the natural cogs that moves the human mind in harmony with the divine order. Then again, one of the most complex considerations of human worth – revealing the limits as well as the generosity of Dante's optimism – are to be found in the poet's continuing portrayal of Virgil (70–19 BC) as his guide in the realm of Purgatory. It was surprising enough to find Virgil in the dark wood of *Inferno* 1; it is even more surprising to find the pagan poet still with Dante on the shores of a distinctly Christian arena. It could easily have been otherwise. Indeed, Dante comes close to electing an alternative guide when he depicts the (again pagan) hero Cato the Younger (95–46 BC) as the guardian of the shore. (See commentary to *Purgatorio* 1.) But Virgil stays and, in some measure, his function is still what it was in the *Inferno*: to assure Dante of the resources that reside in the human mind and human culture, even without the aid of grace and revelation. Thus, the Golden World to which Dante rises in the conclusion of the *cantica* is not only the Garden of Eden but also the world of perfect justice which Dante and Virgil alike believe might be instituted by the rule of a perfect emperor. Virgil's fourth *Eclogue* (c. 39 BC) (to which Dante openly alludes at *Purgatorio* 22: 70–72) provides something of a model, and the final cantos of the work are punctuated by references to the classical myths of Proserpina, the Sybils and the Ovidian tales of Hero and Leander.

At the same time, the position of Virgil has begun to alter. For one thing, he is now portrayed less as the author of the *Aeneid*, laying before Dante a model of heroic behaviour, and more as a prophet and a poet of the pastoral world. Virgil's fourth *Eclogue* is a pastoral poem as well as being, for many, a prophecy of how Christian redemption has been made possible by the birth of Christ. So, too, for Virgil the age of perfect justice will be inaugurated by the birth of a child: the *Eclogue* concludes with lines that urge the child to 'smile' at its mother. Virgil may, then, be accorded the status of a prophet. (See also *Inferno* 20.) But, if he is viewed in this light, it only serves to introduce a further emphasis on the humility, or even limitation, of Virgil's position in the narrative of the *Purgatorio*. The power of a prophet resides in his willingness to act as a vessel of truth to be fulfilled in the future, far beyond his immediate comprehension or even (in Virgil's case) his own capacity ever to enjoy that truth. Similar considerations arise when, at *Purgatorio* 22: 57, Virgil is described as 'the singer of the farming songs' – a reminder that Virgil was the author of the agricultural poems the *Georgics* (29 BC), which concern viticulture, horse-breeding, bee-keeping and general husbandry. This bucolic Virgil may be as much a model of day-to-day humility as of heroism, and his rationality may just as well reside in a certain pragmatic concern with the fruitfulness of ordinary endeavours as in the pursuit of the grand design.

Whether as prophet or pragmatist, Dante's depiction of Virgil in the *Purgatorio* shifts very subtly to accommodate these new emphases, producing some of the most delicate effects of pathos, intimacy, even comedy to be found in the whole *Commedia* (as, particularly, in the conclusion to *Purgatorio* 21). The dominant tone, however, of Virgil's presence is one of melancholia. In Hell, Virgil was in a certain sense at home. Not only did he dwell in Limbo, he was also mythically supposed to have travelled the whole of the expanse of Hell before Dante was entrusted to his charge. But in Purgatory his absolute authority has gone. He is himself as much a stranger as Dante is in the second realm, needing to ask the way and being constantly taken aback by what he sees. His function is still necessary in a pragmatic sense – as he encourages Dante over difficult terrain or engages the penitents in courteous and fruitful conversation. (See, in particular, *Purgatorio* 6, 21 and 22.) But the shadow is indelible. For Virgil – and the rationality, whether principled or pragmatic, that he represents – is not only a stranger in Purgatory but an exile and, worse still, an exile tantalized by the sight of an environment reserved for Christian penitents in which he will never have a footing. It is part of the depth of Dante's characterization of Virgil that he expresses no lament at this, save for certain tight-lipped allusions to his place in Limbo, which are, of course, all the more moving because of their restraint. (See, in particular, *Purgatorio* 3, 6 and 22.) Nor is it difficult to see that in his depiction of Virgil's melancholia Dante introduces many of the vestigial emotions that he must have experienced himself during almost twenty years of exile from his native Florence. Yet the true tragedy lies in the philosophical realization of the limits that Dante now recognizes must always lie around the competence of human rationality.

The problem of why Virgil and other noble pagans should be condemned to Limbo continues to torment Dante until the higher reaches of the *Paradiso* (see especially *Paradiso* 19), and may not be resolved even there. In a more general sense, however, Dante in his second *cantica* continually interlaces his interest in human effort and excellence with a fully religious awareness of the workings of grace, divine providence and submission to the divine will. One indication of this is the appearance in what at first seems to be a wholly natural landscape of angels who interrupt or miraculously advance the journey of mortal protagonists. These interventions, described in varied terms, always display a particular delicacy in the observation of environment, colour and light, as, for instance, in canto 12, lines 88–90:

> To us that lovely creature now advanced,
> white-vestitured, in countenance, it seems,
> trembling in air as does the morning star.

The angels also – as messengers of God – bring to Dante the words of Christ, usually in the form of Latin quotations from the Beatitudes of the Sermon on the Mount. In this regard, they perform a priestly function, and reveal, as does the Christian liturgy, a range of meanings that are unavailable to natural reason. See, for instance, the angel of canto 19, lines 43–51:

> And then I heard: 'Come on! The crossing's here!'
> spoken in tones more soft and generous
> than ever could be heard in mortal shires.
> With open wings, as, seemingly, a swan's,
> the one who'd spoken turned us to the heights
> between two walls within the granite rock.

> He moved his feathers, and he fanned us both,
> affirming that '*qui lugent*' are the blessed.
> To them the gift of consolation comes.

In Purgatory, then, the natural landscape is not entirely natural. It is, rather, one that, particularly when the angels appear, opens up into a realm of visions and symbols. To the religious eye, physical phenomena are often important in themselves but are also important (as Rowan Williams emphasizes) because 'they are more than themselves', and best understood as embodiments of the divine. Virgil, in the end, has no place in such a world. So, at *Purgatorio* 29: 43–57, he is paralysed with incomprehension when the apparently natural forest of the Earthly Paradise begins to transform itself into a liturgical scene, where trees cease to be trees and become instead the golden candlesticks of a ceremonial procession.

In much of this, Dante draws deeply, if indirectly, on the theology which underlay the early Christian development of the doctrine of Purgatory. The intent of this doctrine was to consolidate the Catholic understanding of the unity of all believers – whether living or dead – and, in Aquinas's version, emphasize the efficacy of prayers of intercession. And this is consistent with Dante's constant emphasis in the *Purgatorio* on the primacy of communal existence. Yet, in the hands of the institutional Church, ever more inclined to extend its political and financial grip over the faithful, the same doctrine came to justify, in the course of the thirteenth, fourteenth and fifteenth centuries, something little short of a protection racket in which prayers were to be accompanied by cash payments or the donation of chantry chapels to the fabric of the Church. It is hardly surprising, then, that these abuses led to a fervent attack on the whole concept of Purgatory by Luther and the Reformation protestants of the sixteenth century. Nor is Dante slow to excoriate the papacy of his day for the perverse interpretation they put upon the doctrine. (See, especially, *Purgatorio* 32 and 33.) His response, however, is wholly different from that of Luther. In the *Purgatorio*, as elsewhere, Dante maintains his devotion to the principle of papal tradition,

however corrupt its practice may have become. Just as import-
antly, he never wavers in his conviction that the images made
available to the human mind in the created world may lead us
to the contemplation of God. Some of these are the artistic
images that serve the liturgy of the Church, the value of which,
as will be seen, Dante warmly acknowledges. (See, especially,
cantos 10, 23 and 29–33.) At the same time, he is acutely aware
from the first canto of the *Purgatorio* – with the slow dawning
of its natural light – that the natural sphere is inexhaustibly full
of objects that can reflect the transcendent design of the Creator
of the Universe.

The *Purgatorio* is no less surprising in its narrative and poetic
sensibility than it is in its ethical terms. In canto 1, lines 8–9,
Dante addresses Calliope, the Muse of epic poetry, as if his epic
endeavour were only now beginning. Yet the epic heroes of this
cantica are not warriors, but the humble penitents heroically
performing their God-given labours. And in terms of genre the
Purgatorio is as much a lyric as an epic poem, involving a
markedly original development of the love poetry that Dante
had inherited from his predecessors. (See cantos 24–6.) Dante's
narrative conception finds echoes in pastoral and Romance
literature; compare, for instance, the remote and often en-
chanted island that he pictures here and the island of William
Shakespeare's *The Tempest* (1611). At times, when a tree is
seen growing in the shape of an inverted pyramid, with its aerial
sustenance deriving from Heaven (22: 130–35), or an old man's
beard is illuminated by starlight as brightly as though by the
noon day sun (1: 34–9), the only adequate modern term would
be 'magic realism'.

Given such a rich vein of experimental writing, it is per-
haps not surprising that the *Purgatorio* has exerted a greater
influence over the experimental writers of the twentieth and
twenty-first centuries than the *Inferno*, with its nerve-racking
sublimities, or the *Paradiso*, with its triumphant certainties.
The *Purgatorio*, in both its ethical and its literary aspect, might
almost be described as a work-in-progress, concerned at all
points to respond to movement, process and transition. So, in
Seamus Heaney it can inspire an interest in those 'epiphanic'

moments when an object or detail rises from the flux of ordinary existence to declare an otherwise unknowable meaning or value. In calling his 1991 volume of poetry *Seeing Things*, Heaney identifies, in a manner that is entirely consistent with Dante's view, the ways in which we act best when we see the world around us afresh and are ourselves 'things' defined by our capacity to see. Samuel Beckett draws his interest in the experience of 'waiting' explicitly from Dante's Ante-Purgatory (see commentary to *Purgatorio* 4), and shares with Dante the realization that waiting, however bleak, clears the mind and sharpens the attention to otherwise unnoticeable eddies of sensation and rhythms of language. To T. S. Eliot – perhaps the best interpreter of the *Purgatorio* – the *cantica* offers a way of reconciling our experience of flux and process with the ceaseless but timeless spirit of Christian exploration that he evokes particularly in *Four Quartets* (1943). These are only some of the possibilities that the *Purgatorio* continues to lay before its reader.

Freedom, Penitence and Community: The Ethical Narrative of the *Purgatorio*

At no point in the *Commedia* can Dante's philosophical concerns be separated from the imaginative context in which those concerns are represented. Dante could – and did – write professional philosophy. (See introduction to *Inferno*, pp. xxxiii–xlii.) Yet, in writing the *Commedia*, he chooses to pursue his thoughts and arguments in narrative and poetic form. He dramatizes the implications of philosophical beliefs and errors, partly through the personal histories of the people he encounters and partly through the conversations in which they engage. Scenes of action trace out the trajectories of intellectual purpose. Image and metaphor add depth, nuance and, often, emotional resonance to the merely conceptual outlines of thought. Paraphrase – though necessary and helpful – can never adequately express the full force of Dante's thinking.

Nowhere is this more evident than in the *Purgatorio*. Narrative here is not simply a convenient vehicle for Dante's ethical principles. On the contrary, it is the very form in which these principles are to be practised, through time. We aim to work towards the good in precisely the way that we aim to sustain a coherent story. Purgatory is, after all, a transitional state, where – as in any continuing narrative – lives are still in motion, free from the icy constrictions of Hell, yet still to arrive at the absolute peace of Paradise. There are no absolute conclusions here. We are concerned with lives as they are lived, and with virtues or principles that are expressed in, and explored through, our sympathetic engagement in a process.

This much is already apparent in regard to the two themes of the *cantica* considered so far: penitence and community. Penitence, as Dante views it, does not seek to acquire, as it were, some certificate of sanctity, but rather to enrich the motive of action, impelling the spirit into further action in the ascent of the mountain – and preparing it, finally, to act (in Paradise) in conjunction with God. Community, likewise, requires one's involvement with and fulfilment through the unfolding of other lives. Communities live according to their traditions, images and common languages, drawing on the past, providing for the future and (in Dante's case, as in many others) praying for the dead and the living alike. (An especially rich example of this is offered by *Purgatorio* 23; see the commentary to this canto.)

The same might be said of Dante's third great concern in the *Purgatorio*, his concern with freedom. This theme is established in *Purgatorio* 1, at line 71, where Dante speaks of himself, through Virgil's mouth, as one who goes 'in search of liberty'. Then, in cantos 16–18, which are numerically the three central cantos of the *cantica* (and thus of the whole *Commedia*), he develops a philosophical discourse on the freedom of the will, which is to say the intellectual appetite in which and through which we pursue what we think is good. Finally, in canto 27, at line 140, as Dante is about to enter the Earthly Paradise, Virgil declares that he is at least 'upright, free and whole'. Dante has, through his own climbing of the mountain, displayed to the full the freedom of his own will and is now at liberty to enter the realm of perfect freedom represented by the Earthly Paradise. In none of these cases, however, is freedom offered to

Dante – or to the reader of the *Purgatorio* – merely as a slogan or a comfortable assurance of achievement. Freedom, as an expression of our intellectual appetite, involves a constantly sustained and constantly renewed pursuit of what is good. It is a dynamic rather than a static condition, a way of living rather than a state of rest. And in this sense, freedom, penitence and community are all interconnected. Freedom is expressed in all the movements and activities of mind that are involved in penance, and likewise underlies all those relationships with people into which the penitents choose to enter. Penitence ensures that we make good choices, as part of the communal reciprocations between all those individuals – and eventually God – who have entered the penitential process.

In this light it is significant that when, in canto 1, line 71, Dante is described as one who goes 'in search of liberty' – '*libertà va cercando*' – the syntax of the description should include a gerund, '*cercando*'/'seeking'. This form of the verb – denoting continual action – emphasizes the extent to which the pursuit of liberty is to be seen as a narrative and a process. Nor is the Earthly Paradise the conclusion to that process. As will appear, the most dramatic feature of this climactic episode is Dante's encounter with Beatrice in *Purgatorio* 30 and 31, where she bears forcibly in upon him that there is no good at all – and consequently no freedom – until the human goods we enjoy are seen in the perspective of infinite good. In the Earthly Paradise Dante does not arrive at a final state of spiritual enjoyment. The desire for that good – and the freedom to desire it – are the subject of the *Paradiso*, and much remains unanswered until the reader arrives at that final *cantica*. But even the central cantos of the *Purgatorio* are complicated and impelled by a series of dramatic questions. Why is it that the whole discussion of freedom is conducted in darkness, ending in the second night on the mountain but beginning in a dark smoke suffered by Dante and the penitents alike (*Purgatorio* 16)? Why is it that the figure who introduces the question of freedom, Marco Lombardo, is himself purging the sin of anger and draws on the energies of that anger to enforce his position?

By way of paraphrase, however, this much may be said: that

freedom is a condition of our free will, of our intellectual appetite. And therefore our freedoms must in some measure involve a conscious and intelligent engagement of the mind. This is what Virgil has to offer in the sober and philosophically analytical discussions of *Purgatorio* 17 and 18. He points forward to questions that can only be answered in Paradise by Beatrice (see *Purgatorio* 18: 73–5), but he also offers a clear summary – or paraphrase – of what Marco Lombardo had expounded in his vigorously irascible terms.

The debate in the black smoke is initiated by a question posed by Dante, which, while seemingly naive, has in some ways been the central issue of the whole of the *Commedia* so far: Why is the world a dark wood? Why is it a desert where virtue cannot thrive? Why are we enthralled by sin and confusion? (See *Purgatorio* 16: 58–63.) The reply is given by the penitent in controlled but unmistakably angry terms. The one single reason is the failure of our wills, of that faculty of free choice and self-determination that lies at the heart of our being. We may seek to blame fate, we may suppose that we are determined in some way by the influence of the stars. But we are not. We are free beings, and the responsibility for our lives is entirely our own. (See *Purgatorio* 16: 67–84.)

There are, undoubtedly, menacing implications to this insistence. Damnation, as we have seen in the *Inferno*, only occurs because human beings have abdicated their responsibilities as intelligent creatures. Hell is the product of disordered free will. For all that, Marco's words are consistent with the underlying interest that Purgatory takes in redemptive activity, and, in the first instance, places the possibility of redemption firmly within the competence of human beings themselves: if their own will is the cause of sin, then the remedy for sin must also lie in their own hands. A similar emphasis appears in the conclusion of Marco's speech, especially at canto 16, lines 94–9. Dante is never inclined to stress the helplessness of human beings. On the contrary, he displays at every point a confidence in the power of rational justice to govern our activities and bring them to fruition. And so it is here. However prone to error our human appetites may be, there are laws on which we can fix our minds that can regulate and direct the intellect to a proper appreciation of its best interests. Or rather, there would be such laws if the Imperial principle of justice had not been abandoned by apathetic rulers and confused by the interference of papal ambitions in the secular sphere. (See *Purgatorio* 16: 106–14.) Purgatory offers a solution both to apathy and to the illusions generated by a misguided Church, and stands as a model of what a temporal community might be in its pursuit of freedom.

Neither here nor elsewhere does Dante meditate for long on how original sin can turn even the best of our intentions to disastrous conclusions. (See introduction to *Inferno*, pp. lxxiv–lxxv.) However, he does realize very acutely (and, in the *Paradiso*, joyfully) that human freedom can only be achieved in its fullest form by a return to the presence of God who created the soul in the first place. Thus the whole of Marco's speech needs to be read in the light of the luminous phrases (anticipating the *Paradiso* even in the black smoke of this terrace) that speak, at *Purgatorio* 16: 85–93, of the moment in which the soul leaves the hand of its divine maker:

> Leaving the hand of him who holds it dear
> (before it truly *is*), it weeps and laughs,
> that little simple soul, and baby-plays,
>   as young girls do, and does not know a thing –
> save, being moved by its Maker in joy,
> it willingly turns to every playful thrill.
>   It tastes the flavour, first, of some small good,
> and, fooled by this, it chases down its track,
> unless a brake or guide bends such love back.

Dante's God is a God who loves, desires and delights in existence for its own sake. The human being is first created on a divine impulse of delight. The soul, therefore, will fulfil its own desires most fully when it responds to the initial sense of pleasure that first brought it into being. There is, of course, an admonitory note even here. Precisely because it is impelled by desire and pleasure – and yet is also free to choose the objects on which it exercises its appetite – the 'little simple soul' can and does go tragically astray. None the less, the most fundamental of all our desires remains the will to participate in existence to the fullest extent of our capacities. The goal of any finite creature is to be in harmony with the infinite being from which its own being is derived.

It is this understanding that Virgil goes on to develop in cantos 17 and 18. There is a painful irony here. The God that Marco reveals to be driven by love and desire is precisely the Christian God that Virgil does not know. Nor does it reduce the irony that Virgil should be able to reproduce the logic of Marco's argument, despite the fact that the redemptive implications of this logic cannot have any bearing on his own position in the afterlife. This is what he proceeds to do. The terms in which Virgil conducts his argument are formulaic, stripped of the passionate commitment displayed by Marco. And they make no reference to Christian theology. His concern is with the abstract logic of the relationship between creators and their creations. For all that, it is Virgil, at canto 17, lines 91–3, who leads Dante to see that the true name for any desire for existence is love and that the fullest expression of freedom is also love:

> 'Neither creator nor created thing
> was ever, dearest son, without' (he starts)
> 'the love of mind or nature. You know that.'

In any act of creation, the creator loves the possibility that some particular object should come into being. Conversely, the newly created being will itself be at its most free when it loves and participates most fully in the intentions of its maker. Imagine a potter carefully moulding a pot on his wheel. The action is impelled by the potter's desire that the pot should exist but, once it does exist, it exists most fully, when it fulfils the uses for which it was originally intended. Human beings are (usually) more complicated than pots, and God is more complicated than a human potter. None the less, Virgil's logic holds and produces a particularly surprising turn at lines 94–102. Having declared that love can be 'natural' or conscious – 'of mind' – he goes on to assert:

> The natural love can never go astray.
> The other, though, may err when wrongly aimed,
> or else through too much vigour or the lack.
> Where mind love sets itself on primal good
> and keeps, in secondaries, a due control,
> it cannot be the cause of false delight.
> But when it wrongly twists towards the ill,
> or runs towards the good too fast or slow,
> what's made then works against its maker's plan.

To speak of a 'natural' love would, according to some moralists, imply a base instinct that should in some way be repressed by the conscious mind. But this is not at all Dante's view. Natural love is the instinctual will, the urge to live and to sustain oneself in the existence that the Creator has first granted. This form of love operates in all created things – whether rational or animal or vegetable – and provides an unwavering compass point, directed always towards the development of life, which is never capable of going astray. Desire here, as throughout the *Paradiso* also, is seen as being, on every level, the innate drive that impels all existing things – whether bees as they make honey or fire as it rises (*Purgatorio* 18: 28) or fire rising in flame (*Paradiso* 1: 115–17) – towards their proper goal, which is to nurture to the full the capacity for life with which they have been endowed. All things in existence desire what is good. And 'good' means nothing more nor less than the nourishment that is appropriate to any particular form of life.

Complications, however, arise in the case of human beings. Humans do have both vegetative and animal aspects. Fingernails grow and we experience instinctual appetites. But, unlike other growing things and animals, we also possess consciously intellectual motivations. Thus, for Dante, all that distinguishes a human being from lower forms of life is the possession of will. Will can be defined (according to Aquinas) as 'intellectual appetite', a conscious desire to set our attention on intellectual objects or objectives. It is this appetite that is expressed in, for instance, our love of books or music, or, more importantly, in our love of another person, or ultimately of God. The will is free, in that its motivations are not decided by physical appetite or organic biorhythms (nor, as Marco says, by the influence of the stars – or, as we might say now, by the forces of environment). The will is able to choose the objects of its attention, and pursue these objects with as much or as little energy as it wishes. Yet precisely because it is, for that reason, free, it is also, as Virgil says, capable of error and, in that respect, wholly unlike the natural appetite for life, which can never stray from its life-sustaining goal.

It follows from this that, for Dante, the proper course for the human will to pursue can never lead us to transcend what some might call our lower selves. On the contrary, 'natural' love remains incapable of error. The proper course for consciousness is not that it should seek to repress its lower self, but rather that it should seek to rediscover the energy and direction expressed in the primal will, which is nothing other than a love of life. The human being will love its own, highly complex existence (canto 17, lines 106–8) and seek fulfilment in the sphere of intellectual good with the same zeal that the bee (or even, say, beetroot) seeks fulfilment in its own sphere of existence. If the human being succeeds in this, it will then freely be given credit for collaborating in the creation that the Creator intended it to enjoy. No bee or vegetable will receive such credit. (Nor will any bee or vegetable be condemned for failing to pursue its existential destiny.)

The implications of Virgil's argument have a direct bearing on the plan of the *Purgatorio*, and of the *Commedia* as a whole. Specifically, as Virgil explains at canto 17, lines 106–39, all forms of sin are, at root, merely misdirected forms of love. When intellectual love fails in its perception of what can contribute most to its existence (and is therefore 'good'), it will produce the destructive consequences that are revealed to view on the seven terraces of penance. The proud misguidedly seek to protect their own seeming self-interest. They 'love' to outdo their fellows – and end up hating them. The envious, unsure of their own value, love to see their fellows brought low. The angry, frustrated in their pursuit of a good, will perversely seek to revenge themselves on those who lie in their path. The slothful love good, but not with sufficient zeal. As for the avaricious, the greedy and the lustful, they are all passionately committed to good but, confusedly, to the wrong, or at least a very partial, good of possessions and power. Love is recognized here to be the motive in all sin. But this, as Dante represents it, is a profoundly hopeful doctrine. If it is the case that desire naturally and unerringly impels the human being, then it may also be rediscovered or fanned into fire again by a properly conscious understanding of what it means to love.

Redemption involves no free pardon, nor, for that matter, any simple admission of wrong-doing. It is rather a call to summon up the energies and capacities that were always present and always remain present in the '*anima semplicetta*': 'simple soul' (*Purgatorio* 16: 88). That is what penance involves. Indeed, the very forces that once led to sin can here be wholly redirected, so that pride can become a proper pride in existence, anger a zealous defence of truly lovable goals and lust a passion for self-giving rather than brute possession. Even the apparently mean-minded sins of envy, sloth, avarice and greed (see commentaries on the central cantos 10–26) may reflect psychological traits that can be converted to virtuous applications.

It is at this point, more generally, that a distinction can be developed between damnation in Hell and penitence in Purgatory. For in the *Inferno* Dante contemplates the awful possibility that human beings, precisely because of their intellectual freedom, can choose *not* to live to the full, but rather extinguish within themselves all desire for love – and hence for freedom. Sin here is self-contradiction, as in the sin of apathy (*Inferno* 3), or suicide (*Inferno* 13), or various other forms of self-betrayal and self-hatred which simultaneously destroy both the perpetrator and those who trust in him (*Inferno* 33). In Purgatory, there are penitents who are guilty of particular crimes as vicious as those committed by the damned. But the intellectual appetite for existence, however confused, has not in their case been extinguished. In Paradise (where redeemed sinners are also to be found), this same appetite is given unconstrained scope to pursue the infinite manifestations of goodness.

In the meantime, in the temporal conditions of Purgatory, under the yoke of penance, the exercise of our freedom demands the acceptance of a paradox, which is that there is no freedom that is not also an intelligent recognition of limit. Marco points to this paradox when, at canto 16, line 80, he speaks of us as being 'free subjects' to our better natures. There are obviously political implications here, in that civic order requires submission to the common rule simply as a matter of self-interest. But beyond this, in metaphysical and religious terms, Dante's thinking concerns the very conditions under which we exist at all. There is no existence (save God's) which is not determinate, and, therefore, limited, in the sense that it is formed and shaped in some specific way. Even an amoeba exists within the logic of amoebic existence, as angels do within the logic of angelic existence. So humans exist within their form – and it would not only be impossible but downright absurd for one form of life to seek (in consciously ethical terms, at least) to exist in another form. In this perspective, when one speaks of the freedom of choice, one does not mean (or at least does not merely mean) the choices that face a consumer in a supermarket or at a travel agents. Rather, the concern is with a freedom that allows one to participate in and collaborate fully with the purposes of existence, one's own, that of others and ultimately God's. Penitential suffering represents, therefore, a remedial encounter with the limits that reality has drawn around us in designating our particular form of life.

The dangers and self-destruction that follow when we suppose that we do not have limits were explored in the Ulysses episode of *Inferno* 26. Now, journeying carefully, point by point, under Virgil's tentative guidance, Dante combines the cartography of the mountain with a progressive unfolding of freedom, running in four major phases.

In the opening Cantos, on the shores of Purgatory, freedom is first experienced as freedom from constriction. This experience is a necessary first step in opening the vistas of possibility, but produces only a very rudimentary conception of freedom, which is challenged and expanded even within the space of the first canto. Cato appears here. He is the Roman politician who committed suicide after the battle of Utica rather than live to see an empire under Julius Caesar replace the ancient republic of Rome. It is immediately clear that freedom, as exemplified by Cato, must involve an active willingness to pursue liberty, even to the point of self-sacrifice. And in this respect (though there are complications, which are discussed in the commentary to *Purgatorio* 1), Cato exemplifies a conception of freedom that serves as a model for the equally self-sacrificing pursuit of freedom that the suffering penitents of Purgatory also display. The pagan Cato displays a natural propensity, unassisted by revelation or faith, to accept the paradox that freedom in a full sense depends upon a willingness to accept limitation to the point of pain and martyrdom.

The central cantos of *Purgatorio* (cantos 10–26), pivoting around Marco Lombardo's passionate discussion of freedom, are those in which the freedom to act out our existential potentiality is most fully exercised and trained under the guidance of grace and revelation. Here, Cato's readiness to lose his life as a political martyr in defence of the principles that have made that life worthwhile is translated, point by point, into a Christian understanding of how, in losing life, one gains it. Literally in 'taking pains', the penitent opens up a whole spectrum of intellectual, sensuous and emotional resources. It is notable that Dante, as traveller, before entering this region of Purgatory – which looks like a penitentiary but is in fact a promise of absolute security – should himself be initiated into its paradoxes by receiving the imprint of seven penitential wounds on his brow, in canto 9. The canto is devoted to the rite of passage by which incisions are made in Dante's flesh – representing the seven 'p's that stand for *peccata* (sin) – by an angel who wields a dazzlingly brilliant sword. Yet no sooner are these marks made than, as Dante reaches the end of each terrace, they disappear one by one, wafted away by the wings of subsequent angels. The un-looked-for purpose of this wounding, freely accepted by the penitent Dante, is, paradoxically, to restore the human form to the integrity that it always should have possessed. In the light of redemption, the wound of sin is also the place in which the remedies of purgation are fully realized.

At the same time, the healing of Dante's brow foreshadows a third aspect of freedom, particularly prominent around canto 20 of the *Purgatorio*, that is, the freedom of conversion – a freedom, freely given by God's grace, to change the life one has made for oneself to a life that will last into eternity. Dante is transfigured by the wounds which the angels, as agents of grace, both bestow on him and remove from him. But all penitents on death arrive in Purgatory transfigured as 'new people' (*Purgatorio* 2: 58). As always – as in, especially, the *Vita nuova* – the word 'new' signifies the possibility of wholly unpredicted alterations in our mode of existence, and it is a defining feature of the penitents in Purgatory that they should be open, as the self-enclosed figures of the damned are not, to the epiphanic and revelatory manifestation of new life. So, in cantos 20–22, Dante examines the notion of conversional freedom, and reveals the magnitude of the forces – involving providence no less than the will of the individual – that are brought into play at the conversional moment. Here Dante encounters the one soul who, in his three days on Mount Purgatory, completes his penitential conversion and becomes free to proceed to Paradise. This figure is the Roman poet Statius (*c.* 45–96). And that, already, is a surprise, comparable to discovering Cato on the shores of Purgatory. For while Statius lived in the first decades of the Christian era, there is no record of his ever having been a Christian convert. But Dante's fiction – always ready to pursue a novelty – does not hesitate to invent a Christian story on Statius's behalf. Though never openly confessing his faith, Statius, we find, lived at a time when the womb of history was 'pregnant' (*Purgatorio* 22: 73–87) with the truths of Christian belief. And Statius paid heed, winning himself the opportunity to spend thirteen centuries in Purgatory to expiate his sins.

The conversional rebirth of Statius flouts all historical likelihood and surprises the reader, too, into new attention. A further contribution to this surprise is that the writings of the pagan Virgil are said to have contributed to Statius's conversion even more decisively than the words of the Scriptures. But the forces that operate in any such conversion have, at the opening of the episode (in *Purgatorio* 20: 124–40), already been shown to exceed those that are at work in the biography – or written works – of any single individual. For the announcement of Statius's liberation from penance precipitates an incomprehensible earthquake which shakes the apparently stable structure of Mount Purgatory to its foundations. This transforming moment is seen entirely in terms of the birth of Christ. The earthquake is accompanied by the singing of the 'Gloria' that the angels sang in the heavens at the Nativity (and which subsequently is sung at the Easter Vigil Mass and High Masses outside of Lent), while Dante and Virgil stand looking on in astonishment, as the shepherds did on Christmas night. Every conversion is possible because of the Incarnation, Atonement and Resurrection. In every conversion that occurs within history the creative plan of providence voices itself anew. Our freedom, as individuals within time, are finally secured by a freedom which exists beyond all time.

This rebirth confirms the importance in the later phases of the *Purgatorio* of motifs concerning childhood which began with Marco Lombardo's evocation of the 'little simple soul'. Statius speaks of the facts of life and the generation of the human embryo in *Purgatorio* 25. Dante, as soon as he meets Beatrice in the Earthly Paradise, is reduced to the inarticulate condition of an infant. But this return to childhood anticipates a final aspect of freedom which stands revealed in the final cantos of the poem. This is the freedom (discussed in the final section of this introduction) to abandon oneself entirely, as a child might, to a good which at first seems overwhelming and at all points is beyond one's powers to encompass or explain. The earthquake of *Purgatorio* 20 anticipates the energies that this power of goodness will unleash and suggests the unfamiliar territory that will be uncovered as the solid ground shifts beneath one's feet. It is divine grace that unlocks this power, and grace alone that allows its recipients to meet its impact fully and grow in its resonance.

The Poetics of the *Purgatorio*

Various types of community are depicted in the course of the *Purgatorio*: princes guilty of negligence assembling in the dusk (canto 8); huddles of feeble figures mutually supporting each other like blind beggars in the sun (canto 13); penitents in ritual procession (canto 23); choruses of angels (canto 30). But in the course of the *cantica* a particular interest develops in the communities that poets can create among themselves, either in the literary coteries that were a feature of thirteenth-century Italian culture or, across time, through a reading of the great authors of the classical tradition. It is a characteristic of the *Commedia* that Dante continually reflects upon his own art, not least in its relation to the work of classical poets such as Virgil and Ovid. (See, for instance, *Inferno* 4 and 25.) He is similarly interested, particularly in the *Paradiso*, in the ways in which his reader receives his text and, often, collaborates with him in the pursuit of an ethical or religious meaning.

In the *Purgatorio* Dante displays a particular interest in the unfolding history of thirteenth-century vernacular love poetry. This is not to say that his interest in the *Inferno* in the relation between classical and modern literature disappears. Following Statius's conversional appearance in *Purgatorio* 21, Dante is accompanied on the last stage of his journey by not one but two poets of the classical tradition, Statius and Virgil, and this fiction resuscitates questions of the relationship between Latin and the vernacular that had been in Dante's mind since as early as the *Convivio* and *De Vulgari Eloquentia*. (See introduction to *Inferno*, p. xxxvii, and the commentaries on *Purgatorio* 7, 21–2 and 26.) Still, Dante is a love poet, and his journey in Purgatory will end when he meets his *donna* or courtly 'lady', Beatrice. As early as *Purgatorio* 2, he imagines how, on the shores of the mountain, newly arrived penitents gather to sing one of his own philosophical love lyrics: '*Amor, che nella mente mi ragiona . . .*' ('Love which discourses in my mind . . .'), only to be interrupted by the brusque admonitions of the noble Roman Cato. In a somewhat different, but equally self-reflexive fashion, in canto 9, lines 70–72, as Dante prepares to enter

Purgatory proper and receive the penitential inscription of seven
wounds on his forehead, he calls upon the reader to observe
how his style rises to a more elevated rhetorical level in order
to describe this act of submission and humility. (What is the
relationship, one might ask, between poetic elevation and moral
submission?) So, too, in canto 10, lines 97–9, he refers obliquely
to the success he will soon enjoy in outdoing the achievements
of his predecessors, while also acknowledging how all artistic
achievement is a merely transient example of human pride.

The closer Dante comes to his meeting with Beatrice, the
more his interest turns, contentiously, to the place he holds in
the poetic canon of his own period. For instance, in canto 24,
lines 49–63, a scene occurs in which Dante encounters a poet,
one Bonagiunta da Lucca (*c.*1220–*c.*1290), from the school of
Guittone d'Arezzo (*c.*1235–94) which immediately precedes
(and on Dante's view lags far behind) the Florentine circle of
stilnovisti poets to which Dante himself belonged in his youth.
(See introduction to *Inferno*, pp. xxvii–xxix, and the commen-
tary on this canto.) Disingenuously, he so contrives the
exchange that Bonagiunta is obliged to solicit him for the secret
that explains his success as a *stilnovisti*. The answer is that
Dante is the one who displays a certain spontaneity and fluency
in his writing, always listening to the words that love dictates
within, as shown in lines 52–7:

> And I to him: 'I am just one who, when
> Love breathes in me, takes note and then goes on
> showing the meaning that's ordained within.'
> 'Dear brother, nah I see,' he said, 'the knot
> that kept the Brief, Guittone and me, too,
> from reaching to that sweet new style I hear of.'

Progressing to canto 26, the whole band of penitents whom
Dante now depicts consists of poets, all of them purging the sin
of lust which they have been guilty of in some of its most
flagrant and perverse forms. This group includes the poet Guido
Guinizelli (*c.* 1230–76), to whom Dante refers as the father of
the 'sweet new style' at lines 97–9. (How can he have been

guilty of lust?) But the last sinner of all whom Dante encounters in the other world is Arnaut Daniel (c. 1180–c. 1210), the troubadour poet famous for his particularly complex lyrics, speaking of the frustrations, dangers and purifying effects of love. Arnaut provided Dante with the stimulus and example to write some of his own most elaborate love lyrics, the *Rime Petrose*. (See commentaries to *Inferno* 32 and *Purgatorio* 26.) He says that Arnaut 'crafted the mother tongue with greater skill' (*Purgatorio* 26: 117), clearly recognizing in him, as in Guido, some kind of poetic progenitor or paternal model. Yet Dante also presumes, daringly, to write the words of Arnaut's speech in Arnaut's own vernacular, Occitan. In doing so he mutes the complexity and torment characteristic of Arnaut, but also provides him with lines that are both prayerful and movingly simple.

To some critics, features such as these display a determination – sometimes manipulative – on Dante's part to assert the prestige of his new poem and to establish his own authority within the developing culture of his day. There may well be some truth in this view. In any event, there is a certain comedy to be derived from the picture of Dante involved in the literary rivalries of his time. Yet more important is how he associates literary authority with moral authority, and by doing so continually raises questions concerning the proper ambitions of a poet and the relative virtues of complexity and simplicity in form, or elevation and simplicity in diction. There is clearly in Dante's mind a connection between literary purpose and ethical purpose, and his determination to speak in such a way – whether as prophet, polemicist or philosopher – as to rectify the moral disasters that he sees besetting thirteenth-century Italy, is discernible at every point in his poem.

Yet at no point, least of all in the *Purgatorio*, is authority exercised by Dante in isolation from a self-critical understanding of his own shortcomings and of the developments that have still to take place in the work he is currently engaged upon. In general, humility is an essential principle in Dante's moral and poetic scheme, as it is indeed in the *Paradiso*. But specifically in the *Purgatorio*, Dante's self-criticism runs parallel to the scrutiny that the penitents bring to bear upon themselves in their pursuit of purifying self-knowledge. In canto 9, for example, when Dante speaks of how, as a writer, he must now elevate his style, he also speaks of how, in a still greater act of writing, an angel, as the minister of God, will inscribe penitential wounds on his own brow, marking him with humility at the very moment when his authorial ambitions have begun to soar. Even when displaying his own inventiveness to the full (as, for instance, in cantos 10–12, concerning pride), he still recognizes that all human art, as compared with divine art, is as nothing – and he openly declares, in canto 13, lines 136–8, that he will have to spend a considerable length of time on the terrace of pride for his own pretensions. Even his judgement of the infamous Guittonians is now more guarded in the *Purgatorio* than it was in *Inferno* 23 – or in the *De Vulgari Eloquentia* 2: 4 (1303–5), where Guittone is dismissed as 'a goose imitating an eagle'.

Thus, in the second *cantica* of the *Commedia*, there arises an analogy between the processes of penance and those of poetic composition, which makes it entirely appropriate that the last – and therefore most advanced – penitents on the mountain should all be poets. A poet, bringing his critical eye to bear upon the poetic community and the traditions that he inherits, seeks to advance a common purpose and to expand the possibilities of the language to which he was born. At the same time, under the impulse of his own talents and ambitions, he seeks to refine and define his own meaning and moral purpose. In the composition of a text he devotes a craftsman-like attention, taking pains over the details of word and form. Significantly, the word '*affina*' (discussed above in its connection to penitential purpose) is used by Arnaut Daniel as he concludes his conversation with Dante (*Purgatorio* 26: 148) and chooses to return to the fire that sharpens his ethical aims.

What, then, are the implications of such concerns for our present reading of the *Purgatorio*? The short answer is to compare the relationship between Dante and his reader with that between Virgil and Dante as portrayed in the narrative of the *cantica*. As in the *Inferno*, Virgil is an authority in Purgatory;

yet he is also an explorer in this territory, often out of his depth and always dependent on his conversations with others if he is to succeed in his task. In the same way, the poet Dante is undoubtedly aware of his authority and his superiority to those who have gone before him. Yet he still recognizes that he is in the middle, rather than at the end of a poetic process, and therefore still in need of conversation with others, including his reader, in the development of a linguistic and ethical community.

At this point, one might compare Dante's position with that of T. S. Eliot, a lifelong and often tormented reader of the second *cantica*. It was Eliot who took the phrase '*il miglior fabbro*' (to mean 'the better maker') that Dante applied to Arnaut at *Purgatorio* 26: 117 as the epigraph to *The Waste Land* (1922), applying it to Ezra Pound, and then proceeded to include Dante's description of Arnaut – as one who hides in the fire that 'sharpens them' (*Purgatorio* 26: 148) – as one of the series of fragmentary allusions that concludes his poem. For Eliot, the ability to read the past and gather up fragments against the ruin of contemporary civilization is one of the few resources available to those who live in a wasteland. So, too, Dante in the dark wood of his own exile creates a text of many voices that represents the only community in which he can now hope to thrive. For, as Eliot goes on to say, in his very Dantean essay 'Tradition and the Individual Talent' (1920), the link between tradition and individual talent is indissoluble: poets write not simply from their own experience but also from the experiences stored up and disseminated by their predecessors. Tradition is renewed and handed on to the future by the words of each individual talent. So, too, in *Four Quartets* (1935–42) Eliot imagines a penitential community that stands at the intersection of past, present and future, constantly seeking the precise word that will voice anew the otherwise hidden truths of the 'Word in the Desert', the ultimate truths of an ultimately hidden God. *Little Gidding* in particular explores the ways in which prayer may restore to life a conversation between the living and the dead which otherwise is bound to decay.

This much is entirely consistent with the picture that Dante gives in the *Purgatorio* of a communal order dependent on prayer, self-sacrifice and work, which always seeks to relate the past to the present and both the present and the past to the future. And in this light it is also appropriate that one should, in some measure, read the *Purgatorio*, as one might read *Four Quartets*, for an almost musical patterning of echoes and resonances in word and image and allusion, the more so since many of these resonances – children, gardens, trees, streams – also reverberate in Eliot's text.

Yet there are also differences here between Dante's position and Eliot's. And most of these derive from the wholly different conceptions of the human person – and consequently of the author in relation to his text – that emerge from the works of the two poets. For Eliot, persons are only vestigially present in his writings, as virtual phenomena refracted through caricature names such as Sweeney, Stetson, Prufrock or the 'familiar compound ghost' of *Little Gidding*. Correspondingly, the author (as Eliot argues in 'Tradition and the Individual Talent') is to be regarded as an anonymous presence in the composition of his own texts, only acting as a catalyst in the processes by which tradition refreshes and reconfigures itself. Dante in the *Purgatorio* is no less concerned than he was in the *Inferno* with historical personages, and with the impact he can make, in political as well as literary terms, upon the historical world to which he belongs. Beatrice herself insists in canto 32, line 103, that the purpose of the vision he has received is that he should recount it 'to aid the world that lives all wrong'. To this end, Dante at every point places himself in historical relationship with others, including the readers of his poem. It is therefore shameful, in the eyes of the quick-tempered Marco Lombardo, that at *Purgatorio* 16: 136–8 Dante seems incapable of identifying the long-forgotten (and very obscure) Gherardo (Gerard), whose virtue, according to Marco, deserves to be remembered by anyone who pretends to know what virtue is. Marco's barbed comment must of course be intended for the reader of the *Purgatorio*, who will certainly by now have forgotten who the 'good Gerard' is. The point in the *Purgatorio*, however, is not (as in the *Inferno*) to call historical figures to the bar of judgement. Instead, while creating as great a polyphony of voices as in the first *cantica*, with as great a diversity of characteristics, Dante is seeking to assimilate and also to celebrate the wide range of individuals who have proved likeminded or whose examples have in some way contributed to the progress of his ethical narrative.

A similar distinction can be drawn between Dante's poetics and those of some of his own contemporaries. Many of his acknowledged predecessors in the love poetry tradition (particularly in the Sicilian school, which Dante admired) had written within the fastness of small courtly élites, and cultivated poetic practices which were 'anonymous', to the extent that they depended less upon the affirmation of personal or philosophical truths than upon a skilful artistry in varying traditional tropes and long-established conventions. Few of these poets risked moving into the public arena and testing their voices against history. Of those who did, the most notable was the infamous (to Dante) Guittone d'Arezzo. On the basis of his acknowledged position in the intellectual life of Tuscany, Guittone developed a magisterial public voice capable of expressing powerful political sentiments – and even of defending women's rights. (See also *Purgatorio* 24 and 26.) Dante may, in fact, have owed much more to Guittone in this regard than he was prepared to admit, and possibly conceived his animus against the earlier poet in reaction against that unwanted influence. Yet Guittone was more likely to address himself with an airy rhetoric to the consequences of public events – of battles lost, of political parties discomfited – than to enter into face-to-face encounters with political adversaries or conversation with ethical allies. To that extent, his authority was indeed authoritarian in a way that Dante's never is, and depended upon the univocal utterances of a single self-confident voice rather than the discursive cut-and-thrust that characterizes Dante's meeting with Marco Lombardo. Guittone was not a narrative – or dialogic – poet. His talk was not for the world in its widest sense that lives amiss. His main poetic correspondence was as the dean and arbiter of the coterie to which he gave his name, among its number Bonagiunta da Lucca who appears in *Purgatorio* 24.

A yet more important difference can be observed between, on the one hand, Eliot, Guittone and even the early Dante, and, on the other, the Dante of the *Commedia*. This arises in regard to Dante's all-important representation of Beatrice. There is no figure corresponding to Beatrice in Eliot's poetry, nor anything in Eliot's work – or the work of any other twentieth-century writer – that expresses anything comparable to that confidence in the uniqueness and perfectibility of human beings which Beatrice inspires in Dante. Dante may not be much interested in the novelistic portrayal of realistic character traits, but he is indomitably concerned with the possibility of human excellence. And his concern to celebrate that possibility defines his understanding both of poetry and of people. Nor is there any precedent in the poetry of his own time for the position that Dante constructs in the *Purgatorio*. Some Italian poets of the twelfth century – notably the same Guinizelli who appears in canto 26 of the *Purgatorio* – had tentatively begun to view the *donna* of the courtly love tradition as an angelic figure and to argue that love was the summation of human dignity. Yet none had made the leap that Dante was prepared to make as early as the *Vita nuova* and then decisively accomplishes in *Purgatorio* 30 when he describes his meeting with Beatrice. For Dante, Beatrice is the literal and historical embodiment of what a human being was intended to be – and of what each human being could be if, through purgation or revelation, it understood its relationship with its creator. This is emphatically not to say that Beatrice is Christ or even an angelic presence. In the *Vita nuova*, while still adjusting his own position within the courtly love tradition, Dante at times attempts to define the singularity of Beatrice by surrounding her with scriptural and christological imagery, so that her death can be seen as an indication of Christ's Passion and yet also a promise of resurrection within the providential plan. But in the Earthly Paradise Beatrice emerges from the allegorical shadows, revealing to Dante not a Christian doctrine but a Christian reality, whereby salvation is expressed in life and in the presence of each individual who mirrors – as all can and Beatrice does – the creative love of God.

The great *coup de théâtre* that registers Beatrice's arrival in the Earthly Paradise is, for Dante and for his reader, a moment of conversion – not unlike the moment signified by the earthquake that shakes Purgatory at the liberation of Statius at *Purgatorio* 20. But its significance is underscored, in terms of poetics and conceptions of personhood, by a particular detail in Dante's depiction of the scene, which is that Beatrice actually talks to Dante. No lady in the troubadour or *stil novist* tradition ever talks back to her lover. Nor does Beatrice speak in the *Vita nuova*. But in doing so now, she insists, in extremely vigorous terms, on her own historical and literal reality, almost to the extinction of Dante, where he is reduced in the face of Beatrice to inarticulate sighs and sobs. Moreover, this new development not only advances beyond the earlier love tradition, but also beyond the position that Dante attributes to himself as late as canto 24 of the *Purgatorio*. There, love was said to commune inwardly with the heart of the male lover, dictating with authority the words that, once he had uttered them, would win him prestige within his literary coterie. Now, however, authority shifts outwards to locate itself wholly within the perceptions and language of a historical person other than the poet himself. The whole episode attempts (as far as fiction allows) to depict the abdication of authority on Dante's part.

There are consequences in such a shift, on both a poetic and an ethical plane. In adopting a narrative style, Dante immediately challenges any poetic stance which asserts the self-sufficiency of the single voice, and, likewise, any ethic that asserts the self-sufficient integrity of the ego. For the first time in Italian literature, persons are no longer viewed as single-minded soloists, talking to themselves, to their own consciences or to some admiring group of intellectual companions. Dante's closest associate in his early years, Guido Cavalcanti (*c.* 1250–1301), had strongly encouraged such a view. (See introduction to *Inferno*, pp. xxvii–xxxi.) Rather, they are seen as dependent upon their reciprocal relationship with other beings. A person is constituted as much by the questions that another puts to him – and Beatrice's questions to Dante are especially searching – as by the answers that any single person may presume to give.

There is a theological basis for such a view, since, as Beatrice's presence demonstrates, she is herself a perfect response to the divine question of how we should pursue the lives that we have been given. But theological debate in Dante is largely reserved for the *Paradiso*. The *Purgatorio* concentrates upon the temporal sphere, and our relationship not so much with God as with others in our temporal or trans-temporal community. And on that plane, Dante's own practices in the poetic and ethical sphere are founded upon a self-critical, even penitential view of his status as a person and a poet, constantly modifying the received idea and his own position in the course of his narrative. Thus, the simplest way to view his meeting with Beatrice is to regard it as a piece of confessional writing. It remains, however, to ask what the implications of such a position might be for Dante's readers. How are they meant to view or benefit from this confession?

One answer to this question might be derived from the enviable title of John Freccero's study, *Dante: The Poetics of Conversion* (Cambridge MA, 1986). At all points in the *Purgatorio*, Dante seeks to encourage, if not a direct conversion to Christian understanding, then an attitude of mind and imagination which allows all the details of the created order and the persons he encounters in Purgatory to be seen in a new light. In their often-magical effect, the scenes that unroll here are frequently designed to 'convert' the mind to meanings other than the literal. Mount Purgatory is a place of symbols as well as of physical realities. This need not, however, imply (as Freccero tends to suggest) that we must seek as readers (or as penitents) to transcend our attachments to the earthly world in favour of some purely spiritual flight towards a divine ideal. 'Conversion', rather, implies the ability to see anew the particularity of the order we inhabit and to communicate the pleasure of that order to others. Others – including Beatrice, or even God – have their view of the world, and conversion involves a reconciliation of any single view with the totality of all possible views. Thus the world, revisited in Dante's exploration of the southern hemisphere, becomes a field of communal action, a testing ground which frees, or converts, us from the possessive or acquisitive mode of vision (one might say, 'tunnel vision') of those individuals whom Dante condemns to Hell.

In that respect, it is more appropriate to speak of a poetics of conversation than a poetics of conversion – especially if the word 'con-versation' can be made to carry the implications of its etymological roots, a 'turning' (verse) 'with' (con) others. We receive the conventions by which we see or speak about the world from others in the past and, through conversation, pass them on, in altered form, to others in the future. This understanding of cultural and intellectual collaboration shapes every episode of the second *cantica*. It is, however, most apparent in the attention that Dante pays to scriptural and liturgical, but also classical, allusion. To take a liturgical example, in *Purgatorio* 2: 46–8, as the latest boat-load of penitents arrives on shore of the mountain, they are heard singing the psalm '*In exitu Israel*', with 'all the psalm that's written after this'. Dante records only the first line. Yet the implication must be that the reader will supply from memory the whole of the piece, recording as it does the exodus of the Israelites from bondage in Egypt. It is as if the old text polyphonically accompanies Dante's new version of that text, and that an interlacing thus occurs between the ancient images of exile and deliverance and those which Dante now creates in his vision of purgatorial freedom. For T. S. Eliot and for many other twentieth-century poets, allusions to other texts frequently stand as painful reminders of how fragmentary our common understanding has now become. For Dante, the reverse is true. He calls up, in the rhythms and invention of his narrative, a collaborative attention, in which memory carries forward the old to the new, and confidently hands on the many-stranded product to the interpretations that future readers may reveal. To read the *Purgatorio* is to be fully involved in a community of interpretation.

In no sense, however, is 'conversation' more applicable to the poetics of the *Purgatorio* than in its literal sense. For the details, nuances and implications that matter here most are those that are discerned in the voices of the historical personages whom Dante now chooses to make part of his story. A kind of courtesy is required to allow space and freedom to these voices.

And here, for the reader as for Dante, the poetic concentration on the historical *personae* of the narrative is entirely harmonious with a form of ethical attention to the demands and values embodied in others. It is, indeed, through conversations of this sort that the memory of others (such as the forgotten Gherardo/ Gerard (see above)) and our own capacity for entering into relationship with others is revived. In this sense, one might say that it is through conversations – ultimately, but not only, with God – that human persons are created. And this surely is the implication of one example that appears on the terrace of pride in *Purgatorio* 10.

Here Dante is considering the very sin that isolates the individual from his neighbour through an aggressive pursuit of personal excellence. (See *Purgatorio* 17: 115–17.) And at first sight, it might well seem that the poet has returned to the judgemental posture of the *Inferno*, where punishment always fits the crime: the proud, according to the degree of their arrogance, are all bent down, weighted as they struggle onward by a burden of boulders (*Purgatorio* 10: 106–20). Indeed, these sinners, at first indistinguishable from the rocks they carry, could easily be reduced merely to physical objects and the target of the onlooker's derision. Yet it is precisely any such attitude of derision or judgement that Dante now proceeds to disallow. In this lengthy passage, addressed directly to the reader and then voicing Virgil's admonitions to Dante himself, Dante counsels caution. We are to look not at the punishment but rather at what it leads to – at what it means in the developing story of penitential redemption. This advice occurs even before we have seen the sinners labouring beneath their loads. But then as the eye – now disposed to sympathy – attunes itself to the details of the image, it slowly dawns on the onlooker that these grotesque apparitions – which are compared to the sculptures in human form that sometimes support the roofs of medieval cathedrals (lines 130–32) – are not inanimate stone after all. The eye, as it picks out the human form within this rocky Rorschach blob, is said to 'untwist' the human image from its mineral appearance. In the process, the dead materiality of rock is transformed into the vitality of vegetable growth. But in the same process, the images that initially seemed 'not human forms' (line 113) are finally seen to be human after all, and humans, moreover, who merit as much admiration for the heroism of their labours as they deserve sympathy for the pain it causes them. The act of interpretation which Dante's text encourages has recreated them. Courtesy has here proved creative. In such encounters, 'conversation' emerges as the most characteristic feature of Dante's poetics in the *Purgatorio*.

BEATRICE AND THE EARTHLY PARADISE

No episode in the *Commedia* is more carefully orchestrated or more surprising in its impact than Dante's encounter with Beatrice in the Earthly Paradise, which begins in canto 30 and develops throughout the last four cantos of the *Purgatorio*. Nor does any sequence indicate more fully how Dante's project in the *Commedia* requires him constantly to challenge previous conceptions – be they of poetry or of personhood – which he has received from others, or has developed himself through his own thinking.

At several points Virgil speaks to Dante about Beatrice. In *Inferno* 2, he reports how she commissioned Virgil to assist her forlorn lover, and how she promised to offer praise to God for Virgil's efforts. At *Purgatorio* 6: 47–8 Virgil speaks of how Beatrice waits for Dante, 'smiling, in all her happiness, on the crest'. At 18: 73–5 Virgil refers a question concerning free will forward to Beatrice, who does indeed take up the question in *Paradiso* 4. Then, at *Purgatorio* 27: 35–6, as Dante spends his last night on Mount Purgatory in a vigil which is also an ordeal by fire, Virgil offers encouragement by reminding him that Beatrice is waiting beyond. Yet the expectations aroused in Dante, and the reader, by Virgil's comments prove to be wholly misguided. The Beatrice of the Earthly Paradise is utterly unlike the picture he has painted, and different again from the figure depicted in the *Vita nuova*. Not smiling but fiercely commanding in her demeanour, Beatrice does not congratulate Dante on his manful climb up the mountain, nor does she repeat the promise offered in *Inferno* 2: 73–4 that she will praise Virgil when she returns to Heaven. Indeed, the moment Beatrice appears, Virgil inconspicuously disappears from Dante's side. On discovering this, Dante, deprived of his constant resource, is immediately thrown into confusion, and registers this to the exclusion, momentarily, of any reference to Beatrice, repeating Virgil's name no less than four times in a crescendo of grief at *Purgatorio* 30: 46–51. But that itself earns him a reproof. He should not weep for Virgil. He should not weep for himself and his own sins. In fact he should not weep at all, since the Earthly Paradise is a place where people are happy (*Purgatorio* 30: 75).

The first word that Beatrice speaks in launching this diatribe is Dante's own name (line 55) – recorded here for the only time in the *Commedia*. Where Dante in his lamentation over Virgil had, willingly or not, escaped Beatrice's gaze, he is now inescapably, in his own person, subject to her view and called to fix his attention (though he finds it impossible to do this) on Beatrice, who proceeds insistently to utter her own name, demanding that Dante should recognize her as she truly is: 'Look. I am, truly, I am Beatrice' (line 73). And here again, Virgil proves to have been mistaken. When Dante first entered the Garden, Virgil had assured him that he had completed his moral education and was now 'healthy, upright, free and whole' (*Purgatorio* 27: 140). Now, in a speech sustained over nearly two cantos, Beatrice requires that Dante should recognize in himself the sins for which he has given yet no account, committed after her death when he turned his eyes 'elsewhere'. Under the gaze of Beatrice Dante loses all Virgilian self-control and is reduced to the inarticulate weeping of an infant. At 31: 68, Beatrice sarcastically suggests that Dante should behave like a man ('raise your beard'). And he acknowledges the barb of her comment: he *should* be able to behave like a man. Yet he is not able even to make an audible response to Beatrice's accusations, and she only knows that he accepts them by seeing how his lips form the shape of a 'yes' – a 'sì'.

Eventually, the tempo of the episode changes, and by the end of canto 33 Dante is again 'remade' and 'ready to rise towards the stars'. Yet, even now, he remains a tremulous figure. His vicious memories have been erased, but only by immersion – like a child at baptism – in the river Lethe. And what self-confidence he now commands has come to him through a second immersion, in the river Eunoe, whose waters miraculously restore to him the memory of the good he has done in the course of his life.

So, the point of arrival towards which the narrative of the *Purgatorio* is moving is also a point of crisis, a return which is also a departure, an achievement as disorienting as it is satisfying. Were Dante to follow the suggestion of mythic archetypes, the Earthly Paradise would be a place of eternal and childlike memory. Dante is aware of the power of myth (see 28: 139–41), and his garden is a place that promises an escape from time. Yet memory here also entraps Dante's mind helplessly in its own past, and the forgetfulness that Lethe introduces into his consciousness is an agent of mercy. Recognition (the central factor in so much drama) restores Dante, as it might in a comedy, to the long-lost Beatrice. Yet, simultaneously, this moment of recognition, as in a tragedy, is also a moment of self-knowledge, in which he discovers his own flaws and foolishness. Dante the poet in all of this displays the highest reach of his lyric and epic art. Yet, as protagonist, Dante is deprived of any power at all. And, since both of these Dantes are devoted to the same Beatrice, the reader may well wonder whether it is possible, or fruitful, to draw any distinction between them at all.

Faced with the complexities of this scene, critics over the centuries have usefully emphasized its allegorical character. Recognizing that the *Purgatorio* is a *cantica* of transitions and conversions, many have spoken of the replacement of Virgil as Dante's guide by Beatrice as a radical shift in mentality. Reason is replaced by revelation. Empire is replaced by church, and justice by love. These rapid designations presume we know already what each of these terms means, and take no account of how Dante may be aiming to define them afresh. None the less, there is some merit in the exercise. When, for instance, Beatrice so incisively utters Dante's name at canto 30, line 55, this powerful moment may justifiably be interpreted as one in

which the Church that baptized Dante now reclaims its own.
For Dante, certainly, the Church is ideally the safeguard of
human identity. It is thus an indication of its corruption in
modern times that, in *Inferno* 19, Dante's name should be
ridiculously mistaken by Pope Nicholas V. Beatrice now rem-
edies any such absurdity. In a similar way, arguably, revelation
now leads Dante to an understanding of truths that lie wholly
beyond the scope of reason, in particular those truths of resur-
rection and eternal life which are illustrated by Beatrice's des-
tiny. Having died in the *Vita nuova*, she is triumphantly restored
to life in the Earthly Paradise. Most importantly, the disappear-
ance of Virgilian reason in the face of such truths can be taken
to illustrate the extent to which reason itself can only offer
inadequate and idolatrous conceptions of the ultimate truth.
The last act of a penitent is to cast aside those very conceptions
of good that reason – hitherto the adjudicator of our appetites
– lays before him. Reason may be good, but only as an instru-
ment of inquiry, not as an object of worship.

Readings such as this are invaluable to an understanding of
this episode. Likewise, a proper attention to the construction
of the allegory illustrates once again the irrepressible ambition
to compose in all forms and genres that inspires so much of
Dante's art. The Earthly Paradise draws with the utmost free-
dom on classical sources, such as the myth of Proserpina or the
Ovidian stories of Hero and Leander. Equally, in its diction
and imagery it displays an unrepressed awareness of the ver-
nacular love lyric. Yet it claims confidently to go beyond both,
by virtue of syncretizing the two traditions in the search for a
Christian meaning. The Earthly Paradise represents a quest for,
and a confidence in, the possibility of new significance. Here,
the world of perfected nature becomes an arena for the enact-
ment of religious drama. So, canto 32 is devoted to the overtly
allegorical Masque depicting the tribulations suffered by the
Church throughout its history, where Dante is able, as poet, to
produce – and, as protagonist, to view – with sheer pleasure
the resolution of historical problems that elsewhere in the *Com-
media* would have elicited from him the most venomous of
political diatribes. The allegory of the Earthly Paradise assures

us that there is meaning in all things. Even the vilest manifestations of moral corruption, when displayed in the Masque of the Church, become the subject of intelligent and contemplative reading. And Dante openly rejoices in the ever-proliferating promise of significance. Towards the conclusion of the *Inferno*, especially in canto 32, Dante the poet confesses himself to be frozen by his vision of the meaninglessness to which human beings can reduce their own lives. At the conclusion of the *Purgatorio*, in canto 33, lines 136–41, he declares that he could go on writing in the manner of the Earthly Paradise for ever. In this sense, allegorical constructions by no means confine the reader to single unalterable readings of the author's ideas, but liberate the pleasures of unfettered interpretation.

Yet neither an allegorical reading nor an appeal to theory is sufficient to express Dante's meaning unless due weight is given to the modulations of rhythm and tone that engage the attention of most readers of the episode. Thus the leisurely opening phases of the sequence, particularly in canto 28, may be seen as a parallel to the opening scenes of the *cantica*, on the shores of the mountain. Now on a plateau, Dante and Virgil wander freely through a 'holy forest' (line 2), absorbing the pleasures of a perfected nature which embraces all the senses, as even the ground beneath them exhales shadowy perfumes. Contrasts between this forest and the dark wood of *Inferno* 1 are plain to see. And the frenzied action which characterizes that opening episode is here translated into the free but poised and measured movements of a dance, as (lines 52–7) Dante and Virgil follow the figure who, on the other side of the stream that divides the garden, might be mistaken for Beatrice, as she goes gathering flowers:

> Her feet together, firmly pressed to ground
> as when a *donna* dances, she then turned
> and, scarcely setting foot in front of foot,
>   she turned above the yellow and the red
> of tender flowers, as virgin girls will do
> when they, for decency, dip down their eyes.

In canto 29, the procession begins which brings Beatrice to Dante, and this, on the level of revelation, is analogous to the purposeful mustering of energies that, on the moral level, the penitents of Purgatory proper display in committing themselves to penance. In Beatrice, providential design and human design are brought to a tense point of union. Yet once this meeting has reached its climax in canto 32, another period of waiting, almost of passivity, begins. Strangely, a *cantica* which has so powerfully concerned itself with the discovery of direction and the enactment of purpose concludes with further procession – to which Dante gives less than concentrated attention, at one point (canto 32, lines 63–82) falling into luxurious sleep. In the Masque of the Church, corruptions that would once have excited Dante's most violent polemic are viewed with a certain comic detachment.

The *cantica* finishes, then, almost without a decisive ending, and the keynote of this final phase is provided by the enigmatic words of Christ from John 16:16–19, quoted in Latin at 33:10–12: 'A little while and ye shall not see me: and again, a little while, and ye shall see me [because I go to the Father].' This is, in part, to confirm that, for all the value that Dante attributes to time and history, the temporal life is best characterized as a time of waiting. On this understanding, waiting leads to a concentration rather than a dissipation of attention. And this concentration needs to be the greater in that (following the sense of Saint John's Gospel) the object that takes possession of our minds will come unexpectedly, as an interruption to the apparently settled expectations of ordinary existence. Christ is present, but also absent – on any human understanding of what presence means. Thus the truth of Christ – who, as the Logos, is simply God's truth – requires a mode of thought quite different from those that are employed in negotiating our geographical environment or the field of human relationships. And it is Beatrice, displacing Virgil in *Purgatorio* 30, who brings Dante to a possession of this mode of thought – which, of course, requires nothing other than a total *dis*possession of all familiar ways of knowing.

Returning, then, to canto 30, it is clear that Beatrice, in

demanding that attention is paid to her own unexpected presence, also produces a complete transformation (as Dante always says she does) in Dante's perception of himself. Deprived of the confidence and comfort that Virgil assured him were now his, Dante, on the instant and in his own person, re-enacts the whole process of confession and purgation that he has so far observed being worked out in the lives of *post mortem* penitents. In this single and instantaneous moment of conversion, even the general schemes of Purgatory fall away. Dante's response to Beatrice requires no reference to the exemplary types of vice and virtue that, hitherto, have been presented in the 'whips' and 'bridles' of each terrace. The responses he attributes to himself are particular and personal to the point of being psychosomatic – flinching, flushing, sobbing and murmuring. Pleasure and pain surge through the whole of Dante's being, uniting body and mind in an inarticulable rhythm which at the same time destroys and re-creates him. There is no place for ethical moderation or balance here. The self is delivered up to the mercy of its own extremes of desire and fragility. Nor is the cause of this reaction some judicious representative of a legal or ecclesiastical institution, but simply the presence of another person, seen in the dazzling fullness of her existence.

This, finally, is what it means on Dante's account to encounter the good, and there is much in the final cantos of the *Purgatorio* that anticipates the manner in which Dante will describe his approach to God in the last cantos of the *Paradiso*. For the truth of God is no more an abstraction or intellectual construct than is the truth of a human person – or any presence to which we are loyal or wish to show our love. It is, therefore, with incomparable tragic irony that the new mode of vision that Beatrice instils into Dante should involve the eclipse of the figure of Virgil. Virgil's loyalty to Dante in the course of their journey together has been exemplary. For most readers, too, Virgil – through the sustained concentration of Dante's fiction – has himself become a real object of love. Yet the temperament that Dante attributes to Virgil, in common with the culture to which Virgil belongs, is typified by a reservedness, even a self-defensiveness that has no place in the Christian understanding that Dante has now begun to dramatize. (See commentary on *Inferno* 4.)

This limitation is painfully revealed in the last moment at which Virgil is seen by the reader of the *Commedia*. In *Purgatorio* 29: 52–7 the triumphal procession of revelation shows itself to Dante and Virgil in its full extent and splendour. But the reaction of the two spectators to the same sight are wholly different:

> These fine devices flamed around their heights
> far clearer than the moon in tranquil skies,
> at midnight in the middle of a month.
> Filled full of radiant wonder, I turned round
> to honest Virgil, and he answered me
> with looks no less weighed down by heavy awe.

Here, at precisely the moment that Virgil is 'weighed down', Dante is 'filled full'; where Dante is enlivened by 'wonder', Virgil is stunned by uncomprehending 'heavy awe'. The crucial distinction here is located in the Italian word '*ammirazione*'. Since the *Vita nuova* Dante has increasingly endowed this word with a meaning that relates it (through its roots in the word *mirare* – to concentrate attention) the seeing of miracles and marvels and, supremely, to the miracle of Beatrice's existence. The word does not imply a merely emotional confusion. On the contrary, it denotes that unwavering concentration of intelligence that, in common experience, we bring to bear upon a work of art. In Dante's understanding, however, it is a form of concentration that allows us to appreciate the utterly unique, utterly singular manifestations of reality that human life itself can display when its excellence is fully realized. It is precisely this mode of understanding that Virgil cannot conceive or sustain. It is a mode in which things and persons are 'more than they are', existing in that condition of presence and absence that eludes all definition, generalization or merely linguistic discourse. And any attempt to possess such a singularity in words is likely to blur or contaminate the reality of that singular existence. The only way in which to live with a singularity or 'miracle' is to love it. But Virgil's ethic is not an ethic of love – lovable as he himself may be on Dante's depiction of him. Nor, in his characteristic devotion to discourse – to the 'eloquent words' for which Beatrice first chose him as Dante's guide at *Inferno* 2: 67 – is Virgil able to sharpen his perceptions and achieve the intelligence that resides in sight.

So, defeated, Virgil – or the mentality he represents – disappears from Dante's poem. This is not to say that Dante ever abandons or disprizes the resources of rational discourse. These remain at our disposal, to be employed with the utmost urgency in that communal pursuit of truth which we are bound to follow in the course of our temporal lives. It is, however, a point that will come for Dante (as for Ludwig Wittgenstein famously, at the end of the *Tractatus Logico-Philosophicus* (1922)), when the only intelligent course of action is to cast aside the ladders of sequential discourse and see how we stand, face to face, with the truth of another existence. This is the demand that Beatrice makes upon Dante. For she, like Dante himself and any other human being, is (in Christian truth) the singular creation of a God who created the world and its human inhabitants miraculously out of nothing, each entirely singular, each entirely new. Once the ability to think in these terms is established, Paradise becomes possible, as a realm (for which Virgil has neither the talent nor the appetite) in which Dante at all points will celebrate the *miracle* of the fact that persons, in their absolute diversity, exist at all.

Further Reading

Auerbach, E., *Mimesis: The Representation of Reality in Western Literature* (Princeton, 1953). *Literary Language and Its Public in Late Latin Antiquity and in the Middle Ages* (New York, 1965). These two seminal studies, written with great critical sensitivity, identify crucial issues in regard to Dante's allegory and his relation to classical tradition.)

Barolini, T., *Dante's Poets: Textuality and Truth in the Comedy* (Princeton, 1984).

—, *The Undivine Comedy: Detheologizing Dante* (Princeton, 1992). Interesting attempts to detach Dante's poem from an overinsistence on moral issues and reveal the virtuosity of Dante's fiction in creating a 'hall of mirrors'.)

Boitani, P., *The Tragic and the Sublime in Medieval Literature* (Cambridge, 1989).

—, *The Shadow of Ulysses: Figures of a Myth* (Oxford, 1994). (Highly original studies of issues such as 'recognition' and the search for knowledge as central issues in Dante's poem.)

Boyde, P., *Dante, Philomythes and Philosopher: Man in the Cosmos* (Cambridge, 1981).

—, *Perception and Passion in Dante's 'Comedy'* (Cambridge, 1993). *Human Vices and Human Worth in Dante's Comedy* (Cambridge, 2000). (A magisterial trilogy expounding all the central principles of Dante's philosophical system.)

Curtius, E. R., *European Literature and the Latin Middle Ages* (New York, 1990). (Dante seen as the culminating figure in the tradition of medieval Latinity.)

Davis C. T., *Dante and the Idea of Rome* (Oxford, 1957). (An important study of Dante's political thinking.)

Dronke, P., *Dante and Medieval Latin Traditions* (Cambridge, 1986). (Detailed essays on Dante's use of classical and medieval motifs.)

Eliot, T. S., *Dante* (London, 1929). (Not in itself a particularly illuminating essay, but crucial to an understanding of what concerned Eliot as a poet throughout his long apprenticeship to Dante.)

Fergusson, F., *Dante* (New York, 1966).

—, *Dante's Drama of the Mind: A Modern Reading of the* Purgatorio (Princeton, 1953). (A stimulating introduction by a passionate Dantist.)

Foster, K. *The Two Dantes, and Other Studies* (London, 1977). (The most penetrating study available of Dante's conception of free will and love.)

Freccero, J. (ed.), *Dante: A Collection of Critical Essays* (Englewood Cliffs, 1965).

—, *Dante: The Poetics of Conversion* (Cambridge MA, 1986). (Freccero's edited volume includes extremely important essays on Dante's philosophy of love and learning and also on his poetic experimentalism.)

Gilson, E., *Dante the Philosopher* (London, 1948). (An indispensable study of Dante's political theory, by the most influential medievalist of the twentieth century.)

Hawkins, P., *Dante's Testaments: Essays in Scriptural Imagination* (Stanford CA, 1999). (A study of Dante's indebtedness to the Scriptures, notable for many critical insights.)

Holmes, G., *Dante* (Oxford, 1980). (A concise introduction to the history of Dante's time and also to his political theory.)

Jacoff, R. (ed.), *The Cambridge Companion to Dante* (Cambridge, 1993). (Includes good introductory essays on a range of essential subjects.)

Lansing, R. (ed.), *The Dante Encyclopedia* (New York and London, 2000). (A comprehensive study of Dantean issues, drawing on the best of modern scholarship.)

Le Goff, J., *The Birth of Purgatory* (trans. A. Goldhammer) (London, 1984). (A scholarly account of medieval doctrine which gives great weight to the originality of Dante's conception of Purgatory.)

Mandelstam, O., 'Conversation about Dante', in *The Collected Critical Prose and Letters*, ed. and trans. J. G. Harris (London, 1991). (A poet's account – sometimes extravagant, but always interesting.)

Quinones, R. J., *Dante Alighieri* (Boston, 1979). (A good account, especially of historical themes in the *Commedia*.)

Scott, J. A. *Dante's Political Purgatory*, (Philadelphia, 1996). (A careful account of the political themes in the *Purgatorio*.)

Singleton, C. S., *Journey to Beatrice* (Baltimore, 1977).

Williams, C., *The Figure of Beatrice: A Study in Dante* (London, 1943).

A Note on the Manuscript Tradition

Dante appears to have published parts of the *Commedia* in manuscript form before the work as a whole was completed. The *Inferno* appeared around 1315 and the *Purgatorio* around 1320, a year before the author's death, by which time groups of cantos from the *Paradiso* may also have been available to patrons. No manuscript in Dante's own hand has ever been identified. But the immediate popularity of the work ensured that, from the earliest times, there were a great many copies available. The oldest manuscript of the work complete in all three of its parts appears to have been produced in Florence between 1330 and 1331. The success of this publication is attested by an anecdote in which a Florentine copyist active in the 1330s is said to have made provision for the dowries of his daughters by producing no less than 100 redactions of the *Commedia*. A further wave – of largely de luxe editions, produced in Tuscany, beyond the walls of Florence – began to emerge in the 1350s. This second tradition seems to have been stimulated by the interest that Boccaccio took in Dante's poem. Boccaccio himself seems to have copied out the *Commedia* at least three times, and had one of these delivered to Petrarch in Avignon in 1351. In all, something approaching 900 manuscripts were available before printed editions began to appear in 1472. These editions, too, of which there were many, were quickly sold. They included an octave edition in 1502 from the prestigious house of Aldine – important enough to be pirated in the same year at Lyons. No less than 100 of the early manuscripts were scrupulously illustrated, establishing a collaboration between poet and painter which reached its height in

Botticelli's extraordinarily subtle treatment of all of the cantos of the *Commedia* produced in Florence during the 1480s, and which continued unabated in the works of William Blake, Gustave Doré and Tom Phillips.

The text reproduced in the present volume (with, on a few occasions, silent emendation) is that established by Giorgio Petrocchi in *La commedia secondo l'antica vulgata* (Milan, 1966–7). Petrocchi's text is based on some thirty of the earliest Florentine manuscripts. Debate continues over the detail of some of Petrocchi's readings. However, it is a testimony to the clarity of Dante's thought and style that his copyists seem only rarely to have lapsed in concentration. In very few cases do variant readings lead to significantly different interpretations. This is the more remarkable in that punctuation was negligible in early copies. Dante's use of rhyme and caesurae fulfils most of the functions that are now ascribed to punctuation. The scholarly reader, therefore, of both Petrocchi's text and the present translation may reasonably complain at the very high level of editorial punctuation that these both display. Their justification lies in an attempt to articulate and clarify the subtlety, nuance and polyphonic variety of the author's original voice.

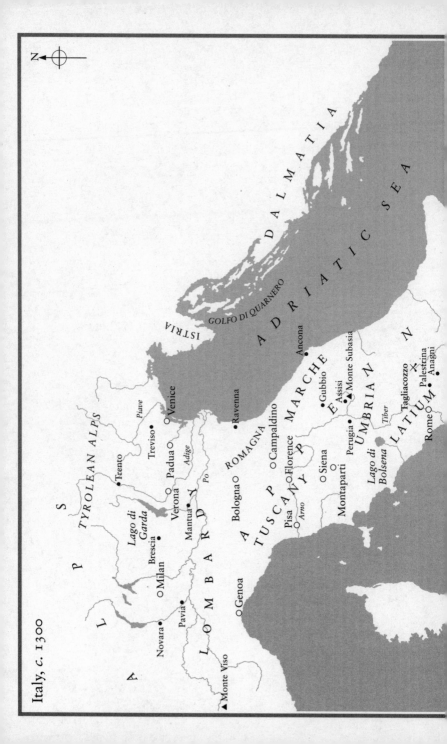

Italy, *c.* 1300

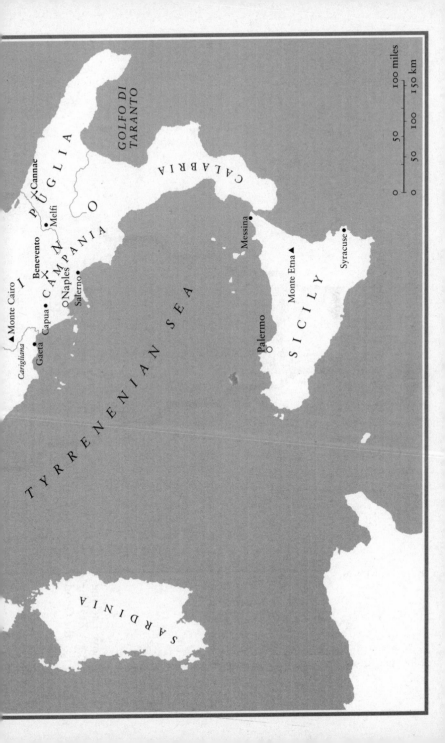

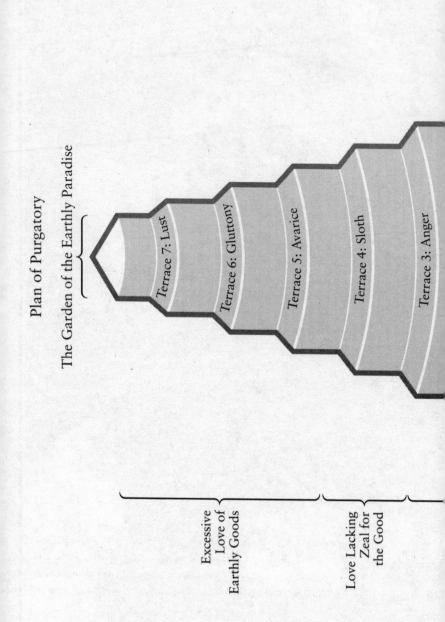

Plan of Purgatory

The Garden of the Earthly Paradise

Terrace 7: Lust

Terrace 6: Gluttony

Terrace 5: Avarice

Terrace 4: Sloth

Terrace 3: Anger

Excessive Love of Earthly Goods

Love Lacking Zeal for the Good

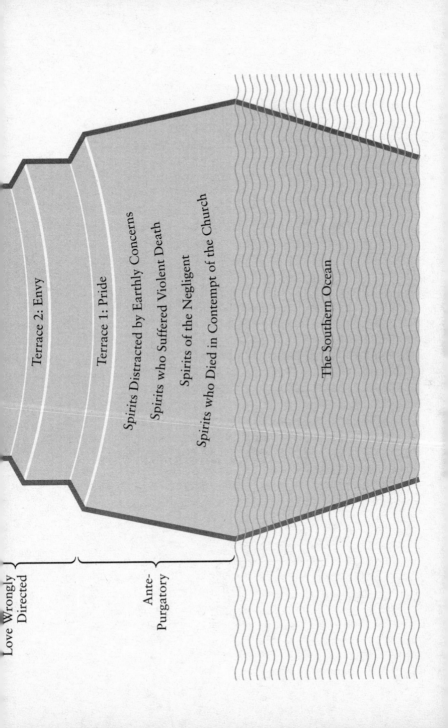

Love Wrongly Directed

Terrace 2: Envy

Terrace 1: Pride

Ante-Purgatory

Spirits Distracted by Earthly Concerns

Spirits who Suffered Violent Death

Spirits of the Negligent

Spirits who Died in Contempt of the Church

The Southern Ocean

Commedia Cantica 2: *Purgatorio*

CANTO 1

1 Per correr miglior acque alza le vele
omai la navicella del mio ingegno,
che lascia dietro a sé mar sì crudele,

4 e canterò di quel secondo regno
dove l'umano spirito si purga
e di salire al ciel diventa degno.

7 Ma qui la morta poesì resurga,
o sante Muse, poi che vostro sono,
e qui Caliopè alquanto surga,

10 seguitando il mio canto con quel suono
di cui le Piche misere sentiro
lo colpo tal, che disperar perdono.

13 Dolce color d'oriental zaffiro
che s'accoglieva nel sereno aspetto
del mezzo, puro infino al primo giro,

16 a li occhi miei ricominciò diletto,
tosto ch'io usci' fuor de l'aura morta
che m'avea contristati li occhi e 'l petto.

19 Lo bel pianeto che d'amar conforta
faceva tutto rider l'oriente,
velando i Pesci, ch'erano in sua scorta.

22 I' mi volsi a man destra e puosi mente
a l'altro polo, e vidi quattro stelle
non viste mai fuor ch'a la prima gente.

25 Goder pareva 'l ciel di lor fiammelle:
Oh settentrional vedovo sito,
poi che privato se' di mirar quelle!

CANTO 1

To race now over better waves, my ship   1
of mind – alive again – hoists sail, and leaves
behind its little keel the gulf that proved so cruel.

And I'll sing, now, about that second realm   4
where human spirits purge themselves from stain,
becoming worthy to ascend to Heaven.

Here, too, dead poetry will rise again.   7*
For now, you sacred Muses, I am yours.
So let Calliope, a little, play her part,

and follow as I sing, with chords that scourged   10
the wretched Magpies (young girls, once) till they
despaired of pardon for their insolence.

Soft hues of sapphire from the orient,   13
collecting gently, marked the circles now
of skies serene from height to horizon.

And this sight – once I left the morbid air,   16
which weighed so heavy on my eyes and heart –
began afresh to bring my eyes delight.

The lovely planet, strengthening to our love,   19*
lit up with laughter all the orient sky,
veiling her escort, Pisces, in bright light.

I turned now to the right. I set my mind   22
up on the southern pole, and saw four stars
that none – save Eve and Adam – ever saw.

The heavens, it seemed, rejoiced in these four gleams.   25
Oh widowed North (your name means seven stars),
how great your lack, to never look on those!

28   Com' io da loro sguardo fui partito,
      un poco me volgendo a l'altro polo,
      là onde 'l Carro già era sparito,

31   vidi presso di me un veglio solo,
      degno di tanta reverenza in vista
      che più non dee a padre alcun figliuolo.

34   Lunga la barba e di pel bianco mista
      portava, a' suoi capelli simigliante,
      de' quai cadeva al petto doppia lista.

37   Li raggi de le quattro luci sante
      fregiavan sì la sua faccia di lume,
      ch'i' 'l vedea come 'l sol fosse davante.

40   'Chi siete voi che contro al cieco fiume
      fuggita avete la pregione etterna?'
      diss' el, movendo quelle oneste piume.

43   'Chi v'ha guidati, o che vi fu lucerna,
      uscendo fuor de la profonda notte
      che sempre nera fa la valle inferna?

46   Son le leggi d'abisso così rotte?
      o è mutato in ciel novo consiglio,
      che, dannati, venite a le mie grotte?'

49   Lo duca mio allor mi diè di piglio,
      e con parole e con mani e con cenni
      reverenti mi fé le gambe e 'l ciglio.

52   Poscia rispuose lui: 'Da me non venni:
      donna scese del ciel, per li cui prieghi
      de la mia compagnia costui sovvenni.

55   Ma da ch'è tuo voler che più si spieghi
      di nostra condizion com' ell' è vera,
      esser non puote il mio che a te si nieghi.

58   Questi non vide mai l'ultima sera;
      ma per la sua follia le fu sì presso
      che molto poco tempo a volger era.

61   Sì com' io dissi, fui mandato ad esso
      per lui campare; e non li era altra via
      che questa per la quale i' mi son messo.

I made my gaze, at last, abandon them,   28*
and turning back to glimpse the other pole –
from which the Wain, already, had gone down –

I saw nearby an old man on his own,   31
deserving (from the air and look he had)
of all respect a son might give his sire.

The beard he wore was long and flecked with white,   34
as, too, the hair that flowed down from his head,
falling upon his breast in double braids.

The rays that shot from those four holy stars   37
adorned his brow with honour so I saw
his face as clear as if the sun shone there.

'And who are you, you fugitives who flee,   40
across the unseeing stream, eternal gaol?'
He spoke, and moved his beard in noble plumes.

'Who was your guide? What lantern led you on   43
beyond those deepest reaches of the night
that make the vale of Hell for ever black?

The laws of the abyss – do these break down?   46
Are counsels newly changed in Heaven's height
so you, the damned, approach my secret hills?'

My leader took me firmly in his grip,   49
and – urging me with gestures, hands and words
to bend my brow and knee in reverence –

'I do not, of myself, come here,' he said.   52
'A lady came from Heaven. And her prayers
led me to help this man, and be his guide.

But since your will is that the truth be told   55
more fully as to what we are and why,
I cannot of my own will say you "nay".

This man has yet to see his final night,   58
but through his own stupidity was close,
and scarcely had the time in which to turn.

Then I was sent, for his sake (as I've said),   61
and found no way to see that he survived,
save that which I have set myself to take.

64   Mostrata ho lui tutta la gente ria,
        e ora intendo mostrar quelli spirti
        che purgan sé sotto la tua balìa.

67   Com' io l'ho tratto saria lungo a dirti;
        de l'alto scende virtù che m'aiuta
        conducerlo a vederti e a udirti.

70   Or ti piaccia gradir la sua venuta:
        libertà va cercando, ch'è sì cara,
        come sa chi per lei vita rifiuta.

73   Tu 'l sai, ché non ti fu per lei amara
        in Utica la morte, ove lasciasti
        la vesta ch'al gran dì sarà sì chiara.

76   Non son li editti etterni per noi guasti,
        ché questi vive e Minòs me non lega,
        ma son del cerchio ove son li occhi casti

79   di Marzia tua, che 'n vista ancor ti priega,
        o santo petto, che per tua la tegni:
        per lo suo amore adunque a noi ti piega.

82   Lasciane andar per li tuoi sette regni;
        grazie riporterò di te a lei,
        se d'esser mentovato là giù degni.'

85   'Marzia piacque tanto a li occhi miei
        mentre ch'i' fu' di là,' diss' elli allora,
        'che quante grazie volse da me, fei.

88   Or che di là dal mal fiume dimora,
        più muover non mi può, per quella legge
        che fatta fu quando me n'usci' fora.

91   Ma se donna del ciel ti move e regge,
        come tu di', non c'è mestier lusinghe:
        bastisi ben che per lei mi richegge.

94   Va dunque, e fa che tu costui ricinghe
        d'un giunco schietto, e che li lavi 'l viso
        sì ch'ogne sucidume quindi stinghe;

97   ché non si converria, l'occhio sorpriso
        d'alcuna nebbia, andar dinanzi al primo
        ministro, ch'è di quei di paradiso.

I have already shown him all the damned,   64
and mean that he should see those spirits now
who, in your care, themselves seek purity.

Too long to say how I have brought him here.   67
But power comes down and strengthens me in this –
to lead him on, to see and hear you speak.

Look kindly on his coming, if you will.   70
He goes in search of liberty. All know –
who gave their life for that – how dear it is.

You know yourself. For, dying in that cause,   73
death had, at Utica, no sting for you.
Your mortal robe, on Judgement Day, will shine.

Eternal laws are not through us made vain.   76*
This man still lives, and Minos binds me not.
I'm from that circle where the modest eyes

of Marcia, your wife, are seen. Eyes turned,   79
she prays, O sacred breast, you keep her still your own.
For love of her, incline to our entreaties.

So let us pass through all your seven realms.   82
I'll take your gracious words to Marcia –
if you will grant we speak of you down there.'

'Once, Marcia,' he said, 'so pleased my eyes,   85
while I was there, that I, in gratitude,
would do for her whatever she might choose.

But now she dwells beyond the evil stream.   88
And therefore, by a law in force since I
came out of it, she cannot move me more.

Yet if in Heaven there is, as you declare,   91
a lady who commands and moves your deeds,
fine words aren't needed. Ask it in her name.

Go, and around this man now bind a belt,   94
formed from a single rush grown straight and smooth,
then wash his features clean of filth and stains.

It cannot be that any eye, still clutched   97
by mist and murkiness, should meet the first
of ministers who'll come from Paradise.

100   Questa isoletta intorno ad imo ad imo,
      là giù colà dove la batte l'onda,
      porta di giunchi sovra 'l molle limo:

103   null'altra pianta che facesse fronda
      o indurasse vi puote aver vita,
      però ch'a le percosse non seconda.

106   Poscia non sia di qua vostra reddita;
      lo sol vi mosterrà, che surge omai,
      prendere il monte a più lieve salita.'

109   Così sparì; e io sù mi levai
      sanza parlare, e tutto mi ritrassi
      al duca mio, e li occhi a lui drizzai.

112   El cominciò: 'Figliuol, segui i miei passi:
      volgianci in dietro, ché di qua dichina
      questa pianura a' suoi termini bassi.'

115   L'alba vinceva l'ora mattutina,
      che fuggia innanzi, sì che di lontano
      conobbi il tremolar de la marina.

118   Noi andavam per lo solingo piano
      com' om che torna a la perduta strada,
      che 'nfino ad essa li pare ire in vano.

121   Quando noi fummo là 've la rugiada
      pugna col sole, per essere in parte
      dove, ad orezza, poco si dirada,

124   ambo le mani in su l'erbetta sparte
      soavemente 'l mio maestro pose:
      ond' io, che fui accorto di sua arte,

127   porsi ver' lui le guance lagrimose;
      ivi mi fece tutto discoverto
      quel color che l'inferno mi nascose.

130   Venimmo poi in sul lito diserto,
      che mai non vide navicar sue acque
      omo che di tornar sia poscia esperto.

133   Quivi mi cinse sì com' altrui piacque:
      oh maraviglia! ché qual elli scelse
      l'umile pianta, cotal si rinacque

136   subitamente là onde l'avelse.

Around this little island, all around   100
its lowest reaches where the breakers beat,
are rushes, borne up by the yielding ooze.

No other plant that comes to leaf or grows   103
to form a rigid stem could ever thrive.
For none of these could bend to take those strokes.

Do not return along the way you came.   106
The sun that rises now will show the way
to take this mountain at a gentler rate.'

So saying, he had gone. Without a word,   109
I rose. And, drawing nearer to my guide,
tight by his side, I set my eyes on him.

And he began: 'Follow my steps, dear son.   112
Let's turn back now. From here the level shore,
in reaching to its boundaries, slopes down.

Dawn was defeating now the last hour sung   115
by night, which fled before it. And far away
I recognized the tremblings of the sea.

Alone, we walked along the open plain,   118
as though, returning to a path we'd lost,
our steps, until we came to that, were vain.

Then, at a place in shadow where the dew   121
still fought against the sun and, cooled by breeze,
had scarcely yet been thinned out into vapour,

my master placed the palms of both his hands,   124
spread wide, lightly and gently on the tender grass.
And I, aware of what his purpose was,

offered my tear-stained cheeks to meet his touch.   127
At which, he made once more entirely clean
the colour that the dark of Hell had hidden.

We then came out across an empty shore   130
that never saw its waters sailed upon
by any man who knew how to return.

There, at another's will, he girded me.   133
And this was marvellous: that, as he chose
that simple plant, another like it rose,

reborn the instant that he plucked it out.   136

CANTO 2

1   Già era 'l sole a l'orizzonte giunto
     lo cui meridian cerchio coverchia
     Ierusalèm col suo più alto punto,

4   e la notte, che opposita a lui cerchia,
     uscia di Gange fuor con le Bilance,
     che le caggion di man quando soverchia,

7   sì che le bianche e le vermiglie guance,
     là dov' i' era, de la bella Aurora
     per troppa etate divenivan rance.

10   Noi eravam lunghesso mare ancora,
     come gente che pensa a suo cammino,
     che va col cuore e col corpo dimora.

13   Ed ecco, qual, sul presso del mattino,
     per li grossi vapor Marte rosseggia
     giù nel ponente sovra 'l suol marino:

16   cotal m'apparve – s'io ancor lo veggia –
     un lume per lo mar venir sì ratto
     che 'l muover suo nessun volar pareggia.

19   Dal qual com' io un poco ebbi ritratto
     l'occhio per domandar lo duca mio,
     rividil più lucente e maggior fatto.

22   Poi d'ogne lato ad esso m'appario
     un non sapeva che bianco, e di sotto
     a poco a poco un altro a lui uscìo.

25   Lo mio maestro ancor non facea motto,
     mentre che i primi bianchi apparver ali;
     allor che ben conobbe il galeotto,

CANTO 2

The sun had reached, already, that horizon   1*
the arc of whose meridian, at its height,
covers Jerusalem as day time ends.

And night, which circles opposite the sun,   4
was rising out of Ganges with the Scales,
which leave her hand, once she has overcome.

So lovely Aurora's cheeks, both red and white,   7
were turning, where I was, to sallow rose
as dawn grew older in the eastern sky.

We went on walking, still beside the sea,   10
as people do when pondering the road.
(Their hearts go forward, though their limbs delay.)

But look! As Mars – surprised, when morning breaks,   13
by thickening vapours – glows to burning red,
low in the west above its ocean floor,

there now appeared (may I see that once more!)   16
a light that came so swift across the sea
that nothing else in flight could equal it.

And, having briefly drawn my eyes away   19
to ask my leader what this light could be,
I saw it now grown greater and more bright.

And then, around it, all appeared to me   22
a something of I-did-not-know pure white,
and, bit by bit, another under that.

As long as these first whitenesses seemed wings,   25
my teacher spoke no word. But when he saw
and recognized who was this galley man:

28   gridò: 'Fa, fa che le ginocchia cali.
      Ecco l'angel di Dio: piega le mani;
      omai vedrai di sì fatti officiali.

31   Vedi che sdegna li argomenti umani,
      sì che remo non vuol né altro velo
      che l'ali sue, tra liti sì lontani.

34   Vedi come l'ha dritte verso 'l cielo,
      trattando l'aere con l'etterne penne,
      che non si mutan come mortal pelo.'

37   Poi, come più e più verso noi venne
      l'uccel divino, più chiaro appariva,
      per che l'occhio da presso nol sostenne,

40   ma chinail giuso; e quei sen venne a riva
      con un vasello snelletto e leggero
      tanto che l'acqua nulla ne 'nghiottiva.

43   Da poppa stava il celestial nocchiero,
      tal che parea beato per descripto;
      e più di cento spirti entro sediero.

46   'In exitu Israel de Aegypto'
      cantavan tutti insieme ad una voce
      con quanto di quel salmo è poscia scripto.

49   Poi fece il segno lor di santa croce,
      ond' ei si gittar tutti in su la piaggia:
      ed el sen gì, come venne, veloce.

52   La turba che rimase lì, selvaggia
      parea del loco, rimirando intorno
      come colui che nove cose assaggia.

55   Da tutte parti saettava il giorno
      lo sol, ch'avea con le saette conte
      di mezzo 'l ciel cacciato Capricorno,

58   quando la nova gente alzò la fronte
      ver' noi, dicendo a noi: 'Se voi sapete,
      mostratene la via di gire al monte.'

61   E Virgilio rispuose: 'Voi credete
      forse che siamo esperti d'esto loco;
      ma noi siam peregrin come voi siete.

'Come now,' he cried out. 'Bend your knees to him!   28
Look there! God's angel! Fold your hands in prayer.
Henceforth, you'll meet this kind of minister.

You see he scorns all human instruments.   31
He needs no oar, nor any other sail
than his own wings, to ply these distant shores.

You see he holds these upright to the skies   34
and, with eternal pinions, fans the air.
These do not shift as human tresses do.'

Then, as he came towards us more and more,   37
that holy bird, he seemed the brighter still.
My eyes could not, close to, sustain the sight.

I bent my eyes. He reached the shore – his boat   40
so swift, so quick, so light, so elegant,
no wave could swallow any part of it.

Celestial, at the stern, the pilot stood –   43
beatitude, it seemed, inscribed on him –
and, ranged within, a hundred spirits more.

'*In exitu Israel de Aegypto*':   46*
they sang this all together, in one voice,
with all the psalm that's written after this.

Then, over them, he made the holy cross,   49
at which they flung themselves upon the shore.
And he, as fast as he had come, went off.

The crowd that now remained, it seemed, was strange,   52
astray there, wondering, looking all around,
as people do, assessing what is new.

On every side the sun shot daylight darts.   55*
Its well-aimed arrows had already chased
the stars of Capricorn from middle sky,

by which time these new people raised their brows,   58
saying to us: 'If you two know this place,
point us the way to go towards the Mount.'

And Virgil answered: 'You may think that we   61
possess experience of where we are.
But we, like you, are pilgrim foreigners.

64   Dianzi venimmo, innanzi a voi un poco,
       per altra via, che fu sì aspra e forte,
       che lo salire omai ne parrà gioco.'

67   L'anime, che si fuor di me accorte,
       per lo spirare, ch'i' era ancor vivo,
       maravigliando diventaro smorte.

70   E come a messagger che porta ulivo
       tragge la gente per udir novelle,
       e di calcar nessun si mostra schivo,

73   così al viso mio s'affisar quelle
       anime fortunate tutte quante,
       quasi obliando d'ire a farsi belle.

76   Io vidi una di lor trarresi avante
       per abbracciarmi, con sì grande affetto
       che mosse me a far lo somigliante.

79   Ohi ombre vane, fuor che ne l'aspetto!
       Tre volte dietro a lei lei mani avvinsi,
       e tante mi tornai con esse al petto.

82   Di maraviglia, credo, mi dipinsi;
       per che l'ombra sorrise e si ritrasse,
       e io, seguendo lei, oltre mi pinsi.

85   Soavemente disse ch'io posasse;
       allor conobbi chi era, e pregai
       che per parlarmi un poco s'arrestasse.

88   Rispuosemi: 'Così com' io t'amai
       nel mortal corpo, così t'amo sciolta:
       però m'arresto; ma tu perché vai?'

91   'Casella mio, per tornar altra volta
       là dov' io son, fo io questo viaggio,'
       diss' io; 'ma a te com' è tanta ora tolta?'

94   Ed elli a me: 'Nessun m'è fatto oltraggio,
       se quei che leva quando e cui li piace,
       più volte m'ha negato esto passaggio;

97   ché di giusto voler lo suo si face:
       veramente da tre mesi elli ha tolto
       chi ha voluto intrar, con tutta pace.

We came a little while before yourselves,   64
taking a different, hard and bitter road.
So now the climb will seem to us a game.'

    The souls who were aware (because I breathed)   67
that I was still alive, now blenched in awe,
and, wondering at the sight, grew very pale.

    And, as around some messenger who bears   70
an olive branch in hand, crowds form to hear
the news – none shy to trample to the fore –

    so these souls, too, stares fixed upon my face,   73
forgetting almost (all so fortunate!)
to go ahead and make themselves more fine.

    And one drew forward now, I saw, to me   76
to take me in his arms with such great warmth
it moved me, so I did the same to him.

    Ah shadows, empty save in how they look!   79
Three times I locked my hands behind his back.
As many times I came back to my breast.

    Wonder, I think, was painted over me.   82
At which the shadow smiled, and so drew back,
while I, pursuing him, pressed further on.

    Gently, he told me I had better stop.   85
And then I knew who this was, so I prayed
that he should speak and pause there for a while.

    His answer came: 'As first in mortal flesh   88
I loved you well, so, freed, I love you now.
And so I stop. But you, why go through here?'

    'Casella!' I said. 'My own! I take this course   91
to come once more where I have now arrived.
But how have you been robbed of so much time?'

    'No one has done me violence,' he said,   94
'if many times my voyage was denied
by Him Who chooses who'll He take, and when.

    For His will stands at one with God's just will.   97
Yet truly for the last three months He's picked,
in utter peace, whoever's wished to board.

100   Ond' io, ch'era ora a la marina vòlto
dove l'acqua di Tevero s'insala,
benignamente fu' da lui ricolto.

103   A quella foce ha elli or dritta l'ala,
però che sempre quivi si ricoglie
qual verso Acheronte non si cala.'

106   E io: 'Se nuova legge non ti toglie
memoria o uso a l'amoroso canto
che mi solea quetar tutte mie voglie,

109   di ciò ti piaccia consolare alquanto
l'anima mia, che, con la sua persona
venendo qui, è affannata tanto!'

112   'Amor che ne la mente mi ragiona'
cominciò elli allor sì dolcemente,
che la dolcezza ancor dentro mi suona.

115   Lo mio maestro e io e quella gente
ch'eran con lui parevan sì contenti,
come a nessun toccasse altro la mente.

118   Noi eravam tutti fissi e attenti
a le sue note; ed ecco il veglio onesto
gridando: 'Che è ciò, spiriti lenti?

121   Qual negligenza, quale stare è questo?
Correte al monte a spogliarvi lo scoglio
ch'esser non lascia a voi Dio manifesto.'

124   Come quando, cogliendo biade o loglio,
li colombi adunati a la pastura,
queti, sanza mostrar l'usato orgoglio,

127   se cosa appare ond' elli abbian paura,
subitamente lasciano star l'esca,
perch' assaliti son da maggior cura:

130   così vid' io quella masnada fresca
lasciar lo canto e fuggir ver' la costa,
com' om che va, né sa dove riesca;

133   né la nostra partita fu men tosta.

So I, who now had gone back to that shore   100*
where Tiber waters turn themselves to salt,
was, in all kindness, taken up by him.

He's set His wings back now towards that gorge,   103
since all who don't descend to Acheron
will always gather at that river mouth.'

And I: 'If no new law has robbed you of   106
your memory or skill in songs of love –
with which you once would calm all my desires –

then, if you'd care to, ease my soul a while.   109
For coming here with still its body's shape,
it is so worn, and weary of the way.

'Love that speaks reasons in my mind to me . . .'   112
So he began, and in a tone so sweet
the sweetness, even now, sounds in my heart.

My teacher, I myself and those who'd come   115
along with him, were so content with this
that nothing touched the mind apart from that.

So there we were, attentive to these notes,   118
entirely still, then calling suddenly,
that stern old man: 'What's this, malingering souls?

What's this neglect, this simply-standing-here?   121
Go run towards the mountain. Shed that skin
which won't let God be manifest to you.'

Compare: when doves, when gleaning grain or weeds,   124
flock all together at their feeding place,
with none of their habitual pride, at peace,

if something they are fearful of appears,   127
then suddenly they'll leave that bait behind,
assailed by greater worries as they are.

In that same way, I saw that fresh new band   130
break off their song and flee towards the cliff,
as people do, not knowing where they'll end.

Our own departure wasn't much less swift.   133

CANTO 3

1   Avvegna che la subitana fuga
dispergesse color per la campagna,
rivolti al monte ove ragion ne fruga,

4   i' mi ristrinsi a la fida compagna:
e come sare' io sanza lui corso?
Chi m'avria tratto su per la montagna?

7   El mi parea da sé stesso rimorso:
o dignitosa coscienza e netta,
come t'è picciol fallo amaro morso!

10   Quando li piedi suoi lasciar la fretta
che l'onestade ad ogn' atto dismaga,
la mente mia, che prima era ristretta,

13   lo 'ntento rallargò, sì come vaga,
e diedi 'l viso mio incontr' al poggio
che 'nverso 'l ciel più alto si dislaga.

16   Lo sol, che dietro fiammeggiava roggio,
rotto m'era dinanzi a la figura
ch'avea in me de' suoi raggi l'appoggio.

19   Io mi volsi dallato, con paura
d'essere abbandonato, quand' io vidi
solo dinanzi a me la terra oscura;

22   e 'l mio conforto: 'Perché pur diffidi?'
a dir mi cominciò tutto rivolto.
'Non credi tu me teco e ch'io ti guidi?

25   Vespero è già colà dov' è sepolto
lo corpo dentro al quale io facea ombra;
Napoli l'ha, e da Brandizio è tolto.

CANTO 3

Although the suddenness with which they fled   1
dispersed the rest across the open plain,
turning towards the Mount, where justice probes,

I drew the closer to my trusted friend.   4
For how, without him, could I run ahead?
And who but he could draw me up that hill?

But he, it seemed, was gnawed by self-reproach.   7
Such dignity of conscience, clear and clean,
bitten so keenly by so slight a fault!

When once his steps had put aside that haste   10
that strips the air of honour from our deeds,
my mind, till now tight-reined within itself,

in eagerness of purpose broadened out.   13
I gave my sight to meet the rising ground,
higher than all, that banks towards the skies.

The sun that flared behind us, brilliant red,   16
broke now in front of me – my silhouette! –
as rays of light lay resting on my form.

I turned around, to one side, fearing I   19
had been abandoned there, seeing ahead
of me alone the earth was dark with shade.

And he, my strength, swung straight around to say: 22
'Why so dismayed and faithless? Don't you know
that I am with you and still guide your steps?

The evening falls where now, within its grave   25*
that body lies in which I cast a shade,
Napoli has it, borne from Brindisi.

28 Ora, se innanzi a me nulla s'aombra,
non ti maravigliar più che d'i cieli,
che l'uno a l'altro raggio non ingombra.

31 A sofferir tormenti, caldi e geli
simili corpi la Virtù dispone
che, come fa, non vuol ch'a noi si sveli.

34 Matto è chi spera che nostra ragione
possa trascorrer la infinita via
che tiene una sustanza in tre persone.

37 State contenti, umana gente, al *quia*;
ché se potuto aveste veder tutto,
mestier non era parturir Maria;

40 e disiar vedeste sanza frutto
tai che sarebbe lor disio quetato,
ch'etternalmente è dato lor per lutto:

43 io dico d'Aristotile e di Plato
e di molt' altri'; e qui chinò la fronte,
e più non disse, e rimase turbato.

46 Noi divenimmo intanto a piè del monte;
quivi trovammo la roccia sì erta
che 'ndarno vi sarien le gambe pronte.

49 Tra Lerice e Turbìa la più diserta,
la più rotta ruina è una scala,
verso di quella, agevole e aperta.

52 'Or chi sa da qual man la costa cala,'
disse 'l maestro mio fermando 'l passo,
'sì che possa salir chi va sanz' ala?'

55 E mentre ch'e' tenendo 'l viso basso
essaminava del cammin la mente,
e io mirava suso intorno al sasso,

58 da man sinistra m'apparì una gente
d'anime, che movieno i piè ver' noi,
e non pareva, sì venian lente.

61 'Leva,' diss' io, 'maestro, li occhi tuoi:
ecco di qua chi ne darà consiglio,
se tu da te medesmo aver nol puoi.'

If nothing now is shadowed at my feet,   28
don't wonder any more than when the rays
the heavens project don't block each other out.

To suffer torments both of heat and chill,   31
the Utmost Power gives bodies, fit for that,
not wishing *how* it does to be revealed.

It's madness if we hope that rational minds   34
should ever follow to its end the road
that one true being in three persons takes.

Content yourselves with *quia*, human kind.   37*
Had you been able to see everything,
Mary need not have laboured to give birth.

You saw the fruitless yearning of those men   40
who might have had that yearning satisfied,
now given them eternally to mourn.

Plato, I mean, and Aristotle, too,   43
and many more with them.' He bowed his head
and said no more, remaining darkly troubled.

We had, meanwhile, now reached the mountain foot.   46
And there we came across a cliff so sheer
that legs, though willing, were quite useless there.

Between Fort Lerici and Turbia   49*
the wildest, steepest scarp would be, compared
with this, an easy stairway, opening clear.

'Now who's to know on which side this cliff sinks' –   52
so stopping in his tracks my teacher said –
'to let us climb, since we have got no wings?'

And while he went along, his head bent low,   55
examining in thought the journey's scheme,
and I, in wonder, gazed around the rock,

a tribe of souls appeared, towards our left,   58
moving in our direction (though their tread came slow
and so it hardly seemed to us they did).

'Lift up your eyes! Look, sir,' I said to him.   61
'There, over there, are some who'll give advice,
if you yourself have nothing to suggest.'

64   Guardò allora, e con libero piglio
        rispuose: 'Andiamo in là, ch'ei vegnon piano;
        e tu ferma la spene, dolce figlio.'

67   Ancora era quel popol di lontano,
        i' dico dopo i nostri mille passi,
        quanto un buon gittator trarria con mano,

70   quando si strinser tutti ai duri massi
        de l'alta ripa e stetter fermi e stretti,
        com' a guardar chi va dubbiando stassi.

73   'O ben finiti, o già spiriti eletti,'
        Virgilio incominciò, 'per quella pace
        ch'i' credo per voi tutti s'aspetti,

76   ditene dove la montagna giace
        sì che possibil sia l'andare in suso;
        ché perder tempo a chi più sa più spiace.'

79   Come le pecorelle escon del chiuso
        a una, a due, a tre, e l'altre stanno
        timidette, atterrando l'occhio e 'l muso,

82   e ciò che fa la prima, e l'altre fanno,
        addossandosi a lei, s'ella s'arresta,
        semplici e quete, e lo 'mperché non sanno:

85   sì vid' io muovere a venir la testa
        di quella mandra fortunata allotta,
        pudica in faccia e ne l'andare onesta.

88   Come color dinanzi vider rotta
        la luce in terra da mio destro canto,
        sì che l'ombra era di me a la grotta,

91   restaro e trasser sé in dietro alquanto,
        e tutti li altri che venieno appresso,
        non sappiendo 'l perché, fenno altrettanto.

94   'Sanza vostra domanda io vi confesso
        che questo è corpo uman che voi vedete,
        per che 'l lume del sole in terra è fesso.

97   Non vi maravigliate, ma credete
        che non sanza virtù che da ciel vegna
        cerchi di soverchiar questa parete.'

He looked across, his face now free from doubt,   64
and answered: 'Let's go there. They come so slow.
And you, dear son, be confident, take heart.'

Those people, when we'd gone a thousand steps,   67
were still, I'd say, as far away from us
as someone with a sling might reach by hand,

when, one and all, they clung to that hard mass   70
of towering rock, and stood there firm and tight,
as travellers, uncertain, glance about.

'You chosen ones, who met your end so well,   73
I ask you,' Virgil started, 'by that peace
which, as I think, is waiting for you all,

please tell us where the mountain angles down   76
to make it possible for us to climb.
For those who know the most, most hate time lost.'

As silly sheep come edging from their fold,   79
one, two and three, the rest all standing there
timidly turning earthwards eyes and snouts,

to do exactly what the first one does,   82
huddling against her if she hesitates,
quiet and meek, not knowing why they do,

so, too, I now saw moving out to me   85
the forward markers of that happy flock,
modest in look and dignified in walk.

When those towards the front saw shattered light   88
falling at my right hand towards the ground
(so that, from me, the shadow reached the cliff),

they stopped and drew themselves a little back.   91
Likewise the rest that followed on from them.
Not knowing why, they did the very same.

'You need not ask. I freely will confess   94
that what you see are truly human limbs.
That's why the sunlight on the earth is split.

Don't wonder at the sight but just believe   97
that, not without some virtue from the skies,
does he attempt to overcome this wall.'

100   Così 'l maestro; e quella gente degna
       'Tornate,' disse, 'intrate innanzi dunque,'
       coi dossi de le man faccendo insegna.

103   E un di loro incominciò: 'Chiunque
       tu se', così andando, volgi 'l viso:
       pon mente se di là mi vedesti unque.'

106   Io mi volsi ver' lui e guardail fiso:
       biondo era e bello e di gentile aspetto,
       ma l'un de' cigli un colpo avea diviso.

109   Quand' io mi fui umilmente disdetto
       d'averlo visto mai, el disse: 'Or vedi,'
       e mostrommi una piaga a sommo 'l petto.

112   Poi sorridendo disse: 'Io son Manfredi,
       nepote di Costanza imperadrice;
       ond' io ti priego che, quando tu riedi,

115   vadi a mia bella figlia, genitrice
       de l'onor di Cicilia e d'Aragona,
       e dichi 'l vero a lei, s'altro si dice.

118   Poscia ch'io ebbi rotta la persona
       di due punte mortali, io mi rendei
       piangendo a quei che volontier perdona.

121   Orribil furon li peccati miei;
       ma la Bontà infinita ha sì gran braccia
       che prende ciò che si rivolge a lei.

124   Se 'l pastor di Cosenza, che a la caccia
       di me fu messo per Clemente allora,
       avesse in Dio ben letta questa faccia,

127   l'ossa del corpo mio sariero ancora
       in co del ponte presso a Benevento,
       sotto la guardia de la grave mora.

130   Or le bagna la pioggia e move il vento
       di fuor dal Regno, quasi lungo 'l Verde,
       dov' e' le trasmutò a lume spento.

133   Per lor maladizion sì non si perde
       che non possa tornar, l'etterno amore,
       mentre che la speranza ha fior del verde.

So said my teacher. And these honoured folk   100
replied: 'Turn back! Go on ahead of us',
and signalled this to us with hands reversed.

And one of them began: 'Whoever you,   103
thus going on your way, may be, turn round
and say if you have ever seen me there.'

I turned to him and fixed him with my gaze.   106
Fair-haired and handsome, with a noble look,
a sword stroke, though, had cut across his brow.

In all humility, I then denied   109
that I, till then, had seen him. 'Look!' he said,
and pointed out a wound high on his chest.'

Then, smiling: 'I am Manfred,' he declared,   112
'grandson to Constance, holy empress.
I pray you, therefore, when you've once returned,

seek out my lovely daughter, who has borne   115*
the honoured crowns of Sicily and Aragon.
Tell her the truth, whatever else is said:

I, broken in my person, had received   118
two mortal wounds and, weeping, gave myself
to Him who, freely, cares to pardon us.

My sins and crimes were horrible to hear.   121
God, though, unendingly is good. His arms
enfold and grasp all those who turn to Him.

And if Cosenza's pastor, who was sent   124*
to hunt me down by Clement (then our pope),
had read aright the face God turned to mine,

my body's bones would still be where they were,   127
near Benevento where the bridge head falls,
guarded by that great cairn of heavy stones.

The rain now bathes them, and they're moved by wind,   130
beyond the Kingdom down the Green Stream's bank
to which he'd carried them with torches dimmed.

No one, while hope shows any hint of green,   133
is lost beyond return to love eternal
merely because the Church has voiced its curse.

136   Vero è che quale in contumacia more
        di Santa Chiesa, ancor ch'al fin si penta,
        star li convein da questa ripa in fore,

139   per ognun tempo ch'elli è stato, trenta,
        in sua presunzion, se tal decreto
        più corto per buon prieghi non diventa.

142   Vedi oggimai se tu mi puoi far lieto,
        revelando a la mia buona Costanza
        come m'hai visto, e anco esto divieto;

145   ché qui per quei di là molto s'avanza.'

It is, however, true that those who die,   136
although repentant, in contempt of Church,
are bound to stay outside this mountain wall
     some thirty times the span of years that they   139
presumed to stand apart – if this decree
is not made shorter by good works of prayer.
     Now see if you can bring me happiness,   142
revealing to my Constance that you've seen
where I am now, and understood this ban.
     For here we greatly gain from those down there.'   145

CANTO 4

1   Quando per dilettanze, o ver per doglie,
    che alcuna virtù nostra comprenda
    l'anima bene ad essa si raccoglie,

4   par ch'a nulla potenza più intenda;
    e questo è contra quello error che crede
    ch'un'anima sovr' altra in noi s'accenda.

7   E però, quando s'ode cosa o vede
    che tegna forte a sé l'anima volta,
    vassene 'l tempo e l'uom non se n'avvede;

10   ch'altra potenza è quella che l'ascolta,
    e altra è quella c'ha l'anima intera:
    questa è quasi legata e quella è sciolta.

13   Di ciò ebb' io esperienza vera,
    udendo quello spirto e ammirando;
    ché ben cinquanta gradi salito era

16   lo sole, e io non m'era accorto, quando
    venimmo ove quell' anime ad una
    gridaro a noi: 'Qui è vostro dimando.'

19   Maggiore aperta molte volte impruna
    con una forcatella di sue spine
    l'uom de la villa quando l'uva imbruna,

22   che non era la calla onde salìne
    lo duca mio, e io appresso, soli,
    come da noi la schiera si partìne.

25   Vassi in Sanleo e discendesi in Noli,
    montasi su in Bismantova e 'n Cacume
    con esso i piè, ma qui convien ch'om voli,

CANTO 4

When, through enjoyment (or indeed through pain)   1
which takes possession of some inner strength,
the soul is gathered up round that alone,

   it can't, it seems, pay heed to other powers.   4
And this refutes the error that maintains
the soul ignites in us in multiples.

   When something, therefore, that is heard or seen   7
holds in its thrall the lower act of soul,
time passes by, and we don't notice it.

   For these are different powers – the one that hears, 10
the one residing in the total soul –
the first (let's say) is bound, the other free.

   I had my own experience of this,   13
hearing that spirit, marvelling at his words.
For now the sun, although I had not seen,

   had risen fully five-times-ten degrees when   16
we arrived where all these souls, as one,
cried out to us: 'It's here, what you demand.'

   A farmer, when the grapes are growing dark,   19
with one scant forkful of his hedging thorn
will often stuff a wider gap than this,

   that corridor through which my lord and guide   22
now climbed – I following behind, alone
since all the company, by now, had gone.

   San Leo you can scale, edge down to Noli,   25*
climb to Bismantova, ascend Cacume.
Feet serve you there. But here you need to fly –

28   dico con l'ale snelle e con le piume
      del gran disio, di retro a quel condotto
      che speranza mi dava e facea lume.

31   Noi salavam per entro 'l sasso rotto,
      e d'ogne lato ne stringea lo stremo,
      e piedi e man volea il suol di sotto.

34   Poi che noi fummo in su l'orlo suppremo
      de l'alta ripa, a la scoperta piaggia,
      'Maestro mio,' diss' io, 'che via faremo?'

37   Ed elli a me: 'Nessun tuo passo caggia;
      pur su al monte dietro a me acquista,
      fin che n'appaia alcuna scorta saggia.'

40   Lo sommo er' alto che vincea la vista,
      e la costa superba più assai
      che da mezzo quadrante a centro lista.

43   Io era lasso, quando cominciai:
      'O dolce padre, volgiti e rimira
      com' io rimango sol, se non restai.'

46   'Figliuol mio,' disse, 'infin quivi ti tira,'
      additandomi un balzo poco in sùe
      che da quel lato il poggio tutto gira.

49   Sì mi spronaron le parole sue
      ch'i' mi sforzai carpando appresso lui,
      tanto che 'l cinghio sotto i piè mi fue.

52   A seder ci ponemmo ivi, ambedui
      vòlti a levante ond' eravam saliti,
      ché suole a riguardar giovare altrui.

55   Li occhi prima drizzai ai bassi liti;
      poscia li alzai al sole, e ammirava
      che da sinistra n'eravam feriti.

58   Ben s'avvide il poeta ch'io stava
      stupido tutto al carro de la luce,
      ove tra noi e Aquilone intrava.

61   Ond' elli a me: 'Se Castore e Poluce
      fossero in compagnia di quello specchio
      che sù e giù del suo lume conduce,

with quickening wings, I mean, and pinions   28
of great desire, behind that leading-on
that offers me all hope and gives me light.

We scrambled through the bore of shattered rock.   31
On every side its edges tightened round.
The ground beneath us called for feet *and* hands.

And when we'd reached the rim above that cliff,   34
and came to where the slope was opening out,
'What path, sir,' I inquired, 'shall we take now?'

And he to me: 'Don't let your footsteps slide.   37
Just follow me. We'll gain ground on this mount
until some escort comes who knows the way.'

The summit was so high it conquered sight.   40
The slope stood proud, its incline far more steep
than (point to centre) forty-five degrees.

I was all in, and so began to say: 43
'Look round, my dearest father. Turn and see,
if you don't stop, I'm stuck here all alone.'

And he said: 'Son, just drag yourself up there,'   46
his finger pointing to a ledge beyond
that ran around the flank of that sheer slope.

His words so stirred me to renewed attempts,   49
I forced myself to track him, hands and knees,
till that encirclement was at my feet.

And there we came and sat, the two of us,   52
turned to the east where we had made our climb
(for looking back will often cheer you up).

I set my eyes on, first, the shores below,   55
then raised them to the sun, and was amazed
to see its light assail us from the left.

The poet noticed that I stood struck dumb   58*
so stupefied to see light's chariot
process between us and the Aquilon.

'If Castor,' he replied, 'and Pollux were   61*
now standing in conjunction with the glass
that draws its mirror light both north and south,

64   tu vedresti il Zodiaco rubecchio
        ancora a l'Orse più stretto rotare,
        se non uscisse fuor del cammin vecchio.

67   Come ciò sia, se 'l vuoi poter pensare,
        dentro raccolto imagina Siòn
        con questo monte in su la terra stare

70   sì ch'amendue hanno un solo orizzòn
        e diversi emisperi; onde la strada
        che mal non seppe carreggiar Fetòn,

73   vedrai come a costui convien che vada
        da l'un, quando a colui da l'altro fianco,
        se lo 'ntelletto tuo ben chiaro bada.'

76   'Certo, maestro mio,' diss' io, 'unquanco
        non vid' io chiaro sì com' io discerno,
        là dove mio ingegno parea manco,

79   che 'l mezzo cerchio del moto superno,
        che si chiama Equatore in alcun' arte,
        e che sempre riman tra 'l sole e 'l verno,

82   per la ragion che di', quinci si parte
        verso settentrion, quanto li Ebrei
        vedevan lui verso la calda parte.

85   Ma se a te piace, volontier saprei
        quanto avemo ad andar; chè 'l poggio sale
        più che salir non posson li occhi miei.'

88   Ed elli a me: 'Questa montagna è tale
        che sempre al cominciar di sotto è grave;
        e quant' om più va sù, e men fa male.

91   Però, quand' ella ti parrà soave
        tanto che sù andar ti fia leggero
        com' a seconda giù andar per nave,

94   allor sarai al fin d'esto sentiero;
        quivi di riposar l'affanno aspetta.
        Più non rispondo, e questo so per vero.'

97   E com' elli ebbe sua parola detta,
        una voce di presso sonò: 'Forse
        che di sedere in pria avrai distretta!'

you then would see the rose-red Zodiac   64
wheel still more tightly round the Ursa stars –
so long as it's not left its former track.

And if you need to get your mind round that,   67*
imagine Zion – harvest that within –
and how that mountain stands upon the globe,

so that, though set in different hemispheres,   70
the same horizon bounds that Mount and this.
From which you'll see (if you think clearly now)

the road where Phaeton had no skill to drive   73
was bound to travel north of that mid-line,
and south, conversely, of Jerusalem.'

'Oh, sir!' I said. 'With such great certitude   76
I've never seen as clearly as I do,
(I've not intelligence enough for that)

how that mid-circle of supernal force   79*
(in certain texts termed "Equatorial")
which always stands between the sun and chill,

veers, for the reason that you gave, as far   82
towards the northern clime of seven stars
as Hebrews see it bend to warmer parts.

But, if you please, I'd really like to know   85
how far we've yet to travel. This slope climbs
higher by far than eyes of mine can go.'

And he: 'This mountain is by nature such   88
that, down below, the start is always hard,
yet hurts far less the more one rises up.

And so when you will find the going smooth,   91
floating as lightly upwards in ascent
as boats that travel down a flowing stream,

you'll then have reached the end of this rough path.   94
Await that point to rest your weariness.
I'll say no more. I know the truth of this.'

The moment he had finished speaking so,   97
a voice rang out close by us: 'Well, perhaps
you'll need a good sit-down before you do.'

100   Al suon di lei ciascun di noi si torse,
       e vedemmo a mancina un gran petrone
       del qual né io né ei prima s'accorse.

103   Là ci traemmo; e ivi eran persone
       che si stavano a l'ombra dietro al sasso
       come l'uom per negghienza a star si pone.

106   E un di lor, che mi sembiava lasso,
       sedeva e abbracciava le ginocchia,
       tenendo 'l viso giù tra esse basso.

109   'O dolce segnor mio,' diss'io, 'adocchia
       colui che mostra sé più negligente
       che se Pigrizia fosse sua serocchia.'

112   Allor si volse a noi e puose mente,
       movendo 'l viso pur su per la coscia,
       e disse: 'Or va tu sù, che se' valente!'

115   Conobbi allor chi era, e quella angoscia
       che m'avacciava un poco ancor la lena
       non m'impedì l'andare a lui; e poscia

118   ch'a lui fu' giunto, alzò la testa a pena,
       dicendo: 'Hai ben veduto come 'l sole
       da l'omero sinistro il carro mena?'

121   Li atti suoi pigri e le corte parole
       mosser le labbra mie un poco a riso;
       poi cominciai: 'Belacqua, a me non dole

124   di te omai; ma dimmi: perché assiso
       quiritto se'? attendi tu iscorta,
       o pur lo modo usato t'ha ripriso?'

127   Ed elli: 'O frate, andar in sù che porta?
       ché non mi lascerebbe ire a' martìri
       l'angel di Dio che siede in su la porta.

130   Prima convien che tanto il ciel m'aggiri
       di fuor da essa quanto fece in vita,
       per ch'io 'ndugiai al fine i buon sospiri,

133   se orazione in prima non m'aita
       che surga sù di cuor che in grazia viva:
       l'altra che val, che 'n ciel non è udita?'

On hearing this, we both of us turned round,   100
and saw, towards our left, a bulky rock
of which, at first, we'd neither been aware.

We drew ourselves across. Some persons there   103
were sitting in the shadow of that stone,
in postures, one might say, of negligence.

And one of those, who seemed to me worn out,   106
was sitting with his arms around his knees,
holding his face bowed heavily between.

'My dearest lord,' I said, 'just look at him –   109
at that one there who seems more negligent
than if his sister were Pure Indolence.'

At this he turned a bit, to pay us heed,   112
moving his cheek to look along his thigh.
'All right,' he said. 'Head up, you big, strong lad!'

I knew then who he was. And all the aches   115
that made my breath still come a little fast
could not prevent me from approaching him.

I reached him and he hardly raised his head,   118
saying: 'You've seen now, have you, how the sun
leads to the left its chariot at your back?'

His curt expressions and his sluggish turns   121
had brought my lips, a little, to a smile.
'Belacqua,' I began, 'I need not now

grieve for you any longer. But say why   124
you're sat down here. You're waiting for a guide?
Or are you back again to your old ways?'

'Brother' he said, 'what point in going up?'   127
God's angel, sitting at the gate up there,
would not admit me to the Penances.

The heavens must circle first around me here   130
the length of time they did around my life
(since I delayed good sighs until my end)

unless, before that, prayer has brought me aid,   133
rising on high from hearts that live in grace.
What else – since Heaven won't hear – is any use?'

136   E già il poeta innanzi mi saliva
           e dicea: 'Vienne omai: vedi ch'è tocco
           meridian dal sole, e a la riva
139   cuopre la notte già col piè Morrocco.'

The poet now was climbing further on,   136
saying: 'Come! Come! The high meridian – look! –
is touched by sun. Along the western shore,
    the foot of night is falling on Maroc.'   139

CANTO 5

1   Io era già da quell' ombre partito
e seguitava l'orme del mio duca,
quando di retro a me, drizzando 'l dito,

4   una gridò: 'Ve' che non par che luca
lo raggio da sinistra a quel di sotto,
e come vivo par che si conduca!'

7   Li occhi rivolsi al suon di questo motto,
e vidile guardar per maraviglia
pur me, pur me, e 'l lume ch'era rotto.

10   'Perché l'animo tuo tanto s'impiglia,'
disse 'l maestro, 'che l'andare allenti?
Che ti fa ciò che quivi si pispiglia?

13   Vien dietro a me, e lascia dir le genti:
sta come torre ferma, che non crolla
già mai la cima per soffiar di venti;

16   ché sempre l'omo in cui pensier rampolla
sovra pensier, da sé dilunga il segno,
perché la foga l'un de l'altro insolla.'

19   Che potea io ridir, se non 'Io vegno'?
Dissilo, alquanto del color consperso
che fa l'uom di perdon talvolta degno.

22   E 'ntanto per la costa di traverso
venivan genti innanzi a noi un poco,
cantando 'Miserere' a verso a verso.

25   Quando s'accorser ch'i' non dava loco
per lo mio corpo al trapassar d'i raggi,
mutar lor canto in un 'oh!' lungo e roco;

CANTO 5

Already some way past the shadow folk,   1
I climbed still onward in my leader's track,
until, below us, one of them burst out:

'See that?' – a finger pointing long – 'The one behind!   4
No sun ray shines, it seems, towards his left!
And doesn't he behave as though alive?'

On hearing these sharp words, I turned my eyes,   7
and saw them gazing in astonishment,
at me – yes, me! – and the broken sunlight.

'Why let your thoughts get tangled up like that?'   10
(My master speaks.) 'It only slows your stride.
And why be bothered by their whisperings?

Keep close behind me. Let them say their say.   13
Stand straight, a mighty tower unwavering,
its height unshaken by such breaths of wind.

When thought is bred too rampantly from thought,   16
then, of himself, a man will miss his mark.
Each mental thrust debilitates the first.'

What answer could I offer, save 'I come'?   19
I said so, sprinkled by that blushing hue
that, on occasion, means we merit pardon.

Meanwhile, across the angle of our climb,   22
there now appeared ahead another group,
intoning, verse by verse, the 'Miserere'.

But when they saw my limbs would not allow   25
a thoroughfare to any ray of light,
they changed their chanting to a long, hoarse 'Oooh!'

28   e due di lor, in forma di messaggi,
        corsero incontr' a noi e dimandarne:
        'Di vostra condizion fatene saggi.'

31   E 'l mio maestro: 'Voi potete andarne
        e ritrarre a color che vi mandaro
        che 'l corpo di costui è vera carne.

34   Se per veder la sua ombra restaro,
        com' io avviso, assai è lor risposto:
        fàccianli onore, ed esser può lor caro.'

37   Vapori accesi non vid' io sì tosto
        di prima notte mai fender sereno,
        né, sol calando, nuvole d'agosto,

40   che color non tornasser suso in meno;
        e, giunti là, con li altri a noi dier volta
        come schiera che scorre sanza freno.

43   'Questa gente che preme a noi è molta,
        e vegnonti a pregar,' disse 'l poeta:
        'però pur va, e in andando ascolta.'

46   'O anima che vai per esser lieta
        con quelle membra con le quai nascesti,'
        venian gridando, 'un poco il passo queta.

49   Guarda s'alcun di noi unqua vedesti,
        sì che di lui di là novella porti:
        deh, perché vai? deh, perché non t'arresti?

52   Noi fummo tutti già per forza morti,
        e peccatori infino a l'ultima ora;
        quivi lume del ciel ne fece accorti,

55   sì che, pentendo e perdonando, fora
        di vita uscimmo a Dio pacificati,
        che del disio di sé veder n'accora.'

58   E io: 'Perché ne' vostri visi guati,
        non riconosco alcun; ma s'a voi piace
        cosa ch'io possa, spiriti ben nati,

61   voi dite, e io farò per quella pace
        che, dietro a' piedi di sì fatta guida,
        di mondo in mondo cercar mi si face.'

Then two, who acted as their nuncios,   28
hurried to meet us with the urgent plea:
'What is your standing here? Please let us know.'

My master answered: 'You may now return   31
and bear to those who sent you this reply:
"This man, in body, is true flesh and bone."'

And if, as I suppose they did, they stopped   34
because they saw that shade, these words should serve.
Let them all honour him. He'll pay them well.'

Vapours, when kindled in night's early hours,   37*
flash across tranquil skies like meteors,
and August clouds are cleft by setting suns.

Yet none I've ever seen went up as quick   40
as these two messengers, who turned, once there,
with all the rest, to us – a herd in rampage.

'They'll come in multitudes,' the poet said,   43
'and mill around and pester you for prayers.
So listen as you go, but still press on.'

'You there, that soul now set for happiness'   46
(they yelled their greeting) 'with your limbs intact
as ever you were born! Slow down a bit!

Look! Is there anyone you've seen before?   49
You might, if so, bear news of them beyond.
Ah! Where to now? Ah! Why don't you stand still?

We all were victims of some violent death,   52
yet sinners till we reached our final hour.
Then Heaven's light dawned and made us see things clear,

so that, repenting and forgiving all,   55
we came from life remade at peace with God,
who heartens our desire to see Him still.'

'I stare into your eyes,' I answered them,   58
'and recognize no single one. Yet you
are spirits born anew to good. And all

you wish – and I can do – I shall. Please say.   61
I swear this by the peace that leads me on
from world to world, pursuing this great guide.'

64   E uno incominciò: 'Ciascun si fida
        del beneficio tuo sanza giurarlo,
        pur che 'l voler nonpossa non ricida.

67   Ond' io, che solo innanzi a li altri parlo,
        ti priego, se mai vedi quel paese
        che siede tra Romagna e quel di Carlo,

70   che tu mi sie d'i tuoi prieghi cortese
        in Fano, sì che ben per me s'adori
        pur ch'i' possa purgar le gravi offese.

73   Quindi fu' io; ma li profondi fóri
        ond' uscì 'l sangue in sul quale io sedea,
        fatti mi fuoro in grembo a li Antenori,

76   là dov' io più sicuro esser credea:
        quel da Esti il fé far, che m'avea in ira
        assai più là che dritto non volea.

79   Ma s'io fosse fuggito inver' la Mira
        quando fu' sovragiunto ad Oriaco,
        ancor sarei di là dove si spira.

82   Corsi al palude, e le cannucce e 'l braco
        m'impigliar sì ch'i' caddi; e lì vid' io
        de le mie vene farsi in terra laco.'

85   Poi disse un altro: 'Deh, se quel disio
        si compia che ti tragge a l'alto monte,
        con buona pietate aiuta il mio!

88   Io fui di Montefeltro, io son Bonconte.
        Giovanna o altri non ha di me cura,
        per ch'io vo tra costor con bassa fronte.'

91   E io a lui: 'Qual forza o qual ventura
        ti traviò sì fuor di Campaldino
        che non si seppe mai tua sepultura?'

94   'Oh!' rispuos' elli, 'a piè del Casentino
        traversa un'acqua c'ha nome l'Archiano,
        che sovra l'Ermo nasce in Appennino.

97   Là 've 'l vocabol suo diventa vano
        arriva' io forato ne la gola,
        fuggendo a piede e sanguinando il piano.

Then one began: 'You need not swear to that.   64
Granted your will is not cut short by "can't",
each of us trusts that you will bring some good.

May I (who'll only speak till others do)   67
entreat you, if you've seen those lands that lie
between Romagna and the realm of Charles,

that you, in all your kindness, pray for me   70
in Fano – so entreaties offered there
may give me strength to cleanse my grievous sins.

I was from Fano. But the hollow wounds   73*
from which the blood by which I lived ran down,
were dealt me by the Antenorians.

I thought my safety was, with them, assured.   76
The Estes got it fixed, their spite to me
exceeding all that justice could require.

If only I had fled towards La Mira   79
– they caught me as I ran to Oriaco –
my place would be where men breathe, even now.

Towards the marsh I ran, where – brackish reeds   82
entwining me – I fell, watching as, in this mire,
a lake spread outwards, forming from my veins.'

'May your desires be met' (another spoke)   85
'that draw you to the mountain height. Then, please,
take pity. In your goodness, aid my own.

I am – once Montefeltran – now Buonconte.   88*
Giovanna does not pray for me. None cares.
And so, among all these, I walk, brow lowered.'

'No one has ever known,' I said, 'your place   91*
of burial. What led you – chance? or was it force? –
away, at Campaldino, from the kill?

'Ah!' he replied. 'A stream – the Archiano – runs   94
across the lower Casentino hills,
born above Hermitage-in-Apennine.

I'd got to where this river's title fails,   97
fleeing on foot, and wounded in my throat,
a line of blood behind me on the plain.

100   Quivi perdei la vista, e la parola
nel nome di Maria finì'; e quivi
caddi e rimase la mia carne sola.

103   Io dirò vero, e tu 'l ridì tra 'vivi:
l'angel di Dio mi prese, e quel d'inferno
gridava: "O tu del ciel, perché mi privi?

106   Tu te ne porti di costui l'etterno
per una lagrimetta che 'l mi toglie:
ma io farò de l'altro altro governo!"

109   Ben sai come ne l'aere si raccoglie
quell' umido vapor che in acqua riede
tosto che sale dove 'l freddo il coglie.

112   Giunse quel mal voler che pur mal chiede
con lo 'ntelletto, e mosse il fummo e 'l vento
per la virtù che sua natura diede.

115   Indi la valle, come 'l dì fu spento,
da Pratomagno al gran giogo coperse
di nebbia, e 'l ciel di sopra fece intento

118   sì che 'l pregno aere in acqua si converse,
la pioggia cadde, e a' fossati venne
di lei ciò che la terra non sofferse;

121   e come ai rivi grandi si convenne,

        ver' lo fiume real tanto veloce
si ruinò, che nulla la ritenne.

124   Lo corpo mio gelato in su la foce
trovò l'Archian rubesto, e quel sospinse
ne l'Arno, e sciolse al mio petto la croce

127   ch'i' fe' di me quando 'l dolor mi vinse.
Voltòmmi per le ripe e per lo fondo;
poi di sua preda mi coperse e cinse.'

130   'Deh, quando tu sarai tornato al mondo
e riposato de la lunga via,'
seguitò 'l terzo spirito al secondo,

And now I lost my sight. And all my words   100
ended in uttering Maria's name.
I fell – my flesh alone remaining there.

But tell the living this – I'll speak the truth –   103
God's angel laid his hands on me. Hell shrieked:
"Why do you rob me, Heavenspawn, of this?

You'd prise him from me for one little tear,   106
and carry off his everlasting part?
Well, I'll rule otherwise the other half!"

Humid evaporations (as you know)   109
collect in air, then, rising to the grip
of freezing air, return to earth as rain.

There now arrived the Evil Urge – who seeks,   112
in mind, for nothing if not ill – and stirred,
through powers its nature gives, wind, murk and fog.

And when the light of day had been put out,   115
he draped the vale in clouds, from Pratomagno
to reach the summit of the mountain range

and made the skies condense till gravid air   118
was turned, once more, to water. Whatever
earth refused to bear ran off in runnels.

And when these streams in torrents were
        conjoined,   121
these rushed towards the sovereign river course
with such great speed that nothing held them back.

The Archiano – furious, in spate – had found   124
my body at its outlet, rigid, chill.
It drove this to the Arno, loosing there

the cross that, lost in agony, my arms had formed.   127
From bank to riverbed, it swirled me round,
then wrapped and hid me in its muddy spoil.'

'When you return, pray Heaven, to the world,   130
and, having rested from long travelling'
(with these few words a third soul joined the group)

133   'ricorditi di me, che son la Pia;
             Siena mi fé, disfecemi Maremma:
             salsi colui che 'nnanellata pria
136   disposando m'avea con la sua gemma.'

'please, do remember me. I am La Pia.   133
Siena made me, unmade by Maremma.
And he knows this who, once I wore his ring,
   took me in marriage with his own bright gem.'   136

CANTO 6

1   Quando si parte il gioco de la zara,
colui che perde si riman dolente,
repetendo le volte, e tristo impara;

4   con l'altro se ne va tutta la gente;
qual va dinanzi, e qual di dietro il prende,
e qual dallato li si reca a mente;

7   el non s'arresta, e questo e quello intende;
a cui porge la man, più non fa pressa,
e così da la calca si difende.

10   Tal era io in quella turba spessa:
volgendo a loro, e qua e là, la faccia
e promettendo, mi sciogliea da essa.

13   Quiv' era l'Aretin che da le braccia
fiere di Ghin di Tacco ebbe la morte,
e l'altro ch'annegò correndo in caccia.

16   Quivi pregava con le mani sporte
Federigo Novello, e quel da Pisa
che fé parer lo buon Marzucco forte.

19   Vidi conte Orso e l'anima divisa
dal corpo suo per astio e per inveggia,
com' e' dicea, non per colpa commisa:

22   Pier da la Broccia dico; e qui proveggia,
mentr' è di qua, la donna di Brabante
sì che però non sia di peggior greggia.

25   Come libero fui da tutte quante
quell' ombre, che pregar pur ch'altri prieghi
sì che s'avacci lor divenir sante,

CANTO 6

When punters split off from some gambling game,   1
the loser stays behind, all misery,
to check the throws once more and, sadly, learn,

   while, with the winner, all the rest go off.   4
Some buttonhole the man, some pluck his tails,
and some his sleeve – 'Just think of me,' they mean.

   Though hearing each of them, he does not pause,   7
his hands fend all away, to make them stop.
So he defends himself from this great press.

   Well, that was me, in that dense crowd of souls,   10
turning my face to this side, then to that.
By promising each one, I got away.

   The Aretine was there who met his end   13 *
at vicious Ghin di Tacco's scything arm,
he, too, who, running with the hunt, had drowned.

   And here as well, with hands stretched out in prayer, 16
was Frederick Novello and that Pisan man
who made the clan Marzucco's power appear.

   I saw Count Orso, and the man whose soul   19
was severed from his limbs, so he declared,
by spite and envy and no crime of his.

   I mean Pierre la Brosse – and, while still there,   22
just let the lady of Brabant (lest she
be herded with the worst for that) take care.

   As soon as I got free from all these shades –   25
who went still praying for another's prayer
to speed them on their way to holiness –

28   io cominciai: 'El par che tu mi nieghi,
        o luce mia, espresso in alcun testo,
        che decreto del Cielo orazion pieghi;

31   e questa gente prega pur di questo:
        sarebbe dunque loro speme vana,
        o non m'è 'l detto tuo ben manifesto?'

34   Ed elli a me: 'La mia scrittura è piana,
        e la speranza di costor non falla,
        se ben si guarda con la mente sana,

37   ché cima di giudicio non s'avvalla
        perché foco d'amor compia in un punto
        ciò che de' sodisfar chi qui s'astalla;

40   e là dov' io fermai cotesto punto
        non s'ammendava, per pregar, difetto,
        perché 'l priego da Dio era disgiunto.

43   Veramente a così alto sospetto
        non ti fermar, se quella nol ti dice
        che lume fia tra 'l vero e lo 'ntelletto.

46   Non so se 'ntendi; io dico di Beatrice:
        tu la vedrai di sopra, in su la vetta
        di questo monte, ridere e felice.'

49   E io: 'Segnore, andiamo a maggior fretta,
        ché già non m'affatico come dianzi,
        e vedi omai che 'l poggio l'ombra getta.'

52   'Noi anderem con questo giorno innanzi,'
        rispuose, 'quanto più potremo omai;
        ma 'l fatto è d'altra forma che non stanzi.

55   Prima che sie là sù, tornar vedrai
        colui che già si cuopre de la costa,
        sì che ' suoi raggi tu romper non fai.

58   Ma vedi là un'anima che, posta
        sola soletta, inverso noi riguarda:
        quella ne 'nsegnerà la via più tosta.'

61   Venimmo a lei: o anima lombarda,
        come ti stavi altera e disdegnosa
        e nel mover de li occhi onesta e tarda!

I thus began: 'It seems that you, my Light,   28
deny overtly in a certain text
that prayers can ever bend what Heaven dictates.

And yet these folk are praying just for that.   31
Could it then be the hopes they have are vain?
Or is it that your words aren't clear to me?'

And he to me: 'The words I write are plain.   34
And yet, if you look closely with sane thought,
the hope that these all have will never fail.

God's justice at its summit does not sink   37
because, in one sharp point, the fire of love
completes what those who dwell here expiate.

So, in the passage where I made this point,   40
no flaw could ever be redeemed by prayer.
For prayer was then not linked or joined to God.

Yet do not, truly, let your question rest   43
until the one who'll come as light between
your intellect and truth declares you may.

I don't know if you take my sense. I mean   46
Beatrice. You'll see her up above,
smiling, in all her happiness, on the crest.'

'My lord,' I said, 'let's move with greater haste.   49
I'm not as wearied as I was before.
And – look – the mountain's casting shadow now.'

'While daylight lasts,' he answered me, 'we'll press   52
our way as far ahead as we still can.
But things have not the shape that you suppose.

Before you reach that height, you'll see return   55
the one who now is hidden by the ridge –
so you cannot, now, break the light he sheds.

But over there you see a soul alone,   58
alone placed there who stares across at us.
This one will teach us what's the quickest way.'

We came towards it. O you Lombard soul!   61
How proud you stood, how haughty in your look,
your moving eye so grave and dignified.

64   Ella non ci dicea alcuna cosa,
        ma lasciavane gir, solo sguardando,
        a guisa di leon quando si posa.

67   Pur Virgilio si trasse a lei, pregando
        che ne mostrasse la miglior salita;
        e quella non rispuose al suo dimando,

70   ma di nostro paese e de la vita
        ci 'nchiese; e 'l dolce duca incominciava:
        'Mantoa . . .' e l'ombra, tutta in sé romita,

73   surse ver' lui del loco ove pria stava,
        dicendo: 'O Mantoano, io son Sordello
        de la tua terra!' e l'un l'altro abbracciava.

76   Ahi serva Italia, di dolore ostello,
        nave sanza nocchiere in gran tempesta,
        non donna di province, ma bordello!

79   Quell' anima gentil fu così presta,
        sol per lo dolce suon de la sua terra,
        di fare al cittadin suo quivi festa;

82   e ora in te non stanno sanza guerra
        li vivi tuoi, e l'un l'altro si rode
        di quei ch'un muro e una fossa serra!

85   Cerca, misera, intorno de le prode
        le tue marine, e poi ti guarda in seno,
        s'alcuna parte in te di pace gode.

88   Che val perché ti racconciasse il freno
        Iustiniano, se la sella è vòta?
        Sanz' esso fora la vergogna meno.

91   Ahi gente che dovresti esser devota
        e lasciar seder Cesare in la sella,
        se bene intendi ciò che Dio ti nota,

94   guarda come esta fiera è fatta fella
        per non esser corretta da li sproni,
        poi che ponesti mano a la predella.

97   O Alberto tedesco, ch'abbandoni
        costei ch'è fatta indomita e selvaggia,
        e dovresti inforcar li suoi arcioni,

The soul did not say anything at all.   64
It let us make our way, still looking on,
as hunting lions do that pause and couch.

But Virgil went across to him, and asked   67
that we be shown a better path to climb.
To this request, the soul made no reply.

About our origins, our towns and lives,   70
he questioned *us*. My thoughtful guide began:
'Mantua . . .' The shade – so dark-cowled, sunk within –

rose up towards him from where first he's been,   73
saying: 'You Mantuan! I am Sordello.
Your fellow citizen.' And each round each flung arms.

You! Vile Italia! Sorrow's resting place!   76
You hulk that no one steers through raging storms!
No sovereign lady, you're a cat house whore!

That noble soul was moved with such great speed   79
to greet his fellow citizen, to hear –
no more than that! – the sweet sound of their home.

Yet those who live within your boundaries   82
stand nowhere free of war. Each gnaws the next,
all locked together by one wall and moat.

Search hard, you wretch, round all your ocean shores   85
then turn towards your heart, and try to see
if any of its parts rejoice in peace.

Why should Justinian have formed your reins?   88*
What use is that? The saddle's riderless.
The shame would be far less were there no curb.

You people! If you only understood   91
what God intends you'd be more reverent,
and let the saddle be great Caesar's seat.

Just look how fierce and cruel the beast's become.   94
No spur to set it on its proper course,
since you, Italia, took the bridle up.

You German Albert! You abandon her,   97*
so hard to handle now, untamed and wild,
you who should sit astride her saddle bows.

100   giusto giudicio da le stelle caggia
       sovra 'l tuo sangue, e sia novo e aperto,
       tal che 'l tuo successor temenza n'aggia!

103   Ch'avete tu e 'l tuo padre sofferto,
       per cupidigia di costà distretti,
       che 'l giardin de lo 'mperio sia diserto.

106   Vieni a veder Montecchi e Cappelletti,
       Monaldi e Filippeschi, uom sanza cura:
       color già tristi, e questi con sospetti!

109   Vien, crudel, vieni, e vedi la pressura
       d'i tuoi gentili, e cura lor magagne;
       e vedrai Santafior com'è oscura!

112   Vieni a veder la tua Roma che piagne
       vedova e sola, e dì e notte chiama:
       'Cesare mio, perché non m'accompagne?'

115   Vieni a veder la gente quanto s'ama!
       E se nulla di noi pietà ti move,
       a vergognarti vien de la tua fama.

118   E se licito m'è, o sommo Giove,
       che fosti in terra per noi crucifisso,
       son li giusti occhi tuoi rivolti altrove?

121   O è preparazion che ne l'abisso
       del tuo consiglio fai per alcun bene
       in tutto de l'accorger nostro scisso?

124   Ché le città d'Italia tutte piene
       son di tiranni, e un Marcel diventa
       ogne villan che parteggiando viene.

127   Fiorenza mia, ben puoi esser contenta
       di questa digression, che non ti tocca,
       mercé del popol tuo che si argomenta.

130   Molti han giustizia in cuore, e tardi scocca
       per non venir sanza consiglio a l'arco;
       ma il popol tuo l'ha in sommo de la bocca.

133   Molti rifiutan lo comune incarco;
       ma il popol tuo solicito risponde
       sanza chiamare, e grida: 'I' mi sobbarco!'

May justice from the stars fall, rightly, down   100
on your tribe's blood. May that come strange and clear,
to make your heir feel all the dread of it.

Held back in Germany by raging greed,   103
your father did – as you now – tolerate
the Empire's garden to lie desolate.

Come! See the Montagues and Capulets,   106*
Monaldi, Filippeschi, reckless men,
some plunged in misery and some in fear!

Come, cruel man, and see the great distress   109*
of all your nobles. Cure them of their warts.
You'll see how Santa Fiora is eclipsed.

Come now, and see that Rome of yours in tears.   112
Widowed and lonely, day and night she weeps:
'Say why, dear Caesar, you're not with me now.'

Come now, and see the love between these folk.   115
And if no pity for us makes you move,
come, be ashamed to know what name you've won.

And if, great Jove, once crucified for us,   118
it is permissible for me to say,
then why are Your just eyes now turned elsewhere?

Or is all this a preparation, formed   121
within the chasm of Your wisdom, for some good
cut off completely from what we can see?

In Italy, the cities are all full   124*
of petty despots. Every country lout
who joins a gang is rebel Marcellus.

Dear Florence, you may well content yourself   127
with this parenthesis, which can't touch you,
all thanks, of course, to your so brilliant crew.

Many, though true at heart, are slow to shoot,   130
for fear, without advice, they'd rush the bow.
But your lot tongue-tip justice all the time.

Many refuse to take on public tasks.   133
But your lot, so solicitous, unasked,
reply with shouts: 'Let me! I'm up for that!'

136   Or ti fa lieta, ché tu hai ben onde:
       tu ricca, tu con pace e tu con senno!
       S'io dico 'l ver, l'effetto nol nasconde.

139   Atene e Lacedèmona, che fenno
       l'antiche leggi e furon sì civili,
       fecero al viver bene un picciol cenno

142   verso di te, che fai tanto sottili
       provedimenti, ch'a mezzo novembre
       non giugne quel che tu d'ottobre fili.

145   Quante volte, del tempo che rimembre,
       legge, moneta, officio e costume
       hai tu mutato, e rinovate membre!

148   E se ben ti ricordi e vedi lume,
       vedrai te somigliante a quella inferma
       che non può trovar posa in su le piume,

151   ma con dar volta suo dolore scherma.

Look happy now. You've every reason to,   136
rich as you are, at peace and oh-so-wise.
The outcome does not hide that I speak true.

Athens and Lacedaemon, which first made   139*
the ancient law, and were so civilized,
made, as to living well, the faintest mark

compared to you who make such delicate   142
provisions in your laws that what you spin
won't reach from mid-October to November's end.

How many times within your memory   145
have you, renewing all your limbs, transformed
duties and laws and coinage and customs?

And if you'll know yourself and see the light,   148
you'll see how like you are to some sick hag,
who finds no comfort on her feather bed,

but shields herself from pain with every squirm.   152

CANTO 7

1   Poscia che l'accoglienze oneste e liete
       furo iterate tre e quattro volte,
       Sordel si trasse e disse: 'Voi chi siete?'

4   'Anzi che a questo monte fosser volte
       l'anime degne di salire a Dio,
       fur l'ossa mie per Ottavian sepolte.

7   Io son Virgilio, e per null' altro rio
       lo ciel perdei che per non aver fé.'
       Così rispuose allora il duca mio.

10   Qual è colui che cosa innanzi sé
       sùbita vede ond' e' si maraviglia,
       che crede e non, dicendo: 'Ella è, non è . . .':

13   tal parve quelli; e poi chinò le ciglia
       e umilmente ritornò ver' lui,
       e abbracciòl là 've 'l minor s'appiglia.

16   'O gloria d'i Latin,' disse, 'per cui
       mostrò ciò che potea la lingua nostra,
       o pregio etterno del loco ond' io fui,

19   qual merito o qual grazia mi ti mostra?
       S'io son d'udir le tue parole degno,
       dimmi se vien d'inferno, e di qual chiostra.'

22   'Per tutt' i cerchi del dolente regno,'
       rispuose lui, 'son io di qua venuto;
       virtù del ciel mi mosse, e con lei vegno.

25   Non per far, ma per non fare ho perduto
       a veder l'alto Sol che tu disiri
       e che fu tardi per me conosciuto.

CANTO 7

Three or four times, with solemn happiness,   1
the welcome each gave each had been renewed
till, drawing back, Sordello said: 'Who *are* you?'

'Before the time that souls were turned, when fit,   4
in dignity, for God, to this great mount,
my bones were buried by Octavian.

I am Vergilius. And for no crime,   7
save lack of faith, I lost the heavenly sky.'
This was the answer that my lord then gave.

Like someone on the sudden who, before   10
his eyes, sees what he can't help marvelling at,
can't credit it but does, and says 'It is . . . It's not . . .',

so did Sordello, and he bent his brow,   13
then, turning back to Virgil, flung once more
his arms round where inferiors embrace.

'You glory of the Latin race,' he said,   16
'through you our tongue was shown what it could do.
Eternal honour of where I, once, was.

What merit or what grace shows you to me?   19
If I am fit to listen to your words,
say – if you come from Hell – what cloister's yours.'

'Through all the circles of the grieving realm   22
I've come,' he answered him, 'and now I'm here.
A power in Heaven first moved me. So I come.

Through nothing I had done but what I'd *not*,   25
my sight lost that great Sun that you desire,
known too belatedly in time for me.

28   Luogo è là giù non tristo di martìri,
        ma di tenebre solo, ove i lamenti
        non suonan come guai, ma son sospiri.

31   Quivi sto io coi pargoli innocenti
        dai denti morsi de la morte avante
        che fosser da l'umana colpa essenti;

34   quivi sto io con quei che le tre sante
        virtù non si vestiro, e sanza vizio
        conobber l'altre e seguir tutte quante.

37   Ma se tu sai e puoi, alcuno indizio
        dà noi per che venir possiam più tosto
        là dove Purgatorio ha dritto inizio.'

40   Rispuose: 'Loco certo non c'è posto;
        licito m'è andar suso e intorno;
        per quanto ir posso, a guida mi t'accosto.

43   Ma vedi già come dichina il giorno,
        e andar sù di notte non si puote;
        però è buon pensar di bel soggiorno.

46   Anime sono a destra qua remote;
        se mi consenti, io ti merrò ad esse,
        e non sanza diletto ti fier note.'

49   'Com' è ciò?' fu risposto. 'Chi volesse
        salir di notte, fora elli impedito
        d'altrui, o non sarria ché non potesse?'

52   E 'l buon Sordello in terra fregò 'l dito,
        dicendo: 'Vedi? sola questa riga
        non varcheresti dopo 'l sol partito:

55   non però ch'altra cosa desse briga,
        che la notturna tenebra, ad ir suso;
        quella col nonpoder la voglia intriga.

58   Ben si poria con lei tornare in giuso
        e passeggiar la costa intorno errando,
        mentre che l'orizzonte il dì tien chiuso.'

61   Allora il mio segnor, quasi ammirando,
        'Menane,' disse, 'dunque là 've dici
        ch'aver si può diletto dimorando.'

There is a place down there not grim with pain   28
but only with sad shades whose deep laments
sound not as screams but melancholy sighs.

I take my place with children – innocents   31
in whom the bite of death set lethal teeth
before they'd been made free of human sin.

And there I stay with all who were not clothed   34
in those three holy virtues – though I knew,
and, guiltless, followed all the other four.

But give us – if you know and can – some sign   37
so we can come more quickly to the place
at which the proper Purgatory begins.'

He answered: 'No fixed ground is given us.   40
I am allowed to travel up and round.
As far as I can go, I'll be your guide.

But look! The day by now is going down.   43
And none by night can ever make the climb.
Better to think of some good resting place.

There are, towards the right, souls hidden here.   46
I'll lead you on to them, if you agree,
and you'll not want for pleasure, knowing them.'

'But how is that?' the answer came. 'Would those   49
who wished to make ascent at night be checked
by someone else, or simply lack the power?'

Sordello drew his finger on the ground,   52
saying – that good man – 'There! You see that line?
You could not cross it once the sun was down.

Not, though, because there's anything to bar   55
your going up, save shadows of the night.
It's that which knots the will in powerlessness.

We could, of course, descend and walk below   58
and, while the far horizons keep day shut,
wander and take a turn around the coast.

My lord, then, as though wondering at these words,   61
replied: 'So lead us on to where, you say,
it's possible to linger in delight.'

64   Poco allungati c'eravam di lici,
        quand' io m'accorsi che 'l monte era scemo,
        a guisa che i vallon li sceman quici.

67   'Colà,' disse quell' ombra, 'n'anderemo
        dove la costa face di sé grembo,
        e là il novo giorno attenderemo.'

70   Tra erto e piano era un sentiero schembo
        che ne condusse in fianco de la lacca,
        là dove più ch'a mezzo muore il lembo.

73   Oro e argento fine, cocco e biacca,
        indaco, legno lucido e sereno,
        fresco smeraldo in l'ora che si fiacca,

76   da l'erba e da li fior, dentr' a quel seno
        posti, ciascun saria di color vinto,
        come dal suo maggiore è vinto il meno.

79   Non avea pur natura ivi dipinto,
        ma di soavità di mille odori
        vi facea uno incognito e indistinto.

82   'Salve, Regina' in sul verde e 'n su' fiori
        quindi seder cantando anime vidi,
        che per la valle non parean di fuori.

85   'Prima che 'l poco sole omai s'annidi,'
        cominciò 'l Mantoan che ci avea vòlti,
        'tra color non vogliate ch'io vi guidi.

88   Di questo balzo meglio li atti e ' volti
        conoscerete voi di tutti quanti,
        che ne la lama giù tra essi accolti.

91   Colui che più siede alto e fa sembianti
        d'aver negletto ciò che far dovea,
        e che non move bocca a li altrui canti,

94   Rodolfo imperador fu, che potea
        sanar le piaghe c'hanno Italia morta,
        sì che tardi per altri si ricrea.

97   L'altro, che ne la vista lui conforta,
        resse la terra dove l'acqua nasce
        che Molta in Albia, e Albia in mar ne porta:

We'd only gone a little way from there   64
when, so I saw, the mountain hollowed out,
as, here, our valleys hollow earthly hills.

'Just over there!' the shade now said to us.   67
'We'll go to where the cliff has formed a lap,
and there await the coming of new day.'

Slanting between the level and the steep,   70
a tight path led us to the dale's low edge –
the bank's rim here diminishing to half.

Gold, finest silver, cochineal, white lead,   73 *
indigo, ebony polished to a sheen,
the freshest emeralds when they've just been split,

each in pure colour would be overcome   76
by all the flowers and grasses in that fold –
as by the greater any lesser is.

Nor had great nature worked in paint alone.   79
She also with a thousand perfumes wrought
a sweetness never known and indistinct.

'*Salve, Regina*'. on the flowering greens,   82
the souls, I saw, not seen beyond the vale,
all sat together as they sang this hymn.

'Until what little sun remains nests down,'   85
the Mantuan who'd led us there began,
'don't ask me to escort you down to them.

You'll better see by staying on this ledge   88
the faces, looks and gestures of these kings
than if you'd been received within their glade.

The one who's seated highest, and (in look)   91 *
neglected what his proper duty urged,
and does not move his lips while others sing,

was Rudolph who, as emperor, could have healed   94
the wounds that did Italia to death
so that no others will revive her soon.

The next, who seems to offer him support,   97
ruled in that country where those waters rise
that bear to Elbe the Moldau and the Elbe to sea.

100   Ottacchero ebbe nome, e ne le fasce
       fu meglio assai che Vincislao suo figlio
       barbuto, cui lussuria e ozio pasce.

103   E quel nasetto che stretto a consiglio
       par con colui c'ha sì benigno aspetto,
       morì fuggendo e disfiorando il giglio:

106   guardate là come si batte il petto!
       L'altro vedete c'ha fatto a la guancia
       de la sua palma, sospirando, letto.

109   Padre e suocero son del mal di Francia:
       sanno la vita sua viziata e lorda,
       e quindi viene il duol che sì li lancia.

112   Quel che par sì membruto e che s'accorda,
       cantando, con colui dal maschio naso,
       d'ogne valor portò cinta la corda;

115   e se re dopo lui fosse rimaso
       lo giovanetto che retro a lui siede,
       ben andava il valor di vaso in vaso,

118   che non si puote dir de l'altre rede:
       Iacomo e Federigo hanno i reami;
       del retaggio miglior nessun possiede.

121   Rade volte risurge per li rami
       l'umana probitate, e questo vole
       quei che la dà, perché da lui si chiami.

124   Anche al nasuto vanno mie parole
       non men ch'a l'altro, Pier, che con lui canta,
       onde Puglia e Proenza già si dole.

127   Tant' è del seme suo minor la pianta
       quanto, più che Beatrice e Margherita,
       Costanza di marito ancor si vanta.

130   Vedete il re de la semplice vita
       seder là solo, Arrigo d'Inghilterra:
       questi ha ne' rami suoi migliore uscita.

133   Quel che più basso tra costor s'atterra,
       guardando in suso, è Guiglielmo marchese,
       per cui e Alessandria e la sua guerra

136   fa pianger Monferrato e Canavese.'

His name was Ottakar – a better prince,   100
even when baby-clothed, than Wenceslaus,
his son who, bearded, grazed on lust and ease.

    And that one – button-nosed – who seems so caught   103
in conversation with the kind-faced man
died, fleeing, as he stripped the lily flower.

    Look at him! how he pounds on his own breast.   106
And see the next who's spread his palm to form
a bed on which to lay his sighing cheek.

    Father these are and in-law to the Ill   109
of France. His vicious, filthy life they know –
and hence the grief transfixing each alike.

    And that lord there – the burly type – who sings   112*
in concert with the one of manly nose,
bore, as his knightly belt, all worth and strength.

    And if that young boy sitting at his back   115
could still, succeeding him, have been the king,
true merit would have flowed from urn to urn –

    which none could argue of his other heirs.   118
For James and Frederick rule his kingdoms now
and no one holds his better heritage.

    It seldom happens that man's probity   121
will rise through every branch. He wills it thus,
so, given from beyond, it's known as His.

    These words go out to that one with the nose   124
no less than to Pier, who sings with him,
whom Puglia and Provence already mourn.

    The tree is that much less than its own seed,   127
as Constance can applaud her husband more
than Marguerite and Beatrice can.

    See there the monarch of the simple life,   130*
Henry of England, sitting all alone.
He in his branches comes much better off.

    The one among them lower, on the ground,   133
is Marquis William, looking to the heights.
For him, the wars of Alessandria

    make Canavese and Montferrat weep.   136

CANTO 8

1   Era già l'ora che volge il disio
ai navicanti e 'ntenerisce il core,
lo dì c'han detto ai dolci amici addio,

4   e che lo novo peregrin d'amore
punge, se ode squilla di lontano
che paia il giorno pianger che si more,

7   quand' io incominciai a render vano
l'udire e a mirare una de l'alme
surta, che l'ascoltar chiedea con mano.

10   Ella giunse e levò ambo le palme,
ficcando li occhi verso l'oriente,
come dicesse a Dio: 'D'altro non calme.'

13   'Te lucis ante' sì devotamente
le uscìo di bocca e con sì dolci note
che fece me a me uscir di mente,

16   e l'altre poi dolcemente e devote
seguitar lei per tutto l'inno intero,
avendo li occhi a le superne rote.

19   Aguzza qui, lettor, ben li occhi al vero,
ché 'l velo è ora ben tanto sottile,
certo, che 'l trapassar dentro è leggero.

22   Io vidi quello essercito gentile
tacito poscia riguardare in sùe,
quasi aspettando, palido e umìle,

25   e vidi uscir de l'alto e scender giùe
due angeli con due spade affocate,
tronche e private de le punte sue.

CANTO 8

It was, by now, the hour that turns to home   1
the longing thoughts of seamen, melting hearts
the day they've said goodbye to dearest friends,

    and when by love the pilgrim, new to this,   4
is pierced to hear, far off, the evening bell
that seems to mourn the dying of the day,

    as I began to blank my hearing out,   7
and gaze in wonder at a single soul
who, risen up, hand raised, asked all to hear.

    This soul, first, joined his palms then lifted them,   10
eyes fixed towards the orient, as though
to say to God: 'For nothing else I care.'

    '*Te lucis ante*' issued from his lips   13
with such devotion and each note so sweet
it made me wander out of conscious thought.

    Then, sweetly and devoutly, all the rest,   16
their eyes all turned to those supernal wheels,
picked up from him and sang the hymn in full.

    Reader, now fix a needle eye on truth.   19
The veil is, after all, so gauzy here
you'll thread it through as lightly as can be.

    I saw the noble army of those souls   22
in silence turn their gaze towards the sky –
as though awaiting something – meek and pale.

    And then I saw, descending from the height,   25
two angels with two swords, each flashing fire,
the point of each was blunt and broken off.

28 Verdi come fogliette pur mo nate
erano in veste, che da verdi penne
percosse traean dietro e ventilate.

31 L'un poco sovra noi a star si venne,
e l'altro scese in l'opposita sponda,
sì che la gente in mezzo si contenne.

34 Ben discernea in lor la testa bionda,
ma ne la faccia l'occhio si smarria,
come virtù ch'a troppo si confonda.

37 'Ambo vegnon del grembo di Maria,'
disse Sordello, 'a guardia de la valle,
per lo serpente che verrà vie via.'

40 Ond' io, che non sapeva per qual calle,
mi volsi intorno, e stretto m'accostai,
tutto gelato, a le fidate spalle.

43 E Sordello anco: 'Or avvalliamo omai
tra le grandi ombre, e parleremo ad esse;
grazioso fia lor vedervi assai.'

46 Solo tre passi credo ch'i' scendesse,
e fui di sotto, e vidi un che mirava
pur me, come conoscer mi volesse.

49 Temp' era già che l'aere s'annerava,
ma non sì che tra li occhi suoi e ' miei
non dichiarisse ciò che pria serrava.

52 Ver' me si fece, e io ver' lui mi fei:
giudice Nin gentil, quanto mi piacque
quando ti vidi non esser tra' rei!

55 Nullo bel salutar tra noi si tacque;
poi dimandò: 'Quant' è che tu venisti
a piè del monte per le lontane acque?'

58 'Oh!' diss' io lui, 'per entro i luoghi tristi
venni stamane, e sono in prima vita,
ancor che l'altra, sì andando, acquisti.'

61 E come fu la mia risposta udita,
Sordello ed elli in dietro si raccolse,
come gente di sùbito smarrita.

As green as are the freshest newborn leaves,   28
so were their garments, fanned by bright, green wings
which, drawn behind them, rustled as they beat.

One came to stand a little from our heads.   31
The other lighted on the farther bank.
The people, thus, were held between the two.

Their hair was blond. And this I clearly saw.   34
But looking at their faces, sight was lost –
as natural powers fail, tested to excess.

'These two,' as now Sordello said, 'have come   37
as guardians of the vale, from Mary's breast,
against the serpent who'll soon pass this way.'

I, ignorant of where the snake would come,   40
span all around and huddled closer up,
frozen with dread, to Virgil's trusted side.

Sordello once again spoke out: 'Let's go   43
and talk down there among those famous shades.
To see you will, for them, be welcome grace.'

Three paces only had I gone, perhaps,   46
and there I was. And one of them, I saw,
stared, wondering who I was, at me (yes, me!).

The time had come when air was turning black –   49
not yet so dark, though, that, between our eyes,
what was first had been locked up should not be clear.

He made towards me, as I did to him.   52
Noble judge Nino, how it pleased me then
to see you weren't among the guilty souls.

No courteous welcome now remained unsaid.   55
'How long,' he asked, 'since, over distant waves,
you reached the foothills that surround this shore?'

'Oh! Through unhappy regions,' I replied,   58
'I came at dawn. I'm still in my first life –
though travelling here, I gain the other, too.'

And once the meaning of my words was heard,   61
he (and Sordello, also) drew away,
as people do when suddenly confused.

64   L'uno a Virgilio e l'altro a un si volse
        che sedea lì, gridando: 'Sù, Currado!
        Vieni a veder che Dio per grazia volse!'

67   Poi, vòlto a me: 'Per quel singular grado
        che tu dei a colui che sì nasconde
        lo suo primo *perché* che non li è guado,

70   quando sarai di là da le larghe onde,
        dì a Giovanna mia che per me chiami
        là dove a li 'nnocenti si risponde.

73   Non credo che la sua madre più m'ami,
        poscia che trasmutò le bianche bende,
        le quai convien che, misera, ancora brami.

76   Per lei assai di lieve si comprende
        quanto in femmina foco d'amor dura,
        se l'occhio o 'l tatto spesso non l'accende.

79   Non le farà sì bella sepultura
        la vipera che ' Melanesi accampa,
        com' avria fatto il gallo di Gallura.'

82   Così dicea, segnato de la stampa
        nel suo aspetto di quel dritto zelo
        che misuratamente in core avvampa.

85   Li occhi miei ghiotti andavan pur al cielo,
        pur là dove le stelle son più tarde,
        sì come rota più presso a lo stelo.

88   E 'l duca mio: 'Figliuol, che là sù guarde?'
        E io a lui: 'A quelle tre facelle
        di che 'l polo di qua tutto quanto arde.'

91   Ond' elli a me: 'Le quattro chiare stelle
        che vedevi staman, son di là basse,
        e queste son salite ov' eran quelle.'

94   Com' ei parlava, e Sordello a sé il trasse,
        dicendo: 'Vedi là 'l nostro avversaro,'
        e drizzò il dito perché 'n là guardasse.

97   Da quella parte onde non ha riparo
        la picciola vallea, era una biscia,
        forse qual diede ad Eva il cibo amaro.

One turned to Virgil, while the other turned   64
to someone sitting there, and cried aloud:
'Conrad, get up! Just see what God's grace wills!'

Then facing me: 'I pray you – by the thanks,   67
so singular, you owe to Him who hides
His first "because" so none can pass that stream,

when once you're back beyond the far-flung sea,   70*
then tell my dear Giovanna she should call,
on my behalf, to where the pure are heard.

I do not think her mother loves me now.   73
For she has changed her widowhood's white veil –
which, wretchedly, she'll yearn for once again.

Because of her, one readily can see   76
how long the fire of love in women lasts,
if eye and touch don't often kindle it.

The viper of the Milanese camp   79
will make for her less splendid burial
than my Gallurian cockerel would have done.'

He said all this, his face marked by the stamp   82
of that true zeal that burned with measured flame
within him in his truest heart of hearts.

My eyes still, avidly, were on the skies   85
fixed where the stars ran slowest in their track,
as wheels do closest to the axle tree.

My guide: 'Dear son, what do you see up there?'   88
'Those three sharp torches,' I replied to him,
'with which the southern pole is all ablaze.'

His answer to me was: 'The four bright stars   91
that you saw just this morning sink down there.
And these have risen now to where they were.'

As he said this, Sordello drew him close,   94
saying: 'Look there! You see? Our enemy!'
He stretched his finger, showing where to look.

From that side where this little valley had   97
no sheltering barrier, a snake appeared,
perhaps like that which fed Eve bitter food.

100   Tra l'erba e ' fior venìa la mala striscia,
       volgendo ad ora ad or la testa, e 'l dosso
       leccando come bestia che si liscia.

103   Io non vidi, e però dicer non posso,
       come mosser li astor celestiali,
       ma vidi ben e l'uno e l'altro mosso.

106   Sentendo fender l'aere a le verdi ali,
       fuggì 'l serpente, e li angeli dier volta,
       suso a le poste rivolando iguali.

109   L'ombra che s'era al giudice raccolta
       quando chiamò, per tutto quello assalto
       punto non fu da me guardare sciolta.

112   'Se la lucerna che ti mena in alto
       truovi nel tuo arbitrio tanta cera
       quant' è mestiere infino al sommo smalto,'

115   cominciò ella, 'se novella vera
       di Val di Magra o di parte vicina
       sai, dillo a me, che già grande là era.

118   Fui chiamato Currado Malaspina;
       non son l'antico, ma di lui discesi;
       a' miei portai l'amor che qui raffina.'

121   'Oh!' diss' io lui, 'per li vostri paesi
       già mai non fui; ma dove si dimora
       per tutta Europa ch'ei non sien palesi?

124   La fama che la vostra casa onora,
       grida i segnori e grida la contrada,
       sì che ne sa chi non vi fu ancora;

127   e io vi giuro, s'io di sopra vada,
       che vostra gente onrata non si sfregia
       del pregio de la borsa e de la spada.

130   Uso e natura sì la privilegia
       che, perché il capo reo il mondo torca,
       sola va dritta e 'l mal cammin dispregia.'

133   Ed elli: 'Or va, ché 'l sol non si ricorca
       sette volte nel letto che 'l Montone
       con tutti e quattro i piè cuopre e inforca,

Through grass and flowers this evil smear came on,   100
rolling its head around from time to time,
licking its back as preening beasts will do.

I did not see – and so I cannot say –   103
how those celestial hawks began to move.
I did, though, see the motion that each made.

Sensing the air ripped open by green wings,   106
the serpent fled and both the angels turned,
flying at equal pace, to their high posts.

The shadow that had drawn, when called, towards   109*
the judge, had not, throughout this whole attack,
at any point released me from his gaze.

'May that great lamp that leads you to the height   112
discern in your free will sufficient wax
to light your way to that flower-studded peak,'

(so he began). 'If you have truthful news   115
of Val di Magra or the neighbouring place,
then tell me. I was once a great man there.

I was, by name, Currado Malaspina,   118
not the great ancient but of his descent.
I bore love – here refined – towards my kin.'

'Oh! I have never been,' I said, 'through lands   121
of yours. Yet who in Europe anywhere
is there to whom your name is not well known?

The fame that brings such lustre to your house   124
exalts your lords, exalts all your domains,
so that all know it, though they've not been there.

I swear to you (so may I reach the heights!)   127
that your much-honoured race goes still unstripped
of worthiness and prize in purse and sword.

Nature and how they act so honours them   130
that, though the world's vile head may twist awry,
they all walk straight, and scorn the evil way.'

And he: 'Go on like that. The sun won't sink   133
within the bed that Ram Stars – all four feet
astraddle – cover, more than seven times

136   che cotesta cortese oppinione
            ti fia chiavata in mezzo de la testa
            con maggior chiovi che d'altrui sermone,
139   se corso di giudicio non s'arresta.'

before the courtesy that you express   136
is nailed within the centre of your brain
with greater nails than hearsay brings to you –
    if judgement is not halted in its course.'   139

CANTO 9

1   La concubina di Titone antico
già s'imbiancava al balco d'oriente,
fuor de le braccia del suo dolce amico;

4   di gemme la sua fronte era lucente,
poste in figura del freddo animale
che con la coda percuote la gente;

7   e la notte, de' passi con che sale,
fatti avea due nel loco ov' eravamo,
e 'l terzo già chinava in giuso l'ale;

10   quand' io, che meco avea di quel d'Adamo,
vinto dal sonno, in su l'erba inchinai
là 've già tutti e cinque sedavamo.

13   Ne l'ora che comincia i tristi lai
la rondinella presso a la mattina,
forse a memoria de' suo' primi guai,

16   e che la mente nostra, peregrina
più da la carne e men da' pensier presa,
a le sue vision quasi è divina,

19   in sogno mi parea veder sospesa
un'aguglia nel ciel con penne d'oro,
con l'ali aperte e a calare intesa,

22   ed esser mi parea là dove fuoro
abbandonati i suoi da Ganimede,
quando fu ratto al sommo consistoro.

25   Fra me pensava: 'Forse questa fiede
pur qui per uso, e forse d'altro loco
disdegna di portarne suso in piede.'

CANTO 9

The concubine of timeworn Tithonus   1*
already on the eastern balcony,
out of her dear love's arms, was glimmering white.

Her forehead shone with gemstones in the form   4
of that chill animal, the Scorpion,
that strikes then stings us with its vicious tail.

The night which rises step by step had now,   7
where we'd arrived, advanced by two of these,
the third already lowering on the wing,

when I – some trace of Adam with me still –   10
conquered by sleep, bowed down towards the grass
where all the five of us had come to sit.

In that hour when the swallow, near to dawn,   13*
begins once more her long sad chant, perhaps
recalling all the miseries she'd borne,

and when our minds like hawks on foreign tracks   16*
furthest from flesh, least caught in their own thoughts,
are near divine in visions that they see,

as in some dream, there hovering, it seemed   19
I saw an eagle in the sky, with plumes of gold,
its wings wide spread, its purpose soon to swoop.

And I, it seemed to me, was where the kin   22
of Ganymede, when he was seized – swept up
towards the highest court – remained abandoned.

Just to myself, 'Perhaps,' I thought, 'this strikes   25*
only by habit here, perhaps it scorns
to carry things from elsewhere in its claws.'

28   Poi mi parea che, poi rotata un poco,
        terribil come fólgor discendesse
        e me rapisse suso infino al foco.

31   Ivi parea che ella e io ardesse,
        e sì lo 'ncendio imaginato cosse
        che convenne che 'l sonno si rompesse.

34   Non altrimenti Achille si riscosse,
        li occhi svegliati rivolgendo in giro
        e non sappiendo là dove si fosse,

37   quando la madre da Chirón a Schiro
        trafuggò lui dormendo in le sue braccia,
        là onde poi li Greci il dipartiro,

40   che mi scoss' io, sì come da la faccia
        mi fuggì 'l sonno, e diventa' ismorto,
        come fa l'uom che spaventato agghiaccia.

43   Dallato m'era solo il mio conforto,
        e 'l sole er' alto già più che due ore,
        e 'l viso m'era a la marina torto.

46   'Non aver tema,' disse il mio segnore;
        'fatti sicur, ché noi semo a buon punto;
        non stringer, ma rallarga ogne vigore.

49   Tu se' omai al Purgatorio giunto:
        vedi là il balzo che 'l chiude dintorno,
        vedi l'entrata là 've par digiunto.

52   Dianzi, ne l'alba che procede al giorno,
        quando l'anima tua dentro dormia
        sovra li fiori ond' è là giù addorno,

55   venne una donna, e disse: "I' son Lucia;
        lasciatemi pigliar costui che dorme:
        sì l'agevolerò per la sua via."

58   Sordel rimase e l'altre genti forme;
        ella ti tolse e, come 'l dì fu chiaro,
        sen venne suso, e io per le sue orme.

61   Qui ti posò, ma pria mi dimostraro
        li occhi suoi belli quella intrata aperta;
        poi ella e 'l sonno ad una se n'andaro.'

And then it seemed that, wheeling slightly round,   28
as terrible as lightning, down it struck
and tore me upwards to the sphere of fire.

And there the eagle and I, it seemed, both blazed.   31
And this imagined fire so scorched and seared
that, yielding, dreaming sleep just had to break.

Not very differently, Achilles woke,   34
his startled eyes now staring all around,
dazed, knowing nothing of where he might be,

his mother having fled with him asleep   37
within her arms from Chiron's care to Skyros.
(The Greeks would, after, make him leave that place.)

So too I shook myself as, from my face,   40
sleep fled, and deathly pale I then became,
turning, as terrified we do, to ice.

Beside me, there was only my great strength.   43
The sun by now was more than two hours high.
My eyes were turned back down towards the sea.

My lord said, 'Have no fear. Be confident.   46
For we have reached a good point in our way.
Do not hold back, but give your strengths free rein.

You've now arrived where Purgatory begins.   49
See over there the wall encircling it.
See there the portal where the wall is breached.

Just now, at dawn which comes before new day,   52
when still your soul was sleeping deep within,
couched on the flowers that ornament that place,

a lady came. She said, "I am Lucia.   55*
Let me take up the man who's sleeping there,
so I can make his journey easier."

Sordello and those noble forms stayed back.   58
She took you up and, once the day shone clear,
she came up here, I following in her steps.

She laid you down. But, first, her lovely eyes   61
displayed to me the entrance open there.
Then she and sleep that instant went away.'

64   A guisa d'uom che 'n dubbio si raccerta
e che muta in conforto sua paura
poi che la verità li è discoperta,

67   mi cambia' io; e come sanza cura
vide me 'l duca mio, su per lo balzo
si mosse, e io di rietro inver' l'altura.

70   Lettor, tu vedi ben com' io innalzo
la mia matera, e però con più arte
non ti maravigliar s' io la rincalzo.

73   Noi ci appressammo, ed eravamo in parte
che là dove pareami prima rotto,
pur come un fesso che muro diparte,

76   vidi una porta, e tre gradi di sotto
per gire ad essa, di color diversi,
e un portier ch'ancor non facea motto.

79   E come l'occhio più e più v'apersi,
vidil seder sovra 'l grado sovrano,
tal ne la faccia ch'io non lo soffersi;

82   e una spada nuda avea in mano,
che reflettea i raggi sì ver' noi,
ch'io dirizzava spesso il viso in vano.

85   'Dite costinci: che volete voi?'
cominciò elli a dire, 'ov' è la scorta?
Guardate che 'l venir sù non vi nòi.'

88   'Donna del ciel, di queste cose accorta,'
rispuose 'l mio maestro a lui, 'pur dianzi
ne disse: "Andate là: quivi è la porta."'

91   'Ed ella i passi vostri in bene avanzi,'
ricominciò il cortese portinaio:
'Venite dunque a' nostri gradi innanzi.'

94   Là ne venimmo; e lo scaglion primaio
bianco marmo era, sì pulito e terso
ch'io mi specchiai in esso qual io paio.

97   Era il secondo tinto più che perso,
d'una petrina ruvida e arsiccia,
crepata per lo lungo e per traverso.

As, doubting, people do when reassured –   64
changing to confidence the fears they had,
once what is true has been revealed to them –

so I, too, changed. And since my leader saw   67
that I had now no cares, he moved to climb,
with me behind him still, the wall towards its height.

You, reader, can now see how here I raise   70
the theme my verse attempts. Don't marvel, then,
if with more craft and art I strengthen it.

We now drew closer, and were in that part   73
where, first, as I had thought, a breach appeared,
as might some fissure that divides a wall.

And now I saw a gate and, leading there,   76
three steps beneath, each coloured differently,
and at that gate a guardian who spoke no word.

And as I opened more my eyes to this,   79
I saw him sitting on the highest stair.
His face was such I could not bear that light.

A naked sword he held within his hand   82
which so reflected sun rays back at me
that many times I fixed my eyes in vain.

'Speak from back there! And say what is your will.'   85
So he began. 'And tell me, where's your guide?
Take care, lest going up should cause you harm.'

'From Heaven, a lady, knowing all these things,   88
told us a short time past,' my teacher answered,
'"Go forward for the gate you seek is here."'

'May she advance your steps in doing well,'   91
once more the courteous guardian began:
'Come forward, therefore, to these stairs of ours.'

And there we came to them. The first great block   94
was marble, white, so burnished and so clean
that I as I appear was mirroired there.

The second, in its tint more dark than perse,   97
was rock – waste, rough to touch and scorched and dry,
cracked both across and upward to its height.

100   Lo terzo, che di sopra s'ammassiccia,
        porfido mi parea, sì fiammeggiante
        come sangue che fuor di vena spiccia.

103   Sovra questo tenea ambo le piante
        l'angel di Dio, sedendo in su la soglia
        che mi sembiava pietra di diamante.

106   Per li tre gradi sù di buona voglia
        mi trasse il duca mio, dicendo: 'Chiedi
        umilemente che 'l serrame scioglia.'

109   Divoto mi gittai a' santi piedi;
        misericordia chiesi e ch'el m'aprisse,
        ma pria nel petto tre volte mi diedi.

112   Sette *P* ne la fronte mi descrisse
        col punton de la spada, e: 'Fa che lavi,
        quando se' dentro, queste piaghe,' disse.

115   Cenere, o terra che secca si cavi,
        d'un color fora col suo vestimento;
        e di sotto da quel trasse due chiavi.

118   L'una era d'oro e l'altra era d'argento;
        pria con la bianca e poscia con la gialla
        fece a la porta sì ch'i' fu' contento.

121   'Quandunque l'una d'este chiavi falla,
        che non si volga dritta per la toppa,'
        diss' elli a noi, 'non s'apre questa calla.

124   Più cara è l'una; ma l'altra vuol troppa
        d'arte e d'ingegno avanti che diserri,
        perch' ella è quella che 'l nodo digroppa.

127   Da Pier le tegno; e dissemi ch'i' erri
        anzi ad aprir ch'a tenerla serrata,
        pur che la gente a' piedi mi s'atterri.'

130   Poi pinse l'uscio a la porta sacrata,
        dicendo: 'Intrate; ma facciovi accorti
        che di fuor torna chi 'n dietro si guata.'

133   E quando fuor ne' cardini distorti
        li spigoli di quella regge sacra,
        che di metallo son sonanti e forti,

The third, which, massively, weighed these two down,   100
was porphyry, it seemed, and flamed as bright
as fresh blood spurting from a severed vein.

And, on this third, the angel of the Lord   103
had placed both feet and sat across the threshold,
which, as it seemed, was adamantine stone.

Up these three steps, impelled by good intent,   106
my leader drew me, saying: 'Humbly ask
that he undo the lock that holds the door.'

I fell devoutly at his holy feet   109
and asked that he, for mercy, open it.
But, first, three times I beat upon my breast.

He then sketched seven 'Ps' across my brow,   112
written with sword point. 'When you're once within,
make sure,' he said, 'you go and wash these scars.'

The vestments that he wore would be, in hue,   115
the same as ash or soil when dug out dry.
Then from beneath his robes he drew two keys.

One key was silver and the other gold.   118*
With first the white, then yellow after that,
he worked the door so I was well content.

'Whenever either of these keys falls short   121
and fails to turn correctly in its lock,
this path,' he said, 'will not then open up.

One is more precious, but the other needs   124
much greater art and skill to make it turn.
This is the one that gets the knot undone.

From Peter I receive these keys – who said,   127
when penitents have bowed down to my feet,
"Err more in opening than in locking out."'

He pushed the panels of the sacred gate,   130
saying: 'Go in. But be aware of this,
that those who look behind return outside.'

And when the pivots of that sacred hall,   133
forged out of resonantly massive steel,
were wrenched around within their housing hinge,

136   non rugghiò sì né si mostrò sì acra
        Tarpea, come tolto le fu il buono
        Metello, per che poi rimase macra.

139   Io mi rivolsi attento al primo tuono,
        e 'Te deum laudamus' mi parea
        udire in voce mista al dolce suono.

142   Tale imagine a punto mi rendea
        ciò ch'io udiva, qual prender si suole
        quando a cantar con organi si stea,

145   ch'or sì or no s'intendon le parole.

no roar was heard, no harsher sound was made,   136*
by Tarpeian doors, when from them honest
Metellus was dragged – doors that were henceforth lean.

I turned, attentive when the thunder broke,   139*
and, seemingly, 'Te Deum laudamus'
was heard, as voices mixed in that sweet tune.

The sounds I heard brought back into my mind   142
the same impression that we often get
when organs play, accompanying a voice.

Now, yes, we hear the words; now, no, we don't.   145

CANTO 10

1   Poi fummo dentro al soglio de la porta,
       che 'l mal amor de l'anime disusa
       perché fa parer dritta la via torta,

4   sonando la senti' esser richiusa;
       e s'io avesse li occhi vòlti ad essa,
       qual fora stata al fallo degna scusa?

7   Noi salavam per una pietra fessa
       che si moveva e d'una e d'altra parte
       sì come l'onda che fugge e s'appressa.

10   'Qui si conviene usare un poco d'arte,'
       cominciò 'l duca mio, 'in accostarsi
       or quinci, or quindi al lato che si parte.'

13   E questo fece i nostri passi scarsi
       tanto che pria lo scemo de la luna
       rigiunse al letto suo per ricorcarsi

16   che noi fossimo fuor di quella cruna.
       Ma quando fummo liberi e aperti,
       sù dove il monte in dietro si rauna,

19   io stancato e amendue incerti
       di nostra via, restammo in su un piano
       solingo più che strade per diserti.

22   Da la sua sponda, ove confina il vano,
       al piè de l'alta ripa che pur sale,
       misurrebbe in tre volte un corpo umano;

25   e quanto l'occhio mio potea trar d'ale,
       or dal sinistro e or dal destro fianco,
       questa cornice mi parea cotale.

CANTO 10

Now, both within the threshold of that gate   1
(our souls won't use it, out of ill-bent love
which makes the crooked way, to us, seem straight)

I heard it closed, resoundingly, again.   4
Yet if I'd turned to set my eyes on that,
what adequate excuse could there have been?

We climbed now through a trough of fissured rock   7
that moved, on either side, this way and that,
as waves do, surging near, then running back.

'We'll need,' my lord began, 'a certain skill   10
to keep together tight against the curve
that, ebbing here and there, avoids the swell.'

This made our footsteps few and hesitant.   13
And so the moon, which now was on the wane,
had reached its bed, to lie once more at rest,

before we'd gone beyond that needle eye.   16
But once we did get free and opened up,
climbing to where the mountain gathered in –

I all worn out and both of us unsure   19
of where to make our way – we paused upon
a road far lonelier than any desert track.

If measured from the edge that marked the void,   22
towards the foot of that still-soaring mount,
the span would be three human body lengths.

And, be it to the left side or the right,   25
as far as eyesight could extend its wings,
the ledge, in circuit, seemed to me the same.

28   Là sù non eran mossi i piè nostri anco,
        quand' io conobbi quella ripa intorno
        che, dritta, di salita aveva manco,

31   esser di marmo candido e addorno
        d'intagli sì, che non pur Policleto
        ma la Natura lì avrebbe scorno.

34   L'angel che venne in terra col decreto
        de la molt' anni lagrimata pace,
        ch'aperse il ciel del suo lungo divieto,

37   dinanzi a noi pareva sì verace
        quivi intagliato in un atto soave,
        che non sembiava imagine che tace.

40   Giurato si saria ch'el dicesse 'Ave!'
        perché iv' era imaginata quella
        ch'ad aprir l'alto Amor volse la chiave,

43   e avea in atto impressa esta favella
        'Ecce ancilla Dei', propriamente
        come figura in cera si suggella.

46   'Non tener pur ad un loco la mente,'
        disse 'l dolce maestro, che m'avea
        da quella parte onde 'l cuore ha la gente.

49   Per ch'i' mi mossi col viso, e vedea
        di retro da Maria, da quella costa
        onde m'era colui che mi movea,

52   un'altra storia ne la roccia imposta;
        per ch'io varcai Virgilio, e fe'mi presso,
        acciò che fosse a li occhi miei disposta.

55   Era intagliato lì nel marmo stesso
        lo carro e 'buoi, traendo l'arca santa,
        per che si teme officio non commesso.

58   Dinanzi parea gente; e tutta quanta,
        partita in sette cori, a' due mie' sensi
        faceva dir l'un: 'No,' l'altro: 'Sì, canta.'

61   Similemente al fummo de li 'ncensi
        che v'era imaginato, li occhi e 'l naso
        e al sì e al no discordi fensi.

We'd still to move our feet towards those heights   28
when I perceived that, all around, the bank –
which, rising straight, lacked any upward route –

was marble, brilliant white, and all adorned   31*
with carved reliefs so fine that Polyclite,
or even Nature, would have there felt scorned.

The angel, reaching earth with that decree   34*
of peace – so wept-for over centuries –
which opened Heaven's long-forbidden gates,

appeared so truthfully before us now,   37
carved in a gesture of pure gentleness,
he did not seem an image keeping silence.

In truth, one might have said he spoke the '*Ave*'.   40
For in that image was the one who turned
the key that opened out the utmost Love.

And from her stance and bearing there shone out   43
(exactly as an imprint sealed in wax)
'*Ecce ancilla Dei*', word for word.

'Don't keep your mind fixed only on one part.'   46
These words my teacher gently spoke to me.
(I held him where all others have their heart.)

And so, in sight, I moved. And I could see,   49
behind Maria, on the side where he,
in urging me to make a move, now stood,

set in the rock, another narrative.   52
Passing by Virgil, I came near to that,
so that it stood displayed before my eyes.

Carved there – in marble, also – was the cart,   55*
with oxen, carrying the Holy Ark
(because of which we dread unsanctioned deeds).

Before the Ark were people, as it seemed,   58
gathered in seven choirs who made my sense –
hearing and sight – say, 'No', and, 'Yes, they sing.'

In that same way, the incense smoke, which there   61
was imaged, worked on eye and nose, so these
were not concordant as to 'no' and 'yes'.

64   Lì precedeva al benedetto vaso,
      trescando alzato, l'umile salmista,
      e più e men che re era in quel caso.

67   Di contra, effigiata ad una vista
      d'un gran palazzo, Micòl ammirava
      sì come donna dispettosa e trista.

70   I' mossi i piè del loco dov' io stava,
      per avvisar da presso un'altra istoria
      che di dietro a Micòl mi biancheggiava.

73   Quiv' era storiata l'alta gloria
      del roman principato, il cui valore
      mosse Gregorio a la sua gran vittoria:

76   i' dico di Traiano imperadore;
      e una vedovella li era al freno,
      di lagrime atteggiata e di dolore.

79   Intorno a lui parea calcato e pieno
      di cavalieri, e l'aguglie ne l'oro
      sovr' essi in vista al vento si movieno.

82   La miserella intra tutti costoro
      pareva dir: 'Segnor, fammi vendetta
      di mio figliuol ch'è morto, ond' io m'accoro!' –

85   ed elli a lei rispondere: 'Or aspetta
      tanto ch'i' torni' – e quella: 'Segnor mio,'
      come persona in cui dolor s'affretta,

88   'se tu non torni?' – ed ei: 'Chi fia dov' io,
      la ti farà' – ed ella: 'L'altrui bene
      a te che fia, se 'l tuo metti in oblio?' –

91   ond' elli: 'Or ti conforta; ch'ei convene
      ch'i' solva il mio dovere anzi ch'i' mova:
      giustizia vuole e pietà mi ritene.'

94   Colui che mai non vide cosa nova
      produsse esto visibile parlare,
      novello a noi perché qui non si trova.

97   Mentr' io mi dilettava di guardare
      l'imagini di tante umilitadi,
      e per lo fabbro loro a veder care,

Before that vessel of all holiness,   64
the humble psalmist danced, his robe tucked up –
both more and less than king in all of this.

Then Michal, opposite, was gazing down,   67
as from some window of the royal court,
an effigy of rancour and disdain.

I turned my feet away from where I'd stood   70
to note another story, close at hand,
its gleam beyond the 'Michal', showing white.

En-storied here was found the glorious deed   73 *
of that high prince of Rome whose prowess moved
Pope Gregory to win great victory.

I speak of Trajan, noble Emperor.   76
A widow there had snatched his horse's rein,
her gestures those of grief and bitter tears.

Around him, surging horsemen, as it seemed,   79
filled all the space. And eagles, wrought in gold,
were seen above, as moving in the wind.

The wretched widow, as these thronged around,   82
was saying, seemingly: 'My lord, avenge
my dearest son. He's dead. That is my heart-wound!'

He, seemingly, replied to her: 'Just wait.   85
I shall return.' And she: 'My lord' – as though
her agony were quickening all the more –

'but if you don't return?' And he: 'The one   88
who's where I am will act.' And she: 'How can
his good be yours when you forget your own?'

Then he: 'Be comforted. It's right that I   91
fulfil, before I move, what I should do.
Justice demands this, and compassion binds.'

The One who sees no thing that's new to Him   94
produced this form of discourse visible –
so new to us, so fresh since not found here.

While I, in all delight, still gazed upon   97
these images of great humility,
more precious being formed by that skilled hand.

100   'Ecco di qua, ma fanno i passi radi,'
       mormorava il poeta, 'molte genti:
       questi ne 'nvieranno a li alti gradi.'

103   Li occhi miei, ch'a mirare eran contenti
       per veder novitadi, ond' e' son vaghi,
       volgendosi ver' lui non furon lenti.

106   Non vo' però, lettor, che tu ti smaghi
       di buon proponimento per udire
       come Dio vuol che 'l debito si paghi.

109   Non attender la forma del martìre:
       pensa la succession, pensa ch'al peggio
       oltre la gran sentenza non può ire.

112   Io cominciai: 'Maestro, quel ch'io veggio
       muovere a noi, non mi sembian persone,
       e non so che, sì nel veder vaneggio.'

115   Ed elli a me: 'La grave condizione
       di lor tormento a terra li rannicchia,
       sì che ' miei occhi pria n'ebber tencione.

118   Ma guarda fiso là, e disviticchia
       col viso quel che vien sotto a quei sassi:
       già scorger puoi come ciascun si picchia.'

121   O superbi cristian, miseri lassi,
       che, de la vista de la mente infermi,
       fidanza avete ne' retrosi passi,

124   non v'accorgete voi che noi siam vermi
       nati a formar l'angelica farfalla
       che vola a la giustizia sanza schermi?

127   Di che l'animo vostro in alto galla,
       poi siete quasi antomata in difetto,
       sì come vermo in cui formazion falla?

130   Come per sostentar solaio o tetto
       per mensola talvolta una figura
       si vede giugner le ginocchia al petto,

133   la qual fa del non ver vera rancura
       nascere 'n chi la vede: così fatti
       vid' io color, quando puosi ben cura.

'Look over here! Although their pace is slow,   100
there are,' the poet murmured, 'people there,
a crowd who'll send us to the steps above.'

My eyes, entranced in wonder, longingly,   103
happily seeking yet new things to see,
turned round towards him, making no delay.

Yet, reader, I'd not have your minds bewitched,   106
hearing how God would have the debt repaid,
or drawn away from your best purposes.

Don't dwell upon the form their sufferings take.   109
Think of what follows, and that, come the worst,
it can't go on beyond the Judgement Day.

'Sir,' I began, 'it seems that what I see,   112
moving towards us, are not human forms.
I cannot tell. I rave. I look in vain.'

'Their grievous mode of punishment' (to me)   115
'so creases them and bends them to the ground
that my eyes, too, first fought at what they see.'

Look, though, and fix your gaze. Let sight untwist   118
the vines of what comes there beneath these stones.
You see already how each beats his breast.'

Proud Christians, wretched and – alas! – so tired,   121
who, feeble in your powers of mental sight,
place so much faith in your own backward tread,

do you not recognize that you are worms   124
born to become angelic butterflies
that fly to justice with no veil between?

Why is it that your thoughts float up so high?   127
You, with your faults, are little more than grubs,
chrysalides (no more!) that lack full form.

As sometimes, bracing up a roof or vault,   130
a figure will be seen as corbel stone
that, bending, joins its two knees to its chest,

at which there's born, in anyone who sees,   133
from this non-truth a truly harsh distress:
that's how I saw them when I gave them thought.

136   Vero è che più e meno eran contratti
        secondo ch'avien più e meno a dosso,
        e qual più pazienza avea ne li atti
139   piangendo parea dicer: 'Più non posso.'

The truth is each was hunched up, less and more,   136
according to his load, some more, some less.
The one who, from his actions, bore the most,
   appeared in tears to pant: 'I can't do more.'   139

CANTO 11

1   'O padre nostro che ne' cieli stai,
non circunscritto, ma per più amore
ch'ai primi effetti di là sù hai,

4   laudato sia 'l tuo nome e 'l tuo valore
da ogne creatura, com' è degno
di render grazie la tuo dolce vapore.

7   Vegna ver' noi la pace del tuo regno,
ché noi ad essa non potem da noi,
s'ella non vien, con tutto nostro ingegno.

10   Come del suo voler li angeli tuoi
fan sacrificio a te, cantando *osanna*,
così facciano li uomini de' suoi.

13   Dà oggi a noi la cotidiana manna,
sanza la qual per questo aspro diserto
a retro va chi più di gir s'affanna.

16   E come noi lo mal ch'avem sofferto
perdoniamo a ciascuno, e tu perdona
benigno, e non guardar lo nostro merto.

19   Nostra virtù, che di legger s'adona,
non spermentar con l'antico avversaro,
ma libera da lui che sì la sprona.

22   Quest' ultima preghiera, segnor caro,
già non si fa per noi, ché non bisogna,
ma per color che dietro a noi restaro.'

25   Così a sé e noi buona ramogna
quell' ombre orando, andavan sotto 'l pondo,
simile a quel che talvolta si sogna,

CANTO 11

'Our Father, dwelling in the heavenly spheres,   1
not circumscribed by these but through that love
which you bear more, on high, to primal things,

Your name, and all the prowess of your might,   4
be praised by every creature. It is fit
to pay all thanks to Your sweet forming power.

May peace, as in Your realm, come down to us.   7
For we ourselves cannot attain to that,
if come it doesn't – not with all our wit.

As all your angels make a sacrifice,   10
singing "*Osanna*", of their wills to you,
so, too, may men make sacrifice of theirs.

Give us this day the manna each day needs.   13
Without that, exiled in this grinding waste,
all travel backwards who strive forwards most.

And just as we, to everyone, forgive   16
the harm we bear, grant generous pardon, too.
And do not look upon what we deserve.

The powers we have (so easily subdued)   19
do not make trial of through the ancient foe,
but free us from the one who is our goad.

This final prayer is made, O dearest Lord,   22
not for ourselves (we now have no such need).
We speak for those behind us, who've remained.'

Then praying, for themselves and us, 'God speed',   25
these shadows made their way beneath such loads
as sometimes in our nightmares can be seen,

28   disparmente angosciate tutte a tondo
        e lasse su per la prima cornice,
        purgando la caligine del mondo.

31   Se di là sempre ben per noi si dice,
        da qua che dire e far per lor si puote
        da quei c'hanno al voler buona radice?

34   Ben si de' loro atar lavar le note
        che portar quinci, sì che mondi e lievi
        possano uscire a le stellate ruote.

37   'Deh, se giustizia e pietà vi disgrievi
        tosto sì che possiate muover l'ala,
        che secondo il disio vostro vi lievi,

40   mostrate da qual mano inver' la scala
        si va più corto; e se c'è più d'un varco,
        quel ne 'nsegnate che men erto cala,

43   ché questi che vien meco, per lo 'ncarco
        de la carne d'Adamo onde si veste,
        al montar sù, contra sua voglia, è parco.'

46   Le lor parole che rendero a queste
        che dette avea colui cu' io seguiva
        non fur da cui venisser manifeste,

49   ma fu detto: 'A man destra per la riva
        con noi venite, e troverete il passo
        possibile a salir persona viva.

52   E s'io non fossi impedito dal sasso
        che la cervice mia superba doma,
        onde portar convienmi il viso basso,

55   cotesti, ch'ancor vive e non si noma,
        guardere' io, per veder s'i' 'l conosco
        e per farlo pietoso a questa soma.

58   Io fui latino e nato d'un gran Tosco:
        Guiglielmo Aldobrandesco fu mio padre;
        non so se 'l nome suo già mai fu vosco.

61   L'antico sangue e l'opere leggiadre
        d'i miei maggior me fer sì arrogante
        che, non pensando a la comune madre,

around and all around on that first ledge,   28
worn-out, tormented (though each differently),
purging away the murky fogs of earth.

If they, in that place, always speak our good,   31
down here what can be said and done for them,
by those whose wills are good in where they root?

We surely ought to help them cleanse the marks   34
that they bore hence – till, light in weight and pure,
they've power to rise towards the wheeling stars.

'May justice and compassion soon relieve   37
this weight from you, so you may move your wings,
which then, as you desire, may lighten you!

So, too, point out to us, to left or right,   40
the shortest way to go towards the stair.
If more than one, teach us the least steep slope.

For this man here who comes along with me,   43
burdened in being clothed with Adam's flesh,
is loath to climb, despite the will to do.'

The words that came, responding now to those   46
that he whom I was following first spoke,
rose from some source not clearly manifest.

But this was said: 'Turn right, and come with us   49
along the bank. You'll find an upward path
where even living persons can ascend.

And were I not impeded by this stone   52
that tames the hauteur of my once-proud neck –
so I am bound to keep my head held low –

I'd raise my eyes to look at this man here –   55
alive still, though unnamed – in case I knew him,
and make him look in pity on my load.

I was Italian, bred of Tuscan stock.   58
Aldobrandesco was my noble sire.
I don't know if his name was known to you.

The ancient lineage and courtly airs   61
of my great forebears wrought such pride in me
that, heedless of the mother we all share,

64   ogn' uomo ebbi in despetto tanto avante
      ch'io ne mori', come i Sanesi sanno,
      e sallo in Campagnatico ogne fante.

67   Io sono Omberto; e non pur a me danno
      superbia fe', ché tutti miei consorti
      ha ella tratti seco nel malanno.

70   E qui convien ch'io questo peso porti
      per lei, tanto che a Dio si sodisfaccia,
      poi ch'io nol fe' tra ' vivi, qui tra ' morti.'

73   Ascoltando chinai in giù la faccia;
      e un di lor, non questi che parlava,
      si torse sotto il peso che li 'mpaccia

76   e videmi e conobbemi e chiamava,
      tenendo li occhi con fatica fisi
      a me che tutto chin con loro andava.

79   'Oh!' diss' io lui, 'non se' tu Oderisi,
      l'onor d'Agobbio e l'onor di quell'arte
      ch'alluminar chiamata è in Parisi?'

82   'Frate,' diss' elli, 'più ridon le carte
      che pennelleggia Franco Bolognese;
      l'onore è tutto or suo, e mio in parte.

85   Ben non sare' io stato sì cortese
      mentre ch'io vissi, per lo gran disio
      de l'eccellenza ove mio core intese.

88   Di tal superbia qui si paga il fio;
      e ancor non sarei qui, se non fosse
      che, possendo peccar, mi volsi a Dio.

91   Oh vana gloria de l'umane posse!
      com' poco verde in su la cima dura,
      se non è giunta da l'etati grosse!

94   Credette Cimabue ne la pittura
      tener lo campo, e ora ha Giotto il grido,
      sì che la fama di colui è scura.

97   Così ha tolto l'uno a l'altro Guido
      la gloria de la lingua, e forse è nato
      chi l'uno e l'altro caccerà del nido.

I so disdained all other men, I died   64
because of that. The Sienese know this,
as do the squads in Campagnatico.

I am Omberto, and my arrogance   67
did harm to me, but not to me alone,
for all my peers were victims of that bane.

Because of this, till God is satisfied,   70
I needs must bear this weight among the dead –
since I did *not* while still with those who live.'

Still listening, I had kept my face bowed low.   73
And one of them – not he who spoke these words –
twisted beneath the load that bore him down.

He saw and recognized, then called to me,   76
holding his eyes, with effort, firmly fixed
on me, bowed down, who went along with him.

'Oh! Aren't you Oderisi?' I replied.   79*
'Great Gubbio's glory, glory of that art,
known to Parisians as design-in-light?'

'Dear man,' he said, 'those pages smile far more   82
that Franco Bolognese smoothly pens.
The honour is all his – and, partly, mine.

Yet while I lived, I'd not, you may be sure,   85
have shown such courtesy. My heart's desire
was excellence. I yearned for that alone.

For arrogance like this one pays a fee.   88
And I'd still not be here if I had not,
while having power to sin, turned back to God.

Oh, what vaingETlorying in human powers!   91*
How short a time the green lasts on the height
unless some cruder, darker age succeeds.

Once, as a painter, Cimabue thought   94
he took the prize. Now "Giotto" is on all lips
and Cimabue's fame is quite eclipsed.

In verse, as well, a second Guido steals   97
all glory from the first. And someone's born,
who'll thrust, perhaps, both Guidos from the nest.

100   Non è il mondan romore altro ch'un fiato
di vento, ch'or vien quinci e or vien quindi,
e muta nome perché muta lato.

103   Che voce avrai tu più, se vecchia scindi
da te la carne, che se fossi morto
anzi che tu lasciassi il "pappo" e 'l "dindi",

106   pria che passin mill' anni? ch'è più corto
spazio a l'etterno ch'un muover di ciglia
al cerchio che più tardi in cielo è torto.

109   Colui che del cammin sì poco piglia
dinanzi a me Toscana sonò tutta;
e ora a pena in Siena sen pispiglia,

112   ond' era sire quando fu distrutta
la rabbia fiorentina, che superba
fu a quel tempo sì com' ora è putta.

115   La vostra nominanza è color d'erba
che viene e va, e quei la discolora
per cui ella esce de la terra acerba.'

118   E io a lui: 'Tuo vero dir m'incora
bona umiltà, e gran tumor m'appiani;
ma chi è quei di cui tu parlavi ora?'

121   'Quelli è,' rispuose, 'Provenzan Salvani,
ed è qui perché fu presuntuoso
a recar Siena tutta a le sue mani.

124   Ito è così e va, sanza riposo,
poi che morì; cotal moneta rende
a sodisfar chi è di là troppo oso.'

127   E io: 'Se quello spirito ch'attende,
pria che si penta, l'orlo de la vita
là giù dimora e qua sù non ascende,

130   se buona orazion lui non aita,
prima che passi tempo quanto visse,
come fu la venuta lui largita?'

133   'Quando vivea più glorioso,' disse,
'liberamente nel Campo di Siena,
ogne vergogna diposta, s'affisse;

The roar of earthly fame is just a breath   100
of wind, blowing from here and then from there,
that changes name in changing origin.

What more renown will you have if you strip   103*
your flesh in age away than if you died
before you'd left off lisping "Din-dins!", "Penth!"

when once a thousand years have passed, a space   106
that falls far short of all eternity –
an eye blink to the slowest turning sphere.

He who, ahead of me, takes such brief strides   109
is one with whom all Tuscany once rang.
His name's now scarcely whispered in Siena,

where he was Lord when Florence, running wild –   112
as proud at that time as it's whorelike now –
was left destroyed and ravaged by the war.

All your renown is coloured like the grass,   115
which comes then goes. And He discolours it
who made it first appear from bitter earth.'

And I to him: 'Your words in truth give heart   118
to good humility, and puncture pride.
But who's this man of whom you spoke just now?'

'Provenzan Salvani' (the answer was).   121
'And he is here because he proudly claimed
to hold Siena wholly in his hands.

And since his death, he's walked as now he walks, 124
without repose. Like all who down there dared,
he pays his debts in full with such-like cash.

And I: 'If any spirit who delays   127
repentance to life's final verge is bound
to dwell below the gate and not ascend

(unless good prayers on his behalf bring aid)   130
until it's passed as much time as it lived,
how was it granted him that he should come?'

'When he could boast, in life, most glorious fame, 133
freely he took a stand,' the answer was,
'in Campo di Siena, free from shame,

136   e lì, per trar l'amico suo di pena
        ch'e' sostenea ne la prigion di Carlo,
        si condusse a tremar per ogne vena.

139   Più non dirò, e scuro so che parlo,
        ma poco tempo andrà, che ' tuoi vicini
        faranno sì che tu potrai chiosarlo.

142   Quest'opera li tolse quei confini.'

and there, to save his friend the punishment –   136
incurred in his imprisonment to Charles –
he brought himself to tremble down each vein.

    I'll say no more (I know I speak dark words,   139
But little time will pass till those near you
will act in ways that mean you can explain).

    Provenzan's deed removed him from those bounds.'   142

CANTO 12

1   Di pari, come buoi che vanno a giogo,
m'andava io con quell' anima carca,
fin che 'l sofferse il dolce pedagogo.

4   Ma quando disse: 'Lascia lui e varca;
ché qui è buon con la vela e coi remi,
quantunque può, ciascun pinger sua barca,'

7   dritto sì come andar vuolsi rife'mi
con la persona, avvegna che i pensieri
mi rimanessero e chinati e scemi.

10 Io m'era mosso, e seguia volontieri
del mio maestro i passi, e amendue
già mostravam com' eravam leggeri;

13 ed el mi disse: 'Volgi li occhi in giùe:
buon ti sarà, per tranquillar la via,
veder lo letto de le piante tue.'

16 Come, perché di lor memoria sia,
sovra i sepolti le tombe terragne
portan segnato quel ch'elli eran pria,

19 onde lì molte volte si ripiagne
per la puntura de la rimembranza,
che solo a' pii dà de le calcagne:

22 sì vid' io lì – ma di miglior sembianza
secondo l'artificio – figurato
quanto per via di fuor del monte avanza.

25 Vedea colui che fu nobil creato
più ch'altra creatura, giù dal cielo
folgoreggiando scender, da l'un lato.

CANTO 12

Paired up, like oxen yoked to move as one,   1
so onward with that burdened soul I went,
as long as he – my dear, kind sir – allowed.

But then he said: 'Leave him and go beyond.   4
The best thing is that each here drives along
his craft, by oar or sail, as best he can.'

I made myself (as, walking, one must do)   7
in person stand up straight. And yet my thoughts
remained in me stripped bare, reduced, bowed low.

I'd now moved on, and followed willingly   10
the footsteps of my teacher. And we two
already showed how light in tread we were.

And then he said: 'Just turn your eyes down there.   13
That will be good for you, to ease the way.
See there the bed on which your paces rest.

Compare: to serve as some memorial   16
for those entombed beneath, our earthly graves
bear signs of what they had been when alive –

at which it often happens that we weep,   19
responding to the spur of memories
which only strike the heel of pious minds.

I now saw carvings there – though finer, far,   22
considering the hand that crafted them –
along the path the mountain cliffs had left.

Mark now, to this side I here saw the one   25 *
nobler-created than all creatures else,
thrown down in flashing thunder fire from Heaven.

28   Vedea Briareo, fitto dal telo
        celestial, giacer da l'altra parte
        grave a la terra per lo mortal gelo.

31   Vedea Timbreo, vedea Pallade e Marte,
        armati ancora, intorno al padre loro,
        mirar le membra d'i Giganti sparte.

34   Vedea Nembròt a piè del gran lavoro,
        quasi smarrito, e riguardar le genti
        che 'n Sennaàr con lui superbi fuoro.

37   O Niobè, con che occhi dolenti
        vedea io te segnata in su la strada,
        tra sette e sette tuoi figliuoli spenti!

40   O Saùl, come in su la propria spada
        quivi parevi morto in Gelboè,
        che poi non sentì pioggia né rugiada!

43   O folle Aragne, sì vedea io te
        già mezza ragna, trista in su li stracci
        de l'opera che mal per te si fé!

46   O Roboàm, già non par che minacci
        quivi 'l tuo segno, ma pien di spavento:
        nel porta un carro, sanza ch'altri il cacci.

49   Mostrava ancor lo duro pavimento
        come Almeon a sua madre fé caro
        parer lo sventurato addornamento.

52   Mostrava come i figli si gittaro
        sovra Sennacherìb dentro dal tempio
        e come, morto lui, quivi il lasciaro.

55   Mostrava la ruina e 'l crudo scempio
        che fé Tamiri, quando disse a Ciro:
        'Sangue sitisti, e io di sangue t'empio.'

58   Mostrava come in rotta si fuggiro
        li Assiri poi che fu morto Oloferne,
        e anche le reliquie del martiro.

61   Vedeva Troia in cenere e in caverne:
        o Iliòn, come te basso e vile
        mostrava il segno che lì si discerne!

Mark this, I witnessed on the other side,   28
pierced by the spear celestial, Briareus,
heavy on earth, laid low in deathly chill.

Mark this, I saw Timbreus, still in arms,   31
and Mars and Pallas round their father's side,
amazed to see the scattered Giantbones.

Mark this, I saw, beneath the tower he'd made,   34
Nimrod, as in confusion. All the tribe
of Shinar – arrogant as him – gazed on.

Ah! Niobe I saw. With grieving eyes,   37
I traced your outline carved within that road,
among your children – seven, then seven – slain.

Ah! Saul, it seemed that you were there, as dead,   40
pierced on Gilboa's hill with your own sword,
feeling no longer showers of rain or dew.

Ah! Mad Arachne, how I saw you there   43
half-turned to spider and the work in shreds
which, once attempted, brought you so much harm.

Ah! Rehoboam, as you're there portrayed,   46
you're not, now, menacing, but full of dread.
A chariot bears you off, though none gives chase.

Now also shown on that hard floor was how   49
Alcmaeon made the fatal ornament
that cost his treacherous mother very dear.

Now was displayed how Sennacherib's sons   52
flung themselves at him in the temple hall,
and how, once dead, they left him there alone.

Now there appeared the chaos, crude and cruel,   55
wrought by Thamyris, who to Cyrus said:
'You thirst for blood. With blood I'll feed you full!'

Now, fleeing, the Assyrians were shown –   58
routed when Holofernes met his death –
and showed the relics of his mortal pain.

Mark this, I saw Troy's ash and hollowed stone.   61
Ah, Ilion! How humbled and how vile,
Now picked out in those signs, you seemed to be!

64   Qual di pennel fu maestro o di stile
        che ritraesse l'ombre e ' tratti ch'ivi
        mirar farieno uno ingegno sottile?

67   Morti li morti e i vivi parean vivi:
        non vide mei di me chi vide il vero
        quant' io calcai, fin che chinato givi.

70   Or superbite, e via col viso altero,
        figliuoli d'Eva: e non chinate il volto
        sì che veggiate il vostro mal sentero!

73   Più era già per noi del monte vòlto,
        e del cammin del sole assai più speso,
        che non stimava l'animo non sciolto,

76   quando colui che sempre innanzi atteso
        andava, cominciò: 'Drizza la testa;
        non è più tempo di gir sì sospeso.

79   Vedi colà un angel che s'appresta
        per venir verso noi, vedi che torna
        dal servigio del dì l'ancella sesta.

82   Di reverenza il viso e li atti addorna,
        sì che i diletti lo 'nviarci in suso;
        pensa che questo dì mai non raggiorna!'

85   Io era ben del suo ammonir uso
        pur di non perder tempo, sì che 'n quella
        materia non potea parlarmi chiuso.

88   A noi venìa la creatura bella,
        biancovestito e ne la faccia quale
        par tremolando mattutina stella.

91   Le braccia aperse, e indi aperse l'ale;
        disse: 'Venite: qui son presso i gradi,
        e agevolemente omai si sale.

94   A questo invito vegnon molto radi:
        o gente umana, per volar sù nata,
        perché a poco vento così cadi?'

97   Menocci ove la roccia era tagliata;
        quivi mi batté l'ali per la fronte;
        poi mi promise sicura l'andata.

What master of the pencil or the brush   64
could reproduce those shadows and those strokes
which, there, would make the sharpest mind admire?

The dead seemed dead, the living seemed alive.   67
And all I trod upon – bowed low – I saw
far truer than had those who'd seen it true.

Strut on, you sons of Eve, with head held high.   70
Display your pride, and do not bend your face
to see the errors of your evil way!

We'd made more distance round the mountainside   73
(spending more time than mind, still bound, supposed,
in following the track the sun observes)

when he – who always kept his mind ahead –   76
began: 'Now straighten up, and lift your brows.
The moment's passed to go caught up like this.

See? Over there! An angel quickens pace.   79
It comes our way. Come! See! See, too, the hour,
sixth handmaid of the day, already turns.

Adorn your eyes and acts with reverence,   82
so he, to his delight, may speed our climb.
Think! This same day will never dawn again.'

I was well used to his admonishments –   85
always 'to waste no time'. So, as to that,
the words he spoke could hardly be obscure.

To us that lovely creature now advanced,   88
white-vestitured, in countenance, it seems,
trembling in air as does the morning star.

Opening his arms, then opening his wings,   91
he said: 'Now come. The steps are very near,
and now the climb could not be easier.

Men, though invited, come too rarely here.   94
O human nature! You are born to fly!
Why fail and fall at, merely, puffs of wind?'

He lead us where the cleft was in the rock.   97
And here he struck his wings across my brow,
then promised me the way ahead was safe.

100   Come a man destra, per salire al monte
        dove siede la chiesa che soggioga
        la ben guidata sopra Rubaconte,

103   si rompe del montar l'ardita foga
        per le scalee che si fero ad etade
        ch'era sicuro il quaderno e la doga:

106   così s'allenta la ripa che cade
        quivi ben ratta da l'altro girone;
        ma quinci e quindi l'alta pietra rade.

109   Noi volgendo ivi le nostre persone,
        'Beati pauperes spiritu!' voci
        cantaron sì che nol diria sermone.

112   Ahi quanto son diverse quelle foci
        da l'infernali! ché quivi per canti
        s'entra, e là giù per lamenti feroci.

115   Già montavam su per li scaglion santi
        ed esser mi parea troppo più lieve
        che per lo pian non mi parea davanti.

118   Ond' io: 'Maestro, dì, qual cosa greve
        levata s'è da me, che nulla quasi
        per me fatica, andando, si riceve?'

121   Rispuose: 'Quando i P che son rimasi
        ancor nel volto tuo, presso che stinti,
        saranno, come l'un, del tutto rasi,

124   fier li tuoi piè dal buon voler sì vinti
        che non pur non fatica sentiranno,
        ma fia diletto loro esser sù pinti.'

127   Allor fec' io come color che vanno
        con cosa in capo non da lor saputa,
        se non che ' cenni altrui sospecciar fanno,

130   per che la mano ad accertar s'aiuta,
        e cerca e truova e quello officio adempie
        che non si può fornir per la veduta:

133   e con le dita de la destra scempie
        trovai pur sei le lettere che 'ncise
        quel da le chiavi a me sovra le tempie,

136   a che guardando, il mio duca sorrise.

Compare: to scale the hill towards that church   100*
which dominates the city (so well-ruled!)
that stands around the Rubaconte bridge,

rightwards the vaunting angle of the climb   103
is broken by a stairway built in times
when chronicles and balances were true.

Like this, the bank which falls so steeply here   106
from where the next ring stands was gradual,
though all around the high rock shaved its sides.

While turning (we two persons) to that slope   109*
voices sang out: 'Beati pauperes',
as no mere speech could properly relate.

How different from the thoroughfares of Hell   112
are those through which we passed. For here with songs
we enter, there with fierce lamentations.

We were, by now, ascending that great stair.   115
And I, it seemed, was lighter now by far
than I had seemed while still on level ground.

So, 'Tell me, sir,' I said, 'what weight has now   118
been lifted from me, so I almost feel
no strain at all in walking on my way?'

He answered: 'When the "P"s that mark your brow,   121
remaining still, though growing now more faint,
have all (as is the first) been sheared away,

your steps will then be conquered by good will   124
and, being thus impelled towards the heights,
will feel no strain but only sheer delight.'

And then I did what anyone would do   127
with something on their head – they can't tell what –
but, seeing people point, peer up suspiciously,

then raise a hand to help them be quite sure,   130
to search around, to find and do the job
that sight had been unable to complete.

So now my right-hand fingers found reduced   133
the letters there inscribed to merely six
of those the angel with the keys had cut.

My leader, watching as I did so, smiled.   136

CANTO 13

1   Noi eravamo al sommo de la scala,
dove secondamente si risega
lo monte che salendo altrui dismala.

4   Ivi così una cornice lega
dintorno il poggio come la primaia,
se non che l'arco suo più tosto piega.

7   Ombra non li è nè segno che si paia:
parsi la ripa e parsi la via schietta
col livido color de la petraia.

10   'Se qui per dimandar gente s'aspetta,'
ragionava il poeta, 'io temo forse
che troppo avrà d'indugio nostra eletta.'

13   Poi fisamente al sole li occhi porse;
fece del destro lato a muover centro,
e la sinistra parte di sé torse.

16   'O dolce lume a cui fidanza i' entro
per lo novo cammin, tu ne conduci,'
dicea, 'come condur si vuol quinc' entro.

19   Tu scaldi il mondo, tu sovr' esso luci:
s'altra ragione in contrario non ponta,
esser dien sempre li tuoi raggi duci.'

22   Quanto di qua per un migliaio si conta,
tanto di là eravam noi già iti,
con poco tempo, per la voglia pronta;

25   e verso noi volar furon sentiti,
non però visti, spiriti parlando
a la mensa d'amor cortesi inviti.

CANTO 13

We now were at the summit of the stair.   1
The mountain there – which, as one climbs, takes ill
away – is chiselled back a second time.

  And so there's, here, a ledge around the slope,   4
which binds it, as the first ledge also did,
except that now the arc curves faster in.

  Shade? There's none here, nor any sign to see.   7
The cliffs show bare. The path looks shorn of marks,
save only for its stones of liverish blue.

  'I fear,' the poet said, considering this,   10
'our choice of route may well be long delayed
if we wait here for someone we can ask.'

  Firmly, he fixed his eyes towards the sun.   13
He made a fulcrum of his right-hand side,
and moved his left around that central point.

  'You, sweetest light, in trusting you I now,'   16
he said, 'embark upon this strange new road.
Guide us, as guidance must be here required.

  You warm the world. You shine out over it.   19
Your rays, where counter reasons have no weight,
must always lead with their authority.'

  The distance of a mile (as earth miles count)   22
we travelled now from where we'd been before –
our will so quick – in little time at all.

  Then, unseen, flying towards us were heard   25
the voices of spirits, all delivering
a courteous welcome to the feast of love.

28   La prima voce che passò volando
      'Vinum non habent!' altamente disse
      e dietro a noi l'andò reiterando.

31   E prima che del tutto non si udisse
      per allungarsi, un altra 'I' sono Oreste!'
      passò gridando, e anco non s'affisse.

34   'Oh!' diss' io, 'padre, che voci son queste?'
      E com' io domandai, ecco la terza
      dicendo: 'Amate da cui male aveste!'

37   E 'l buon maestro: 'Questo cinghio sferza
      la colpa de la invidia, e però sono
      tratte d'amor le corde de la ferza.

40   Lo fren vuol esser del contrario suono;
      credo che l'udirai, per mio avviso,
      prima che giunghi al passo del perdono.

43   Ma ficca li occhi per l'aere ben fiso,
      e vedrai gente innanzi a noi sedersi,
      e ciascun è lungo la grotta assiso.'

46   Allora più che prima li occhi apersi;
      guarda'mi innanzi e vidi ombre con manti
      al color de la pietra non diversi.

49   E poi che fummo un poco più avanti,
      udia gridar: 'Maria, ora per noi!'
      gridar 'Michele!' e 'Pietro!' e 'Tutti santi!'

52   Non credo che per terra vada ancoi
      omo sì duro che non fosse punto
      per compassion di quel ch'i' vidi poi,

55   ché, quando fui sì presso di lor giunto
      che li atti loro a me venivan certi,
      per li occhi fui di grave dolor munto.

58   Di vil ciliccio mi parean coperti,
      e l'un sofferia l'altro con la spalla,
      e tutti da la ripa eran sofferti.

61   Così li ciechi a cui la roba falla
      stanno a' perdoni a chieder lor bisogna,
      e l'uno il capo sopra a l'altro avvalla

The first voice, fleeting past, declared aloud,   28*
'*Vinum non habent*!' ('Look, they have no wine!'),
and then went on behind us, echoing that.

And then, before it wholly was not heard,   31
so distancing, another voice went by,
declared, '*I'm* Orestes!' and did not stay.

'Father,' I said, 'what voices can these be   34
and, as I asked, there came – just look! – a third,
saying: 'Love those by whom you suffer harm.'

'This confine scourges,' my good teacher said,   37
'the sin of envious hate. And so the skeins
that form the stinging lash vibrate with love.

The bridle will elicit different notes.   40
And these, I think, as far as I can tell,
you'll hear before you reach the pardon-pass.

But fix your eyes intently through the air.   43
You'll see some people sitting there ahead,
each in their place along the mountain wall.'

My eyes far wider than before, I looked   46
and saw in front of us a group of shades,
their cloaks in hue no different from the rock.

And when we were a little further on,   49
I heard them calling: 'Mary, pray for us.'
'Michael!' they cried. 'Saint Peter! All the saints!'

I can't believe that anyone on earth   52
could be so hard that pity, at the sight
that I saw now, would not have pierced him through.

For when at last I'd come up close to them,   55
and saw for certain what these people did,
I spurted from my eyes the milk of grief.

A poor hair shirt appeared to blanket each.   58
Each let the other lean against his side,
and all were let to lean against the cliff.

In that same way, the blind, for lack of things,   61
stand begging for their needs on Pardon Days,
the head of one bent low above the next,

64   perché 'n altrui pietà tosto si pogna,
      non pur per lo sonar de le parole
      ma per la vista, che non meno agogna.

67   E come a li orbi non approda il sole,
      così a l'ombre quivi ond' io parlo ora
      luce del ciel di sé largir non vole:

70   ché a tutti un fil di ferro i cigli fóra
      e cusce, sì come a sparvier selvaggio
      si fa però che queto non dimora.

73   A me pareva, andando, fare oltraggio
      veggendo altrui, non essendo veduto:
      per ch'io mi volsi al mio consiglio saggio.

76   Ben sapev' ei che volea dir lo muto,
      e però non attese mia dimanda
      ma disse: 'Parla, e sie breve e arguto.'

79   Virgilio mi venìa da quella banda
      de la cornice onde cader si puote,
      perché da nulla sponda s'inghirlanda;

82   da l'altra parte m'eran le divote
      ombre, che per l'orribile costura
      premevan sì che bagnavan le gote.

85   Volsimi a loro, e: 'O gente sicura,'
      incominciai, 'di veder l'alto Lume
      che 'l disio vostro solo ha in sua cura,

88   se tosto grazia resolva le schiume
      di vostra coscienza, sì che chiaro
      per essa scenda de la mente il fiume,

91   ditemi, ché mi fia grazioso e caro,
      s'anima è qui tra voi che sia latina,
      e forse lei sarà buon s'i' l'apparo.'

94   'O frate mio, ciascuna è cittadina
      d'una vera città; ma tu vuo' dire
      che vivesse in Italia peregrina.'

97   Questo mi parve per risposta udire
      più innanzi alquanto che là dov' io stava,
      ond' io mi feci ancor più là sentire.

to gain from others pity for their plight   64
not only through the sound of their sad words
but also through the sight, which ached no less.

　　And as the sun grants nothing to the blind,   67
so, to the shadows that I speak of now,
the light of heaven bestowed no generous ray.

　　For all their eyelids, pierced by iron wires,   70
were sewn up like an untamed sparrow hawk's
when, restively, it won't keep calm and still.

　　To me, it seemed an outrage to walk by   73
seeing those others who did not see me.
And so I turned to where wise counsels were.

　　He knew full well what, mute, I meant to say.   76
And so he did not wait to hear my words.
'Speak out,' he said, 'but briefly, to the point.'

　　Virgil beside me took the outer strip   79
(where, since there is no verge to garland it,
one might too easily have tumbled down)

　　while, on my other side, in constant prayer,   82
were shadows who, through dreadful sutures, squeezed
a press of tears to rinse and bathe their cheeks.

　　To these I turned. 'You, who are confident,'   85
so I began, 'to see the Light Supreme –
which your desires are set upon alone –

　　may grace soon clarify the scum that blurs   88
your consciences, and let the streams of mind descend –
with all of memory's power – through you once more.

　　Tell me – I'd hold your answer very dear –   91
if any soul among you is Italian.
It may, if I hear that, go well for him.'

　　'We are, dear brother, now all citizens   94
of one true place. But you must mean:
". . . who winged his pilgrim life through Italy".'

　　This, in reply, I seemed to hear proceed   97
from somewhere just ahead of where I stood.
So further on I made my voice be heard.

100   Tra l'altre vidi un'ombra ch'aspettava
           in vista; e se volesse alcun dir 'Come?'
           lo mento a guisa d'orbo in sù levava.

103   'Spirto,' diss' io, 'che per salir ti dome,
           se tu se' quelli che mi rispondesti,
           fammiti conto o per luogo o per nome.'

106   'Io fui sanese,' rispuose, 'e con questi
           altri rimendo qui la vita ria,
           lagrimando a colui che sé ne presti.

109   Savia non fui, avvegna che Sapìa
           fossi chiamata, e fui de l'altrui danni
           più lieta assai che di ventura mia.

112   E perché tu non creda ch'io t'inganni,
           odi s'i' fui, com' io ti dico, folle,
           già discendendo l'arco d'i miei anni.

115   Eran li cittadin miei presso a Colle
           in campo giunti co' loro avversari,
           e io pregava Iddio di quel ch'e' volle.

118   Rotti fuor quivi e vòlti ne li amari
           passi di fuga; e veggendo la caccia,
           letizia presi a tutte altre dispari,

121   tanto ch'io volsi in sù l'ardita faccia,
           gridando a Dio: "Omai più non ti temo!"
           come fé 'l merlo per poca bonaccia.

124   Pace volli con Dio in su lo stremo
           de la mia vita, e ancor non sarebbe
           lo mio dover per penitenza scemo,

127   se ciò non fosse ch'a memoria m'ebbe
           Pier Pettinaio in sue sante orazioni,
           a cui di me per caritate increbbe.

130   Ma tu chi se', che nostre condizioni
           vai dimandando, e porti li occhi sciolti,
           sì com' io credo, e spirando ragioni?'

133   'Li occhi,' diss' io, 'mi fieno ancor qui tolti,
           ma picciol tempo, ché poca è l'offesa
           fatta per esser con invidia vòlti.

Among the rest, I saw a shadow seem   100
to wait as though to say to me, 'Well, how?'
tilting its chin up as the sightless do.

'Spirit,' I said, 'you train yourself to rise.   103
If you're the one who just replied to me,
then make it known. Tell me your name and place.'

'I' (so the answer came) 'was Sienese,   106
and here repair the wicked life I led,
weeping so He will grant Himself to us.

Sapia (though not sapient) I was called.   109
And I, to witness other people's harm,
felt joy far more than at my own good luck.

Listen. Don't think that this is mere deceit.   112
Was I (then sinking down my arc of years)
as crazy as I've said I was, or not?

My fellow Sienese near Colle cliff   115
were joined in battle with their enemies.
And God, I prayed, would do what He then did.

Routed here, shattered, they'd turned in bitter   118
footfalls of flight. And, seeing them hunted,
sheer happiness seized me, beyond compare,

so great I turned my reckless face on high,   121*
yelling at God: "I'll fear you never more!" –
just like the blackbird in a sunny spell.

Then, coming to the utmost edge of life,   124
I sought my peace with God. And even now,
my dues would not, in penance, have been paid

had I not been remembered in the prayers   127*
that Peter Pettinaio so devoutly made
in heartfelt charity on my behalf.

But who are you, to make your way round here   130
inquiring as to us – with, still, I'm sure,
your eyes unbound, and breathing when you speak?'

'My eyes,' I said, 'will only briefly here   133
be taken from me. For the harm is small
that they, pursuing envy, might have done.

136   Troppa è più la paura ond' è sospesa
l'anima mia del tormento di sotto,
che già lo 'ncarco di là giù mi pesa.'

139   Ed ella a me: 'Chi t'ha dunque condotto
qua sù tra noi, se giù ritornar credi?'
E io: 'Costui ch'è meco e non fa motto.

142   E vivo sono; e però mi richiedi,
spirito eletto, se tu vuo' ch'i' mova
di là per te ancor li mortai piedi.'

145   'Oh, questa è a udir sì cosa nuova,'
rispuose, 'che gran segno è che Dio t'ami;
però col priego tuo talor mi giova.

148   E cheggioti per quel che tu più brami,
se mai calchi la terra di Toscana,
che a' miei propinqui tu ben mi rinfami.

151   Tu li vedrai tra quella gente vana
che spera in Talamone, e perderagli
più di speranza ch'a trovar la Diana;

154   ma più vi perderanno li ammiragli.'

Far greater fear holds sway within my soul   136
of tortures suffered on the ridge below.
The burdens of that place already press.'

And she: 'Who, then, has led you up to us,   139
when you are certain that you'll head back down?'
'This one,' I said, 'with me, who speaks no word.

I am alive. And so please ask of me,   142
you chosen spirit, if you'd have me move
my living tread on earth to serve your needs.'

'Well, that's,' she said, 'a strange new thing to hear,   145
a great sign of the love God bears to you.
Do help me sometimes when you say your prayers.

I beg of you, by that for which you yearn,   148
if you should ever tread on Tuscan soil,
make my name good for those most near to me.

You'll find them with that empty-headed crowd   151*
whose hopes are set on Talamone's port.
They'll lose more there than tracing Dian's source.

The venturers, though, will come off much the worse.'   154

CANTO 14

1   'Chi è costui che 'l nostro monte cerchia
     prima che morte li abbia dato il volo,
     e apre li occhi a sua voglia e coverchia?'

4   'Non so chi sia, ma so che non è solo;
     domandal tu che più li t'avvicini,
     e dolcemente, sì che parli, acco'lo.'

7   Così due spirti, l'uno a l'altro chini,
     ragionavan di me ivi a man dritta;
     poi fer li visi, per dirmi, supini,

10   e disse l'uno: 'O anima che fitta
     nel corpo ancora inver' lo ciel ten vai,
     per carità ne consola e ne ditta

13   onde vieni e chi se'; ché tu ne fai
     tanto maravigliar de la tua grazia
     quanto vuol cosa che non fu più mai.'

16   E io: 'Per mezza Toscana si spazia
     un fiumicel che nasce in Falterona,
     e cento miglia di corso nol sazia.

19   Di sovr' esso rech' io questa persona;
     dirvi chi sia saria parlare indarno,
     ché 'l nome mio ancor molto non suona.'

22   'Se ben lo 'ntendimento tuo accarno
     con lo 'ntelletto,' allora mi rispuose
     quei che diceva pria, 'tu parli d'Arno.'

25   E l'altro disse lui: 'Perché nascose
     questi il vocabol di quella riviera,
     pur com' om fa de l'orribili cose?'

CANTO 14

'Who's this one here who's circling round our Hill   1
before Death's given him the right to fly,
opening his eyes and closing them at will?'

    'I don't know who, but know he's not alone.   4
You ask, since you are closer up to him.
And treat him gently so he'll speak to us.'

    Two spirits – each one leaning on the next –   7*
thus talked about me on the right-hand side,
then laid their heads back to have words with me.

    And one now said: 'O you, that soul who goes,   10
still fixed in mortal limb, towards the skies,
gives us, in charity, some ease and say

    what place you're from, and who it is you are.   13
You make us marvel at the grace you've gained –
as much as *must* be at things never known.'

    And I: 'Through Tuscany, a ranging stream   16*
cuts down from Falterona where it's born –
its course not sated for a hundred miles.

    I bring this body from that river's bank.   19
There'd be no point in saying who I am.
My name, as yet, produces no great sound.'

    'If, in my thoughts, I swoop on what you mean,'   22
he then replied to me (the first to speak),
'you are, I take it, talking of the Arno.'

    'But why,' the other asked, 'did he then hide   25
the name that designates that flowing stream,
as people do with something that they dread?'

28   E l'ombra che di ciò domandata era
si sdebitò così: 'Non so, ma degno
ben è che 'l nome di tal valle pèra:

31   ché dal principio suo, ov' è sì pregno
l'alpestro monte ond' è tronco Peloro
che 'n pochi luoghi passa oltra quel segno,

34   infin là 've si rende per ristoro
di quel che 'l ciel de la marina asciuga,
ond' hanno i fiumi ciò che va con loro,

37   vertù così per nimica si fuga
da tutti come biscia, o per sventura
del luogo o per mal uso che li fruga;

40   ond' hanno sì mutata lor natura
li abitator de la misera valle,
che par che Circe li avesse in pastura.

43   Tra brutti porci, più degni di galle
che d'altro cibo fatto in uman uso,
dirizza prima il suo povero calle.

46   Botoli trova poi, venendo giuso,
ringhiosi più che non chiede lor possa,
e da lor disdegnosa torce il muso.

49   Vassi caggendo, e quant' ella più 'ngrossa,
tanto più trova di can farsi lupi
la maladetta e sventurata fossa.

52   Discesa poi per più pelaghi cupi,
trova le volpi, sì piene di froda
che non temono ingegno che le occùpi.

55   Né lascerò di dir perch' altri m'oda;
e buon sarà costui, s'ancor s'ammenta
di ciò che vero spirto mi disnoda.

58   Io veggio tuo nepote che diventa
cacciator di quei lupi in su la riva
del fiero fiume, e tutti li sgomenta.

61   Vende la carne loro essendo viva;
poscia li ancide come antica belva;
molti di vita e sé di pregio priva.

To which, in offering a due reply,   28
that shade first-questioned answered: 'I don't know.
It's right, though, that that valley's name should die.

For from its origin, where those sheer hills   31*
(Pelorus was dissevered from that chain)
that breed more streams than many others do,

down to the estuary where yet once more   34
it pays back what the skies dry from the sea
(rivers derive their onward spate from that)

virtue is fled by all – an enemy!   37
a hateful snake! – either because that place
is fated so, or pierced by wickedness.

The people dwelling in that wretched vale   40*
are changed in nature to the point at which
it seems that Circe might provide their swill.

Through brute swine, firstly, who far more deserve   43
acorns for food than any human dish,
it points the channel of its meagre path.

Then, coming down, it lights on mongrel dogs   46
snarling far worse than ever they can bite.
From these it turns its snout in high disdain.

So ever downwards – and the more it swells   49
so much the more does this accursed ditch
hit upon bitches now transformed to wolves.

Then, having sunk through many a stagnant lake,   52
it finds out foxes that, so full of guile,
fear not at all that they might be out-tricked.

Nor shall I cease to speak since this one hears.   55
It will be good for him if he attends
to what true spirit here unknots for me.

I see your little nephew now become   58
a hunter of those wolf packs on the bank
of that fierce stream, and he confounds them all.

He sells their flesh while this is still alive,   61
then slays them like mere cattle past their prime.
Many of life, himself of praise he robs.

64   Sanguinoso esce de la trista selva;
        lasciala tal che di qui a mille anni
        ne lo stato primaio non si rinselva.'

67   Com' a l'annunzio di dogliosi danni
        si turba il viso di colui ch'ascolta,
        da qual che parte il periglio l'assanni:

70   così vid' io l'altr' anima, che volta
        stava a udir, turbarsi e farsi trista
        poi ch'ebbe la parola a sé raccolta.

73   Lo dir de l'una e de l'altra la vista
        mi fer voglioso di saper lor nomi,
        e dimanda ne fei con prieghi mista;

76   per che lo spirto che di pria parlòmi
        ricominciò: 'Tu vuo' ch'io mi deduca
        nel fare a te ciò che tu far non vuo'mi.

79   Ma da che Dio in te vuol che traluca
        tanto sua grazia, non ti sarò scarso:
        però sappi ch'io fui Guido del Duca.

82   Fu il sangue mio d'invidia sì riarso
        che, se veduto avesse uom farsi lieto,
        visto m'avresti di livore sparso:

85   di mia semente cotal paglia mieto.
        O gente umana, perché poni 'l core
        là 'v' è mestier di consorte divieto?

88   Questi è Rinier, questi è 'l pregio e l'onore
        de la casa da Calboli, ove nullo
        fatto s'è reda poi del suo valore.

91   E non pur lo suo sangue è fatto brullo,
        tra 'l Po e 'l monte e la marina e 'l Reno,
        del ben richesto al vero e al trastullo:

94   ché dentro a questi termini è ripieno
        di venenosi sterpi, sì che tardi
        per coltivare omai verrebber meno.

97   Ov' è 'l buon Lizio e Arrigo Mainardi?
        Pier Traversaro e Guido di Carpigna?
        Oh Romagnuoli tornati in bastardi!

He comes out bloodied from that dismal wood,   64
and leaves it so, a thousand years from now,
it won't rebranch and reach its primal state.'

As at announcements of some grievous harm,   67
whatever side the fangs of peril strike,
the faces of those listening will grow grim,

so did I see that other soul, who'd turned,   70
setting his mind to hear, cloud and grow sad,
in garnering up these words to his own heart.

The speech of one and how the other looked   73
made me the keener to be told their names,
and so, with prayers as well, I made request.

At which the spirit who first spoke to me   76
began once more: 'You'd have me bring myself
to do for you what you'll not do for me.

But since God wills that such great grace should shine   79
through all your being, I'll not grudge you this.
Know, then, that I was Guido del Duca.

My blood so fired itself with envious thoughts   82
that, if I saw some man transformed by joy,
you'd then have seen me flushed to liver green.

From such a sowing I now reap the straw.   85
You human creatures, why repose your hearts
where you are banned from mutual exchange?

This is Rinieri of the Calboli –   88
the honour of that House, their pride. No one
lays claim, as heir, to all his proven worth.

Nor has his blood alone – between the Po,   91
the hill, the sea and Reno – turned to waste,
stripped of the good that truth and pleasure need.

For all within these confines now is full   94
of poisonous thickets, so it's now too late
for cultivation to reduce their grip.

Where is good Lizio, Arrigo Mainardi?   97*
Pier Traversaro and Guido di Carpigna?
Oh, Romagnuoli, you're all bastards now.

100   Quando in Bologna un Fabbro si ralligna?
       quando in Faenza un Bernardin di Fosco,
       verga gentil di picciola gramigna?

103   Non ti maravigliar s'io piango, Tosco,
       quando rimembro, con Guido da Prata,
       Ugolin d'Azzo che vivette nosco,

106   Federigo Tignoso e sua brigata,
       la casa Traversara e li Anastagi
       (e l'una gente e l'altra è diretata),

109   le donne e ' cavalier, li affanni e li agi
       che ne 'nvogliava amore e cortesia
       là dove i cuor son fatti sì malvagi.

112   O Bretinoro, ché non fuggi via,
       poi che gita se n'è la tua famiglia
       e molta gente per non esser ria?

115   Ben fa Bagnacaval, che non rifiglia;
       e mal fa Castrocaro, e peggio Conio,
       che di figliar tai conti più s'impiglia.

118   Ben faranno i Pagan da che 'l demonio
       lor sen girà, ma non però che puro
       già mai rimagna d'essi testimonio.

121   O Ugolin de' Fantolin, sicuro
       è 'l nome tuo, da che più non s'aspetta
       chi far lo possa, tralignando, scuro.

124   Ma va via, Tosco, omai, ch'or mi diletta
       troppo di pianger più che di parlare,
       sì m'ha nostra ragion la mente stretta.'

127   Noi sapavam che quell' anime care
       ci sentivano andar; però, tacendo,
       facean noi del cammin confidare.

130   Poi fummo fatti soli procedendo,
       folgore parve, quando l'aere fende,
       voce che giunse di contra, dicendo:

133   'Ancideràmmi qualunque m'apprende!'
       e fuggì come tuon che si dilegua,
       se sùbito la nuvola scoscende.

When in Bologna is a Fabbro bred?   100
When in Faience a Bernadin di Fosco
(branching so nobly from mere creeping weeds)?

Don't marvel, Tuscan, if you see me weep   103
when I call back to mind, with Guido Prata,
Ugolin d'Azzo (who once lived with us),

Frederick Tignoso and his circle, too,   106
the Traversara house, the Anastagians,
(these last two having no descendants now),

the knights and ladies, all the toil and ease   109
that love and courtesy once made us seek,
where now all hearts are criminal and base.

O Bretinoro, why not take to heel,   112*
since your whole family has gone its way,
as others do, eluding vice and ignominy.

Bagnacaval, it's good you don't re-child,   115
and bad for Castrocaro – far worse Conio! –
so tangled up in childing worthless lords.

The clan Pagani, once their demon's gone,   118
will do quite well, but not so well that pure
account of them will ever now remain.

O Ugolino of the Fantolines,   121
your name is safe since none, demeaning you,
is now expected who could dim your fame.

But, Tuscan, you had better pass along.   124
To weep delights me more than words now can.
This talk has wrung my mind with such distress.'

We knew those well-loved souls could hear our tread. 127
Therefore, their silence, as we went our way,
gave us the confidence to take that path.

So, going on, when once we were alone,   130
just like a thunder bolt that rends the air,
a voice rang out towards us, saying this:

'They'll murder me whoever captures me!'   133*
then fled like thunder when it fades away,
the clouds abruptly being torn apart.

136   Come da lei l'udir nostro ebbe triegua,
        ed ecco l'altra con sì gran fracasso
        che somigliò tonar che tosto segua:

139   'Io sono Aglauro, che divenni sasso!'
        e allor, per ristringermi al poeta,
        in destro feci, e non innanzi, il passo.

142   Già era l'aura d'ogne parte queta;
        ed el mi disse: 'Quel fu 'l duro camo
        che dovria l'uom tener dentro a sua meta.

145   Ma voi prendete l'esca, sì che l'amo
        de l'antico avversaro a sé vi tira,
        e però poco val freno o richiamo.

148   Chiamavi 'l cielo e 'ntorno vi si gira,
        mostrandovi le sue bellezze etterne,
        e l'occhio vostro pur a terra mira:

151   onde vi batte chi tutto discerne.'

Then, as our hearing gained some peace from that –   136
just see! – a second with as great a crash
seemed then at once to follow that first peal.

'I am Aglauros, who became a stone!'   139
And then, to get up closer to the poet,
I stepped not forwards but towards the right.

The air was quiet now on every side   142
and, 'That was the restraint' (so Virgil said)
'that ought to keep mankind within due bounds.

You take the bait, though. So the well-barbed hook   145
of our old enemy will draw you in.
And that's why checks and lures have little power.

The heavens wheel around and summon you,   148
displaying to your eyes eternal charms.
Yet your gaze fixes merely on the ground.

For that, He strikes you down who sees all clear.'   151

CANTO 15

1   Quanto tra l'ultimar de l'ora terza
      e 'l principio del dì par de la spera
      che sempre a guisa di fanciullo scherza,

4   tanto pareva già inver' la sera
      essere al sol del suo corso rimaso:
      vespero là, e qui mezza notte era.

7   E i raggi ne ferien per mezzo 'l naso,
      perché per noi girato era sì 'l monte
      che già dritti andavamo inver' l'occaso,

10   quand' io senti' a me gravar la fronte
      a lo splendore assai più che di prima,
      e stupor m'eran le cose non conte;

13   ond' io levai le mani inver' la cima
      de le mie ciglia e fecimi 'l solecchio,
      che del soverchio visibile lima.

16   Come quando da l'acqua o da lo specchio
      salta lo raggio a l'opposta parte,
      salendo su per lo modo parecchio

19   a quel che scende, e tanto si diparte
      dal cader de la pietra in igual tratta,
      sì come mostra esperïenza e arte:

22   così mi parve da luce rifratta
      quivi dinanzi a me esser percosso,
      per che a fuggir la mia vista fu ratta.

25   'Che è quel, dolce padre, a che non posso
      schermar lo viso tanto che mi vaglia,'
      diss' io, 'e pare inver' noi esser mosso?'

CANTO 15

As much time as the childlike circle plays   1*
between the third hour at its ultimate
and when the day had first begun to rise,

remained, it seemed – till evening – for the sun   4
to travel and complete its onward way.
There it was vespers (midnight in our clime).

The sun's rays struck us straight along the nose.   7
For now the mountain had, by us, been turned
so that we went direct towards the west.

But then I felt my forehead weighted down   10
by splendour far more bright than first there'd been.
It dazed me, wondering at these untold things.

And so, towards the peak of my two brows   13
I raised my hands and shaped myself a shield
to pare these too great visibles away.

Compare: from water or reflective glass   16*
a ray of light leaps back as opposite,
rising exactly in the same degree

(as tests and theory demonstrate) against   19
a plumb-stone line as when it first descends,
equal as measured from that vertical.

It seemed that I was struck by some such light   22
that broke, reflected back, ahead of me,
causing my eyes, in flight, to speed away.

'My gentle father, what is this?' I said.   25
'I can't protect my eyes from it enough.
It moves, it seems, towards us all the time.'

28   'Non ti maravigliar s'ancor t'abbaglia
         la famiglia del cielo,' a me rispuose;
         'messo è che viene ad invitar ch'om saglia.

31   Tosto sarà ch'a veder queste cose
         non ti fia grave, ma fieti diletto
         quanto natura a sentir ti dispuose.'

34   Poi giunti fummo a l'angel benedetto,
         con lieta voce disse: 'Intrate quinci
         ad un scaleo vie men che li altri eretto.'

37   Noi montavam, già partiti di linci,
         e 'Beati misericordes!' fue
         cantato retro, e 'Godi, tu che vinci!'

40   Lo mio maestro e io soli amendue
         suso andavarmo; e io pensai, andando,
         prode acquistar ne le parole sue;

43   e drizza'mi a lui, sì dimandando:
         'Che volse dir lo spirto di Romagna,
         e "divieto" e "consorte" menzionando?'

46   Per ch'elli a me: 'Di sua maggior magagna
         conosce il danno, e però non s'ammiri
         se ne riprende perché men si piagna.

49   Perchè s'appuntano i vostri disiri
         dove per compagnia parte si scema,
         invidia move il mantaco a' sospiri.

52   Ma se l'amor de la spera supprema
         torcesse in suso il disiderio vostro,
         non vi sarebbe al petto quella tema:

55   ché, per quanti si dice più lì "nostro",
         tanto possiede più di ben ciascuno,
         e più di caritate arde in quel chiostro.'

58   'Io son d'esser contento più digiuno,'
         diss' io, 'che se mi fosse pria taciuto,
         e più di dubbio ne la mente aduno.

61   Com' esser puote ch'un ben, distribuito
         in più possedítor, faccia più ricchi
         di sé che se da pochi è posseduto?'

'Don't marvel,' he replied to me, 'if still   28
the family of the heavens bedazzle you.
This comes as messenger, to bid us climb.

And soon to see such things as these will bring   31
not stupor, but delight to you as great
as you by nature are disposed to feel.'

And when we'd come to where the angel was,   34
the blessed creature said in tones of joy:
'Enter this stair – less steep than those before.'

And climbing now (the angel left below)   37*
behind us, 'Beati misericordes!'
and 'Rejoice! You conqueror!' were sung.

Together, my teacher and I alone   40
proceeded upward and, while going on,
I thought I'd gain some profit from his words,

so turned to him, demanding he should say: 43
'What did that spirit of Romagna mean
to speak of "mutual exchange" and "bans"?'

'He knows the damage done by his main flaw.   46
Don't therefore be surprised,' he said, 'if he
chides us, to lessen penitential tears.

Because your human longings point to where   49
portions grow smaller in shared fellowship,
meanness of mind must make the bellows sigh.

If love, though, seeking for the utmost sphere,   52
should ever wrench your longings to the skies,
such fears would have no place within your breast.

For, there, the more that we can speak of "ours",   55
the more each one possesses of the good
and, in that cloister, caritas burns brighter.'

'I hunger more for satisfaction now   58
than if,' I said, 'you'd not said anything.
I gather in my mind still greater doubt.

How can it be that good distributed   61
to many owners makes, in that respect,
each one far richer than if few had shared?'

64   Ed elli a me: 'Però che tu rificchi
         la mente pur a le cose terrene,
         di vera luce tenebre dispicchi.

67   Quello infinito e ineffabil Bene
         che là sù è, così corre ad amore
         com' a lucido corpo raggio vène.

70   Tanto si dà quanto trova d'ardore,
         sì che quantunque carità si stende,
         cresce sovr' essa l'etterno Valore.

73   E quanta gente più là sù s'intende,
         più v'è da bene amare, e più vi s'ama,
         e come specchio l'uno a l'altro rende.

76   E se la mia ragion non ti disfama,
         vedrai Beatrice, ed ella pienamente
         ti torrà questa e ciascun' altra brama.

79   Procaccia pur che tosto sieno spente,
         come son già le due, le cinque piaghe
         che si richiudon per esser dolente.'

82   Com' io voleva dicer: 'Tu m'appaghe,'
         vidimi giunto in su l'altro girone,
         sì che tacer mi fer le luci vaghe.

85   Ivi mi parve in una visione
         estatica di sùbito esser tratto
         e vedere in un tempio più persone,

88   e una donna, in su l'entrar, con atto
         dolce di madre, dicer: 'Figliuol mio,
         perché hai tu così verso noi fatto?

91   Ecco, dolenti, lo tuo padre e io
         ti cercavamo.' E come qui si tacque,
         ciò che pareva prima, dispario.

94   Indi m'apparve un'altra, con quell'acque
         giù per le gote che 'l dolor distilla
         quando di gran dispetto in altrui nacque,

97   e dir: 'Se tu se' sire de la villa
         del cui nome ne' dèi fu tanta lite
         e onde ogne scïenza disfavilla,

'You thrust your mind,' he answered, 'back down there   64
and, thinking still in terms of earthly things,
you tease out darkness from the light of truth.

The Good that – infinite beyond all words –   67
is there above will run to love like rays
of light that come to anything that shines.

It gives itself proportioned to the fire,   70
so that, as far as *caritas* extends,
eternal Worth increases over it.

The more there are who fix their minds up there,   73
the more good love there is – and more to love –
and each (as might a mirror) gives to each.

And if these words of mine don't slake your thirst,   76
you'll see Beatrice. And she, all in all,
will ease this craving – as she'll others, too.

Press forward, then. For these five wounds that heal,   79
through all the pain they bring, will soon
be gone, as are by now the other two.'

Intending here to say: 'You've fed me well',   82
I saw that I had reached the upper ring.
And there my eyes, entranced, now silenced me.

For, in a sudden-seeing ecstasy,   85*
I was, it seemed, caught up and made to see
a temple, many thronging all around.

There at the door a lady stood who said –   88
sweet in her manner as a mother is:
'Why, dearest son, have you done this to us?

Look at how, grieving, your father and I   91
have searched for you!' And she falling silent,
what first appeared now disappeared from view.

A second woman now appeared to me.   94
Her cheeks were washed with streams that grief distils
when grief is born in us from angry scorn.

'If you,' she said, 'are lord of that great place   97
whose name caused so much strife among the gods,
and yet from which all knowledge sparkles out,

100   vendica te di quelle braccia ardite
           ch'abbracciar nostra figlia, o Pisistràto.'
           E 'l segnor mi parea benigno e mite

103   risponder lei con viso temperato:
           'Che farem noi a chi mal ne disira,
           se quei che ci ama è per noi condannato?'

106   Poi vidi genti accese in foco d'ira
           con pietre un giovinetto ancider, forte
           gridando a sé pur: 'Martira, martira!'

109   E lui vedea chinarsi, per la morte
           che l'aggravava già, inver' la terra,
           ma de li occhi facea sempre al ciel porte,

112   orando a l'alto Sire, in tanta guerra,
           che perdonasse a' suoi persecutori,
           con quello aspetto che pietà diserra.

115   Quando l'anima mia tornò di fòri
           a le cose che son fuor di lei vere,
           io riconobbi i miei non falsi errori.

118   Lo duca mio, che mi potea vedere
           far sì com' om che dal sonno si slega,
           disse: 'Che hai, che non ti puoi tenere,

121   ma se' venuto più che mezza lega
           velando li occhi e con le gambe avvolte,
           a guisa di chi vino o sonno piega?'

124   'O dolce padre mio, se tu m'ascolte,
           io ti dirò,' diss' io, 'ciò che m'apparve
           quando le gambe mi furon sì tolte.'

127   Ed ei: 'Se tu avessi cento larve
           sovra la faccia, non mi sarian chiuse
           le tue cogitazion, quantunque parve.

130   Ciò che vedesti fu perché non scuse
           d'aprir lo core a l'acque de la pace
           che da l'etterno fonte son diffuse.

take vengeance on those hands, Pisistratus,   100
that clasped our daughter in their rash embrace.'
That lord, to me, seemed mild and generous

and – temperate in expression – answered her: 103
'What shall we do to those that wish us ill
if those that love us are condemned by us?'

I saw, next, crowds enflamed in fires of wrath,   106
all yelling out to all a loud 'Kill! Kill!',
stoning a young man to the point of death.

And he, I saw, bowed down towards the earth   109
as death imposed on him its heavy weight,
yet still he bore his eyes towards the skies

(his look that look which opens pity's lock)   112
praying in so much strife that Heaven's Lord
should pardon those who'd hunted him to death.

When once my soul turned outwards once again   115
to beings truly there outside itself,
I'd strayed, I saw, towards not-false error.

My leader, who could see that I behaved   118
like someone who has just escaped from sleep,
exclaimed: 'What's wrong? Why can't you stand
        straight up?

You've come along for half a mile or more   121
veiling your eyes, your legs turned all askew,
like someone in the grip of sleep or drink.'

'My dearest father, if you'll hear me out,   124
I'll tell you what appeared to me,' I said,
'during the time my legs were snatched from me.'

'Had you a thousand masks around your face,   127
your thinking,' he replied, 'would not, to me,
be hidden, even in the least degree.

You've seen these things. So you'll have no excuse   130
if you don't give your heart to streams of peace
which spread out from their everlasting source.

133   Non dimandai: "Che hai?" per quel che face
chi guarda pur con l'occhio che non vede,
quando disanimato il corpo giace,

136   ma dimandai per darti forza al piede:
così frugar conviensi i pigri, lenti
ad usar lor vigilia quando riede.'

139   Noi andavam per lo vespero, attenti
oltre quanto potean li occhi allungarsi
contra i raggi seròtini e lucenti.

142   Ed ecco a poco a poco un fummo farsi
verso di noi come la notte oscuro;
né da quello era loco da cansarsi.

145   Questo ne tolse li occhi e l'aere puro.

I did not ask, "What's wrong?" as those might do   133
who only see with eyes that do not see,
staring at bodies that are drained of life,

but rather asked to give your stride more strength.   136
You need to prod the indolent like this,
slow as they are to use their waking powers.'

Walking towards the setting sun, we stretched   139
to see as far beyond as eyes could reach
against the brilliance of the evening rays.

Then, bit by bit, a rising cloud of smoke,   142
as dark as night, began to form ahead.
There was no way for us to turn aside.

It took from us our eyesight and pure air.   145

CANTO 16

1   Buio d'inferno e di notte privata
d'ogne pianeto, sotto pover cielo,
quant' esser può di nuvol tenebrata,

4   non fece al viso mio sì grosso velo
come quel fummo ch'ivi ci coperse,
né a sentir di così aspro pelo

7   che l'occhio stare aperto non sofferse;
onde la scorta mia saputa e fida
mi s'accostò e l'omero m'offerse.

10   Sì come cieco va dietro a sua guida
per non smarrirsi e per non dar di cozzo
in cosa che 'l molesti o forse ancida:

13   m'andava io per l'aere amaro e sozzo,
ascoltando il mio duca, che diceva
pur: 'Guarda che da me tu non sia mozzo.'

16   Io sentia voci, e ciascuna pareva
pregar per pace e per misericordia
l'Agnel di Dio che le peccata leva.

19   Pur 'Agnus Dei' eran le loro essordia;
una parola in tutte era e un modo,
sì che parea tra esse ogne concordia.

22   'Quei sono spirti, maestro, ch'i' odo?'
diss' io. Ed elli a me: 'Tu vero apprendi,
e d'iracundia van solvendo il nodo.'

25   'Or tu chi se' che 'l nostro fummo fendi,
e di noi parli pur come se tue
partissi ancor lo tempo per calendi?'

CANTO 16

Darkness in Hell, or any night stripped bare   1
of planets under impoverished skies
(a pall of clouds as dense as these could be),

    has never formed, for me, as thick a veil   4
as did the smoke that now surrounded us,
or stretched a weave so rasping in its feel

    that eyes could not stay open to its touch.   7
Therefore, my guide, as ever wise and true,
came to my side, his shoulder lending aid.

    And, as a blind man goes behind his guide –   10
for fear he'll wander or collide with things
that might well maim him or, perhaps, could kill –

    I, too, went on through acrid, filthy air,   13
attending to my leader, who would say,
'Take care. Don't get cut off!' repeatedly.

    I now heard voices. And it seemed that each   16
was praying to the Lamb of God, who takes
all sin away, for mercy and for peace.

    The words they uttered first were '*Agnus Dei*' –   19
the self-same text and tune from all of them,
so that, it seemed, at heart they sang as one.

    'Are these all spirits, sir, that I can hear?'   22
I spoke. He answered: 'Yes. In that you're right.
And anger is the knot they're working free.'

    'And who are you, that cleave our smoke-filled air, 25*
and speaks of us as though (if this could be)
you still divided time by month and year?'

28   Così per una voce detto fue;
        onde 'l maestro mio disse: 'Rispondi,
        e domanda se quinci si va sùe.'

31   E io: 'O creatura che ti mondi
        per tornar bella a colui che ti fece,
        maraviglia udirai, se mi secondi.'

34   'Io ti seguiterò quanto mi lece,'
        rispuose, 'e, se veder fummo non lascia,
        l'udir ci terrà giunti in quella vece.'

37   Allora incominciai: 'Con quella fascia
        che la morte dissolve men vo suso,
        e venni qui per l'infernale ambascia.

40   E se Dio m'ha in sua grazia rinchiuso
        tanto che vuol ch'i' veggia la sua corte
        per modo tutto fuor del moderno uso,

43   non mi celar chi fosti anzi la morte,
        ma dilmi, e dimmi s'i' vo bene al varco,
        e tue parole fier le nostre scorte.'

46   'Lombardo fui, e fu' chiamato Marco,
        del mondo seppi, e quel valore amai
        al quale ha or ciascun disteso l'arco.

49   Per montar sù dirittamente vai.'
        Così rispuose, e soggiunse: 'I' ti prego
        che per me prieghi quando sù sarai.'

52   E io a lui: 'Per fede mi ti lego
        di far ciò che mi chiedi; ma io scoppio
        dentro ad un dubbio, s'io non me ne spiego.

55   Prima era scempio, e ora è fatto doppio
        ne la sentenza tua, che mi fa certo,
        qui e altrove, quello ov' io l'accoppio.

58   Lo mondo è ben così tutto diserto
        d'ogne virtue come tu mi sone,
        e di malizia gravido e coverto;

61   ma priego che m'addite la cagione,
        sì ch'i' la veggia e ch'i' la mostri altrui;
        ché nel cielo uno, e un qua giù la pone.'

These words were those that one voice uttered now.   28
At which my teacher said to me: 'Reply.
Ask them if we can make our climb from here.'

    And I: 'My fellow creature, who now wash   31
to go once more in beauty to your maker,
you, if you follow close, will hear of wonders.'

    'I'll follow you as far as I'm allowed.   34
And if,' he said, 'the smoke won't let us see,
hearing instead will keep us closely joined.'

    'Still swaddled in the clothes that death dissolves'   37
(so I began) 'I make my way above,
and come here from the agonies of Hell.

    And if God circles me with such great grace   40
that I, as He desires, should see His court,
in ways beyond what men of our day know,

    then do not hide who you were till your death,   43
but speak and tell me: am I near the rise?
And your words only will become our guide.'

    'I was a Lombard, and my name was Mark.   46
I knew the world and loved that noble worth
at which all now aim slack and unslung bows.

    To make your climb, just take the straight way on.'   49
He answered thus, and added then: 'I pray
that you should pray for me, when you're up there.'

    And I to him: 'Through faith I bind myself   52
to do what you demand. And yet I burst,
if you will not explain, with one great doubt.

    Though simple to begin with, what you say   55
has made doubt double now. That makes me sure
I'm right to couple things heard here and elsewhere.

    The world is, truly, as your words declare,   58
a sterile place where every virtue fails –
pregnant with viciousness that blankets all.

    Point me, I beg you, to the reason why,   61
so I can see and then show others, too.
Some place the cause in stars, some here below.'

64   Alto sospir, che duolo strinse in 'uhi!'
        mise fuor prima; e poi cominciò: 'Frate,
        lo mondo è cieco, e tu vien ben da lui.

67   Voi che vivete ogne cagion recate
        pur suso al cielo, pur come se tutto
        movesse seco di necessitate.

70   Se così fosse, in voi fora distrutto
        libero arbitrio, e non fora giustizia
        per ben letizia, e per male aver lutto.

73   Lo cielo i vostri movimenti inizia;
        non dico tutti, ma, posto ch'i' 'l dica,
        lume v'è dato a bene e a malizia,

76   e libero voler, che, se fatica
        ne le prime battaglie col ciel dura,
        poi vince tutto, se ben si notrica.

79   A maggior forza e a miglior natura
        liberi soggiacete, e quella cria
        la mente in voi, che 'l ciel non ha in sua cura.

82   Però se 'l mondo presente disvia
        in voi è la cagione, in voi si cheggia,
        e io te ne sarò or vera spia.

85   Esce di mano a lui che la vagheggia
        prima che sia, a guisa di fanciulla
        che piangendo e ridendo pargoleggia,

88   l'anima semplicetta, che sa nulla,
        salvo che, mossa da lieto fattore,
        volontier torna a ciò che la trastulla.

91   Di picciol bene in pria sente sapore;
        quivi s'inganna, e dietro ad esso corre
        se guida o fren non torce suo amore.

94   Onde convenne legge per fren porre;
        convenne rege aver che discernesse
        de la vera cittade almen la torre.

97   Le leggi son, ma chi pon mano ad esse?
        Nullo, però che 'l pastor che procede
        rugumar può, ma non ha l'unghie fesse;

A long, deep sigh that grief dragged out to 'Uhi'   64
he uttered first, then 'Brother,' he began,
'the world is blind, and, yes, that's where *you're* from.

You, living there, derive the cause of all   67
straight from the stars alone, as if, alone,
these made all move in mere necessity.

Yet were that so, in you would be destroyed   70
the freedom of your will – and justice fail
in giving good its joy and grief its ill.

The stars initiate your vital moves.   73*
I don't say all. And yet suppose I did,
you're given light to know what's good and bad,

and free will, too, which if it can endure   76
beyond its early battles with the stars,
and if it's nourished well, will conquer all.

Of better nature and of greater power   79
you are free subjects. And you have a mind
that planets cannot rule or stars concern.

So if the present world has gone astray,   82
the reason lies in you, in you it's sought,
and I, on your behalf, will spy it out.

Leaving the hand of him who holds it dear   85
(before it truly *is*), it weeps and laughs,
that little simple soul, and baby-plays,

as young girls do, and does not know a thing –   88
except, being moved by its Maker in joy,
it willingly turns to every playful thrill.

It tastes the flavour, first, of some small good,   91
and, fooled by this, it chases down its track,
unless a brake or guide bends such love back.

So law is needed to apply this brake.   94
A king is needed, with the skill to see
the towers of that true city, at the least.

The laws are there. Who sets his hand to these?   97*
There's no one. For the shepherd out ahead,
though he can chew the cud, has not split hooves.

100 per che la gente, che sua guida vede
pur a quel ben fedire ond' ella è ghiotta,
di quel si pasce e più oltre non chiede.

103 Ben puoi veder che la mala condotta
è la cagion che 'l mondo ha fatto reo,
e non natura che 'n voi sia corrotta.

106 Soleva Roma, che 'l buon mondo feo,
due soli aver, che l'una e l'altra strada
facean vedere, e del mondo e di Deo.

109 L'un l'altro ha spento, ed è giunta la spada
col pasturale, e l'un con l'altro insieme
per viva forza mal convien che vada,

112 però che, giunti, l'un l'altro non teme:
se non mi credi, pon mente a la spiga,
ch'ogn' erba si conosce per lo seme.

115 In sul paese ch'Adice e Po riga
solea valore e cortesia trovarsi
prima che Federigo avesse briga;

118 or può sicuramente indi passarsi
per qualunque lasciasse per vergogna
di ragionar coi buoni o d'appressarsi.

121 Ben v'èn tre vecchi ancora in cui rampogna
l'antica età la nova, e par lor tardo
che Dio a miglior vita li ripogna:

124 Currado da Palazzo e 'l buon Gherardo
e Guido da Castel, che mei si noma,
francescamente, il semplice Lombardo.

127 Dì oggimai che la Chiesa di Roma,
per confondere in sé due reggimenti,
cade nel fango, e sé brutta e la soma.'

130 'O Marco mio,' diss' io, 'bene argomenti,
e or discerno perché dal retaggio
li figli di Levì furono essenti.

133 Ma qual Gherardo è quel che tu per saggio
di' ch'è rimaso de la gente spenta
in rimprovèro del secol selvaggio?'

So people, when they see their leader snatch   100
at those same goods that greedily *they* crave,
graze on just those, and do not seek beyond.

So – as you may well see – bad government   103
is why the world is so malignant now.
It's not that nature is corrupt in you.

Once, Rome, which made this world for us pure good,   106*
had two suns in its sky. And these made known
both roads to take, the world's and that of God.

One sun has snuffed the other out. The sword   109
is joined now to the shepherd's crook. And ill
is bound to follow when force links these two.

For, once they're joined, there can't be mutual dread.   112
And if you don't believe this, think of crops,
where grass is known according to its seed.

Before the Emperor Frederick was opposed,   115*
in regions washed by Po and Adige
all courtesy and prowess could be found.

Now anyone is safe to travel through   118
who might avoid, from sheer embarrassment,
speech or encounters with good, honest men.

There are, it's true, three old ones there in whom   121
times now long gone rebuke the new. To them,
in granting better life, God seems too slow.

Currado da Palazzo, good Gherardo   124*
and Guido da Castello, better named
the "honest Lombard" – as French travellers do.

So you can say this now: the Church of Rome,   127
by mingling in itself two forms of rule,
falls in the mud, befouling self and load.'

'Dear Mark,' I said, 'your argument runs well.   130*
And now I see why Levi's priestly sons
were all excluded from inheritance.

But who's that "Gerard" whom you say remains   133
as pattern of an age that is no more,
to speak reproaches to our savage time?'

136   'O tuo parlar m'inganna, o el mi tenta,'
        rispuose a me, 'ché, parlandomi tosco,
        par che del buon Gherardo nulla senta.

139   Per altro sopranome io nol conosco,
        s'io nol togliessi da sua figlia Gaia.
        Dio sia con voi, ché più non vegno vosco.

142   Vedi l'albór che per lo fummo raia
        già biancheggiare, e me convien partirmi –
        l'angelo è ivi – prima ch'io li paia.'

145   Così tornò, e più non volle udirmi.

'Your words are meant to test,' so he replied,   136
'or else to have me on. You're speaking Tuscan,
yet have no clue, it seems, about good Gerard!

I know no other name by which he's known –   139
unless I draw it from his daughter's shame.
May God go with you. I can't come along.

You see that bright gleam, dawning through the smoke,   142
already whitening. I must now go back –
the angel's there – before I'm shown to him.'

He turned, and would not hear me any more.   145

CANTO 17

1   Ricorditi, lettor, se mai ne l'alpe
ti colse nebbia per la qual vedessi
non altrimenti che per pelle talpe,

4   come, quando i vapori umidi e spessi
a diradar cominciansi, la spera
del sol debilemente entra per essi,

7   e fia la tua imagine leggera
in giugnere a veder com' io rividi
lo sole in pria, che già nel corcar era.

10   Sì, pareggiando i miei co' passi fidi
del mio maestro, usci' fuor di tal nube
ai raggi morti già ne' bassi lidi.

13   O imaginativa, che ne rube
talvolta sì di fuor ch'om non s'accorge
perché dintorno suonin mille tube,

16   chi move te, se 'l senso non ti porge?
Moveti lume che nel ciel s'informa,
per sé o per voler che giù lo scorge.

19   De l'empiezza di lei che mutò forma
ne l'uccel ch'a cantar più si diletta
ne l'imagine mia apparve l'orma,

22   e qui fu la mia mente sì ristretta
dentro da sé che di fuor non venìa
cosa che fosse allor da lei ricetta.

25   Poi piovve dentro a l'alta fantasia
un crucifisso, dispettoso e fero
ne la sua vista, e cotal si moria;

CANTO 17

Reader, recall, if ever in the hills   1
a fog has caught you so you couldn't see
(or only as a mole does through its skin),

    then how, as vapours, clinging, damp and dense,   4
begin to dissipate, the sun's round disc
enters, and feebly makes its way through these.

    From this, you'll easily be brought to see,   7
in your imagination, how I saw
the sun again, already setting now.

    So, levelling with my teacher's trusted steps,   10
I came out from that cloud, along with him,
to rays, down on the shore, already dead.

    Imagination, you at times will steal   13*
the outer world from us so we can't tell
(even if horns in thousands blare around)

    who makes you move when sense does not provide.   16
It's light that moves you, formed in heavenly spheres
by Will, which guides it down, or else *per se*.

    The godless wrath of one who changed her form   19*
to be that bird which most delights in song
appeared, and left its footprint on my brain.

    My mind was now so clenched upon itself   22
that nothing was received within its bounds
that might have come from outside or beyond.

    And then, within these high imaginings,   25
one crucified rained down. He, in his gaze,
was fierce and full of scorn and, like that, died.

28   intorno ad esso era il grande Assuero,
        Estèr sua sposa e 'l giusto Mardoceo,
        che fu al dire e al far così intero.

31   E come questa imagine rompeo
        sé per sé stessa, a guisa d'una bulla
        cui manca l'acqua sotto qual si feo,

34   surse in mia visione una fanciulla
        piangendo forte, e dicea: 'O regina,
        perché per ira hai voluto esser nulla?

37   Ancisa t'hai per non perder Lavina:
        or m'hai perduta! Io son essa che lutto,
        madre, a la tua pria ch'a l'altrui ruina.'

40   Come si frange il sonno ove di butto
        nova luce percuote il viso chiuso,
        che fratto guizza pria che muoia tutto:

43   così l'imaginar mio cadde giuso
        tosto che lume il volto mi percosse,
        maggior assai che quel ch'è in nostro uso.

46   I' mi volgea per veder ov' io fosse,
        quando una voce disse: 'Qui si monta,'
        che da ogne altro intento mi rimosse,

49   e fece la mia voglia tanto pronta
        di riguardar chi era che parlava
        che mai non posa, se non si raffronta.

52   Ma come al sol, che nostra vista grava
        e per soverchio sua figura vela,
        così la mia virtù quivi mancava.

55   'Questo è divino spirito, che ne la
        via da ir sù ne drizza sanza prego,
        e col suo lume sé medesmo cela.

58   Sì fa con noi come l'uom si fa sego,
        ché quale aspetta prego e l'uopo vede,
        malignamente già si mette al nego.

61   Or accordiamo a tanto invito il piede;
        procacciam di salir pria che s'abbui,
        ché poi non si poria, se 'l dì non riede.'

Around him were the great Ahasuerus,   28
Esther (his wife) and honest Mordecai,
who showed such probity in word and deed.

This image of itself now burst – as might   31
some rising bubble when the water fails,
beneath the surface where it first filled out.

And then, within my vision, there rose up   34
a girl who, weeping fiercely, said: 'Great Queen!
Why wish yourself as nothing in your wrath?

To keep – not lose – Lavinia, you slew yourself.   37
You've lost me now, dear mother. This is me.
I mourn yours more than any other's doom.'

As sleep is shattered when some strange new light   40
strikes, on the sudden, at our closed-up eye,
then flickers for a moment till it dies,

so, too, these images I saw crashed down,   43
as, now, a light struck hard against my face,
greater by far than those to which we're used.

I turned around to see where I might be.   46
At which, a voice spoke out: 'You go up here.'
This distanced me from any other thought,

and wrought in me that great desire to see   49
'Who was it that said this to me?' which won't
admit of rest until we're face to face.

But, as when sun weighs heavy on our sight   52
and veils its shape in overwhelming glare,
so did my inner powers at this fall short.

'This spirit is divine. Before we've asked,   55
it indicates the way to go above,
and hides itself within the light it gives.

It treats us as we like to treat ourselves.   58
For those who see a need yet wait for prayers
ill-willingly stand ready to refuse.

To this great welcome let us tune our pace   61
and strive to climb before the darkness falls –
we cannot, otherwise, till day returns.'

64   Così disse il mio duca, e io con lui
        volgemmo i nostri passi ad una scala;
        e tosto ch'io al primo grado fui,

67   senti'mi presso quasi un muover d'ala
        e ventarmi nel viso e dir: '*Beati*
        pacifici, che son sanz' ira mala!'

70   Già eran sovra noi tanto levati
        li ultimi raggi, che la notte segue,
        che le stelle apparivan da più lati.

73   'O virtù mia, perché sì ti dilegue?'
        fra me stesso dicea, ché mi sentiva
        la possa de le gambe posta in triegue.

76   Noi eravam dove più non saliva
        la scala sù, ed eravamo affissi
        pur come nave ch'a la piaggia arriva.

79   E io attesi un poco, s'io udissi
        alcuna cosa nel novo girone;
        poi mi volsi al maestro mio e dissi:

82   'Dolce mio padre, dì, quale offensione
        si purga qui nel giro dove semo?
        Se i piè si stanno, non stea tuo sermone.'

85   Ed elli a me: 'L'amor del bene, scemo
        del suo dover, quiritta si ristora;
        qui si ribatte il mal tardato remo.

88   Ma perché più aperto intendi ancora,
        volgi la mente a me, e prenderai
        alcun buon frutto di nostra dimora.

91   Né creator né creatura mai,'
        cominciò el, 'figliuol, fu sanza amore,
        o naturale o d'animo, e tu 'l sai.

94   Lo naturale è sempre sanza errore,
        ma l'altro puote errar per male obietto
        o per troppo o per poco di vigore.

97   Mentre ch'elli è nel primo ben diretto
        e ne' secondi sé stesso misura,
        esser non può cagion di mal diletto,

So said my leader and, along with him,   64
I turned my step to make towards a stair.
As soon, though, as I reached its lowest tread,

I felt close by a movement as of wings,   67*
a fanning at my face and words: '*Beati
pacifici* – of violent wrath they're free.'

By now the final rays, pursued by night,   70
had risen over us, and gone so far
that stars in many parts appeared to view.

'My strengths and powers! Why do you slip away?'   73
(I said within myself.) 'A truce, I feel,
has been imposed upon my striding thighs.'

We'd got to where the stairway rose no more.   76
And there we stuck – as fixedly as ships
that beach themselves, arriving at the shore.

I waited for a while, in case I heard   79
some sign in this new ring of anything,
then, turning to my teacher, I said now:

'My dearest teacher, tell me what offence   82
is purged within the circle where we are.
Our feet stand still. Don't let your words do so.'

'The love of good,' he said, 'when this falls short   85
of what it ought to be, is here restored.
The oar that wrongly slackened strikes once more.

But, so you may more plainly understand,   88
turn, pay attention and, from this short wait,
you'll carry off some truly worthwhile fruit.

Neither creator nor created thing   91*
was ever, dearest son, without' (he starts)
'the love of mind or nature. You know that.

The natural love can never go astray.   94
The other, though, may err when wrongly aimed,
or else through too much vigour or the lack.

Where mind-love sets itself on primal good   97
and keeps, in secondaries, a due control,
it cannot be the cause of false delight.

100   ma quando al mal si torce, o con più cura,
      o con men che non dee corre nel bene,
      contra 'l fattore adovra sua fattura.

103   Quinci comprender puoi ch'esser convene
      amor sementa in voi d'ogne virtute
      e d'ogne operazion che merta pene.

106   Or, perché mai non può da la salute
      amor del suo subietto volger viso,
      da l'odio proprio son le cose tute;

109   e perché intender non si può diviso,
      e per sé stante, alcuno esser dal primo,
      da quello odiare ogne effetto è deciso.

112   Resta, se dividendo bene stimo,
      che 'l mal che s'ama è del prossimo, ed esso
      amor nasce in tre modi in vostro limo.

115   È chi, per esser suo vicin soppresso,
      spera eccellenza, e sol per questo brama
      ch'el sia di sua grandezza in basso messo;

118   è chi podere, grazia, onore e fama
      teme di perder perch'altri sormonti,
      onde s'attrista sì che 'l contrario ama;

121   ed è chi per ingiuria par ch'aonti
      sì che si fa de la vendetta ghiotto,
      e tal convien che 'l male altrui impronti:

124   questo triforme amor qua giù di sotto
      si piange. Or vo' che tu de l'altro intende,
      che corre al ben con ordine corrotto.

127   Ciascun confusamente un bene apprende
      nel qual si queti l'animo, e disira,
      per che di giugner lui ciascun contende.

130   Se lento amore a lui veder vi tira
      o a lui acquistar, questa cornice,
      dopo giusto penter, ve ne martira.

133   Altro ben è che non fa l'uom felice;
      non è felicità, non è la buona
      essenza, d'ogne ben frutto e radice.

But when it wrongly twists towards the ill,   100
or runs towards the good too fast or slow,
what's made then works against its maker's plan.

Hence, of necessity, you'll understand   103
that love must be the seed of all good powers,
as, too, of penalties your deeds deserve.

Now, since love cannot turn its face away   106
from that which greets it with a promised health,
all things are safe from hatred of themselves,

and since no being can be understood   109
as independent, separate, from the First,
effects, decidedly, can't hate their source.

Restat: if I've prepared the ground aright,   112*
the ill we love must be our *neighbour's* harm.
Such "love" is born in three ways from your slime.

Some hope, by keeping all their neighbours down,   115
that they'll excel. They yearn for that alone –
to see them brought from high to low estate.

Then, some will fear that, if another mounts,   118
they'll lose all honour, fame and grace and power,
so, grieving at success, love what it's not.

And some, it seems, when hurt, bear such a grudge   121
that they crave only to exact revenge –
which means they seek to speed another's harm.

This tri-formed love is wept for down below.   124
But now I'd have you understand the next
which runs, in broken order, after good.

We all, confusedly, conceive a good,   127
desiring that our hearts may rest in that.
And each will strive to make their way to it.

If love is slack in drawing you to view –   130
or win – that good, then this ledge, where we're now,
after your fit repentance, martyrs you.

And other goods will not bring happiness,   133
not happy in themselves, nor that good source
of being, seed and flower of all that's good.

136   L'amor ch'ad esso troppo s'abbandona
          di sovr' a noi si piange per tre cerchi;
          ma come tripartito si ragiona,
139   tacciolo, acciò che tu per te ne cerchi.'

The love that gives itself too much to these   136
is wept for in the circles still above.
But why "tripartite" I shall not here say,
    so you can seek the reason for yourself.'   139

CANTO 18

1   Posto avea fine al suo ragionamento
l'alto dottore, e attento guardava
ne la mia vista s'io parea contento;

4   e io, cui nova sete ancor frugava,
di fuor tacea a dentro dicea: 'Forse
lo troppo dimandar ch'io fo li grava.'

7   Ma quel padre verace, che s'accorse
del timido voler che non s'apriva,
parlando di parlare ardir mi porse.

10   Ond' io: 'Maestro, il mio veder s'avviva
sì nel tuo lume ch'io discerno chiaro
quanto la tua ragion parta o descriva.

13   Però ti prego, dolce padre caro,
che mi dimostri amore, a cui reduci
ogne buono operare e 'l suo contraro.'

16   'Drizza,' disse, 'ver' me l'agute luci
de lo 'ntelletto, e fieti manifesto
l'error de' ciechi che si fanno duci.

19   L'animo, ch'è creato ad amar presto,
ad ogne cosa è mobile che piace,
tosto che dal piacere in atto è desto.

22   Vostra apprensiva da esser verace
tragge intenzione, e dentro a voi la spiega,
sì che l'animo ad essa volger face;

25   e se rivolto inver' di lei si piega,
quel piegare è amor, quell' è natura
che per piacer di novo in voi si lega.

CANTO 18

That great authority concluded here.   1
Attentively, he looked me in the face,
to see if I was pleased and satisfied.

   And I (a new thirst searching through my brain)   4
was silent outwardly but said within:
'Too many questions may, perhaps, annoy him.'

   He, though, true father that he was, had seen   7
this hesitant desire unopened yet,
and, speaking, gave me courage to speak out.

   'My power to see,' I said, 'in your light, sir,   10
grows bright, alive in me, so – yes – I'm clear
on every point your words define and stress.

   And so, my dear, kind father, I entreat   13
that you expound for me that love to which
you trace all good acts and their opposite.'

   'Direct on me,' he said, 'your mind's sharp light.   16
And I shall make quite evident to you
the error of the blind – who claim they lead.

   The mind, which is created quick to love,   19
when roused by pleasure into conscious act
will tend towards such things as give delight.

   From things that truly are, your *apprehensio*   22
draws out an image which it then unfolds
within you, so that mind turns round to it.

   If mind, once having turned, inclines to that,   25
this bending is called love – and "nature", too –
bound up in you afresh by pleasure's knot.

28   Poi, come 'l foco movesi in altura
      per la sua forma, ch'è nata a salire
      là dove più in sua matera dura,

31   così l'animo preso entra in disire,
      ch'è moto spiritale, e mai non posa
      fin che la cosa amata il fa gioire.

34   Or ti puote apparer quant' è nascosa
      la veritate a la gente ch'avvera
      ciascun amore in sé laudabil cosa;

37   però che forse appar la sua matera
      sempre esser buona, ma non ciascun segno
      è buono, ancor che buona sia la cera.'

40   'Le tue parole e 'l mio seguace ingegno,'
      rispuos' io lui, 'm'hanno amor discoverto,
      ma ciò m'ha fatto di dubbiar più pregno;

43   ché, s'amore è di fuori a noi offerto,
      e l'anima non va con altro piede,
      se dritta o torta va non è suo merto.'

46   Ed elli a me: 'Quanto ragion qui vede,
      dir ti poss' io; da indi in là t'aspetta
      pur a Beatrice, ch'è opra di fede.

49   Ogne forma sustanzial, che setta
      è da matera ed è con lei unita,
      specifica vertute ha in sé colletta,

52   la qual sanza operar non è sentita
      né si dimostra mai che per effetto,
      come per verdi fronde in pianta vita.

55   Però, là onde vegna lo 'ntelletto
      de le prime notizie, omo non sape,
      e de' primi appetibili l'affetto,

58   che sono in voi sì come studio in ape
      di far lo mele; e questa prima voglia
      merto di lode o di biasmo non cape.

61   Or perché a questa ogn' altra si raccoglia,
      innata v'è la virtù che consiglia
      e de l'assenso de' tener la soglia.

And then, as fire moves upwards to the heights   28
(by virtue of its form, it's born to rise
to where it may, as matter, most endure),

so minds, when captured, pass into desire –   31
a motion of the spirit that won't pause
until the thing it loves has yielded joy.

From which, it's clear, you'll find how far truth hides 34
from those who think it true that all love is –
in all its types – deserving of our praise,

perhaps because its matter, seemingly,   37
is always good. Yet, grant the wax is good,
the seal need not be so in every print.'

'Your words (and, walking in their track, my wits)   40
disclose to me what love is,' I replied.
'Yet this, for me, gives birth to greater doubt.

If love is just an offering from *outside*,   43
and souls go forward on no other foot,
then going right or wrong involves no merit.'

'I can, as far as reason sees, respond.   46
Beyond that, faith's required' (so he to me)
'and you must therefore wait for Beatrice.

Forms of substantiality (distinct   49
from matter, though at one with that) collect,
each one within itself, specific powers.

These powers, unless they act, are not perceived,   52
nor are they known except by their effects –
as life appears in plants when leaves are green.

No one can, therefore, see from where there comes   55
the sense of primal concepts that we have,
nor our desire for prime desirables.

These are in you as is the urge in bees   58*
to make their honey. And this primal will
cannot be credited with blame or praise.

To group all other wills around the first,   61
there is a counselling power innate in you
that's meant to guard the threshold of consent.

64   Quest' è 'l principio là onde si piglia
        ragion di meritare in voi, secondo
        che buoni e rei amori accoglie e viglia.

67   Color che ragionando andaro al fondo
        s'accorser d'esta innata libertate;
        però moralità lasciaro al mondo.

70   Onde, poniam che di necessitate
        surga ogne amor che dentro a voi s'accende,
        di ritenerlo è in voi la podestate.

73   La nobile virtù Beatrice intende
        per lo libero arbitrio, e però guarda
        che l'abbi a mente, s'a parlar ten prende.'

76   La luna, quasi a mezza notte tarda,
        facea le stelle a noi parer più rade,
        fatta com' un secchion che tuttor arda;

79   e correa contra 'l ciel per quelle strade
        che 'l sole infiamma allor che quel da Roma
        tra ' Sardi e ' Corsi il vede quando cade.

82   E quell' ombra gentil, per cui si noma
        Pietola più che villa mantoana,
        del mio carcar diposta avea la soma;

85   per ch'io, che la ragione aperta e piana
        sovra le mie quistioni avea ricolta,
        stava com' om che sonnolento vana.

88   Ma questa sonnolenza mi fu tolta
        subitamente da gente che dopo
        le nostre spalle a noi era già volta.

91   E quale Ismeno già vide e Asopo
        lungo di sé di notte furia e calca,
        pur che i Teban di Bacco avesser uopo:

94   cotal per quel giron suo passo falca,
        per quel ch'io vidi di color venendo,
        cui buon volere e giusto amor cavalca.

97   Tosto fur sovr' a noi, perché correndo
        si movea tutta quella turba magna,
        e due dinanzi gridavan piangendo:

This is the principle from which derives   64
the inward rationale of just desert
that stores or winnows good love from what's bad.

And those who argued all things to the core   67
took notice of this inborn liberty,
and so bequeathed to us a moral rule.

Suppose that love, then, of necessity   70
does rise in you, when once its fire begins,
you have within the power to rein it back.

This power, which Beatrice understands,   73
is freedom of the will. And so take care
that, if she speaks of it, it's in your mind.'

The moon at almost midnight, slow to rise   76
(formed like a copper bucket burnished red),
now made the stars seem fewer in the sky,

and ran against the heavens around those roads   79*
where sunlight flames when anyone in Rome
observes it set between the Sards and Corsicans.

That noble shade, for whom Pietola   82*
is named above all other Mantuan towns,
had now laid down the burden I'd imposed.

So, having harvested his plain, frank words –   85
which answered all the questions I had had –
I stood like someone in a drowsy blank.

But all such drowsiness was borne away   88
by people who had suddenly appeared,
swinging towards us from behind our backs.

As once the Asop and Ismenus saw,   91*
whenever Thebans needed Bacchus's aid,
orgies at night, feet pounding by their banks,

so here – from what I saw as these came on –   94
they, too, ran scything round the mountain's curve,
spurred on and ridden by good love and will.

Soon they were on us. For they moved at speed,   97
racing towards us, that great multitude.
And two ahead were shouting, weepingly.

100   'Maria corse con fretta a la montagna!'
        e: 'Cesare, per soggiogare Ilerda,
        punse Marsilia e poi corse in Ispagna!'

103   'Ratto, ratto, che 'l tempo non si perda
        per poco amor,' gridavan li altri appresso,
        'che studio di ben far grazia rinverda!'

106   'O gente in cui fervore aguto adesso
        ricompie forse negligenza e indugio
        da voi per tepidezza in ben far messo,

109   questi che vive, e certo i' non vi bugio,
        vuole andar sù, pur che 'l sol ne riluca:
        però ne dite ond' è presso il pertugio.'

112   Parole furon queste del mio duca;
        e un di quelli spirti disse: 'Vieni
        di retro a noi, e troverai la buca.

115   Noi siam di voglia a muoverci sì pieni,
        che restar non potem; però perdona,
        se villania nostra giustizia tieni.

118   Io fui abate in San Zeno a Verona
        sotto lo' mperio del buon Barbarossa,
        di cui dolente ancor Milan ragiona.

121   E tale ha già l'un piè dentro la fossa
        che tosto piangerà quel monastero
        e tristo fia d'avere avuta possa:

124   perché suo figlio, mal del corpo intero
        e de la mente peggio, e che mal nacque,
        ha posto in loco di suo pastor vero.'

127   Io non so se più disse o s'ei si tacque,
        tant' era già di là da noi trascorso,
        ma questo intesi, e ritener mi piacque.

130   E quei che m'era ad ogne uopo soccorso
        disse: 'Volgiti qua: vedine due
        venir dando a l'accidia di morso.'

133   Di retro a tutti dicean: 'Prima fue
        morta la gente a cui il mar s'aperse,
        che vedesse Iordan le rede sue!'

'Maria hastened up to Juda's hill!'   100*
And, 'Caesar, bringing Lerida to heel,
struck at Marseilles and then ran into Spain.'

'Quick! Quick! Let's lose no time through lack of love!'   103
so all of those behind now shouted out.
'For zeal in doing good turns grace new green.'

'You people, whose keen fervour now repays   106
some negligence or else delay of yours,
through tepidness in acting for the good,

this man (he's living, and I tell no lie)   109
desires, when sunlight shines on us again,
to go on up. So where's the closest gap?'

These were the words my leader spoke to them.   112
And one among these spirits now replied:
'Come! Follow us and you'll soon find that hole.

Full of desire to move ourselves along,   115
we cannot pause. And therefore, pardon us,
if what for us is right, seems crass and wrong.

When Barbarossa ruled – that good, true lord   118
of whom Milan still speaks with pain and grief –
I, at Verona, was San Zeno's Dom.

And there's a man with one foot in the grave   121
who'll bitterly bewail that abbey soon,
and grieve the power that he had over it.

For he, where one true shepherd should have been,   124
has placed his son, diseased throughout his frame,
and worse than sick in mind, a bastard born.'

He'd run so far beyond us by this time,   127
I don't know if his words went on or ceased.
This much I heeded and would gladly keep.

And he who helps me in my every need   130
said now: 'Turn round, and look at these two here,
who, fast approaching, put the bite on sloth.'

Behind the rest, these two were calling: 'First,   133*
before the river Jordan saw their heirs,
all those for whom the sea had opened, died!'

136   E: 'Quella che l'affanno non sofferse
        fino a la fine col figlio d'Anchise,
        sé stessa a vita sanza gloria offerse!'

139   Poi quando fuor da noi tanto divise
        quell' ombre che veder più non potiersi,
        novo pensiero dentro a me si mise,

142   del qual più altri nacquero e diversi;
        e tanto d'uno in altro vaneggiai
        che li occhi per vaghezza ricopersi,

145   e 'l pensamento in sogno trasmutai.

And: 'Those who couldn't bear until the end   136
the labours that Anchises' son endured,
submitted to a life where honour lacked.'

Then, when these shades had split so far from us   139
that neither any more could be observed,
a new thought set itself within my mind,

from which were born yet other, differing thoughts.   142
And so I wandered round from this to that
and, dozing off, I gladly closed my eyes,

transforming all my thinking into dream.   145

1 Ne l'ora che non può 'l calor diurno
   intepidar più ' l freddo de la luna,
   vinto da terra e talor da Saturno,

4   quando i geomanti lor Maggior Fortuna
   veggiono in oriente, innanzi a l'alba,
   surger per via che poco le sta bruna,

7   mi venne in sogno una femmina balba,
   ne li occhi guercia e sovra i piè distorta,
   con le man monche, e di colore scialba.

10   Io la mirava; e come 'l sol conforta
   le fredde membra che la notte aggrava,
   così lo sguardo mio le facea scorta

13   la lingua, e poscia tutta la drizzava
   in poco d'ora, e lo smarrito volto,
   com' amor vuol, così le colorava.

16   Poi ch'ell' avea 'l parlar così disciolto,
   cominciava a cantar sì che con pena
   da lei avrei mio intento rivolto.

19   'Io son,' cantava, 'io son dolce serena,
   che ' marinari in mezzo mar dismago,
   tanto son di piacere a sentir piena.

22   Io volsi Ulisse del suo cammin, vago
   al canto mio, e qual meco s'ausa
   rado sen parte, sì tutto l'appago!'

25   Ancor non era sua bocca richiusa
   quand' una donna apparve santa e presta
   lunghesso me per far colei confusa.

CANTO 19

Now, at that hour when daytime heat cannot –   1
vanquished by earth and, sometimes, Saturn's rays –
sustain its warmth against the chilling moon,

   when geomancers in the east trace out,   4*
before the dawn their signs of Greater Fortune
(the path these climb is only briefly dark),

   there came, dreaming, to me a stammering crone,   7
cross-eyed and crooked on her crippled feet,
her hands mere stumps, and drained and pale in look.

   I gazed at her. Then, as to frozen limbs   10
when night has weighed them down, the sun gives strength,
likewise my staring made her free, long-tongued,

   to speak, and drew her, in the briefest space,   13
erect in every limb, giving the hue
that love desires to her blurred, pallid face.

   And once her powers of speech were thus untied,   16
she then began to sing, so I could not,
except with pain, have drawn my eyes away.

   'I am,' she sang, 'I am the lovely siren.   19
So full of pleasure to the ear my tune
that mariners I magic in mid-ocean.

   And Ulysses, entranced to hear my song,   22
I turned off course. Rarely do those who've learned
my ways depart. I bring them full content.'

   And then, before that mouth closed up once more,   25
a lady – holy and alert – appeared
and, at my side, she crushed the other's power.

28   'O Virgilio, Virgilio, chi è questa?'
        fieramente dicea; ed el venìa
        con li occhi fitti pur in quella onesta.

31   L'altra prendea, e dinanzi l'apria,
        fendendo i drappi, e mostravami 'l ventre;
        quel mi svegliò col puzzo che n'uscia.

34   Io mossi li occhi, e 'l buon maestro: 'Almen tre
        voci t'ho messe!' dicea, 'Surgi e vieni:
        troviam l'aperta per la qual tu entre.'

37   Sù mi levai, e tutti eran già pieni
        de l'alto dì i giron del sacro monte,
        e andavam col sol novo a le reni.

40   Seguendo lui, portava la mia fronte
        come colui che l'ha di pensier carca,
        che fa di sé un mezzo arco di ponte,

43   quand' io udi': 'Venite: qui si varca,'
        parlare in modo soave e benigno,
        qual non si sente in questa mortal marca.

46   Con l'ali aperte, che parean di cigno,
        volseci in sù colui che sì parlonne,
        tra due pareti del duro macigno.

49   Mosse le penne poi e ventilonne,
        'qui lugent' affermando esser 'beati,
        ch'avran di consolar l'anime donne.'

52   'Che hai che pur inver' la terra guati?'
        la guida mia incominciò a dirmi,
        poco amendue da l'angel sormontati.

55   E io: 'Con tanta sospeccion fa irmi
        novella vision ch'a sé mi piega
        sì ch'io non posso dal pensar partirmi.'

58   'Vedesti,' disse, 'quell'antica strega
        che sola sovr' a noi omai si piagne;
        vedesti come l'uom da lei si slega.

61   Bastiti, e batti a terra le calcagne;
        li occhi rivolgi al logoro che gira
        lo rege etterno con le rote magne.'

'Virgil! O Virgil!' – in the harshest tones –   28
'Who's that?' she said. And he approached, eyes set,
unwavering, on her true nobility.

He seized the Siren, ripping down her dress,   31
opened the front of her, displayed her guts,
and that, with all its stench, now woke me up.

I swung my eyes around. 'Three times, at least,   34
I've voiced this. Come!' (My generous teacher spoke.)
'Get up! Let's find an opening you can take.'

Up I now got. And all the circles round   37
the holy hill were full of highest day.
We went along, the new sun at our backs.

Now following in his track, I bore my brow   40
as people do when – loaded down with thought –
they make themselves the half-arch of a bridge.

And then I heard: 'Come on! The crossing's here!'   43
spoken in tones more soft and generous
than ever could be heard in mortal shires.

With open wings, as, seemingly, a swan's,   46
the one who'd spoken turned us to the heights
between two walls within the granite rock.

He moved his feathers and he fanned us both,   49*
affirming that '*qui lugent*' are the blessed.
To them the gift of consolation comes.

'What's got to you? You still stare at the ground.'   52
When once beyond the angel, climbing on,
these were the words with which my guide began.

'I'm made to make my way in so much doubt   55
by that weird vision – which so wraps me up
I just can't leave off thinking back to it.'

'You saw,' he said to me, 'the ancient witch.   58
For her the penitents above us weep.
You saw how men are loosened from her grip.

Let that suffice. So strike your heels to earth   61
and turn your eyes to see the lure that's spun
in mighty wheels by one eternal king.

64   Quale 'l falcon, che prima a' piè si mira,
        indi si volge al grido e si protende
        per lo disio del pasto che là il tira,

67   tal mi fec' io; e tal, quanto si fende
        la roccia per dar via a chi va suso,
        n'andai infin dove 'l cerchiar si prende.

70   Com' io nel quinto giro fui dischiuso,
        vidi gente per esso che piangea
        giacendo a terra, tutta volta in giuso.

73   'Adhaesit pavimento anima mea!'
        sentia dir lor, con sì alti sospiri
        che la parola a pena s'intendea.

76   'O eletti di Dio, li cui soffriri
        e giustizia e speranza fa men duri,
        drizzate noi verso li alti saliri.'

79   'Se voi venite dal giacer sicuri,
        e volete trovar la via più tosto,
        le vostre destre sien sempre di fòri.'

82   Così pregò 'l poeta, e sì risposto
        poco dinanzi a noi ne fu; per ch'io
        nel parlare avvisai l'altro nascosto,

85   e volsi li occhi a li occhi al segnor mio,
        ond' elli m'assentì con lieto cenno
        ciò che chiedea la vista del disio.

88   Poi ch'io potei di me fare a mio senno,
        trassimi sovra quella creatura
        le cui parole pria notar mi fenno,

91   dicendo, 'Spirto in cui pianger matura
        quel sanza 'l quale a Dio tornar non pòssi,
        sosta un poco per me tua maggior cura.

94   Chi fosti, e perché vòlti avete i dossi
        al sù, mi dì, e se vuo' ch'io t'impetri
        cosa di là, ond' io vivendo mossi.'

97   Ed elli a me: 'Perché i nostri diretri
        rivolga il cielo a sé, saprai; ma prima
        scias quod ego fui successor Petri.

A falcon, first, looks down towards its feet,   64
then, being called, will turn and stretch full length,
drawn by desire to reach the offered food.

And so did I. Through one split span of rock,   67
which served as entrance to the upward path,
I went to where the ring above begins.

Now loosed out on to circle number five,   70
I saw there people all around who wept,
each turned face downwards, lying on the earth.

'*Adhaesit pavimento anima mea!*'   73*
I heard them say this, but sighing deep
so what they said was hardly understood.

'You chosen ones of God whose sufferings are,   76
by hope and justice, made less hard to bear,
direct me to the steep way we must climb.'

'If you come here exempt from lying flat,   79
and wish to find the quickest way ahead,
your right hands will be always to the out.'

This was the poet's prayer, and thus – a bit   82
ahead of us – the answer came. And I,
on hearing this, knew where the rest were hid.

I turned my eyes to meet my lord's own eyes.   85
And he assented with a happy sign
to what my face displayed as its desire.

So, being free to act as I saw fit,   88
I drew myself across and stood above
that being whose words first had made me note,

saying: 'You spirit who, in tears, matures   91
that without which no soul can turn to God,
for my sake, leave awhile your greater care.

Who were you? Tell me that, and why you've turned   94
your backs above – and what you'd have me beg
on your behalf, returning whence I moved.'

'Why Heaven should turn our rears against itself   97*
you'll shortly know,' he said to me. 'But first
scias quod ego fui successor Petri.

100   Intra Siestri e Chiaveri s'adima
       una fiumana bella, e del suo nome
       lo titol del mio sangue fa sua cima.

103   Un mese e poco più prova' io come
       pesa il gran manto a chi dal fango il guarda,
       che piuma sembran tutte l'altre some.

106   La mia conversione, omè! fu tarda;
       ma, come fatto fui roman pastore,
       così scopersi la vita bugiarda.

109   Vidi che lì non s'acquetava il core,
       né più salir potiesi in quella vita:
       per che di questa in me s'accese amore.

112   Fino a quel punto misera e partita
       da Dio anima fui, del tutto avara;
       or, come vedi, qui ne son punita.

115   Quel ch'avarizia fa, qui si dichiara
       in purgazion de l'anime converse,
       e nulla pena il monte ha più amara.

118   Sì come l'occhio nostro non s'aderse
       in alto, fisso a le cose terrene,
       così giustizia qui a terra il merse.

121   Come avarizia spense a ciascun bene
       lo nostro amore, onde operar perdési,
       così giustizia qui stretti ne tène,

124   ne' piedi e ne le man legati e presi;
       e quanto fia piacer del giusto Sire,
       tanto staremo immobili e distesi.'

127   Io m'era inginocchiato e volea dire,
       ma com' io cominciai ed el s'accorse,
       solo ascoltando, del mio reverire:

130   'Qual cagion,' disse, 'in giù così ti torse?'
       E io a lui: 'Per vostra dignitate
       mia coscienza dritto mi rimorse.'

133   'Drizza le gambe, lèvati sù, frate!'
       rispuose; 'non errar: conservo sono
       teco e con li altri ad una Podestate.

Between Siestri and Chiavari   100*
a lovely stream descends, and from its name
my blood derives the height of all its claims.

A month, no more than that, I knew the weight   103
of keeping papal garments from the mud.
Compared with that, all loads are feather light.

My own conversion was, alas, too late.   106
And yet, made shepherd of the Roman flock,
the lies of life revealed themselves to me.

I saw the heart will never rest in these.   109
And I could not rise higher in that life.
So love of *this* life then caught fire in me.

I was, until that point, a wretched soul.   112
Divorced from God, my all was avarice.
And I am punished, as you see, for that.

What avarice will do is now made clear   115
through penance in these souls, inverted so.
The mountain has no pain more harsh than this.

Because our eyes were fixed on earthly things,   118
at no point raised to look towards the heights,
so justice sinks them here within the earth.

Since avarice extinguished all our love   121
for any good – and so good works were lost –
justice here holds us tight within its grip.

We're captives, bound at both our hands and feet,   124
and here stretched out, unmoving, we shall stay,
as long as our just Lord may think it right.'

I'd fallen to my knees and meant to speak.   127
But he, as soon as I'd begun, took note –
simply on hearing my respectful bow.

'What makes you twist like that?' he said to me,   130
and I to him: 'Aware of your high rank,
my conscience bit me when I stood erect.'

'Straighten your knee, my brother. Just get up!   133
Make no mistake. I am – along with you
and all – co-servant of one single Power.

136   Se mai quel santo evangelico suono
        che dice 'neque nubent' intendesti,
        ben puoi veder perch' io così ragiono.

139   Vattene omai, non vo' che più t'arresti,
        ché la tua stanza mio pianger disagia,
        col qual maturo ciò che tu dicesti.

142   Nepote ho io di là c'ha nome Alagia,
        buona da sé, pur che la nostra casa
        non faccia lei per essempro malvagia;

145   e questa sola di là m'è rimasa.'

If ever you have heard aright the sound   136*
of Holy Gospel in '*neque nubent*'
then you can see why I should argue thus.

Now go away. I'd not delay you more.   139
You, standing there, upset the tears I shed,
by which I ripen penance as you said.

I have, down there, a niece. Her name's Alagia,   142*
good in herself – provided that our house
does not, by bad example, make her worse.

And she alone is left of me back there.'   145

CANTO 20

1   Contra miglior voler voler mal pugna:
    onde contra 'l piacer mio, per piacerli,
    trassi de l'acqua non sazia la spugna.

4   Mossimi, e 'l duca mio si mosse per li
    luoghi spediti pur lungo la roccia,
    come si va per muro stretto a' merli,

7   ché la gente che fonde a goccia a goccia
    per li occhi il mal che tutto 'l mondo occupa,
    da l'altra parte in fuor troppo s'approccia.

10 Maladetta sie tu, antica lupa,
    che più che tutte l'altre bestie hai preda
    per la tua fame sanza fine cupa!

13 O ciel, nel cui girar par che si creda
    le condizion di qua giù trasmutarsi,
    quando verrà per cui questa disceda?

16 Noi andavam con passi lenti e scarsi,
    e io attento a l'ombre, ch'i' sentia
    pietosamente piangere e lagnarsi;

19 e per ventura udi': 'Dolce Maria!'
    dinanzi a noi chiamar così nel pianto
    come fa donna che in parturir sia,

22 e seguitar: 'Povera fosti tanto
    quanto veder si può per quello ospizio
    dove sponesti il tuo portato santo.'

25 Seguentemente intesi: 'O buon Fabrizio,
    con povertà volesti anzi virtute
    che gran ricchezza posseder con vizio.'

CANTO 20

Against a better will, will can't well fight.   1
And so, against what pleased me, pleasing *him*,
I drew the sponge still thirsty from the stream.

I moved myself. My leader moved through those   4
free spaces that, around the cliff, remained –
tightly, as by some castle's battlements –

since all those people, melting drop by drop,   7
in tears, the ill that holds the world in thrall,
encroached too far upon the outer part.

Curses on you, you wolf bitch, ages old!   10
You snatch more prey than all the other beasts,
endlessly hollow in your hungering.

You heavens, whose revolutions, we believe,   13
alter the way things are with us down here,
when will He come to put this wolf to flight?

We went our way with slow, restricted tread,   16
I listening to the shadows whom I heard
weeping in piteously sharp distress,

and chanced to hear ahead of us the cry,   19*
'Sweet Mary!' uttered in those floods of tears
that women scream when labouring at a birth.

The voice went on: 'What poverty you knew   22
we all can see from that poor lodging house
in which you laid your holy burden down.'

Then, following this: 'O good Fabrizio,   25
you chose the way of honest penury
above the treasures that were stained with vice.'

28   Queste parole m'eran sì piaciute
        ch'io mi trassi oltre per aver contezza
        di quello spirto onde parean venute.

31   Esso parlava ancor de la larghezza
        che fece Niccolò a le pulcelle
        per condurre ad onor lor giovinezza.

34   'O anima che tanto ben favelle,
        dimmi chi fosti,' dissi, 'e perché sola
        tu queste degne lode rinovelle.

37   Non fia sanza mercé la tua parola,
        s'io ritorno a compiér lo cammin corto
        di quella vita ch'al termine vola.'

40   Ed elli: 'Io ti dirò, non per conforto
        ch'io attenda di là, ma perché tanta
        grazia in te luce prima che sie morto.

43   Io fui radice de la mala pianta
        che la terra cristiana tutta aduggia,
        sì che buon frutto rado se ne schianta.

46   Ma se Doagio, Lilla, Guanto e Bruggia
        potesser, tosto ne saria vendetta,
        e io la cheggio a lui che tutto giuggia.

49   Chiamato fui di là Ugo Ciappetta;
        di me son nati i Filippi e i Luigi
        per cui novellamente è Francia retta.

52   Figliuol fu' io d'un beccaio di Parigi;
        quando li regi antichi venner meno
        tutti, fuor ch'un renduto in panni bigi,

55   trova'mi stretto ne le mani il freno
        del governo del regno, e tanta possa
        di nuovo acquisto, e sì d'amici pieno,

58   ch'a la corona vedova promossa
        la testa di mio figlio fu, del quale
        cominciar di costor le sacrate ossa.

61   Mentre che la gran dota provenzale
        al sangue mio non tolse la vergogna,
        poco valea ma pur non facea male.

To me, these words had such a pleasing sound   28
that I pressed forward to be clear about
the spirit who, it seemed, had spoken them.

He still was speaking of the generous gifts   31
that Nicholas once made to those young girls,
to save the honour of their threatened youth.

'O soul! Your words shed light on so much good.   34
Tell me,' I said, 'who were you – and why *you*
alone renew these words of worthy praise.

If I return to finish that short road   37
of life on earth which flies towards its end,
your answer won't remain without reward.'

'I'll say,' he answered, '(though support from there   40
I *don't* expect) because in you yourself,
before your death, so great a grace shines forth.

I was the root from which that sick weed grows   43
that overshadows every Christian land,
so that it's rare to strip good fruit from it.

If Douai, though, or Ghent or Bruges or Lille   46*
could get their way, then vengeance would be swift.
I pray for it from Him who judges all.

I was, down there, called Hugh Capet once.   49*
From me were born those Louis and Philippes
by whom in these new days our France is ruled.

I was from Paris, and a butcher's son.   52
And when the line of ancient kings died out –
all gone, save one who wears a monk's dark cowl –

I found my hands were tight around the reins   55
that govern in that realm, and so empowered
in making that new gain, with friends so full,

that, to the widowed crown my son's own head   58
received advancement. And from him began
our lineage of consecrated bones.

Until that splendid dowry of Provence   61
deprived my blood of any sense of shame,
they didn't do much good – nor much great harm.

64   Lì cominciò con forza e con menzogna
la sua rapina; e poscia, per ammenda,
Pontì e Normandia prese e Guascogna.

67   Carlo venne in Italia, e, per ammenda,
vittima fé di Curradino; e poi
ripinse al ciel Tommaso, per ammenda.

70   Tempo vegg' io, non molto dopo ancoi,
che tragge un altro Carlo fuor di Francia
per far conoscer meglio e sé e ' suoi.

73   Sanz' arme n'esce e solo con la lancia
con la qual giostrò Giuda, e quella ponta
sì ch'a Fiorenza fa scoppiar la pancia.

76   Quindi non terra, ma peccato e onta
guadagnerà, per sé tanto più grave
quanto più lieve simil danno conta.

79   L'altro, che già uscì preso di nave,
veggio vender sua figlia e patteggiarne
come fanno i corsar de l'altre schiave.

82   O avarizia, che puoi tu più farne,
poscia c'ha' il mio sangue a te sì tratto
che non si cura de la propria carne?

85   Perché men paia il mal futuro e 'l fatto,
veggio in Alagna intrar lo fiordaliso
e nel vicario suo Cristo esser catto.

88   Veggiolo un'altra volta esser deriso,
veggio rinovellar l'aceto e 'l fiele,
e tra vivi ladroni esser anciso.

91   Veggio il novo Pilato sì crudele
che ciò nol sazia, ma sanza decreto
portar nel Tempio le cupide vele.

94   O Segnor mio, quando sarò io lieto
a veder la vendetta che, nascosa,
fa dolce l'ira tua nel tuo secreto?

97   Ciò ch'io dicea di quell' unica sposa
de lo Spirito Santo e che ti fece
verso me volger per alcuna chiosa,

There, there began, with violence and with lies,   64*
their course of plunderings. And to put things right,
Ponthieu they seized, then Norman lands, then Gascon.

Then Charles reached Italy. To put things right,   67
he sacrificed young Conradin, then sent
Saint Thomas to the skies, to put things right.

I see a time, not very far from now,   70*
that brings another Carlo out of France
to make his clan and him the better known.

Unarmed he comes. And simply with that lance   73
that Judas jousted with, he aims then stabs
the guts of Florence till the belly bursts.

From this, his profit will be no mere land,   76
but sin and shame – the heavier for him
the more he counts as light the harm he does.

The other – captured, once, on board his ship –   79*
I now see sells his daughter, bargaining
as pirates do in deals for female slaves.

O avarice! What more harm can you do?   82
You've got my blood so firmly in your grip,
it takes no thought about its own kin's flesh.

To make its past and future crimes seem less,   85*
I see the fleur-de-lys besiege Anagni,
and Christ recaptured in his vicar's form.

I see them mocking him a second time.   88
I see renewed the vinegar and gall.
I see him slain again with living thieves.

I see renewed a Pilate who's so cruel,   91
unsatisfied, he bears with no just cause
his greedy saints towards the Temple walls.

My Lord and God! When shall I see in joy   94
that just revenge that, hidden to our view,
makes anger in your secret counsels sweet?

Those words I spoke about the one true Bride   97
of God's Own Spirit – those that made you turn,
seeking from me some further commentary –

100   tanto è risposto a tutte nostre prece
        quanto 'l dì dura; ma com' el s'annotta,
        contrario suon prendemo in quella vece.

103   Noi repetiam Pigmalïòn allotta,
        cui traditore e ladro e paricida
        fece la voglia sua de l'oro ghiotta,

106   e la miseria de l'avaro Mida
        che seguì a la sua dimanda gorda,
        per la qual sempre convien che si rida.

109   Del folle Acàn ciascun poi si ricorda,
        come furò le spoglie, sì che l'ira
        di Iosuè qui par ch'ancor lo morda.

112   Indi accusiam col marito Saffira;
        lodiamo i calci ch'ebbe Eliodoro;
        e in infamia tutto 'l monte gira

115   Polinestòr ch'ancise Polidoro;
        ultimamente ci si grida: "Crasso,
        dilci, che 'l sai: di che sapore è l'oro?"

118   Talor parla l'uno alto e l'altro basso,
        secondo l'affezion ch'ad ir ci sprona
        ora a maggiore e ora a minor passo:

121   però al ben che 'l dì ci si ragiona
        dianzi non era io sol, ma qui da presso
        non alzava la voce altra persona.'

124   Noi eravam partiti già da esso
        e brigavam di soverchiar la strada
        tanto quanto al poder n'era permesso,

127   quand' io senti', come cosa che cada,
        tremar lo monte, onde mi prese un gelo
        qual prender suol colui ch'a morte vada.

130   Certo non si scoteo sì forte Delo,
        pria che Latona in lei facesse 'l nido
        a parturir li due occhi del cielo.

133   Poi cominciò da tutte parti un grido
        tal, che 'l maestro inverso me si feo,
        dicendo: 'Non dubbiar, mentr' io ti guido.'

respond, while daylight lasts, to all our prayers.   100
But as the darkness of the night sets in
we then sound out the contrary tune.

   We now call back to mind Pygmalion,   103*
whose hankering after gold made his will turn
to treachery and theft and parricide.

   Then, too, the misery of miser Midas,   106
caused by that gluttonous demand of his,
for which he'll always be ridiculous.

   Then each recalls mad Achan's escapade,   109
and how he stole the spoils of Jericho –
so Joshua's anger seems to gnaw him still.

   We blame Sapphira, and her husband, too,   112
and praise the hooves that trampled Heliodore.
And round the mount, in notoriety,

   goes Polymnestor who slew Polydore.   115
Then finally our cry of "Crassus!" comes.
"You know. So tell us! What's the taste of gold?"

   These words are spoken high or sometimes low,   118
responding to the urge that makes us move,
spurred to a greater or a lesser pace.

   In telling – as, by day, we do – the best,   121
I was not, earlier, the only one.
But no one else nearby had raised their voice.'

   We'd gone from him by now and, moving on,   124
struggled, as far as we were given strength,
to overcome the hardships of that road,

   when, as though things were crashing down, I heard   127
the mountain tremble. And I felt the chill
that all will suffer when they come to die.

   Delos itself did not so fiercely shake   130*
before Latona made a nest of it
to bring to birth the two eyes of the sky.

   On every side there then began this cry   133
(my teacher turned around to me to say,
'While I'm your guide, you need not be afraid'):

136   'Gloria in excelsis' tutti 'Deo!'
       dicean, per quel ch'io da' vicin compresi,
       onde intender lo grido si poteo.

139   No' istavamo immobili e sospesi,
       come i pastor che prima udir quel canto,
       fin che 'l tremar cessò ed el compiési.

142   Poi ripigliammo nostro cammin santo,
       guardando l'ombre che giacean per terra,
       tornate già in su l'usato pianto.

145   Nulla ignoranza mai con tanta guerra
       mi fé desideroso di sapere,
       se la memoria mia in ciò non erra,

148   quanta pareami allor, pensando, avere;
       né per la fretta dimandare er' oso,
       né per me lì potea cosa vedere:

151   così m'andava timido e pensoso.

'*Gloria in excelsis Deo*!' and all   136*
were speaking out these words, so I could tell
the meaning of the cry from those close to.

We stood unmoving, caught there in suspense –   139
as were the shepherds who first heard this song –
until the tremor ceased and all was done.

And then once more we took our holy path,   142
looking at those that lay there on the earth
who'd gone back, now, to their familiar tears.

Never has ignorance with so much force   145
(if, in my memory, I do not err)
driven me in my keen desire to know,

as now it seemed to, thinking and thinking.   148
Nor had I dared, in all our haste, to ask.
Nor, for my part, could I see anything.

So, timid, deep in thought, I travelled on.   151

CANTO 21

1   La sete natural che mai non sazia,
se non con l'acqua onde la femminetta
samaritana domandò la grazia,

4   mi travagliava, e pungeami la fretta
per la 'mpacciata via dietro al mio duca,
e condoleami a la giusta vendetta.

7   Ed ecco, sì come ne scrive Luca
che Cristo apparve a' due ch'erano in via,
già surto fuor de la sepulcral buca,

10   ci apparve un'ombra, e dietro a noi venìa
dal piè guardando la turba che giace,
né ci addemmo di lei, sì parlò pria,

13   dicendo: 'O frati miei, Dio vi dea pace.'
Noi ci volgemmo sùbiti, e Virgilio
rendéli 'l cenno ch'a ciò si conface;

16   poi cominciò: 'Nel beato concilio
ti ponga in pace la verace corte,
che me rilega ne l'etterno essilio.'

19   'Come?' diss' elli, e parte andavam forte:
'Se voi siete ombre che Dio sù non degni,
chi v'ha per la sua scala tanto scorte?'

22   E 'l dottor mio: 'Se tu riguardi a' segni
che questi porta e che l'angel profila,
ben vedrai che coi buon convien ch'e' regni.

25   Ma perché lei che dì e notte fila
non li avea tratta ancora la conocchia
che Cloto impone a ciascuno e compila,

CANTO 21

The natural thirst that never can be slaked   1*
save by those waters that, as gracious gift,
the widowed, bright Samaritan demanded once,

toiled in me now, while hurry spurred my steps,   4
behind my leader, round the cluttered path,
mourning within to see that just revenge.

And look! As in his gospel Luke describes   7
how Christ, when risen from the hollow tomb,
appeared to two who travelled on their way –

a shadow from behind us now appeared.   10
Still looking at the crowd around our feet,
we didn't notice till it spoke and said:

'May God, my brothers, bring to you His peace.'   13
We turned round suddenly. And Virgil made
a fitting gesture to reply to this.

Then he began: 'May that true government   16
which keeps me bound in exile endlessly
grant you a place within that happy court.'

'What's that?' he said, as we still hurried on.   19
'If you are shades that God won't let ascend,
who, then, has led you up this stair so far?'

'If you observe,' my teacher said, 'those signs   22
that he bears and the angel traces out,
you'll see it's right that he reigns with the good.

But since the fate that spins thread day and night   25*
has not, in his case, yet drawn out the skein
that Clotho casts and spins for every life,

28   l'anima sua, ch'è tua e mia serocchia,
     venendo sù non potea venir sola,
     però ch'al nostro modo non adocchia.

31   Ond' io fui tratto fuor de l'ampia gola
     d'inferno per mostrarli, e mosterrolli
     oltre, quanto 'l potrà menar mia scola.

34   Ma dimmi, se tu sai, perché tai crolli
     diè dianzi 'l monte, e perché tutto ad una
     parve gridare infino a' suoi piè molli.'

37   Sì mi diè, dimandando, per la cruna
     del mio disio, che pur con la speranza
     si fece la mia sete men digiuna.

40   Quei cominciò: 'Cosa non è che sanza
     ordine senta la religione
     de la montagna, o che sia fuor d'usanza.

43   Libero è qui da ogne alterazione:
     di quel che 'l ciel da sé in sé riceve
     esser ci puote, e non d'altro, cagione.

46   Per che non pioggia, non grando, non neve,
     non rugiada, non brina più sù cade
     che la scaletta di tre gradi breve;

49   nuvole spesse non paion né rade,
     né coruscar, né figlia di Taumante,
     che di là cangia sovente contrade;

52   secco vapor non surge più avante
     ch'al sommo d'i tre gradi ch'io parlai,
     dov' ha 'l vicario di Pietro le piante.

55   Trema forse più giù poco o assai,
     ma per vento che 'n terra si nasconda,
     non so come, qua sù non tremò mai.

58   Tremaci quando alcuna anima monda
     sentesi, sì che surga o che si mova
     per salir sù, e tal grido seconda.

61   De la mondizia sol voler fa prova
     che, tutto libero a mutar convento,
     l'alma sorprende, e di voler le giova.

his soul – a sister to both yours and mine –   28
though coming here cannot come on its own.
Its eyes as yet don't see as our eyes do.

And I was therefore drawn from Hell's wide throat   31
to show him – and I've still to show him more –
as much as my own schooling will allow.

But if you're able, tell me why the mount   34
shuddered just now so hard, and why it seemed
to cry, down to its plashy foot, as one.'

In asking this, he pierced the needle's eye   37
of all I longed to know. And so my thirst,
through hope alone, became less keen in me.

'There's nothing that this mountain's holy law   40
consents to,' so the other now began,
'that's lacking order or irregular.

This place is free from every kind of change.   43
Only what Heaven, of itself, receives
can act here as a cause, and nothing else.

Therefore no showers of rain, nor hail or snow   46
no dew or hoar frost ever falls above
that little stairway with its three brief steps.

No clouds here – whether rare or dense – appear,   49*
no glint of lightning nor the rainbow child
of Thaumas, there so often changing place.

And dry evaporations do not rise   52
beyond the third and highest of those steps –
I spoke of them – where Peter's vicar stands.

Tremors occur below (some small, perhaps;   55
some great). At these heights, though, no tremor comes
from winds that hide (I can't tell why) in earth.

Tremors strike here when any soul feels pure   58
and rises, newly cleansed, to start its climb.
And that cry follows as the soul ascends.

The will alone gives proof of purity   61
when, wholly free to change its sacred place,
it aids and sweeps the soul up, willing well.

64   Prima vuol ben, ma non lascia il talento
che divina giustizia, contra voglia,
come fu al peccar, pone al tormento.

67   E io, che son giaciuto a questa doglia
cinquecent' anni e più, pur mo sentii
libera volontà di miglior soglia:

70   però sentisti il tremoto e li pii
spiriti per lo monte render lode
a quel Segnor che tosto sù li 'nvii.'

73   Così ne disse; e però ch'el si gode
tanto del ber quant' è grande la sete,
non saprei dir quant' el mi fece prode.

76   E 'l savio duca: 'Omai veggio la rete
che qui vi 'mpiglia e come si scalappia,
perché ci trema, e di che congaudete.

79   Ora chi fosti piacciati ch'io sappia,
e perché tanti secoli giaciuto
qui se', ne le parole tue mi cappia.'

82   'Nel tempo che 'l buon Tito, con l'aiuto
del sommo Rege, vendicò le fóra
ond' uscì 'l sangue per Giuda venduto,

85   col nome che più dura e più onora
ero io di là,' rispuose quello spirto,
'famoso assai, ma non con fede ancora.

88   Tanto fu dolce mio vocale spirto
che tolosano a sé mi trasse Roma,
dove mertai le tempie ornar di mirto.

91   Stazio la gente ancor di là mi noma;
cantai di Tebe e poi del grande Achille,
ma caddi in via con la seconda soma.

94   Al mio ardor fuor seme le faville,
che mi scaldar, de la divina fiamma
onde sono allumati più di mille:

97   de l'Eneida, dico, la qual mamma
fummi e fummi nutrice poetando:
sanz' essa non fermai peso di dramma.

The soul till then indeed had willed ascent.   64
But, set against that will there is the bent –
which God instils – for pain as sin's equivalent.

And I, who've lain five hundred years and more   67
in that same pain, have only felt just now
the freedom of the better way ahead.

That's why you felt and heard those tremors here,   70
and spirits round the mountain rendering praise,
so God, our Lord, might send them higher soon.'

He said these things to us. And since we take   73
a joy in drinking equal to our thirst,
I could not say what benefit he'd brought.

My lord, in wisdom: 'Now I see the net   76
that here entangles you – and your escape –
why there are tremors here, why all rejoice.

Now tell me, at your pleasure, so I'll know,   79
who were you? And your words, please, will include
why you have lain so many centuries here.'

'In those days when good Titus, by the aid   82*
of our exalted King, avenged the wounds
from which the blood that Judas sold had sprung,

I was,' the spirit answered, 'well renowned.   85
My name down there was that which most endures,
and honours most – not yet, though, of the Faith.

My voice in spirit breathed so sweet that Rome   88*
took me to her own heart from French Toulouse,
where merit dressed my brow with myrtle leaves.

My name was Statius to the people there.   91
I sang of Thebes and then of great Achilles,
but stumbled carrying that second load.

The seed my ardour sprang from was a spark   94
which warmed me through of that most sacred flame
from which a thousand, and yet more, are lit.

I'm speaking of the *Aeneid* – a mum   97
to me, to me my nurse in poetry.
Without that, I'd not weigh a single gram.

100   E per esser vivuto di là quando
        visse Virgilio, assentirei un sole
        più che non deggio al mio uscir di bando.'

103   Volser Virgilio a me queste parole
        che viso che, tacendo, disse 'Taci';
        ma non può tutto la virtù che vuole,

106   ché riso e pianto son tanto seguaci
        a la passion di che ciascun si spicca,
        che men seguon voler ne' più veraci.

109   Io pur sorrisi come l'uom ch'ammicca;
        per che l'ombra si tacque e riguardommi
        ne li occhi, ove 'l sembiante più si ficca,

112   e: 'Se tanto labore in bene assommi,'
        disse, 'perché la tua faccia testeso
        un lampeggiar di riso dimostrommi?'

115   Or son io d'una parte e d'altra preso:
        l'una mi fa tacer, l'altra scongiura
        ch'io dica; ond' io sospiro, e sono inteso

118   dal mio maestro, e: 'Non aver paura,'
        mi dice, 'di parlar, ma parla e digli
        quel ch'e' dimanda con cotanta cura.'

121   Ond' io: 'Forse che tu ti maravigli,
        antico spirto, del rider ch'io fei;
        ma più d'ammirazion vo' che ti pigli.

124   Questi che guida in alto li occhi miei
        è quel Virgilio dal qual tu togliesti
        forte a cantar de li uomini e d'i dèi.

127   Se cagion altra al mio rider credesti,
        lasciala per non vera, ed esser credi
        quelle parole che di lui dicesti.'

130   Già s'inchinava ad abbracciar li piedi
        al mio dottor, ma el li disse: 'Frate,
        non far, ché tu se' ombra e ombra vedi.'

133   Ed ei, surgendo: 'Or puoi la quantitate
        comprender de l'amor ch'a te mi scalda,
        quand' io dismento nostra vanitate,

136   trattando l'ombre come cosa salda.'

And could I live back then when Virgil lived,   100
I would agree to pass, beyond the due
that brought me out of exile, one year's sun.'

These words turned Virgil round to me – his look   103
saying, unspeakingly: 'Be silent now!'
But will power can't do everything it wills.

For tears and laughter follow on so close   106
to those emotions from which each act springs
that these least follow *will* in those most true.

And so I smiled, as though to give a hint.   109
At which the shade fell silent and just stared,
straight in my eyes where what we feel shows most.

'I wish that all your toil may come to good   112
Why did your features, though, display to me
just now,' he said, 'that sudden flashing smile?'

So I was caught on this side and on that.   115
One urges silence while the other calls
for words from me. I sigh. I'm understood

by him, my teacher. 'Do not fear to speak.   118
Speak out,' he said to me, 'and tell him all
that he so urgently desires to know.'

At which, 'You ancient spirit,' I began,   121
you're wondering maybe why you see me smile.
I'd have you gripped with yet more wonderment.

The one who guides my eyes towards the heights   124
is that same Virgil that you drew upon
to sing so strong of deities and men.

If you suppose I'd other cause to smile,   127
put that aside. It is not true. And think
those words you spoke of him were cause enough.'

He'd bowed at once to clasp my teacher's feet.   130
But he, in that embrace, said: 'Brother, don't!
You are a shadow and you see a shade.'

And he, in rising: 'Now you grasp how great   133
the love that warms my heart for you must be,
when I dismiss from mind our emptiness,

treating a shadow as a thing of weight.'   136

CANTO 22

1   Già era l'angel dietro a noi rimaso,
l'angel che n'avea vòlti al sesto giro,
avendomi dal viso un colpo raso,

4   e quei c'hanno a giustizia lor disiro
detto n'avea '*beati*', e le sue voci
con '*sitiunt*', sanz' altro, ciò forniro.

7   E io più lieve che per l'altre foci
m'andava, sì che sanz' alcun labore
seguiva in sù li spiriti veloci,

10   quando Virgilio incominciò: 'Amore,
acceso di virtù, sempre altro accese,
pur che la fiamma sua paresse fòre;

13   onde da l'ora che tra noi discese
nel limbo de lo 'nferno Giovenale,
che la tua affezion mi fé palese,

16   mia benvoglienza inverso te fu quale
più strinse mai di non vista persona,
sì ch'or mi parran corte queste scale.

19   Ma dimmi, e come amico mi perdona
se troppa sicurtà m'allarga il freno,
e come amico omai meco ragiona:

22   come poté trovar dentro al tuo seno
loco avarizia, tra cotanto senno
di quanto per tua cura fosti pieno?'

25   Queste parole Stazio mover fenno
un poco a riso pria; poscia rispuose:
'Ogne tuo dir d'amor m'è caro cenno.

CANTO 22

The angel had by now been left behind –   1
that angel who had turned us to Gyre Six,
once having shaved my brow of one more wound.

Those souls who thirst for justice he had named   4*
as 'blessed'. His words as far as *sitiunt*–
but not beyond that verse – had filled this out.

And, flowing lighter than through other bays,   7
I went along and, free from any toil,
followed those rapid spirits on their way.

Virgil, meanwhile, began to speak: 'Pure love,   10
provided that its flame shows outwardly,
kindled in virtue, kindles answering love.

So, from the time that Juvenal came down   13*
to dwell among us on the fringe of Hell,
and made your feeling for me plain to see,

my own good will to you has gripped me more   16
than any for a person yet unseen.
These stairs will seem, then, short for me to climb.

But tell me – and, in friendship, pardon this,   19
if too much confidence sets free my reins –
and speak with me as friendship now permits:

how could it be that in your breast, so full   22
of all the wisdom that your learning won,
a place was found for avarice as well?'

Statius, on hearing this, was moved to smile   25
(a little, anyway), but then replied:
'As marks of love, I value all your words.

28   Veramente più volte appaion cose
che danno a dubitar falsa matera
per le vere ragion che son nascose.

31   La tua dimanda tuo creder m'avvera
esser ch'i' fossi avaro in l'altra vita,
forse per quella cerchia dov' io era.

34   Or sappi ch'avarizia fu partita
troppo da me, e questa dismisura
migliaia di lunari hanno punita.

37   E se non fosse ch'io drizzai mia cura
quand' io intesi là dove tu chiame,
crucciato quasi a l'umana natura:

40   "Perché non reggi tu, o sacra fame
de l'oro, l'appetito de' mortali?"
voltando sentirei le giostre grame.

43   Allor m'accorsi che troppo aprir l'ali
potean le mani a spendere, e pente'mi
così di quel come de li altri mali.

46   Quanti risurgeran coi crini scemi
per ignoranza, che di questa pecca
toglie 'l penter vivendo e ne li stremi!

49   E sappie che la colpa che rimbecca
per dritta opposizione alcun peccato,
con esso insieme qui suo verde secca:

52   però, s'io son tra quella gente stato
che piange l'avarizia, per purgarmi,
per lo contrario suo m'è incontrato.'

55   'Or quando tu cantasti le crude armi
de la doppia trestizia di Giocasta,'
disse 'l cantor de' buccolici carmi,

58   'per quello che Cliò teco lì tasta,
non par che ti facesse ancor fedele
la fede, sanza qual ben far non basta.

61   Se così è, qual sole o quai candele
ti stenebraron sì che tu drizzasti
poscia di retro al pescator le vele?'

It's true, though, that the way things often look   28
provides false substance for our searching doubts,
the real considerations lying hid.

Your question verifies that you believe –   31
viewing, perhaps, the circle where I was –
that I was "grasping" in the other life.

Please understand that avarice, for me,   34
ran too far off. My own extreme – the opposite –
was punished over many thousand moons.

Had I not set my spending urge to rights,   37
and seen the meaning of the line you shout
in, almost, agony at human ways:

"You, awestruck hungering for gold! Why not   40*
impose a rule on mortal appetite?"
I'd feel the rumbling turns of that grim duel.

With that, I realized our hands can wing   43
too openly in wild expense, and so
for that repented, as for all my sins.

How many will rise up with hair cropped short   46
through ignorance of vice, which takes away
repentance while we live, or at life's end.

Know, too, the guilt that butts at any sin,   49
directly counter to that first offence,
is drained here, with it, of its rampant green.

And so, if I have been (to purge my sins)   52
among those men who weep for avarice,
this came my way by rule of contraries.'

'When first you sang of vicious wars between   55*
the twofold sadness that Jocasta bore,'
so said the singer of the farming songs,

'to read the notes that Clio strikes from you,   58
it does not seem that you had then become
faithful in faith – without which good must fail.

If that is so, what sun or candlelight   61*
dispelled your shadows so that you could set
your sails to track the fisherman aright?'

64   Ed elli a lui: 'Tu prima m'inviasti
        verso Parnaso a ber ne le sue grotte,
        e prima appresso Dio m'alluminasti.

67   Facesti come quei che va di notte,
        che porta il lume dietro e sé non giova,
        ma dopo sé fa le persone dotte,

70   quando dicesti: "Secol si rinova;
        torna giustizia e primo tempo umano,
        e progenie scende da ciel nova."

73   Per te poeta fui, per te cristiano:
        ma perché veggi mei ciò ch'io disegno,
        a colorare stenderò la mano.

76   Già era 'l mondo tutto quanto pregno
        de la vera credenza, seminata
        per li messaggi de l'etterno regno,

79   e la parola tua sopra toccata
        si consonava a' nuovi predicanti,
        ond' io a visitarli presi usata.

82   Vennermi mi poi parendo tanto santi
        che, quando Domizian li perseguette,
        sanza mio lagrimar non fur lor pianti,

85   e mentre che di là per me si stette
        io li sovvenni, e i lor dritti costumi
        fer dispregiare a me tutte altre sette.

88   E pria ch'io conducessi i Greci a' fiumi
        di Tebe poetando, ebb' io battesmo;
        ma per paura chiuso cristian fu' mi,

91   lungamente mostrando paganesmo;
        e questa tepidezza il quarto cerchio
        cerchiar mi fé più che 'l quarto centesmo.

94   Tu dunque, che levato hai il coperchio
        che m'ascondeva quanto bene io dico,
        mentre che del salire avem soverchio

97   dimmi dov' è Terrenzio nostro antico,
        Cecilio e Plauto e Varro, se lo sai;
        dimmi se son dannati, e in qual vico.'

'You,' he replied, 'first beckoned me to drink   64
from springs that rise in high Parnassian glades.
And you first lit the way for me to God.

   You acted then like someone who, at night,   67
bears at his back a lamp – no use to him,
but teaching those the way who come behind

   when once you said: "The years begin anew,   70
justice returns, so, too, Man's earliest time.
A new race, born of Heaven, now descends."

   I was, through you, a poet and a Christian, too.   73
But, so you'll better see what I intend,
I'll stretch my hand to colour in this sketch.

   The world, by then, was pregnant, all entire,   76
with true belief – an understanding sown
by messengers of God's eternal realm.

   And your words (which were touched on just above)   79
sang, with new preachers, to a single tune.
I therefore took to visiting these men.

   And these soon came to seem to me such saints   82 *
that, when Domitian's persecution struck
their weeping did not lack for my own tears.

   And while on earth I lived my given time,   85
I aided them. And their right-thinking ways
made me look down on other cults in scorn.

   Even before, in verse, I'd led the Greeks   88 *
to drink the Theban stream, I'd been baptized,
but still, from fear, concealed my Christian faith,

   displaying all that time a pagan face.   91 *
And this luke-warmness made me circle round
more than four hundred years on Terrace Four.

   But tell me – you who lifted up the veil   94
that hid from me the good of which I speak –
while still some way remains for us to climb,

   where, if you know, is ancient Terence now?   97 *
Plautus, Cecilius and Varro, too?
Tell me if these are damned, and where they walk.'

100   'Costoro e Persio e io e altri assai,'
rispuose il duca mio, 'siam con quel Greco
che le Muse lattar più ch'altri mai

103   nel primo cinghio del carcere cieco;
spesse fiate ragioniam del monte
che sempre ha le nutrice nostre seco.

106   Euripide v'è nosco e Antifonte,
Simonide, Agatone e altri piùe
Greci che già di lauro ornar la fronte.

109   Quivi si veggion de le genti tue
Antigone, Deifile e Argia,
e Ismene sì trista come fue.

112   Védeisi quella che mostrò Langia;
èvvi la figlia di Tiresia e Teti,
e con le suore sue Deidamia.'

115   Tacevansi ambedue già li poeti,
di novo attenti a riguardar dintorno,
liberi dal salire e da' pareti,

118   e già le quattro ancelle eran del giorno
rimase a dietro, e la quinta era al temo,
drizzando pur in sù l'ardente corno,

121   quando il mio duca: 'Io credo ch'a lo stremo
le destre spalle volger ne convegna,
girando il monte come far solemo.'

124   Così l'usanza fu lì nostra insegna,
e prendemmo la via con men sospetto
per l'assentir di quell'anima degna.

127   Elli givan dinanzi, e io soletto
di retro, e ascoltava i lor sermoni,
ch'a poetar mi davano intelletto.

130   Ma tosto ruppe le dolci ragioni
un alber che trovammo in mezza strada,
con pomi a odorar soavi e buoni;

133   e come abete in alto si digrada
di ramo in ramo, così quello in giuso,
cred' io perché persona sù non vada.

'All these, and Persius,' my leader said,   100
'myself and more are there beside that Greek
who, more than all, the Muses fed with milk,

    within Ring One of that unseeing gaol.   103
And many times we speak of that great peak
which always keeps our nurses on its slopes.

    Euripides is with us, Antiphon,   106
Simonides and Agathon, and Greeks
who crowned their brows with laurels, many more.

    And seen there, too (all named within your verse),   109*
Deiphile, Antigone and Argia,
Ismene also, grieving as she did.

    She, too, is seen who spied out Langia's stream.   112
The daughter of Tiresias is there,
Thetis and, with her sisters, Deidamia.'

    The poets both fell silent and, anew,   115
free from the climb and tight surrounds of wall,
gave all their thoughts to looking round about.

    Already, of the handmaids of the sun   118*
four were behind. The fifth was at the pole,
stretching its burning point towards the height.

    My leader now: 'I think that we should turn   121
our right sides to the far extremity,
and circle round the mount, as we are wont.'

    So habit was the flag we followed there.   124
We took the chosen path with lesser doubt
since that most worthy soul gave his assent.

    They made their way, I all alone behind.   127
And as we went, I listened to their talk –
which made me see what writing verse can mean.

    But then (a sudden break to soothing words!)   130
we found there, in the middle of the road,
a tree – its fruits, in perfume, good and sweet.

    As fir trees rise and lessen, by degrees,   133
from branch to branch, so this – but lessening *down*,
lest anyone, I'd say, should try to climb.

136   Dal lato onde 'l cammin nostro era chiuso,
        cadea de l'alta roccia un liquor chiaro
        e si spandeva per le foglie suso.

139   Li due poeti a l'alber s'appressaro,
        e una voce per entro le fronde
        gridò: 'Di questo cibo avrete caro.'

142   Poi disse: 'Più pensava Maria onde
        fosser le nozze orrevoli e intere
        ch'a la sua bocca, ch'or per voi risponde.

145   E le Romane antiche per lor bere
        contente furon d'acqua; e Daniello
        dispregiò cibo e acquistò savere.

148   Lo secol primo quant' oro fu bello:
        fé savorose con fame le ghiande,
        e nettare con sete ogne ruscello.

151   Mele e locuste furon le vivande
        che nodriro il Batista nel diserto,
        per ch'elli è glorioso e tanto grande

154   quanto per lo Vangelio v'è aperto.'

And, to the side, where rock walls closed our path,   136
clear liquids streaming off the towering cliff
sprinkled across the surface of the leaves.

Both poets now drew nearer to that tree,   139
and then, within its leaves, a voice cried out:
'Of this dear food you'll know the bitter dearth.'

And then it said: 'Maria thought far more   142*
of how the wedding might be full and fine
than of that mouth by which she prays for you.

And Roman women were, in ancient times,   145
content to drink plain water. Daniel, too,
despising food, gained greatly in true thought.

The primal age – as lovely, once, as gold –   148
made acorns, through long fasting, good to taste,
and, thirsting, nectar of each rivulet.

Honey and locust were the nourishment   151
that fed the Baptist in the wilderness.
How glorious and great he is, for that
    is made quite clear in the Evangelist.'   154

CANTO 23

1   Mentre che li occhi per la fronda verde
    ficcava io, sì come far suole
    chi dietro a li uccellin sua vita perde,

4   lo più che padre mi dicea: 'Figliuole,
    vienne oramai, ché 'l tempo che n'è imposto
    più utilmente compartir si vuole.'

7   Io volsi 'l viso, e 'l passo non men tosto,
    appresso i savi, che parlavan sìe
    che l'andar mi facean di nullo costo.

10 Ed ecco piangere e cantar s'udìe
    'Labia mea, Domine', per modo
    tal che diletto e doglia parturìe.

13 'O dolce padre, che è quel ch'i' odo?'
    comincia' io; ed elli: 'Ombre che vanno
    forse di lor dover solvendo il nodo.'

16 Sì come i peregrin pensosi fanno,
    giugnendo per cammin gente non nota,
    che si volgono ad essa e non restanno:

19 così di retro a noi, più tosto mota,
    venendo e trapassando ci ammirava
    d'anime turba tacita e devota.

22 Ne li occhi era ciascuna oscura e cava,
    palida ne la faccia e tanto scema
    che da l'ossa la pelle s'informava:

25 non credo che così a buccia strema
    Erisittone fosse fatto secco
    per digiunar, quando più n'ebbe tema.

CANTO 23

While I, through these green boughs, fixed searching sight 1
(as might some hunter tracking little birds,
who spends his life in vain on that pursuit),

  my more-than-father spoke. 'Dear son,' he said, 4
'do come along. The time appointed us
should be more usefully divided out.'

  I turned my eyes (my footsteps came as fast) 7
to track that learned pair, who, talking on,
made going with them free, for me, of cost.

  And then, just look! Both tears and songs were heard – 10
'*Labia mea, Domine*', so tuned
it brought both happiness and pain to birth.

  'My sweetest father, what is this I hear?' 13
so I began. And he: 'These may be shades,
who go unknotting what their debts have tied.'

  As pilgrims do when, deep in thought, they meet 16
a group along their path that they don't know
and, though they turn towards it, still don't stop,

  so, now, behind us, moving with more speed, 19
a throng of spirits, silent and devout,
reaching and overtaking us, gazed back.

  Each one was dark and hollow round the eyes, 22
pallid in feature, and so gaunt and waste
their skin was formed to show the very bone.

  Erysichthon, as I can well believe, 25*
was not so dry and shrivelled round his rind
when, hungering, his dread was at its height.

28   Io dicea fra me stesso pensando: 'Ecco
la gente che perdé Ierusalemme,
quando Maria nel figlio diè di becco.'

31   Parean l'occhiaie anella sanza gemme:
chi nel viso de li uomini legge *omo*
ben avria quivi conosciuta l'emme.

34   Chi crederebbe che l'odor d'un pomo
sì governasse, generando brama,
e quel d'un'acqua, non sappiendo como?

37   Già era in ammirar che sì li affama,
per la cagione ancor non manifesta
di lor magrezza e di lor trista squama,

40   ed ecco del profondo de la testa
volse a me li occhi un'ombra e guardò fiso;
poi gridò forte: 'Qual grazia m'è questa!'

43   Mai non l'avrei riconosciuto al viso,
ma ne la voce sua mi fu palese
ciò che l'aspetto in sé avea conquiso.

46   Questa favilla tutta mi raccese
mia conoscenza a la cangiata labbia,
e ravvisai la faccia di Forese.

49   'Deh, non contendere a l'asciutta scabbia
che mi scolora,' pregava, 'la pelle,
né a difetto di carne ch'io abbia,

52   ma dimmi il ver di te, dì chi son quelle
due anime che là ti fanno scorta:
non rimaner che tu non mi favelle!'

55   'La faccia tua, ch'io lagrimai già morta,
mi dà di pianger mo non minor doglia,'
rispuos' io lui, 'veggendola sì torta.

58   Però mi dì, per Dio, che sì vi sfoglia:
non mi far dir mentr' io mi maraviglio,
ché mal può dir chi è pien d'altra voglia.'

61   Ed elli a me: 'De l'etterno Consiglio
cade vertù ne l'acqua e ne la pianta
rimasa dietro, ond' io sì m'assottiglio.

And I, in thought, was saying to myself,   28
'Just look! The folk who lost Jerusalem
when starving Mary pecked her son to death.

The sockets of their eyes seemed gemless rings,   31
and those who read Man's 'OMO' in Man's face
would clearly have seen 'M' in all of these.

Who would have thought the scent of some mere fruit   34
could work to make a craving grow like this,
and water, too – unless he knew the 'how'.

Already wondering what had starved them so,   37
I saw no reason that could well explain
such thinness and those dreadful scales of skin.

Then, look! A shadow turned its eyes on me,   40
deep in its skull, and, peering fixedly,
cried out aloud: 'For me, how great a grace!'

I never would have known him from his face.   43
But in his voice, all now was shown to me
that had, in feature, been destroyed and lost.

That spark for me rekindled at a stroke   46
clear recognition of those much-changed lips,
and once again I saw Forese's face.

'Don't boggle so to see these dried-up scabs,   49
which drain the colour from my skin,' he begged,
'nor that I have so great a lack of flesh.

But speak out. Tell the truth about yourself,   52
and who these two souls are that act as guides.
Don't stand there, holding back the spark of words.'

'That face of yours I wept for once in death   55
now gives me,' I replied, 'as painfully,
a cause to weep, seeing it here so wrenched awry.

But tell me, in God's name, what strips your leaves?   58
Don't make me, wonderstruck, attempt to talk.
No one, desiring other things, speaks well.'

'There falls,' he said, 'from the Eternal Mind   61
a virtue in that water and that tree –
back there – which sharpens me and pares me down.

64   Tutta esta gente che piangendo canta,
        per seguitar la gola oltra misura,
        in fama e 'n sete qui si rifà santa.

67   Di bere e di mangiar n'accende cura
        l'odor ch'esce del pomo e de lo sprazzo
        che si distende su per sua verdura.

70   E non pur una volta, questo spazzo
        girando, si rinfresca nostra pena:
        io dico pena, e dovria dir sollazzo,

73   ché quella voglia a li alberi ci mena
        che menò Cristo lieto a dire "Elì",
        quando ne liberò con la sua vena.'

76   E io a lui: 'Forese, da quel dì
        nel qual mutasti mondo a miglior vita,
        cinqu' anni non son vòlti infino a qui.

79   Se prima fu la possa in te finita
        di peccar più che sovvenisse l'ora
        del buon dolor ch'a Dio ne rimarita,

82   come se' tu qua sù venuto ancora?
        Io ti credea trovar là giù di sotto
        dove tempo per tempo si ristora.'

85   Ond' elli a me: 'Sì tosto m'ha condotto
        a ber lo dolce assenzo d'i martìri
        la Nella mia con suo pianger dirotto.

88   Con suoi prieghi devoti e con sospiri
        tratto m'ha de la costa ove s'aspetta,
        e liberato m'ha de li altri giri.

91   Tanto è a Dio più cara e più diletta
        la vedovella mia, che molto amai,
        quanto in bene operare è più soletta,

94   ché la Barbagia di Sardigna assai
        ne le femmine sue più è pudica
        che la Barbagia dov' io la lasciai.

97   O dolce frate, che vuo' tu ch'io dica?
        Tempo futuro m'è già nel cospetto
        cui non sarà quest' ora molto antica,

And all these people, weeping as they sing,   64
because their gullets led them past all norms,
are here remade as holy, thirsting, hungering.

Cravings to eat and drink are fired in us   67
by perfumes from that fruit and from the spray
that spreads in fans above the greenery.

Nor once alone, in circling round this space,   70
is agony and pain refreshed in us.
I call it pain. Rightly, I should say solace.

For that same yearning leads us to the tree   73*
that led Christ, in his joy, to say "Elì",
when through his open veins he made us free.'

And I to him: 'Forese, from that day   76
that you exchanged your world for better life,
no more than five years have, till now, gone by.

If your capacity to sin was dead   79
before there came to you that holy hour
of penance that remarries souls to God,

how can it be that you've got here so quick?   82
I thought that I should find you there below,
where restitution comes to time through time.'

'To drink sweet wormwood in this rightful pain   85
I'm brought,' he now replied, 'so rapidly
by broken tears that my dear Nella shed.

With her devoted prayers and heartfelt sighs,   88
she's drawn me from that shore where spirits wait,
and freed me from the other circles, too.

My little widow, whom I loved so well,   91
to God is dearer still, and better loved,
since she so stands alone in doing good.

For, as to womenfolk, Barbagian Sards   94*
are far more chaste and modest in their ways
than is that Barbary I left her in.

What, dearest brother, would you have me say?   97
A future time, already in my sight,
will come (when our time's still not history),

100   nel qual sarà in pergamo interdetto
        a le sfacciate donne fiorentine
        l'andar mostrando con le poppe il petto.

103   Quai barbare fuor mai, quai saracine,
        cui bisognasse, per farle ir coperte,
        o spiritali o altre discipline?

106   Ma se le svergognate fosser certe
        di quel che 'l ciel veloce loro ammanna,
        già per urlare avrian le bocche aperte,

109   ché, se l'antiveder qui non m'inganna,
        prima fien triste che le guance impeli
        colui che mo si consola con nanna.

112   Deh, frate, or fa che più non mi ti celi!
        Vedi che non pur io, ma questa gente
        tutta rimira là dove 'l sol veli.'

115   Per ch'io a lui: 'Se tu riduci a mente
        qual fosti meco e qual io teco fui,
        ancor fia grave il memorar presente.

118   Di quella vita mi volse costui
        che mi va innanzi l'altr' ier, quando tonda
        vi si mostrò la suora di colui' –

121   e 'l sol mostrai. 'Costui per la profonda
        notte menato m'ha d'i veri morti
        con questa vera carne che 'l seconda.

124   Indi m'han tratto sù li suoi conforti,
        salendo e rigirando la montagna
        che drizza voi che 'l mondo fece torti.

127   Tanto dice di farmi sua compagna
        che io sarò là dove fia Beatrice;
        quivi convien che sanza lui rimagna.

130   Virgilio è questi che così mi dice' –
        e addita'lo – 'e quest' altro è quell' ombra
        per cui si scosse dianzi ogne pendice

133   lo vostro regno, che da sé lo sgombra.'

when, from the pulpit, there'll be issued bans   100
forbidding bare-faced Florence girls to go
with blatant breasts and both their boobs on show.

What mere barbarians or Saracens   103
required a priest or threat of on-spot fines
to make them cover up when they go out!

If, though, these brazen creatures only guessed   106
what Heaven so swiftly will bring down on them,
then they'd already howl with open mouths.

For if, foreseeing this, I'm not beguiled,   109
they'll come to grief before the cheek grows hair
on any boy now rocked by lullabies.

So, brother, don't still hide yourself from me.   112
You see? It's all of us, not me alone,
who gaze in wonder where you veil the sun.'

'If you bring back to mind,' I now replied,   115
'what you were once to me and I to you,
the memory of that will still be sore.

I, from that life, was turned away by him   118*
who walks ahead of me the other day,
when she, his sister' (here I point the sun)

'showed full and round. He, through the utmost depths   121
of night and all the truly dead has been
a guide to me, who follow in true flesh.

Now his encouragements have drawn me up,   124
ascending here and circling all round
this mount that straightens what the world distorts.

He will, he says, be in my company   127
until I'm there where Beatrice is.
And when I am, I must then be without him.

Virgil it is who tells me all of this.'   130
(I point him out.) 'That other is the shade
for whom just now, in loosing him, your realm

was shaken in its every slope and cliff.'   133

1 Né 'l dir l'andar, né l'andar lui più lento
facea, ma ragionando andavam forte,
sì come nave pinta da buon vento;

4 e l'ombre, che parean cose rimorte,
per le fosse de li occhi ammirazione
traean di me, di mio vivere accorte.

7 E io, continuando al mio sermone,
dissi: 'Ella sen va sù forse più tarda
che non farebbe, per altrui cagione.

10 Ma dimmi, se tu sai, dov' è Piccarda?
Dimmi s'io veggio da notar persona
tra questa gente che sì mi riguarda.'

13 'La mia sorella, che tra bella e buona
non so qual fosse più, triunfa lieta
ne l'alto Olimpo già di sua corona.'

16 Sì disse prima, e poi: 'Qui non si vieta
di nominar ciascun, da ch'è sì munta
nostra sembianza via per la dieta.

19 Questi' – e mostrò col dito – 'è Bonagiunta,
Bonagiunta da Lucca; e quella faccia
di là da lui, più che l'altre trapunta,

22 ebbe la santa Chiesa in le sue braccia:
dal Torso fu, e purga per digiuno
l'anguille di Bolsena e la vernaccia.'

25 Molti altri mi nomò ad uno ad uno,
e del nomar parean tutti contenti,
sì ch'io però non vidi un atto bruno.

CANTO 24

Our words did not slow down our steps (nor stride   1
end speech). So on we went, talking apace,
like ships when driven by a favouring wind.

And all those shades, who looked like things twice dead,   4
wondered – the sockets of their eyes dug out –
as they looked on, to see me there alive.

And I, continuing my former theme: 7
'Statius's soul climbs slower than it would,
perhaps by reason of another's need.

But tell me: where's Piccarda – if you know?   10
And tell me, too, among those souls who gaze
at me, are any that I ought to note?'

'My sister (was she more – I do not know –   13
in beauty than in goodness?) triumphs now,
crowned on Olympian heights, in happiness.'

This first, and then he said: 'Since we're milked dry,   16
by fasting, of the way that once we seemed,
it's not forbidden that we each be named.

And this' (he pointed out) 'is Bonagiunta,   19*
Bonagiunta of Lucca. And, further on,
that face more raddled than are all the rest

held tight our Holy Church in his embrace.   22
He came from Tours, and purges by this fast,
Bolsena eels and flagons of vernaccia.'

Then, one by one, he named me many more.   25
And these, it seemed, were happy to be named.
I got no dark looks from them when they were.

28   Vidi per fame a vòto usar li denti
        Ubaldin da la Pila e Bonifazio,
        che pasturò col rocco molte genti.

31   Vidi messer Marchese, ch'ebbe spazio
        già di bere a Forlì con men secchezza,
        e sì fu tal che non si sentì sazio.

34   Ma come fa chi guarda e poi s'apprezza
        più d'un che d'altro, fei a quel di Lucca,
        che più parea di me voler contezza.

37   El mormorava, e non so che 'Gentucca'
        sentiv' io là ov' el sentia la piaga
        de la giustizia che sì li pilucca.

40   'O anima,' diss' io, 'che par sì vaga
        di parlar meco, fa sì ch'io t'intenda,
        e te e me col tuo parlare appaga.'

43   'Femmina è nata, e non porta ancor benda,'
        cominciò el, 'che ti farà piacere
        la mia città, come ch'om la riprenda.

46   Tu te n'andrai con questo antivedere;
        se nel mio mormorar prendesti errore,
        dichiareranti ancor le cose vere.

49   Ma dì s'i' veggio qui colui che fòre
        trasse le nove rime, cominciando:
        "Donne ch'avete intelletto d'amore"?

52   E io a lui: 'I' mi son un che, quando
        Amor mi spira, noto, e a quel modo
        ch'e' ditta dentro vo significando.'

55   'O frate, issa vegg' io,' diss' elli, 'il nodo
        che 'l Notaro e Guittone e me ritenne
        di qua dal dolce stil novo ch'i' odo.

58   Io veggio ben come le vostre penne
        di retro al dittator sen vanno strette,
        che de le nostre certo non avvenne;

61   e qual più a riguardar oltre si mette,
        non vede più da l'uno a l'altro stilo.'
        E quasi contentato si tacette.

I saw there, plying teeth on empty air,   28
Ubaldin da la Pila and that Boniface
who pastured many with his castled crook.

I saw Sir Marquis, who had far more space   31
to drink at Forlí (being far less parched),
a man who never felt he'd had his fill.

But, as our glance will scan around then prize   34
one above all, so I with that Lucchese –
seeming the keenest to be known by me.

And he, I heard, was murmuring – I don't know . . .   37
something: 'Gentucca'? – where he felt the wound
of justice as it plucked and nibbled him.

'You seem, dear soul, to long to speak with me.   40
So make me understand your sense,' I said,
'and, speaking, satisfy the two of us.'

'A woman's born (not yet grown-up in dress)'   43
(so he began) 'who'll make my native place
a joy for you, although men talk it down.

You'll leave here carrying this prophecy.   46
And if my murmurings made you mistake,
then true events will make their meaning clear.

But tell me: do I see the man who drew   49
those new rhymes forth, whose opening line ran so:
"Ladies, who have intelligence of love . . ."'?'

And I to him: 'I am just one who, when   52
Love breathes in me, takes note and then goes on
showing the meaning that's ordained within.'

'Dear brother, nah I see,' he said, 'the knot   55*
that kept the Brief, Guittone and me, too,
from reaching to that sweet new style I hear of.

I see how close behind the power that speaks   58*
your winged pens fly, transcribing what he says –
which certainly our own pens never did.

Strive as you might to see, between our styles,   61
some greater difference, you'll not see it here.'
And then, as though content, he said no more.

64   Come li augei che vernan lungo 'l Nilo
        alcuna volta in aere fanno schiera,
        poi volan più a fretta e vanno in filo:

67   così tutta la gente che lì era,
        volgendo 'l viso, raffrettò suo passo,
        e per magrezza e per voler leggera.

70   E come l'uom che di trottare è lasso
        lascia andar li compagni e si passeggia
        fin che si sfoghi l'affollar del casso:

73   sì lasciò trapassar la santa greggia
        Forese, e dietro meco sen veniva,
        dicendo: 'Quando fia ch'io ti riveggia?'

76   'Non so,' rispuos' io lui, 'quant' io mi viva,
        ma già non fia il tornar mio tantosto
        ch'io non sia col voler prima a la riva,

79   però che 'l loco u' fui a viver posto
        di giorno in giorno più di ben si spolpa,
        e a trista ruina par disposto.'

82   'Or va,' diss' el: 'ché quei che più n'ha colpa
        vegg' io a coda d'una bestia tratto
        inver' la valle ove mai non si scolpa.

85   La bestia ad ogne passo va più ratto,
        crescendo sempre, fin ch'ella il percuote,
        e lascia il corpo vilmente disfatto.

88   Non hanno molto a volger quelle ruote' –
        e drizzò li occhi al ciel – 'che ti fia chiaro
        ciò che 'l mio dir più dichiarar non puote.

91   Tu ti rimani omai, ché 'l tempo è caro
        in questo regno, sì ch'io perdo troppo
        venendo teco sì a paro a paro.'

94   Qual esce alcuna volta di gualoppo
        lo cavalier di schiera che cavalchi,
        e va per farsi onor del primo intoppo:

97   tal si partì da noi con maggior valchi,
        e io rimasi in via con esso i due
        che fuor del mondo sì gran marescalchi.

As birds that pass their winters by the Nile   64*
will rise at times and gather on the air,
then fly, more rapidly, to form a line,
   so now the crowd of people who were there   67
all turned their faces and increased their stride,
light-footed, driven by desire (and thin!).
   And then, like someone tired of trotting on   70
who lets the pack go by and takes his time
until the heaving of his chest is done,
   Forese, too, now left the holy flock.   73
As these raced off, he followed in my track,
saying: 'So when shall I see *you* again?'
   'How long I'll live,' I answered, 'I don't know.   76
But my return will not be sooner than
desire already brings me to this shore.
   For that place where it falls to me to live   79
grows, day by day, less meaty as to good,
and sets its mind on ruin and despair.'
   'That's right,' he said. 'I see who's most to blame   82
dragged at a horse's tail towards the ditch
where no one, ever, can be free of sin.
   That beast rampages faster with each step,   85
accelerating always, till it strikes
and leaves his broken corpse a mangled mess.
   Those wheels' (he fixed his eyes upon the stars)   88
'have little left to run till you see clear
the things that I, in words, cannot declare.
   You stay behind. For time is precious here.   91
Coming along with you and keeping step,
I, in this realm, already lose too much.'
   Knights gallop out at times from charging troops,   94
intending, as they leave the rest behind,
to claim the honours of an opening duel.
   So off he went from us at greater pace,   97
and I remained, still travelling with those two
who in the world were such great dignitaries.

100   E quando innanzi a noi intrato fue
       che li occhi miei si fero a lui seguaci
       come la mente a le parole sue,

103   parvermi i rami gravidi e vivaci
       d'un altro pomo, e non molto lontani,
       per esser pur allora vòlto in laci.

106   Vidi gente sott' esso alzar le mani
       e gridar non so che verso le fronde:
       quasi bramosi fantolini e vani

109   che pregano, e 'l pregato non risponde,
       ma, per fare esser ben la voglia acuta,
       tien alto lor disio e nol nasconde.

112   Poi si partì sì come ricreduta,

       e noi venimmo al grande arbore adesso,
       che tanti prieghi e lagrime rifiuta.

115   'Trapassate oltre sanza farvi presso:
       legno è più sù che fu morso da Eva,
       e questa pianta sì levò da esso.'

118   Sì tra le frasche non so chi diceva,
       per che Virgilio e Stazio e io, ristretti,
       oltre andavam dal lato che si leva.

121   'Ricordivi,' dicea, 'd'i maladetti
       nei nuvoli formati, che, satolli,

       Teseo combatter co' doppi petti,

124   e de li Ebrei ch'al ber si mostrar molli,
       per che no i volle Gedeon compagni
       quando inver' Madian discese i colli.'

127   Sì, accostati a l'un d'i due vivagni,
       passammo, udendo colpe de la gola
       seguite già da miseri guadagni.

130   Poi, rallargati per la strada sola,
       ben mille passi e più ci portar oltre,
       contemplando ciascun sanza parola.

And when he'd gone so far ahead of us   100
that eyesight strained to follow in his track
(as did my mind to understand his words),

there then appeared to me, ripe-branched and bright,   103
a second fruit tree, not so far from us,
just there, around the bend that we'd now turned.

Beneath, I saw a group that raised their hands   106
and called towards the leaves I-don't-know-what,
like silly, over-eager little tots,

who plead – although their target won't respond   109
but rather seeks to whet their appetite,
dangling, unhidden, what they want aloft.

Then off they went (as though they'd changed their
        minds).   112
And we ourselves arrived at that great tree
which turned aside so many tears and prayers.

'Move further on, and don't get drawn to that.   115
There's, higher up, the tree that Eve once bit.
This tree is raised from it, and flourishes.'

Someone – I don't know who – among its sprigs   118
spoke this. So Virgil, Statius and myself
closed ranks, to pass by on the rising side.

'Recall those curséd ones,' the voice went on,   121*
'the centaurs, formed from cloud, who once, when
        gorged,
fought against Theseus with doubled chests.

Recall those Hebrews, softened so by drink   124
that Gideon would not take them in his ranks
when he swept down on Midian from the hills.

So, tightly pressed against the near-side verge,   127
we passed along and heard how sins of greed
were followed once by miserable rewards.

Then, broadening out, we found an empty road.   130
A thousand paces bore us on (and more),
each of us silent, each contemplative.

133   'Che andate pensando sì voi sol tre?'
         sùbita voce disse, ond' io mi scossi
         come fan bestie spaventate e poltre.

136   Drizzai la testa per veder chi fossi,
         e già mai non si videro in fornace
         vetri o metalli sì lucenti e rossi

139   com' io vidi un che dicea: 'S'a voi piace
         montare in sù, qui si convien dar volta:
         quinci si va chi vuole andar per pace.'

142   L'aspetto suo m'avea la vista tolta,
         per ch'io mi volsi dietro a' miei dottori
         com' om che va secondo ch'elli ascolta.

145   E quale, annunziatrice de li albóri,
         l'aura di maggio movesi e olezza,
         tutta impregnata da l'erba e da' fiori:

148   tal mi senti' un vento dar per mezza
         la fronte, e ben senti' mover la piuma,
         che fé sentir d'ambrosia l'orezza,

151   e senti' dir: 'Beati cui alluma
         tanto di grazia che l'amor del gusto
         nel petto lor troppo disir non fuma,

154   esuriendo sempre quanto è giusto.'

'And what are you three thinking as you go?'   133
A sudden voice said this – at which I shied
in terror like an untamed animal.

I raised my head to see who this might be.   136
And in no furnace was there ever seen
metal or glass that glowed as bright and red

as now I saw one, saying: 'If you wish   139
to get up there, then here's where you must turn.
All seeking peace are bound to take this path.'

The blazing face had robbed me of my sight.   142
And so behind my teachers I went on
as someone will when led by what he hears.

And as the breeze in May – first messenger   145
of whitening dawn – is moved in fragrant waves,
pregnant with grasses, greenery and flowers,

so here I sensed, mid-brow, wind touching me,   148
and sensed the moving feathers of a wing
that brought ambrosial senses to the air,

and made me sense the words: 'The truly blessed   151
are lit with so much grace that in their hearts
a love of food fumes forth no false desire,

esurient always for the good and true.'   154

CANTO 25

1   Ora era onde 'l salir non volea storpio,
       ché 'l sole avea il cerchio di merigge
       lasciato al Tauro e la notte a lo Scorpio,

4   per che, come fa l'uom che non s'affigge
       ma vassi a la via sua che che li appaia,
       se di bisogno stimolo il trafigge:

7   così intrammo noi per la callaia,
       uno innanzi altro prendendo la scala
       che per artezza i salitor dispaia.

10   E quale il cicognin che leva l'ala
       per voglia di volare, e non s'attenta
       d'abbandonar lo nido, e giù la cala:

13   tal era io con voglia accesa e spenta
       di dimandar, venendo infino a l'atto
       che fa colui ch'a dicer s'argomenta.

16   Non lasciò, per l'andar che fosse ratto,
       lo dolce padre mio, ma disse: 'Scocca
       l'arco del dir, che 'nfino al ferro hai tratto.'

19   Allor sicuramente apri' la bocca
       e cominciai: 'Come si può far magro
       là dove l'uopo di nodrir non tocca?'

22   'Se t'ammentassi come Meleagro
       si consumò al consumar d'un stizzo,
       non fora,' disse, 'a te questo sì agro,

25   e se pensassi come al vostro guizzo
       guizza dentro a lo specchio vostra image,
       ciò che par duro ti parrebbe vizzo.

CANTO 25

The hour would not allow a crippled climb.   1*
The sun had now abandoned to the Bull
its noon-time ring, and night to Scorpio.

    And so, like people who will not stay put   4
but, driven forward by some piercing need,
go on, whatever comes before their eyes,

    so here we entered on a passageway   7
(so narrow it uncouples those who climb),
clambering in single file to mount the stair.

    Compare: a fledgling stork will lift its wings.   10*
It wants to fly but still dares not attempt
to leave the nest, so sinks back down again.

    That was me, too – the urge to ask, alight   13
and yet snuffed out, arriving at the *look*
(no more) of someone who intends to speak.

    My dearest father, though the pace was quick,   16
did not hold back, but said: 'Let loose your bow.
You've drawn that arrow to its iron tip.'

    Now, confident, I opened up my lips.   19
'Where there's no need for nourishment,' I said,
'how can it be that people get so thin?'

    'Were you to call to mind how Meleager –   22*
a log consumed by fire – consumed himself,
then this,' he said, 'would not seem sour to you.

    And if you thought how, when you writhe around,   25
your image in a mirror also writhes,
what seems so hard would seem a hoary truth.

28   Ma perché dentro a tuo voler t'adage,
        ecco qui Stazio, e io lui chiamo e prego
        che sia or sanator de le tue piage.'

31   'Se la veduta etterna li dislego,'
        rispuose Stazio, 'là dove tu sie,
        discolpi me non potert' io far nego.'

34   Poi cominciò: 'Se le parole mie,
        figlio, la mente tua guarda e riceve,
        lume ti fiero al come che tu die.

37   Sangue perfetto, che poi non si beve
        da l'assetate vene e si rimane
        quasi alimento che di mensa leve,

40   prende nel core a tutte membra umane
        virtute informativa, come quello
        ch'a farsi quelle per le vene vane.

43   Ancor digesto, scende ov' è più bello
        tacer che dire; e quindi poscia geme
        sovr' altrui sangue in natural vasello.

46   Ivi s'accoglie l'uno e l'altro insieme,
        l'un disposto a patire e l'altro a fare,
        per lo perfetto loco onde si preme;

49   e, giunto lui, comincia ad operare
        coagulando prima, e poi avviva
        ciò che per sua matera fé constare.

52   Anima fatta la virtute attiva
        qual d'una pianta, in tanto differente
        che questa è in via e quella è già a riva,

55   tanto ovra poi che già si move e sente
        come spungo marino, e indi imprende
        ad organar le posse ond' è semente:

58   or si spiega, figliuolo, or si distende
        la virtù ch'è dal cor del generante,
        dove natura a tutte membra intende.

61   Ma come d'animal divegna fante
        non vedi tu ancor: quest' è tal punto
        che più savio di te fé già errante,

To make you, though, at ease in your desires,   28
Statius is here, look. I now call on him,
begging he be the healer of your wounds.'

Statius responded: 'If, for him, I free –   31
with you still here – a vista of eternity,
let this be my excuse: I can't say no.'

He then began: 'My son, if in your mind   34
you gather up and guard my words to you,
they'll be a light that shows the "how" you seek.

Pure, perfect blood – which never will be drunk   37
by thirsting veins – remains behind untouched,
as might some dish that's carried from the feast,

and gains there, in the heart, a power to mould   40
the limbs and organs of new embryos –
as blood runs through our veins to form our own.

This blood, distilled as sperm, descends to where   43
(more decent not to say) its droplets run
within the natural cup to other blood.

These two bloods meet and gather, each with each.   46
Menstrum is passive. But the other acts –
the perfect place it's pressed from causes that –

and, once arrived, begins to do its work,   49
first to coagulate, and then to bring
the matter that it first made dense to life.

The active virtue, which is now a soul,   52
much like a plant (though differing in this point,
that plant souls stay as plants while this moves on),

continues in its work, to move and feel,   55
as do aquatic sponges, then begins
to form the organs for the powers it seeds.

And now, my dearest son, the power that flows   58
out of the father's heart (where nature plans
for every organ) stretching, spreads to all.

This creature will become a speaking child.   61
Yet *how*, you don't yet see. And this same point
led someone far more wise than you astray,

64   sì che per sua dottrina fé disgiunto
        da l'anima il possibile intelletto,
        perché da lui non vide organo assunto.

67   Apri a la verità che viene il petto,
        e sappi che, sì tosto come al feto
        l'articular del cerebro è perfetto,

70   lo Motor primo a lui si volge, lieto
        sovra tant' arte di natura, e spira
        spirito novo, di vertù repleto,

73   che ciò che trova attivo quivi tira
        in sua sustanzia, e fassi un'alma sola,
        che vive e sente e sé in sé rigira.

76   E perché meno ammiri la parola,
        guarda il calor del sol che si fa vino,
        giunto a l'omor che de la vite cola.

79   Quando Làchesis non ha più del lino,
        solvesi da la carne, e in virtute
        ne porta seco e l'umano e 'l divino:

82   l'altre potenze tutte quante mute;
        memoria, intelligenza e volontade
        in atto molto più che prima agute.

85   Sanza restarsi, per sé stessa cade
        mirabilmente a l'una de le rive;
        quivi conosce prima le sue strade.

88   Tosto che loco lì la circunscrive,
        la virtù formativa raggia intorno
        così e quanto ne le membra vive.

91   E come l'aere, quand' è ben piorno,
        per l'altrui raggio che 'n sé si reflette,
        di diversi color diventa addorno:

94   così l'aere vicin quivi si mette
        in quella forma che in lui suggella
        virtüalmente l'alma che ristette;

97   e simigliante poi a la fiammella,
        che segue il foco là 'vunque si muta,
        segue lo spirto sua forma novella.

who in his teachings set the soul apart   64
from *intellectus* as *possibilis*,
finding no organ taken up by that.

Open your heart. Receive the coming truth.   67
Know this: when once the foetal brain is brought
to full articulation in the womb,

the Primal Cause of Motion turns in joy   70
to see so much of Nature's art, and breathes
new breath of spirit filled with power within,

which draws all active elements it finds   73
into its being and thus forms one soul
which lives and feels and turns as conscious self.

And – so you'll wonder less at what I say –   76
look at how solar warmth transforms to wine
when joined with juices flowing from the grape.

And when Lachesis cannot spin more thread,   79*
the soul leaves flesh and carries, by its power,
both human and divine along with it.

But memory, intelligence and will,   82*
since all the other powers are silent now,
become, in act, much keener than before.

Unrestingly, it falls, by its own will –   85
a miracle! – on one of these two shores,
and here first knows the paths it has to take.

As soon as it is circumscribed by place,   88
the power that forms it radiates around
in size and shape as in its living limbs.

And as the air, when drenched with vaporous rain,   91
is soon adorned with many different hues,
from other rays reflected in the haze,

so when the soul has reached this point of rest,   94
the air around it gathers in the form
that virtual powers of soul impress on it.

And, as some little flame pursues the fire   97
and follows where its changing heat may lead,
so this new form will go where spirit goes.

100   Però che quindi ha poscia sua paruta,
      è chiamata ombra; e quindi organa poi
      ciascun sentire infino a la veduta.

103   Quindi parliamo e quindi ridiam noi;
      quindi facciam le lagrime e ' sospiri
      che per lo monte aver sentiti puoi.

106   Secondo che ci affliggono i disiri
      e li altri affetti, l'ombra si figura,
      e quest' è la cagion di che tu miri.'

109   E già venuto a l'ultima tortura
      s'era per noi e vòlto a man destra,
      ed eravamo attenti ad altra cura.

112   Quivi la ripa fiamma in fuor balestra,
      e la cornice spira fiato in suso
      che la reflette e via da lei sequestra,

115   ond' ir ne convenia dal lato schiuso
      ad uno ad uno, e io temea 'l foco
      quinci, e quindi temeva cader giuso.

118   Lo duca mio dicea: 'Per questo loco
      si vuol tenere a li occhi stretto il freno,
      però ch'error potrebbesi per poco.'

121   'Summae Deus clementiae', nel seno
      al grande ardore allora udi' cantando,
      che di volger mi fé caler non meno,

124   e vidi spirti per la fiamma andando,
      per ch'io guardava loro e a' miei passi,
      compartendo la vista a quando a quando.

127   Appresso il fine ch'a quell' inno fassi,
      gridavano alto: 'Virum non cognosco!'
      indi ricominciavan l'inno, bassi.

130   Finitolo, anco gridavano: 'Al bosco
      si tenne Diana ed Elice caccionne,
      che di Venere avea sentito il tòsco.'

133   Indi al cantar tornavano; indi donne
      gridavano e mariti che fuor casti,
      come virtute e matrimonio imponne.

And since in this way soul appears to view,   100
that's called soul's shade. And from this there will form
the organs of all sense, including sight.

And that is how we speak and how we laugh,   103
and how we form our tears and all those sighs
that you may well have heard around this hill.

As our desires and other feelings form,   106
the shade accordingly configures them.
And that's the cause of what you wonder at.'

Our path had brought us, turning to the right,   109
to reach the final twist of punishment,
and we were now intent on new concerns.

The bank here shot out blazing bolts of flame.   112
And round the edge there breathed an upward wind
that bent these flames back, keeping them at bay.

So, one by one, we had to make our way   115
along the unprotected outer rim.
I feared the fire there. Here I feared the fall.

Meanwhile, my leader said: 'In such a place   118
we need to keep a strict check on our eyes.
It wouldn't be too hard for them to stray.'

And then I heard: '*Summae Deus clementiae*'   121
singing within the heart of that great blaze,
which made me – no less watchfully – turn round.

I saw there spirits walking in the flames.   124
At which I looked at both my steps and them,
dividing my attentions, here then there.

And, when the ending of the hymn had come,   127*
they cried aloud, '*Virum non cognosco*!'
then, singing low, began the hymn again.

That finished, they all cried once more: 'Diana,   130
guarding her woodlands, drove out Helice
who'd felt what bitter poison Venus sends.'

And yet again they now began their song,   133
then called on men and women who were chaste –
as virtue and our marriages demand.

136   E questo modo credo che lor basti
         per tutto il tempo che 'l foco li abbruscia:
         con tal cura conviene e con tai pasti
139   che la piaga da sezzo si ricuscia.

This form of song will serve for them, I think,   136
throughout the time the fire is scorching them.
With this concern and fed by foods like this,
   sin's final wound is sewn up once again.   139

CANTO 26

1   Mentre che sì per l'orlo, uno innanzi altro,
ce n'andavamo, e spesso il buon maestro
diceami: 'Guarda: giovi ch'io ti scaltro,'

4   feriami il sole in su l'omero destro,
che già raggiando tutto l'occidente
mutava in bianco aspetto di cilestro,

7   e io facea con l'ombra più rovente
parer la fiamma; e pur a tanto indizio
vidi molt' ombre, andando, poner mente.

10 Questa fu la cagion che diede inizio
loro a parlar di me, e cominciarsi
a dir: 'Colui non par corpo fittizio.'

13 Poi verso me quanto potean farsi
certi si fero, sempre con riguardo
di non uscir dove non fosser arsi.

16 'O tu che vai, non per esser più tardo
ma forse reverente, a li altri dopo,
rispondi a me, che 'n sete e 'n foco ardo.

19 Né solo a me la tua risposta è uopo,
ché tutti questi n'hanno maggior sete
che d'acqua fredda Indo o Etiopo.

22 Dinne com' è che fai di te parete
al sol, pur come tu non fossi ancora
di morte intrato dentro da la rete.'

25 Sì mi parlava un d'essi, e io mi fóra
già manifesto, s'io non fossi atteso
ad altra novità ch'apparve allora:

CANTO 26

While on, in single file, we went around   1
the rim – my trusted teacher saying often:
'Careful! I'll point the dangers out. Attend!' –

the sun was beating on my right-hand side,   4
its rays illuminating all the west,
changing its face from clearest blue to white.

And I, in casting shadows on the flame,   7
made fire seem fiercer. Then many shades,
I saw, at that one hint, while walking on,

gave thought, and came, because of that,   10
to say of me their say. So they began:
'He does not seem, in body, fiction-formed.'

And then, as far towards me as they could,   13
they pressed to make quite sure – with constant care
lest any come where they should *not* be burned.

'You there (who, following the other two,   16
aren't slow, maybe, but mean to show respect)
please answer me. I burn in fire and thirst.

Nor will your answer serve for me alone.   19
For all of us are thirsting more for this
than Ethiopes or Indians for cool streams.

Tell us: how do you make yourself a wall   22
to shield the sun, as if you had not yet
entered within the trammels of death's net?'

These words from one of them. And I'd have said   25
already who I was, except my mind
was set on something new that now appeared.

28   ché per lo mezzo del cammino acceso
      venne gente col viso incontro a questa,
      la qual mi fece a rimirar sospeso.

31   Lì veggio d'ogne parte farsi presta
      ciascun' ombra e basciarsi una con una
      sanza restar, contente a brieve festa:

34   così per entro loro schiera bruna
      s'ammusa l'una con l'altra formica,
      forse a spiar lor via e lor fortuna.

37   Tosto che parton l'accoglienza amica,
      prima che 'l primo passo lì trascorra,
      sopragridar ciascuna s'affatica,

40   la nova gente: 'Soddoma e Gomorra!'
      e l'altra: 'Ne la vacca entra Pasife
      perché 'l torello a sua lussuria corra!'

43   Poi, come grue ch'a le montagne Rife
      volasser parte, e parte inver' l'arene,
      queste del gel, quelle del sole schife:

46   l'una gente sen va, l'altra sen vène;
      e tornan lagrimando a' primi canti
      e al gridar che più lor si convene;

49   e raccostansi a me, come davanti,
      essi medesmi che m'avean pregato,
      attenti ad ascoltar ne' lor sembianti.

52   Io, che due volte avea visto lor grato,
      incominciai: 'O anime sicure
      d'aver, quando che sia, di pace stato,

55   non son rimase acerbe né mature
      le membra mie di là, ma son qui meco
      col sangue suo e con le sue giunture.

58   Quinci sù vo per non esser più cieco;
      donna è di sopra che m'acquista grazia,
      per che 'l mortal per vostro mondo reco.

61   Ma se la vostra maggior voglia sazia
      tosto divegna, sì che 'l ciel v'alberghi
      ch'è pien d'amore e più ampio si spazia,

For down the middle of the blazing path,   28
facing the first, there came another group.
This made me pause in answering, and gaze.

I saw on either side the shadows kiss.   31
They did not cease, however, in their course,
each one content to keep the frolic brief.

In that same way, within their darkening ranks,   34
ants nuzzle other ants, when columns meet,
to scout the road ahead or spy on fate.

These friends, once parted from their warm embrace,   37
before their forward steps can speed them on,
strain, each one louder than the next, to yell

(the new arrivals), 'Sodom! Gomorrah!'   40*
'Into the cow' (the rest) 'went Pasiphae
to let the bull calf run his lust in her.'

As flocks of cranes divide – some flying north   43*
to find the Riphean steeps, while some seek sand
(the second can't stand chill; the former, sun),

one lot went off, the other went off, too,   46
all turning, weeping, to their former song,
each to the slogan that most suited them.

Then those same souls who'd pleaded with me first   49
came to my side, as they had done before
and, from the look of them, were keen to hear.

And I (who'd now seen twice what they found good)   52
began: 'You souls, quite certain to arrive –
whenever that time comes – at perfect peace,

my living limbs have not remained back there,   55
not aged and ripe, nor youthful green. They're here.
They travel with me, blood and joints entire.

I make this climb to be no longer blind.   58
A lady up above besought this grace
that through your world I bear my mortal part.

Yet – may your greater longing soon be fed,   61
so that you come to lodge at rest in Heaven,
which, ranging wide and free, is full of peace –

64   ditemi, acciò ch'ancor carta ne verghi:
chi siete voi, e chi è quella turba
che se ne va di retro a' vostri terghi?'

67   Non altrimenti stupido si turba
lo montanaro e rimirando ammuta,
quando rozzo e salvatico s'inurba,

70   che ciascun' ombra fece in sua paruta;
ma poi che furon di stupore scarche,
lo qual ne li alti cuor tosto s'attuta:

73   'Beato te, che de le nostre marche,'
ricominciò colei che pria m'inchiese,
'per morir meglio, esperienza imbarche!

76   La gente che non vien con noi offese
di ciò per che già Cesar triunfando
"Regina" contra sé chiamar s'intese;

79   però si parton "Soddoma" gridando,
rimproverando a sé com' hai udito,
e aiutan l'arsura vergognando.

82   Nostro peccato fu ermafrodito,
ma perché non servammo umana legge,
seguendo come bestie l'appetito,

85   in obbrobrio di noi per noi si legge,
quando partinci, il nome di colei
che s'imbestiò ne le 'mbestiate schegge.

88   Or sai nostri atti e di che fummo rei;
se forse a nome vuo' saper chi semo,
tempo non è di dire, e non saprei.

91   Farotti ben di me volere scemo:
son Guido Guinizelli, e già mi purgo
per ben dolermi prima ch'a lo stremo.'

94   Quali ne la tristizia di Ligurgo
si fer due figli a riveder la madre,
tal mi fec' io – ma non a tanto insurgo –

97   quand' io odo nomar sé stesso il padre
mio e de li altri, miei miglior, che mai
rime d'amor usar dolci e leggiadre,

'tell me, so I may rule a page for this,   64
who might you be, and who's within that crowd
that's going on its way behind your backs?'

These shadows in appearance now all stood   67*
as mountain yokels stand – no differently –
in dumbstruck stupefaction, staring round,

when, red-necked, rough, they make it, first, to town.   70
But once they'd set astonishment aside
(it's quickly blunted in a noble heart),

'Blessèd be you, who round our border lands,'   73
the shade who first had questioned me began,
'haul in experience for your better death!

Those folk who do not follow in our track   76*
offended as did Caesar – who once heard
"You queen!", when triumphing, yelled out at him.

Then they, as they depart, are crying, "Sodom!"   79
to castigate themselves as you have heard,
bringing self-shame to aid the scorching fire.

Our sin, by contrast, was hermaphrodite.   82*
And since we paid no heed to human law –
choosing to follow bestial appetites –

ourselves we read out our opprobrium,   85
speaking, on leaving here, the name of one
who made herself a beast in beastlike planks.

So now you know our guilt and what we did.   88
But if you seek to know us each by name,
there is no time – and I don't know them all.

I shall diminish what you want of me.   91
I'm Guido Guinizelli. Since I mourned
my sins before my end, I'm here made clean.'

Like those two sons, who, when Lycurgus grieved,   94*
were made to see their mother once again,
so I became (though I don't reach those heights),

listening as now he named himself, the sire   97
of me and all those (better men) who ever
wrote about love in sweet and well-poised rhyme.

100   e sanza udire e dir pensoso andai
        lunga fiata rimirando lui,
        né, per lo foco, in là più m'appressai.

103   Poi che di riguardar pasciuto fui,
        tutto m'offersi pronto al suo servigio
        con l'affermar che fa credere altrui.

106   Ed elli a me: 'Tu lasci tal vestigio
        per quel ch'i' odo in me, e tanto chiaro,
        che Leté nol può tòrre né far bigio.

109   Ma se le tue parole or ver giuraro,
        dimmi che è cagion per che dimostri
        nel dire e nel guardar d'avermi caro.'

112   E io a lui: 'Li dolci detti vostri,
        che, quanto durerà l'uso moderno,
        faranno cari ancora i loro incostri.'

115   'O frate,' disse, 'questi ch'io ti cerno
        col dito,' e additò un spirto innanzi,
        'fu miglior fabbro del parlar materno.

118   Versi d'amore e prose di romanzi
        soverchiò tutti, e lascia dir li stolti
        che quel di Lemosì credon ch'avanzi.

121   A voce più ch'al ver drizzan li volti,
        e così ferman sua oppinione
        prima ch'arte o ragion per lor s'ascolti.

124   Così fer molti antichi di Guittone,
        di grido in grido pur lui dando pregio,
        fin che l'ha vinto il ver con più persone.

127   Or se tu hai sì ampio privilegio
        che licito ti sia l'andare al chiostro
        nel quale è Cristo abate del collegio,

130   falli per me un dir d'un paternostro,
        quanto bisogna a noi di questo mondo,
        dove poter peccar non è più nostro.'

133   Poi, forse per dar luogo altrui secondo
        che presso avea, disparve per lo foco
        come per l'acqua il pesce andando al fondo.

Hearing and saying nothing, deep in thought,   100
I walked a while, just marvelling at him,
yet did not – since the fire was there – draw near.

Then, having pastured fully on that gaze,   103
I gave myself entirely to his service,
with gestures of the kind that win good faith.

To me he said: 'Through what I hear, you leave   106
so clear a trace and footprint in my mind,
Lethe won't cancel it or make it fade.

But, if the oath you took just now holds true,   109
tell me, why is it that, in word and look,
you show so frankly that you hold me dear?'

And I to him: 'That smooth, sweet verse you wrote   112
will make its very ink most dearly prized
as long as present usage still endures.'

'Brother,' he said, 'the one I single out'   115
(his finger pointing to a soul ahead)
'crafted the mother tongue with greater skill.

Lyrics of love, in prose the French Romance –   118
all these he far surpassed. Let idiots talk,
rating that poet from Limoges ahead.

Their gaze is turned to chatter more than truth.   121
They settle their opinions long before
reason or art is heard within their thoughts.

That's what they did with Fra Guittone once,   124
proclaiming, on and on, his proven worth
until, with many more, the truth won through.

Now since you're granted generous privilege   127
to pass within those cloistered corridors,
where Christ is abbot of the brotherhood,

then say a *Paternoster* for me there –   130
as much, at least, as we, in this world, need –
where no ability to sin is ours.'

Maybe to give another, nearby, space,   133
he disappeared at this point through the fire,
as fish do going to the water's depth.

136   Io mi fei al mostrato innanzi un poco,
          e dissi ch'al suo nome il mio disire
          apparecchiava grazioso loco.

139   El cominciò liberamente a dire:
          'Tan m'abellis vostre cortes deman,
          qu'ieu no me puesc ni voill a vos cobrire.

142   Ieu sui Arnaut, que plor e vau cantan;
          consiros vei la passada folor,
          e vei jausen lo joi qu'esper denan.

145   Ara vos prec, per aquella valor
          que vos guida al som de l'escalina,
          sovenha vos a temps de ma dolor.'

148   Poi s'ascose nel foco che li affina.

I made towards the soul he'd pointed out,   136
and said that my desires were gratefully
disposed to find a fit place for his name.

   And, free and open, he began to speak: 139*
'*Tan m'abellis vostre cortes deman,*
qu'ieu no me puesc ni voill a vos cobrire,

   Ieu sui Arnaut, que plor e vau cantan;   142
consiros vei la passada folor,
e vei jausen lo joi qu'esper denan.

   Ara vos prec, per aquella valor   145
que vos guida al som de l'escalina,
sovenha vos a temps de ma dolor.'

   He hid then in the fire that sharpens them.   148

CANTO 27

1   Sì come quando i primi raggi vibra
là dove il suo Fattor lo sangue sparse,
cadendo Ibero sotto l'alta Libra

4   e l'onde in Gange da nona riarse:
sì stava il sole, onde 'l giorno sen giva,
come l'angel di Dio lieto ci apparse.

7   Fuor de la fiamma stava in su la riva
e cantava 'Beati mundo corde!'
in voce assai più che la nostra viva.

10   Poscia: 'Più non si va, se pria non morde,
anime sante, il foco: intrate in esso,
e al cantar di là non siate sorde,'

13   ci disse come noi li fummo presso;
per ch'io divenni tal, quando lo 'ntesi,
qual è colui che ne la fossa è messo.

16   In su le man commesse mi protesi,
guardando il foco e imaginando forte
umani corpi già veduti accesi.

19   Volsersi verso me le buone scorte,
e Virgilio mi disse: 'Figliuol mio,
qui può esser tormento, ma non morte.

22   Ricorditi, ricorditi! E se io
sovresso Gerion ti guidai salvo,
che farò presso più a Dio?

25   Credi per certo che se dentro a l'alvo
di questa fiamma stessi ben mille anni,
non ti potrebbe far d'un capel calvo.

CANTO 27

As when it strikes its first vibrating rays   1*
where once its own Creator shed His blood
(the river Ebro falling under Libra's height,

  while Ganges' waves are scorched by noon-time heat)   4
at *that* degree the sun now stood. So day
was leaving when, in joy, God's angel showed.

  Beyond the flame, he stood there on the bank,   7*
and sang the words '*Beati mundo corde*!',
his voice – far more than ours can be – alive.

  And then: 'None can, you holy souls, proceed   10
until the fire has bitten them. Go in.
And do not turn deaf ears to what is sung!'

  he said to us, as we came near to him.   13
And I became, on seeing what he meant,
as though, still living, placed within a tomb.

  Over my suppliant hands entwined, I leaned   16
just staring at the fire, imagining
bodies of human beings I'd seen burn.

  And both my trusted guides now turned to me.   19
And Virgil spoke, to say: 'My dearest son,
here may be agony but never death.

  Remember this! Remember! And if I   22
led you to safety on Geryon's back,
what will I do when now so close to God?

  Believe this. And be sure. Were you to stay   25
a thousand years or more wombed in this fire,
you'd not be made the balder by one hair.

28   E se tu forse credi ch'io t'inganni,
      fatti ver' lei, e fatti far credenza
      con le tue mani al lembo d'i tuoi panni.

31   Pon giù omai, pon giù ogne temenza,
      volgiti in qua e vieni: entra sicuro!'
      E io pur fermo e contra coscienza.

34   Quando mi vide star pur fermo e duro,
      turbato un poco disse: 'Or vedi, figlio:
      tra Beatrice e te è questo muro.'

37   Come al nome di Tisbe aperse il ciglio
      Piramo in su la morte e riguardolla,
      allor che 'l gelso diventò vermiglio:

40   così, la mia durezza fatta solla,
      mi volsi al savio duca, udendo il nome
      che ne la mente sempre mi rampolla.

43   Ond' ei crollò la fronte e disse: 'Come,
      volenci star di qua?' Indi sorrise
      come al fanciul si fa ch'è vinto al pome.

46   Poi dentro al foco innanzi mi si mise,
      pregando Stazio che venisse retro,
      che pria per lunga strada ci divise.

49   Sì com' fui dentro, in un bogliente vetro
      gittato mi sarei per rinfrescarmi,
      tant' era ivi lo 'ncendio sanza metro.

52   Lo dolce padre mio per confortarmi
      pur di Beatrice ragionando andava,
      dicendo: 'Li occhi suoi già veder parmi.'

55   Guidavaci una voce che cantava
      di là; e noi, attenti pur a lei,
      venimmo fuor là ove si montava.

58   'Venite, benedicti Patris mei!'
      sonò dentro a un lume che lì era,
      tal che mi vinse e guardar nol potei.

61   'Lo sol sen va,' soggiunse, 'e vien la sera:
      non v'arrestate, ma studiate il passo
      mentre che l'occidente non si annera.'

And if, perhaps, you think I'm tricking you,   28
approach the fire and reassure yourself,
trying with your own hands your garment's hem.

Have done, I say, have done with fearfulness.   31
Turn this way. Come and enter safely in!'
But I, against all conscience, stood stock still.

And when he saw me stiff and obstinate,   34
he said, a little troubled: 'Look, my son,
between Beatrice and you there's just this wall.'

As Pyramus, on hearing Thisbe's name,   37*
opened his eyelids at the point of death,
and (mulberries turning crimson) gazed at her,

so, too – my obstinacy softening now –   40
I turned to hear her name, which, growing still,
thrives in my thinking to my guide, so wise.

Saying 'What's this?' he shook his head. 'Would you   43
prefer we stayed on this side?' Then he smiled
as though to see a child won round by apples.

Ahead of me, he went to meet the fire,   46
and begged that Statius, who had walked the road
so long between us, now take up the rear.

And, once within, I could have flung myself –   49
the heat that fire produced was measureless –
for coolness, in a vat of boiling glass.

To strengthen me, my sweetest father spoke,   52
as on he went, of Beatrice always,
saying, 'It seems I see her eyes already.'

And, guiding us, a voice sang from beyond.   55
So we, attending only to that voice,
came out and saw where now we could ascend.

'Venite, benedicti Patris mei!'   58*
sounded within what little light there was.
This overcame me and I could not look.

'The sun departs,' he added. 'Evening comes.   61
Don't stop. Think hard about your speed. Keep up,
as long as western skies have not turned dark.'

64 Dritta salia la via per entro 'l sasso
verso tal parte ch'io tagliava i raggi
dinanzi a me del sol, ch'era già basso.

67 E di pochi scaglion levammo i saggi,
che 'l sol corcar, per l'ombra che si spense,
sentimmo dietro e io e li miei saggi.

70 E pria che 'n tutte le sue parti immense
fosse orizzonte fatto d'un aspetto,
e notte avesse tutte sue dispense,

73 ciascun di noi d'un grado fece letto;
ché la natura del monte ci affranse
la possa del salir più e 'l diletto.

76 Quali si stanno ruminando manse
le capre, state rapide e proterve
sovra le cime avante che sien pranse,

79 tacite a l'ombra, mentre che 'l sol ferve,
guardate dal pastor, che 'n su la verga
poggiato s'è e lor di posa serve:

82 e quale il mandrian che fòri alberga
lungo il peculio suo queto pernotta,
guardando perché fiera non lo sperga:

85 tali eravamo tutti e tre allotta,
io come capra ed ei come pastori,
fasciati quinci e quindi d'alta grotta.

88 Poco parer potea lì del di fòri,
ma per quel poco vedea io le stelle
di lor solere e più chiare e maggiori.

91 Sì ruminando e sì mirando in quelle,
mi prese il sonno, il sonno che sovente,
anzi che 'l fatto sia, sa le novelle.

94 Ne l'ora, credo, che de l'oriente
prima raggiò nel monte Citerea,
che di foco d'amor par sempre ardente,

97 giovane e bella in sogno mi parea
donna vedere andar per una landa
cogliendo fiori, e cantando dicea:

The pathway through the rock rose sheer and straight –   64
and angled so I cut, ahead of me,
the rays of sunlight, which had now sunk low.

The steps the sages and myself assayed   67
were few until – my shadow petering out –
we sensed the sun behind us laid to rest.

Before the sky's horizon had assumed   70
one look in all its vast unmeasured parts
(night gathering all within its lawful bounds)

on separate stairs we each had made our beds.   73
The mountain by its natural law had wrecked
our power to climb and all delight in that.

Compare: goats, ruminating, mildly stand   76
where first, before they'd fed, they raced above
the summits of the hills, eager, untamed,

now, while the sun seethes, muted in the shade –   79
their herdsman watching over them, leaning
against his stick, so they can safely rest.

And shepherds, too, will lodge outdoors beside   82
their flocks, and calmly spend the night on guard,
so predators can't come to scatter them.

That is what, now, all three of us were like –   85
they as my shepherds and the she-goat, me –
tucked up on either side by towering rock.

Little was visible of things beyond.   88
Yet, by that 'little' I could see the stars
brighter than usual, and of greater size.

So, ruminating, wondering so at these,   91
sleep grasped me now – that sleep which often will,
before the fact appears, tell all that's new.

At that hour, so I think, when, from the east,   94*
Cytherea casts her first rays on the hill
(seeming to blaze, as always, in love's fire),

lovely and young, a *donna* in a dream   97
appeared to me and walked along the lea,
plucking its flowers and singing as she said:

100   'Sappia qualunque il mio nome dimanda
          ch'i' mi son Lia, e vo movendo intorno
          le belle mani a farmi una ghirlanda.

103   Per piacermi a lo specchio qui m'addorno,
          ma mia suora Rachel mai non si smaga
          dal suo miraglio, e siede tutto giorno.

106   Ell' è d'i suoi belli occhi veder vaga
          com' io de l'addornarmi con le mani:
          lei lo vedere e me l'ovrare appaga.'

109   E già per li splendori antelucani,
          che tanto a' pellegrin surgon più grati
          quanto, tornando, albergan men lontani,

112   le tenebre fuggian da tutti lati,
          e 'l sonno mio con esse: ond' io leva'mi,
          veggendo i gran maestri già levati.

115   'Quel dolce pome che per tanti rami
          cercando va la cura de' mortali
          oggi porrà in pace le tue fami.'

118   Virgilio inverso me queste cotali
          parole usò, e mai non furo strenne
          che fosser di piacere a queste iguali.

121   Tanto voler sopra voler mi venne
          de l'esser sù ch'ad ogne passo poi
          al volo mi sentia crescer le penne.

124   Come la scala tutta sotto noi
          fu corsa, e fummo in su 'l grado superno,
          in me ficcò Virgilio li occhi suoi

127   e disse: 'Il temporal foco e l'etterno
          veduto hai, figlio, e se' venuto in parte
          dov' io per me più oltre non discerno.

130   Tratto t'ho qui con ingegno e con arte;
          lo tuo piacere omai prendi per duce:
          fuor se' de l'erte vie, fuor se' de l'arte.

133   Vedi lo sol che 'n fronte ti riluce,
          vedi l'erbette, i fiori e li arbuscelli
          che qui la terra sol da sé produce.

'Let anyone who asks me for my name   100
know I am Leah, and my lovely hands
fashion my garland as I move them round.

   I dress here so my mirror gives me joy.   103
My sister Rachel, though, entranced, won't cease
to sit all day in wonder at her glass.

   She yearns to see her own delightful eyes,   106
as I desire to dress by my own hands.
Seeing, for her, is all – as doing is for me.

   Driven before bright antelucan rays   109*
(which pilgrims, in returning, welcome more
since now they've lodged one night less far from home),

   shadowy dark now fled on every side   112
and, with these shades, my sleep. At which I rose,
and saw my masters were already up.

   'The sweetest apple that the mortal heart   115
seeks in the branches with such urgency
today will offer all your cravings peace.'

   These words were those that Virgil used on me.   118
And never had such tokens of good luck
been equal in the pleasure that they gave.

   Desire beyond desire came over me   121
to be up there. And so, at every pace,
my plumage grew, I felt, more quick to fly.

   Below us now, the stair had run its course,   124
and we were on the highest of the steps.
Then, firmly, Virgil fixed his eyes on me,

   saying: 'The temporal and eternal fires   127
you've seen, my son, and now you're in a place
where I, through my own powers, can tell no more.

   I've drawn you here by skill and searching mind.   130
Now take what pleases you to be your guide.
You're now beyond the steeps, beyond all straits.

   The sun, you see, is shining on your brow.   133
You see the bushes, fresh, young grass, and flowers.
The earth by its own powers brings this to be.

136   Mentre che vegnan lieti li occhi belli
       che lagrimando a te venir mi fenno,
       seder ti puoi e puoi andar tra elli.

139   Non aspettar mio dir più né mio cenno:
       libero, dritto e sano è tuo arbitrio,
       e fallo fora non fare a suo senno.

142   Per ch'io te sovra te corono e mitrio.'

   Until, in joy, those lovely eyes appear   136
that, weeping, made me come to be your guide,
through these you may go walking, or may sit.
   No longer look to me for signs or word.   139
Your will is healthy, upright, free and whole.
And not to heed that sense would be a fault.
   Lord of yourself, I crown and mitre you.'   142

CANTO 28

1   Vago già di cercar dentro e dintorno
la divina foresta spessa e viva,
ch'a li occhi temperava il novo giorno,

4   sanza più aspettar lasciai la riva,
prendendo la campagna lento lento
su per lo suol che d'ogne parte auliva.

7   Un'aura dolce, sanza mutamento
avere in sé, mi feria per la fronte
non di più colpo che soave vento,

10   per cui le fronde tremolando pronte
tutte quante piegavano a la parte
u' la prim' ombra gitta il santo monte,

13   non però dal loro esser dritto sparte
tanto, che li augelletti per le cime
lasciasser d'operare ogne lor arte;

16   ma con piena letizia l'ore prime
cantando ricevieno intra le foglie,
che tenevan bordone a le sue rime:

19   tal qual di ramo in ramo si raccoglie
per la pineta in su 'l lito di Chiassi,
quand' Eolo scilocco fuor discioglie.

22   Già m'avean trasportato i lenti passi
dentro a la selva antica tanto ch'io
non potea rivedere ond' io mi 'ntrassi,

25   ed ecco più andar mi tolse un rio
che 'nver' sinistra con sue picciole onde
piegava l'erba che 'n sua ripa uscìo.

CANTO 28

Aching to search, now, in and all around   1
that holy forest, dense, alive and bright,
which tempered to my eyes the newborn day,

  not pausing anymore, I left the verge,   4
treading in slow, slow steps across the field.
The earth below breathed scent on every side.

  A gentle breeze, unchanging in itself,   7
struck on my forehead, yet with no more force
than would the smoothest of our changing winds.

  To this the branches, trembling in response,   10
yielded, all bending to the place at which
the sacred mountain casts its earliest shade,

  and yet not leaning so far out of true   13
that fledglings perched among the topmost boughs
were forced to leave the practice of their trade.

  But, full of happiness, they greet the dawn,   16
singing among the foliage which holds
a steady undertone to all their tunes –

  as in those notes that gather, branch by branch,   19*
through all the pines along Ravenna's shore
when, from the south, sciroccos start to blow.

  My steady steps by now had carried me   22
so deep within the ancient wood that I
could not see back to where I'd entered first.

  Look there! A brook held back my onward pace.   25
Its course was leftward, and its little waves
swayed all the grass that rose along its banks.

28   Tutte l'acque che son di qua più monde
parrieno avere in sé mistura alcuna
verso di quella, che nulla nasconde,

31   avvegna che si mova bruna bruna
sotto l'ombra perpetua, che mai
raggiar non lascia sole ivi né luna.

34   Coi piè ristetti e con li occhi passai
di là dal fiumicello, per mirare
la gran variazion d'i freschi mai;

37   e là m'apparve – sì com' elli appare
subitamente cosa che disvia
per maraviglia tutto altro pensare –

40   una donna soletta che si gia
e cantando e scegliendo fior da fiore
ond' era pinta tutta la sua via.

43   'Deh, bella donna che a' raggi d'amore
ti scaldi, s'i' vo' credere a' sembianti,
che soglion esser testimon del core,

46   vegnati in voglia di trarreti avanti,'
diss' io a lei, 'verso questa rivera
tanto ch'io possa intender che tu canti.

49   Tu mi fai rimembrar dove e qual era
Proserpina nel tempo che perdette
la madre lei, ed ella primavera.'

52   Come si volge, con le piante strette
a terra e intra sé, donna che balli,
e piede innanzi piede a pena mette:

55   volsesi in su i vermigli e in su i gialli
fioretti verso me, non altrimenti
che vergine che li occhi onesti avvalli,

58   e fece i prieghi miei esser contenti,
sì appressando sé che 'l dolce suono
veniva a me co' suoi intendimenti.

61   Tosto che fu là dove l'erbe sono
bagnate già da l'onde del bel fiume,
di levar li occhi suoi mi fece dono.

The purest waters that down here may flow   28
would seem to have admixtures in their depths
compared with those, which don't hide anything.

And yet these waters move dark, dark beneath   31
a shadow that's perpetual and allows
no ray of sun or moonlight ever through.

My pace here checked, I passed in sight alone   34
beyond that stream, to see and wonder at
these May-things in abundance varying.

And then appeared to me – as things appear   37
that suddenly in wonder will deflect
the claims of every other thought we have –

a *donna* all alone who walked along,   40
singing and choosing flowers to pluck from flowers
that painted all the way she went upon.

'Lady, you warm yourself in rays of love,   43
or so I think, to see your lovely looks –
these usually bear witness to the heart.

May you incline, in will, to move more close,'   46
sighing I said, 'towards this flowing stream,
so I may understand the song you sing.

You make me call to mind Proserpina,   49
both where and what she was – when she lost Spring
and her own mother lost all sight of her.'

Her feet together, firmly pressed to ground   52
as when a *donna* dances, she then turned
and, scarcely setting foot in front of foot,

she turned above the yellow and the red   55
of tender flowers, as virgin girls will do
when they, for decency, dip down their eyes.

Then she in full responded to my prayers,   58
bringing herself so near that that sweet sound
came to me, with the meanings that it bore.

And now, the moment she'd arrived at where   61
the grass was bathed by waves from that fine stream,
she made a gift to me: she raised her eyes.

64   Non credo che splendesse tanto lume
        sotto le ciglia a Venere, trafitta
        dal figlio fuor di tutto suo costume.

67   Ella ridea da l'altra riva, dritta,
        trattando più color con le sue mani,
        che l'alta terra sanza seme gitta.

70   Tre passi ci facea il fiume lontani,
        ma Elesponto – là 've passò Serse,
        ancora freno a tutti orgogli umani –

73   più odio da Leandro non sofferse
        per mareggiare intra Sesto e Abido,
        che quel da me perch' allor non s'aperse.

76   'Voi siete nuovi, e forse perch' io rido,'
        cominciò ella, 'in questo luogo eletto
        a l'umana natura per suo nido,

79   maravigliando tienvi alcun sospetto;
        ma luce rende il salmo *Delectasti*,
        che puote disnebbiar vostro intelletto.

82   E tu che se' dinanzi e mi pregasti,
        dì s'altro vuoli udir, ch'i' venni presta
        ad ogne tua question tanto che basti.'

85   'L'acqua,' diss' io, 'e 'l suon de la foresta
        impugnan dentro a me novella fede
        di cosa ch'io udi' contraria a questa.'

88   Ond' ella: 'Io dicerò come procede
        per sua cagion ciò ch'ammirar ti face,
        e purgherò la nebbia che ti fiede.

91   Lo sommo Ben, che solo esso a sé piace,
        fé l'uom buono e a bene, e questo loco
        diede per arr' a lui d'etterna pace.

94   Per sua difalta qui dimorò poco;
        per sua difalta in pianto e in affanno
        cambiò onesto riso e dolce gioco.

97   Perché 'l turbar che sotto da sé fanno
        l'essalazion de l'acqua e de la terra,
        che quanto posson dietro al calor vanno,

I do not think so great a light shone out   64*
beneath the brows of Venus when her son
pierced her with love beyond his usual stroke.

　　She stood there, laughing, on the other bank   67
arranging many colours in her hands,
strewn by the mighty earth without a seed.

　　The river kept us still three steps apart.   70*
And yet the Hellespont where Xerxes passed
(a bridle still on all our human pride)

　　did not so much incur Leander's hate,   73
when oceans raged from Sest to Abydos,
as this did mine because it would not part.

　　'You are both new,' she now began to say,   76
'in this place, chosen for the human race
to make its nest. And you stand wondering,

　　perhaps because I smile, caught up in doubt.   79
The psalm, though, '*Delectasti*' sheds a light
that may dispel the clouds around your mind.

　　And you who begged me speak – the one ahead –   82
say if there's any more you wish to hear.
I'll quickly come to answer you in full.'

　　'These waters, and the sound the forest makes,   85
battle within me with a newborn faith
in something I've heard contrary to this.'

　　At which she said: 'I'll tell you, then, the cause   88
from which those things you wonder at derive,
and thus will purge the fog that strikes at you.

　　The Highest Good – alone its own delight –   91
made human beings good and fit for good,
and gave this place as pledge of endless peace.

　　Through his own fault, Man did not dwell here long.   94
Through his own fault, to weeping and to grief
he changed his noble laughter and sweet play.

　　Water and earth below breathe vapours out   97
that search, as fully as they can, for heat,
and this induces turbulence down there.

100   a l'uomo non facesse alcuna guerra,
        questo monte salìo verso 'l ciel tanto,
        e libero n'è d'indi ove si serra.

103   Or perché in circuito tutto quanto
        l'aere si volge con la prima volta,
        se non li è rotto il cerchio d'alcun canto,

106   in questa altezza ch'è tutta disciolta
        ne l'aere vivo, tal moto percuote,
        e fa sonar la selva perch' è folta;

109   e la percossa pianta tanto puote

        che de la sua virtute l'aura impregna
        e quella poi, girando, intorno scuote;

112   e l'altra terra, secondo ch'è degna
        per sé e per suo ciel, concepe e figlia
        di diverse virtù diverse legna.

115   Non parrebbe di là poi maraviglia,
        udito questo, quando alcuna pianta
        sanza seme palese vi s'appiglia.

118   E saper dei che la campagna santa
        dove tu se' d'ogne semenza è piena,
        e frutto ha in sé che di là non si schianta.

121   L'acqua che vedi non surge di vena
        che ristori vapor che gel converta,
        come fiume ch'acquista e perde lena,

124   ma esce di fontana salda e certa
        che tanto dal voler di Dio riprende
        quant' ella versa da due parti aperta.

127   Da questa parte con virtù discende
        che toglie altrui memoria del peccato;
        da l'altra d'ogne ben fatto la rende.

130   Quinci Letè, così da l'altro lato
        Eunoè si chiama, e non adopra
        se quinci e quindi pria non è gustato:

Yet, so that these should bring no harm to men,   100
this mountain climbs and reaches to the sky,
free of these swirls from where the gate is locked.

But now, because the circling sphere of air,   103*
if that's not interrupted in some part,
turns altogether as the heavens turn,

that motion, unconstrained in living air,   106
will strike directly on this utmost peak
and make the forest, being dense, sound out.

And plants here, when they're struck, have such great
        strength   109
that, with its natural power they seed the breeze,
which then, in circling round, will scatter this.

The other hemisphere – as far as soil   112
is right, and climate suits – conceives and bears
plants in variety with various powers.

And hearing this, it would not seem, down there,   115
a source of wonder if a plant takes root
without there being, visibly, a seed.

And you should know that all this holy field   118
is filled where you are now with every seed,
and here has fruits which, there, are never plucked.

The water that you see is from no well   121
(as rivers are that gain and lose in force)
that's freshly filled when ice condenses mist,

but issues, sure and steady, from a spring   124
that gathers all it has from God's own will,
which then it pours out, opening in two parts.

It flows, in this part, down with all its power   127
to take the memory of sin away,
restoring, on the other, all good done.

Its name is Lethe here, Eunoe there.   130*
Until a taste is had on either side,
the influence it has won't take effect.

133   a tutti altri sapori esto è di sopra.
       E avvegna ch'assai possa esser sazia
       la sete tua perch' io più non ti scuopra,

136   darotti un corollario ancor per grazia,
       né credo che 'l mio dir ti sia men caro
       se oltre promession teco si spazia.

139   Quelli ch'anticamente poetaro
       l'età de l'oro e suo stato felice,
       forse in Parnaso esto loco sognaro.

142   Qui fu innocente l'umana radice;
       qui primavera sempre e ogne frutto;
       nettare è questo di che ciascun dice.'

145   Io mi rivolsi 'n dietro allora tutto
       a' miei poeti, e vidi che con riso
       udito avean l'ultimo costrutto;

148   poi a la bella donna torna' il viso.

This savour is above all other tastes   133
and – though your thirst would none the less be slaked
if I disclosed to you no more than this –

I'll add one footnote, out of grace and thanks.   136
(I cannot think you'll hold my words less dear
if these soar out beyond my promised theme.)

Those who, in times long gone, composed those poems   139*
that sang the Age of Gold and all its joys
thought, maybe here's Parnassus when they dreamed.

Here, once, the root of man was innocent.   142
Here, there is always spring and every fruit.
And that's the nectar they all speak about.'

I swung around to face my poets there,   145
and both (as I could tell) had smiled to hear
the meaning of the words that she'd spelled out.

I then turned back to see that lovely girl.   148

CANTO 29

1   Cantando come donna innamorata,
continuò col fin di sue parole:
'*Beati quorum tecta sunt peccata.*'

4   E come ninfe che si givan sole
per le salvatiche ombre, disiando
qual di veder, qual di fuggir lo sole,

7   allor si mosse contra 'l fiume, andando
su per la riva, e io pari di lei,
picciol passo con picciol seguitando.

10   Non eran cento tra ' suoi passi e' miei,
quando le ripe igualmente dier volta,
per modo ch'a levante mi rendei.

13   Né ancor fu così nostra via molta,
quando la donna tutta a me si torse,
dicendo: 'Frate mio, guarda e ascolta.'

16   Ed ecco un lustro sùbito trascorse
da tutte parti per la gran foresta,
tal che di balenar mi mise in forse.

19   Ma perché 'l balenar, come vien, resta,
e quel, durando, più e più splendeva,
nel mio pensier dicea: 'Che cosa è questa?'

22   E una melodia dolce correva
per l'aere luminoso, onde buon zelo
mi fé riprender l'ardimento d'Eva,

25   che là dove ubidia la terra e 'l cielo,
femmina, sola e pur testé formata,
non sofferse di star sotto alcun velo,

CANTO 29

Singing as might some *donna* deep in love,   1*
she then went on and brought an end to words:
'*Beati quorum tecta sunt peccata.*'

And then, as nymphs who, once, would go alone   4
through woodland shadows longing, some of them,
to see the sun while others fled its rays,

she moved, against the course that clear stream ran,   7
walking along her bank while I kept up,
with small steps too, pursuing her small pace.

Before a hundred steps had gone (to count   10
both hers and mine) the banks on either side
curved equally, so I was facing east.

Nor did our path continue so for long,   13
until the lady turned direct to me,
saying: 'Dear brother, just watch and listen.'

And look! A sudden radiance, darting all   16
around, pierced that great forest through and through,
at which I thought that lightning may have struck.

But lightning, when it comes, is quenched at once,   19
where this, enduring, shone out more and more.
So I was left, thought muttering: 'What is this?'

And then, through all that luminous air, there ran   22
a melody so fine that purest zeal
made me reprove the recklessness of Eve.

Where earth and Heaven displayed obedience,   25
a woman, one alone, formed only now,
was not content to stay beneath the veil.

28   sotto 'l qual se divota fosse stata
        avrei quelle ineffabili delizie
        sentite prima e più lunga fiata.

31   Mentr' io m'andava tra tante primizie
        de l'etterno piacer tutto sospeso,
        e disioso ancora a più letizie,

34   dinanzi a noi tal quale un foco acceso
        ci si fé l'aere sotto i verdi rami,
        e 'l dolce suon per canti era già inteso.

37   O sacrosante Vergini, se fami,
        freddi o vigilie mai per voi soffersi,
        cagion mi sprona ch'io mercé vi chiami:

40   or convien che Elicona per me versi,
        e Uranìe m'aiuti col suo coro
        forti cose a pensar mettere in versi.

43   Poco più oltre, sette alberi d'oro
        falsava nel parere il lungo tratto
        del mezzo ch'era ancor tra noi e loro;

46   ma quand' i' fui sì presso di lor fatto
        che l'obietto comun, che 'l senso inganna,
        non perdea per distanza alcun suo atto,

49   la virtù ch'a ragion discorso ammanna
        sì com' elli eran candelabri apprese,
        e ne le voci del cantare 'Osanna.'

52   Di sopra fiammeggiava il bello arnese,
        più chiaro assai che luna per sereno
        di mezza notte nel suo mezzo mese.

55   Io mi rivolsi d'ammirazion pieno
        al buon Virgilio, ed esso mi rispuose
        con vista carca di stupor non meno.

58   Indi rendei l'aspetto a l'alte cose
        che si movieno incontr' a noi sì tardi
        che foran vinte da novelle spose.

61   La donna mi sgridò: 'Perché pur ardi
        sì ne l'affetto de le vive luci,
        e ciò che vien di retro a lor non guardi?'

Had she in true devotion stayed beneath,   28
I should have known these pleasures, past all speech,
far sooner and enjoyed them at more length.

While on I went among these primal fruits,   31
the pleasures yielded by eternity,
caught up, desiring yet more happiness,

ahead of us, beneath the branching green,   34
the air blazed up like newly kindled fire,
and that sweet sound was clearly heard as song.

You holy virgin Muses, if, for you,   37*
I've ever suffered vigils, fast or cold,
there's now all reason to beseech your aid.

Now Helicon must pour in streams for me,   40
Urania with her choirs assist me here,
to put in verse things hardly thinkable.

Just further on were seven trees of gold –   43*
that semblance given them, mistakenly,
by distance that, between us, intervened.

But when I'd got so near to them that now   46
(far off, aspectuals can fool our sense)
these things lost nothing of their proper form,

that power that sends (as manna) rational thought,   49
discerned that these were candle-bearing staves,
and heard 'Hosanna' in that singing voice.

These fine devices flamed around their heights   52
far clearer than the moon in tranquil skies,
at midnight in the middle of a month.

Filled full of radiant wonder, I turned round   55
to honest Virgil, and he answered me
with looks no less weighed down by heavy awe.

I then restored my gaze to those high things   58
that came towards us now and moved so slow
that new-wed brides would quickly have gone past.

The lady reprimanded me: 'Why burn,   61
so moved, to see alone these living lights
and fail to look at what comes after them?'

64   Genti vid' io allor, come a lor duci
        venire appresso, vestite di bianco,
        e tal candor di qua già mai non fuci.

67   L'acqua imprendea dal sinistro fianco,
        e rendea me la mia sinistra costa,
        s'io riguardava in lei, come specchio anco.

70   Quand' io da la mia riva ebbi tal posta
        che solo il fiume mi facea distante,
        per veder meglio ai passi diedi sosta,

73   e vidi le fiammelle andar davante,
        lasciando dietro a sé l'aere dipinto,
        e di tratti pennelli avean sembiante,

76   sì che lì sopra rimanea distinto
        di sette liste, tutte in quei colori
        onde fa l'arco il Sole e Delia il cinto.

79   Questi ostendali in dietro eran maggiori
        che la mia vista, e, quanto a mio avviso,
        diece passi distavan quei di fori.

82   Sotto così bel ciel com' io diviso,
        ventiquattro segnori, a due a due,
        coronati venien di fiordaliso.

85   Tutti cantavan: 'Benedicta tue
        ne le figlie d'Adamo, e benedette
        sieno in etterno le bellezze tue!'

88   Poscia che i fiori e l'altre fresche erbette
        a rimpetto di me da l'altra sponda
        libere fuor da quelle genti elette,

91   sì come luce luce in ciel seconda,
        vennero appresso lor quattro animali,
        coronati ciascun di verde fronda.

94   Ognuno era pennuto di sei ali;
        le penne piene d'occhi, e li occhi d'Argo,
        se fosser vivi, sarebber cotali.

97   A descriver lor forme più non spargo
        rime, lettor, ch'altra spesa mi strigne
        tanto ch'a questa non posso esser largo;

I then saw people guided by the flames,   64
now coming near to us. Their robes were white,
of brilliant purity not seen down here.

The water to my left reflected fire,   67
and rendered back to me, if I looked down,
as mirrors do, the sight of my left side.

When, on my own bank, I had reached a place   70
where I was distanced only by the stream,
I brought my steps to rest, to see them well.

I saw those flames, diminishing, move on,   73
leaving behind a paint stroke in the air,
as though they all drew pennants after them,

so that, above them, there were seven streams,   76*
their colours those the Sun makes with its bow
or else the girdle of the Delian moon.

These pennants stretched far back beyond my sight.   79
The outer two, as far as I could tell,
were drawn on through the air ten steps apart.

And under this fine sky, as here described,   82*
were elders – twenty-four – who walked in pairs,
and each of them was crowned with *fleurs-de-lys*.

And all of these were singing: 'You among   85
the daughters born to Adam are *benedicta*,
your beauty blessed to all eternity.'

And when, across from me, the other bank –   88
with all its flowers and other fresh young growth –
was free of these, who were the chosen ones,

as light lights up in sequence through the sky,   91*
there came behind them now four animals,
and each of these was crowned with boughs of green.

And each was fledged and feathered with six wings.   94
These feathers all were peacock-eyed. The eyes
of Argus would, if they still lived, be like this.

I'll scatter, reader, no more rhymes to trace   97
what these forms were. Other expenditure
constrains me. I cannot be generous.

100   ma leggi Ezechiele, che li dipigne
    come li vide da la fredda parte
    venir con vento e con nube e con igne,

103   e quali i troverai ne le sue carte
    tali eran quivi, salvo ch'a le penne
    Giovanni è meco e da lui si diparte.

106   Lo spazio dentro a lor quattro contenne
    un carro, in su due rote, triunfale,
    ch'al collo d'un grifon tirato venne.

109   Esso tendeva in sù l'una e l'altra ale
    tra la mezzana e le tre e tre liste
    sì ch'a nulla, fendendo, facea male;

112   tanto salivan che non eran viste.
    Le membra d'oro avea quant' era uccello,
    e bianche l'altre, di vermiglio miste.

115   Non che Roma di carro così bello
    rallegrasse Affricano o vero Augusto,
    ma quel del Sol saria pover con ello:

118   quel del Sol, che sviando fu combusto
    per l'orazion de la Terra devota,
    quando fu Giove arcanamente giusto.

121   Tre donne in giro da la destra rota
    venian danzando, l'una tanto rossa
    ch'a pena fora dentro al foco nota;

124   l'altr' era come se le carni e l'ossa
    fossero state di smeraldo fatte;
    la terza parea neve testé mossa;

127   e or parean da la bianca tratte,
    or da la rossa, e dal canto di questa
    l'altre toglien l'andare e tarde e ratte.

130   Da la sinistra quattro facean festa,
    in porpore vestite, dietro al modo
    d'una di lor ch'avea tre occhi in testa.

133   Appresso tutto il pertrattato nodo
    vidi due vecchi in abito dispari,
    ma pari in atto e onesto e sodo.

But read Ezekiel, who paints them all   100
as once he saw them, coming from cold climes
in whirlwinds, towering clouds and folds of fire.

And as you'll find them written on his page,   103
so were they there, except that, as to wings,
Saint John is with me, and departs from him.

The space that lay between these four contained   106
a two-wheeled chariot in triumphal state.
A gryphon drew it, harnessed at the neck.

This gryphon held his two wings stretched on high   109
between the middle band and three and three,
so that, in cleaving air, he did no harm.

These wings rose higher than the eye could see.   112
The bird-limbs of that form were all of gold,
the others white, commingling with bright red.

Not only did not Rome cheer Scipio   115*
with such fine chariots (or Caesar, even!)
the Sun itself beside that would look poor –

the Sun that burned to nothing when it strayed   118
(here Jove for his dark reasons once proved just)
in answer to the prayers of pious earth.

Beside the right-hand wheel, three ladies came,   121
all dancing in a ring, the first so red
that she, in fire, would hardly have been seen,

the next as if her very bones and flesh   124
were fashioned from the freshest emerald,
the third like snow just fallen from the sky.

Their steps were drawn, it seems, by, first, the white,   127
then red, and from the song that this one sang
the others took their tempo, fast or slow.

Four ladies to the left, all purple-clothed,   130
rejoiced in following the melody
of one of them, whose brow displayed three eyes.

Then, close within the track of this tight knot,   133
I saw two elders, differing in their garb,
but equal in demeanour, grave and firm

136   L'un si mostrava alcun de' famigliari
di quel sommo Ipocràte che Natura
a li animali fé ch'ell' ha più cari;

139   mostrava l'altro la contraria cura
con una spada lucida e aguta,
tal che di qua dal rio mi fé paura.

142   Poi vidi quattro in umile paruta,
e di retro da tutti un vecchio solo
venir dormendo, con la faccia arguta.

145   E questi sette col primaio stuolo
erano abituati, ma di gigli
dintorno al capo non facean brolo,

148   anzi di rose e d'altri fior vermigli;
giurato avria poco lontano aspetto
che tutti ardesser di sopra da' cigli.

151   E quando il carro a me fu a rimpetto,
un tuon s'udì, e quelle genti degne
parvero aver l'andar più interdetto,

154   fermandosi ivi con le prime insegne.

One showed himself a close familiar   136
of great Hippocrates, whom Nature formed
to serve the creatures that she loved the best.

The other showed the opposite concern,   139
a well-honed sword in hand – so bright and keen
it brought me terror from beyond the stream.

I then saw four, each one with humble looks,   142
and after these, an old man all alone,
who came as though still sleeping, face alert.

These seven were clothed as was the first brigade   145
except that, as they came, around their heads,
they wore no garland formed of lilia,

but roses, rather, and vermilion flowers.   148
And, standing just a short way off, you'd swear
that all, above their brows, bore searing fire.

When, now, that chariot stood facing me,   151
thunder was heard. These people of great worth
were banned, it seemed, from going further on.

With standards to the fore, they halted there.   154

CANTO 30

1   Quando il Settentrione del primo cielo,
che né occaso mai seppe né orto
né d'altra nebbia che di colpa velo,

4   e che faceva lì ciascuno accorto
di suo dover, come 'l più basso face
qual temon gira per venire a porto,

7   fermo s'affisse, la gente verace
venuta prima tra 'l grifone ed esso,
al carro volse sé come a sua pace,

10   e un di loro, quasi da ciel messo,
'*Veni, sponsa, de Libano!*' cantando
gridò tre volte, e tutti li altri appresso.

13   Quali i beati al novissimo bando
surgeran presti ognun di sua caverna,
la revestita voce alleluiando:

16   cotali in su la divina basterna
si levar cento, *ad vocem tanti senis*,
ministri e messaggier di vita etterna.

19   Tutti dicean: '*Benedictus qui venis!*'
e, fior gittando e di sopra e dintorno,
'*Manibus*, oh, *date lilia plenis!*'

22   Io vidi già nel cominciar del giorno
la parte oriental tutta rosata
e l'altro ciel di bel sereno addorno,

25   e la faccia del sol nascere ombrata,
sì che per temperanza di vapori
l'occhio la sostenea lunga fiata:

CANTO 30

Those Seven Polar Stars that constellate   1
the highest sphere, and never knowing nadir
or zenith, veiled by the murk of sin alone,

those stars that make the souls, in Heaven, aware   4
of what is right (as, by our Wain, down here,
a helmsman turns his wheel to steer for port)

stopped and stood firm. The people of the truth –   7
who marched between the Gryphon and these stars –
turned, as though each found peace, towards the chariot.

And one of them, as sent from Heaven, cried out: 10
'*Veni, sponsa, de Libano!*' singing
(the others followed on) this verse three times.

As when the Last New Day is heralded,   13
and happy souls will rise keen from their caves,
dressed in new voice, to echo 'Alleluia'

so now, *ad vocem tanti senis*, there arose   16
above the hallowed chariot a hundred
angels, all bearing news of eternal life.

They spoke thus: '*Benedictus qui venis!*'   19
and, strewing petals upward and around:
'*Manibus, oh date lilia plenis!*'

I saw, once, at the opening of the day,   22
the orient sky in colour all clear rose,
the western height still robed in tranquil blue,

and then the sun newborn, with shadowed face,   25
hazy, in vapours that so tempered it
that eyes could tolerate its light a while.

28   così, dentro una nuvola di fiori
        che da le mani angeliche saliva
        e ricadeva in giù dentro e di fòri,

31   sovra candido vel cinta d'uliva
        donna m'apparve, sotto verde manto
        vestita di color di fiamma viva.

34   E lo spirito mio, che già cotanto
        tempo era stato ch'a la sua presenza
        non era di stupor tremando affranto,

37   sanza de li occhi aver più conoscenza,
        per occulta virtù che da lei mosse
        d'antico amor sentì la gran potenza.

40   Tosto che ne la vista mi percosse
        l'alta virtù che già m'avea trafitto
        prima ch'io fuor di puerizia fosse,

43   volsimi a la sinistra col respitto
        col quale il fantolin corre a la mamma
        quando ha paura o quando elli è afflitto,

46   per dicere a Virgilio: 'Men che dramma
        di sangue m'è rimaso che non tremi:
        conosco i segni de l'antica fiamma!'

49   Ma Virgilio n'avea lasciati scemi
        di se – Virgilio, dolcissimo patre,
        Virgilio, a cui per mia salute die'mi –,

52   né quantunque perdeo l'antica matre
        valse a le guance nette di rugiada
        che, lagrimando, non tornasser atre.

55   'Dante, perché Virgilio se ne vada,
        non pianger anco, non piangere ancora,
        ché pianger ti conven per altra spada.'

58   Quasi ammiraglio che in poppa e in prora
        viene a veder la gente che ministra
        per li altri legni, e a ben far l'incora:

61   in su la sponda del carro sinistra,
        quando mi volsi al suon del nome mio,
        che di necessità qui si registra,

So now, beyond a drifting cloud of flowers   28
(which rose up, arching, from the angels' hands,
then fell within and round the chariot),

    seen through a veil, pure white, and olive-crowned,   31
a lady now appeared to me. Her robe was green,
her dress the colour of a living flame.

    And I, in spirit, who so long had not   34
been, trembling in her presence, wracked by awe,
began again to tremble at her glance

    (without more evidence that eyes could bring,   37
but darkly, through the good that flowed from her),
sensing the ancient power of what love was.

    But on the instant that it struck my sight –   40
this power, this virtue, that had pierced me through
before I'd even left my boyhood state –

    I turned aside (and leftwards) meaning now,   43
with all the hope and deference of some child
that runs when hurt or frightened to its mum,

    to say to Virgil: 'There is not one gram   46
of blood in me that does not tremble now.
I recognize the signs of ancient flame.'

    But Virgil was not there. Our lack alone   49
was left where once he'd been. Virgil, dear sire,
Virgil – to him I'd run to save my soul.

    Nor could the All our primal mother lost,   52
ensure my cheeks – which he once washed with dew –
should not again be sullied with dark tears.

    'Dante, that Virgil is no longer here,   55
do not yet weep, do not yet weep for that.
A different sword cut, first, must make you weep.'

    From stern to prow, some admiral will pace   58
to see how well, in other hulls, his captains fare,
and seek to hearten them to do their best.

    So, almost (left along the chariot),   61*
turning now to hear my own name voiced
(I here record it of necessity),

64   vidi la donna che pria m'appario
      velata sotto l'angelica festa
      drizzar li occhi ver' me di qua dal rio,

67   tutto che 'l vel che le scendea di testa,
      cerchiato de le fronde di Minerva,
      non la lasciasse parer manifesta.

70   Regalmente ne l'atto ancor proterva,
      continuò come colui che dice
      e 'l più caldo parlar dietro reserva:

73   'Guardaci ben! Ben son, ben son Beatrice.
      Come degnasti d'accedere al monte?
      non sapei tu che qui è l'uom felice?'

76   Li occhi mi cadder giù nel chiaro fonte,
      ma, veggendomi in esso, i trassi a l'erba,
      tanta vergogna mi gravò la fronte:

79   così la madre al figlio par superba
      com' ella parve a me, perché d'amaro
      sente il sapor de la pietade acerba.

82   Ella si tacque, e li angeli cantaro
      di sùbito: 'In te, Domine, speravi,'
      ma oltre 'pedes meos' non passaro.

85   Sì come neve tra le vive travi
      per lo dosso d'Italia si congela,
      soffiata e stretta da li venti schiavi,

88   poi, liquefatta, in sé stessa trapela
      pur che la terra che perde ombra spiri,
      sì che par foco fonder la candela:

91   così fui sanza lagrime e sospiri
      anzi 'l cantar di quei che notan sempre
      dietro a le note de li etterni giri;

94   ma poi che 'ntesi ne le dolci tempre
      lor compatire a me – par che se detto
      avesser: 'Donna, perché sì lo stempre?' –

97   lo gel che m'era intorno al cor ristretto
      spirito e acqua fessi, e con angoscia
      de la bocca e de li occhi uscì del petto.

I saw my *donna* – who'd at first appeared   64
hidden in garlands of angelic joy –
fix, from beyond the brook, her eyes on me,

though still the veil descending from her brows,   67
encircled with Minerva's olive fronds,
did not allow, distinctly, any sight of her.

Her look was stern and proud. With sovereign strength,   70
she then went on, and spoke as though she still
held back, until the last, her fieriest words.

'Look. I am, truly, I am Beatrice.   73
What right had you to venture to this mount?
Did you not know that all are happy here?'

My eyes fell, glancing to the spring-clear brook,   76
but, seeing *me* in that, shame bent my brow.
I dragged my gaze back to the grassy bank.

A mother, to her son, looks stern and proud.   79
So she appeared to me. For true concern
is bitter to the taste and quick to sting.

She did not speak; but suddenly, as one,   82
the angels sang: '*In te, Domine, speravi*',
but did not go beyond the '*pedes meos*'.

Compare: the snow that falls through growing eaves   85
freezes the spine of Italy in drifts
blown and compacted by Slavonian winds.

But when the southern lands (where shadow fails)   88
breathe once again, within itself it thaws,
then trickles down, as candles melt in flames.

So, too, until those beings sang – their notes   91
are all concordant with the heavenly spheres –
I'd been there uttering no sigh or tear.

And yet, on hearing, through these harmonies,   94
their pity on me (for it seemed they'd said:
'Why, *donna*, cause him discord such as this?'),

the ice, so tightly stretched around my core,   97
turned now to breath and water, issuing,
at mouth and eye, in spasms from my heart.

100   Ella, pur ferma in su la detta coscia
        del carro stando, a le sustanze pie
        volse le sue parole così poscia:

103   'Voi vigilate ne l'etterno die,
        sì che notte né sonno a voi non fura
        passo che faccia il secol per sue vie;

106   onde la mia risposta è con più cura
        che m'intenda colui che di là piagne,
        perché sia colpa e duol d'una misura.

109   Non pur per ovra de le rote magne
        che drizzan ciascun seme ad alcun fine,
        secondo che le stelle son compagne,

112   ma per larghezza di grazie divine,
        che sì alti vapori hanno a lor piova
        che nostre viste là non van vicine,

115   questi fu tal ne la sua vita nova,
        virtualmente, ch'ogne abito destro
        fatto averebbe in lui mirabil prova.

118   Ma tanto più maligno e più silvestro
        si fa 'l terren col mal seme e non cólto,
        quant' elli ha più di buon vigor terrestro.

121   Alcun tempo il sostenni col mio volto:
        mostrando li occhi giovanetti a lui,
        meco il menava in dritta parte vòlto.

124   Sì tosto come in su la soglia fui
        di mia seconda etade e mutai vita,
        questi si tolse a me e diessi altrui:

127   quando di carne a spirto era salita,
        e bellezza e virtù cresciuta m'era,
        fu' io a lui men cara e men gradita,

130   e volse i passi suoi per via non vera,
        imagini di ben seguendo false,
        che nulla promession rendono intera.

133   Né l'impetrare ispirazion mi valse,
        con le quali e in sogno e altrimenti
        lo rivocai, sì poco a lui ne calse!

Then she (still leftwards on the chariot),   100
unmoved and standing firm, addressed her words
to these true beings, so compassionate:

'You wake, in vigil, through eternal day.   103
So neither night nor sleep can steal from you
a single step that time takes, travelling by.

Thus, answering, my greater care must be   106
that he, in tears there, grasps what I intend,
and brings to balance all his grief and guilt.

Not only by the work of Heaven's great wheels   109
that send, with its companion stars, each seed
along the road towards its rightful end,

but also by those holy generosities   112
that rain in grace from clouded powers so high
that human sight can come in no way near,

this man through all his new life, fresh and young,   115
in virtual power was one who might have proved,
in all of his behaviour, wonderful.

Yet there, on earth, the richer soil may be,   118
the more – untilled or sown with evil seed –
its vigour turns to wilderness and bane.

I, looking on, sustained him for a time.   121
My eyes, when bright with youth, I turned to him,
and led him with me on the road to truth.

Then, on the threshold of my second age,   124
I changed, took different life, and he at once
drew back and yielded to another's glance.

Risen from body into spirit-form,   127
my goodness, power and beauty grew more strong.
Yet I to him was then less dear, less pleasing.

He turned his steps to paths that were not true.   130
He followed images of failing good
which cannot meet, in full, their promises.

And when I prayed that he might be inspired,   133
seeking to call him back – by dreams and other ways –
all *that* came to nothing. He paid little heed.

136   Tanto giù cadde che tutti argomenti
         a la salute sua eran già corti,
         fuor che mostrarli le perdute genti.

139   Per questo visitai l'uscio d'i morti,
         e a colui che l'ha qua sù condotto
         li preghi miei, piangendo, furon porti.

142   Alto fato di Dio sarebbe rotto
         se Letè si passasse e tal vivanda
         fosse gustata sanza alcuno scotto

145   di pentimento che lagrime spanda.'

He fell so far that every other means   136
to save this man, by now, came short, unless
he saw, himself, those people who are lost.

I went, then, to the doorway of the dead,   139
and, weeping, my entreaties there were borne
to one who, since, has brought him to these heights.

God's high decree would shatter, though, if he   142
should pass by the Lethe and go on to taste
the food of life, yet leave unpaid the tax

of penitence, which pours out flowing tears.'   145

CANTO 31

1   'O tu che se' di là dal fiume sacro,'
volgendo suo parlare a me per punta,
che pur per taglio m'era paruto acro,

4   ricominciò, seguendo sanza cunta:
'Dì, dì se questo è vero: a tanta accusa
tua confession conviene esser congiunta.'

7   Era la mia virtù tanto confusa
che la voce si mosse e pria si spense
che da li organi suoi fosse dischiusa.

10   Poco sofferse, poi disse: 'Che pense?
Rispondi a me, ché le memorie triste
in te non sono ancor da l'acqua offense.'

13   Confusione e paura insieme miste
mi pinsero un tal 'sì' fuor de la bocca
al quale intender fuor mestier le viste.

16   Come balestro frange, quando scocca
da troppa tesa, la sua corda e l'arco,
e con men foga l'asta il segno tocca:

19   sì scoppia' io sottesso grave carco,
fuori sgorgando lagrime e sospiri,
e la voce allentò per lo suo varco.

22   Ond' ella a me: 'Per entro i mie' disiri,
che ti menavano ad amar lo Bene
di là dal qual non è a che s'aspiri,

25   quai fossi attraversati o quai catene
trovasti, per che del passare innanzi
dovessiti così spogliar la spene?

CANTO 31

'You, who are there beyond the sacred stream,'   1
turning the sword point of her words on me
(the edge alone had seemed quite keen enough),

    so, without lapse continuing, she began,   4
'Say, say, if this is true. To such a charge
your own confession needs to be conjoined.'

    My natural powers by now were so confused   7
that voice began to move, and yet gave out
before it cleared the larynx and the throat.

    She bore this for a while, and then she said: 10
'Respond to me. Your wretched memories
have not been struck through yet by Lethe's stream.'

    Fear and confusion, intermixed in me,   13
drove from my lips a 'yes' so hard to hear
it needed sight to make it understood.

    A crossbow triggered under too much stress   16
snaps its own string and splinters at the arc.
Its shaft thus hits the target with less force.

    I burst in that same way beneath the load   19
and, shedding streams of sighs and sobs and tears,
my voice came slack and slow along its course.

    And so: 'In your desire for me,' she said,   22
'which then was leading you to love the Good
beyond which we cannot aspire to reach,

    what ditches or what chains across your path   25
did you discover that led you to strip
the hopes you had of getting further on?

28   E quali agevolezze o quali avanzi
      ne la fronte de li altri si mostraro,
      per che dovessi lor passeggiare anzi?'

31   Dopo la tratta d'un sospiro amaro,
      a pena ebbi la voce che rispuose,
      e le labbra a fatica la formaro;

34   piangendo dissi: 'Le presenti cose
      col falso lor piacer volser miei passi
      tosto che 'l vostro viso si nascose.'

37   Ed ella: 'Se tacessi o se negassi
      ciò che confessi, non fora men nota
      la colpa tua: da tal giudice sassi!

40   Ma quando scoppia de la propria gota
      l'accusa del peccato, in nostra corte
      rivolge sé contra 'l taglio la rota.

43   Tuttavia, perché mo vergogna porte
      del tuo errore, e perché altra volta,
      udendo le serene, sie più forte,

46   pon giù il seme del piangere, e ascolta:
      sì udirai come in contraria parte
      mover dovieti mia carne sepolta.

49   Mai non t'appresentò natura o arte
      piacer quanto le belle membra in ch'io
      rinchiusa fui, e sono in terra sparte;

52   e se 'l sommo piacer sì ti fallio
      per la mia morte, qual cosa mortale
      dovea poi trarre te nel suo disio?

55   Ben ti dovevi, per lo primo strale
      de le cose fallaci, levar suso
      di retro a me, che non era più tale.

58   Non ti dovea gravar le penne in giuso,
      ad aspettar più colpo, o pargoletta
      o altra novità con sì breve uso.

61   Novo augelletto due o tre aspetta,
      ma dinanzi da li occhi d'i pennuti
      rete si spiega indarno o si saetta.'

What easements, profits, gain or benefit   28
displayed themselves to you on other brows
that you preferred to flounce within their sight?'

I drew the bitterest of sighs, but then   31
I hardly had the voice left to respond.
My lips were labouring to give form to words.

Weeping, I said: 'Mere things of here and now   34
and their false pleasures turned my steps away
the moment that your face had hid itself.'

'Had you,' she said, 'been silent, or denied   37
what you confess, your guilt would equally
have been observed. It's known to such a judge!

But when the plea of guilty, in this court,   40
bursts, freely uttered, from the sinner's cheek,
the grindstone here will turn against the blade.

And yet – so you may bear the proper shame   43
your error brings and, hearing, once again,
the siren call you may show greater strength –

put to one side the seed that nurtures tears.   46
Listen and hear how down a different path
my flesh, when buried, should have made you move.

Never had art or nature shown to you   49
such beauty and delight as did those limbs,
in which I was enclosed, now strewn in earth.

And if that great delight, because I died,   52
did fail for you, what other dying thing
should then have drawn you to desire of it?

Pierced by the arrows of fallacious things,   55
you should at once have raised yourself on high,
to follow me, I being none such now.

You ought not to have weighed your feathers down   58*
just waiting to be stricken by some girl,
or other novelty of short-lived use.

A newborn chick will take a blow or two.   61
But arrows fly, and nets are spread in vain,
before the eyes of any fully fledged.'

64   Quali fanciulli, vergognando, muti
        con li occhi a terra stannosi, ascoltando
        e sé riconoscendo e ripentuti:

67   tal mi stav' io; ed ella disse: 'Quando
        per udir se' dolente, alza la barba,
        e prenderai più doglia riguardando.'

70   Con men di resistenza si dibarba
        robusto cerro, o vero al nostral vento
        o vero a quel de la terra di Iarba,

73   ch'io non levai al suo comando il mento;
        e quando per la barba il viso chiese,
        ben conobbi il velen de l'argomento.

76   E come la mia faccia si distese,
        posarsi quelle prime creature
        da loro aspersion l'occhio comprese;

79   e le mie luci, ancor poco sicure,
        vider Beatrice volta in su la fiera
        ch'è sola una persona in due nature.

82   Sotto 'l suo velo e oltre la rivera
        vincer pariemi più sé stessa antica,
        vincer che l'altre qui, quand' ella c'era.

85   Di penter sì mi punse ivi l'ortica
        che di tutte altre cose qual mi torse
        più nel suo amor, più mi si fé nemica.

88   Tanta riconoscenza il cor mi morse
        ch'io caddi vinto, e quale allora femmi
        salsi colei che la cagion mi porse.

91   Poi, quando il cor virtù di fuor rendemmi,
        la donna ch'io avea trovata sola
        sopra me vidi, e dicea: 'Tiemmi, tiemmi!'

94   Tratto m'avea nel fiume infin la gola,
        e tirandosi me dietro sen giva
        sovresso l'acqua, lieve come scola.

97   Quando fui presso a la beata riva,
        'Asperges me' sì dolcemente udissi
        che nol so rimembrar, non ch'io lo scriva.

As little boys who stand there dumb with shame,   64
eyes on the ground and listening to what's said,
aware – very sorry – of what they are,
    so I, too, simply stood. And she said: 'Since   67
you grieve at what you're hearing, raise your beard
and, looking up, you'll feel still greater pain.'
    With less resistance some well-sinewed oak   70
is rooted out by northern winds of ours,
or blasts from savage Iarbas' Libyan realm,
    than I at her command raised up my chin.   73
And when she spoke of 'beard' (to name my face),
I knew the venom that her meaning bore.
    But as I stretched to show my face to her,   76
those primal creatures, as my eyes observed,
had ceased in scattering their arc of flowers.
    Those lights of mine, still very far from sure,   79
saw Beatrice turn towards the beast,
being two natures and, in person, one.
    Beneath her veil, beyond the flowing stream,   82
she overcame, it seemed, what once she'd been,
when once, as here, she overcame all women.
    The nettle of remorse now stung so sharp,   85
whatever else had drawn me most to love
became for me my utmost enemy.
    It gnawed my heart – the consciousness of this –   88*
that, overwhelmed, I fell. What I became,
she knows who is the cause of why I did.
    Then when my heart gave back my outward powers,   91
the *donna* whom I'd found there all alone,
I saw above me, saying: 'Grip me! Grip!'
    She'd drawn me up to throat height in the stream,   94
and, pulling me behind her, went her way
across the wave as light as any skiff.
    And then, when I approached the blessed shore,   97
'*Asperges me*' was heard, so sweetly sung
I can't remember it, still less can write.

100   La bella donna ne le braccia aprissi,
       abbracciommi la testa e mi sommerse,
       ove convenne ch'io l'acqua inghiottissi.

103   Indi mi tolse e bagnato m'offerse
       dentro a la danza de le quattro belle,
       e ciascuna del braccio mi coperse.

106   'Noi siam qui ninfe e nel ciel siamo stelle;
       pria che Beatrice discendesse al mondo,
       fummo ordinate a lei per sue ancelle.

109   Merrenti a li occhi suoi, ma nel giocondo
       lume ch'è dentro aguzzeranno i tuoi
       le tre di là, che miran più profondo.'

112   Così cantando cominciaro, e poi
       al petto del grifon seco menarmi,
       ove Beatrice stava vòlta a noi.

115   Disser: 'Fa che le viste non risparmi:
       posto t'avem dinanzi a li smeraldi
       ond' Amor già ti trasse le sue armi.'

118   Mille disiri più che fiamma caldi
       strinsermi li occhi a li occhi rilucenti,
       che pur sopra 'l grifone stavan saldi.

121   Come in lo specchio il sol, non altrimenti
       la doppia fiera dentro vi raggiava
       or con altri, or con altri reggimenti.

124   Pensa, lettor, s'io mi maravigliava
       quando vedea la cosa in sé star queta,
       e ne l'idolo suo si trasmutava!

127   Mentre che piena di stupore e lieta
       l'anima mia gustava di quel cibo
       che, saziando di sé, di sé asseta,

130   sé dimostrando di più alto tribo
       ne li atti, l'altre tre si fero avanti,
       danzando al loro angelico caribo.

133   'Volgi, Beatrice, volgi li occhi santi,'
       era la sua canzone, 'al tuo fedele,
       che per vederti ha mossi passi tanti!

That lovely lady, opening wide her arms,   100
circled my head, submerging me so far
I could not help but swallow from the stream.

From there she took and led me, bathed, still wet,   103
to join the dance of those four lovely ones.
And each one raised an arm to cover me.

'We, here, are nymphs and, in the heavens, stars,   106
given to Beatrice as her maids,
before she first descended to the world.

We'll lead you to her eyes. Yet to that light,   109
so jubilant, within, those three beyond –
their gaze still deeper – will make yours more keen.'

So, singing, they began and, moving on,   112
they brought me with them to the Gryphon's breast,
where, turned towards us, Beatrice stood.

'Make sure,' they said, 'you do not spare your eyes.   115
We've placed you here before these emeralds,
from which Love aimed his arrows at you once.'

A thousand longings, fiercer far than flame,   118
wrestled my eyes to her eyes, shining back,
fixed on the Gryphon, never unwavering.

No differently from sun in mirror glass,   121*
the twyform beast shone rays into her eyes,
displaying one and then the other kind.

Reader, just think how great my wonder was   124
to see that creature stilled within itself
and yet – within that icon – altering.

And, while astounded, yet so full of joy,   127
my soul received the savour of the food
that feeds us full and makes us thirst for more,

the other three who showed, in all they did,   130*
that they were scions of a greater tribe
came forward, to their angel's chant, *en loure*.

'Turn, Beatrice, turn your holy eyes'   133
(their song went thus) 'on your most faithful one
who, for your sight, has moved so many steps.

136 Per grazia, fa noi grazia che disvele
a lui la bocca tua, sì che discerna
la seconda bellezza che tu cele.'

139 O isplendor di viva luce etterna:
chi palido si fece sotto l'ombra
sì di Parnaso, o bevve in sua cisterna,

142 che non paresse aver la mente ingombra,
tentando a render te qual tu paresti
là dove armonizzando il ciel t'adombra,

145 quando ne l'aere aperto ti solvesti?

In grace, we beg, do us the grace to lift   136
the veil that veils your lips so he can tell
the second beauty that you still conceal.'
    Splendour of living and eternal light!   139
Who would not seem – though pale from studying
deep in Parnassian shade, whose wells he drinks –
    still to be much encumbered in his mind,   142
endeavouring to draw what you then seemed,
where heavens in harmony alone enshadow you,
    as you came forth and showed yourself in air?   145

CANTO 32

1   Tant' eran li occhi miei fissi e attenti
    a disbramarsi la decenne sete,
    che li altri sensi m'eran tutti spenti.

4   Ed essi quinci e quindi avien parete
    di non caler – così lo santo riso
    a sé traéli con l'antica rete! –

7   quando per forza mi fu vòlto il viso
    ver' la sinistra mia da quelle dee,
    perch' io udi' da loro un 'Troppo fiso!'

10 e la disposizion ch'a veder èe
    ne li occhi pur testé dal sol percossi,
    sanza la vista alquanto esser mi fée.

13 Ma poi ch'al poco il viso riformossi –
    e dico 'al poco' per rispetto al molto
    sensibile, onde a forza mi rimossi –

16 vidi 'n sul braccio destro esser rivolto
    lo glorioso essercito, e tornarsi
    col sole e con le sette fiamme al volto.

19 Come sotto li scudi per salvarsi
    volgesi schiera e sé gira col segno,
    prima che possa tutta in sé mutarsi:

22 quella milizia del celeste regno
    che procedeva, tutta trapassonne
    pria che piegasse il carro il primo legno.

25 Indi a le rote si tornar le donne,
    e 'l grifon mosse il benedetto carco,
    sì che però nulla penna crollonne.

CANTO 32

My eyes were now so fixedly intent   1
to free themselves from that decade-long thirst
that every sense but sight had been eclipsed.

   This side and that, my eyes were walled about   4
with 'I-don't-care-at-all' (the holy smile
so drew them to it with its age-old net!),

   when, by sheer force, my face was turned around   7
towards my left by all those deities,
hearing from them a 'Far too fixedly!'

   And that debility that's found in eyes   10
when just now stricken by a blinding sun
here left me, for some moments, without sight.

   But when my eye refocused on the less   13*
(the 'less' I mean in contrast to that great
thing seen from which, with strain, I'd turned away)

   the glorious army had, I saw, right-wheeled –   16
those seven flames ahead – to face the sun,
and so to make its march towards the east.

   As, to protect itself, a squadron turns,   19
wheeling beneath its shields around the flag,
till every man has made a turnabout,

   so, too, those troops of that celestial realm   22
that marched in front went by us, rank by rank,
before the chariot had turned its pole.

   The *donne* then went back beside its wheels.   25
The Gryphon drew its blessèd burden on.
And not a single feather stirred or fell.

28   La bella donna che mi trasse al varco,
        e Stazio e io seguitavam la rota
        che fé l'orbita sua con minore arco.

31   Sì passeggiando l'alta selva vòta,
        colpa di quella ch'al serpente crese,
        temprava i passi un'angelica nota.

34   Forse in tre voli tanto spazio prese
        disfrenata saetta quanto eramo
        rimossi, quando Beatrice scese.

37   Io senti' mormorare a tutti 'Adamo';
        poi cerchiaro una pianta dispogliata
        di foglie e d'altra fronda in ciascun ramo.

40   La coma sua, che tanto si dilata
        più quanto più è sù, fora da l'Indi
        ne' boschi lor per altezza ammirata.

43   'Beato se', grifon, che non discindi
        col becco d'esto legno dolce al gusto,
        poscia che mal si torce il ventre quindi.'

46   Così dintorno a l'albero robusto
        gridaron li altri; e l'animal binato:
        'Sì si conserva il seme d'ogne giusto.'

49   E vòlto al temo ch'elli avea tirato,
        trasselo al piè de la vedova frasca
        e quel di lei a lei lasciò legato.

52   Come le nostre piante, quando casca
        giù la gran luce mischiata con quella
        che raggia dietro a la celeste lasca,

55   turgide fansi, e poi si rinovella
        di suo color ciascuna, pria che 'l sole
        giunga li suoi corsier sotto altra stella:

58   men che di rose e più che di viole
        colore aprendo, s'innovò la pianta,
        che prima avea le ramora sì sole.

61   Io non lo 'ntesi, né qui non si canta
        l'inno che quella gente allor cantaro,
        né la nota soffersi tutta quanta.

The lovely one who'd drawn me through the pass,   28
Statius and I now followed at that wheel
which, in its orbit, traced the lesser arc.

So passing through that deep yet empty grove   31
(the fault of her who trusted in the snake),
our steps were measured to the angel song.

The distance that, perhaps, we travelled so,   34
was three flights of an arrow when discharged.
And Beatrice now, at last, came down.

I heard them murmur 'Adam', all as one.   37
And then they circled round a leafless tree.
Its every branch was stripped of greenery.

The crested peak which broadens out the more   40
the more it rises, would, for height, inspire
wonder in Hindus in their own great woods.

'Blessèd are you, the Gryphon. With your beak   43
you did not spoil this wood, so sweet to taste.
For, after tasting, bellies writhe, all sick.'

Around the mighty tree they made this cry.   46
And then the creature, two-formed in its birth:
'In this way, all that's true and just is saved.'

Then, turned towards the pole he'd drawn before,   49
towards the foot of that long-widowed sprig,
he tugged it and then left it bound to that.

Compare: in spring the great light of the sun   52
cascades on earthly trees conjoined with that
which shines out following the astral Carp.

These trees then swell. The colour is renewed,   55
in each and all, before the sun moves on
to yoke its horses to some other star.

So did this tree, whose boughs had hung bereft,   58
take on new strength, in colour opening
to more than violet and to less than rose.

I did not understand (it's not sung here)   61
the hymn these people sang, nor could I bear
in full the beauty of its harmonies.

64   S'io potessi ritrar come assonnaro
        li occhi spietati udendo di Siringa –
        li occhi a cui pur vegghiar costò sì caro –

67   come pintor che con essempro pinga
        disegnerei com' io m'addormentai,
        ma qual vuol sia che l'assonnar ben finga.

70   Però trascorro a quando mi svegliai,
        e dico ch'un splendor mi squarciò 'l velo
        del sonno, e un chiamar: 'Surgi: che fai?'

73   Quali a veder de' fioretti del melo
        che del suo pome li angeli fa ghiotti
        e perpetue nozze fa nel cielo,

76   Pietro e Giovanni e Iacopo, condotti
        e vinti, ritornaro a la parola
        da la qual furon maggior sonni rotti,

79   e videro scemata loro scuola
        così di Moisè come d'Elia,
        e al maestro suo cangiata stola:

82   tal torna' io, e vidi quella pia
        sovra me starsi che conducitrice
        fu de' miei passi lungo 'l fiume pria.

85   E tutto in dubbio dissi: 'Ov' è Beatrice?'
        Ond' ella: 'Vedi lei sotto la fronda
        nova sedere in su la sua radice.

88   Vedi la compagnia che la circonda;
        li altri dopo 'l grifon sen vanno suso
        con più dolce canzone e più profonda.'

91   E se più fu lo suo parlar diffuso
        non so, però che già ne li occhi m'era
        quella ch'ad altro intender m'avea chiuso.

94   Sola sedeasi in su la terra vera,
        come guardia lasciata lì del plaustro
        che legar vidi a la biforme fera.

97   In cerchio le facevan di sé claustro
        le sette ninfe, con quei lumi in mano
        che son sicuri d'Aquilone e d'Austro.

If I could trace the drowsiness that came   64
on hearing Syrinx sung to ruthless eyes –
those eyes that wakefulness cost very dear –

then, from that model, as a painter paints,   67
I'd draw in my design how I now slept.
But that needs someone who can feign sleep well.

So I speed on to when I came awake,   70*
and say how splendour tore apart sleep's veil
and this cry: 'Rise! What *are* you doing there?'

When brought to see the budding apple flowers   73
which make the angels greedy for their fruit,
and makes in Heaven perpetual marriage feast,

Peter and James and John were overcome   76
but, waking once again, they heard that word
which shattered greater sleeps than theirs had been,

and saw the school they'd sat in two souls short –   79
since Moses and Elijah both had gone –
their teacher with his robe now much transformed.

So, too, I woke, and saw, above me there,   82
the one who in compassion led my steps
along the river sometime earlier.

And, full of doubt, I said: 'Where's Beatrice?'   85
At which, 'See there,' she said, 'beneath the leaves –
now new – she's seated on the root of that.

And see the company that encircles her!   88
The rest behind the Gryphon go on high,
singing a deeper, ever sweeter song.'

And if her speech flowed further on than this,   91
I do not know. My eyes were set, by now,
on her. She'd closed my mind to other thoughts.

Alone, she sat upon that one true earth   94
as guard, left there to watch the chariot
which, as I'd seen, the two-form beast had tied.

The seven nymphs encloistered her around   97*
and in their hands all carried lights, secure
from Aquilonian or Austral winds.

100   'Qui sarai tu poco tempo silvano;
      e sarai meco sanza fine cive
      di quella Roma onde Cristo è romano.

103   Però, in pro del mondo che mal vive,
      al carro tieni or li occhi, e quel che vedi,
      ritornato di là, fa che tu scrive.'

106   Così Beatrice; e io, che tutto ai piedi
      d'i suoi comandamenti era divoto,
      la mente e li occhi ov' ella volle diedi.

109   Non scese mai con sì veloce moto
      foco di spessa nube quando piove
      da quel confine che più va remoto,

112   com' io vidi calar l'uccel di Giove
      per l'alber giù, rompendo de la scorza,
      non che d'i fiori e de le foglie nove,

115   e ferì 'l carro di tutta sua forza,
      ond' el piegò come nave in fortuna,
      vinta da l'onda or da poggia, or da orza.

118   Poscia vidi avventarsi ne la cuna
      del triunfal veiculo una volpe
      che d'ogne pasto buon parea digiuna;

121   ma, riprendendo lei di laide colpe,
      la donna mia la volse in tanta futa
      quanto sofferser l'ossa sanza polpe.

124   Poscia per indi ond' era pria venuta,
      l'aguglia vidi scender giù ne l'arca
      del carro e lasciar lei di sé pennuta;

127   e qual esce di cuor che si rammarca,
      tal voce uscì del cielo, e cotal disse:
      'O navicella mia, com' mal se' carca!'

130   Poi parve a me che la terra s'aprisse
      tr'ambo le ruote, e vidi uscirne un drago
      che per lo carro sù la coda fisse;

133   e come vespa che ritragge l'ago,
      a sé traendo la coda maligna,
      trasse del fondo, e gissen vago vago.

'With me a while you'll be a woodsman here   100
and then, with me, a citizen eternally
in that new Rome where Christ is Roman, too.

And so, to aid the world that lives all wrong,   103
keep your eyes firmly on the chariot.
And what you see write down when you go back.'

Thus Beatrice. I myself, devout,   106
touching the feet of all that she ordained,
gave eye and mind to where she said I should.

No fire that rains from regions farthest off   109*
has, from the densest vapours, struck
as rapidly in motion as I saw

the Eagle, bird of Jupiter, swoop down   112
straight through the tree, to rip off all its bark –
the flowers as well, and all its new green leaves.

It struck the chariot with all its force,   115
making it lurch – a ship in jeopardy,
vanquished by windward and then leeward gusts.

Within the cradle of the Victory Car   118
I saw a vixen headlong hurl herself,
starving, it seemed, for any healthy food.

And yet, reproving all her loathsome faults,   121
my lady sent that vixen off in flight –
or such flight as her fleshless bones could bear.

But then from where the Eagle first had come,   124
I saw it swoop down on the chariot-ark
and leave it feathered as it was itself.

And then, as coming from some grieving heart,   127
a voice came from the heavens. And this voice said:
'My little ship, what ill load weighs you down!'

And then, it seemed, the earth beneath both wheels   130
gaped wide. I saw a dragon coming out
that thrust its tail deep in the Chariot.

And then, as wasps do, drawing out their sting,   133
so did the dragon its malignant tail –
tearing out planks – then went off, wandering.

136   Quel che rimase, come da gramigna
       vivace terra, da la piuma – offerta
       forse con intenzion sana e benigna –

139   si ricoperse, e funne ricoperta
       e l'una e l'altra rota e 'l temo, in tanto
       che più tiene un sospir la bocca aperta.

142   Trasformato così, 'l dificio santo
       mise fuor teste per le parti sue,
       tre sovra 'l temo e una in ciascun canto.

145   Le prime eran cornute come bue,
       ma le quattro un sol corno avean per fronte:
       simile mostro visto ancor non fue.

148   Sicura, quasi rocca in alto monte,
       seder sovresso una puttana sciolta
       m'apparve con le ciglia intorno pronte;

151   e come perché non li fosse tolta,
       vidi di costa a lei dritto un gigante,
       e basciavansi insieme alcuna volta.

154   Ma perché l'occhio cupido e vagante
       a me rivolse, quel feroce drudo
       la flagellò dal capo infin le piante;

157   poi, di sospetto pieno e d'ira crudo,
       disciolse il mostro e trassel per la selva
       tanto che sol di lei mi fece scudo

160   a la puttana e a la nova belva.

What wood remained, like grass in living earth,   136
with eagle feathers – offered, as may be
with generous purpose kindly meant to heal –

covered itself once more and covered all,   139
both wheels and pole, within the time it takes
for open mouths to breathe the longest sigh.

Then, so transformed, the sacred structure sent   142
new heads out all along its many parts,
three on the pole and one on all four sides.

The first three heads were horned as oxen are.   145
The four, though, on their brows bore single horns.
No monster like this ever has been seen.

As confident as strongholds in the hills,   148
sitting there now, a loose-wrapped whore appeared,
her flickering lashes quick to look around.

And then I saw a giant standing by,   151
lest she should ever lift her eyes from him.
And every now and then these two would kiss.

But since her wandering and cupidinous eye   154
was turned on me, that rabid paramour
whipped her ferociously from head to foot.

Then, full of jealousy and raw, wild wrath,   157
he loosed the beast and led it through the wood,
so far the wood itself now formed a shield

between the whore and weird new beast and me.   160

CANTO 33

1   '*Deus, venerunt gentes,*' alternando
or tre or quattro dolce salmodia,
le donne incominciaro, e lagrimando,

4   e Beatrice sospirosa e pia
quelle ascoltava, sì fatta che poco
più a la croce si cambiò Maria.

7   Ma poi che l'altre vergini dier loco
a lei di dir, levata dritta in pè
rispuose, colorata come foco:

10 '*Modicum, et non videbitis me*;
et iterum, sorelle mie dilette,
modicum, et vos videbitis me.'

13 Poi le si mise innanzi tutte e sette,
e dopo sé, solo accennando, mosse
me e la donna e 'l savio che ristette.

16 Così sen giva, e non credo che fosse
lo decimo suo passo in terra posto,
quando con li occhi li occhi mi percosse,

19 e con tranquillo aspetto: 'Vien più tosto,'
mi disse, 'tanto che, s'io parlo teco,
ad ascoltarmi tu sie ben disposto.'

22 Sì com' io fui com' io dovea seco,
dissemi: 'Frate, perché non t'attenti
a domandarmi omai venendo meco?'

25 Come a color che troppo reverenti
dinanzi a suo maggior parlando sono,
che non traggon la voce viva ai denti,

CANTO 33

'*Deus, venerunt gentes*,' – alternating   1
three, then four – the seven *donne*, weeping
gently, sweetly, began to chant that psalm.

  And Beatrice, sighing in compassion,   4
listened and changed, to hear them, hardly less
then Mary did when she stood by the Cross.

  But when those other virgins granted her   7
a place to speak, she, rising to her feet,
responded, fiery in her colour, thus:

  '*Modicum, et non videbitis me*;   10
et iterum, my most beloved sisters,
modicum, et vos videbitis me.'

  She then sent all those seven on ahead   13
and, with one gesture, brought along behind
myself, the lady and the sage who'd stayed.

  And so she went her way, but had not placed   16
her tenth step on the earth (or so I think)
before her glance had pierced me, eye to eye.

  And, calm in countenance, 'Come on. Be quick,   19
so if I choose,' she said, 'to speak to you,
you'll be well placed to hear what I may say.'

  As soon as I was with her, as I ought,   22
'Dear brother, now you're walking by my side,
why don't you seek to question me?' she said.

  It happened now to me (it often does   25
to those too reverent with superiors,
who can't get living voice behind their teeth)

28   avvenne a me, che sanza intero suono
incominciai: 'Madonna, mia bisogna
voi conoscete, e ciò ch'ad essa è buono.'

31   Ed ella a me: 'Da tema e da vergogna
voglio che tu omai ti disviluppe,
sì che non parli più com' om che sogna.

34   Sappi che 'l vaso che 'l serpente ruppe
fu e non è; ma chi n'ha colpa, creda
che vendetta di Dio non teme suppe.

37   Non sarà tutto tempo sanza reda
l'aguglia che lasciò le penne al carro,
per che divenne mostro e poscia preda,

40   ch'io veggio certamente, e però il narro,
a darne tempo già stelle propinque,
secure d'ogn' intoppo e d'ogne sbarro,

43   nel quale un cinquecento diece e cinque,
messo di Dio, anciderà la fuia
con quel gigante che con lei delinque.

46   E forse che la mia narrazion, buia
qual Temi e Sfinge, men ti persuade,
perch' a lor modo lo 'ntelletto attuia,

49   ma tosto fier li fatti le Naiade
che solveranno questo enigma forte
sanza danno di pecore o di biade.

52   Tu nota, e sì come da me son porte
così queste parole segna a' vivi
del viver ch'è un correre a la morte.

55   E aggi a mente, quando tu le scrivi,
di non celar qual hai vista la pianta
ch'è or due volte dirubata quivi.

58   Qualunque ruba quella o quella schianta
con bestemmia di fatto offende a Dio,
che solo a l'uso suo la creò santa.

61   Per morder quella, in pena e in disio
cinquemilia anni e più l'anima prima
bramò colui che 'l morso in sé punio.

that I began without a full, clear sound: 28
'My lady, what your need is, you well know,
and also what is good to meet that need.'

    And she to me: 'From dread and shame alike,   31
I'd have you now at once unknot yourself,
so you no longer speak as in a dream.

    Know this: the vessel that the serpent broke   34*
was and is not. But let the guilty one
be sure God's vengeance need not fear grave-sops.

    The eagle, leaving feathers on the Cart –   37
through which it, first, was monster then the prey –
will not for ever be without an heir.

    I see with certainty, and therefore say   40
that stars, secure from obstacle or bar,
are drawing near to give to us the hour

    in which will come FIVE HUNDRED TEN AND FIVE   43
as messenger of God to slay that thief –
the giant, too, whom she makes mischief with.

    It may be that my narrative – as dark   46*
as those of Themis and the Sphinx – will blunt
(as theirs did), not persuade your intellect.

    Yet real events will soon prove Naiades,   49
who'll free you from this enigmatic knot
yet bring no harm to grazing sheep or grain.

    Take note and, as these words are borne from me,   52
inscribe them for a sign to those who live
the life that rapidly runs on to death.

    And take good care, when you write all this down,   55
that you don't hide how you have seen the tree,
twice over now, stripped bare and robbed of green.

    Whoever steals from it, or tears its trunk   58
blasphemes, by doing so, against the God
who made it sacred for His use alone.

    Five thousand years and more, the first of souls –   61
condemned to yearning pain for biting it –
hungered for Him whose own self scourged that bite.

64   Dorme lo 'ngegno tuo, se non estima
per singular cagione essere eccelsa
lei tanto e sì travolta ne la cima.

67   E se stati non fossero acqua d'Elsa
li pensier vani intorno a la tua mente,
e 'l piacer loro un Piramo a la gelsa,

70   per tante circostanze solamente
la giustizia di Dio ne l'interdetto
conosceresti a l'arbor moralmente.

73   Ma perch' io veggio te ne lo 'ntelletto
fatto di pietra e, impetrato, tinto
sì che t'abbaglia il lume del mio detto,

76   voglio anco – e se non scritto, almen dipinto –
che 'l te ne porti dentro a te per quello
che si reca il bordon di palma cinto.'

79   E io: 'Sì come cera da suggello,
che la figura impressa non trasmuta,
segnato è or da voi lo mio cervello.

82   Ma perché tanto sovra mia veduta
vostra parola disiata vola,
che più la perde quanto più s'aiuta?'

85   'Perché conoschi,' disse, 'quella scuola
c'hai seguitata, e veggi sua dottrina
come può seguitar la mia parola,

88   e veggi vostra via da la divina
distar contanto quanto si discorda
de terra il ciel che più alto festina.'

91   Ond' io rispuosi lei: 'Non mi ricorda
ch'i' straniasse me già mai da voi,
né honne coscienza che rimorda.'

94   'E se tu ricordar non te ne puoi,'
sorridendo rispuose, 'or ti rammenta
come bevesti di Letè ancoi;

97   e se dal fummo foco s'argomenta,
cotesta oblivion chiaro conchiude
colpa ne la tua voglia altrove attenta.

Your wits lie sleeping if you do not judge   64
that soaring height, inverted at the top,
to be occasioned by some unique cause.

And if, around your mind, your own vain thoughts   67*
had not been calcifying Elsa streams,
their joys like Pyramus to mulberries,

then, from its many attributes alone,   70
you, in this allegory, might well have seen
that tree to be God's justice known in bans.

But since I see that you, in intellect,   73
are turned to stone and petrified, pure black,
hence dazzled by the light of what I say,

I wish, as well, that you'll bear this within –   76
at least as image, not yet written script –
as pilgrims bring their staves back wreathed with palms.'

And I: 'No less than wax, I'll bear the print   79
and never change the shape impressed on it,
seeing my brain has now been signed by you.

But why so far above my powers of sight   82
does your word, so much longed for, take its flight
so that the more it strives it loses more?'

'I ask,' she said, 'so you will know how far   85
that school of yours can follow what I say,
and see what its philosophy can do,

and also that you see how all your ways   88
diverge, as distant from the ways of God
as your world is, untuned, from swiftest spheres.'

'I cannot call to mind,' I answered her,   91
'that I have ever been estranged from you.
My conscience sets sharp teeth in me for that.'

'And if you cannot bring that back to mind,'   94
smiling, she answered me, 'then just recall
you've drunk, this very day, from Lethe's stream.

And if, when smoke appears, it proves there's fire, 97
then this oblivion will itself conclude
that guilt once drew your will away, elsewhere.

100   Veramente oramai saranno nude
le mie parole quanto converrassi
quelle scovrire a la tua vista rude.'

103   E più corusco e con più lenti passi
teneva il sole il cerchio di merigge,
che qua e là, come li aspetti, fassi,

106   quando s'affisser, sì come s'affigge
chi va dinanzi a gente per iscorta,
se trova novitate o sue vestigge,

109   le sette donne al fin d'un'ombra smorta,
qual sotto foglie verdi e rami nigri
sovra suoi freddi rivi l'alpe porta.

112   Dinanzi ad esse Eufratès e Tigri
veder mi parve uscir d'una fontana
e, quasi amici, dipartirsi pigri.

115   'O luce, o gloria de la gente umana,
che acqua è questa che qui si dispiega
da un principio e sé da sé lontana?'

118   Per cotal priego detto mi fu: 'Priega
Matelda che 'l ti dica.' E qui rispuose,
come fa chi da colpa si dislega,

121   la bella donna: 'Questo e altre cose
dette li son per me, e son sicura
che l'acqua di Letè non gliel nascose.'

124   E Beatrice: 'Forse maggior cura,
che spesse volte la memoria priva,
fatt' ha la mente sua ne li occhi oscura.

127   Ma vedi Eunoè che là diriva:
menalo ad esso e, come tu se' usa,
la tramortita sua virtù ravviva.'

130   Come anima gentil, che non fa scusa
ma fa sua voglia de la voglia altrui
tosto che è per segno fuor dischiusa:

133   così, poi che da essa preso fui,
la bella donna mossesi, e a Stazio
donnescamente disse: 'Vien con lui.'

My words must be as naked, after this,   100
as far as they may fittingly unveil
themselves to your as-yet-untutored sight.'
    Its spark more brilliant and with slower step,   103
the sun now held the circle of the noon,
which moves (from what one sees) from side to side,
    when, stopping – as a guide will stop, who goes   106
before the rest as escort if he finds
some novelty or traces of the strange –
    the *donne* reached the edges of that shade   109
cast, as in mountains, over chilly streams
beneath green leaves and boughs of ebony.
    Ahead of them, as from a single spring,   112
it seemed I saw the Tigris and Euphrates
rise and then part, like friends, reluctantly.
    'You light and glory of the human race,   115
what are these waters that, from their one sole source,
rise up then, spreading, distance each from each?'
    To this demand: 'Best ask,' the answer came,   118
'Matelda. She'll reply to you.' She did –
meaning, it seemed, to free herself from blame,
    saying, that lovely lady: 'I have told him why.   121
Both this – I'm sure of it – and other things
are not concealed from him by Lethe's stream.'
    And Beatrice: 'Maybe greater cares –   124
which often take the memory away –
have made his mind grow darker in its view.
    But see Eunoe, which is flowing there.   127
Lead him to that. And, as you always do,
bring back his fainting, half-dead powers to life.'
    As noble souls incline to do – they make   130
another's will, without excuse, *their* will
as soon as any sign of that appears –
    so, too, when I was taken by the hand,   133
the lovely lady made her way and said
to Statius, as a *donna* does: 'Come, too.'

136   S'io avessi, lettor, più lungo spazio
       da scrivere, i' pur cantere' in parte
       lo dolce ber che mai non m'avria sazio,

139   ma perché piene son tutte le carte
       ordite a questa cantica seconda,
       non mi lascia più ir lo fren de l'arte.

142   Io ritornai da la santissima onda
       rifatto sì come piante novelle
       rinovellate di novella fronda,

145   puro e disposto a salire a le stelle.

If, reader, I'd more space in which to write,   136
then I should sing in part about that drink,
so sweet I'd never have my fill of it.

However, since these pages now are full,   139
prepared by rights to take the second song,
the reins of art won't let me pass beyond.

I came back from that holiest of waves   142
remade, refreshed as any new tree is,
renewed, refreshed with foliage anew,

    pure and prepared to rise towards the stars.   145

Commentaries and Notes

Under the notes for each canto, the reader will find broadly factual explanations, references and cross-references to texts cited by Dante that are worth reading alongside Dante's own. An asterisk alongside the line number in the main English text refers to the beginning of the *terzina* in which a reference occurs. Sometimes this points to a sequence of *terzine* in which, by consolidating these references, readers may discern some pattern of concerns – with, say, the minutiae of thirteenth-century politics – that will better emerge than in a strictly line-by-line treatment. This edition attempts to disturb as little as possible the narrative flow of Dante's poem. Where a pattern or point of critical interest has been pointed up, the explanatory note is subsumed into the interpretative commentary which precedes the notes and marked by bold type. Traditional annotations in sequential form are to be found in the excellent editions by Robert Durling and Ronald Martinez (Oxford, 2003) and the well-conceived apparatus by David Higgins in his commentary on C. H. Sissons's translation (London, 1980). To both of these editions the present editor is glad to acknowledge a warm debt of gratitude. Quotations from the Bible are, unless otherwise stated, from the Authorized Version.

CANTO 1

*Dawn rises in Purgatory. Dante encounters Cato,
guardian of the mountain, and, at Cato's command,
Virgil binds Dante with a reed plucked from the
seashore.*

Commentary

If you turn directly from the *Inferno* to the *Purgatorio* (as ideally
you should, since the *Commedia* is a connected narrative), you will
experience to the full the effect of disorientation, but also of refresh-
ment and new freedom, that Dante creates in *Purgatorio* 1. However,
save for a few backward glances to Hell, all of them veiled and oblique
(as at **lines 3, 88** and **118–36**), Dante does not insist upon this contin-
uity but rather invites his readers to explore for themselves the differ-
ences between the second realm and the first. The scene here ought to
be familiar. It is simply a description of the daily rising of the dawn
on the natural topography of a south seas beach. Yet, after the subter-
ranean experiences of the *Inferno*, with its multitudinous distortions
of natural light and design, such familiar details and natural processes
have themselves become unfamiliar. Likewise, Dante's verse here
enters new, yet very accessible, territory. His rhythms are more rapid
and lightly stressed than before. 'I'll sing' at **line 4** is in the future
tense, as if to indicate new horizons, hopes and possibilities. The
imagery of this canto evokes the phenomena of change, process, regen-
eration and return. Dawn is perceived not as a sudden dayburst, but
as a slow suffusion of ever clearer blue (**13–18**). Reeds, when plucked
from the ebb and flow of the tide, immediately grow back into new
life (**134–6**). Dante is only now 'returning' to the path he had lost
(**119–20**), as if the journey since he entered the Dark Wood of *Inferno*
1 and into Hell had been merely a waste of time.

It can be calculated that the action of *Purgatorio* 1 takes place at
around 5.30 a.m. on Easter Day 1300. Thus, behind all the references
that the canto makes to regeneration and rebirth there is the realization
that all life and all redemption depends upon Christ's Resurrection
from the dead. Likewise, the stars that shine in the southern sky (**23**)
(a constellation invented by Dante) point to the providential purpose
of purgation, which is to recover the innocence and purity of under-
standing that was first possessed by Adam and Eve. They alone have
seen these stars (**24**), from the vantage point of the Garden of Eden,

which is located on the summit of Mount Purgatory. Dante's ultimate task in this *cantica* is to recover that original vision.

References to the Christian scheme of redemption are no more explicit in *Purgatorio* 1 than are the references to Hell. The time of day is established by purely astronomical reference to the movement of the planets (19–21). Geographically, but intellectually as well, the first canto (like all of the nine preliminary cantos of the second *cantica*) occupies a hinterland where there are no absolute points of reference and in which exploration, inquiry and path-finding are the dominant modes of action, involving the reader no less than the figures depicted in Dante's narrative. It is thus remarkable (but entirely characteristic of Dante, who consistently leads himself and his reader into problematic encounters) that the main protagonists in *Purgatorio* 1 are two pagans – Virgil and Cato the younger – who would seem to have no place in a realm reserved for Christian penitents, and who engage in an edgy and mutually uncomprehending conversation (40–108). It is immediately clear that, even in the *Purgatorio*, Dante has no intention of abandoning his belief that classical culture and classical ethics have a perennial contribution to make to the advancement of Christian purposes and Christian poetry. But the problems still remain. In what way is Virgil still qualified to be Dante's guide? More acutely, how can Cato be qualified to act (on his own account at line 48) as the guardian of these cliffs, which he possessively describes as 'my', when he is not only a pagan but also a suicide (as are the damned of *Inferno* 13) and a rebel against the imperial cause which Dante so strongly supported? Indeed, one of the last sights in the *Inferno*, as Dante records it, is that of Cato's political allies, Brutus and Cassius, dangling alongside Judas Iscariot from the jaws of Satan (64–7). What has changed?

Historically, Marcus Porcius Cato Uticensis (95–46 BC) was descended from a senatorial family famous for its rigorous defence of ancient Roman values. To him, Julius Caesar's ambition to establish his own imperial power would have seemed the equivalent of enslavement, and his death by his own hand after the battle at Utica, near Carthage can readily be viewed as a Stoic affirmation of the freedom of conscience. Dante responds warmly to Cato's example. In his early philosophical treatise the *Convivio* – written before the poet's imperial sympathies were fully formed – Dante says that Cato is illuminated by an especial light of divine goodness, and supremely demonstrates – as all Romans should – a capacity for self-sacrifice, ensuring that justice and the public good should always be of paramount importance. (See *Convivio* 4: 5 and 4: 27.) In *Convivio* 4: 28 Cato is even compared allegorically to God. In that passage, Dante refers (as he does here at lines 85-7) to the story of how Cato's wife Marcia willingly returns to him, after a second marriage, in her final years. So, too, the soul in the last phase of its existence on earth should turn to the contemplation of God. No mention is made in the *Convivio* of Cato's suicide. However, in *De Monarchia* 2: 5 – possibly written after the *Purgatorio* – Cato's suicide is seen as an act, not of cowardice or evasion (which would certainly attract condemnation), but rather of self-sacrifice, which stands among the many signs and 'miracles' that demonstrate how Rome has been chosen providentially to foster righteousness in the world.

Up to a point, the Cato of *Purgatorio* 1 is compatible with the figure who appears in Dante's minor works. The four stars that cast a light as bright as the sun on Cato's features (37-9) are regularly taken to symbolize how the four cardinal virtues, wisdom, courage, temperance and justice – which can be displayed even without the inspiration of grace – are supremely exemplified in Cato, and certainly have a place in the ethical programme that Dante intends to follow in the *Purgatorio*. Rational virtue, whether illustrated by Cato or by Virgil, will not be overthrown here but exercised and fulfilled on the way to the perfected realm of justice which lies at the top of Mount Purgatory. The very act of self-sacrifice may be seen as 'rational' – as the expression of a mind aware of, and capable of, the heroic devotion that political justice may at times demand, and in that respect, too, a model for the appetite that the penitents display in their hungering for righteousness.

None of this, however, diminishes the surprise that Cato's presence in Purgatory arouses. Nor should it. By introducing Cato, Dante signals a wholly new dimension that is about to reveal itself in the ethical vision of the *Commedia*. In the speeches that Dante attributes to Cato, he displays an appropriately stern, even Stoic adherence to the conception of law, crying out at the sight of Dante and Virgil: 'The laws of the abyss – do these break down?' (46). Yet, ironically – even comically – Cato shows no awareness whatsoever of how the laws of eternity have been broken in his case. From this point on, Dante – without retracting his commitment to the rationality of justice – reveals progressively how ethical principles derive from the Christian understanding of God's unexpected but liberating action, in the person of Christ, and, on this foundation, these principles encourage a flourishing of human possibilities which would lie imprisoned even under the rule of the most rational institutions of justice. Dante's own poem, which in the *Inferno* had been so harshly committed to the ethics of judgement, becomes now a work where the cultivation of excellence is its primary objective.

Virgil's presence in Purgatory is not as permanent as Cato's appears to be (since Cato at **line 48** seems to regard himself as the permanent guardian of the cliffs of the mountain). Virgil, having travelled for three days in the light and dark of the slopes for the benefit of his pupil, will eventually return to the Limbo region from which he first departed to guide Dante on his journey. From this feature of Virgil's story there flows a perception (acutely expressed in *Purgatorio* 3 and 6) of the fragility of his character and, equally, of the rational competence which he has hitherto exemplified. In **lines 85–7**, as again at *Purgatorio* 2: 120, he suffers a rebuke from the austere Cato – and feels it keenly (*Purgatorio* 3: 7–9). Yet this rebuke again is as much an indication of Cato's limitations as of Virgil's. With notable inflexibility, Cato refuses to be swayed by any flattering mention of his wife Marcia – who as a pagan like Virgil, is destined for the eternally unchanging condition of Limbo. Likewise, it is only with some bemusement that Cato responds (**91–3**) to Virgil's mention of the favour that Dante enjoys in Beatrice's eyes. This recalls the complex but sensitive reply that Virgil gives to Beatrice in *Inferno* 2: 76–84, and *Purgatorio* 6, 17 and 27, in which Virgil readily invokes Beatrice's name to encourage Dante further in his quest. For the moment, Cato's ethical attitude of mind stands revealed as one which – in so far as it favours rule – also resists or is deaf to the impact of surprises that overthrow the general rule and, likewise, excludes any response to ambiguity and the demands of emotion and sensibility.

By contrast, the mentality that Dante attributes to Virgil, particularly in the final phase of this canto (**112–36**), is one which – deriving precisely from Virgil's foreign-ness, as an exile in Purgatory – combines pragmatism with humility, and aesthetic sensibility with an attention to the particular requirements of place and person. Submitting to Cato's command, Virgil leads Dante down to the deserted shore to bind him, as mark of humility, with one of the reeds that grow along the water's edge (**133–6**). The reader's eye follows in Virgil's track, and is brought from the airy contemplation of the sky with which the canto began to a minute observation of the processes observable on the ground in the gradual evaporation of dewdrops from the shadowy parts of the beach (**121–3**). Touch, texture and sensations are brought into play as, with a ritual gesture, Virgil spreads his hands into the dew and proceeds to cleanse Dante's face and forehead of the grime of Hell. There is, unmistakably, a priestly aspect to Virgil's action, which points to a feature of the *Purgatorio* that will strengthen in cantos 3 and 5. The Church on earth may fail, but it is still possible to draw upon the resources of a new rationality – a newfound perception of the small things of creation in all their brilliance – and recover by doing so the nature that sin has irrationally abandoned.

These suggestions are confirmed by the final lines of the canto (130–36), which directly allude to the last line of *Inferno* 26: 'until once more the sea closed over us'. In that canto, Dante depicts the last exploratory voyage of the classical hero Ulysses who, seeking experience of the world, its vice and its virtues, has arrived in the southern hemisphere, only to be denied landfall and end up wrecked on the shores of Mount Purgatory. It is to Ulysses that Dante alludes in **lines 130–32** when he declares that no one who has seen these shores before has ever returned to tell the tale. Dante is distinguished from Ulysses exactly in his capacity to benefit from the experience of purgation. But Ulysses as a pagan is also to be distinguished from Cato and Virgil. His pursuit of knowledge reflects nothing of that self-sacrificing concern with conscience and the public good that inspires Cato's moral severity. Nor is knowledge for Ulysses – in the grip of intellectual hubris – at all comparable to that knowledge, born of detail, touch and sensation, that is evident in Virgil's actions. Dante's own journey, and the poem that records it, draws towards its conclusion in *Paradiso* 27 with a last reference to Ulysses, in which he too passes all natural boundaries in his approach towards God. Until that time, and especially in the *Purgatorio*, Dante's gradual advance draws upon the disciplined regularity that Cato exemplifies, but also upon an aptitude, such as Virgil displays here, for attention to the detail of a world which, since the Resurrection, is always in a process of regeneration.

Notes

7–12 Calliope is the Muse of epic poetry. The 'Magpies' referred to here appear in Ovid's *Metamorphoses* 5: 294–678, in which the daughters of Pierus challenge the Muses to a singing contest and, even though they lose, persist in their defiance and as their punishment are transformed into magpies. (Compare *Paradiso* 1: 19–21 for a similarly violent reference to the contests between mortal musicians and the gods.)

19–21 The 'lovely' planet is Venus, whose brilliance here rises in company with but outshines, or 'veils', the constellation Pisces. Venus is both the morning and the evening star, and Dante seems to be mistaken about the position of the planet in April 1300, when it would in fact have risen in the evening.

28–30 The constellation referred to here is Charles' Wain, otherwise known as the Plough, which is located in Ursa Major.

76–84   For Limbo, see *Inferno* 4, and for Minos, see *Inferno* 5. Dante's account of Marcia and her relation to Cato may derive from Lucan's *Pharsalia* 2.

CANTO 2

The arrival of penitents in a boat impelled by an angel. Dante meets Casella. The singing of a canzone composed by Dante.

Commentary

Whereas the first canto of the *Purgatorio* is illuminated by the slow return of natural light, canto 2 opens with a sudden display of supernatural illumination which, with growing intensity (13–48), distracts attention from the steady advance of the dawn. This light is initially beyond comprehension, an 'I-did-not-know-what' (23) of whiteness which cannot be accounted for in the astronomic terms that are employed in lines 1–6. Here, as in *Inferno* 8, 9 and 31, Dante shows a scientific interest in the workings of sense perception and optical effect. But this interest is now only part of a narrative crescendo that traces the action of the eye from a blurred first impression to the precise outline of an angel and a boat (travelling, mysteriously, without oar or sail) and, finally, to a closeness of view in which ecstatic brilliance defeats comprehension.

At line 30 Virgil declares that, from now on, Dante must accustom himself to such moments of revelation; angels will make significant appearances at the conclusions of every episode from cantos 10 to canto 26 of the *cantica*. The *Purgatorio*, though concerned with the redemption and fulfilment of the natural world, also acknowledges that temporal nature depends upon and is impelled by forces of grace which derive directly from the will of God. This dependency is registered in canto 2 and, throughout Dante's narrative in the *Purgatorio*, by moments of epiphany where a greater light shines on the objects of the natural world to reveal their ultimate significance. (Compare *Purgatorio* 29: 43–8.)

Against the dynamic background of both natural process and angelic intervention, *Purgatorio* 2 continues to concern itself, like the Cato episode of canto 1, with the effects of unaccountable liberation, but differs from the first canto in that it focuses upon Dante and his Christian contemporaries rather than figures from the classical past, and also introduces a consideration of music and poetry alongside the ethical concerns of the previous sequence.

The boat that the angel brings to shore is laden with souls, including one of Dante's friends, the musician Casella (fl. 1282) who, at line 112, begins to perform one of Dante's own early lyrics. Dante is surprised that Casella should have arrived so swiftly at Purgatory (91–3), and the penitents themselves are shown to be amazed by the newness and strangeness of their redemption (52–4). But the psalm that Casella and all his companions are singing as they arrive (46) points to the repeated action of providence in human history, celebrating the deliverance of the Israelites from servitude in Egypt – which here stands, typologically, as an indication of our deliverance from sin. (Compare *Convivio* 2: 1, 7.) More specifically, Casella's arrival is attributed at lines 91–9 to the pardon or plenary indulgence that was granted in the jubilee year of 1300 (effective from Christmas 1299) to all who travelled to Rome and visited certain specific churches. There is remarkable evidence here – paralleling Dante's treatment of Cato in *Purgatorio* 1 – of a new flexibility in Dante's ethical stance. The pope who proclaimed this jubilee, Pope Boniface VIII (*c.* 1235–1303), is the object of Dante's unremitting hatred. Indeed, the last occasion on which Dante mentioned the jubilee was in *Inferno* 18 where he compares the manic discipline exercised by the devils of the lower regions of Hell to the systems of crowd control employed in Rome throughout 1300. In the *Purgatorio* Dante's contempt for papal corruption continues unabated (see, especially, cantos 3, 32 and 33), yet, despite the failings of its ministers, the Church remains, for Dante, the vessel of grace and redemption, miraculously able to secure an 'exodus' from sin. (Compare *Purgatorio* 20.)

The angel disappears at line 51 to allow the bewildered new arrivals – Dante as well as the boatload of souls – to discover their own orientation and to negotiate between themselves the way ahead. There is an intimacy about these exchanges which is not to be found in the earlier conversation between Virgil and Cato. There is also, at lines 70–87, an early example of a subtlety in the handling of emotional tone and the play of sensation that become characteristic of the *Purgatorio*, especially in its opening cantos. (Compare cantos 3 and 5; also canto 25.) At lines 76–81 Dante alludes to a melancholic scene in Virgil's *Aeneid* 6: 700–702, in which Aeneas attempts to embrace the shade of his father Anchises, but fails as his physical arms prove unable to grasp the insubstantial ghost. Momentarily, there is a comparable note of sadness in Dante's lines. Yet the 'empty' shadow of Casella finally smiles at Dante's baffled attempts at an embrace (83). The circumstances in Purgatory are wholly different from those in Virgil's underworld. Mysteries here are part of a redemptive scheme, and the interplay of spirit and body does not betoken loss or frustration, but rather the ultimate, if mysterious, significance of both spirit and body in the other world.

Song also endures. At line 106, Dante establishes that the 'new law' of Purgatory has not taken away Casella's capacity for music, despite the disapproval that Cato expresses at lines 118–23. The scene began with singing, and already the psalm of line 46 suggests the value that can attach itself to art in a fully religious perspective. By intoning the psalm, the penitents associate themselves with a tradition, constantly renewed, that goes back to the origins of Jewish history. Moreover, the psalm is said at line 48 to continue, verse by verse, beyond the first line that is quoted here. It is as if Dante imagines the text of the Latin psalm to be recited in the memory of his reader as a polyphonic accompaniment to the vernacular verses of his own canto. So, too, at many other points in the *Purgatorio* (in complete contrast to the *Inferno*, which is dominated by adversarial aggression) one voice supports and augments another, while texts acknowledge their sources and intertexts.

As to the second, vernacular song (112), Dante is alluding here directly to his own '*Amor che ne la mente mi ragiona*' (*Convivio* 3), but, while celebrating the importance of that lyric, he also significantly departs from it in both theme and style. In the *Convivio*, this *canzone* speaks of the way in which the human mind can contemplate the wisdom of God as displayed in the structure of the created universe. This theme is of central importance in Dante's thinking, and will continue to be so as late as *Paradiso* 10. The *Purgatorio* has already signalled its undiminished significance in depicting the harmony of natural order in canto 1 and the impulse of angelic intelligence in canto 2. Yet there are also modifications now to the implication of Dante's original poem. Originally, it is unlikely that '*Amor che ne la mente mi ragiona*' would have been set to music. It was, rather, intended as a contribution to the elite poetic circles seemingly initiated in Florence by Guido Cavalcanti (*c.* 1255–1300) (see *Inferno* 10) and devoted to the development of philosophical and scientific discussion. A further difference now is that the *canzone* is located within a distinctly religious framework, and is seen as a contribution to the communal experience of salvation, drawing together the otherwise disoriented penitents in an act of collective attention. Cato mistakes (or can only perceive) such attention as negligence and, on his understanding, it is reasonable to insist that the pursuit of virtue is a laborious and painstaking endeavour. For much of the *Purgatorio* it is precisely that. Yet the contemplation of harmony, and the pleasure that flows from it, will be, in the Earthly Paradise, the condition to which all penitence points.

A final feature distinguishes '*Amor che ne la mente mi ragiona*' from the poetry of the *Purgatorio*. In the *canzone* as it appears in the *Convivio* Dante's attention is fixed on the large circlings of the universe and on the astral influences that affect the workings of the cosmos. He often speaks of this with rapturously elevated diction, as when he pictures the way in which the created order is centred lovingly on wisdom (represented here as a courtly lady):

> *Non vede il sol, che tutto 'l mondo gira*
> *cosa tanto gentil, quanto in quell'ora*
> *che luce ne la parte ove dimora*
> *la donna, di cui dire Amore mi face*

(The sun as it circles round the whole world never sees anything so fine and noble as in that hour when it shines in the place where my lady dwells of whom Love makes me speak.)

Convivio 3:19–22

In contrast, the narrative style that Dante has developed in the *Commedia* demands that evidence of divine wisdom be sought in the precise observation of terrestrial detail. It is as important now to observe the behaviour of doves in a field as the movements of the heavens, as Dante does at lines 124–9 in the simile which describes the response of the penitents to Cato's harsh injunctions. It is possible that the reference to doves already carries some of the symbolic associations, suggesting grace and peace, that surround such references in, say, *Paradiso* 25: 19–24. There are certainly contrasts to be drawn between this passage and *Inferno* 5: 82–5, where, far from adopting a realistic concern with the activities of doves gathering chaff and weeds in the field, the simile evokes the vague, if beautiful, sentimentality that surrounds the appearance of Francesca. As in *Purgatorio* 1, where the details of the physical universe – its dew and its grass – contribute directly to Dante's onward journey, so now the minutiae of animal and human behaviour also have a contribution to make as eloquent as any law or abstract principle.

Notes

1–9 Time in Purgatory is told in relation to the time of day in Jerusalem. As night falls over Jerusalem, so day begins to dawn ('Aurora') in Purgatory. The mouth of the Ganges marks the extreme of the known world. Libra – the Balance or Scales – disappears from the night sky ('leaves her hand') at the autumn equinox, when nights become longer than days.

46–8 The opening words of Psalm 114, the first few lines of which are:

> When Israel went out of Egypt, the house of Jacob from a people of strange language; Judah was his sanctuary, and Israel his dominion. The sea saw it, and fled: Jordan was driven back. The mountains skipped like rams and the little hills like lambs . . .

55–7 At dawn the constellation Capricorn was located directly above Purgatory. Capricorn descends as the sun rises with Aries, the Ram.

100–105 Dante imagines that the voyage to Purgatory begins at the mouth of the river Tiber, near Rome. Contrast with the passage of the damned souls in Hell, which will take them to the infernal river Acheron. (For the formation of rivers in the other world, see *Inferno* 14: 97–120.)

CANTO 3

Virgil speaks of why Dante alone casts a shadow in Purgatory. The excommunicates appear, among them King Manfred.

Commentary

Canto 3 of the *Purgatorio* is among the subtlest cantos of the *Commedia*. Its tonalities shift constantly from violence and disruption to evocations of doubt and moments of delight. The phase of the canto that runs from line 25 to line 45 (ending with a 'darkly troubled' Virgil) is predominantly tragic, whereas that which runs from line 73 to line 145 (and ends with a smiling Prince Manfred) displays its own restrained but exhilarating form of comedy. At times it is elegiac, at times pastoral in character. Simultaneously Dante here focuses on

some of the major themes that are to occupy his attention in the
Ante-Purgatory – the sequence from canto 1 to canto 9 which is set
outside the realm where purgation is actively pursued. The penitents
in canto 3 are the excommunicates – those who have died outside the
embrace of the Church, having failed to reconcile themselves with, or
benefit from, the teachings or demands of the ecclesiastical community.
There can be no doubt that Dante attaches value to the guidance of
the Church, especially when it is directed toward the saving of souls.
(See his treatment of the jubilee in *Purgatorio* 2.) So there can be doubt
that for Dante excommunication is a serious matter. Yet in canto 3,
aware as he always is of the failings to which the Church of his
day was prone, the question also arises as to whether the formal
prohibitions uttered by the Church – possibly for its own political
advantage – are absolute in their implications. All the excommunicates
that Dante meets in the episode are destined to enter Purgatory and,
eventually, Paradise. They must simply wait – like the penitents of
cantos 4–9 – outside the arena of Purgatory proper, suffering no pain
except frustration and disorientation as, for the time being, they are
excluded from the pursuit of their heartfelt moral intentions. The
dominant concern of canto 3 is with the mysteries that determine
whether we should be included or excluded from the community of
the redeemed.

The most problematic statement of this issue emerges at line 103
with the appearance of Manfred. Manfred (*c.* 1232–66) was not only
the illegitimate son of the Emperor Frederick II (1194–1250) – whom
the thirteenth-century Church frequently referred to as the Anti-Christ
– but was himself excommunicated on three separate occasions, twice
by Pope Alexander IV in 1258 and again by Pope Urban IV in 1261.
As with Cato – and, to some degree, Casella – Manfred's presence
in Purgatory challenges any simple conception of moral norms and
regulatory codes. Yet the challenge is driven to an extreme, even
scandalous degree at lines 106–8, in which Dante all but explicitly
compares the figure of Manfred – blond, handsome, with the scars
from which he died still plain to see – to the risen Christ: where Christ
showed his wounds to the doubting Saint Thomas (at Luke 24: 40
and John 20: 27), Manfred calls upon the uncomprehending Dante to
acknowledge his own wholly unexpected salvation.

The daring of Dante's treatment in some measure reflects a political
motive. Manfred was the last representative in Italy of the cause of
the Holy Roman Empire to which Dante himself was committed. He
acted as regent to the legitimate heirs of Frederick II, and was as deeply
involved as his father in political contests with the Church. Eventually,

Manfred had himself crowned king of Sicily, in August 1258. But the Church had its own favoured candidate, Charles of Anjou (1227–85), who was also crowned king of Sicily, at Saint Peter's, Rome in 1263. In the ensuing struggles between Manfred and Charles, Manfred was slain at the battle of Benevento in 1266. (For Charles of Anjou, see notes below and *Purgatorio* 6 and 7.) But for Dante the Imperial cause that Manfred represented was more than a mere expression of territorial or military power. The one remedy, as he increasingly believed, for his own unjust exile from Florence was the restoration of Imperial justice throughout Italy, even though, with the defeat of Manfred, its cause ebbed rapidly away. But Dante's hopes for the Empire went far beyond the realm of contemporary politics. In his political philosophy (which was still developing as he wrote the early cantos of the *Purgatorio*), Dante finally argues that the Holy Roman Empire was instituted by God to bring peace to all parts of the world, and consistently views the political aspirations of the contemporary Church as an obstacle to the realization of this divine intention. His treatment of Manfred in canto 3 ignores the contemporary rumours (or Church propaganda) that represented Manfred as a murderer and a libertine, and daringly celebrates the favour which, in his view, God will always show to the standard-bearers of temporal justice.

This political reading, however, should not be allowed to over-shadow other issues raised by the canto, or the subtlety of its tonal spectrum. In particular, a question arises at lines 25–45 which, tragic in character, remains unresolved and continues to haunt the comic surprises that are sprung with the appearance of the smiling Manfred. For if Manfred is saved, then why not Virgil? Virgil, too, as the author of the *Aeneid*, is, supremely, a representative of Imperial justice. What justice is there in his being excluded from salvation and relegated, as he movingly recalls in lines 40–45, to Limbo? There are questions here concerning the (seeming) contradictions in Dante's thinking between his view of Imperial justice and his view of divine justice that recur in the *Commedia* and emerge even as late as *Paradiso* 19 and 20. But in the present sequence no solution is offered. Instead, Dante attributes to Virgil, an exile from salvation, something of the emotions of incomprehensible loss which he must have experienced in his own exile from Florence. And the questions that Virgil's position in the canto stimulates become more acute when one takes into account that the third protagonist of this scene, Dante himself, is enjoying as a remedy for his exile the unaccountable privilege of journeying in bodily form through a realm reserved for purely spiritual beings.

It is on the figure of Dante that the canto initially focuses. The sudden flight of the new arrivals, under the lash of Cato's reprimand, leaves Dante exposed, confused and directionless (1–9) in an unfamiliar landscape, seeking comfort from the equally troubled Virgil. His confidence begins to return at lines 10–15, yet it is immediately shattered at lines 16–21 by a sudden and violent effect born of the perception of sunlight and shadow. In contrast to the sweet or 'soft' ('*dolce*') dawn light of canto 1, the sun is now a fiery red and searingly hot. The alliterations at lines 16–17 on the 'r' of '*roggio*' ('burning red') and '*rotto*' ('broken'), along with the enjambment between these lines, intensify this effect. And the shadow that Dante now sees in front of him precipitates a range of conflicting emotions, all focused upon questions of exclusion and inclusion, privilege and rejection. Dante, seeing only one shadow on the ground – his own – is terrified. Is he after all alone in Purgatory? And what right has a man still in his bodily form to enter here and impede, or even 'break' the beams of rising light? Is not the shadow itself an indication of a residual taint or slur?

To relieve Dante of these doubts, Virgil now utters a speech (22–44) which, on the surface, is calmly philosophical, yet, when due attention is paid to its rhythms and tones, gives disturbing evidence of his own exclusion from salvation – so that, by line 45, he is left so deeply sunk in melancholic thoughts that, temporarily, he cannot serve as Dante's guide. (Dante himself sees the way forward at line 61.) In paraphrase, Virgil explains that only Dante possesses a physical body in Purgatory, since the dead only have ghost bodies, as Dante's experience with Casella has already made clear. He also traces this fact to the mysterious working of the Trinity, which creates these virtual bodies so that the physical effects of penance can be experienced to the full. Characteristically, Virgil says nothing of the physical pleasures that will be granted in the Earthly Paradise. (Compare and contrast *Purgatorio* 25: 79–108.) It is worth noting that these apparently theological considerations provide a justification (disingenuously or playfully, some may say) for Dante's whole narrative, which requires that the actors in the *Purgatorio* possess a physical presence. At the same time, Virgil's deference to the mysteries of the Trinity reflects an abiding concern on Dante's part with the limits of rational thinking. When, at line 37, Virgil declares that human beings should content themselves with the '*quia*', he employs a term from scholastic logic to demand that reason limit itself to subjects that lie within its proper competence to discuss – to explore, that is, the way things actually *are* in the world, not *why* they are like that. This need not be seen as a restrictive pronouncement, though it does prohibit the pointless and ultimately destructive curiosity displayed by Ulysses in *Inferno* 26. If Virgil, who is himself a pagan, can understand this point, then there is every reason why Ulysses should as well, and, positively, Virgil's words are an encouragement to a precise and productive investigation of our relationship with our natural environment. (Compare with Thomas Aquinas in *Paradiso* 13: 112–42.)

None the less, there is an evident strain in Virgil's speech. A note of curt irritation is heard in **lines 34–6**, declaring that it is 'madness' to suppose that we can ever penetrate the 'why' of eternal mystery. And, in calming Dante's doubts, Virgil is obliged to put himself in an exposed position. Here, in explaining why Dante's possession of a body is a privilege, he is driven to the plangent and elegiac confession that his own body lies interred in the shadows of a grave in Naples (25–7). Moreover, in discussing those mysteries that save Dante but condemn him and his fellow pagans to perpetual excommunication, there is a discernible distaste beneath Virgil's neutral tone. Speaking of the Incarnation, Virgil is obliged to mention the name of Christ's mother, Mary (38). But this simple or homely feminine name is uttered without decoration or enthusiasm and, in that respect, is in marked contrast to the namings of Aristotle and Plato (43), incomprehensibly condemned along with Virgil to Limbo, yet resonant with honour and intellectual dignity.

At **line 45** Virgil is left weighed down by his unspoken meditations, as the path leads to an apparently unscalable cliff. It is Dante now who takes the initiative for the onward progress of their journey, pointing out a group of penitents a thousand steps in the far distance (67–9). Here, too, a shift begins through which the mysteries of providence are viewed in a fully Christian perspective as a source of joy, redemption and even comedy.

In the second phase of the canto, 'not knowing' (a phrase used twice, at **lines 84** and **93**), along with humility, becomes a part of the remedy for exclusion. And here the extended comparison at **lines 79–84** between the excommunicates and sheep leaving a sheepfold is especially telling. The Christian associations of this simile are obvious: those who are excommunicated from the fold – the lost sheep – are now to be gathered in and brought to salvation. This, however, is not Dante's principal emphasis. Instead, he stresses the communal action of the flock – their huddling together, their timidity at *leaving* (rather than *entering*) the fold – to establish a conversation with Dante and Virgil. The simplicity and apparent ignorance of the penitents draw them into a relationship, one with another, as a remedy for their fear of the unknown and the confusions of excommunication.

Furthermore, this realistic and precise simile illustrates what it means for a mind to 'content itself' with *what* things are like rather than to inquire, presumptuously, *why* they should be so. Few of Dante's similes can match this in its attention to the details of movement – 'one, two, and three', 'timidly turning earthwards eyes and snouts' – or of texture – 'backs huddling ['*addossondosi*'] against backs'.

Yet these, after all, are not sheep but penitents. At line 85 it becomes clear that the pastoral simile has been used as a way of preparing the eye of the reader for a significant re-engagement with human figures. At line 87 these figures are restored to the dignity of fully human action. But this is a dignity that accepts the simplicity and humility first observed in the sheep to which they are compared as the underlying condition of their new merit.

It is (comically) incongruous that Manfred should be one of these 'sheep'. He retains the flamboyant beauty of form for which he was famous in his lifetime. And the marks on his body, though in one aspect indications of mortal fragility, are also the marks by which he may be identified and recognized even in the spiritual world. Here Dante consolidates a theme which first appeared in the canto when Dante's own body cast its shadow on the ground. Properly understood, the physical form of the human being is an inalienable part of its identity. Manfred's papal opponents were aware of this when, maliciously, they disposed of his corpse (scattering the cairn of stones that Manfred's military enemies had erected to honour him) so that no cult should grow up around his resting place (124–32). Here, too, a further contrast emerges between the pagan and the Christian worlds. Virgil's body, like Manfred's, was transported from the place where he died – from Brindisi to Naples (27). This removal had been intended by the Emperor Augustus as a celebration of Virgil's achievements. Yet it has done nothing to redeem Virgil from the exile he suffers in Limbo. Dante, for all his subtle pleading on behalf of the pagan, never imagines that the absolute ban can ever be lifted, at least in any way that human beings can comprehend. There is no possibility that prayer will be effective in this case. (Compare *Purgatorio* 6: 28–48.) Yet the encounter between Manfred and Dante with which canto 3 concludes is alive with the possibility that individuals can be drawn together in a new community of intercession. Manfred tells his story so that Dante, travelling back to the world, should be able to report the news of Manfred's redemption to his daughter, referred to here with the utmost simplicity and affection (115–17, 142–4).

Notes

25-7 The Emperor Augustus had Virgil's body transported in from Brindisi, where Virgil died in 19 BC, to Naples for an honourable burial.

37 *Quia* is a term drawn from technical argumentation in scholastic philosophy. The implication here is that human beings should not concern themselves with speculative questions as to *why* things exist, but confine themselves to the examination of things as they actually *do* exist.

49-51 Lerici (just north of La Spezia) and Turbia (east of Nice) are towns lying at opposite ends of Liguria. The cliffs of these two towns go straight into the sea but landslips provide some pathways.

115-16 Manfred's grandmother (d. 1198) was queen of Sicily and wife of the Emperor Henry VI (1165-97). Manfred's daughter was Constance (d. 1302) by his first wife, Beatrice of Savoy. Constance married Peter III of Aragon (1239-85), who laid claim through her to the throne of Sicily. (See notes to *Purgatorio* 7: 91-111; *Paradiso* 8: 72-5.)

124-32 Charles of Anjou (see *Purgatorio* 7 and 20), on defeating Manfred at the battle of Benevento and thus destroying the Imperial cause in Italy, had him buried honourably (though not in consecrated ground) under a cairn of stones. Pope Clement IV (d. 1268) ordered the bishop of Cosenza in Calabria to exhume the body and throw it irrecoverably over the border of the kingdom of Naples which is marked by the river Verde. (Significantly, green ('*verde*') is the colour of hope; also Manfred is said to have preferred green clothing.) The same pope confirmed Charles's claim to the crown of Sicily and Naples.

CANTO 4

*Dante and Virgil begin to climb Mount Purgatory
and encounter Dante's Florentine acquaintance
Belacqua among those who have delayed their final
acts of repentance.*

Commentary

At **lines 97–139** of canto 4, Dante describes his encounter with a figure as unlike the heroic and politically vigorous Manfred as it is possible to be. This is Belacqua (d. 1299?), who, according to fourteenth-century commentators, was an acquaintance of Dante's from Florence, a maker of musical instruments notorious for his indolence (though also for his witty repartee). Belacqua is still apparently indulging that vice when Dante finds him sitting in the shadow of a great boulder on the mountainside (100–105). There are, however, thematic connections between cantos 3 and 4. The theme of bodily identity introduced in the description of Manfred's warrior scars in the previous canto expands in the present 4 to include a consideration of the relationship that exists between body and mind, each cooperating with the other in the pursuit of virtue. Canto 4 also focuses upon the value that Dante attributes to time, in particular to the ways in which time may be wasted or properly employed in our ethical undertakings. In this respect it prepares the reader for issues that will be addressed in canto 5, which concerns those who have only repented at the moment of death.

The Belacqua episode is the culmination of a well-orchestrated thematic development. And at first sight canto 4 is, above all things, a celebration of intellectual ambition. Certainly, its first two phases contain some of the most taxingly intellectual poetry of the early *Purgatorio*. The first of these (1–12) reflects a controversy which originally arose between Platonists and Aristotelians over the nature (and number) of the human soul. For Plato, there were three souls that governed the activities of the human being – the vegetative, the animal and the rational, ascending in such a way that the rational could assert its superiority over and transcend its lower counterparts. For Aristotle, on the other hand, there was only one soul, though this single soul possessed three distinct functions pertaining to the activities of growth and instinct (in which humans are involved, as are plants and animals), as well as the activities of reason which are unique to the human being. It is Aristotle that Dante follows in these lines (though the compression of his thinking leads to a certain confusion over the metaphors of binding and loosing, which at **lines 3–8** refer to the soul in its single nature and at **lines 10–12** mean the three separate functions of the single soul). To paraphrase: When one aspect of the soul is engaged in thought, the unified soul still continues to carry along with it the other two functions – as here Dante continues to move along his path. Thought does not transcend what might in platonic terms be considered its 'lower' functions. Aristotelian unity continues to operate, even when, physically, we do not notice the passing of time. Here, as at every point in his thinking, Dante follows Aristotle and Aristotle's Christian followers in asserting that the soul, or '*anima*' in Latin and Italian, is nothing more or less than the power which 'animates' a specific form of life – which in human beings is always an *embodied* form of life. (See introduction to *Inferno*, pp. lii–liii.)

The second passage of philosophy (**61–9**) offers an astronomical account of where Dante, on his journey through Purgatory, now stands within the coordinates of space and time. This discussion has an immediate bearing on the developing logic of the narrative. The reader of the *Purgatorio* – supplied with introductory maps and plans – is aware from the first that Purgatory is located in the southern hemisphere, whereas Dante as traveller only becomes fully aware of it – and of its implications – in the course of this canto. At **lines 55–7** he is astonished to see the sun rising on the northern rather than the southern horizon. Yet this position is only astonishing if one doesn't know that Mount Purgatory is in the southern hemisphere. Virgil now proceeds to remind Dante of the logic of existence on a terrestrial globe. On that understanding, there has not, as Dante first suspected, been any breach of the laws of nature. Astronomical science ensures that he can determine his position in harmony with the workings of the cosmos.

The science that Virgil has to relate is expressed in a rhetoric which is rich in its references to mythology and enthusiastic in the sustained rhythms of its syntax. When at lines **76–84** Dante offers a paraphrase of Virgil's lesson, he adopts a similarly elevated form of diction. There can be no doubt that an enthusiasm for intellectual and scientific debate is a permanent feature of Dante's thinking. His mind is literally 'in love' with the technical questions that arise in describing the universal system. (See also *Purgatorio* 2: 112.) This interest is evident in all parts of the *Convivio* (as, for example, at *Convivio* 2: 3) and persists deep into the *Paradiso*. To that extent, canto 4 has so far confirmed the sovereignty of intellect.

For all that, at **lines 85-7** there is something of the over-diligent or ingratiating student in the words that Dante here attributes to himself. Equally, there is a comic hint of down-to-earth apprehension as he attempts to assess how far he has still to climb up the precipitous mountain. Virgil offers him a moment of moralizing consolation – pointing out that the climb can only get easier as it proceeds (88–96). But then, at **line 98** a voice enters which directly challenges the intellectual 'certitude' (76) that Dante and Virgil had complacently (and, up to a point, rightly) been cultivating, with an emphatically mocking 'perhaps'. With this, Dante's gaze – hitherto focused on the heights and far horizons – is redirected downwards to a realm of ambiguities, to the shadows of a great boulder and to the people lying there who protect themselves in *seeming* indolence (103–5, 109–11) from the heat of the day.

From this point on, canto 4 concerns itself with details that might easily be supposed to carry negative connotations. Darkness, physical matter, corporeality – these are the key notes of the lines with which this canto concludes (**127–39**). Yet in the course of Dante's relaxed and markedly humorous conversation with Belacqua, it emerges that an attention to phenomena such as these is as significant as any intellectual attention to the movement of the heavens. Belacqua is proved right to have insisted on the physical limitations that Dante as traveller needs to observe. It is consistent with Dante's Christian thinking that he should reject any dualistic division of the world into light and dark, matter and spirit, mind and body. All things are redeemable. It is likewise consistent with his Aristotelianism that a precise observation of the world around us – which is possible only when we wait and take care – should contribute directly to the pursuit of an ultimate truth. For Aristotle, as for Christians, the human being is an *embodied* being.

At **lines 123–5** Dante expresses relief at finding Belacqua in Purgatory. It could have been otherwise. The first sinners that Dante encountered in Hell (see *Inferno* 3) were guilty of a lethargy apparently similar to that of which Belacqua stands accused. But whereas in Hell Dante described a group of anonymous and physically repellent figures, his descriptions of Belacqua display concentration and carefulness, as at **lines 112–13**, where he traces the heavy movement with which Belacqua, supporting his head on his thigh, looks sideways and askance at the new arrivals. (The word pictures of these lines recalls the painting style of Giotto in their sensitivity to realistic effects of volume and weight.) This, however, is a recognition scene and not a scene of judgement. And the relationship between the two interlocutors is reciprocal and equal. Dante recognizes in Belacqua the self-same laziness of gesture and tight-lipped, though sharp-witted speech (121–2) that contemporary anecdote attributes to him, and reacts to this with a smile rather than judgemental contempt. Conversely, through Belacqua's eyes, Dante appears to represent himself, with equal mockery, as someone inclined to stretch intellectually beyond the boundaries of his physical strength (114), and to be obsessively interested in the intricacies of scientific theory (119–20).

It is part of the comedy of canto 4 that unexpected parallels should arise between its opening and concluding phases. Where the sun appears, at first, to be in the wrong position in the sky, so the indolent Belacqua appears, at first, to be in the wrong domain of the other world – in Purgatory rather than in Hell. But astronomical logic can explain the former, and the logic of redemption can explain the latter. Here, as elsewhere in the *Commedia*, comedy has a liberating effect, allowing a view of the wholly unexpected. However, in the final lines of the canto, the tone darkens. At lines 127–35 Belacqua speaks about time, but about time as an ethical and penitential, rather than astronomical, phenomenon. If Belacqua is sitting where he is, the reason is not, after all, that he has resumed his old habit of indolence. It is because he has an exact understanding of the laws that govern progress up the purgatorial mountain. Having delayed appropriate repentance on earth, he must now pass an equivalent length of time in Ante-Purgatory before proceeding, as he longs to do, to the active pursuit of virtue (127–32). Here the same attitudes that on earth betrayed Belacqua's lethargy are put to the service of a new understanding. Indolence now expresses itself as true patience. So, the slow, laborious rhythms of limb and word that are characteristic of Belacqua remain, but here provide a solemn ground bass to his acceptance of the time that he must still spend in waiting.

Waiting is as important to Dante as any vigorous advance might be. Lucifer, at *Paradiso* 19: 46–8, is said to have fallen into sin precisely because he refused to 'wait for light'. Ulysses, in *Inferno* 26, chooses not to wait for his death at home in Ithaca but to pursue an eventually disastrous ambition for yet more 'experience' (*Inferno* 26: 116). In Belacqua Dante celebrates the ways in which 'waiting' may reveal the value of time as a means of connecting intelligence to the immediate demands of the physical environment in which it is embodied. (It is no accident that Samuel Beckett carried the Belacqua episode in mind throughout his career.) And when time is, potentially, of such value, it is not to be wasted.

As the canto ends, Virgil's voice at lines 137–9 abandons the elevated science and rhetoric of his earlier speech to adopt the new logic suggested by Belacqua's intervention. Time here is told by a human measure in which day and night are personified: the meridian is 'touched' by the sun; the 'foot of night' falling on Morocco.

Notes

25–6 San Leo is a mountain fortress near Urbino. Noli is a city on the Ligurian coast, which is reached via a stairway cut in the cliff. 'Bismantova' probably refers to a fortress that once sat on a crag near Canossa in Emilia. Cacume is a peak near Anagni.

58–60 Aquilon is the North Pole. (See diagram opposite.)

61–6 Castor and Pollux are the twins of the constellation Gemini. The sun moves through this constellation in May and June. The 'Ursa stars' are Ursa Major and Ursa Minor, otherwise known as the Bears. The sun is a 'mirror' in so far as it reflects God's power into the universe. That part of the Zodiac which is heated by the sun is 'rose-red'. It 'wheels' as the sun moves north along the ecliptic, reaching further across the sky each day at noon. To paraphrase: If the present month were May or June, you would see the sun moving still further towards the north.

67–75 Jerusalem (Zion) in the northern hemisphere stands diametrically opposite Purgatory in the southern hemisphere.

79–83 These lines refer to the celestial equator which stands at 90 degrees from the North and South Poles. It is around this that the daily revolutions of the heavens take place. (See diagram opposite.) The seven stars form part of the constellation Ursa Major, seen in the northern sky. Reference to these stars regularly signifies the northern regions, as in the Italian adjective *settentrionale*.

CANTO 5

Among those who have delayed repentance, Dante meets three figures who have all suffered violent deaths and only at the moment of death have turned to God.

Commentary

The value of time is an issue in canto 5 as it was in the preceding canto. However, whereas in canto 4 Dante focused on the long durations of indolence and patience, his concern in canto 5 is with minutes and

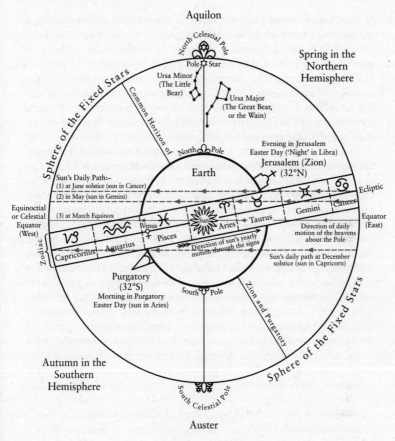

Aquilon

Spring in the
Northern
Hemisphere

North Celestial Pole

Pole Star

Ursa Minor
(The Little
Bear)

Ursa Major
(The Great Bear,
or the Wain)

Sphere of the Fixed Stars

Common Horizon of

North Pole

Earth

Evening in Jerusalem
Easter Day ('Night' in Libra)
Jerusalem (Zion)
(32°N)

Sun's Daily Path:-
(1) at June solstice (sun in Cancer)

(2) in May (sun in Gemini)

(3) at March Equinox

Ecliptic

Equinoctial
or Celestial
Equator
(West)

Gemini

Cancer

Equator
(East)

Venus

Sun

Aries

Taurus

Direction of daily
motion of the heavens
about the Pole

Zodiac

Capricornus

Aquarius

Pisces

Direction of sun's yearly
motion through the signs

Sun's daily path at December
solstice (sun in Capricorn)

Purgatory
(32°S)

Morning in Purgatory
Easter Day (sun in Aries)

South Pole

Zion and Purgatory

Sphere of the Fixed Stars

Autumn in the
Southern
Hemisphere

South Celestial Pole

Auster

Path of the Sun

seconds – instants of time, all but infinitely divisible. The penitents here are those who repented only in the last moment of their earthly lives. Yet a split-second repentance is seen to be sufficient for their salvation. That single instant can outweigh all the innumerable moments that, until that point, have been allowed to pass unregarded. In the case of the three figures whom Dante pictures here, an understanding of this was, tragically, only realized at the moment of their violent deaths.

The narrative of the fifth canto captures this tragedy in a sequence of three separate episodes (64–84, 85–129 and 130–36), each marked, in complete contrast to the leisurely conversations of canto 4, by a violence and intensity of effect. However, in the opening section of the canto (1–57), attention is directed, as it was at the opening of canto 3, to the person of Dante, to his bodily form and to his position of privilege in Purgatory. Here, implicitly, an answer is offered to the question of violence on earth. The body that suffers violence is also the body that is redeemed and resurrected by association with the resurrection of Christ after his suffering on the Cross. It is this understanding that the penitents in this canto achieved at the moment of their death, notably in the case of the second penitent, the warrior Buonconte da Montefeltro, whose final act, as described at **lines 124–9**, is to lock his arms across his body in the form of a cross. Here, as throughout the *Purgatorio* (and also, occasionally, in the *Inferno*), the presence of Dante in the other world is emblematic of the salvation that is offered to all human beings through the Resurrection. (Compare *Purgatorio* 3, 22 and 26; also *Inferno* 12 and 28.) Thus, the figures that Dante was speaking to in the previous canto finally recognize his bodily presence at **lines 1–6**, one of them pointing a long finger after him as he begins to climb further up the slope. This recognition is belated, as fits the temperament of the late repentants. But the same recognition is borne in immediately upon the next group that Dante encounters in, again, an act that corresponds to the impetuosity of their characters. **Lines 22–7** introduce the only note of comedy into a canto which is otherwise devoted to violent depictions of violent death. The group that now approaches is singing, appropriately, the penitential psalm *Miserere*, invoking God's forgiveness of their sins:

> Have mercy upon me, O God, according to thy loving kindness: according unto the multitude of thy tender mercies blot out my transgressions. Wash me thoroughly from mine iniquity, and cleanse me from my sin.
>
> Psalms 51: 1–2

Yet these solemn devotions are on the instant interrupted by the sight of Dante's shadow, and the chanting breaks off into a confused and discordant 'Oooh!' (27) This moment of surprise, however, reflects the underlying meaning of the episode more fully than the ritual singing of the psalm. From a Christian perspective, there is no need for the pitiful sentiments that the psalm expresses. Mercy, beyond the mere forgiveness of sins, has already been displayed in the redemptive actions of Christ. Salvation, as betokened by Dante's presence in this scene, will extend to the resurrection of the human being in its bodily identity.

This said, the canto now goes on to picture the harshest realities of lives on earth, subject always to catastrophe and unexpected extinction, to a world of uncertainty and change. This is the world of thirteenth-century Italy, seen as a place of treachery, internecine warfare and domestic murder. It is a world, at lines 103–23, in which even the physical processes of nature are seen as expressions of satanic power.

The first penitent to tell his story (64–83) – a tragedy precipitated by a combination of treachery and mistaken directions – is Jacopo di Uguccione del Cassero (*c.* 1260–98) from Fano on the Adriatic coast, who allied himself with the Florentine Guelfs and, in 1288, marched in a campaign in which Dante himself took part against the city of Arezzo. Jacopo was chief magistrate of Rimini in 1294 and of Bologna in 1296, during which time he opposed the ambitions of Azzo VIII of Este (d. 1308). (See notes to *Inferno* 12: 106–38.) While travelling through Paduan territory *en route* for Milan, where he was to take up a similar office, he was ambushed at Oriaco and scandalously murdered by Azzo's henchmen ('Antenorians' (75)). Dante's narrative focuses on Jacopo's headlong flight from his pursuers, and on the simple mistake he made that led to his death. Reaching a fork in the road, Jacopo disastrously chose to go south into the swampy territory of the Venetian lagoons. Here the rush of the narrative slows down to reflect Jacopo slowly becoming entangled in the reeds and mud, where he is mortally wounded. In the hypnotic lines 83–4, Jacopo gazes at the flow of blood issuing from his wounds as if it were no longer his own but merely a slick of liquid mingling with the sodden surface of the marsh.

The second episode (85–129), though as violent as the first, unrolls more slowly and is more complex, particularly in its reference back to a parallel episode in *Inferno* 27. The protagonist in this case is Buonconte da Montefeltro (*c.* 1250–89), a Ghibelline general – and the son of Guido da Montefeltro, who appears in *Inferno* 27 – who died leading the armies of Arezzo against the Florentine Guelfs at the battle of Campaldino in 1289. Dante (and Jacopo del Cassero, also) fought in this battle on the Florentine side. It is this which gives point to Dante's inquiry at lines 91–3 as to why Buonconte's body was never discovered on the battlefield and initiates Buonconte's own account of his final hours.

At the same time, Dante's interest in his one-time enemy and his decision to place him in Purgatory suggests how far the poet has advanced in writing the second *cantica* beyond the sometimes-partisan scheme of judgement that he followed in the *Inferno*. This change of heart is likewise emphasized by the parallels that Dante draws between the stories of Buonconte, the son, and Guido, the father. In *Inferno* 27 Dante condemns Guido as a treacherously manipulative politician. He admired this man once, but, having learnt of the intrigues between Guido and Pope Boniface VIII, he retracts that good opinion. Guido is shown receiving an assurance of pardon from the corrupt pope and, in horrified surprise, cannot understand why, despite this pardon, he is snatched at his death from the gates of Heaven to be deposited in the depths of Hell. The case of Buonconte is exactly the reverse. In common with Manfred in *Purgatorio* 3, Buonconte dies without any formal blessing from the Church. Yet the last words that he utters are spontaneously words of faith (100–101), which are enough to defeat the claims that the Devil has over him. He is transported to salvation, despite the violence and frustrated anger Satan displays towards him (103–8).

The contrast between father and son that Dante sets up here has far-reaching implications. Guido is a man of reason; his son is a man of action. But the arguments and stratagems that Guido devises entangle him in a web of self-deception, and are of no significance compared with the single, simple word that Buonconte utters at the moment of his death. The corridors of power that Guido inhabits as a politician lead only to an ill-fated alliance with a corrupt pope. Buonconte is caught in the surge and stress of the natural world, yet derives from his involvement in that world an intensity, a violence of concentrated devotion that matches and counters the violence of battle. Guido has all the time he could wish to settle his account with God. Buonconte has only an instant. Yet into this instant he concentrates a lifetime of understanding and secures his own salvation.

The drama in Buonconte's case unrolls in two phases. The first (94–102) describes his disappearance from the battlefield, wounded in the throat and dragging himself some two miles across open country. Where Jacopo's lifeblood seeps away into a blur of muddy waters, Buonconte's wound leaves a continuous line of blood on the plain (99) until he reaches the river into which his body falls. There is no pious sentiment in his final, fading utterance of the word 'Maria'. It is the climax, rather, of all the heroic energy that otherwise he would have expended in battle. In the second phase, the body, now lifeless, continues to express this heroic determination. Satan conjures up a storm in the Apennines in which all the destructive forces of the natural world are summoned to unloose the cross that Buonconte's arms have formed across his chest now in the grip of *rigor mortis*. The sphere of nature – which, for Dante, usually offers evidence of divine order – is here, at least momentarily, seen in terms of its mutability and anarchic power (**128–9**). But, as always, Dante refuses to envisage any merely spiritual transcendence of the natural realm. In Buonconte's case, as with Dante earlier in the canto, it is the human body which reveals the significance that endures in spite of Satan's depredations. It is true – and realistic enough – that the crossed arms of Buonconte's corpse are eventually forced to relinquish their hold (**124–6**) as the mountain stream sweeps into the river Arno. By that time, however, the body has sufficiently testified to the cross and given meaning to the otherwise senseless conflict into which Buonconte has been swept.

In contrast to the heroics of the preceding episode, canto 5 concludes on a dying fall, with a coda (**130–36**) uttered by a delicate but by no means fragile feminine voice. This is Pia dei Tolomei, who married Nello dei Pannocchieschi, a member of the lesser nobility in the Sienese Maremma (a notoriously swampy and insalubrious region in southern Tuscany) and was murdered by her husband in 1295. It is well worth comparing Dante's treatment of La Pia with his characterization of Francesca in *Inferno* 5 and of Piccarda, who speaks of *caritas* in *Paradiso* 3. To La Pia, Dante attributes a restrained clarity of utterance which is wholly absent from Francesca, while, in contrast to Piccarda, she retains a wistful, though unreproachful memory of her tragic marriage and the rings that sealed it.

Notes

37–9 Lightning was said by Aristotle to be caused by particles of fire (vapours) in the atmosphere. (Compare *Inferno* 14: 35.)

73–5 '*Antenori*' ('Antenorians') here means Paduans. Antenor, who according to legend betrayed Troy to the Greeks, was also said to have founded Padua. Antenora is the deepest circle of treachery in Hell. (See *Inferno* 32–3.)

88–9 Giovanna was Buonconte's wife.

91–6 Campaldino is situated in the Casentino, a mountainous region of Tuscany east of Florence, forming a plain between the Apennine peaks of Giogana and Pratomagno. The Hermitage is the monastery above Camaldoli, situated on Giogana.

115–16 Mount Pratomagno lies in the south-west of the Casentino.

CANTO 6

*A discussion of the efficacy of prayer. Dante and
Virgil encounter Sordello. Dante launches a diatribe
against the political confusion of Italy resulting from
a lack of support for the Imperial cause.*

Commentary

The violence and agitations of tone that emerged in canto 5 continue
throughout the four major phases into which canto 6 divides. In
particular, the final phase – running for almost half the canto, from
line 76 – is an attack launched by Dante, in his authorial voice, on the
anarchic condition of political life in thirteenth-century Italy, where
violence and agitation have become the norm.

The opening phase (1–24) is linked directly to the stories of sudden
death recorded in canto 5 and provides, at lines 13–24, a rapid and
much compressed account of beheadings, clan murders and politically
motivated executions. (See notes below.) It starts strikingly with a
simile, sustained over three *terzine*, in which Dante – on his way to
salvation while still in his bodily form – compares himself to a success-
ful gambler who is harassed after the game by losers begging for a share
of his winnings. For twelve lines, the poet (with his usual attention to
the minute details of gesture and facial expression) realistically pictures
the embarrassments and distractions of the gambler's uncomfortable
progress. Disconcertingly, the winnings in question here are Dante's
spiritual success, and the share for which the penitents are begging is
prayer from those on earth who might be able, by their intercessions,
to speed the penitents through Purgatory (26–7). Prayer is one of the
most important themes in the *Purgatorio*, reflecting Dante's belief that
time and eternity, the living and the dead, are linked by a common
devotion to God. Yet such certainties waver momentarily here, as if
Dante were suddenly questioning whether the privileges assured by
prayer were distinguishable from the capriciousness of chance and the
accidents that emerge in games of hazard.

The second phase of the canto (28–48) confirms this interrogative
note. Free at last from the fretful attentions of the penitents, Dante
ruminatively raises, once more, a doubt over the authority and spiritual
fate of his mentor, Virgil. Virgil, it seems, declared in the *Aeneid*
6: 373–6 that prayer could be of no avail in influencing the will of the

gods (28–30). Yet the irritations that Dante has just suffered only arise because the penitents believe that prayer can be effective.

What is at stake here? If Virgil as the author of the *Aeneid* is right, then Christian understanding is mistaken. If Virgil is wrong, then the reliance that Dante has placed upon him – as an exemplary poet no less than as a leader on his fictional journey – may seem seriously misguided. The answer he receives from Virgil is, at first glance, careful and judicious. In Virgil's own time – which is to say, before the Incarnation and Atonement – prayer was indeed invalid (40–41). But Christ's entry into the world changed the situation entirely. This analysis solves the immediate problem and restores Virgil's reputation as a rational guide, always considerate for his pupil's intellectual well-being. The irony is that, in giving this answer, Virgil is obliged to acknowledge that he himself was born in an era when Christian truth was unavailable. In serving Dante's interests and in defending the truthfulness of his own literary text, Virgil indicates once more (as in *Purgatorio* 3: 25–45) the brute fact of his own alienation from God's mercy. Dante attributes no bitterness to Virgil. Indeed, Virgil's recognition of his own limitations is expressed at **lines 43–8** as part of his encouragement for Dante to lay aside his doubts: since Virgil cannot say everything on the subject, Dante should await the illuminating explanations that Beatrice will eventually offer. Dante reacts enthusiastically to the promise offered by these words. Yet the ever-recurrent question remains unvoiced for the moment: is it any more than a matter of chance that Virgil should have lived and died before prayer became valid?

In the third phase of the canto (52–75), a new set of themes begins to emerge. Hitherto, over the last three cantos, Dante has been particularly concerned with the effects of time and the use we make of time in our earthly or penitential lives. This interest does not disappear. The next group of penitents whom Dante will encounter (though not until canto 7, line 84) are the negligent princes of thirteenth-century Europe who, in Dante's view, have wasted the time and opportunity they had to promote the cause of justice. However, as Dante approaches the valley in the mountainside where these princes are now at rest, he begins to combine an attention to time with one to space. From this point until the end of canto 9, the narrative of the *Purgatorio* is punctuated by references to geographical locations, to homes and resting places (even to beds) and, conversely, to those experiences of exile or of disturbance in the political arena that threaten our established boundaries.

At **lines 52–7**, Virgil darkly alludes to the coming of night. Dante does not yet realize, in the still sunlit scene that he will have to spend three nights on the mountain before he reaches Beatrice. Virgil wants to make as much progress as he can. But soon he will need to find a place to rest. Seeking a guide through this still unfamiliar location, he approaches a soul sitting alone on the mountainside. Here, the tempo and focus of the episode immediately change, becoming tense with arrested, concentrated energy. The solitary figure to whom Virgil addresses himself appears to be at rest. Yet he defends the space around him from intrusion with the nervous ferocity of a couching lion (**66**) and, far from offering any immediate assistance, deflects Virgil's inquiries and breaks his silence with an aggressive question of his own: where do you come from? (**70–71**).

This figure (not named until **line 74**) proves to be the poet Sordello (*c.* 1200–*c.* 1269), who was born at Goito near Mantua and emigrated to the court of Provence in 1229, fleeing a scandal which probably involved an adulterous liaison with Cunizza da Romano, the wife of his feudal lord. (Cunizza occupies an important place in Heaven – see *Paradiso* 9: 22–66.) Sordello prospered in his adopted country, was knighted and endowed with lands in both northern and southern Italy. His extant poetry is all written in the Occitan language. And, most famously, these poems include the *Lament for Blacatz* (1237), declaring that now his patron Blacatz is dead, his heart should be cut out so that the great nobles 'who now live disheartened', can eat it – 'and then they'll have heart enough!'

It seems likely that Sordello's *Lament* was in Dante's mind as he approached the question of faint-hearted kingship and, specifically, when he wrote the polemical verses that constitute the second half of canto 6. But Sordello's response to Virgil at **lines 74–5** expresses a passionate concern with native place which finds no parallel in the writings of this émigré poet. When asked where he comes from, Virgil manages to utter no more than the single word 'Mantua' (he, too, having been born in Mantuan territory) before Sordello abandons all his previous aloofness and, embracing Virgil, reveals his identity, even though Virgil does not reveal his own name until *Purgatorio* 7: 7.

At this point the action of the episode freezes, as the Florentine Dante prepares – against the tableau of the Mantuan embrace – to begin his assault on the political confusions of latter-day Italy. But this tableau (involving, as will canto 7, a revisionary interpretation of Sordello's historical career) has already made a point of the utmost significance for Dante's political thinking in the *Commedia*: our attachment to the place of our birth is ineradicable, and if only our local territories were safe from partisan strife, they would be free to foster the generosity of spirit that prevails between Sordello and Virgil (79–81). In *De Monarchia* Dante looks to the Empire as the means of securing peace on earth, hence, in cantos 6–7, he attacks the apathy of the princes of his day in refusing to respond to the legitimate, even sacred claims of Imperial over-lordship (88–93). None the less, the aim of Imperial government is to restore good order in the local arena of the city states, so that the spaces enclosed within urban walls and moats are no longer places where one citizen 'gnaws' at another (82–4). (Compare the importance of the city as discussed in *Paradiso* 15–18.)

Dante as poet now summons up the energies that are lacking in the rulers of his day. This passage is clearly in part an exercise in the art of rhetoric, displaying many of the effects of compression, emphatic duplication and exclamation which were taught by late medieval handbooks, while also showing affinities to Occitan types of polemical or satirical poetry such as the *sirventese*. But Dante goes far beyond his models in the vigour of his political commitment and in the visual sweep and energy with which he establishes his geographical target. Surveying the Italian peninsula from coast to coast, from north to south, he reveals in each place the partisan strife or petty tyrannies that prevail in its bosom (85–7) – in what ought to be the garden of the Empire. At one point, his eye turns to God, angrily asking why divine justice does not provide a remedy, and contemplating the possibility that the apparent triumph of evil is an apocalyptic preparation for the imposition of the remedy that will come when God's justice is revealed at the Last Judgement (118–23). But neither here nor elsewhere in the *Commedia* does Dante remove responsibility for their own affairs from human beings themselves. (See especially *Purgatorio* 16.)

It is the failure of such responsibility that finally draws Dante's attention back to Florence (124–48). Here, in tones of high sarcasm, he pictures a people who, unlike others, actually long to assume the offices of state, but do so in a mood of confused and chaotic energy. The consequence is that laws which should be governed by eternal principles of justice are constantly tampered with, being changed from one month to the next as one party, then another comes into power. (Dante's own exile can be seen as the result of laws that were dictated by the triumphant Black Guelfs against the defeated Whites.) Florence prides itself on its own civilized interest in matters of justice. But talk of justice here becomes mere intellectual chatter. The very bed in which Florence lies – which should be the place of comfort and rest –

is a squalid sickbed, disturbed by ungoverned tossing and turning. Italy is no longer a court in which beauty, elegance and good order thrive. It has become a '*bordello*' (76–8). Florence – where Beatrice once lived – has become a diseased and moribund hag (146–8).

Notes

13–24 It is not certain whom Dante intends by 'the Aretine' here, though it may be Benincasa da Laterino, who was beheaded around 1297 by the notorious highwayman Ghin di Tacco of Siena. Federigo Novello was a member of the Tuscan clan of the Conti Guidi and was killed around 1290 by a member of the Guelf Bostoli faction of Arezzo. The Pisan man is the son of Marzucco degli Scornigiani, whose murderer was forgiven by his father. Count Orso degli Alberti was murdered in 1286 by his cousin in the course of a long-lasting family feud. Pierre la Brosse became chamberlain to Philip III of France (1245–85). When Pierre accused Philip's queen of poisoning the heir to the throne, Philip's son by his first wife, he was arrested and hanged in 1278.

88–93 The Roman Emperor Justinian (AD 482–565) appears among the blessed in *Paradiso* 6, where he is celebrated for his achievement in codifying the Roman law. It is this body of law that rulers in Dante's day are accused of ignoring. The 'saddle's riderless' in that, since the time of Frederick II (see introduction to *Inferno*, p. xvii), no Holy Roman Emperor had taken an active interest in the government of Italian affairs. For Rudolph, see notes to *Purgatorio* 7: 97–111.

97–105 Albert I of Habsburg (1255–1308) was elected Holy Roman Emperor in 1298 but remained uncrowned, and here stands accused (in common with his father Rudolph I (1218–91)) of abandoning his rightful domains to political confusion. Albert was murdered on 1 May 1308 by his nephew John of Swabia. His successor was Henry VII (1275–1313), on whom Dante pinned his (disappointed) hopes for the restoration of Imperial rule in Italy.

103–11 The four families mentioned here were all involved in the rivalry between the Guelf and the Gibellines in thirteenth-century Italy. The Montecchi (here translated as Montagues) were Ghibellines from Verona, while the Cappelletti (here Capulets) were Guelfs from Cremona. The Monaldi and Filippeschi fought for control of Orvieto, the former being Guelf, the latter Ghibelline.

Santa Fiora is a town which lay under the control of the Ghibelline Aldobrandeschi (condemned for pride in *Purgatorio* 11: 52–72) until he was defeated by the Sienese in 1301.

109–17   Compare Dante's rhetoric in this passage with Virgil's account of the admonition that Jupiter directs at Aeneas in *Aeneid* 4: 272–6.

124–6   'Marcellus' refers to Marcus Claudius Marcellus (consul 51 BC), an opponent of Julius Caesar (see Lucan, *Pharsalia* 1: 313), and thus the prototype for the rebel against Imperial authority.

139–41   In his *Institutes* 1: 2: 10 Justinian recognizes Athens and Sparta (Lacedaemon) as the cities that first established both common and statutory law.

CANTO 7

Virgil identifies himself to Sordello, who speaks of how journeying at night is impossible in Purgatory. Entry into the vale of princes.

Commentary

With the opening lines of canto 7 the main narrative of the *Purgatorio* begins again, as, to renewed astonishment on Sordello's part, Virgil declares his name. Attention shifts from directly political questions to questions concerning language and poetry – though, for Dante, poetry, language and politics tend to be interconnected.

Implicit in Sordello's deference to Virgil, once his name is declared (7), is an understanding of the relation between Latin and the vernacular which reflects, in abbreviated form, many of the concerns that Dante expressed in his theoretical work the *De Vulgari Eloquentia*. The vernacular tongues need to learn from Latin how syntax and rhetorical ornamentation are properly structured and deployed. In this sense, Virgil shows 'our tongue . . . what it could do' (17). Latin, and in particular Virgil's Latin, demonstrates the underlying rules which govern the use of language in any vernacular form. (Hebrew and Greek, in Dante's view, provide similarly 'grammatical' and rhetorical models.) However, this is not to say that vernacular poets should simply imitate Latin usage, and certainly not that they should prefer writing in Latin to writing in their own tongue. On the contrary, the understanding of how language works which Latin teaches allows the poet to elicit from the vernacular those latent qualities which will remain undiscovered until he has learnt how to apply the rules of art to his native tongue. (In a comparable way, the rule of Imperial justice, Dante would maintain, would stimulate city states to bring their own local forms of existence to fruition.)

The result of such discipline, as Dante argues in *De Vulgari Eloquenti* 2, will be the creation of a '*Volgare Illustre*' ('Illustrious Vernacular') – an elevated and disciplined form of the vernacular which is 'illustrious' in that it sheds an honourable light on those who use it and on those readers who appreciate the poet's art. This will be a courtly language, but not primarily in the sense of being a language spoken at a particular court. There is, after all – as *Purgatorio* 6 makes plain – no true court in Italy where such a language could be learned. The *Volgare Illustre* is 'courtly' in the sense that it is created by the most sophisticated poetic intellects as they engage with the most elevated of moral themes and develop a language through which they can share the best of their thoughts. A bond is thus established between particularly eminent authors which will constitute the beginning of a new 'courtly' order, an order built essentially on the foundations of intellectual respect.

Among the most important poems that Dante wrote in the *Volgare Illustre* is one which has strong affinities with *Purgatorio* 7. This is Dante's *canzone* '*Tre donne intorno al cor . . .*' ('Three ladies around my heart . . .'), written in the early years of his banishment from Florence. Three ladies – representing three aspects of the virtue of justice – seek out the exiled Dante in the wilderness and weep with him over the disappearance of justice from the world. Hearing their lamentations, Dante declares that his exile must be considered an honour when it wins him such companions. In its concluding lines, the *canzone* speaks of itself as an exile going out into the desert where it will attract the attention of other '*amici di virtù*' – 'friends of virtue' – who, in true courtliness, will recognize the merits that the poem displays. It is notable that in *Paradiso* 8 and 9, in an episode in which he encounters Cunizza, Sordello's mistress, Dante alludes to the way in which another of his *canzone* in the *Volgare Illustre* won him the friendship of the Prince Carlo Martello when the prince arrived in Florence on a royal progress.

There are many similarities between '*Tre donne . . .*' and *Purgatorio* 7. Like canto 6, canto 7 is set in a hinterland outside the valley of princes which the travellers only approach at lines 43–6. And as 'friends of virtue', Virgil, Sordello and Dante here form a group of their own in this uncertain territory. It is significant that Virgil at lines

28–36 speaks of his condition as a dweller in Limbo far more directly than he does anywhere else in the *Commedia* (though compare *Purgatorio* 21: 31–3 and 22: 100–115). The courtliness that prevails among like-minded poets overcomes the exile that they all, in their different ways, experience, and allows Virgil an emotional eloquence which elsewhere (as in *Purgatorio* 3 and 5) remains repressed.

There are, however, differences between the earlier poem and the *Purgatorio* sequence. Dante is now writing a narrative work rather than a highly wrought lyrical poem. Three historical figures replace the three allegorical ladies. And, as always in the *Commedia*, the historical reality of the figures whom he portrays stimulates Dante to make judgements and discriminations which, in the *Purgatorio*, are likely to be delicately balanced between criticism and praise.

The depiction of Sordello is an instance of this. Sordello is not, after all, a perfect model for Dante, or for any other vernacular poet. He abandoned his native Italian in favour of Occitan – and, in *Inferno* 15, Dante has already shown his disapproval of those who deliberately desert their own linguistic roots. Sordello is in Purgatory, and one of the lessons he apparently needs to learn here is that he must recover an appropriate sense of his native place. That much is evident in his response to the word 'Mantua'. This, too, may explain why, at lines 49–60, Sordello is given a speech that (in common with Belacqua's final speech in canto 4) insists upon the observance of limit. But where Belacqua spoke of temporal limit, Sordello – continuing the interest that Dante now shows in the delineation of space – speaks of a law that forbids any further movement at night. He draws a line in the earth and, in contrast to his willingness in life to leave his native territory, he now insists that, when night falls, that line simply cannot be crossed. The travellers are bound to rest within the confines that have been allocated to them. It is there they rest and gather their strengths.

The vale of princes is reached at lines 64–6. This is a protected region, held within a 'lap' (68) or womb hollowed out in the mountainside, and in an important sense it stands as a prefiguration of the Earthly Paradise on the summit of Mount Purgatory – where Dante speaks of the perfect nature that we could enjoy if perfect justice reigned on the earth. But the vale is also a court. The princes at line 82 are heard singing a hymn to the Virgin Mary – the '*Salve, Regina*' ('Hail to the Queen') – as queen of the court of the redeemed. (Compare Mary's role in *Paradiso* 23.) In the twilight, flowers take on the brilliant colours of jewels and precious materials (73–82). There is, however, a certain decadence about the description here that distinguishes it from the descriptions of supremely natural vitality in the Earthly Paradise sequence. This is appropriate. The princes within the valley have been guilty of a certain languor and self-indulgence that still remains with them.

Dante does not go down to join this courtly company until canto 8, lines 43–8. In the conclusion to canto 7, he is still looking down from the lip of the valley (88–90). This gives the poet an advantage, and in some measure the concluding sequence of the canto offers a parallel to the diatribe of canto 6. Dante proceeds to identify and satirize a number of rulers whose negligence led to disaster, or whose heirs failed to live up to the good example of their fathers. (See notes below for details.) There is, however, a difference. Dante's concern now is less with the general confusion of the political arena and more with individuals who, despite their own failings or the failings of their descendants, are still heading for salvation. It is on the physical gestures and distinguishing marks of these individuals that he now concentrates. There is one who does not move his lips to the communal hymn-singing (91–3). One prince is 'burly' in figure (112–14), another lolls with his chin in his palm (107–8), while three times (103, 113 and 124), and to comic effect, Dante identifies particular princes by the size of their noses.

Notes

73–8   These lines may interestingly be viewed as a *plazer* – a lyric form in which the poet rhetorically constructs a list of things that give pleasure. (See Durling and Martinez, p. 120.)

91–111   Rudolph of Hapsburg (1218–91) was elected emperor in 1291, but would not come to Italy to be crowned. Ottakar II of Bohemia (*c.* 1230–78) (whose realms are designated here by the courses of the rivers Moldau and Elbe) was in life an especially dangerous opponent of Rudolph – whom in Purgatory he now comforts. Wenceslaus II was Ottakar's successor (ruling from 1278 to 1305) and son-in-law to the Emperor Rudolph. The 'button-nosed' prince is Philip III the Bold (1245–85), who succeeded Louis IX (1214–70) as king of France in 1270. When Angevin rule in Sicily was ended by the Aragonese during the rebellion known as the Sicilian Vespers in 1282, Philip's fleet was defeated in the gulf of Rosas by that of Peter III of Aragon (1239–85). This defeat may be implied in the reference to stripping the lily flower – since the lily appears on the French royal coat of arms. Line 104 refers to Henry I (the Fat), king of Navarre between 1270 and 1274. Henry's daughter married Philip IV of France (1268–1314; reigned from 1285), the 'Ill' or 'plague' of France, who was thus son-in-law to Henry and son to Philip III, who are the two figures described in lines 106–8. The crimes of Philip IV included a military attack on Pope Boniface VIII. (See *Purgatorio* 20: 46, 66, 85–90, and the notes to that canto.) For other criticisms of Philip, see *Inferno* 19: 87 and *Paradiso* 19: 118–20.

112–29   The 'burly type' is Peter III of Aragon. The marriage of his daughter to King Manfred (*Purgatorio* 3: 115–16) provided him with a claim to the Sicilian crown which he made good at the time of the Sicilian Vespers. (For the Sicilian Vespers, see also *Purgatorio* 20: 70–78 and *Paradiso* 8: 73–5.) Lines 115–20 refer to Peter's sons and heirs. The 'young boy' (line 115) is probably Peter's eldest son, Alfonso III the Magnificent, who died in 1291 after a reign of only six years. Peter's second and third sons are here accused of degeneracy. James (line 119) is James II (the Just), king of Catalonia and Sicily from 1285 to 1295 and king of Aragon from 1291 until his death in 1327. James was forced to abandon control of Sicily in 1296 when the Sicilians renounced their allegiance to him and his puppet government and installed his younger brother Frederick (also mentioned here) as king. (See *Purgatorio* 3: 115–16, and *Paradiso* 19: 131 and 20: 63.) The king with the 'manly nose' (line 113; compare with line 124) is Charles I of Anjou (1226–85). Though receiving only a cursory mention here, Charles was a figure of great importance in the history of mid-thirteenth-century Italy, frequently mentioned by Dante, who, despite the fact that he advances Charles to Purgatory in this *cantica*, deplored his politics. Son of Louis VIII of France and Blanche of Castile and brother of Louis IX, Charles married Beatrice of Provence in 1246, thus becoming count of Provence. (See notes to *Purgatorio* 20.) His realm became still greater when on the death of Beatrice he married Margaret of Burgundy. (See *Purgatorio* 20: 61–6). In 1266–7 he defeated Manfred and Conradino, thus also becoming king of Naples and Sicily. (See *Purgatorio* 3: 124–9.) Charles, like Peter III, suffered unworthy heirs, particularly Charles II of Anjou, who inherited Naples (Apulia) and Provence in 1285. For a manifestation of Dante's consistent antipathy to the second Charles, see *Purgatorio* 20: 70–78. The sense of lines 127–9 is that the sons of Charles I are as inferior to him as Charles I was inferior to Peter III of Aragon – to the same extent that Constance values her husband Peter more than Beatrice and Margaret (the two wives of Charles) value Charles himself.

130–36 The 'monarch of the simple life' is Henry III of England (1216–72). His offspring is Edward I, who reigned at the time the *Commedia* is set, in 1300. (See also *Paradiso* 19: 121–3.) William VII (1254–92), marquis of Monteferrato, served as Imperial representative but took advantage of political disorder to subject the cities of Lombardy to his rule. He moved his allegiances from Charles of Anjou when Charles attempted to subjugate Lombardy. Eventually, William was captured while attacking Alessandria in 1290 and died after being put on display in a cage. William's marquisate extended from Monferrato (lying between the Po and the Ligurian Apennines) to Canavese (between the Pennine and Graian Alps in north-west Italy). William's son attacked Alessandria, whose citizens, aided by the Visconti clan of Milan, counterattacked Monteferrato and other towns in William's marquisate, which is why Canavese and Monteferrato now 'weep'.

CANTO 8

While Dante speaks to Nino Visconti and Conrad Malaspina, the vale of princes is defended by angels from the incursions of the satanic serpent.

Commentary

The hymn that the negligent princes were singing when Dante first went down to meet them at canto 7, line 82 was the '*Salve, Regina*', which calls upon the Virgin Mary to aid the prayers of those who live as exiles from their original state of innocence:

> To you we cry, poor banished children of Eve.
> To you we send up our sighs, mourning and weeping
> in this valley of tears.
> Turn then, most gracious advocate,
> your merciful eyes toward us.
> And after our exile,
> show us the fruit of your womb, Jesus.

The references in this hymn to a lost Eden and to exile are exactly paralleled in Dante's depiction of the vale of princes, where he contemplates not only the confusions in Italy that led to his own exile but conceives the vale itself as an anticipation of the Earthly Paradise to which penance will assure his own (temporary) return. In canto 7, Dante's concern has been predominantly with the political questions that first stirred his attention in canto 6. Now, in canto 8, Dante's attention turns to the religious scheme that underlies, and promises a solution to, these disasters. God's final judgement has not yet been delivered (*Purgatorio* 6: 118–20). However, until that comes, the hopes expressed in the Marian hymn remain. Waiting is seen as a state of prayer and of a continuing inward pilgrimage.

In canto 8 the space defined by the Vale of the Princes becomes a liturgical space, resonating with the hymns and prayers that now express a confidence in God's providential plan. Night has not yet fallen, and its gradual onset is marked at **lines 1–7** and **49–51**. But '*Te lucis ante*', the hymn sung at **line 13**, commits the souls to the safekeeping of God in the faith that they will be protected from the delusions and phantasms that night can bring with it:

> To You before the end of light we pray, O Lord,
> creator of all things, that You watch over and protect us.
> Keep far from us the dream and fantasies of night,
> defeat our enemy, so that our bodies may remain without taint.

In keeping with this, canto 8 offers a piece of religious theatre in which, according to Dante's invention, a serpent nightly enters the vale, as if in repetition of the temptation in the Garden of Eden, but is driven away by angels coming from the bosom of Mary. The re-enactment of this drama is performed in two phases of the canto, at **lines 22–39** and at **85–108**. But interleaved with the unrolling manifestation of providential power are two intimate conversations, at **lines 64–84** and **109–39**, that draw attention back to the disturbed arena of earthly life, looking no longer at the grand political picture but at the ways in which ordinary houses and homes (and palaces) can be places of either distress or comfort.

The first two *terzine* of canto 8 speak of journeys away from home. These lines designate the arrival of the evening hours. But whereas in other cantos the passage of time is denoted by the movements of the heavens, here Dante's references are to the emotional clock, to the feelings of homesickness and of yearning that arise at dusk in the hearts of seafarers and pilgrims as their thoughts are drawn back to the shores they have left or are driven forward to the goals they have set themselves. In miniature, these two verses reflect the forces impelling the whole of the *Purgatorio* – a desire to return to where one came from, and a determination to advance the pursuit of one's ultimate goals. In the Earthly Paradise, it will be found that these two impulses are the same: our ultimate goal is to *return* to the state of innocence that humanity was originally intended to enjoy. However, the soul in Purgatory, as on earth, is still on a journey. At nightfall, the journeying sailors and pilgrims may relax. But their desires, longings and memories become even more acute. In the same way, Dante cannot now make any physical progress up the mountainside. Nor are there any external signs to guide him on his path – there are no references here to astronomical features. But the mind can still turn inward on itself and recover its deepest impulses. This is particularly evident in Dante's second night on the mountain, described in cantos 17 and 18. (See commentary on these cantos.) But a similar meditation is initiated in canto 8 by the graphic evocation of natural feelings – the tug of friendship, the chiming of the bell for the evening office of Compline which pierces the heart and stimulates its religious purposes.

The canto's highly suggestive opening lines, famous for their sonority and lyrical cadence, are, however, only the prelude to a more concentrated meditation which begins at lines 7–9. Here again the human being is the focus of attention, as a single, anonymous figure rises up to begin, on behalf of his fellows among the negligent princes, the *'Te lucis ante terminum'*. The figure calls for attention with the solemn gesture of line 10 and directs our gaze. However, the guidance offered here is not derived from geography, factual information or even argument; it is that which resides in ceremonial and liturgical action, where a group re-establishes its relationship with itself and with God. The simple posture of this priest-like presence carries a complex significance, as liturgy always does, in which the normal co-ordinates of time and space are re-interpreted by reference to the unfolding of providential purpose. The singer looks to the east; that is to say, he peers deeper into the gathering darkness. But the east is where the sun will eventually rise on the following day. The darkness (as, later, in canto 16) tests the faith of the celebrant in an unseen power that will ensure the return of light.

The opening *terzine* of canto 8 drew attention to the horizontal trajectories of any physical journey on earth. The *'Te lucis'* passage also stresses the horizontal east–west axis. But – pursuing a liturgical re-interpretation of earthly experiences – the canto also concerns itself with the vertical axis, as that which symbolically points to the action of those divine realities that lie beyond earthly phenomena. The singer attracts Dante's attention when he rises from the lethargic group around him. Now, at lines 16–24, Dante's eye is irresistibly drawn upwards to note the first phase in the dramatic spectacle that unrolls here every night. The reader, too, is called upon to sharpen the eye and pay particular attention to the meaning that lies hidden here (19–21). But the veil of allegory is 'gauzy', thin and diaphanous. Attention, then, is not to be rigorously tested here. Rather, the eye is invited, with appropriate confidence, into the playing-out of a providential enigma. The meaning is clear: just as the sun will return each day, so each night the princes, inhabiting an Eden of their own, will be assured that they are safe from the dangers that first arose in the original Eden. The snake makes its appearance at lines 97–102, but the angels are already at their post. Their wings are green (the colour of hope), and flutter brilliantly against the gathering darkness. Their swords recall the flaming sword that the angel wielded as it banished Adam and Eve from the Garden of Eden. But these swords are blunt, in token of how little they will be needed.

As this providential drama develops, an everyday but extremely courtly conversation draws Dante's attention back to the ground, where two speakers – recognizing as always Dante's privileged position – urgently wish to talk to him. The first of these is Nino Visconti (d. 1296), a figure of considerable importance in the public life of thirteenth-century Tuscany and the son of a daughter of Count Ugolino who appears in *Inferno* 33. He became judge (or chief magistrate) of Galluria in Sardinia and collaborated with Count Ugolino in the government of Pisa, but fled the city when his grandfather joined the Ghibellines. After this, between 1288 and 1293, he was frequently to be found in Florence, where, as seems likely, Dante became acquainted with him.

There is a marked contrast between Nino's intimate conversation here and the silent scene in *Inferno* 33 in which his grandfather dies of hunger along with his four sons. That scene – an appalling parody of family dependencies – traced to a tragic conclusion the political treacheries in which Ugolino had been involved. Nino, too, speaks of family, but of women members rather than of men folk, and of the emotions of loss and hope that his wife and daughter inspire in him. His wife (73–81) has been caught up in the power play of the period. At Nino's death, she abandoned 'my Gallurian cockerel', which was the emblem of Nino's clan, and married into the Visconti clan of Milan, whose emblem was a viper. (See notes below.) Nino's melancholy at losing the affection of his wife is registered in **line 73**, in which he states simply that he does not think she 'loves me now'. But the point of reference in this moment of desolation is his daughter Giovanna, on whose prayers and constancy his progress up through Purgatory in part depends.

After the intervention of the angels, canto 8 concludes (**109–39**) with reference to a safe haven where Dante was to find refuge in the early years of his exile from Florence. The figure who now engages the traveller is Conrad (Currado) Malaspina (d. 1294), marquis of Villafranca. Dante stayed with the Malaspina family for a time and in 1306 was chosen to represent them in successful peace negotiations with the bishop of Luni. In 1307 or 1308 Dante addressed his fourth epistle to Moroello Malaspina, speaking in grateful terms of Moroello's hospitality. Here, in what might seem like a piece of courtly flattery, the poet identifies and celebrates the principles on which a true court, if that could ever exist, should be established (**127**). It is a place of honour, where old virtues are maintained (**130**). (See also *Purgatorio* 14.) It is also a place where protection, comparable to that offered by the angels in the vale of princes, is extended to the exile.

Notes

70–81 Giovanna, daughter of Nino Visconti and Beatrice d'Este, was orphaned on the death of her father in 1296, and later married Rizzardo da Camino. (See *Paradiso* 9: 49–51.) Nino's wife was Beatrice, daughter of the infamous Obizzo d'Este (1247–93). (See *Inferno* 12: 111 and 18: 55–7.) After Nino's death in about 1300, while still wearing the white fillets of widowhood Beatrice married the Ghibelline ruler of Milan, Galeazzo Visconti, but came to regret this when her new husband was driven out of Milan and into poverty in 1302. She returned to Milan when her son Azzo was recalled in 1328.

109–39 The Malaspina family controlled the Lunigiana region – between Tuscany, Liguria and Lombardy – from their ancestral home in Val di Magra. Where Dante so often sees division and enmity within families (compare *Purgatorio* 14), he seems to see in the Malaspinas an example of great solidarity persisting over the generations. For an equally eloquent passage in praise of Dante's patrons, see *Paradiso* 17: 70–92, in which Dante eulogizes at length about the Della Scala family of Verona.

CANTO 9

*Dante dreams of being lifted to the skies by a golden
eagle. On waking, he discovers that he has been
carried to the gate of Purgatory, where the angel
guarding the gate inscribes the letter 'P' seven times
on his brow, to signify the seven capital vices which
have now to be purged.*

Commentary

Previous cantos have depicted Dante among the various groups of
penitents travelling through the Ante-Purgatory, and have shown him
either entering into these groups, praying on their behalf or demon-
strating the grace that God displays in making his journey possible.
Canto 9, however, focuses attention on Dante alone, at a moment of
crisis as he approaches the gate that leads to the realm of purgatorial
suffering. This canto, in common with the *Purgatorio* at large, is
concerned with the experience of transition, and crystallizes many of
the concerns that animate both preceding and succeeding sequences.
Arriving at the gate is the decisive moment at which those who have
hitherto been excluded (or exiled) from salvation receive assurance of
their place in the providential scheme. (Compare the emphasis on exile
and homecoming in cantos 3, 4 and 6.) This homecoming, however, is
fraught with tensions and paradox. It involves the active and conscious
acceptance of the sufferings of the penances which are displayed from
canto 10 to canto 26. And at the canto's climactic moment (112–14),
seven wounds are inscribed on Dante's forehead by the angel who
guards the gate, to signify the seven capital vices which are successively
purged on the terraces of the mountain.

There are readings of canto 9 which regard it as an allegory of the
act of confession. Such interpretations apply particularly to lines 76–
108, where Dante climbs the three steps leading to the gate, signifying
the three stages of confession. However, readings such as this do little
to represent the imaginative and emotional complexity of a sequence
that in its first phase (1–42) is dominated by a terrifying dream and
in its second (76–108) by the threat which seems to hang over Dante
as he approaches the angel with its dazzling sword. Dante here has
summoned from the depths of his subconscious the anxieties and
premonitions that accompany the crossing of any threshold. The scene
depicts an initiation ceremony or rite of passage in which (as might be

expected from the meaning attached to bodily marks in cantos 3 and 5) the scarring and decoration of the human body is as significant as any act of mind or will.

The full force of canto 9 derives from its subtext and the implications of its imagery. For instance, whereas, by the end of the canto, Dante is carrying the seven penitential 'P's as wounds on his forehead, the canto begins with a languorous, even erotic description of the moon dawn – 'The concubine of timeworn Tithonus' – rising from the bed of the sea with the stars of the constellation Scorpio dangling on her forehead. Nor is that all. The dawn unwillingly *leaves* her bed to encounter the chill of the morning hour and the long-drawn-out rhythms of line 2 ('*già s'imbiancava al balco d'oriente*'/'already on the eastern balcony') replicate the rhythms of stretching and yawning. But Dante *goes in* to the gate accompanied by sounds which grate upon, yet simultaneously soothe his nerves – the roar of rusty hinges mingling with the singing of a hymn (133–45). Throughout the canto, physical and often conflicting sensations are vividly evoked, as are effects of danger and distress. The bed from which the concubine arises is the ocean – warm as a bed, chilly as an element – and on the warm convex of her brow, her jewels (4–6) are shaped in the form of 'that chill animal, the Scorpion, that strikes then stings us with its vicious tail'. The sword that the angel holds initially seems no less dangerous than the scorpion. Its blade reflects a piercing light into Dante's eyes (82–4), and the marble stair that Dante climbs at lines 94–105 is textured and coloured in contrasting mirror sheens, blacks and red.

There are further contrasts between the two halves of the canto: the first half is punctuated by references to pagan mythology; the second by the liturgical images of Christian ritual. The references to Tithonus, Ganymede, Achilles, Chiron and Skyros at lines 1, 23, 34 and 38 are replaced by a concentration on the single figure of the angel, who is also a priestly presence, carrying beneath his ash-coloured cloak the keys that open the way, through confession, to absolution. The hymn of praise '*Te Deum*' (140) replaces the lamentations of the swallow (or, in some readings, nightingale) (13–15) which allude to an Ovidian story of rape, infanticide and cannibalism. (See notes below.) Bodies, subject to violence in the world of pagan myth, carry, in the second half, the same significance that attaches to the stigmata that Saint Francis received in imitation of Christ.

In this light, canto 9 not only depicts the entry of Dante into the Christian fold but also represents (subtextually) a movement from the culture of the pagan world to that of a world redeemed by the coming of Christ. (Other sequences in the *Commedia* enact this transition, too

– notably *Inferno* 8 and 9.) Indeed, in lines 10–12 Dante refers to the fallen state of Adam, whose body (as a result of his original sin) weighs humanity down, until redemption comes. So, too, at lines 70–72 Dante marks the solemnity of the transition by addressing the reader directly and, in a canto concerned with 'ascent' in many forms, drawing attention to its elevated style and moral seriousness.

Two events in canto 9 bring about this transition. One is the wounding of Dante's brow at line 112. Firstly, however, there is the dream that Dante has at lines 19–42. Here, at first sight, there is a concentration of the violence and sharp interplay of conflicting sensations that characterizes the opening of the canto. In his dream, Dante imagines himself carried up to Heaven as violently as Ganymede was carried up by the eagle of Jupiter in Ovid's *Metamorphoses* 10. The terror with which he seems to see the eagle suspended above – in a slow circling and lightning descent emphasized by the rhythms of the verse (28–9) – is matched by sensations of burning fire (30) as the eagle and its prey pass through the upper heavens. Heat and cold, pallor and trembling shock accompany Dante's sudden awakening (40–42). The eagle, however, is not merely a destructive force. For Dante, it is always a symbol of justice and also for the Imperial power which the pagan world at its best bequeaths to subsequent ages. From canto 6 Dante has been intensely concerned with the absence of Imperial justice in the politics of his day. Thus the dream realistically reflects his obsessions of the previous day and also suggests that – terrifying as it may be to submit to justice – this submission is none the less a precondition of entry into Purgatory. In its active phase, the penitential life is seen, throughout the *Commedia*, as being in part an attempt to conform to the demands of justice. (See, for instance, *Purgatorio* 21: 64–6.)

For all that, the dream of the eagle is not the final reality. On waking, Dante finds that all that he had experienced was nothing other than the heat of the sun rising in the dawn sky. Virgil – himself the representative of Imperial justice – explains to him what has happened to Dante in a simple narrative sequence (46–63). Virgil further explains, in more lyrical phrases that Dante, now arriving at the steps that lead to the gate of Purgatory, was lifted there, not by an eagle after all, but by a Christian saint, his own patron Saint Lucy (Lucia) – whose name means 'light'. The heat that he experienced in his dream was in fact the light of revelation. The significance of this re-interpretation is considerable. Justice, in Dante's view, is always the supreme virtue. But behind justice, and equally necessary for salvation, is divine love and the grace through which love is channelled.

Saint Lucy expresses the action of grace, the wholly unexpected libera-
tion that underlies our eventual freedom. (Compare *Inferno* 2: 97–
100; *Paradiso* 20 and the notes to these cantos.)

However, the actions of grace do not diminish individuals' responsi-
bility for their own actions. And now the canto begins to concern
itself with the waking terror that Dante experiences as he climbs the
final steps by himself towards the angel at their summit (79–81). At
each step, his self-possession is challenged as deeply as it was in the
rape that his dream had envisaged. His eyes are unendurably dazzled
by the brightness of the angel's face and of the reflections from the
angel's sword (81–4). Yet still he moves upwards, even though the
very steps he is treading threaten his composure and put his identity
into question (94–6). These lines re-enact the experience of con-
fession, in which the single self submits to the understanding that the
Church conceives of its sins and capabilities. But, as an initiation
rite, the liturgical implications of Dante's action are spelled out in
sensations of light and colour and feel no less vivid than those which
appeared in the first half of the canto.

The first step is so brightly polished that it gives back a more than
perfect reflection of Dante's features. Here Dante experiences his own
self as it truly is, yet as though the self were now detached from its
own safe-keeping and incorporated into the substance of the precious
stone. Notable here is the (untranslatable) word play at **line 96** (*'ch'io
mi specchiai in esso qual io paio'*) where the personal pronoun *io* – 'I'
– forms part of the word *paio* – 'I appear'. (The word 'mirroired' in
the translation is an attempt to capture something of the density of
this phrase – and would be more successful if 'mi' could be pronounced
as 'me'.) Identity is an illusion. Yet identity, once committed to the
substance of the eternal rock, is assured of permanence. Then all signs
of identity are erased as Dante confronts the second step, which is
black, rough and cracked in the form of a cross (97–9). Here, selfhood
is abandoned. Yet simultaneously that abandonment leads to an
implicit identification of the penitent with the self-abandonment of
Christ on the Cross. Finally (**102**), Dante comes to a step as brilliantly
red as 'fresh blood spurting from a severed vein'. In the context of the
wounds that seem to be threatened by the angel's sword, this phrase
carries an especial menace. Yet again, however, the reference suggests
the restoration of bodily life in a palpitating, vulnerable reality that
neither the first step nor the second had envisaged.

When, at **lines 112–14**, the wounds are finally inscribed on Dante's
brow, they are not what was expected. Despite the preceding suspense,
blood does not spurt here. Instead, the description speaks of a gentle,

almost featherlike pen stroke, and the angel's words are concerned less with the impact of the wound than with washing and healing. This exactly parallels the experience of the dream, in which the apparent violence of the eagle's descent is simply a mask for the remedial actions of Saint Lucy. It also prepares for certain ambiguities of sense experience which emerge in the final phase of this canto (133–45) and assume further importance in canto 10.

In appearance and dress, like the three steps that he guards, the angel has presented a picture of contrasting impressions, wearing an ash-grey cloak (as a sign of humility) yet drawing from beneath it keys of silver and gold (115–120). Now, such visual contrasts are replaced by aural contrasts. The gate of Purgatory grinds and echoes as it swings open, as though on rusty hinges while the sounds of the 'Te Deum' are heard. A simile here (136–8) recalls the age of pagan conflict: at the foot of the Tarpeian rock was the public treasury of Rome when its guardian, Metellus, attempted to defend it from attack. Julius Caesar drove him away and, forcing the door of the treasury, proceeded to loot it. This reference is consistent with the reference to jewels and precious materials that punctuate canto 9. At the same time, an obvious contrast is suggested between the riches that Caesar stole and the spiritual wealth that Purgatory holds for the penitent. But as the world of power yields to the world of penitential humility, so, too, the self abandons self-assertion and enters a sphere in which its most fundamental perceptions are to be reshaped and re-created. The harsh strenuousness with which the gate opens is registered in the syntax and onomatopoeia of lines 133–8. But so is the sweetness of the hymn, to the extent that the ear is caught between 'yes' and 'no' (145) – sometimes confident that it hears the singing voices, at other times not. (Compare *Purgatorio* 10: 58–63.) Where the canto began with the vague and unresolved emotions aroused by the moon dawn, so it ends on a note of uncertainty. But this uncertainty – entirely characteristic of Purgatory, as a transitional state – is the uncertainty of a continuing process in which the self will eventually see itself in a new light.

Notes

1–9   There has been some scholarly debate as to whether Dante is referring here to the dawn of the moon or the dawn of the sun. However, the reference to the constellation Scorpio indicates that the time is 9 p.m.

13–24 In *Metamorphoses* 6: 424–674 Ovid tells of how Philomela was raped by Tereus, the husband of her sister, Procne. Tereus cuts out Philomela's tongue to prevent her identifying him. But she weaves a tapestry which depicts the scene and sends it to her sister, who, in revenge, murders Tereus's son Itys, cooks him and feeds him to his father. When Tereus discovers what his food is made of he pursues both Philomela and Procne, but, before he can murder them, all three are transformed into birds. Tereus becomes a hoopoe, Procne (following the commentator Servius) becomes a swallow and Philomela (whose name means 'lover of song') becomes a nightingale. (Compare *Purgatorio* 17: 19–21.) *Metamorphoses* 10: 155–61 retells the classical legend of how Jupiter falls in love with the beautiful boy Ganymede, descends on him in the form of an eagle and carries him to Heaven to be the cupbearer to the gods.

16   The adjective *peregrinas*, as Dante uses it here, suspended in an unusually prominent position at the end of this line, carries three possible meanings: 'pilgrim', 'stranger' (or 'wanderer') and 'falcon'. All three meanings are relevant here, to Dante's pilgrim state in a foreign land and to his readiness to ascend in his pursuit of purity. (For comparisons between the spirit and hawks and falcons, see *Purgatorio* 14: 148–51 and 19: 61–9.) References to birds are frequent in the first half of canto 9. The canto is also marked at every point by ambiguities and unresolved meanings, reflecting its character as a transitional sequence. Interpretations in the sequence are still in the process of being discovered.

25–33 Geoffrey Chaucer wrote a comic pastiche of this episode in *The House of Fame* 2 (1379–80) (though Dante already – with his '*Forse*'/'Perhaps' – presents a momentarily comic picture as he attempts to convince himself that the eagle is here simply as a matter of routine and not to seek him out).

55–7   For Saint Lucy (Lucia), see *Inferno* 2: 100 and *Convivio* 3:9, 15–16.

118–29 These are the keys entrusted to Saint Peter by Christ in Matthew 16: 19. The gold key represents the power of the Church, gained by Christ's Atonement, to forgive sins. The silver key represents the intelligence and discretion needed to unlock the hardness of the human heart.

136–8 The story of Caesar's assault on the treasury is told in Lucan's *Pharsalia* 3: 153–68.

139–41 The '*Te Deum*' ('We praise you, O God') is said to date back to the fourth century AD, and was supposedly sung spontaneously by Saint Augustine and Saint Ambrose at the former's baptism.

Subsequently the hymn has been sung when novices first leave the world to enter a religious order.

CANTO 10

On the terrace where pride is being purged, Dante and Virgil first come to see examples of humility carved on the cliff face of the mountain, and then encounter the first group of penitents.

Commentary

Once he has entered the gate of Purgatory, Dante encounters (as described in cantos 10–12) those penitents whose sin on earth had been pride in either self and family, in achievement or in personal power. Pride, in Dante's scheme, is the most deep-rooted of all the seven capital vices, and all other sins are a consequence of mistaken self-regard. (Dante admits his own propensity to this failing at *Purgatorio* 13: 133–8.) However, it is no part of his ethical scheme in the second *cantica* simply to condemn the past failings of the penitents. He is equally concerned with the ways in which the virtue that stands in opposition to any particular vice may be brought to fulfilment. In this case the virtue is humility, which is illustrated first in the wall carvings that he observes at lines 28–99. For Dante, it is through humility rather than pride that our moral excellence is fully displayed.

In the *Inferno* Dante did not deal directly with the question of pride – since the scheme of sins in Hell follows a classical rather than a Christian programme. He did, however, produce at various points certain intense portraits of self-obsession and a violent disregard for others (including God) in the pagans Capaneus and Ulysses (see *Inferno* 14 and 26) and contemporary Christians such as Farinata (*Inferno* 10) and Vanni Fucci (*Inferno* 24). The difference now lies not only in Dante's concern to analyse humility as well as pride, but also in a narrative style that abandons a concentration on single individuals and single episodes in favour of an interest in groups, and the construction of a sequence of cantos (running until canto 12) in which many voices can be introduced and many facets of the moral issue fully explored. These long sequences (which are to be found from this point on throughout the *Purgatorio*) also allow metaphor and subtext to play as large a part in the development of Dante's conception of any one sin as do explicit moral judgements or dramatic characterizations.

Pride – one of the greatest themes in western literature – can be understood in many ways. The Greeks speak of Promethean hubris, which leads human beings to battle for their rights against aggressive gods. The Old Testament, especially in Ecclesiastes, reveals the vanity of any human ambition to build its fame or fortune on the shifting sands of a mutable world. Dante by no means ignores either of these earlier conceptions. However, his purpose is not to destroy or criticize human aspiration but, rather, to discover proper ground on which excellence can be established, and even to acknowledge that, in certain respects, pride itself can be a virtue.

A clear indication of Dante's thinking is to be found in the definition of pride that he provides in *Purgatorio* 17: 115–20:

> Some hope, by keeping all their neighbours down,
> that they'll excel. They yearn for that alone –
> to see them brought from high to low estate.
> Then, some will fear that, if another mounts,
> they'll lose all honour, fame and grace and power,
> so, grieving at success, love what it's not.

Pride is here defined not as an offence against God but as an offence against our neighbours. Pride is a pursuit of excellence and (in common with all sin, on the account that Dante offers here) is merely a yearning for goodness which goes astray. In this case, the perversity resides in the belief that we can only achieve excellence for ourselves by disparaging or doing down our fellow human beings. It is an offence against the communal pursuit of good. In Purgatory, the penitents have a chance to repair the damage they have done by cultivating the virtue of humility, which, again, implies an attitude of co-operation with one's fellows rather than simply deference to the divine.

Further nuances are introduced by a closely connected nexus of images, referring to rock, weightiness, air, lightness and art. Rock provides the form of penance that the proud now undergo, and in one sense this is (as it might also be in the *Inferno*) a form of *contrapasso*, or even divine revenge: the proud labour under great boulders, in so far as they have unduly exalted themselves and are now laid low. But rock is also symbolic of faith: to be at one with the rock is to recover the solidarity that faith makes possible with both God and others who are working out their lives in that same shared faith. In contrast to the references to rocky material, there are continual references to flight, lightness, the movement of wind. At times, as in *Purgatorio* 11: 100–102, the brush of the wind to and fro can point to the vanity of ambitions. Yet these references also point, in a positive sense, to the success that the penitents can look forward to when, freed from their penance, they will be able to fly towards God: we are chrysalises born to become angelic butterflies that fly to justice with no veil between (124–9).

The third, and most notable, feature of the pride sequence is its concern with art. Art can be seen as a source of pride in those who create it, and is taken as such in *Purgatorio* 11: 71–142, where an illuminator of manuscripts speaks of his own pride in his art and also comments on the constantly changing fashions and tastes that make any trust in such achievements ridiculous. Conversely, the examples of the virtue of humility (and the examples of the vice that are found in canto 12) are sculpted by the art of God on the rock face itself. Here, too, a double meaning can be discerned. On the one hand is the idea that art – especially as a form of reality – is only for God to create. This is an important point. The art of Dante's time had begun to display an appetite for the realistic representation of the world. Dante's own art speaks realistically and descriptively of this world, too. Yet any suggestion that such imitations of reality could challenge divine art may be viewed as pride. In that sense the works displayed on the terrace wall are reminders of the nature of truly religious art, which points always beyond itself and establishes a perspective of worship. At the same time, there is a recognition here of the peculiar aesthetic pleasure to be had from the play of illusion and reality. We see the heaviness of rock being turned at every point into the most rarefied of effects – of smoke rising, of dew falling, of spider webs. (See especially *Purgatorio* 10: 55–63 and 12: 40–45.) Rock ceases to be an impediment and becomes the material of a new, vivid kind of life.

The possible transformation of matter, not into something more spiritual but into finer and more animated forms of matter, corresponds to the underlying meaning of purgation, which does not transcend matter but rather rediscovers its finest possibilities. Here, too, as throughout the *Purgatorio*, the figure of the Virgin Mary provides a central example of virtue in the scheme of 'whips' and 'bridles'. She is plainly an example of humility – as elsewhere she is of generosity. But she is so only because she is also the fullest expression of the embodiment of God in physical form, revealing what human beings are capable of in their corporeal natures. This is a theme that grows stronger in Dante especially towards the end of the *Paradiso*. (See Commentaries to *Paradiso* 23 and 33.) But there is also here a mode of vision that is particularly important in the pride cantos, a cultivation of ambiguity. Dante twice emphasizes that the senses are caught between the 'yes' and the 'no' as they look at these reliefs (58–63; compare *Purgatorio* 9: 145). This may rightly be seen as an indication of the frailty of the physical perception – of the 'feeble . . . powers of mental sight' that are referred to at line 122. But that frailty or subjection to illusion is also one of the ways in which we come to appreciate the illusions of art – an appreciation which itself sharpens and refines our perceptions. At lines 124–9, Dante employs his own metrical art to similar effect, where, at first sight, he is uttering the most severely moralistic attack on pride: we are no more than grubs or worms. Yet to interpret this as his final conclusion would be to ignore the enjambment which leads us, against expectation, to see that, just as a 'worm' is the latent form of a butterfly, so too the acknowledgement of our apparently debased position in the created order is a preparation for our entry into the realm of the angels.

Dante's interest in the re-creative shifting of material forms is evident from the opening phase of the canto. Here, at lines 7–9, climbing through a winding breach in the cliff face, he describes the rock in terms of ocean waves, constantly surging forward and receding. However, the importance of this concern reveals itself most fully in the concluding phase of the canto (106–39). Here, the reader's attention shifts from figures carved on fine stone walls to the strange sight of heavy, unworked boulders which initially look like architectural gargoyles or corbel stones but are moving before Dante's eyes and prove to be the living, human figures of penitents labouring beneath their loads. Stone had previously been made to flutter or smoke through the effect of divinely created illusions. Now it moves by virtue of heroic physical effort. Dante's own eye and that of the reader (who is addressed at unusual length at lines 106–11) is called upon to engage with the ambiguity of this apparition and release from it a proper appreciation of those fellow human beings who seem at first not to have human forms at all (112–14).

In the introduction to this volume, it has been argued that this episode is characteristic of the *Purgatorio* at large in envisaging the re-creation of human dignity through appropriate human regard. However, the ambiguity that drew the onlooker into an appreciation of divine art similarly now operates to readjust our understanding of the penitents themselves. The human mind may be infirm in its perceptions (121–3), but that infirmity also makes us more sympathetic to others. Humility is not humiliation, but a rediscovery of our human interdependency.

The last line of the canto offers a particularly subtle illustration of how this process works. The onomatopoeia suggests at first that Dante the realist is here attempting mimetically and comically to evoke the stress, strain and shortness of breath that the labour of the penance produces. But then the *trompe l'oeil* begins to register. The penitents only *seem* to be uttering these words. And what they say is out of keeping with their actions. Saying they can't go on, they go on. Their experience of weakness is simultaneously an indication of strength. In this sense, when at line 121 Dante addresses 'Proud Christians', he is not simply reprimanding pride but indicating that the penitents have rediscovered the grounds for pride in their Christian penance.

Notes

31–3 Polyclitus (*c.* 452–412 BC) was, along with Phidias, the most famous of the Greek sculptors, known to Dante through references in Cicero's writings.

34–54 These lines refer to the Annunciation, in which the Virgin Mary submits to the divine will and accepts her role as the mother of God. Luke 1: 38: 'And Mary said, Behold the handmaid of the Lord; be it unto me according to thy word . . .'

55–69 Having brought the Ark of the Covenant into Jerusalem, King David dances in humility before it (tucking up his robe and so displaying his naked legs), and is despised by his wife Michal (lines 67–9) for his undignified display. (See also 2 Samuel 6: 2.) Uzziah sins by presumptuously touching the Ark when it seems about to fall. (See 1 Chronicles 13:9.)

73–93 These lines refer to the humility of the Emperor Trajan (d. 117), who was persuaded (according to John of Salisbury's *Policraticus* (1159) and other medieval texts) to postpone a military campaign at the behest of a widow whose son had just been murdered and to pursue the justice that she claimed. For acts such as this, Trajan, although he died as a pagan, has a place of honour in Heaven (see *Paradiso* 20), his salvation having been secured by the intercession of Pope Gregory the Great (*c.* 540–604). The legend suggests that Gregory had seen Trajan's act of charity depicted on Trajan's column (which stood close to Gregory's palace on the Celian Hill in Rome) and prayed so movingly for the emperor's salvation that he was restored to life long enough for him to become a Christian.

CANTO 11

The proud (continued). Dante speaks with Omberto
Aldobrandeschi, known for his pride in family, and
with Oderisi da Gubbio, an illuminator of
manuscripts who concludes the canto by speaking of
the humility displayed by the Sienese nobleman
Provenzan Salvani.

Commentary

The figures who in canto 10 were scarcely distinguishable from the rocks under which they laboured become fully recognizable as human beings in canto 11 through the conversations they hold with Dante. Though still bent beneath their loads, two penitents speak to Dante, both displaying the subtlety of characterization to which readers of Dante's *Inferno* are accustomed. The first speaks of the destructive pride he used to take in his noble birth (46–72). The second speaks of his own pride – and that of many others – in his artistic achievement (82–142), and concludes with a celebration of the humility shown on one occasion by Provenzan Salvani, a Sienese leader notorious throughout his life for his pride in the exercise of power.

The canto begins, however, with the Lord's Prayer, rewritten by Dante in terms that reflect his philosophical interests and the demands of his narrative fiction. The simple language of the original prayer is heightened at lines 2–3 by the complex idea that God is infinite and not 'circumscribed', except by the love that He willingly displays to the angels – the 'primal things'. At line 6 a reference to God's creative spirit is introduced with the technical term *'vapore'* – 'forming power' – in a sentence which may well have been influenced by the Preface of the Mass: 'It is right to give him thanks and praise.' At lines 22–4, Dante adapts the sentiments of the prayer to the conditions that prevail in his own (imagined) Purgatory: the penitents, having being reconciled with God, can no longer be threatened by temptation. So, if they pray to be 'delivered from evil', the prayer must be uttered for those who are still journeying through their earthly lives.

It is useful to consider whether, in presuming to edit and expand the scriptural text, Dante is already exhibiting a species of pride in his own intellect and poetic powers. (Compare with his rewriting of the Creed in *Paradiso* 24: 130–47.) That would be consistent with the interest he has shown throughout the pride sequence in the relation between human and divine art. At the same time (and on the evidence of canto 10), there can be no question here of brash self-affirmation on Dante's part. He conceives these lines as a chorus, uttered by all the as-yet anonymous penitents. All language for Dante is communal. It is the foundation of social and intellectual existence that we should be understood in our words by other persons, and should seek to develop that understanding through the development of language. These principles inform much of Dante's theoretical writings, especially the *De Vulgari Eloquentia*. Particularly in its opening chapters (*De Vulgari Eloquentia* 1: 4–5), Dante also argues that prayer is the fundamental condition of all language. The first word that Adam spoke was the word 'God', addressed to God in a spirit of praise for the happiness of existence that human beings were intended to enjoy, thus initiating the conversation with divine reality that articulates that happiness. So, too, in the early cantos of the *Purgatorio* prayer has been seen repeatedly as the means by which the community of believers is drawn together in the furtherance of God's redemptive purpose. If Dante does now rewrite the '*Pater Noster*', it is as likely that he is attempting to demonstrate his active participation in that community (31–6) as that he wishes, divisively, to assert his own artistic prowess.

Pride impedes any full participation in existence. And the pride particularly in human endeavour and art that was displayed in the building of the Tower of Babel (see the commentary to *Inferno* 31; also *Purgatorio* 12: 34–6) led directly to the loss of a common language and the confusion of competing tongues. Mount Purgatory offers the opportunity to rebuild Babel on a more secure foundation, nowhere more so than in the present sequence, where the communal labour of penance is viewed as an expression of productive humility. Once the opening prayer has established the appropriate conditions for discourse, the conversations can begin, and the especial subtlety of these is that, far from offering rigid examples of repentance, they reveal, in tone and reference, a continual interweaving of pride and humility, of attitudes still evolving and of earthly tendencies not yet wholly overcome.

Courtesies are exchanged at **lines 37–57** between Dante and the penitents, still bent beneath their boulders. The first speaker is Omberto Aldobrandeschi, son of Guglielmo Aldobrandesco, scion of a powerful family from south Tuscany and lord of Campagnatico who fought against Siena and the Empire in alliance with the Papacy in 1243. Omberto was assassinated by the Sienese in 1259. Omberto's words here (despite his humiliating penance) are dignified, forthright and sustained. At **lines 58–60** a resonance of pride is given to the weighty and balanced words with which he identifies himself and to the utterance of his father's magnificent (nine-syllabled) name. But at lines 67–9 the same dignity is heard in his unwavering confession of the damage that his pride has done to himself and those around him.

A second and more complex conversation takes place between line 79 and the conclusion of the canto. The protagonist here – whom Dante seems to have been acquainted with in life – is Oderisi da Gubbio (c. 1240–99), an illuminator of manuscripts and a friend of the painter Giotto di Bondone (1267–1337), who is said to have been employed in the Vatican Library by Pope Boniface VIII. The decision to give the otherwise obscure Oderisi a prominent position in his poem represents a remarkable leap of the imagination. Oderisi, despite his obscurity, is here elected to deliver the great sermon of lines 91–108, deriving from the book of Ecclesiastes, which speaks of the vanity of vanities and the transience of all human greatness. Symbolically, too, his presence has much to contribute. As an illuminator of manuscripts, Oderisi was a craftsman in one of the minor arts – this art itself being an art of the 'margins', working at the service of the text to which his illustrations were applied. All art, especially in a religious perspective, might be viewed as a decoration in the margin of a transcendent text. And the same might be said of the verbal decorations that Dante introduced, at the beginning of the canto, into the traditional wording of the 'Pater Noster'.

Running through the opening exchanges between Oderisi and Dante (79–90) is a discernible vein of comedy. Gubbio – Oderisi's home town – is referred to in Dante's Italian text by an honorific and Latinate locution 'Agobbio'. Yet the city is nothing more than a provincial hill town in the mountains of north-east Italy, which makes it all the more incongruous, and presumptuous, that it should be twinned in this verse with metropolitan Paris. Similarly, Oderisi may humbly admit the superior skills of his contemporary and competitor, Franco Bolognese. But at line 84 he cannot resist claiming that, 'partly' at least, the honour remains his own.

At line 91 Oderisi's speech becomes more solemn. The sentiments of the speech are now directly drawn from Ecclesiastes. All flesh is grass, all honour and glory will pass away. Yet even here there is a lightness of rhythm and a delicacy of coloration in the imagery that creates an ornamental tracery around these sombre thoughts. The fading grass is touched with a little green at its tip (91–3). The 'breath of wind' that bears away all human renown (100–101) is evoked with artful onomatopoeia in the Italian text in a verse which is thrown out of balance by the enjambment of line 100 and by repetitive fluctuations, which displace the caesura here, of 'from here, and then from there'. Art and reputation are subject to endless alteration. Yet it is sometimes supposed that in lines 94–9 Dante was expressing his confidence in the steady advance of artistic achievement. These lines certainly indicate that he was alert to the changing fashions of his day. In the visual sphere, the (relatively) realistic art of Giotto is said to have replaced the (relatively) iconic art of his master Cimabue (1240–1302). In the sphere of poetry, he sees, within his own literary circle, how Guido Cavalcanti (c. 1255–1300) displaced Guido Guinizelli (d. before 1276). (See Commentary to Purgatorio 26, where this same theme is treated further.) It also seems likely that when Dante refers to a third poet, already born who will supersede both of these Guidos, he is modestly, perhaps, referring to himself. Yet it would be hard to argue that Dante means here to celebrate progress for its own sake. His moral lesson is unambiguous. These variations in artistic taste are simply evidence of what he described in canto 10 at line 122 as 'our feeble . . . powers of mental sight'. Now, at lines 103–8, he declares that, no matter how long we live, the honours we achieve will amount to no more than those which are ours when, as infants, we are still talking baby talk. (Dante does not necessarily disparage the simplicity of baby talk.) (See commentary on Paradiso 33).

For all that, the final phase of the canto (121–42) records a story – which is a story of humility – that does deserve to endure. Here again there is a telling incongruity. The story concerns the ferociously aristocratic politician Provenzan Salvani (c. 1220–69). Yet it appears on the lips of a mere artisan, speaking from the margins of political history. This appears entirely appropriate, though. The conflicts and posturings of history fade to reveal, as the only thing worth recording, the moral example offered by a single individual.

Provenzan Salvani at his height exercised tyrannical power over Siena. He was responsible for the military expansion of the city which led to the absorption of the lands of Omberto Aldobrandeschi (see above). He was associated with Farinata (Inferno 10) in the Ghibelline cause, and supported the proposal (which Farinata opposed) that, after the battle of Montaperti in 1260, Florence should be razed to the ground. Provenzan was captured by the Florentines and beheaded at the battle of Colle di Val d'Elsa (1269). (See Purgatorio 13: 106–38.) The act of humility that wins Provenzan an entry into Purgatory concerns his willingness to save a close friend who had been captured at the battle of Tagliacozzo (1268). To pay the required ransom, Provenzano dressed in sackcloth and went begging through the streets of Siena.

The canto concludes (139–42) with an ominous hint from Oderisi that Dante should heed Provenzano's example. Dante, too, when his exile comes will know what it means to beg humbly for one's daily bread.

Notes

79–81   The term Oderisi uses here for the illumination of manuscripts, '*alluminar*', is formed from the French word *enluminer* and thus preserves a reference to light. The more usual word in Italian is *miniare*, derived from the noun *minio*, meaning 'red cinnabar'.

91–3   Compare here, and the while of Oderisi's speech with the sentiments expressed, particularly, in Ecclesiastes 1: 4 and 6: 11.

103–8   Dante's text uses here the baby word for 'food'/'*pappo*', and '*dindi*' for '*denaro*'/'money'. The astrological reference that follows refers to the movement of the fixed stars which, on Dante's reckoning, move imperceptibly 360 degrees in the course of 36,000 years. This complete revolution was referred to by Plato as 'The Great Year'.

CANTO 12

Examples of pride carved in the marble pathway of the mountain. An angel brushes one of the penitential marks from Dante's brow.

Commentary

In two ways, canto 12 concentrates particular attention on Dante himself. The first phase of the canto (1–72) is built around a complex piece of word play which many critics have judged to be the most artificial and self-advertising passages in the whole *Commedia*, and which certainly draws attention to the poet's virtuosity. The second phase (73–136) focuses on Dante as protagonist, describing – in an especially fluent and delicate fashion – how an angel brushes Dante's brow with its wing and erases one of the wounds that he received at the gate of Purgatory.

The artificiality of the opening phase is most obviously exemplified by the acrostic of lines 25–63, in which in the Italian the word *VOM* (an abbreviated form of '*uomo*', here translated as 'MAN') is spelled out progressively by the initial letters of twelve *terzine*. Its final appearance is in the 'V', 'O' and 'M' that open in turn the three lines of the thirteenth *terzina*. In fact, Dante has substituted the initial 'U' with a 'V' to make possible a four-fold repetition of '*Vedea*' – 'I saw', to be followed by a four-fold repetition of the grief-stricken exclamation '*O*', and the '*Mostrava*' – '[the pavement] showed . . .' that concludes the spelling of '*UOM*'.

It would be reasonable to think of this as mere contrivance on Dante's part were it not for the fact that the pride sequence has, throughout, been sensitive to the relationship between pride and art. And, in this light (as with the version of the Lord's Prayer that opens canto 11) the acrostic verses – which in any case contain some brilliant narrative vignettes – have an important part to play in the developing theme. The section is, in the first place, a brilliantly tragic summary of what MAN is, defining mankind in the perspective of pride that runs from Satan's fall, through an allusion to Nimrod, builder of Babel, to the myths of pride as it is punished in Greek legend and the Hebrew Scriptures. (See Notes below.) This is the history of a precipitous and apparently unstoppable fall from grace, emphasized graphically by the tumble of initial letters down the side of the page. Yet if one keeps in mind the inter-relationship of horizontal and vertical axes – whereby the usual sequence of reading from left to right is interrupted by the vertical accent of these initials – a different and redemptive reading begins to emerge. These *terzine* certainly describe a descent. At the same time, Dante's narrative, as he describes it step by step, is the narrative of an ascent which, in taking the penitential path towards the summit, enacts the process by which sin can be redeemed (70–72). For readers, too, the contemplation of these examples in sequence is clearly intended to contribute to a moral understanding of how the forces of sin and redemption that underlie their temporal lives are always inter-related and intersect.

In this episode, then, as also in the 'whips' and 'bridles' on each successive terrace of Purgatory, there is a strong connection to be drawn between art and morality. It would wrong, however, to suppose that Dante was interested merely in the didactic message of these vivid stories-within-the-story. In this regard, as in every other, morality for Dante is a means of liberating the human mind from its self-imposed restrictions, by bringing it to concentrate on the essential factors in its own existence. Even in the highly disciplined reading which the *UOM* passage demands, scenes are framed by the rectilinear outline of the paving stones and by the numerical regularity of Dante's verse. Like any artistic discipline, this framing produces its own effect of aesthetic and imaginative intensity. At line 27, there is the excitement of the single word '*folgoreggiando*'/'thunderbolting' – a neologism invented for the occasion – with which Dante describes Satan's spectacular fall from Heaven. So, too, as in the description of incense carved in stone at canto 10, lines 61–3, a purely aesthetic pleasure in illusion arises at the thought of stone being cut to produce effects of spider webs or dew on a suicide's sword (40–45). It is as if the tread of the foot on the pavement could contribute as much as any effort of mind to Dante's progress and moral insight. The sequence ends in a daring summary of the whole disastrous history of Troy in a single *terzina* (61–3), where particularly solemn and sonorous lines speak of the ashes and hollow ruins of the fallen city.

Such freedom of sensuous and imaginative response is especially evident in the second half of the canto, where Dante's narrative runs free from the linear axes that governed its opening phase. At lines 79–99, he describes his encounter with the angel who removes the first of the penitential letters from his forehead. This angel is described in marked contrast to the severe figure that guarded the gate in canto 9. The effect now is of liberation and refreshment, evoked by the fluent rhythms and alliterative filigree of lines 88–90, where the angel appears, dressed in white, its face trembling with light like the morning star. The rigidity of stone is here replaced by movement, light and breeze.

In a similar way, the concluding phase of the canto (115–36) is playfully free in its representation of Dante himself. The steepness of his climb is expressed in a comparison between the stairways of Purgatory and the steps that once led to San Miniato in Florence ('that church which dominates the city'), and Dante does not miss the opportunity to allude to the corruption that is evident there. But, for once, his tone is only lightly ironic in its reference to that 'well-ruled' city. (Compare *Inferno* 26: 1–6.) Nor is there any self-congratulation in the picture he offers of himself as a man now well on his way to Heaven. The conclusion is comic, capturing the absurdity of a situation in which Dante only slowly realizes that a letter has been cancelled from his brow. At lines 127–35 he is described trying to squint up to his forehead, which he cannot see, like someone walking down the streets without knowing that he has something ridiculous perched on his head (except that in Dante's case something is unaccountably missing rather than present). The canto ends with Virgil (very unusually) smiling at Dante's puzzlement.

Notes

25–63 The examples of pride begin with Satan and his fall from Heaven. Then comes Briareus, one of the Titans or giants who were defeated in their challenge to the gods. (See Ovid, *Metamorphoses* 1: 151–62 and *Inferno* 31.) Mars and Pallas are referred to at line 32 as fighting alongside their father Zeus. Nimrod is the builder of the Tower of Babel. (See Genesis 10: 9–10, 11: 1–9 and *Inferno* 31: 46–81.) Niobe boasted that her seven sons and seven daughters made her superior to Latona, who only had two children, Apollo (here referred to as Timbreus) and Diana. Latona sent her children to murder Niobe's children. Niobe was transformed into a stone from which tears continually ooze. (See Ovid, *Metamorphoses* 6: 142–312.) Saul, first king of Israel, fell on his sword after his defeat at the battle of Gilboa, during which three of his sons were slain. (See 1 Samuel 31: 1–6.) Arachne challenged Athene to a competition in tapestry-weaving and, when she proved to be the winner, was turned by Athene into a spider. (See Ovid, *Metamorphoses* 6: 1–145.) Rehoboam, king of Israel, was unwilling to lift the taxes imposed on his people by his father Solomon. The Israelites rose up in revolt and stoned Rehoboam's general Adoram to death, at which the king fled. (See 1 Kings 12: 1–19.) Erpyle, Alcmaeon's mother, was bribed with a necklace to betray her husband Amphiaraus and was murdered in revenge by her son Alcmaeon. (See Statius, *Thebaid* 2: 265–305 and 4: 187–212; also *Inferno* 20: 32–6 and *Paradiso* 4: 103–5.) Sennacherib, king of Assyria (704–631 BC) was murdered by his sons after his defeat in a campaign against Israel. (See 2 Kings 18: 13–37, 19: 1–37.) These are the words attributed to Thamyris, queen of the Scythians, who took revenge on Cyrus II (founder of the Persian empire) for the murder of her son by decapitating him and flinging his head into a container full of blood. (See Orosius, *Adversus Paganos Historia* 2: 7, 6.) Holofernes, general to the Assyrian king Nebuchadnezzar, was decapitated by the Jewish widow Judith while besieging Bethulia. (See the apocryphal Book of Judith 8–14.) Troy is designated by the name of Ilion, its great palace tower. (See Virgil, *Aeneid* 2 and Ovid, *Metamorphoses* 15: 422–5.)

100–105 On a hill above Florence there stands the ancient church of San Miniato al Monte, which is approached by a particularly steep stairway. The Rubaconte bridge over the Arno, named after the official who first began its construction, was later called the

Ponte alle Grazie. In the times when this bridge was built (around 1237), Florence was free from the scandals which later affected it, which included (in 1299) the tampering with official records and (in 1283) the selling of salt by monopolists with dishonest measures.

109–11 'Blessed are the poor in heart' (Matthew 5: 6).

CANTO 13

Envy. Examples of generosity carried on airborne voices. The envious are compared to blind beggars. Dante meets Sapia of Siena.

Commentary

For what reason is envy – or *'invidia'* – a sin? The view that Dante develops of envy in cantos 13 and 14 is closely akin to, and just as original as, the view he takes of pride in the previous cantos. In canto 17, lines 118–20, he writes of envy:

> Then, some will fear that, if another mounts,
> they'll lose all honour, fame and grace and power,
> so, grieving at success, love what it's not.

On this understanding, where pride misapprehends the excellence that we can achieve in isolation from our fellow humans, the envious, convinced of their own lack of excellence, fear and seek to destroy it wherever it appears, even when such excellence comes as a manifestation of God's goodness. Placed almost as low on Mount Purgatory as pride itself is, envy appears not primarily as a desire for material goods, but as a depression of mind scarcely less pernicious than manic self-exaggeration. The proud overvalue their own excellence. The envious – better referred to as the 'invidious' – refuse to acknowledge excellence in any form, whether displayed by others or themselves. This understanding is offered here with particular subtlety by the case of Sapia at lines 106–32. Born around 1210 and dying at some point between 1274 and 1289, Sapia was the aunt of the Sienese grandee Provenzan Salvani. (See *Purgatorio* 11: 121–38.) Here she describes her temperament as being so eroded by envy that she would rejoice more in the misfortunes of others than at any good fortune she might herself enjoy. She offers a particular example. As she neared the end of her life, she was present at the battle of Colle di Val d'Elsa, in which the Sienese, under her nephew Provenzano, were routed by the Florentines. Looking down on the battlefield from the great cliff where the town of Colle is located (14 miles north-west of Siena), she prayed (for no reason save a delight in destruction) that God would bring defeat upon her own compatriots. Her prayer was granted, and her relish over this disaster is captured at **lines 118–20** in the long-drawn-out rhythms (effected by enjambment in Dante's Italian) that speak of the '*amari/passi di fuga*' – 'bitter footfalls of flight' – that describe the retreat of her fellow citizens. The attention given in line 118 by virtue of enjambment to the word '*amari*' – 'bitter' – which is closely akin to *amare*, meaning 'to love', allows a momentary perception of how her sin (like all sin) is a perversion of love. (See commentary to cantos 17 and 18.) But her irrationality reaches its climax when she turns her eyes – which have been looking down on the battlefield – upwards in a challenge to God (**124–6**), declaring that, since God has apparently granted her prayer, she need no longer fear Him. Envy hardens her to the real nature of divine love. And she is only redeemed from such self-absorption by the prayers offered on her behalf by Peter Pettinaio (**127–9**), a lay Franciscan and hermit, known as 'the comb-seller'.

At **line 109** Sapia introduces herself by alluding to the pun implied in her name: 'Sapia' being a form of '*savia*', meaning 'wise'. Her failure of wisdom displays itself in her refusal to acknowledge the perspectives of generous feeling and harmony that the natural world can open up. The natural world is itself an expression of the divine wisdom that created it and, in picturing Sapia – raised to the skies by her physical position on the cliffs of Colle di Val d'Elsa as well as by her crazy exultations – Dante points to the deeper disorder, in the senses as well as in the emotions, that envy engenders. '*Invidia*' isolates the sinner from any proper appreciation of the generosity that this world itself displays in the light, warmth and refreshment that it offers. It is a part of the penance that the envious undergo that they should be blind and wholly dependent on the presence and good will of others.

This may explain why the imagery of cantos 13 and 14 evokes the elements of the natural world (in particular earth and air), in contrast to cantos 10–12, where art and craft were important considerations. This becomes apparent first in Virgil's address to the sun at **lines 16–21**. Where the works of art of canto 12 gave direction to Dante's advance, there are no marks or signposts at all on this terrace of the mountain (**7–9**). But Virgil – who is himself a manifestation of wisdom and described as such, for example, at *Inferno* 11: 91–3 – takes his bearings from the sun, emphasizing its warmth as well as its trustworthy position in the sky. But as well as this illuminated rationalism, the passage carries suggestions – very relevant to the treatment of envy – of Saint Francis's 'Hymn of Brother Sun':

> May you be praised, my Lord, with all your creatures
> And most of all by our brother Sun,
> By whom we are illuminated every day.
> For he is fair and radiant with great splendour
> And bears your likeness, O highest one.

For Saint Francis, our understanding of God's wisdom and our relationship to other beings in the created order is born of humility and poverty. (Compare *Paradiso* 11 and its commentary.) Dante offers his own version of this in the envy sequence. At first sight, the penance that the envious undergo is peculiarly humiliating. Lines 58–84 describe the penitents as beggars indistinguishable at first – because of their drab and coarsely textured dress – from the rock against which they are leaning. And they are all horribly blinded: their eyelids have been stitched to their cheeks by iron wires. This punishment suggests the psychological character of envy, which is not only a depressive malaise but also a sin that operates through the eye as the sinner looks suspiciously and critically at the qualities possessed by their fellows. (The Latin word '*in*-vidia' – both 'peering *into*' and '*not* seeing at all' – suggests a similar lack of moral vision.) Yet, as in canto 10, lines 106–11, the present canto does not encourage any vengeful (or invidious) delight in the exactitude of the *contrapasso*. On the contrary, as Dante picks out these figures from the rocky background – as if they were now equivalent to the works of art he observed on the previous terrace – the positive attributes of the penance begin to emerge. The sinners are not only dependent on the benevolence of the passer-by, but are also supportive of each other, thereby mustering that understanding of universal relationship that Saint Francis's hymn expresses but envy denies. Even the terrible penance allotted to them points to the promise implicit in their present suffering (as Dante does at lines 85–7). At lines 72–3, he compares this penance to the 'seeling' of a sparrow hawk's eyes (sometimes with a silk thread, and supposedly without pain) which was intended to tame the bird and make it dependent on its master. Yet the simile of the sparrow hawk also contains the symbolism that Dante invariably attaches to the hunting bird. (Compare *Purgatorio* 19: 64–7 and *Paradiso* 19: 34–9.) The bird is inherently noble, and its nobility is only enhanced when it participates in sport with its master. Properly disciplined, the sparrow hawk is all the freer to fly in pursuit of appropriate goods. An eventual airiness is discerned in and through the demeaning surface of the penance.

A delicate responsiveness to the present suffering and eventual excellence of the penitents is generated throughout the narrative of the canto. The examples of virtue which are offered at lines 28–33 suggest the sensitive and finally self-sacrificing nature of generosity. The first alludes to the reactions of the Virgin at the Marriage at Cana, when she alerted the attention of her son to the diminishing supply of appropriate wine. The second recalls the friendship of Orestes and Pylades which led each of these friends, when captured by the tyrant of Tauris, to claim to be that same 'Orestes' whom the tyrant (never having met Orestes himself) wished to put to death. The third refers to Christ's demand in the Sermon on the Mount that we should 'Love our neighbours and do good to those that hate us'. But it is also an act of generosity to the blind that these examples should come in an appeal to their hearing. Here (as at the end of canto 14) voices vibrate through the air with a rapid, percussive rhythm that sharpens and animates the ear – of the reader no less than the penitents.

Then Dante, too, displays his own form of courtesy to the sinners. The compassion that he feels at lines 52–3 is not an inert emotion. Rather, it translates itself into a courtesy, at lines 85–7, which is founded on the particular courtesy of attitude which is described at lines 73–5. To Dante it here seems outrageous that he should be able to see the sinners when they cannot see. Each must be open to the scrutiny of the others, not in the hypercritical spirit of envy, but in that perception of need and of intrinsic value that lies at the heart of human community.

In its conclusion (148–54), the canto returns to the day-to-day affairs of Siena, as Sapia, in the typically acid tones of the envious, speaks of the stupidity of the Sienese, particularly in matters of commercial enterprise, and invidiously distinguishes her own family at lines 151–4 from those who have come off badly in their ill-judged investments.

Notes

28–36 The words of Mary, '*Vinum non habent*!' – 'They have no wine!', refer to the story told in John 2: 1–12. Dante would have known the story of Orestes and Pylades from Cicero's *De Amicitia* 7: 24. Christ's command that we should love our enemies appears in Matthew 5: 43–5.

121–3 In what may have been a thirteenth-century Tuscan proverb, the blackbird begins to twitter, mistakenly supposing that a single fine day in mid-winter is the beginning of spring.

127–9 Peter Pettinaio (d. 1289) was a hermit and tertiary of the Franciscan order who had once been a comb-seller. He was revered by the Sienese, who erected a tomb for him in the church of San Francesco and in 1328 instituted a feast in his honour.

151–4 These lines refer to two instances of business and financial ventures that went disastrously wrong. (Dante attributes similarly hare-brained schemes to the Sienese in *Inferno* 29.) One is the idea of buying the port of Talamone from the count of Santafiora to give Siena trading access to the sea. The other was an attempt to locate a water supply in the Diana, an underground stream. The Italian word '*ammiraglio*' could be applied to both the captains of ships and general contractors.

CANTO 14

The envious continued. Guido del Duca inveighs
against the corruption of the present age in Tuscany
and the decline of courtly virtue in the Romagna.

Commentary

Is it conceivable that envy can be transformed into a productive disposition? Pride, in cantos 10–12, is shown to be legitimate when it is understood as pride in a God-given excellence. In canto 16 anger will be converted from rage to zeal. Meanness of mind would hardly seem to promise so much. Yet it is precisely this promise that Dante carries to a conclusion in canto 14.

The canto begins, as does no other in the *Commedia*, in the middle of a conversation between two as-yet unidentified voices. These voices display traces of an envious temperament. They speak in a subdued whisper, manifesting edgy discomfort at the appearance of a newcomer and an acutely sensitive awareness of the privileges he possesses which they do not: he seems to be alive and to open and close his eyes as they – with their eyes stitched up – are unable to do (1–3). Here, the social unease of the penitents, as if attempting to defend their territory against the interloper, combines with a heightened sharpness of sense perception. If they are blind, how do these speakers know that Dante's eyelids are moving? It is as if (in compen-

sation for their lack of sight) they are capable of hearing this move-
ment. So, too, at lines 127–9, as Dante takes leave of the invidious,
an especially delicate moment, combining generosity and courtesy,
occurs which could only come about because of this same sharpness
of hearing. Dante, seeing the penitents deeply engaged in their medi-
tations, does not wish to disturb them. So he moves away in silence,
even though he does not know whether he should go to the left or to
the right. Yet he is confident that they can hear his footsteps and are
sensitive enough to know whether he is taking the right or the wrong
way forward. He is also sufficiently confident of their good will to
know that, if he were going wrong, the penitents would tell him so.
They remain silent. So Dante is sure he is on the right track. The
meditation, too, remains unbroken. In the space of two lines, Dante
has pictured an action which expresses the reciprocity of concern that
lies at the opposite pole from envy.

Lines 10–15 (in common with the central sections of canto 13)
display a courtliness in which invidious observations are repressed as
the speaker acknowledges and defers to the particular characteristics
and privileges of his interlocutor. And in the second half of the canto,
courtesy will itself become a theme as the speaker bewails the deca-
dence of life in the courts of contemporary Romagna, in south-east
Italy. (See especially lines 109–12.) But, first, at lines 16–30, Dante
begins to trace a transformation which sees the energy and critical
sensitivity that reside in the envious temperament transformed into
moral vision and scathing diatribe.

Dante's reply to the courtesies of the penitent is itself courtly in its
rhetoric – marked by periphrases and elegant flourishes which mod-
estly conceal his own name and that of the city from which he comes
(17–21). But the penitent – later to identify himself with equal modesty
as a certain Guido del Duca (see notes) – immediately suspects an
evasion here, and swoops on the truth behind Dante's words: Dante
comes from Florence, the city on the river Arno, and is too ashamed
to confess himself a native of so corrupt a place. The violence of this
intuition is enforced in Italian by the snarl of rhyme between 'Arno'
and 'accarno' – 'accarno' meaning 'I set my teeth into the flesh of . . .',
as a bird might strike its talons into its prey. Under the impulse of this
new asperity, Guido now turns all his rhetoric to an attack on the
corruptions of Tuscany, tracing them down the course of the river
Arno from its unpolluted origins in the Apennines through ever-
increasing manifestations of human wickedness.

Though Guido is blind, his indignation opens up a visionary land-
scape of mesmerizing clarity. Lines 34–6 speak of the natural process

by which water vapour is taken from the sea and returned in the form of river water. But at lines 37–9 this process is immediately contrasted with the perversity of human beings who flee from virtue as if virtue were a serpent. A reference here to the serpent of the Garden of Eden is at once apparent, and the scene becomes one in which the original purity of the world is yet again corrupted by human malice. This comes to its climax in lines 58–71. Here, Guido speaks of the nephew of his silently weeping companion. But this nephew is no comfortingly domestic figure. Though unnamed, he can be identified as Fulcieri dei Paolucci da Calboli (c. 1270–c. 1340), military governor of Florence in 1303 and a Guelf supporter of the papal cause, who is reported to have persecuted, tortured and killed White Guelfs of Dante's party at the behest of the Black Guelfs. Now, in his menacing anonymity, Fulcieri becomes an archetypal embodiment of cruelty, coming out blood-stained from an ancient forest which his actions have so despoiled that it will not recover its primal vigour in less than a thousand years. Faced with the knowledge that his own family has produced this demonic force, Rinieri flinches and garners up the pain that Guido's prophecy causes him. Here, as elsewhere (notably in *Purgatorio* 20), purgation proves to be a matter less of physical pain than of mental pain, induced (as it was for Dante in the *Inferno*) by a contemplation of the heart of darkness.

In Guido's first speech, the energies that might have been directed, on earth, to acts of envy and spite are here devoted to a penitential purpose. Then, in lines 76–90, the reverse of envy is displayed in the generosity and courtesy that Guido proceeds to show to his silent fellow penitent Rinieri and to Dante himself. However, the second of Guido's monologues reverts to the offensive in a wide-ranging attack on the ungenerosity of the modern age. The golden age of courtliness and true courtesy is over – the age of 'knights and ladies, all the toil and ease/that love and courtesy once made us seek' (109–10). And this, in Dante's scheme, is no trivial loss. Court life, chivalry and the refinement of moral perception that such a life encourages promote a recognition of excellence in the deeds of its members. But this can easily be destroyed. In fact, envy is the characteristic vice of a false court. (See *Inferno* 13: 64–6.) But a recognition of courtly elegance has a crucial part to play in making the other virtues that an individual may possess accessible and attractive to those around. It is for this reason that among the 'moral' *canzoni* that Dante wrote before he began the *Commedia* – including 'Tre donne . . .', the great *canzone* concerning justice that is discussed in the commentary to *Purgatorio* 7, one is wholly devoted to the virtue of '*leggiadria*', which is to say 'lightness of touch' or even 'charm'. This virtue is like the sun (especially as evoked by Virgil in *Purgatorio* 13: 16–21), illuminating the world and making virtue thrive:

> Al gran pianeta è tutta simigliante
> che dal levante
> avante   infino a tanto che s'asconde
> co li bei raggi infonde
> vita e vertù qua giuso
> ne la matera sì com' è disposto.

([*This virtue*] is truly like the mighty planet that, from the time it rises in the east until it hides away, sends down with its lovely rays power and life into matter as matter was firstly disposed.)

'Poscia ch' Amor . . .', 96–111

But all such courtesy, in Guido's view, has disappeared from the world, and with it any possibility of identifying examples of individual excellence. Guido's great catalogue of names from the past (97–111) plucks momentarily from oblivion the courtly figures of his own generation. Then, returning to the theme he touched on first in speaking of Fulcieri, Guido expands the range of his diatribe to a terrible cry that calls for an end to all child-bearing and procreation. When virtue fails and there is no environment in which it might be celebrated, it is better that humanity should cease to be. It is good that many families which were once courtly but are now degenerate should be on the point of extinction (112–23). Their descendants only disgrace the names of their ancestors.

The violence of Guido's tone is echoed in the thunder claps at lines 130–41 that announce the restraining examples of envy. These are the more powerful in that they break in upon Dante's silent and courteous departure from the penitents. But the canto ends with a re-affirmation of the value of elegance and nobility on a more elevated plane than the decadent families of Italy could conceive. In lines 148–51 Virgil energetically urges Dante to fix his eye on the circling of the planetary spheres as evidence of eternal beauty. These are the 'lures' on which the mind must fix. And in employing this hunting metaphor Dante recalls his description of the blind penitents as hawks being trained by the sewing-up of their eyelids. That temporary blinding will make the hawk, like the penitent, more responsive to the call of its master, when engaged in the courtly art of falconry. Without such discernment, Virgil concludes, the soul will be beaten down by the power of a divinity that discerns the potential excellence and beauty of all created things.

Notes

7–9   The speakers are later identified as: firstly, Guido del Duca (*c.* 1170–*c.* 1250), a Ghibelline nobleman from Bretinoro (mentioned at line 112) in the Romagna, who was chief magistrate of Rimini in 1199; and, secondly, Rineiri dei Paolucci da Calboli (*c.* 1225–96), Guelf leader of the Romagna, who was chief magistrate of various cities in northern Italy and uncle of Fulcieri, mentioned at lines 58–71. (See commentary above.)

16–18   The Arno rises south of Mount Falterona in the Apennines.

31–3   The Apennines were thought once to have extended into Sicily, continuing to Mount Pelorus on that island, until they were broken off by an earthquake.

40–45   The witch Circe, daughter of the sun, changed the followers of Ulysses into swine. (See Ovid, *Metamorphoses* 14: 248.)

97–111   This is a catalogue of honourable but sometimes obscure figures from the age preceding Dante's own. (At canto 16: 138, Dante is criticized for not knowing the name of the long-dead Gherardo.) Lizio (fl. 1260) was a Guelf from Valbona whose family controlled certain abbeys in that area and who fought with Rinieri (see above) against the Ghibellines of Forli. Arrigo Mainardi – a friend of Guido del Duca (see above) and, like him, a native of Bretinoro – is known to have died around 1228. Pier Traversaro (1145–1225) was a Ghibelline lord of Ravenna and ally of the Emperor. In 1170 Piero and Arrigo were held prisoner together by the citizens of Faenza. Guido di Carpigna (d. 1283), a Guelf opponent of Frederick II, was chief magistrate of Ravenna in 1251. Fabbro de' Lambertazzi (d. 1259) was leader of the Ghibellines in the Romagna and Bologna. Bernardin di Fosco rose from humble origins to become a leader in Faenza, which he defended against Frederick II. Guido da Prata was probably a dignitary of Ravenna in the early thirteenth century. Ugolino d'Azzo (d. 1293) was probably a member of the Tuscan Ubaldini who settled in the Romagna. Federigo Tignoso was a nobleman associated with the Traversari of Ravenna in the early thirteenth century. The Traversari and Anastagi were Ghibelline (and Byzantine) clans important in Ravenna.

112–23   Bretinoro was a castle near Forli held by the Manardi family, who had become extinct by 1300. The Ghibelline family of

Malvicini were counts of Bagnacavallo but were also nearly extinct in 1300. The degenerate Ghibelline counts of Castrocaro in the region of Imola were, however, thriving at this time, as were the Guelf counts of Conio in the same region. The Pagani, Ghibelline lords of Imola and Faenza at the end of the thirteenth century, produced a particularly vicious offspring in Maghinardo, known as 'the demon'. (See *Inferno* 27: 50–51.) The speech concludes with praise for Ugolino dei Fantolini (d. 1278), a Guelf nobleman of Cerfugano and of castles near Faenza, whose line died out (and therefore can no longer be disgraced) when his sons were killed in campaigns against Guido da Montefeltro. (See *Inferno* 27.)

133–41 Cain murders his brother Abel out of envy and utters these words when he receives God's curse. (See Genesis 4: 14.) The story of Aglauros is told by Ovid in *Metamorphoses* 2: 708–832. She envies her sister Herse, with whom Mercury is in love. She is eventually turned, by Mercury, into a statue of murky-hued stone.

CANTO 15

Dante, leaving the circle of the envious, has the second penitential mark removed from his forehead, and, moving to the circle of the angry, experiences visions displaying the virtue of mildness.

Commentary

Canto 15, describing Dante's journey from the circles of envy to the circles of anger, falls into two parts. The first of these, at lines 1–81, is dominated by three different kinds of light, the light of the sun in late afternoon (1–9), the light that emanates from the angel who arrives at line 11 to cleanse Dante's brow of a second wound, and the action of divine light as discussed by Virgil at lines 64–78. The second part, lines 82–145, depicts three acts of inner vision which present to Dante the examples of the virtue opposite to the vice of anger – meekness or the clarity of mind that makes peace possible. The penance of anger (142–5) calls for the penitents to be deprived of sight, as were the envious – in this case by being enfolded in an impenetrable black smoke. Suffering the same condition, Dante receives the necessary illustrations of vice and virtue inwardly, in a series of scenes which narrate (as in the 'sudden-seeing rapture' of line 85) the often disturbing and distressing events narrated in these examples.

The canto opens playfully, with a comparison of the sun's path (which changes from day to day when seen from any one latitude) as being like a child skipping from point to point. From this moment on, the metaphor of the child will become increasingly important in the *Purgatorio* (as, next, at canto 16, lines 85–90), sometimes expressing the distraction to which human wills are subject but, more frequently, pointing to an original innocence which, if lost, can still be recovered through penance. Now, three hours before sunset, as the sun begins to decline – its light weighing directly on Dante's brow (10) – an angel appears to remove from the brow the second mark of sin and make possible Dante's own advance towards the recovery of innocence. Here, as in cantos 2 and 28, Dante envisages an interplay of natural and supernatural light. For the moment, he does not attempt to describe the constant impact of eternal light: indeed, he shields his eyes from it to remain in relative darkness. Instead, the impact of the angel's appearance is described – with an exact attention to the science of optics – in terms of natural phenomena (16–21), observing how light, when it strikes a reflective surface, is reflected back at the same angle (measured from the exact vertical referred to at line 21) as the angle of its first impact. The linguistic interest lies in a brilliant precision of syntax which allows the scientific analysis to make its full effect while at no point diminishing the appeal to the imagination of various kinds of light.

At lines 67–75, light becomes a metaphor for the action of divine love. The absolute and infinite generosity of God flows into any receptive creature in the way that light flows into any transparent object. The particular mistake of the envious is to suppose that the quantity of divine love is, somehow, finite. They mistakenly believe that if others display the excellence of divine love, the supply of illuminating virtue will be diminished, and consequently they begrudge any such manifestation. This passage insists upon the logic that governs the relationship between an infinite Creator and a finite creature, and stands as a premonition of themes, images and forms of poetic argument that will come to their climax in the *Paradiso*, especially in its second canto. It also anticipates the great philosophical discussions at the centre of the *Purgatorio* that will begin in canto 16 and only conclude in canto 18. In all of these discussions, Virgil's position will be particularly sensitive. In one sense, he is here at the height of his powers; and through his mouth, Dante will produce (as in the present passage) some of his most lucid philosophical poetry in what the critic

Giovanni Getto has called 'the poetry of intelligence'. At the same time, Virgil is made to admit, at lines 76–8, that his careful and rationally formed explanations may not satisfy Dante, and that Beatrice – still beyond – may be needed to give a different and fuller account. (Compare *Purgatorio* 18: 73–5.) For Dante, rationality in its highest form is also most likely to recognize the limitations of rationality.

At its limit, reason must yield to the authority of other spiritual resources. Thus the second half of the canto moves inward to a region of ecstatic vision in which, beyond any scientific or rational explanation, the mind is enraptured and informed by powers beyond itself. In reference to this state, at lines 133–5, Dante speaks of 'eyes that do not see'. Paradoxically, these unseeing eyes are the eyes of physical vision, contrasted with the eyes of the mind. The eyes of the mind will often operate most fully when blinded – as they are for most of the next three cantos – to the phenomena of the external world.

The truths to which Dante's visions introduce him are far from consoling. All three offer examples of gentleness – but gentleness too deeply intertwined with mystery, even with violence, for a mind such as Virgil's to comprehend. The first vision depicts Mary looking for the child Jesus when he appears to have wandered off and got lost. Mary and Joseph discover Christ in the temple discoursing with the temple elders and teachers, and Mary's response, in the words that Dante attributes to her at line 90–92, display a certain maternal gentleness. But, with accurate realism, they also betray a distress and parental annoyance, and an incomprehension of the destiny that is evolving in their growing child. Christ's reply in the Scriptures (though not recorded in Dante's text) insists likewise – with something of the hurtful truculence of an adolescent – that he is bound to devote himself to his mission as the Son of God. His human parents 'understood not the saying which he spake unto them' (Luke 2: 50).

The second example – providing the lengthy narrative of lines 94–105 – pictures anger on a domestic level pacified by a kindliness which is also firm and incisive in its effect. Pisistratus (*c.* 607–528 BC), ruler of Athens, discovers that his daughter has been kissed in the public market place by a young man who is in love with her. Pisistratus's wife is incensed and asks that the youth should be punished. To which, in a spirit of conjugal dissension, Pisistratus replies: 'What shall we do to those that wish us ill/if those that love us are condemned by us?'

The final scene is one where zeal, murder, martyrdom and the submission of a saint to the mystery of suffering all intermingle. Saint Stephen is the earliest of the Christian martyrs, dying in the first year of the Christian era (probably in AD 36). Accused of heresy in the councils of the Jews, Stephen persists in his belief and preaches sermons that denounce the pride of the Israelites. A mob is roused in Jerusalem, who pursue him (in Dante's dramatic and somewhat altered version) with cries of 'Kill, kill!', which recall the calls for Christ's crucifixion (Luke 23: 21). He dies, according to the Acts of the Apostles, asking forgiveness for his persecutors and saying, in words that recall Christ's final words on the Cross: 'Lord Jesus, receive my spirit' (Acts 7: 59).

In the coda to the canto, there is a moment almost of anger, certainly of incomprehension, on Virgil's part as he sees the – to him – inexplicable rapture into which Dante has been drawn. (Compare the quarrels depicted in *Inferno* 30.) This is momentarily eased as Virgil mind-reads Dante's thoughts. But the canto ends ominously with the arrival of the dark smoke. Even before the natural night alluded to at the beginning has fallen, darkness – representing sin, violence and confusion – will have deprived Dante of sight and the benefits of the clear natural air. Virgil's ability to read Dante's thoughts when natural sight is no longer available proves to be an important emblem of reason's power in this canto. An equal part is played by zeal, by the pent-up violence of rapture, by anger and vision.

Notes

1–6 The time is three hours before sunset. In liturgical terms, this is the hour of Vespers. In astronomical terms, the angle of the sun above the horizon is the same now as it was a full three hours from the beginning of the day. If it is three hours until sunset in Purgatory, it is three hours before sunrise in Jerusalem. Since Florence ('our clime') is 45 degrees west of Jerusalem, it is midnight in that city. The circle of the sun plays like a child in that, during the course of any one year, it changes latitude and follows different paths according to the hour and the season.

16–24 These lines draw on the theorem, known since the time of Euclid's *Optics*, that the angle of reflection is equal to the angle of incidence. In medieval optics the terms 'reflection' and 'refraction' were not clearly distinguished. Dante, as traveller, mistakenly assumes that the laws of reflection apply to the light emanating from the angel – where in fact the angel is a medium through which the light of God is refracted.

37–9 These lines refer to the fifth Beatitude: 'Blessed are the merciful' (Matthew 5: 7). Mercy, according to Aquinas, is one of the virtues that stand in opposition to envy.

85–114 The episode of Christ in the temple is related in Luke 2: 42–
51. The story of Pisistratus is told in Valerius Maximus, *Facta et
dicta memorabilia* 5:1. The naming of Athens, referred to at
line 98, was the cause of a dispute between Pallas Athene and
Poseidon, as related in Ovid, *Metamorphoses* 6: 70–82. The
story of Stephen, the first Christian martyr, appears in Acts 6: 6–
15 and 7: 54–60.

CANTO 16

*Anger. Dante encounters Marco Lombardo, who –
purging the sin of anger – identifies the abuse of free
will as the source of human misery and insists upon
the proper exercise of law as a remedy.*

Commentary

The sequence of cantos from 16 to 18 that form, numerically, the
centre of the *Purgatorio* (and thus of the whole *Commedia*) address
some of the most central issues in Dante's philosophy. Beginning with
the references to divine love in canto 15, lines 67–72, Dante proceeds
in canto 16 to deal with questions concerning the freedom of the will
and law (as the expression of a communal will). In canto 17 – in
discourses attributed to Virgil – he speaks of the relationship between
the Creator and created beings and also of the nature of sin. Continu-
ing this discussion, he proceeds, in canto 18, to a consideration of love
and freedom.

An outline of Dante's thinking on these issues is to be found in the
general introduction to *Inferno*, pp. li–lvii and the introduction to the
present volume. However, neither here nor anywhere else can Dante's
thinking be seen in isolation from the dramatic and narrative context
in which it is set.

Two particular questions immediately spring to mind. Why is it,
firstly, that Dante locates an extremely rigorous and sometimes highly
technical debate in a scene of complete darkness? Canto 16 evokes the
impenetrable black smoke – first mentioned at the conclusion of canto
15 – which provides the penance for anger. But even when Dante
leaves this darkness at canto 17, lines 4–6, the scene he enters is not
one of sunlit normality – his eyes at this point are violently seized by
ecstatic visions – and by line 70 of that canto, evening is falling on the
second day of his penitential journey. Virgil's discourses on freedom

and love take place during a night illuminated only by strange moon-light, which shines in the sky like 'a copper bucket burnished red'. (See *Purgatorio* 18: 77.)

Secondly, how appropriate is it that a discussion of love and freedom should be initiated by a voice which is still recognizably afflicted by the sin of anger? And why is it that the conclusion of this discussion (at *Purgatorio* 18: 88–145) coincides with the brief but intense depic-tion of the slothful purging their sin by running wildly through the night around their terrace on the mountain?

Some answers immediately suggest themselves. Darkness, most obviously, symbolizes sin, and from the vantage point of Purgatory Dante now revisits the question which has occupied him since he first entered the dark wood of *Inferno* 1: why is the world a moral desert, deprived of all virtue (58–64); and what possible remedies are there for this apparent disaster? Strikingly, Dante describes the penitential smoke as being worse than any of the fumes of Hell. But, as in all penance, a remedy lies in a conscious engagement with the agony of the problem. At lines 64–84, Dante's interlocutor, Marco Lombardo (*c.* 1250–*c.* 1290), a minor noble probably from the Venetian terri-tories, insists that human beings alone are responsible for the disasters that have befallen them. His tone is angry and aggressive. Yet if human beings are themselves the cause of their own misfortunes, they can also provide the remedy. Law exists, after all (97–111), and, though no one pays attention to it, they *could*, and, if they did, they would be able to safeguard justice and moral freedom for all.

Here Dante – in the person of Marco Lombardo – expresses the main principles of his political thinking, which always points to the ways in which peace and order can be restored to the world through the implementation of Imperial justice. Yet he does not ignore the possibility of religiously minded solutions. Within the redemptive ethos of Purgatory, even darkness may produce its own kind of light. To reason in darkness may be to see with a clearer eye than when one is mesmerized by the detail of the external world. In *Paradiso* 26, where Dante also speaks of divine charity, that discussion, too, takes place in darkness – Dante having been temporarily blinded in his external senses by the radiance of the saints in Heaven. The same understanding seems to hold good there as in *Purgatorio* 16: we shall only perceive the peculiar logic of love when the eye abandons its apparently rational grip on earthly logic. It is true that the speaker in *Purgatorio* 17 and 18 is Virgil, and the darkness in which the discourse is conducted cannot fail to suggest, pathetically, the limitations from which his reasoning suffers – as a pagan to whom the full meaning of divine charity has never been revealed. None the less, the Christian Marco speaks of an inner light (75) that guides us to the discernment of good and ill. It is in darkness that this light is inwardly most visible.

Similar considerations arise in analysing why anger is associated with these philosophical debates. On the one hand, anger is, for Dante, an utter abandonment of rational control, a descent into bestial violence which leads – in the words of Pope Gregory the Great who, around the year 600, first devised the list of seven capital vices – 'to brawling, pride, uproar, indignation and blasphemy' (*Magna Moralia* 31: 45). The black smoke of the penance stands as a metaphor for such confusions. On the other hand, repentance for anger must clearly involve the rebuilding of a rational intelligence and the cultivation of precisely that submission to law that would inhibit 'brawling' and 'uproar'. It is thus crucial to Marco's argument – and to the ethics of the *Purgatorio* at large – that our true freedom should reside not in violence or the destruction of social bonds but in the free subjection of our wills (80) to the needs and demands of others. It is in this spirit that Marco – with vehemence reminiscent of his sins on earth – defends the rule of law and, more importantly, attempts, albeit abrasively, to serve Dante by answering his heartfelt questions. Here, too – as in the exercise of reason in darkness – there is a religious dimension. For if the temperamental dispositions of pride and envy can all be turned to good effect, so, likewise, can anger when it manifests itself as zeal or wholehearted commitment to a truth. Thus, discussing the type of anger which 'moves against vices', Aquinas writes:

> The passion of anger is useful, just like all the other movements of the sense appetites, in that it enables one to execute more promptly what reason dictates. Otherwise the sense appetites would exist to no purpose in man.
>
> *Summa Theologiae* 2a–2ae, 158, 1, ad.2; 8, ad.2

This is a particularly crucial doctrine for a poet such as Dante, who is constantly moved to polemical violence – evident even in the *Paradiso*, as, for example, at canto 27, lines 19–27, where he assaults the corruptions of the contemporary Church. In the context of the *Purgatorio*, Marco stands as a mirror image or perhaps even an *alter ego* of Dante himself, mustering – for criticism as well as approval – the passion for truth that Dante displays as much in his political epistles as in the fiction of the *Commedia*. There are similar grounds for Dante's treatment of sloth at the conclusion of this sequence. Time and energy cannot be frittered away. Once the truth is seen, it needs to be pursued to the utmost of one's powers.

Canto 16 draws Dante's philosophical interests into impressive combination with effects of voice, tone and imagery. Evoking the impact of the acrid black smoke – which forces the eyes to close and thus creates a double darkness – lines 1–15 speak of a perilous advance in which the travellers might, at any moment, encounter some unknown harm or even something that 'could kill'. The syntax of the passage is disturbed and apprehensive, its diction harsh – rhyming in Italian, at lines 11–15, on '*cozzo*' ('things'), '*sozzo*' ('filthy') and '*mozzo*' ('cut off') in a way that recalls some of the harsher passages of the *Inferno*. The blind lead the blind here, with only words to provide a means of connection. But the tightly formed duo of Dante and his rational guide, Virgil, is joined also in the attempt to maintain their threatened solidarity by voices singing deep within the fumes. And the hymn they are singing offers hope (beyond the hopes that right-minded community can generate) of a divine answer to the darkness of sin. This hymn is the '*Agnus Dei*' – 'Lamb of God that takes away the sins of the world' – sung when communion in the Eucharist begins (19). The words recall the sacrificial involvement in history that led Christ to His crucifixion. They also recall that the response of the Christian God to the outrage of sin was not anger but an act of love, accepting in his own person the burden of human guilt.

However – as is characteristic of Dante – religious hope is allowed to fade into the subtext of the canto, so that the reader's attention can fall upon how human beings themselves might work out their own salvation. Single selves – in an isolation that anger can only exacerbate – now seek, for their own good, salvation from other selves who share their darkness.

As Dante imagines the unseen presence of his own *alter ego*, the first exchanges are courteous. But Marco speaks already with pent-up indignation at the decadence of the modern world (47–8); and Dante too is bursting (53) with a desire to know why the world has become so corrupt. At line 64 Marco's righteous anger breaks through, and, heaving an all-but-comic sigh, he incriminates Dante, as well as the world at large, for his blindness to the obvious truth. You really do come from that world. And it is you, along with all other human beings, who are responsible for the disaster. The truth is that we cannot blame the stars for our fate. Nothing predetermines us to untruth and violence. It is true that the stars may have some influence on our temperaments (73–8) – and in the *Paradiso*, particularly at canto 22, Dante makes clear why it is important to allow a degree of astral influence. But the prime truth – which Dante examines in all its aspects throughout the next three cantos – is that we do possess free will, which is the intellectual appetite that allows us to be discerning in pursuit of our goals and desires.

In the course of this argument, Marco's voice shifts from antagonistic anger to an impassioned but lyrical contemplation of his theme. Particularly in lines 67–9, there is a notable patterning of alliterations and internal half-rhymes – on 'v' and 't', and '-ete' and '-ate' – along with an energetic repetition of 'pur' for emphasis (68) which, here as throughout, makes Marco's speech seem far more than an abstract statement of philosophical principle. (Contrast Virgil's voice at Purgatorio 17: 91–6.) This ensures that the 'necessity' which Marco wishes to deny is uttered (in its emphatic rhyming position) with all the scorn that, by now, one would expect of the angry penitent. A similarly energetic stress is produced by the enjambment that precedes the key phrase 'libero voler'/'free will' at line 76.

The lyricism and linguistic inventiveness that Dante brings to this philosophical manifesto is most apparent at lines 85–90 in his account of the 'little simple soul'. Dante's Italian is here marked by neologisms such as 'pargoleggia' – 'playing like a child' – and by daring choices of word, such as 'trastulla' at line 90, translated here as 'playful thrill', which could be used of the kind of game that a grandfather might play with his grandchildren. Elegant and exact use is made of the subjunctive 'sia' at line 86, to denote the as-yet-unrealized possibility of existence that the soul first enjoys in the mind of God. Throughout, internal rhymes and alliterations – '-etto', '-ieto', 'fatt-' – interweave with sonorous vowels – '-ui', '-ulla' – to generate both resonance and agility of movement.

At line 97, the character of the verse changes. Here Marco begins to assert the importance of law as a check on misguided forms of love, and simultaneously mounts an attack on the Church for interfering in the Imperial administration of divine law. His language now becomes prophetic, scathingly satirical and, like many prophecies, deeply obscure: the city of Rome once had two suns in its sky – the Empire and the Papacy – but now it has only one, the power of the pope (106–8). The sword is now dangerously united with the bishop's crook (109–11). The pope, as pastor, chews the cud but does not have a cloven hoof (97–9). (For the references in these lines, see notes below.)

Marco's voice does not relax in the final phase of the canto (115–45). However, it does shift its aim away from Rome itself to trace the destructive reverberations of Roman politics on the territories around the capital. Philosophy and prophecy here give way to an angry old man's denunciation of the modern world – comparable to Guido del Duca's diatribe in canto 14. In witheringly sarcastic phrases, Marco declares that the northern parts of Italy, from which he himself hails, have become so decadent that anyone who is embarrassed by displays of virtue may safely travel through them without fear of blushing. The tone lightens a little at **lines 130–38**, as the poet Dante allows the same sarcasm to be directed at his own *persona*. Certain men of Marco's generation, already longing for death, manage to maintain the habits of virtue. Yet Dante, it seems, has never heard of them, and this to Marco is, still further, a sign of degeneracy. He ends the interview with brusque impatience when, seeing a light dawning beyond the darkness, he plunges once more into the depths of the black smoke – the symbol of both his angry obfuscation of mind and his righteous indignation.

Notes

25–7 The Italian text speaks of telling time *'per calendi'*, which is to say by the civil calendar employed in ancient Rome and still in use in thirteenth-century Italy.

73–5 To assess how far Dante is prepared to admit the influence of the stars, see *Paradiso* 22: 111–17.

97–9 Dante draws his metaphor from the dietary laws of the Jews, as laid down in Leviticus 11: 3–4, which stipulates:

> Whatsoever parteth the hoof, and is cloven footed, and cheweth the cud, among the beasts, that shall ye eat. Nevertheless these shall ye not eat of them that chew the cud, or of them that divide the hoof: as the camel, because he cheweth the cud, but divideth not the hoof; he is unclean unto you.

106–8 Papal propaganda argued that the Empire was subject to the Papacy and stood in the same relation to the Church as the moon does to the sun. However, believing that Church and Empire are equal agents of God's will, Dante speaks here and elsewhere of Rome uniquely possessing two suns in its sky. (Compare *De Monarchia* 3:4 and *Epistle* 5: 1.3.)

115–17 The land watered by the Adige and the Po rivers comprises most of northern Italy, in particular Lombardy–Emilia and the march of Treviso. These territories began to oppose the Emperor Frederick II (see introduction to *Inferno*, p. xvii) in the 1220s, and thus contributed to the disastrous (in Dante's view) diminution of Imperial power in Italy.

124–6 Currado da Palazzo served as representative of Charles I of Anjou in Florence in 1276 and was captain of the Guelfs in 1277, becoming *podestà* (or chief magistrate) of Piacenza in 1288. Gherardo da Camino is known to have been captain-general of Treviso from 1283. He was a supporter of the White Guelfs and was a patron of poets. Gherardo's daughter Gaia married Tolberto da Cammino in 1311. Sources differ as to whether she lived a notoriously wicked or a famously virtuous life. Guido da Castello (c. 1235–c. 1316) was a member of the noble Roberti family of Reggio Emilia, and is 'better named/the "honest Lombard"' by the French because of his honesty in dealing with French travellers who passed through Lombardy.

130–32 The reference is to Numbers 18: 20–24, in which the tribe of Levi is established as the source of priests among the Jews but is denied any territorial portion of the Promised Land.

CANTOS 17 AND 18

Visions of anger punished. The arrival at the terrace of sloth. Virgil, in canto 17, discusses the bonds of love between creator and creature and outlines the seven capital vices. In canto 18, Virgil, continuing his discussion, speaks of the nature of love. The penitent slothful appear. Visions of zeal.

Commentary

The second part of canto 17 (17: 91–139) and the first half of canto 18 (18: 1–75) develop themes, concerning the freedom of the will, which were first raised by Marco Lombardo in canto 16 and offer a philosophical account of sin, freedom and love that is central to all Dante's thinking. The speaker throughout is Virgil, responding to Dante's questions, and his style is cool and rational. In a number of ways these themes anticipate the thinking that will underlie the *Paradiso*, as well as providing a guide to the moral system of the *Purgatorio*. (To arrive at a complete account of the issues raised in cantos 17 and 18, it is useful to read them in conjunction with *Purgatorio* 25.)

In these two cantos, as in canto 16, philosophy is embodied in a narrative and imaginative context that cannot be ignored in any full reading. As will be seen, it is significant that this discussion largely takes place during Dante's second night on the mountain, and also that it is introduced by a sequence of waking dreams, displaying examples of anger as violent as the examples of mildness that began the episode. It is equally significant that the second half of canto 18 deals, in an unusually abbreviated sequence, with the sin of sloth, and shows the slothful penitents running through the night with clamorous and unnatural energy. There is, however, drama, too, in Virgil's speeches. And it should not be thought – as it was once – that for Dante there is any division between poetry and philosophy. The clarity and balance that he attributes to Virgil are reflected in a language that replicates the processes of effective thought, even though Virgil (or natural reason) is at the limit of his powers.

Like Marco Lombardo in canto 16 when he speaks of the relationship between the 'little simple soul' and its maker, Virgil is concerned in cantos 17 and 18 with the relationship between God and the human being, with love both of God and of lesser goods, and with our freedoms of mind and will – which involve both the freedom to sin and also the freedom to live in the light of the ultimate good that underlies our existence. (See introduction pp. xxvii–xxxiii.) However, where Marco speaks with angry enthusiasm, attempting to bring his listener to a new and urgent understanding, Virgil goes back, coolly and therapeutically, to the first logical principles of which his pupil must already be aware – as at 17: 93: 'You know that.' It is a matter of logic that a bond of love exists between any creator and the objects which that creator makes. To paraphrase: The true craftsman or artist wishes that a certain object should come into existence. When that object arrives at existence, then, in pleasing the eye of its maker and fulfilling its intended function, it might be said to 'love' the existence it has been given and the maker that first gave it that existence. The lines that express this thought (17: 91–3) are characterized by balanced rhythms, clear syntax and an emphatic observance of the etymological link between 'creat-or'/'creator' and 'creat-ura'/'creat-ed'. Yet there is also a subdued pathos here. Virgil may understand the logic, and it may be useful as a point of Socratic pedagogy to lead Dante back to first principles, but, as a pagan, he cannot know the Christian God as a personal creator or benefit from any such relationship. Here – as in his first words at *Inferno* 1: 67 ('*Non omo* . . .') – Virgil's words begin here with a negative ('Né . . . né'/'Neither . . . nor'), rejecting all confusing appeals to emotion so as to clarify the mind of his pupil, yet implicitly acknowledging that his own experience of this truth remains in the negative, as a merely formulaic understanding. There is also an impulse of repressed tenderness in these lines, as Virgil, addressing Dante as his dearest (or, in Italian, 'little') son ('*figliuol*'), demonstrates a feeling for the bond between creator and creature which, for him, can only be sustained in terms of intellectual conversation with his pupil.

Pursuing his initial logic, Virgil speaks of the relationship within the human psyche between natural and intellectual love. Both types of love have their part to play in our pursuit of good. There is no suggestion that by 'natural love' (17: 94) Virgil here means to indicate some instinctual or lower urge that needs to be repressed. On the contrary, 'natural love' here is the love of, and desire for, existence which is unconsciously present in all created things – whether vegetative, animal or rational – and unfailingly operates within them, impelling them towards the fulfilment of their goals in existence. Dante never ceases to celebrate the action of this 'natural love' (see, for instance, *Paradiso* 1: 109–42), and there are echoes throughout the present sequence of Virgil's initial proposition. But intellectual love is another matter. This in its rational (rather than angelic) form is unique to human creatures. And, properly exercised, intellectual love can lead us consciously to appreciate our position in the scheme of existence. We shall be given credit by our Creator for having done so, and condemned if we fail to do so. In this sense – though there are problems here which Dante goes on to address in canto 18 – we are free (as vegetables and animals are *not*) to form our own place in existence and collaborate in our own making. But we are also free to work against our maker (17: 102). This, in the final analysis, is an illogical thing to do. But it is the origin of sin. And, in parallel with Marco's account of how the 'little simple soul' can be distracted from God by lesser goods (*Purgatorio* 16: 91–3), Virgil proceeds in the concluding part of canto 17 to discuss the ways in which sin can lead the soul away from its natural orientation.

Sin, as Virgil presents it, is not directly an offence against God but rather against ourselves, in so far as rational love chooses to ignore the promptings of the natural love that, unfailingly, impels our existences. In fact, even in committing sin, when rational love abandons its innate sense of direction, we are still, confusedly, seeking an ultimate good (17: 127–9). This confusion also distorts our perception of the many lesser goods – the legitimate pleasures of the world – which rightly have their own contribution to make to our lives. In sin, however, we lose the capacity to recognize how destructive – and self-destructive – our misapplied freedom might be. Love in its natural

form can never seek its own destruction (17: 106–8), since by defi-
nition all things have a natural disposition to sustain themselves in
existence. We are thus safe from self-hatred. Equally, we know, as
rational beings, that we do not bring ourselves to life or are ever
wholly 'independent, separate' (17: 109). And since the source of our
existence is God, we, strictly speaking, cannot hate God either. (In the
Inferno 3, where 'the good of intellect' has been entirely lost, the sins
of suicide and blasphemy are represented as delusional expressions of
hatred against self and hatred of the divine.) So sin, in the worst cases
– as in pride, envy and anger – is hatred displaced in its destructive
effects from ourselves and God towards our neighbour. And sin in
every form is a misapprehension of inherent goodness.

The scheme that Virgil offers at 17: 115–26, detailing the nature of
the seven capital vices, corresponds to the scheme that Dante adopts
in the *Purgatorio*, where, terrace by terrace, the effects of these seven
vices are fully dramatized. However, Virgil's words are an attempt to
re-invigorate the exercise of rational love, and to provide a point of
reference for all the surrounding sequences of the narrative. Pride,
envy and anger, as we have seen in previous commentaries, mistake
the true nature of excellence. Pride directs itself in hatred against a
neighbour in the mistaken belief that one person's good requires that
it be exalted above all others. Envy, somewhat similarly, yearns for
the destruction of all forms of excellence, for fear of being over-
shadowed by any of them. Anger perceives the damage that others
wrongfully inflict upon the good, and mistakenly seeks to take revenge
for that wrong – as if two wrongs could make a right. Sloth – which
is the fourth of the vices, and is to be purged on the terrace at which
Dante has now arrived – is a particular case which emphasizes that
sin can be the result of ill-regulated love, whereby we do not set our
minds with sufficient zeal to pursue the course along which natural
love impels us. The remaining three sins are greed (an excessive love
of things), avarice (an excessive love of power and money), and lust
(an excessive love of persons). These are dealt with only cursorily at
17: 124–7. Here, as with sloth, there is a misregulation of our energies,
expressed in these cases as excess, and, in each case, the mind appre-
hends a good – in things, in social efficiency, or in persons – but
distorts the good by making it an end in itself. These goods are only
good when seen in the perspective of the divine goodness that created
them. Dante is left to work out this diagnosis for himself. The canto
ends with that question in mind, stimulating further inquiry on the
part of Virgil's pupil.

In canto 18, the first question that Dante raises concerns love and the ways in which love arises in the human mind. The answer that Virgil gives (18: 22–39) is strictly philosophical. His words in large part represent a return – in more abstract terms – to the vivid account that Marco Lombardo gave of how the childlike soul – created out of God's delight in its existence – is misguidedly impelled towards lesser pleasures. However, Virgil makes no reference to the divine Creator here. His concern is largely with the ways in which the mind receives stimuli from the world around us and translates our physical experience of external things into intellectual love. (In canto 19 Dante considers the ways in which, inwardly, the mind may itself generate sin through self-delusion.)

This account leads to a further question that Dante raises at 18: 40–45. In concentrating on the mechanics of perception, the impression may have been made that love arises merely as response to external stimuli, and that we are therefore conditioned by externals in our conception of love. In which case, are we free at all when we experience love? We know from Marco Lombardo's words at canto 16, lines 64–78 that we are not finally influenced by any astral determination. But could it be that love exerts its own subtler form of deterministic influence? This was a question that arose in many forms in early Italian poetry – which was almost obsessively concerned with the effects of love, and which Dante himself represented dramatically in the case of Francesca in *Inferno* 5. Now, Virgil clear-headedly analyses the issues that lay beneath Francesca's confusions. There are questions here – as Virgil acknowledges before providing his response – which can only fully be answered by Beatrice, who, in the *Paradiso*, will demonstrate what it means to live in free communion with the generosity of divine love. (See *Paradiso* 3–5, especially 5: 19–24.) For the moment, however, he is concerned to identify a capacity in the human mind that actively censors and controls our inclinations to love and consciously reconciles (as the previous canto envisaged) our conscious decisions with the pre-conscious activity of our natural love.

Throughout, this discussion (still taking place in the dark) recalls Marco Lombardo's previous insistence that we possess an inner light which allows us to discern the inner impulses of our nature. The action of the mind and the interaction of one mind with another are spoken of constantly in metaphors of luminosity (18: 10–18). The canto is also highly technical in its terminology and argumentation, as well as being far more compressed than many comparable pieces of philosophy would be. Dante as poet here enters into debate, no doubt deliberately, with contemporaries such as Guido Cavalcanti who had also attempted to reconcile philosophy with poetry. (Compare with *Purgatorio* 25.) It is likewise an indication of how mind can speak to mind across time (regardless of revelation) that Dante throughout follows a broadly Aristotelian conception of the mind and its various operations.

The modern reader may feel less confident than Dante that connections such as this can be made. From the first, some attention needs to be paid (here and for the rest of the *Commedia*) to terms and conceptions – such as free will and even love – that may now have altered their meaning. (For an expert view of these issues, see P. Boyde, *Perception and Passion in Dante's Comedy* (1993).)

In 18: 19–20 the argument draws its principles from Aristotle's *De Anima* and from scholastic followers of the Aristotelian school. The process of 'apprehension' is one that humans share with all other forms of animal life and is a direct response to impressions received from external things (which are said, at 18: 22, to be true in that they do not exist as a result only of such mental activity as Dante describes in, say, *Purgatorio* 19: 7–15). Apprehension takes place in the 'common sense' – which, for scholastics, was a physical organ thought to be located in the frontal lobe of the brain. The common sense is 'common' in so far as it is able to create a synthesis from the various sensations that are conducted along the nerves from external stimuli. In the act of apprehension, these disparate impressions are drawn together in terms of such general features as shape, size and number. (These features are described as 'common sensibles' so as to distinguish them from such specific manifestations of sensation as colour, sound, odour, taste and texture.) This composite is usually referred to as an 'image'. Apprehension then delivers the image to the centre of the brain where a distinct faculty 'estimates' the image. It is important again to emphasize that this 'estimation' takes place in all animals, and equally important to emphasize that the 'estimation' performed will tell the animal that performs it whether the object ahead of it is good or bad for it, whether it is something to be feared and avoided or something that will prove nutritious, comfortable or in some other way pleasurable. The mind thus forms 'intentions' – which are 'intent' on what is good or bad about the object. To love something 'intentionally' is thus rightly and inevitably rooted in our animal nature, and, if we take seriously Dante's conception of 'natural love', it will not seem strange to say that even good and bad, in their primary sense, refer not to abstract moral qualities but rather to those properties in an object that are likely to contribute to, or else damage, the proper operation of specific modes of existence. Good nourishes us, as good soil nourishes a plant. Bad contaminates us, as poisoned water might. It is true that human beings, endowed with rational as well as animal attributes, have more complex natures to nourish or protect than do animals or vegetables. Still, the principle remains the same, and may even be compared (18: 28–30) to the natural actions of fire burning upwards. (Compare, again, *Paradiso* 1.) So, when the human mind 'inclines' consciously to what pleases it, the desire for that object will be entirely legitimate. This is love, and love will be satisfied when the objects of its intentions (18: 33) is reached and feeds it to the full.

It should not, however, be supposed that human minds – or even the minds of animals – are unerring or immune to error. This itself is a philosophical error which Dante probably attributes, at 18: 34–6, to the Epicurean school of philosophy. The 'wax' to which he refers at 18: 37–9 may be taken to mean the raw material of the senses, while the 'seal' is the perceptual machinery which has already been discussed. The metaphor of wax and seal derives from Aristotle's *De Anima* 2: 12: 42a and was also taken up by scholastic philosophers such as Aquinas and Albertus Magnus. Both the material and the process are inherently good – in the sense that they contribute to the furtherance of existence. But in particular situations, the seal applied to this wax may waver and produce a false result – and animals are as capable of making mistakes as human beings are. (Virgil does not say why this wavering occurs. But in *Paradiso* 13: 76–8 Dante speaks of how nature is an artist whose hand, in the fallen state of the world, may sometimes tremble in applying its intended signature.)

After receiving an answer so rigorously concerned with the natural workings of the mind, Dante's next question seeks assurance that our specifically human freedom of choice remains, and that, consequently, just rewards may be allocated after an assessment of our conscious decisions (18: 40–45). As before, Virgil says nothing directly about the actions of divine justice, nor about grace, redemption or charity. His approach is again philosophical, indeed scientific, and aims to demonstrate this by inductive reasoning from observable evidence. Our freedom is to be inferred from the way that human beings act. The argument concludes with a reference to how the moral laws that were first worked out by classical philosophers depend upon the existence of the inward freedom that Dante is now asking to have defined (18: 67–9). Moral laws are possible only because we are free and responsible beings. But in arguing this case, Virgil recognizes that there are areas of thought – eventually to be filled by the certainties of revealed religion – in which invisible realities can properly be known by arguments from visible effects.

The terms of this argument are once more Aristotelian in origin, and three in particular will henceforth be of especial importance whenever Dante debates the structure of created things. These are 'substance', 'form' and '*virtù*'. (Compare, for instance, the account of the creation of the world offered in *Paradiso* 29. See also the glossary to the *Paradiso*.) 'Substance' for Dante and his scholastic sources emphatically does not mean, as in modern usage, a material substance, but is rather the potentiality to be an independent, 'subsisting' being. 'Form' is the shaping power (which might now be explained as DNA) that gives a specific character to independently existing beings. '*Virtù*' does not refer solely to moral virtue but also means the power imbued in all members of a species to operate in conformity with their specific nature. In the case of human beings, this power is the discursive intellect. (See *Purgatorio* 25: 67–75.)

Applying these terms in canto 17, Virgil first of all establishes that the characteristic actions of the 'form' and '*virtù*' that make each specific thing what it is cannot themselves be seen but are known only from their effects. This is true of trees, where the virtue of growth as such cannot be seen, but the green of their foliage, as the result of that growth, can be seen, and growth inferred from that. It is the same with the action of the human will on which our freedom depends (18: 55–60). A more fully theological understanding of where the mind comes from and how it operates is offered in *Purgatorio* 25. But working within his philosophical limit, Virgil here posits – but does not name – a set of 'primal concepts', or 'prime desirables'. These are ultimate realities such as beauty, truth and goodness. The mind, set on these intellectual compass points, shows its powers of ratiocination by working towards the unknown from the known. In that respect, ratiocinative action is analogous to the unseen power that drives bees to make honey. But in bees that power is a direct expression of the primal will. In human beings, whose minds are consciously set upon the '*primi appetibili*', there exists a power which allows them to collect all their thoughts into one to move in harmony with their primal natures as unerringly as the zealous (but not conscious) bee might do in making honey. This power provides the measure which can be applied to all possibly divergent thoughts and which thus acts as a censor or arbiter of intellectual aims. We are, according to Virgil's account, free in so far as we can apply this censor (18: 70–75).

Contrasted with the quiet tones that Virgil adopts are the waking visions that appear in 17: 13–39 and the frantic energy displayed by the slothful at 18: 97–145. The visions mark the point at which Dante emerges from the dark smoke of the terrace of anger to find that the sun is already setting. The slothful appear at the point when Dante, exhausted, is about to fall asleep for a second time in his journey up the mountain. These passages contain, respectively, the 'bridle' appropriate to anger and the 'whip' that offers examples of zeal to the slothful. The stories told here in miniature, to exemplify the dangers of anger, refer to events of extreme and destructive violence. (See notes below.) There is a correspondingly violent energy in the examples of zeal. Here Dante yokes together two decisions – each carried through with courageous vigour – that completely changed the world. One is the decision of the Virgin Mary to accept her role as the mother of God. The other – an example taken from the Roman civil wars – depicts the military ruthlessness of Julius Caesar in a campaign that laid the foundation of the Roman empire.

Each set of examples contributes to the philosophical themes that the sequence pursues. In the examples of anger, the inner light of which Marco speaks at canto 16, line 75 is shown to be stimulated by illuminations deriving directly from the heavens. It can be ignited even when the natural light of day has disappeared, and can endow us with a power to contemplate the most tragic instances of human destructiveness. This does not, however, take away the urgent responsibility that human beings must bear – as exemplified in the decisions of Caesar and the Virgin Mary – in directing their natural energies to productive ends.

This second point is also made by the one encounter that Dante manages to have with the slothful as they rush by him (18: 91–3) as rapturously noisy as crowds taking part in a drunken bacchic orgy. Drawing Dante and Virgil along into the stampede, a single figure speaks (18: 114–26). This is a certain Gerard (d. 1187), who was abbot of the opulent and strategically powerful abbey of San Zeno in Verona (a city in which Dante spent several years of his exile). Little is known about Gerard. He did, however, serve as abbot during the reign of the Emperor Frederick Barbarossa (1122–90). And his words here express an understanding of how power may be both rightly and wrongly used. It may be that Dante implicitly criticizes Gerard for the sloth that the luxuries of monastic life could induce. (See *Paradiso* 21: 130–42.) Yet the abbot can see how appropriate it was for Barbarossa, in 1167, to exert his imperial power against the rebellious Milanese (18: 118–20). He can also recognize, at 18: 121–6, the corrupt example offered by Alberto della Scala (d. 1301), the local overlord of Verona, who installed his illegitimate son as abbot of San

Zeno. Alberto already has 'one foot in the grave'. He was mortally ill in 1300 – the date at which Dante's journey through the other world takes place – and died in 1301. Alberto's two legitimate sons, Bartolommeo and Can Grande, became Dante's patrons, of whom he speaks with elevated praise in *Paradiso* 17: 70–92.

Notes to canto 17

13–16   The German philosopher and theologian Albert Magnus writes of the imagination in Aristotle's *De somno et vigilia* 3: 1.8–9:

> The celestial forms directed at us, when touching our bodies, move them with great strength and impress their powers, though they are not perceived because of the tumult of outward distractions. When the soul is separated from the senses, in whatever way, then the motions are perceived.
>
> Quoted in T. Gregory, *Mundana sapientia* (Rome, 1992)

19–39   Three examples of anger are offered here. The first refers to the story of Philomel and Procne, involving infanticide and cannibalism. (See notes to canto 9.) Dante's source – much compressed and altered – is *Metamorphoses* 6: 412–676. The second is drawn from Esther 3–7, 10. Here, the 'one crucified' is Haman, chief minister of Ahasuerus, king of Persia, whose wife is the Jewish queen Esther, daughter of Mordecai. When Mordecai refuses to bow to Haman, Haman orders all the Jews in Persia to be exterminated. Esther intervenes and persuades Ahasuerus to execute Haman. The third is the story of Lavinia, drawn from the *Aeneid* 7: 341–53 and 12: 595–607. Lavinia, daughter of the king of Latium, was promised as wife to Aeneas (who fought against the realm of Latium) in preference to Turnus. Amata, Lavinia's mother, is incensed by this decision, having vowed never to agree to such a marriage, and kills herself.

67–9   'Blessed are the peacemakers' (Matthew 5: 9).

91–6   In a similar vein, Saint Thomas Aquinas writes:

> God, as he is the universal good from which all natural goods depend, is naturally loved by all.
>
> *Summa Theologiae* 1a q. 60a. 5 and 4

and:

As natural cognition is always true, so natural love is always right, since natural love is nothing other than the natural inclination grafted in us by the author of nature.

Summa Theologiae 1a q. 60 a. 1 and 3

Aristotle had written: 'We are lords of our own actions, in so far as we can choose this or that' (*Nichomachean Ethics* 3, 2 1111b). (Compare with *Purgatorio* 27: 142.)

112 The technical term *restat* draws attention to the method of scholastic argument that Dante attributes to Virgil, and means roughly 'after careful analysis there remains . . .'

Notes to canto 18

58–60 Virgil's natural imagery here recalls the language of his *Georgics*, which are poems concerning various forms of farming, including bee-keeping.

79–81 The moon travelling from west to east (and thus in a direction opposite the daily motion of the heavens) has reached the same point in the Zodiac that the sun occupies when, viewed from Rome, it sets between Corsica and Sardinia.

82–4 Pietola (in Roman times known as Andes) is the village near Mantua where Virgil was born. (Compare *Purgatorio* 6: 72.)

91–3 The rivers Ismenus and Asopus ran close to Thebes, where Bacchus was worshipped in the ecstatic dances of the Bacchantes.

100–111 The 'whips' and 'bridles' of sloth are abbreviated, and though, as in every other case, they appear at the beginning and end of the episode, this episode is so short that it occupies only the last 57 lines of the canto. The encouraging examples at the beginning, at line 100, refer firstly to the excitement and urgency with which the Virgin Mary, after the Annunciation, ran to tell her cousin Elisabeth about her pregnancy. (See Luke 1: 39–40.) The second refers to an episode from the Roman civil wars, as recounted in Julius Caesar's *De Bello Civili* 1: 34–87 and Lucan's *Pharsalia* 3: 453–5, which is probably the source of Dante's wording. In 49 BC Caesar showed characteristic rapidity and decisiveness when he organized the siege of Marseilles (held by his opponent Pompey), and then marched his legions into northern Spain, conquering Pompey's stronghold at Ilerda (modern Lerida), securing, within forty days, the whole western region of the Roman world.

133–8 The 'bridles', as examples of feebleness of spirit, refer to

Numbers 14: 20–23, where the Israelites who are shown to have offended God by their lack of faith are prevented from living long enough to enter the Promised Land. The second, parallel example refers to the *Aeneid* 5: 604–776. As Aeneas is journeying to his own 'promised land', the women among his band of refugees set fire to his ships – on the anniversary of the death of Aeneas's father – in the hope of ending their wanderings. Jupiter extinguishes the flames with a rainstorm. Those who are unwilling to travel with Aeneas are left behind in Sicily in disgrace.

CANTO 19

Dante dreams of the Siren and witnesses the exposure of her fallaciousness. The avaricious, including Pope Hadrian V, engaged in their penance.

Commentary

The long darkness that reigns over the central sequences of the *Purgatorio* begins to be broken in the opening phase of canto 19 by a dream (not, as in previous cantos, a waking vision) that disturbs the fitful sleep of Dante's second night on the mountain. This dream brings before Dante's eyes (7–24) a figure who is, at first, repellently distorted in all her limbs and features, but is then transformed by the attention she receives into a figure who, in richly erotic rhythms, claims that she is the Siren who once led Ulysses astray. (See *Inferno* 26). At **line 26**, an unnamed lady appears who alerts Virgil (as perceived, still, in Dante's dream) to the danger into which Dante's half-conscious mind is falling. Finally (in one of the very few passages of the *Commedia* that remotely displays any repugnance over sexuality), Dante dreams at **lines 31–3** that Virgil strips the Siren and reveals the stench that issues from her sexual parts. On awakening, however, these fevered imaginings immediately fade and, as in the dream of *Purgatorio* 9, the facts concealed beneath the fantasy prove to be, simply, that Virgil, in urgent but temperate terms, has already three times at least told Dante to wake up (34–6).

In one respect, the early parts of the dream (as also in *Purgatorio* 9) represent an internalization – or a summary in imaginative form – of the issues that have occupied Dante's mind in the preceding sequence of the poem. Where the will fails to exercise a fully conscious understanding of its own best aims and purposes, it becomes hallucinated by the attraction of lesser things. Sin is nothing but a confused apprehension of the good. To this fundamental diagnosis, however, Dante now adds a strong emphasis on the complicity of the human intelligence in the misapprehension of good. It is through Dante's mistaken gaze – applying to the Siren the sort of attention that only Beatrice merits – that the self-evident deficiencies of the Siren are transformed into an imagined attraction. There remains, even so, the miraculous orientation to the true good which is here represented by the lady who speaks to Virgil. She is not Beatrice, but anticipates the role that Beatrice will perform in the Earthly Paradise. It is equally true that the faculty of rational discrimination – as represented by Virgil – remains alert and capable of restoring us to our proper, waking strengths.

In a second respect, the dream (which, in its representation of the lady, is as much a vision as a dream) points forwards as well as back. (Compare the truly visionary dream of *Purgatorio* 27.) In particular, the sequence introduces a theme that will come increasingly into prominence over the next three cantos, the theme of conversion. By canto 21, Dante will be ready to recount (or rather, invent) the story of the conversion of the Roman poet Statius. But, having established that free will is the central factor in human personality, Dante now goes on to explore an ultimate freedom that is located at the intersection of will and divine grace, whereby the mind is able to free itself entirely from the hold of ingrained habits – be they sensuous, emotional or intellectual – and embark entirely upon a new life. The transformations that the mind performs in its misguided attention to the Siren are evidence of a capacity for malignant and retrograde conversion. But, together, the lady and Virgil represent a wholly different capacity, through which Dante as the protagonist can proceed out of the darkness towards the broad daylight of the third day on the mountain (37–42), and to an unambiguously trustworthy encounter with an angel – who, in contrast to the Siren, has wings as white as a swan's (46).

The central factor in the experience of conversion is a change in the definition and orientation of selfhood. Notably, the first person pronoun 'I' – '*io*' in Italian – is both emphatic and peculiarly shifting in the Siren's seductive song, providing a slurred refrain – '*cantav(a i)o*' – at line 19 which resolves into the four indistinct 'm's of line 20: '*che 'marinari in mezzo mar dismago*'. This may be contrasted directly with the clear articulate insistence on her own selfhood that characterizes Beatrice's first address to Dante at *Purgatorio* 30: 73. Whereas the Siren attempts to entangle Dante in the cocoon of his own half-realized urges and compulsions, Beatrice (partly anticipated by the lady of the second dream) insists that Dante's attention should be directed outward to beings other than himself, to her own being and that of the divinity she reflects. A self is constituted out of not only its own satisfactions but also out of its responsiveness to all beings in the created and uncreated universe. Conversion is not a single event but the freedom to pursue and continually refresh that responsiveness. So it is that Dante concludes the second phase of the canto at lines 64–9 with a comparison between himself and a hunting falcon. (Compare *Purgatorio* 14: 148–51; also *Paradiso* 19: 61–9.) The cloying indulgence of his dream disappears in the sharply drawn simile of a falcon preparing to fly in pursuit of appropriate food. Air, flight, keenness of concentration are all evoked, as the bird begins to launch itself (as Dante will in the *Paradiso*) around the varied horizons of the created order.

The third phase of the canto (70–145) offers a subtle psychological close-up of conversion at work in a senior member of the Church hierarchy, Pope Innocent IV's nephew Ottobono dei Fieschi (*c.* 1215–76), who became Hadrian V in 1276, dying after only 38 days in office. The Church is properly the custodian of conversion and of those who seek constant renewal of their devotion to God through the liturgy and the sacraments. To Dante, the Church of his time had failed disastrously to fulfil this office, and canto 19 of the *Inferno* traces in grotesquely comic terms the loss of personal identity that ensues when the Church fails to maintain a responsibility for the new life it offers. For the most part, the Church of Dante's day is condemned bitterly for pursuing, quite differently, a conversion in the direction of the Siren that leads it to devote all its attention, avariciously, to the winning of material treasure and possessions. Of all the popes mentioned in the *Commedia*, Hadrian is one of only two (from the contemporary, as opposed to the primitive Church) who are not consigned to Hell. None the less, Hadrian admits that, until he assumed the papal office, he had been guilty of avarice. Avarice is the sin for which penance is performed in this circle of Purgatory and, throughout Hadrian's long and tormented speech, he still struggles with the residual effects of this failing. But his physical posture, face down, deprived of any sight of the sky, is both the worst of punishments and a sign of his being 'turned around' or converted. Singing a verse from Psalm 118 (73), Hadrian displays his obsession with the things of the earth, but transforms this into penitential awareness. As he speaks of his belated conversion on earth (106), his sense of the material advantages that he at one time sought struggles painfully with the effects of conscience which, in his case and in his alone, first dawned on him when, at his election, he arrived at a true understanding of the Church. His speech is marked by phrases of Latin Scripture. These can be seen as marks of both piety and also an authoritarian affirmation of dignity and power. But his whole purpose in Purgatory is to recover a sense of justice – and a proper sense of proportion in the distribution of temporal goods. (See commentaries on *Inferno* 6 and *Purgatorio* 23.) This can be achieved only by an act of absolute dispossession (115–26). So, brusquely, he rejects any attempt on Dante's part to show him the honour due to his office (127–41). What remains (in contrast to the distractions generated by the Siren) is the thought that his virtuous niece Alagia might pray for him.

Notes

4–6   Geomancy involves the drawing of omens from signs made in the earth, usually by the random tapping of sticks on sand. The Greater Fortune, thought to be the most favourable sign, is seen when these marks resemble six of the stars in the constellations Aquarius and Pisces.

49–51   '*Qui lugent*' is the Latin text of the second beatitude of the Sermon on the Mount (Matthew 5: 4): '[Blessed are those] who mourn.'

73–5   'I cleave to the ground.' These lines quote Psalm 119: 25, which in Latin reads '*pavimento*' where the Hebrew text may be rendered more accurately as 'dust'. This verse, in the commentary tradition, was taken as a warning against any attachment to riches.

97–9   The magisterial Latin phrase may be translated as: 'Know that I was the successor of Peter.'

100–102   The river Lavagna runs between Sestri Levante and Chiavari in Liguria. Hadrian's family, the Fieschi of Genoa, were counts of Lavagna.

136–8   These words – to be translated as 'neither shall they marry' – are spoken by Jesus to the Saduccees (who denied physical resurrection of the body) in Matthew 22: 30, and may here be taken to mean that in Heaven there will be no social ranks.

142–5   These lines refer to Alagia dei Fieschi, daughter of Ottobono's brother Niccolò, married to Moroello Malaspina of the Lunigiana, whose guest Dante had been around 1306. (See notes to *Purgatorio* 8.) Women of the Fieschi clan were otherwise notorious for their licentiousness.

CANTO 20

Avarice. Dante listens to Hugo Capet's attack on the political ambitions of the French. Mount Purgatory is shaken by an earthquake.

Commentary

Where canto 19 concentrates on the spiritual biography of a pope, canto 20 focuses on a political figure, Hugo Capet (*c.* 940–96), founder of the Capetian dynasty in France. Hugo utters a long lament (40–123), penitential in spirit and satirical in tone, on the crimes perpetrated by his descendants. He, like Pope Hadrian, is purging the sin of avarice, and avarice is the 'sick weed' which those who came after him cultivated, to the extent that it now 'overshadows every Christian land' (43–4). There is no historical reason to suggest that Hugo ever repented of his actions in establishing the Capetian legacy or was converted, as Pope Hadrian was, at any point in his earthly life. However, in a canto heavy with ironic devices, it may be considered a stroke of polemical irony on Dante's part to give Hugo so central a role, emphasizing precisely how much Hugo Capet had to answer for, even if he did not himself know it.

Hugo's speech is particularly concerned, at **lines 61–93**, with the involvement of French princes in the politics of thirteenth-century Italy (which Dante deplored) and their sometimes stormy alliance with the papacy against the Empire. In these lines particular prominence is given to Charles I of Anjou (1226–85), the youngest child of Louis VIII of France. The turning point in Charles's fortunes came in 1246 when, through marriage, he became count of Provence. It was at this point, too (61–3), that Capetian power – hitherto malignant but ineffectual – began to menace Italy. Supported by Pope Clement IV, Charles was invested as king of Sicily in 1266. But this favour brought Charles, on behalf of the papacy, into direct conflict with the Hohenstauffen rulers of Sicily descended from Emperor Frederick II – whose Imperial cause Dante broadly supported. Though Charles, like Hugo, is granted a place in Purgatory (*Purgatorio* 7: 113), his campaigns in the Italian peninsula led ultimately to the extinction of Imperial claims. (See commentary to *Purgatorio* 3.) Further destabilization followed (70–78), particularly in the 'Sicilian Vespers' of 1282, a revolt in which the Sicilian populace rose against their French overlords and installed an Aragonese dynasty under Peter III. (Compare *Purgatorio* 7: 112 and *Paradiso* 8: 73–5.)

At every point in canto 20, avarice is identified as the driving force in the ambitions of the Capetian dynasty, which ranged from Sicily to Normandy and to the Low Countries (46–8, 64–6). With hindsight, one may see the expansionist programme pursued by the Capetians as the remote beginnings of a modern nation state, fuelled by the resources of a particular economy and expanding under the impetus of territorial gain. But national ambition of this sort stood in direct opposition to Dante's demand for a universal and divinely sanctioned Empire. The Emperor, ruling all by right was, for Dante, logically incapable of avarice and consequently able to uphold perfect justice in the distribution of earthly goods. The political appetites of the French were, by contrast, those of the 'wolf bitch' (10), endlessly famished, never satisfied and always disruptive of the welfare of those around them. (Compare with the wolf of avarice in *Inferno* 1, who is opposed by Virgil's Imperial vision and by the promise that a mysterious defender of justice, the '*veltro*' or 'hound', will eventually put the wolf to flight.)

Despite the political detail of canto 20, the primary contrast that Dante pursues here is not that between France and Empire as historical powers. His concern is to open the widest of religious perspectives, measuring the malignant advance of avariciously partisan policies against the providential purposes of the Christian God, who entered history and redeemed it from the grip of sin through the Incarnation and Atonement. (Compare *Paradiso* 6 and 7.) It is part of Hugo's penitential conversion that he should now be able to recognize the workings of these purposes. The dramatic design of the canto sustains at all points Dante's own vision of history. In his view, the Empire is the vessel of divine justice. But so is the individual. In acts of conversion such as Hugo now exemplifies, the individual comes to understand, in a moment of revelation, the divine power that operates beneath the troubled surface of the temporal universe.

This is especially evident in the dramatic conclusion. At lines 127–8 the mountain of Purgatory begins to tremble in the grip of an earthquake. Hitherto, the mountain has provided a firm footing for the endeavours of the penitents and Dante as traveller. Now an intervention occurs, the revelation of a divine action which is beyond the comprehension of the human mind and yet is the foundation on which our temporal being and activities are bound to depend. From the first lines of the canto (especially lines 19–21) penance has been compared to childbirth (a motif that is connected to the recurrent references to children in the *Purgatorio* from canto 15 onwards). Purgation, in its positive aspect, is viewed as a way of bringing new life to birth, as a form of conversion. But this birth depends upon another birth, which is the redemptive birth of Christ in the Incarnation. And it is Christ's Nativity that is recalled at the conclusion of the canto when, as the mountain shakes, Dante compares the event directly (136–41) to the moment at which, at Luke 8: 20, the shepherds in the fields at the first Christmas were stopped in their tracks by the sound of the angels singing '*Gloria in excelsis Deo*'. The new life for which the penitents strive will only come about because a divine birth has interrupted the seemingly inevitable advance of decadence and corruption in the earthly sphere.

Canto 20 is remarkable for the double narrative it maintains between historical sequence and a dawning awareness of providential purpose. At lines 13–15, for instance, Dante appeals directly to the heavens, which circle above and beyond the affairs of history, to intervene and save humanity from the violent onward march of those affairs. Similarly, at lines 94–6, the poet invokes the vengeance of God, which still lies hidden to his view. Still more notable is the recognition that, if Christ is constantly being reborn in history, then so, too, is He being constantly recrucified by the mistaken actions of temporal creatures. Thus, the ill-doings of the Capetians are seen to produce nothing less than a second crucifixion (88–93). At the hands of Hugo's successors, Christ's representative on earth, the pope, is assaulted and Hugo sees again Christ mocked, sees again the vinegar and gall of the crucifixion, and sees again Christ hanging on the Cross between living thieves. The pope in question is the execrable Boniface VIII. (See notes below.) But the sanctity of his office (as in *Purgatorio* 2) remains unassailable, and it is that which is violated in the events described here.

The imagery, diction and often very complex rhetoric of canto 20 exactly reflect the double perspective of Dante's theme. (Compare this passage with Dante's diatribe against Italy in *Purgatorio* 6: 76–148.) An implicit contrast arises between the circlings, which symbolize the ultimate harmony and perfection of divine action (as at lines 13–15), and the linear sequences in which history, under the impulsion of avarice, becomes an endless and pointless reiteration of destructive events. Avarice is pictured here at lines 10–12 exactly as it was in the first canto of the *Inferno* – a famished wolf making a repetitive and frustrating assault on human appetites. Until the vigorous liberation that comes with the earthquake and the '*Gloria*' of its conclusion, repetition is a notable feature of the rhetoric and diction of Dante's text. In lines 1–2 the repetitions of '*voler*' and '*piacer/piacerli*' – 'will' and 'pleasure' – produce a stressful paralysis at odds with the usual implications of these two key words which elsewhere indicate our capacity for, and enjoyment of, moral freedom. Rhythmic movement is, likewise, inhibited by the double '*mossimi*' and '*mosse*' of line 4: 'I moved myself. My leader moved . . .' Footsteps throughout the canto are either slow and infrequent (16) or reduced to immobile suspense (139). The tears of the penitents flow 'drop by drop' at line 7. The lessons in virtue come in sequence – '*seguentemente*' – at line 25. Most strikingly, the whole line of French kings is reduced, in the sarcastic rhetoric of their forebear Hugh, to a mere sequence of 'Louis and Philippes' (50), while their violence and treachery is recorded in the bitterly ironic account of how, to make amends for one bad deed, they simply do another '*per ammenda*'/'To put things right' (64–9). There is no natural growth, only a mechanical onward march of anonymous figures, bent only on possession.

In his depiction of Hugo, Dante offers a particularly searching dramatization of what penitence truly means. The core of Hugo's suffering is mental rather than physical. (Compare the speech of Guido del Duca in *Purgatorio* 14.) Often Hugo speaks in prophetic terms, laying his mind open to truths which lie beyond the limited horizons that obsessive avarice imposes on the intellect. This exposure to the truth is painful. But it is also an act in which the sinner assumes responsibility for both his own sins and the sins of others. So here, for the only time in the *Purgatorio*, the relevant examples of vice and virtue (22–7 and 103–17) are enunciated on behalf of all by a single penitent, in this case Hugo himself. At the same time, this agonizing meditation also assimilates the penitent to Christ and the redemptive suffering on the Cross. (Compare *Purgatorio* 23: 73–5.) The tensions between human and divine purpose are realized anew, and so too, in the wholly unexpected rebirth to which this realization points, history is itself resurrected on new foundations.

Notes

19–33　The examples of willing poverty are, firstly, the Virgin Mary, who gave birth to Christ in a stable (Luke 2: 7). The second example is Gaius Fabricius Luscinus, Roman general and consul in 282 BC, who refused a bribe offered him by Pyrrhus, mercenary leader of the Samnites, intending to lead him to betray Rome. Fabricius subsequently died in poverty and was buried at the expense of the State, which also paid the dowries of his daughters. (Compare *De Monarchia* 2: 5 11.) The third example is Saint Nicholas, the third–fourth-century bishop of Myra in modern Turkey, who saved the three daughters of an impoverished nobleman from prostitution by dropping gold through their window, and thus providing them with dowries.

46–8 Between 1297 and 1304 the Capetian Philip IV the Fair (1268–1314) invaded these Flemish towns, often using treachery to attain his ends, as when he promised the count of Flanders liberty in exchange for the surrender of Ghent and promptly broke his word, imprisoning the count. Vengeance came in 1302 when the Flemish defeated the French at the battle of Courtrai. (Compare *Purgatorio* 7: 109 and *Paradiso* 19: 118–20.)

49–60 Hugo was never himself king but was powerful enough to act as kingmaker on behalf of his son Robert II the Pious (972–1031). (Hugh was '*cappato*' or Ciappetta, in the sense of being a lay abbot, and possibly because he inherited the *cape* of Saint Martin, the popular saint who divided his cloak with a beggar.) The Capetian dynasty replaced the Carolingians in 987–8 (line 53) and ruled until 1328, seven years after Dante's death. Hugh's ascent from humble Parisian origins was a legend widespread in Dante's day, though in fact Hugh and his father were dukes of the Franks and counts of Paris and Orléans. With only two exceptions, the monarchs of this dynasty were named Philip or Louis (four of the former, five of the latter).

64–9 Normandy, Ponthieu, Gascony and Aquitaine had been in English hands until they were re-appropriated, the first two from King John in 1206, the latter two from Edward I in 1294. Charles I of Anjou, during his Italian campaigns, first defeated Manfred in 1266 (see *Purgatorio* 3: 118–29) and then kidnapped Conradin, grandson of Frederick II, and ended the Hohenstauffen dynasty by having him publicly beheaded in Naples in 1268. It was rumoured (baselessly) that when Saint Thomas Aquinas, who came from a southern Italian family, threatened to reveal the truth about Charles's behaviour he was poisoned by agents of Charles.

70–78 The prophecy foretells the entry of Charles of Valois (1270–1325), brother of Philip the Fair, into Italy in 1301, with the intention of recovering Sicily for the French kingdom. Charles allied himself with Pope Boniface VIII and favoured the Florentine Black Guelfs in the coup that ousted Dante's White Guelf party – an event referred to here as the bursting of the Florentine 'belly'.

79–81 The 'other' Charles – the second of that name (see *Purgatorio* 7: 126) (1248–1309), son of Charles I and king of Naples, was captured during the war of the 'Sicilian Vespers' by Ruggiero di Lauria (*c.* 1245–1305), the admiral of the Aragon claimant, and imprisoned from 1284 to 1287. Though he was crowned king of Sicily in 1289, he never exerted control over the realm. Charles II (represented as a pirate at line 79) is condemned here for arranging an advantageous marriage between his daughter Beatrice and the infamous Azzo VIII d'Este (d. 1308) (see *Inferno* 18: 55–7.)

85–96 These lines (linked to the crucifixion of Christ) record the quarrels that broke out between Philip the Fair and Boniface VIII concerning a papal ban on payments by the French priesthood to the French exchequer. Despite Dante's contempt for Boniface, he maintains an understanding of the papal office as the true representative of Christ, and, at lines 91–3, Philip is referred to as a new Pilate in abandoning Boniface, as Pontius Pilate abandoned Christ, to the mercy of a violent mob. When, in September 1303, Boniface was threatening to excommunicate Philip, Philip's agent Guillaume de Nogaret (*c.* 1260–1313) – here identified by the 'fleur-de-lys' – seized the pope at the papal palace of Anagni, to the south-west of Rome. Boniface was rescued by the townspeople but died – presumably of trauma – within a month. The papacy itself now fell under French control, and removed to Avignon in 1309 under the papacy of Clement V. In 1307 Philip IV accused the Knights Templar of heresy and acquired their enormous wealth – and remission of his enormous debts to them – when, in 1312, Pope Clement V (who as pope was titular sovereign of the Templars) suppressed the Order.

103–17 Pygmalion, king of Tyre, murdered his uncle Sychaeus (husband of his sister Dido) in an act here referred to as parricide. (See *Aeneid* 1: 340–59.) The story of Midas, king of Phrygia, occurs in *Metamorphoses* 11: 85–179. Midas asks Bacchus that all he touches should be turned to gold, and repents when his food is transformed in this way. The soldier Achan appears in Joshua 7. Having pilfered the booty won at Jericho, including a 'wedge of gold' Achan is stoned to death by his comrades-in-arms (Joshua 7: 25–6). In Acts 5: 1–11, Sapphira and her husband Ananias, members of the early Christian community, keep back for themselves some part of the profit on a land transaction and, when accused by Saint Peter, fall down dead. Heliodorus was the treasurer of the Syrian King Seleucus IV, referred to in 2 Maccabees 3: 2. When ordered to steal the treasury of the temple in Jerusalem, he was assailed and struck down by the hooves of a mysterious horse and rider. Priam, king of Troy, entrusted his son Polydorus, along with a great weight of gold, to Polymnestor, king of Thrace, who, when Troy fell, treacherously murdered the boy and retained the gold. (See *Aeneid* 3: 19; *Metamorphoses* 13: 429. Compare *Inferno* 30: 13–21.) Crassus (115–53 BC), third member of the triumvirate of Rome, along with Julius Caesar and Pompey, was famous for his riches. Defeated by the Parthians in 59 BC, he was killed while attempting to surrender, and the king of the Parthians had molten gold poured into his corpse's mouth. (See Cicero, *De Officiis* 1: 30.)

130–32 Delos, the birthplace of Apollo and Diana, was originally a floating island, unstable and subject to earthquakes. However, because it proved to be a place of shelter for Latona, mother of Apollo and Diana, Apollo ensured that the island should be made to stand firm. (See *Aeneid* 3: 73–7.)

136–8 'Glory to God in the highest!' The '*Gloria*' is here associated with the Nativity (Luke 2: 14). In the liturgical year, the '*Gloria*' is omitted from the liturgy during Lent, and sung for the first time once more at the Easter Vigil. Birth and resurrection are thus simultaneously signified by this hymn.

CANTOS 21 AND 22

*Dante discovers that the earthquake in Purgatory
announced the end of Statius's purgation. Statius
comes to accompany Dante to the Earthly Paradise,
and discusses the influence that Virgil exerted over his
poetry and Christian belief. Arriving at the terrace of
gluttony the three travellers come across a second tree
from which examples of moderation are heard.*

Commentary

Dante's concern with avarice, beginning in canto 20, continues through that canto and the next until, in cantos 21 and 22, his interest shifts again, towards the consideration of greed which occupies cantos

23 and 24. No fewer than five cantos, therefore, are devoted to the theme of cupidity, first in its effect on public life and, secondly, in its personal manifestation. This is not surprising, considering that Dante views cupidity as the direct antithesis of justice and a principle cause of social division. (See, especially, the commentary on *Inferno* 6.) His violent attack on avarice in *Purgatorio* 20 recalls the language of the *Inferno* and is evidence of a polemical attitude that will prevail until the very end of the *Paradiso*. So, too, at 22: 46–51 direct reference is made to the punishments reserved for avarice in *Inferno* 7, and there is much talk (as at 22: 55–81) of the ways in which Paradise (or the Golden World) may be lost through cupidity and regained through Christ's redemptive act.

For all that, Dante's treatment of the sin in this sequence is notably oblique. In fact, the main character in cantos 21 and 22, the Latin poet Statius (*c.* 45–*c.* 96), is not guilty of cupidity at all but rather of its opposite, an overgenerous prodigality in buying and giving. So when Dante expresses his surprise on hearing at 22: 19–45 that Statius might have been guilty of a sin as demeaning as avarice, it is explained, in Aristotelian terms, that, in departing from the golden mean of virtue, a prodigal expenditure on goods is as culpable as the inclination to hoard or consume them.

As directly moral questions fade into the background, so other themes come into prominence. One is the theme of conversion. As is now revealed, the earthquake of canto 20 signals the moment in Purgatory when Statius is finally converted from a penitential state to one in which he awaits beatification. So, too, in the story offered at 22: 76–93, Statius is represented as a pagan who was converted to Christianity in the earliest years of the Christian era. A second theme, which continues to be important for the remainder of the *Purgatorio*, concerns the relationship between sacred and secular literature and the contribution that poetry (of any era) may make to the pursuit of spiritual truth.

Connecting all these themes is a rich strand of imagery and mythic reference which leads forward to the point in canto 28 when Dante arrives at the Earthly Paradise (which Adam and Eve enjoyed before cupidity led to banishment), but also points back in repeated allusions to the classical myths of the Golden Age. (This age was 'golden' precisely because greed was unknown, while hunger and thirst – as Dante says at 22: 148–50 – made all foods keenly appreciated.) Most significant of all is the central position that Dante gives throughout this episode to the version of this myth that Virgil offers in his fourth *Eclogue*. This pastoral poem was regularly supposed in the Middle

Ages to prophesy the birth of Christ, and bears resemblances to the book of Isaiah in the picture it offers of an age of peace restored. Virgil here speaks of how the birth of a child will issue in an age of perfect justice, when the earth will effortlessly bear all the fruits we need. Greed and labour will both be unnecessary:

> But for you, young boy, the first fruits of the earth without any ploughing will pour abundantly forth. Wandering ivy will be everywhere, with a scattering of berries and lotus mingling with smiling acanthus. The she goats will bring home their milk of their own accord . . . The ram in the meadow will change his fleece of itself first to reddish purple, then to saffron yellow. Vermilion will freely clothe the lambs at pasture.
>
> Virgil, *Eclogue* 4: 17–22 and 43–4

At 22: 70–74 Dante offers an Italian translation from the opening lines of the same *Eclogue*: '*magnus ab integro saeclorum nascitur ordo/iam redit et Virgo, redeunt Saturnia regna.*' From this point on, the canto registers the change that has occurred in Virgil's function as Dante's guide from the time throughout the *Inferno* when his task was to lay before Dante an example of epic heroism. Virgil's role is now that of a prophet. The text of the *Eclogue* also contributes to the imagery of childhood and natural generation with which Dante is concerned from *Purgatorio* 16 to the conclusion of the *cantica*. However, as will be seen, Dante is far from accepting in unmodified form either the ethical or poetic implications of Virgil's vision. His own understanding develops in significant counterpoint with Virgil's – which allows, for instance, no allusion to the penitential labour that precedes Dante's own recovery of the Golden World. And Virgil certainly finds no place in his Golden World for the illuminating influence of a courtly *donna* such as Beatrice.

Associated with Dante's freedom in his treatment of Virgil's *Eclogue* are the two other major concerns of canto 21: conversion and poetry. Nothing is more striking in cantos 21 and 22 than the claim attributed to Statius at 21: 94–9 that it was through Virgil's influence that he became a successful poet, and through Virgil's influence, too, that he was converted to Christianity. A reading of the *Aeneid* inspired him to write his two epic poems, the *Thebaid* and the unfinished *Achilleid* (22: 64–72). A reading of the fourth *Eclogue* harmonized so well with the words of the early Christian preacher that Statius was won over to the new religion. During the persecutions initiated by the Domitian (Emperor Diocletian (*c.* 245–*c.* 312)), his sympathy and respect for his co-religionists greatly increased, but he was still too timid and luke warm to make his conversion public – for which reason, even before arriving on the terrace of avarice, he spent many centuries in the lower rungs of the mountain, where those who wasted their time on earth are confined (22: 92–3).

Statius lived in the early years of the Christian era. There is, however, no independent evidence whatsoever to corroborate Dante's account of his change of heart. Why should Dante have invented this fiction and, subsequently, have given Statius such an authoritative role in the narrative of the *Purgatorio*?

One answer must be that the poet wished to raise, as so many times elsewhere, the question of Virgil's damnation. Much is said here, as in *Purgatorio* 6, about the state of Limbo, where many great poets of the past are confined along with Virgil. But, if Virgil can contribute to the salvation of others such as Statius (and the Dante of *Inferno* 1), why can he not save himself? Virgil's predicament is movingly defined at 22: 67–9, where he is described as one who 'at night,/bears at his back a lamp – no use to him,/but teaching those the way who come behind'.

In the course of the next four cantos, a partial answer to the question of Virgil's exclusion from salvation begins to suggest itself. For Statius's poetry is wholly different in its subject from Virgil's, and the difference lies in a terrible perception of evil (comparable to Dante's own in the *Inferno*), an understanding of the heart of darkness which Virgil never countenances but which itself reveals a desperate need for salvation. Virgil in the *Aeneid* describes a journey away from the ruins of Troy which leads, triumphantly, to the founding of Rome and to the subsequent glories of the Augustan era in which he lived. Statius, on the other hand, in his *Thebaid* goes back – with a certain appetite for spectacle and horror – to the world of ancient Greece, and tells of the conflict in Thebes between the incestuously conceived children of Oedipus and Jocasta. For Dante (who makes frequent reference to Statius's work in the *Inferno*) the corrupt city of Thebes is always viewed as a type of Hell (most notably in the Ugolino episode of *Inferno* 33: 88–9). Knowing the depths of human depravity, Statius knows the need for repentance and restoration. Virgil is impelled by no such appalling knowledge.

It is significant, then, that Statius should be given, in his most important speech in the *Purgatorio*, in canto 25, the account of procreation and the development of the human foetus. Here, at last, he is allowed to contemplate, in contrast to his previous vision of corruption, the pure unsullied workings of nature as God intended them to be. However, in the present episode, the difference that Dante sees between Virgil's position and Statius's extends to a subtle distinction between their linguistic styles and, further, to a distinction between their respective styles and Dante's own as he composes the scene in which they appear together. (Compare the similar trio of considerations that arises between Virgil, Sordello and Dante in *Purgatorio* 6 and 7.)

Consider, firstly, the central passage of 21: 43–60. On Dante's behalf, Virgil seeks to know what the cause of the earthquake was. As always, his words are clear and precisely formulated. Yet he is now well past the point (*Purgatorio* 18: 73–5) at which he openly acknowledged the limitations of his own understanding, and 21: 33 repeats that acknowledgement. There is, of course, no natural or meteorological reason why the mountain should shake. The event is the expression of a redemptive act, in which a religious expiation is fulfilled. So the language of 21: 34–6 is terse, unenthusiastic and pointing downwards, to the 'plashy' shores around the foot of Mount Purgatory. In contrast, Statius speaks with a vibrant lyricism and decoration of phrase which gives the passage at 21: 43–60 a distinctive style. This is a dramatic reflection of his new status as a redeemed Christian, alive with new understanding. It also reflects, however, some of the differences between the characteristics of Virgil's *Aeneid*, which is prevailingly sober and ethically serious, and the much more decorated Latin that Statius developed at his later point in the development of Latin poetry. If, in moral terms, Dante attributes prodigality to Statius, this may well be because he discerns in his poetry, as have many subsequent critics, a certain luxuriousness and indulgence in effect which could itself be described as 'prodigal'. Dante now writes a skilful pastiche of such a style, as for instance in 21: 50, where the rainbow is personified as the 'daughter of Thaumas', and where the Italian rhyme on the '-*ante*' of '*Taumante*' produces both a grandeur of reference and a delicate tracery of phonetic effect.

A notable difference arises between Virgil and Statius as represented in the *Commedia* is the way in which the negative '*non*' is used in their speeches. As was seen particularly in *Purgatorio* 17: 91 ('Neither creator nor created thing'), the negative is, in Virgil's mouth, an indication simultaneously of his self-effacingness and his intellectual discipline. In Statius's speech the repeated '*non*' of 21: 49–50 is related to a willingness to accept, in a very relaxed spirit, that certain causes must remain unknown (21: 57). However, it also produces a rhetorical and rhythmic pleasure of its own, as in the description of the absence of meteorological variation on the upper slopes of the mountain (21: 43), which evokes over two lines a rarefied state which can only be grasped through the absence of natural phenomena: 'no showers of rain, nor hail or snow,/no dew or hoar frost . . .' (46–7).

The paradox in Statius's speech is that, in describing a state which is both natural and yet free from natural change, his words produce through repetition a flickering tremor of rhythm and lexical decoration. The repeated use of the verb '*tremare*': 'to tremble' (21: 55, 57, 58) is an indication of this. Here, Dante attributes to Statius a word that, from the first chapter of the *Vita nuova*, has been of considerable significance in his own thinking. The mysterious influence of Beatrice – and of God's action on him through Beatrice – is registered by this word. (Compare *Purgatorio* 30: 34–48.) The beginning of any 'new life' such as Statius's entry into salvation is likely to be associated with the birth pangs that shake identity to its core and demand wholly unexpected responses. Where Virgil is constantly stable in his speech, the 'tremors' of which Statius speaks (21: 78) – and which he brings to life in the alliterative progress of the sequence – associate him directly with Dante's own apprehension of how 'new life' begins.

As a character, Dante is silent throughout this episode. Towards the end of the canto, at 21: 104, Virgil demands that he should be so, while in the following canto he represents himself as a student listening in on the elevated conversations – concerning poetry and history – that take place between the two masters of classical poetry. The irony is, however, that Dante's own narrative is here more than usually free and inventive. One indication of this is his willingness to play fast and loose with the known facts of Statius's historical life and to turn him, against all expectation, into a Christian. So, too, the whole discussion of weather conditions in upper Purgatory enlists the two classical poets in an explanation of what is nothing more than Dante's fictional construction. The passage may have symbolic implications in suggesting the relation between God and His creation. (Compare *Purgatorio* 27: 97–111.) It is also an expression of Dante's ceaseless interest in scientific observation and hypothesis. But it remains a reflection of interests which have no counterpart in Virgil's own writing or in Statius's. Just as importantly, canto 21 begins (as canto 22 will end) with references to the Scriptures which are likewise out of keeping with the historical registers of classical Latin verse.

Thus, 21: 1–3 refers to a particularly intimate conversation conducted in colloquial terms between Jesus and a Samaritan woman whom he discovers drawing water from a well. More striking still is the daring with which, at 21: 7–10, Dante compares his meeting with Statius to the incident in which the disciples, on meeting the resurrected Christ on the road to Emmaus, fail to recognize Him. Just as in *Purgatorio* 3 Manfred is daringly assimilated to Christ, so in *Purgatorio* 21 is the poet Statius.

From this point on, a third register of diction – in which simplicity and humility of phrase is the dominant note – interweaves with the elevated voices that Dante creates for Virgil and Statius. This may firstly be seen at 21: 91–102, where, without yet knowing that he is addressing Virgil himself, Statius speaks in lofty terms of the influence that the *Aeneid* has exerted over his own poetry. The metaphors are noble expressions of the 'ardour' of inspiration, the sowing of stylistic 'seeds' and 'a thousand' of flames. Yet with a single word this high-flown strain is brought down to the simplest of levels. The word is '*mamma*' – 'mum'. Moreover, the enjambment of 21: 97–8 enhances the effect of the word and modulates from the articulate and resonant language of the preceding passage into a murmur of infantile sounds, eliding one into the other: '*fummi e fummi . . .*': literally, 'was to me and was to me . . .'

The word '*mamma*' is one which punctuates, with apparent incongruity, some of most elevated moments in Dante's text as, for instance, at *Paradiso* 14: 64 and, comparably, in the '*mamella*' of *Paradiso* 33: 108. So, too, the dramatic moment in *Purgatorio* 30: 43–8, where Dante first recognizes that he is in the presence of Beatrice, is marked by the same rhyme words as occur here: '*fiamma/mamma/dramma*' ('flame'/'mummy'/'gram') – though now in the altered order: '*mamma/dramma/fiamma*'. This is no accident, but rather an indication that Dante is engaging once more (as he did in *Purgatorio* 6) with issues that were first raised in the *De Vulgari Eloquentia*. There Dante defined the vernacular tongue as the language that we learn at the breast of our nurse or mother. It is literally our mother tongue. (See also Commentary on *Purgatorio* 26.) Now Statius describes Virgil as his 'nurse' (21: 98). But this implies a far greater appreciation in the *Purgatorio* of the mother tongue in its most basic form than appeared in the *De Vulgari Eloquentia*, even though this work stands as a defence of native Italian. In the earlier work, Dante did not in fact think of Latin as a natural language at all. It was instead (and, of course, against all historical evidence) a language invented by philosophers to serve the demands of intellectual argument and public debate. What is more, the *Volgare Illustre*, which vernacular poets were required to develop in learning the lessons that Latin had to teach, was itself elevated, refined and courtly in its forms and diction. In the *Commedia*, however, Dante has clearly relaxed that view. (See a comparable relaxation discussed in the commentary to *Paradiso* 26.)

Latin, as a 'nurse', now shares some of the characteristics of a mother tongue. And in the *Commedia*, from the *Inferno* to the *Paradiso*, Dante's practice is to allow the simplest and sometimes even the crudest forms of the vernacular to carry meanings that the highest levels of language would not be able to encompass.

This is particularly evident in the final section of the canto, at 21: 103–36. Here, in what is, perhaps, the most movingly comic moment of the whole *Commedia*, there occurs the long-delayed recognition on Statius's part that he is face to face with the very Virgil whom he has been so eloquently praising. It is not, however, eloquence that produces this recognition but an orchestration that involves the most rudimentary forms of language, including gesture, the psychosomatic expressions of body language, even silence itself. At 21: 94, Statius's warm praise of Virgil as a poet rises to its climax. The characteristically retiring Virgil does not want his identity to be known. But there is no rhetoric that he can fall back on, only sign language, communicating in and through the silence he wishes to maintain. So it is with a gesture that he insists that Dante be silent, 'saying, unspeakingly: "Be silent now!"' (21: 104).

Dante, generously delighted by the praise of his master, cannot, psychosomatically, repress a spontaneous smile – 'For tears and laughter follow on so close/to those emotions from which each act springs/ that these least follow *will* in those most true' (21: 106–8). But smiles – as the *De Vulgari Eloquentia* warned – are ambiguous, and Statius is confused, even irritated and offended, by this apparent failure on Dante's part to take his elaborate rhetoric seriously. It is at this point that Virgil, in response to the ambiguity of the situation, relents. To defuse the increasingly embarrassing situation, he allows Dante to reveal his identity. At this point, Statius drops to his knees in reverence. With his usual modesty, Virgil attempts to deflect this spontaneous embrace, reminding Statius that they are both shades (21: 131–2). Statius himself turns this negative dextrously into a further encomium. But the tableau, with all its competing suggestions of sadness, comedy and heartfelt celebration, remains for the reader more telling than any of Statius's words might be.

Canto 22 opens with an understated reference to the ceremony in which the fifth penitential wound is removed from Dante's forehead. Neither Dante nor any explicitly Christian reference have a dominant part to play in the conversation that now ensues between Virgil and Statius. Even in describing his conversion, Statius tends to be concerned less with doctrine or the substance of Christian belief than with the agitated and dangerous atmosphere of early Christian Rome, 'pregnant' with the seed of the new faith (22: 76–8) and convulsed by the concealments to which fear of persecution has led.

Otherwise, the canto brings to mind two conditions to which the minds of the two classical poets are particularly attuned. One is the state of Limbo, to which the great writers of the pre-Christian era are confined (22: 94–108). (Compare *Inferno* 4: 133–44.) The other is the Greek world depicted in Statius's poems, where, especially in Thebes, corruption seemed endemic (22: 109–14). (See also notes below.) These are matters that Statius and Virgil speak of like friends (22: 19–21) and with the detachment, at times, of cultural historians, while Dante, in silent attention, acts the good student (22: 127–9).

At 22: 130, however, there comes 'a sudden break to soothing words', as a visual rather than linguistic sign interrupts the progress of the poets. This sign is constituted by the first of two trees that mark the beginning and end of Dante's encounter with the gluttons. These trees, though rooted in the ground, taper strangely like inverted pyramids. They immediately take on symbolic considerations that are explored further in canto 23. The trees are grown from seed generated in the Earthly Paradise (*Purgatorio* 24: 117), and their shape is clearly intended to deter any such presumptuous attempt to 'climb' that led Adam and Eve to their fall. At the same time, the pleasures of the senses are sharply aroused by the freshness of the perfumes that come from these trees which are constantly sprayed by a shower of water from the cliffside. The penance of the gluttons is to experience this pleasure without being able to satisfy their appetite for it. But the promise is also implied here of the legitimate pleasure that will be experienced once penance is concluded. The voices that come out of the foliage, citing examples of restraint, point to this ultimate, if paradoxical consummation. These are voices wholly different from those that Virgil and Statius have been given hitherto in this canto: they are voices that speak of simplicity, of well-tempered appetites shown as much by Roman women in ancient times as by male heroes (22: 145–6), and of an asceticism, such as that of Saint John the Baptist, which leads through the desert to yet further revelation (22: 151–4).

Notes to Canto 21

1–10 At John 4: 4–26, Jesus engages in a long and spirited conversation with a woman of Samaria – and therefore from a people alien to the Jews – in the course of which Jesus extends the offer of the waters of grace even to those (like the Samaritan woman and, implicitly, Statius) who are not of the chosen race. Jesus concludes:

> God is a Spirit: and they that worship him must worship him in spirit and in truth.
>   The woman saith unto him, I know that Messiah cometh, which is called Christ: when he is come, he will tell us all things.
>   Jesus saith unto her, I that speak unto thee am he.

At Luke 24: 13–32, after his resurrection Jesus encounters two disciples on the road to Emmaus, who do not recognize Him until He breaks bread eucharistically at supper.

25–7 The three Fates are Clotho, Lachesis and Atropos, who respectively allot the thread of a person's life, spin it and cut it off.

49–51 'Thaumas's daughter' is the rainbow. (See *Metamorphoses* 14: 845.)

82–4 The Emperor Titus (AD 39–81) is said to be 'good' in that he is thought to have carried out God's will, avenging the death of Christ by his brutal destruction of Jerusalem in AD 70. Dante returns to this theme in *Paradiso* 6.

88–93 Dante follows a common medieval misreading in supposing that Statius was born in Toulouse. In fact he was born, in about AD 45, in Naples, under the full name of Publius Papinius Statius. (Some critics have discerned in 'Statius' an appropriate pun on the Latin *status* – meaning 'a delaying'.) Throughout Dante speaks of Statius's epic poetry, notably ignoring – in a context where Virgil's pastoral poetry is stressed – Statius's own pastoral *Silvae*.

Notes to Canto 22

4–5 The fourth Beatitude to which Dante here refers speaks of those who hunger and thirst after justice (Matthew 5: 6). Dante attributes a 'thirst' to the avaricious and prodigal, thus (unusually) dividing the Scriptural verse so as to attribute a 'hunger' to the penitent gluttons of the next terrace.

13–15 The poet Juvenal (AD *c*. 60–*c*. 130) is famous for his satires against the extravagant vices of Imperial Rome (although he also writes scornfully of Statius at *Satires* 7: 82).

40–48 Statius here quotes the *Aeneid* 3: 55–8, in which Aeneas condemns the avarice that induced Polymnestor to murder the boy Polydorus (see also *Purgatorio* 20: 115 and *Inferno* 13: 31–51), crying out against the '*auri sacra fames*' – where '*sacra fames*' could be translated as both 'an accursed hunger' for gold ('*auri*') and 'a sacred hunger'. In keeping with his emphatic Aristotelianism in this sequence, it seems that, for Dante, an appetite for riches may be productive (a divine as well as a cursed appetite) if it follows rule or measure. The reference to 'hair cropped short' at line 46 directly recalls the punishment reserved for avarice and prodigality in *Inferno* 7. In *Purgatorio* the same penance 'drains' both sins of their original vitality.

55–60 Jocasta, queen of Thebes, unwittingly married her own son Oedipus. The sons born to their incestuous liaison were Eteocles and Polynices, who became sworn enemies. (See Statius, *Thebaid* 12.) Clio is the Muse of history, whom Statius calls upon in *Thebaid* 1: 41–2.

61–3 The 'fisherman' is Saint Peter. (See Mark 1: 16–17.)

82–4 Domitian, emperor of Rome AD 81–96, initiated a particularly severe persecution of Christians.

88–91 These lines refer to the episode in Statius's *Thebaid* 4: 670–844 where the Greek armies marching on Thebes are close to dying of thirst when Hypsipyle leads them to the one stream still flowing, the Langia. (See also line 112 below.)

91–3 It can be calculated that before spending 500 years in purging his prodigality, Statius had spent 400 years purging his 'lukewarmness'. Where he was for the other 300 years in the period since his death, Dante does not say.

97–108 The Latin authors mentioned here, given that Dante does not know their work directly, are likely to have come to his attention through his reading of Cicero, Horace and Saint Jerome. Most of this catalogue consists of comic dramatists and satirists. Terence (d. 159 BC) was a writer of comedies (see *Inferno* 18: 133–5), as were Caecilius (d. *c.* 166 BC) and Plautus (d. 184 BC). 'Varro' is unknown (and may be the result of a misreading), save from references in Horace's works. Persius (d. AD 62) was a satirist not directly known to Dante. The second part of the list transfers attention to Greek authors whom Dante, not knowing Greek, would have heard about through his reading of Cicero. Most of these are tragedians and dramatists, except Simonides, a lyric poet (556–447 BC). Of the works of Euripides (484–406 BC), eighteen tragedies survive, along with fragments of sixty more. Agathon (448–402 BC) was a friend of Socrates and Plato who speaks in Plato's *Symposium*, but nothing of his work survives.

Antiphon was a poet at the court of Dionysius I of Sicily (405–367 BC).

109–14 These lines refer to Greeks who are protagonists in poems by Statius. Antigone and Ismene are the daughters of Oedipus and Jocasta. Antigone dies immured at the order of Creon. Ismene witnessed the murder of all her family and her lover Cyrrheus (line 111). Deiphile is the wife of Tydeus. (See *Inferno* 32: 130.)

Argia is the daughter of Deiphile and wife of Polynices. The 'one who spied out Langia's stream' is Hypsipyle, who at *Inferno* 18: 92 is mentioned as the deserted lover of Jason and is also referred to in *Purgatorio* 26: 94–6. The daughter of the Theban seer Tiresias is Manto, who, confusingly, is placed among the soothsayers in *Inferno* 20. In Statius's *Achilleid*, Thetis is Achilles' mother and Deidamia his wife. (See *Inferno* 26: 52–4.)

118–20 The handmaids of the sun are the passing hours of the day. It is now within the fifth hour of the day.

142–54 The virtue of restraint is illustrated by the Virgin Mary at the Marriage at Cana; she prays for us and so thought less of the needs of her own appetite (hence the 'mouth' that intercedes on behalf of all Christians) than that of others. (See John 2: 1–11 and compare *Purgatorio* 12: 29.) The legendary restraint shown by the women of ancient Rome is recorded by Aquinas in *Summa Theologiae* 2a 2ae q. 149 a. 4. Daniel at Nebuchadnezzar's court persuades the children of Israel to live on lentils and water. 'As for these four children God gave them knowledge and skill in all learning and wisdom: and Daniel had understanding in all visions and dreams' (Daniel 1: 17). The 'primal age' is the Golden Age. (See *Metamorphoses* 1: 89–150.) In Matthew 3: 4, Saint John the Baptist is described as living off honey and locusts. At Luke 7: 28, Jesus says of Saint John: 'there is not a greater prophet than John the Baptist'.

CANTO 23

The penance for gluttony. Dante's meeting with his
one-time friend Forese Donati, who speaks out
against the corrupt manners of modern Florence.

Commentary

Cantos 21 and 22 concentrated on the relationship between two
Roman poets. By contrast, the focus of cantos 23 and 24 – concerning
the penance allotted for gluttony – falls upon Dante's relationship
with Florentines and other Tuscans, mostly of his own generation.
Where Dante had been concerned in his depiction of Statius with the
history of the early Church, in canto 23 he turns his attention to the
willing acts of personal penance which reconcile the penitent to the
redemptive sacrifice of Christ on the Cross. Here, though, as in the pre-
vious two cantos (as also cantos 24 and 26), the subtext of the sequence
concerns the writing of poetry and its relation to the developing revela-
tion of Christian understanding. The emphasis now falls more upon
the traditions of vernacular love poetry, to which Dante's early writ-
ings belonged, than upon the ancient authors of epics and eclogues.

The gluttons, circling the great tree which was discovered at the
close of canto 22, find that its perfumes only serve to sharpen their
hunger. Yet, at lines 73–5, as one of these figures declares, the same
willing purpose leads them to that tree – and to the suffering it causes
– as led Christ 'in his joy' to the tree of the Cross. This pain, experi-
enced in the agonies of personal appetite, is said to be (as are all the
penances of Purgatory) a 'solace' in that it re-unites the sinner with
Christ. In expressing this paradox, Dante daringly employs the word
sollazzo which, from the beginning of the love poetry tradition in
Provence, was frequently used to express the satisfaction, sexual and
otherwise, to be had between a lover and his courtly mistress. Dante's
oxymoron here reflects the contradictions that were commonly to be
found in early love poetry, where love can be represented as a 'chilling
fire' or 'a welcome malady'. But now, as elsewhere in canto 23, such
turns of phrase are re-applied to express the tensions of religious
experience. Pain is 'refreshed' at lines 70–72, as if it were water or the
promise of a fertile season to those who are stricken by drought. The
fundamental contradiction of a divine maker who is glad to accept
agony and desolation produces a scene which is, simultaneously, litur-

gical, in the constant circling of the emblematic tree, and as painfully realistic as a film of a column of famine victims.

The principle encounter in canto 23 occurs between Dante and his close personal friend Forese Donati (c. 1260– before 1296), a distant cousin of his wife Gemma Donati. Forese is not known for any sustained work of poetry, but historically the closeness of his relationship with Dante is attested by an exchange of scurrilous banter – in the form of a *tenzone*, or poetic dialogue, in which they trade spectacular insults – that took place between the two. Forese, so Dante's poem implies, is hopeless in bed and, in any case, his wife Nella has a perpetual cold and does nothing, even on a summer night, except wear socks and cough. Dante, according to Forese, will end up wearing a smock in a pauper's hospital. In any case, his father was a moneylender. Forese, according to Dante, is a scar-faced thief, the bastard son of a licentious mother whose supposed father stands in the same relationship to Forese 'as Joseph did to Christ': '*che gli appartien quanto Giosepp' a Cristo*'. Nowhere, except in the depths of *Inferno* 29 and 30, does Dante display comparable violence of sentiment and diction.

Yet such violence is wholly absent from the exchanges imagined in *Purgatorio* 23. On the contrary, at lines 115–17, there are hints of shame at what the relationship between these two Florentine friends had been – sometimes taken to suggest a homoerotic relationship. In keeping with the prevailing themes of the *Purgatorio*, repentance is represented as a way of restoring, through a participation in God's redemptive action, the communal relationships that have been fragmented by sin. In common with many of the greatest moments in the *Commedia*, the meeting between Dante and Forese is a recognition scene – and as such it deserves to be compared with the tragically frustrated meeting that takes place between Dante and his Florentine mentor, Brunetto Latini, in *Inferno* 15. Here, as with Brunetto, the distorting effects of punishment make it impossible for Dante to recognize the sinner. But the effects of penance are different from those of damnation. Forese is initially unrecognizable since his face is hollowed out by the starvation that he has suffered, along with all the penitent gluttons. This detail clearly refers back, in altered fashion, to the *tenzone*, where Dante spoke disparagingly of Forese's 'scarred' face. Now, though the scarring remains, there is no disparagement, but rather renewed sympathy and a perception of the significance of Forese's suffering. Caricature gives way to the extremely moving parallel that Dante draws between his present emotions and those he experienced when he saw Forese's face at the point of his early death (55–7). Another tragic, even heroic comparison is drawn between the features of the penitent and those of the Jews who suffered famine in the siege of Jerusalem by Roman forces, which culminated in the destruction of the temple in AD 70.

Most important of all is the reference to the three letters of the alphabet that can be read in Forese's starving features, 'O M O' (31–2). Dante here alludes to a familiar medieval notion which declared that the word 'man' – in Italian, '*omo*' – could be read in the bone structure of the human face. The brow and nose can be seen as an 'M', the sockets of the eyes form the two 'O's. Such body art reminds the reader that Dante's own brow is still inscribed with the two 'P's that have yet to be removed. But the symbolism is also significant in thematic terms and in respect of the narrative development of the canto.

Thematically, the device alerts the reader to the nature of both greed and penance. Greed obscures the proper outline of our humanity. Penance clarifies what it is to be human and brings the penitent back to that understanding, revealing the general nature of 'man' that is written in our being. This is a matter of justice. Dante always sees greed as the direct opposite of justice. (See commentary on *Inferno* 6.) Justice is the highest virtue that human beings are capable of, and ensures that one individual lives in well-proportioned relationship with another. Gluttons, in seeking more than their share, distort that balance. The penitential inscription on their faces insists that, through their suffering, the penitents acknowledge and participate once more in the common character of all human beings. At the same time, in terms of the drama of the canto, this emphasis prepares for the moment at which Dante recognizes the particular presence of his friend Forese. When he dealt with the sin of gluttony in *Inferno* 6, Dante was unable to recognize the man to whom he was speaking, even though, in this case, too, he was addressing a Florentine acquaintance. Now the restoration of humanity, through an appetite for justice, makes possible a general recognition of Forese that develops at lines 40–48 into a precise perception of his identity. As in some puzzle photograph – where a familiar object is pictured from an unfamiliar angle – recognition suddenly dawns when a verbal hint is offered, translating the general shape into a well-focused particular. As Forese speaks, Dante's eye re-organizes his first impressions. The sentence reaches its climax with Forese's name, satisfyingly and firmly locked into the rhyming position.

Throughout canto 23, perception oscillates between the surreal and the real, between symbolic imaginings and colloquial conversation. For instance, in lines 85–111 the canto's attention turns from the ritual scene that the penitents enact to the streets of thirteenth-century Florence, where a lack of measure or integrity in personal behaviour betokens and contributes to a deeper malaise. Forese's own greed, as an expression of injustice, is just one indication of this. But his speech takes as its target the fashionable Florentine women whose immodesty in dress makes the city more barbarous than the luxurious Orient or the wildest regions of Sardinia. There is an unmistakably misogynistic strand in this passage. Moreover, its language and abrasive tone at times recall Forese's prophecies in the *tenzone* of the sorry end to which the 'pauper' Dante would come: 'A future time . . . will come' when spiritual and legal penalties will fall on the heads of the 'bare-faced' and 'brazen' women of Florence. But the passage voices anew some of the principal concerns of the rest of the canto. In the case of both Forese and Dante, the penitential scars that they bear are marks of identity and bring ethical significance to their bodily natures. But the women are anonymous, and Dante's adjective '*sfacciate*' – which literally means 'faceless' – suggests that, in their devotion to fashionable dress, they lose the expressive and particular aspect of the human anatomy which registers individuality and emotion. They make themselves caricatures of what people truly are, and exemplify the same moral degeneracy in Florence that is also indicated by the unmeasured greed and avarice of its citizens. In *Paradiso* 16, where Dante speaks of an age in which Florence was wholly at peace with itself, the austerity with which Florentine women dressed is taken to be an expression of civic harmony.

A further contrast also arises between the Florentine 'fashionisti' and the two women actually named in canto 23, Beatrice and Nella. In some measure, Beatrice is always for Dante an image of what Florence at its best can offer to the world, through the simplicity, poise and dignity he attributes to her. Yet here, at line 128, it is the unadorned normality with which she is named that counts, expressing the reality of the person to whom Dante devotes his attention. Likewise Nella – viciously derided in the *tenzone* – is now mentioned with a respect and affection which wholly displace the cartoon figure of the earlier poems and the self-generated distortions of her shameless sister Florentines. Nella stands in the same relation to Forese as Beatrice does to Dante, giving purpose and direction to his purgatorial life. This is expressed, in entirely realistic terms, as the cause of Forese's rapid advancement in Purgatory. It is Nella's prayers, her affections and her forebearance towards her husband (188–90) which have brought him – as Beatrice will bring Dante – back to an understanding of his better nature.

Finally, the prayers on Forese's behalf which are central to Nella's story (paralleled by Dante's own concerns for him here) point to a concern with the language of religion that has been present in canto 23 since the penitents at lines 10–12 brought to birth in pain and delight the hymn '*Labia mea*': 'O Lord, open Thou our lips and our mouths shall shew forth Thy praise.' An obvious contrast arises here between the misuse of 'lips' of which the gluttons, in their earthly lives, have been guilty and the possibilities that they now pursue through prayer and praise (and, in Forese's case, at lines 106–11, through acts of prophecy). But a similar contrast also arises between praise and prayer, on the one hand, and, on the other, the insults that were offered in the *tenzone* (and indeed in Forese's assault on the Florentine women, and even in Dante's first perception of Forese's distorted appearance here). The language of prayer and praise opens up the perspective of redemption. Dante first realized this in the *Vita nuova* where, developing a 'praise style' – his '*stile della loda*' – in which to celebrate Beatrice, he came to see that his praise also revealed, in the fact of her existence, the purposes of the God who created her. A similar understanding of praise is explored in *Purgatorio* 24 and 26. It is, however, on Nella that the present canto concentrates – not on a courtly *donna* but rather on a simple, domestic figure whose ordinary identity is as worthy of attention as Beatrice's. Piercing the mask that gluttony or crudity of appetite or violence of language creates around the human person, the language of praise reveals, in a clear, disinterested way, the co-operation that is possible between providential purpose and all those particular human persons who are involved in its advancement.

Notes

25–30   Erisichthon, prince of Thessaly, cut down a sacred oak which had within it a wood nymph and, as punishment, was made to suffer a hunger so terrible that he finally consumed his own body. The story is told by Ovid in *Metamorphoses* 8: 738–808, to which Dante's phrases here closely correspond. The second reference is to the siege of Jerusalem by the Romans in AD 70, at the command of the Emperor Titus, as described by Flavius Josephus in *De Bello Judaico* 6 (*c*. AD 75). During this siege, a Jewish woman by the name of Mary was driven to eat her own child. (See also Paulus Orosius, *Historiae Adversum Paganos* 7: 9 (417).)

73–5 These lines refer to the words of Christ on the Cross, recorded
      at Matthew 27: 46, 50 (also Mark 15: 34), a quotation from
      Psalm 22:1: '*Eli, Eli, lama sabacthani*?' ('My God, my God, why
      hast thou forsaken me?')

94–6 The Barbarigia is a mountainous region in central Sardinia,
      noted for the barbarity of its inhabitants.

118–20 The allusion here is to the moon, Diana, twin sister of Apollo,
      the sun.

CANTO 24

Among the gluttonous, Dante meets the poet
Bonagiunta da Lucca, and speaks of his poetic
success, as well as of the deficiencies of earlier poets.
Forese Donati continues the conversation that began
in the previous canto, speaking of his saintly sister
and of his brother Corso who is to die violently and
be dragged to Hell.

Commentary

At **lines 19–63** of canto 24 Dante imagines a conversation between
himself and a penitent who, like Forese, suffers emaciation in expiating
the sin of gluttony and who, unlike Forese, occupies a recognized
place in the traditions of vernacular love poetry. This is Bonagiunta
Orbicciani degli Overardi (*c.* 1220–*c.* 1300), a judge and notary from
Lucca in Tuscany, a city of which Dante spoke with contempt for the
corruption of its public life in *Inferno* 21 and 22. In the course of
their conversation, Dante draws a distinction between the successful
principles on which his own early poetry was founded and the con-
straints of style that deny to Bonagiunta any comparable success.
Bonagiunta is made to confess that his own writings are affected by a
certain knottiness (**55**), probably of rhetorical exaggeration. They
share this defect (**56**) with the poetry of Guittone d'Arezzo (*c.* 1230–
94, see introduction to *Inferno*, p. xxvi and *Purgatorio* 26), whom
historically Bonagiunta acknowledged as master, and the early Sicilian
poet and lawyer or 'Brief', Giacomo da Lentini (*c.* 1200–*c.* 1250).
Bonagiunta quotes the first line of his poem from the *Vita nuova*
20: '*Donne ch'avete intelletto d'amore . . .*' (**line 51**), which in the *Vita*
nuova itself is said to inaugurate Dante's characteristic 'praise style'.
Commenting on this line, Dante now offers an explanation of his

practice which is regularly cited as the key to the poetics of his early
love poetry. While Bonagiunta and others like him are given to wordy
display, Dante follows the dictates of the heart: love speaks in him
and he, as poet, faithfully records love's promptings in praise of his
lady. Thus, Dante claims a degree of spontaneity in his writing but
equally stresses the humility which makes him an accurate scribe of
the revelations that love inspires. 'Praise' develops in Dante's writing
to the point at which it becomes the dominant mode of his poetry in
the *Paradiso*. It is in praise of others that we unknot our obsession
with ourselves (as in any burst of spontaneous applause), and acknow-
ledge an inspiration or illumination that comes from beyond. (See
introduction to the *Paradiso*.)

In the *De Vulgari Eloquentia* 2: 6: 8, Dante had already condemned
Guittone and his poetic school for ambitions unsupported by talent or
self-discipline, and in *Purgatorio* 26: 124–6 he again attacks Guittone
himself for the inflated reputation he enjoyed in the middle of the
thirteenth century. There are hints here of literary squabbles in which
Dante (to some eyes) protests too much, and may even be concealing
a greater debt to Guittone's example, as a moralist and poetic arbiter,
than he is willing to admit. In *Purgatorio* 24, however, his approach
to Bonagiunta – in keeping with the generally conciliatory ethos of the
second *cantica* – is more delicately registered. Bonagiunta is, after all,
a penitent, and he, like Forese, is among those who are singing the
hymn 'O Lord, open Thou our lips and our mouths shall shew forth
Thy praise'. Lips which were once given to gluttony – or, in poetic
terms, might overambitiously have 'bitten off more than they can
chew' – are now devoted to the praise of God. Nor is it accurate,
either here or in *Purgatorio* 26, to suppose that Dante's definition of
his own poetic achievements applies exactly to the poetics that he is
developing in the *cantica*. Rather, as in the repentance he shows
towards Forese, Dante locates his words to Bonagiunta in a context –
to be confirmed by canto 26 – in which the onward march of poetic
tradition is seen to involve the Dante of the *Commedia* in a continuing
re-assessment of what poetry can and should achieve. This is not to
diminish Dante's undoubted awareness of his own superior gifts; it is
to suggest (as the *Paradiso* will confirm) that humility in the face of
unfolding revelation and the reciprocal influences of poetic practice
are always at the heart of Dante's achievement.

It is consistent with Dante's attention to both the coherence and
subsequent development of his poetic style that the opening phase of
canto 24 – which also adds a further note to his long conversation
with Forese – should include a modified and extended version of the

praise style he first developed in the *Vita nuova*. At lines 13–15, Forese answers a question concerning his sister, Piccarda, who will occupy an important place in *Paradiso* 3, and, in celebrating her virtues, produces a verse which, in its enjambments and alliterative patternings, is more fluent and lyrical than any verse that Dante devoted to Beatrice in the *Vita nuova*. It is true that at lines 20–24 Forese shifts back to the satirical harshness of tone that characterized the conclusion of canto 23, identifying among his companions a gluttonous if penitent cleric noted for his appetite for eels and fine wine. He also speaks with prophetic venom at lines 82–7 of a third member of his family, Corso Donati – a Black Guelf and one of Dante's bitterest enemies – who is rushing headlong to Hell (thus ensuring, uniquely, that the Donati family have members in each of the three realms of the other world). In praising Piccarda, however, Forese registers the distance that he has travelled (and Dante is travelling) from the violence and greed that characterize Florence. Here, as always, the praise style speaks of a pure and disinterested love which stands at the opposite pole from any violent desire to possess or destroy. Praise in its fullest sense acknowledges that the speaker recognizes that true value lies beyond the confines of his own being, and that the value of the speaker resides precisely in reflecting that ungraspable reality, whether of Nella, of Beatrice or of God. It is, therefore, appropriate that canto 24 should be punctuated by references to 'not knowing'. Piccarda possesses both beauty and goodness – 'was she more – I do not know – in beauty than in goodness?' says Forese. Bonagiunta is discovered at line 37 muttering a feminine but otherwise unidentifiable name ('I don't know. Something: Gentucca?': *'non so che "Gentucca"'*). In a similar vein, Bonagiunta speaks of an unnamed woman of Lucca (43–5) who, apparently, will give Dante support in the early years of his exile. Then, at line 76, Dante confesses to Forese his own ignorance (*'non so . . .'*) as to the length of days that God will allow him still to live on earth. In each case, the speaker points to a mystery still unfolding, while also admitting a dependence on the praiseworthy figures who illuminate the darkness of that mystery.

Dante distinguishes himself from Bonagiunta and the Guittonian school in regard to their respective conceptions of poetry and praise. But canto 24 also registers some of the specific developments that have occurred in Dante's style since he began the *Commedia*. The give-and-take of the conversation with Bonagiunta emphasizes how far Dante has progressed beyond the univocal, self-regarding lyrics that even he was inclined to write while he still remained within the lyric tradition. In the *Commedia* he creates a drama of competing voices. Meaning is to be established and recorded through dialogue with others. At the same time, the opening lines of the canto, pointing to the unimpeded connection between speech and physical progress, emphasize the extent to which Dante, unlike any of his predecessors, is a narrative poet, constantly concerned with onward motions and sequences of action. This canto, like the previous one, is subsequently marked by a considerable interest in the tempi and dynamics of action, as, for instance, at lines 70–73, and then at lines 94–6, where Forese is first seen to slow his pace as though out of breath, and then to charge onwards like a knight in battle.

In the final phase of the canto, however, from line 106, the agitation of movement and the to-and-fro of conversation recompose into the contemplation of a second tree (like the tree of canto 22, this is an inverted pyramid) which stops the travellers in their tracks and concentrates their attention on the examples of gluttony that are spoken, as penitential curbs, from the midst of its mysterious branches, which 'turned aside so many tears and prayers'. The scriptural and classical legends add to the stylistic palette of the canto, drawing on registers far beyond those of the vernacular conversations. Silence then falls as the three poets, Virgil, Statius and Dante, progress for a thousand paces meditating 'without a word' (130–32) until a further strange and challenging sight attracts their attention. Words now yield to revelatory vision, as the angel appears who is to erase the penultimate mark from Dante's brow. This angel is another figure who, like Beatrice or 'Gentucca', cannot be fully possessed in human language or even by steady perception (142). But in registering such a mysterious influence, Dante produces one of the most refined and yet sensuous pieces of writing in the whole *Commedia* – repeating the verb '*sentir*'/'to sense' four times over in as many lines (148–51). Out of the fire, redder than any furnace of metal or glass (compare *Purgatorio* 27: 49–51), come ambrosial breezes, wafted by the feathers of the angel's wings. The contradictions of sense experience and texture that Dante here evokes recall the oxymorons of canto 23. The synaesthesia of these contrary impressions also anticipates the sensual pleasures that Dante describes on his entry into the Earthly Paradise in cantos 27 and 28. But, in its immediate context, the passage offers a significant contrast to the disordered appetites that he has seen purged in the episode of the penitent gluttons. The conclusion to which he comes does not suggest that the pursuit of transcendent truth leads in any way to an abdication of our physical natures. The goal, rather, is a poise and dynamic harmony, stimulated by our sense of what always lies beyond. Thus the last lines of the canto – in which Dante

presumes to write his own elaborate version of the fourth Beatitude –
speak in richly elevated terms of a hungering which is continual but
simultaneously just and measured.

Notes

19–33 The first person being alluded to here is Pope Martin IV (in
        office 1281–5), one-time treasurer of the cathedral of Tours.
        Dante has already criticized this pope in *Purgatorio* 20: 67 and
        would certainly have disapproved of his meddling in Italian poli-
        tics. Now he finds reasons of his own for allowing Martin's
        salvation – somewhat as he retracts here his earlier sweeping
        condemnation of the Guittonian school. Bolsena is a lake near
        Viterbo famous for its eels. Martin is thought to have had eels
        drowned as a delicacy in the vernaccia wine. Ubaldino da la Pila
        (d. 1291) was father of the notorious Archbishop Ruggieri who
        is cannibalistically consumed by Ugolino in *Inferno* 33. This
        Boniface (to be distinguished from Dante's great enemy, Pope
        Boniface VIII) was archbishop of Ravenna between 1274 and
        1295. The bishop's crook in Ravenna is not hook-shaped but
        carries a rook (as in the chess piece) at its extremity. Line 31
        refers to Messer Marchese degli Argoglesi from Forli, who was
        related to the da Polenta clan of Ravenna, Dante's patrons.

55   Bonagiunta here employs the archaism or dialectic word for
        'now', *issa* – as in English it might be 'nah' or 'noo'. (Compare
        Inferno 23: 7. Like *Purgatorio* 24, *Inferno* 23 contains certain
        anti-Guittonian elements.) This might be seen as an attempt to
        mark his speech with a certain provincialism. Similarly, at line
        43, he fails to employ the courtly term *donna* or 'lady', in favour
        of the coarser term '*femmina*' – 'woman'.

58–60 In speaking of love dictating to him, Dante alludes to an office
        of high importance in medieval courts, where the '*dittator*' or
        'dictator' was a man trained in eloquence who often acted as head
        of the administrative council and drafted all legal documents,
        dictating them to lesser officials.

64–6   For the importance of this bird simile in the vernacular love
        poetry, see commentary on *Purgatorio* 26.

121–6 The first of the two examples of gluttony are the centaurs, who
        drunkenly attempted to rape the women guests at the wedding of
        Pirithous and Hippodamia, but were defeated by Theseus and
        the Lapiths. (See *Metamorphoses* 12: 210–535.) The second
        example is drawn from Judges 7, in which Gideon, the Hebrew

general, forbids certain of his soldiers who have yielded to their physical appetites from participating in the battle against Midian and sharing the spoils of victory.

CANTO 25

On the way to the final terrace of Purgatory, where the lustful are purged, Statius explains how the foetus develops in the womb from conception to birth.

Commentary

The path to the final terrace of Mount Purgatory is so narrow that Dante, Virgil and Statius are forced to climb in single file. Neither this, however, nor the rapid pace of the climb prevents Virgil from sensing that Dante – compared at lines 10–12 to a fledgling stork rising and falling on its nest – has a question in mind which he can hardly bring himself to utter: why is that the penitent gluttons are so emaciated when, being spirit bodies, they have no need of nourishment (19–21)? Virgil's answer is as tentative as Dante's repressed inquiry. He offers two very obscure analogies. One (22–4) is drawn from the myths of Ovid's *Metamorphoses* 8: 260–525, which tells how Meleager's life was connected, by decree of the Fates, to the continued existence of a log which his mother had snatched from the fire at birth but flung back into the flames when in later life he murdered his mother's brothers. As a consequence, Meleager died. The second (25–7) suggests that the penitent's body reflects the actions of the mind in the way that a mirror reflects the actions of a body. These allusions vaguely suggest that our lives must be seen as, simultaneously, our own (as in our bodily forms) and not our own (as in a mirror image), and likewise may depend upon principles beyond ourselves, as Meleager's life depended upon the log to which it was linked. These suggestions are significant in that they introduce a canto in which human beings will be seen, body and soul, as directly dependent upon the will of a divine Creator. It is, however, equally significant that Virgil, who himself does not know God directly, lacks the competence to address the issue more clearly. He now refers Dante's question to the recently redeemed Statius, who proceeds at lines 31–108 to base his answer on a highly technical consideration of how the human foetus develops in the womb.

It is likely that modern readers will experience difficulties with this exposition. Here (as at various points in the *Paradiso*, notably canto 2) Dante attempts to reconcile his poetic with his scientific concerns in a manner which has few, if any, parallels in subsequent literature. By his own lights he succeeds, producing an argument which is both vigorous in its syntax and rich in its imagery. The modern reader will hardly be helped by the fact that the physiology which Dante here adopts is drawn from Aristotle. It predates the discovery of the circulation of the blood – and, as science, is plainly wrong. What is more, Dante's argument unquestioningly accepts the Aristotelian view that, in the procreation of children, the active principle is male while the female principle is entirely passive.

For all that, the discussion remains, in Dante's own terms, one of the most significant in the *Commedia*. In philosophical terms it brings to a conclusion the considerations that began in *Purgatorio* 16, when he first spoke of the relationship between God, as the joyful Creator, and the childlike order of his creation, though focusing now on our physical more than our intellectual participation in that order. The canto also has a contribution to make to the concern with poetry that began with the arrival of Statius alongside Virgil in canto 21 and continues with the appearance of vernacular poets in cantos 24 and 26. It may indeed be argued that Dante's purpose in composing such an arduous piece of scientific verse was in part to assert his own position in the tradition, and to outdo both his classical predecessors and his contemporaries in intellectual rigour and ambition.

Since canto 21, where Dante invented the story of Statius's conversion to Christianity, Dante has claimed the right to re-interpret classical history and, in particular, to investigate significant differences between Virgil's position and that of Statius. In attributing the discussion of Aristotelian biology to Statius, Dante continues the comparison. Three major differences can be observed. The first is that Statius benefits from a revelation of divine purposes which are a closed book to Virgil. This would be an unremarkable distinction, save that here in canto 25 – and against most modern preconceptions – it appears that science can be explored most effectively when God's purposes are taken into account. It is precisely because Statius has come to see the uniqueness and value of life that he can give his detailed account of the biological mechanism that God has ultimately set in motion (70–72). This is the second difference between Statius and Virgil, whose interventions in this canto are meagre in comparison. Virgil's deficiencies are in part those that he shares with Ovid, in relying upon the literary suggestions of myth. (Compare *Inferno* 25 and *Paradiso* 9 and the commentaries on these cantos.) Science, in an age where divine truth has been revealed, can replace mere myth. It can also replace the ill-focused reliance that Virgil here places on observation, as in his reference to mirrored reflections. Thirdly, as was suggested in the commentary to cantos 21 and 22, Statius, unlike Virgil, pursues in his *Thebaid* a vision of violence and corruption, and that vision may be seen as the impulse that drove him to embrace the redemptive doctrines of Christianity. Now, having spoken in his own poetry of the incestuous confusions that arose in Thebes through the marriage of Oedipus and Jocasta, Statius is called upon – as a form of redemptive reward – to speak of procreation in its natural and unpolluted form.

In parallel with his claim to adjudicate between the classical poets, Dante also claims the right, as a philosopher, to enter into a debate that involved the inheritors of Aristotle along with certain medical writers such as the Persian Avicenna (980–1037) and the ancient Greek Galen (AD 129–200). The terms of this debate are drawn largely from Aristotle's *On the Generation of Animals*. But certain divergences arose among Aristotle's followers. On a number of relatively minor points Dante tends to favour the views of Albertus Magnus over those of Saint Thomas Aquinas. But the major and explicit disagreement, at **lines 61–6**, is with the great Islamic philosopher Averroes (Ibn-Rushd (*c.* 1126–*c.* 1198)), whose theories were also attacked many times over by Aquinas. There is no violent condemnation here. Dante speaks with the same respect for this great philosopher that he showed in his mention of him in Limbo (*Inferno* 4: 144). None the less, the point at issue here is crucial. As will be seen, Averroes' position would, if taken to its conclusion, entail a denial of personal immortality. A belief in such immortality is central both to Dante's theology – especially as crystallized in his love for Beatrice who is shortly to re-appear in Dante's sight undiminished by her early death – and also to the fictional story which, from the first, has envisaged his own bodily encounter with the spirit bodies that Statius now undertakes to explain.

The argument runs in three phases. The first (**37–60**) explains the physiological and biological operations that may be observed in the development of any mammal within the womb. The second (**61–78**) looks at the unique conditions that pertain in the development of a human being. The third (**79–108**) addresses Dante's initial question concerning the emaciation of the penitent gluttons.

Lines 37–45 describe the process by which, in any animal, food becomes blood and blood becomes semen. On the Aristotelian view, food is received in the stomach where body heat causes it to divide into a nutritious substance, known as 'chyle', and waste matter, which is expelled as excrement. Chyle then passes to the liver where 'imperfect' – though still nutritious – blood is formed. Some of this blood then passes into the right ventricle of the heart, where it comes into contact with air from the lungs and becomes the 'perfect' blood that Dante here refers to at **line 37**. This blood possesses a power which is formative in that it can be transformed into the tissues and organs of the body. However, in the sexually mature adult, a small part of this perfect blood remains in the heart and undergoes a third and final refinement. It is this small remainder that Dante refers to at **line 39**, in a somewhat strained simile, as food carried away from a banquet – thereby emphasizing, at least, that there is a continuous connection between what we eat and what we are.

The formative power of perfect blood is intensified in the course of this final transformation, so that now it can actually transmit form and generate new and independent forms of life. In the case of females, where natural warmth is supposed to be lacking, this final form of 'perfect' blood is menstrual, and possesses the power to assume, but not initiate, independent forms of life. In the male, perfect blood in its final form descends to the testicles ('more decent not to say') and becomes semen.

When active semen joins with the receptive menstrual blood, a coagulation or clotting occurs, brought about by the activity of sperm, and the embryo begins to develop as described in **lines 47–60**. In becoming a human foetus, the embryo will pass through a number of different phases, from the vegetative or nutritive phase to an animal form of life. Tracking these phases, Statius pays particular attention, at **lines 55–7**, to the phase in which the embryo is comparable to a sea sponge – the sponge being a standard example in Aristotelian biology of a form that has some sensation without possessing organs or limbs. It is important to note that when the term *anima* – 'soul' – is used here (as at **line 52**) it is employed, in a way discussed in the commentaries to *Purgatorio* 4, 17 and 18, to mean the 'animating' principle that gives shape, or, as one might now say, genetic character to any form of life which is capable of growth, be it vegetable, animal or rational. It is not only human beings that have souls, as Aristotle understands the word 'soul'. A sea sponge, on this account, would have its own kind of soul.

It is in his description of this process, as it proceeds over the next seven months, that Dante favours the views of Albertus Magnus over those of Aquinas. Broadly speaking, Aquinas emphasized the discontinuities in the development of the embryo as it moves from one stage to another, whereas Albertus looked to the continuity between these stages of growth. (The details of this debate need not concern us, but see P. Boyde, *Dante, Philomythes and Philosopher* (1981), pp. 270–95 for further discussion.) However, Dante, in his emphasis on continuity, does prepare for the crucial point in his own argument, which is the radical discontinuity that exists in the human being between its vegetative and animal phases and its final human form.

It is this that is discussed in lines 61–78 and here, too, that Dante's radical disagreement with Averroes comes into play. The process of embryonic generation is now complete. The limbs are formed, and so is the foetal brain. However, we do not yet know (61–6) how humans come to possess an intellect, and are thus able to participate in an intellectual experience which associates them with the angels and ultimately with God. The distinction between human beings and other forms of animal life resides in the possession of an intellect. Animals possess cognition of particular objects and thus may have a mental image of a stone as being large, heavy or brown. (Compare the discussion of intellection in the commentary to *Purgatorio* 18.) What they do not have, according to Aristotle and Dante, is conceptual understanding of size, weight and colour. Human beings are capable of such understanding, and their capacity for it is usually referred to as the *intellectus possibilis* (65). This capacity is not to be located in any particular organ of the body. Vision is an activity of the eye, hearing of the ear. But intellectual understanding is an abstraction which makes abstraction itself a possibility. It is by this that we give meaning to the experiences that our physical faculties deliver. It is by intellection, too, that we attain self-conscious knowledge of our own existence and, as Statius emphasizes, the ability to communicate in speech (61–3). So in what way is this intellect acquired and how are its powers exercised?

It is here that Dante confronts the radical difference between his own position and that of Averroes. Responding to Aristotle's argument that intellect cannot be located in any particular organ, Averroes came to the conclusion that the soul must be entirely separable from the particular physical form that a human being assumes, existing as a separable substance, somewhat in the manner of a pure neo-Platonic intelligence. In this case (to quote Boyde, p. 277), 'knowledge could be rented but not owned. Each individual could participate in the pool of intellect', but intellect was not in any way an essential part of its individuality. Nor would the intellective soul enjoy personal immortality. At death, the *intellectus possibilis* returned to the communal pool of intelligence.

No view could be less consistent with Dante's own. The Aristotelianism that Dante himself espouses insists that the human soul is the animating form of a physical form of life and inseparable from the body of a particular individual. (See introduction to *Inferno*, pp. lii–lvii.) His theology is sustained by the belief – first inspired by Beatrice's death – that human beings live beyond their earthly death. The dramatic fiction of his poem involves at all points conversation with individuals who retain the marks of their intellectual and physical lives. So, a great deal depends upon the rebuttal of Averroes which Statius now utters. With appropriate solemnity of phrase (67–72), Statius prepares to open up the truth, and for the first time brings God, the 'Primal Cause of Motion', into consideration. So far Statius has described the development until the point where it is complete in all its organs and limbs, as well as (Dante emphasizes) in its brain. But at this point God looks down on the excellent work that biological process has performed and breathes into it an intellective soul which renders it a new and particular human individual. This human being remains in certain aspects a vegetative and animal being. However, as was established in the opening lines of canto 4, there are not three animating principles at work in the individual but only one, which draws all others into its sphere of operations and exerts a self-conscious influence over all its activities, cerebral, animal or vegetative (75). This soul, henceforth, can never be separated from the human being, nor can the body be seen (as Virgil suggests at lines 25–7) merely as a mirror image of the soul. As the heat of the sun combines with the juice of grapes to make wine (77–8) and can never, afterwards, be distinguished from the wine itself, so the rational soul, granted by divine intervention, works in the individual as the absolute ground of what that individual is.

Running through the first two phases of Statius's discussion is a distinction between two ways in which creatures come into existence: the mode of 'generation' and the mode of 'creation'. God works in both modes. But in 'generation' he works through 'Nature's art' (71). Having created nature in the first place, God then allows the laws of nature – physical, chemical and biological – to take their course. He operates, in this case, at one remove, though, through the instruments of natural cause and effect. In 'creation', however, God works *sanza mezzo* – literally, 'without intermediary' – bringing creatures into life through the direct act of his will. (Compare *Paradiso* 7: 142–4; also *Paradiso* 13 and 14.) In the first phase of his speech, Statius has described a process of generation, in which the foetus develops according to the laws that govern growth in all vegetative or animal creatures.

But the second phase describes an act of creation in which the particular soul issues (as Dante has already said at *Purgatorio* 16) directly from the hand of God. God emphatically rejoices in the generative work of nature. It is only when nature has displayed its greatness to the full that He then 'creates' the individual by bestowing on this being the gift of an intellective soul.

The view which Dante expresses here, while standing in complete contrast to Averroes, also forms the foundation for some of his most characteristic beliefs. In the first place, human beings are unique in the universe precisely because they are the product both of generation and creation. Animals are the product purely of natural generation. Angels are the product purely of God's creative act. But Dante never imagines that human beings will ever become angels or, for that matter, descend to the level of animals. Their role is to live fully in their unique form of existence. And, at the resurrection of the dead, they will return to the flesh and live in the fullness that only a being which is both generated and created can enjoy. Thus, as Dante argues in *Paradiso* 7: 124–44, the physical attributes, which in other generated beings will eventually pass away, are assured eternal existence by virtue of the intrinsic connection that exists between the intellective soul and the matter (or, as it were, 'grape juice') that this created being animates.

In the *Purgatorio*, Dante does not advance quite as clearly to this conclusion as he does in *Paradiso* 7. However, the closer he draws to Beatrice in the Earthly Paradise, the closer he comes to a realization of how complete and triumphant our possession of immortal existence will be. Moreover, in Statius's words, there is already a perceptible shift in diction that leads away even from Aristotle towards a fully theological understanding of the issue. To speak of God breathing life into the human being (70–72) alerts us to the action of a God who from the book of Genesis onwards is believed to have created all life out of nothing. But emphatically this is not to speak of God as a merely mechanical device, the ultimate source of power, the battery of the universe. Nature remains its own engine. It is rather to indicate in the act of creation a wholly mysterious but wholly personal interest on the part of the Creator in His own creatures. The crucial word here is *'lieto'* – 'happy', translated here as 'in joy' at **line 70**, which also appears at *Purgatorio* 16: 89 and 23: 74. The Christian God is a God who delights in existence, and is even happy to suffer the desolation of the Cross so as to ensure that his creatures enjoy existence in its fullest expression. Delight is an engagement of the conscious mind as it devotes itself to the complexity or value of some great design. And delight is particularly acute when it perceives harmony or compatibility or likeness. So God, in creating human beings, bestows his own likeness on them, as if to enjoy their existence all the more. Thus, at line 75, Statius speaks of the threefold action of a self-conscious being, as he will speak later (82) of the three faculties that characteristically distinguish human operations – memory, understanding and will. It is the possession of these faculties that ensures the autonomy and freedom of human beings (as discussed in *Purgatorio* 16–18), and, in being free, human beings resemble their Creator – who need not have created them in the first place and whom they, if they choose, can wholly ignore. But the threefold operation of these attributes also reflects the threefold activity of God in the Trinity, which directs, receives and sustains the 'love that moves the sun and other stars' (*Paradiso* 33: 145). In realizing that, even as generated beings, they are part of that motion, human beings rediscover their similitude to the divine.

One implication of this view is that intellect is not simply a power that allows us to analyse or control the working of the generated cosmos, but actually admits us, in delight, to a direct participation in the workings of the Trinity. Dante will not pursue this understanding until he arrives at the *Paradiso* – where it is particularly significant in cantos 10–15 and in canto 29. Obliquely, however, it has a contribution to make to the final phase of Statius's speech here (79–108), where he finally offers a direct, though highly decorated, answer to Dante's initial question. If the penitent gluttons do display the physical signs of starvation, this is because, at their deaths, they experienced a new form of birth which parallels but reverses the process by which an embryo becomes a human child. Where previously the process was initiated and carried through by generative action, it is now the *created* soul of the intellect that governs all. This soul is indelibly in place, and, coming now into the presence of its Creator, it grows yet more intense in its operations than before (82–4). These operations include – since the human soul is one single entity – all the operations that hitherto have been displayed in physical movements and psychosomatic action. But now the soul radiates its own self-consciousness into a semblance of physical matter, which can register even smiles and tears that are naturally part of a human existence. (Compare *Purgatorio* 21: 106–8.) So, too, (though Dante does not say this explicitly here) the intellect in its desires and feelings (106–8) is primarily tuned to the will of God, and so registers, in all its being, the physical consequences that flow from a love of God's justice. (Compare commentary on *Purgatorio* 23.) Where justice demands that the body lives by the measure that God has used in creating it, the penitents now willingly shed the excrescences that their gluttony in life has generated.

By now, Statius's argument has entered the sphere of hypothesis, and even of exuberant science – or (theological) fiction, as Dante with evident delight develops a justification for his own narrative inventions. The verse is full of metaphors, classical allusions and scintillating imagery, reflecting in some measure the highly mannered style that Dante attributes to Statius in *Purgatorio* 21 and 22, where images of rainbows and references to the Fates are also to be found. Here, too, Dante prepares for a contrast between his own achievements and the vernacular poets who will appear in canto 26. Not only is he capable of a philosophical sophistication which none of his contemporaries could muster, but he has also a wider acquaintance with classical style and rhetorical usage. However, the final phase of the canto (109–39) adds a further consideration which is relevant to the themes of canto 25 and to the treatment of lust which follows in canto 26. The path is suddenly very dangerous (115–17), with a precipice on one side and on the other the fire surrounding the summit of the mountain in which the lustful perform their penance. But Dante, too, must pass through this fire on his way to Beatrice. So, suddenly, after the philosophical abstraction of Statius's discourse, the canto now speaks of vertigo and violent sensations which directly affect Dante as he travels forward, and associate him with the last group of sinners he will meet. Then, out of the flame, comes first the sound of a hymn and then the examples of chastity which mark the entry into the final terrace. The hymn is the seventh-century '*Summae Deus clementiae*', usually sung late on a Saturday night in preparation for the Sabbath:

> O God of highest mercy, maker and ruler of these earthly workings, one in substance and in persons three, majestic Trinity in Unity. In love do graciously accept our songs mingled with our prayerful weeping, and so that, free at heart from stain and error, we may delight more fully in Thee. Burn out our loins and livers, diseased. And with appropriate fire put away all sinful lust, so that it may ever after be girded up. As we all interrupt the hours of night with our singing, so may we be enriched beyond desire with the riches of our homeland. Hear our prayer, Almighty King. And hear our praises while we sing, adoring with the heavenly choirs, the Father, Son and Holy Ghost.

The relevance of this to the lustful is immediately obvious. This is a prayer for sexual restraint, its message confirmed by the examples (133–5) which conclude the canto in praise of married love. The tradition to which the poets of the next canto and Dante himself all belong is one which, even in its most refined forms, praises the courtly *donna*, who is never the wife of her devotee. Beatrice was not, of course, Dante's wife. Yet the point here is not simply to preach a lesson in conjugal fidelity. Dante, rather, is beginning to consider how human love may conjoin and collaborate with the divine love that is first displayed in the Trinity. '*Summae Deus clementiae*' is first and last concerned with the action of the Trinity, with God as the maker of the universal system and with the delight that is possible when we come home to our proper place in the divine order. And sexuality, far from being repressed, is viewed here – and, by implication, in Dante's text – as a way of furthering divine action in the sphere of generated and created existence. This is precisely what the sexual activity that Statius describes is aimed to do in the generation of children who are also the recipients of God's creative breath. Beyond that, too, there is the mystic marriage which Dante (like none of his contemporaries) will prefigure in his meeting with Beatrice. This is the alternative to the lust which Dante is about to speak of. The human soul will eventually return to its origins in a marriage which is also a rebirth. None of Dante's contemporaries in the Languedoc or in Italy envisaged any such point of arrival for human love. Yet it is precisely this – a marriage and a rebirth – that Dante depicts when in *Purgatorio* 30 he describes his return to the presence of Beatrice.

Notes

1–3   The time designated by this reference is around 2 p.m. in Purgatory and 2 a.m. in Jerusalem.

10–12   Compare this simile with the references to birds in *Purgatorio* 24: 64–6 and 26: 43–5.

22–4   Here and throughout the canto there are certain precise parallels with *Inferno* 25. In that canto, Dante presents an appalling parody of procreation, whereby the bodies of thieves are forced to intermingle, producing, however, not children but monstrosities that have no form or identity at all, which are neither 'two' nor 'one' nor any kind of recognizable new being. In *Inferno* 25 Dante consciously seeks to outdo the spectacular and often erotic narratives of metamorphosis that Ovid offers. From the allusion to Meleager here, Ovid is again in Dante's mind and continues to be so in *Purgatorio* 26, where the penitents are the lustful. But now, if Dante outdoes the classical author, he does so through a sympathetic, even celebratory rewriting of Statius's life and works. And the underlying philosophy of this canto stands in complete contrast to the Lucretian philosophy of the *Metamorphoses*. Change and flux are, in Dante's thinking, not endless processes but rather expressions of form directed to an appropriate end, assured by God – and, in the case of the human being, eternally assured. Compared even with the *Inferno* there is no frustrated play upon nothingness, unity and duality. All processes in the human being resemble the process of love enacted in the Trinity and are devoted to the furtherance of new forms of life.

79–81 For Lachesis, see note to *Purgatorio* 21: 25–7.

82–4 Durling and Martinez speak, in a valuable note to their edition of *Purgatorio* (2003), of a tradition going back to Saint Augustine's *De Trinitate* 10: 11, 18 (400–416), which saw the three intellectual powers as the 'seal' of the Holy Trinity, impressed upon the human being.

127–39 The examples of chastity are drawn, firstly, from the words of the Virgin Mary to the Archangel Gabriel in Luke 1: 34: 'I know not a man'. The second comes from *Metamorphoses* 2: 401–507, which tells the story of Helice (or Callisto), a nymph of Diana's company who is raped and made pregnant by Jupiter, then driven from Diana's woods so that she cannot corrupt their purity. When Callisto gives birth to a son, she is transformed by the jealous Juno into a bear. But Jupiter further transforms her and her son into the constellations of the Bear, Ursa Major and Ursa Minor.

CANTO 26

The lustful. Dante meets with Guido Guinizelli – whom he acknowledges as the father of the sweet new style – and the Occitan poet Arnaut Daniel.

Commentary

Throughout canto 26 Dante continues, as he did in cantos 23 and 24, to concern himself with the past achievements of vernacular culture and to display, in counterpoint to that theme, his own poetic development as he proceeds towards his meeting with Beatrice. There are, likewise, connections between this canto and canto 25. Where the previous canto had spoken of biological procreation, this one speaks of poetic and intellectual inheritance. Of the two main characters who appear in canto 26, one is described, at lines 97–8, as the 'sire', or *father*, of the sweet new style (with which Dante's early poetry was associated); the other is introduced, at line 117, as a better maker of the *mother* tongue. Yet, in celebrating these figures, Dante also acknowledges that poetry is capable of perverting the highest conceptions of love. These two poets, like all the penitents on the final terrace, have been guilty of lust. This means that, in some way, Dante considers them to have misapprehended the relationship that exists between people, distorting the sexual and ethical principles that underlie such relationships. Nor does Dante hesitate to summon from his own imagination, at lines 40–42, a disturbing evocation of sexual violence, with hectic and violent references to the sins of Sodom and Gomorrah and to bestialism. Moreover, while his conversations here are courteous – and at times ornate in their diction, to the point of artificiality – he also alludes to, and indulges in, the literary in-fighting that can be a feature of any cultural élite (see lines 121–6). At two points (lines 96 and 98) Dante confesses the superiority of past poetic achievements to his own. The reader must judge whether these lines are meant to be sincere or are themselves an example of rhetorical modesty.

The first of the two poets – who leads the discussion for most of this canto – is Guido Guinizelli, an academic jurist and judge from Bologna. In his early years, Guinizelli had been associated with Guittone's circle of poets, and was reproved by Bonagiunta da Lucca (see canto 24) for 'changing his master's style' in favour of a supposedly oversubtle interest in matters of intellectual debate. To Dante, on the contrary, Guinizelli was responsible for a new and elevated conception of love, expressed with greater fluency than Guittone could command, particularly in the *canzone* '*Al cor gentil . . .*', which begins:

> *Al cor gentil rempaira sempre amore*
> *come l'ausello in selva a la verdure;*
> *Né fe' amor anti che gentil core,*
> *né gentil core anti ch'amor, natura.*

(Love always returns to the noble heart, as does the bird in the woodlands to the foliage. Nor did nature create love before it made the noble heart, or the noble heart before it created love.)

These lines directly inspired Dante's own conviction, expressed in the sonnet '*Amor e 'l cor gentil sono una cosa . . .*' (*Vita nuova* 20), that love is the defining feature of true nobility, and that love itself can only exist where the heart is truly noble.

In the *Vita nuova*, Guinizelli's example seems to have liberated Dante from the melancholy influence of Guido Cavalcanti, who saw love as a power that was often in conflict with the best of human capabilities (see introduction to *Inferno*, pp. xxvii–xxxiii), and led him to develop the praise style to which he alludes in *Purgatorio* 24. In the *Commedia*, too, especially in the opening simile of *Paradiso* 23, Dante's continuing debt is apparent in a highly developed version of the metaphor with which Guinizelli's famous *canzone* begins. It seems hard, therefore, to explain why Guinizelli should appear among those who, in their lives, were guilty of lust or followed 'bestial appetites' (82–4). It would be equally hard, however, to argue that Guinizelli himself fully understood the consequences of the position that his verses suggested to Dante. In particular, the last stanza of his poem retracts the enthusiastic implication that the love of an earthly woman might be harmonious with the love of God. But it is this extreme conclusion to which Dante moves at the end of the *Purgatorio*, where his vision of Beatrice, in style and theme, goes far beyond anything that Guinizelli was capable of. All love poetry that fails to make that connection is in danger of treating human love as merely a form of lust.

In the case of the second poet to whom Dante alludes here, it is easier to see why he should have entered a revisionary judgement of his literary ancestor. This figure (introduced at **lines 115–17**) is Arnaut Daniel (*c.* 1140–*c.* 1190), to whom Dante has previously made frequent and admiring reference, for instance in *De Vulgari Eloquentia* 2: 2; 2: 6; 2: 13. Arnaut was born at Ribérac, in the Dordogne. He was active at the court of Richard Coeur de Lion at Poitiers and was possibly a friend of the poet Bertran de Born (*c.* 1140 – before 1215), whom Dante also praises in the *De Vulgari Eloquentia* but then chooses to place in Hell. (See commentary on *Inferno* 28. See also *Paradiso* 8, where the Occitan poet and bishop Folco of Marseilles (d. 1231) appears in Heaven, thus ensuring that one Occitan poet appears in each of the three realms of the afterlife.) Seventeen of Arnaut's eighteen extant poems are *canzoni*. The *canzone* is, technically, a highly elaborate form, usually devoted in theme to the subject of courtly love in its most extreme manifestations. And some of Arnaut's contemporaries found the poet's work obscure. The *canzone* was precisely the form, however, that Dante adopted for himself at the time of *De Vulgari Eloquentia* and recommended to others who wished to elevate their native vernaculars. For Dante, it was through the *canzone*'s complex rhymes, associated in Arnaut's writing with vivid and sometimes far-fetched imagery, that the mother tongue could be made coherent, harmonious and capable of dealing with serious ethical subjects.

An example of Arnaut's virtuosity is to be found in the *canzone* 'Lo ferm voler . . .', which concludes:

> For thus my soul cleaves and clings with its nail to her, as close as the bark to the rod. For she is to me joy's tower, and palace and bedroom, and I love her more than I do cousin and uncle. Hence in Paradise will my soul have twofold joy, if ever a man through fine loving enters.
>
> Arnaut sends his song of fingernail and uncle for the pleasure of her who arms him with his rod to his desired One who with merit in bedroom enters.

The two extremes of love are explored in the course of this poem. On the one hand, there is a recognition of the madness and frustration into which sexual desire can throw the lover. On the other, there is an awareness that desire can transcend itself, refining the lover (as loyalty to clan or family can never do) to the point at which he merits an entry into 'Paradise' – whether sexual or spiritual. Throughout, Arnaut, in this 'song of fingernail and uncle', maintains a running pun on the words 'ongle' and 'oncle' ('fingernail' and 'uncle') in rhyming positions, creating formal harmony while simultaneously evoking an experience of obsession and frustration.

In certain of Dante's early poems similar experiences are expressed through similarly formal experiments. Among his *Rime Petrose*, dedicated to a 'stony' and resistant *donna* (see commentary on *Inferno* 32), there is, for instance, the *sestina* 'Al poco giorno . . .', in which the poet describes his imprisonment as a lover within the 'winter' of unrequited passion, and where, in the six verses of this poem, the same six rhyme words occur in each stanza, shifted by strict permutation into six different positions within successive stanzas. But in the *Commedia* Dante has developed a simpler and more balanced form, and the implications of this development are revealed in the way in which he now revises Arnaut's mode of speech. As nowhere else in the *Commedia*, Dante attempts to write a speech in the native language of the character he is depicting. This may be seen as a celebration of the mother tongue that Arnaut elaborated to such a degree of perfection. These verses also identify a regular feature of Arnaut's own writing, which is that, at the conclusion of his *canzoni*, he tends to name himself as author and present himself to view, with the recurrent phrase 'Ieu sui Arnaut'/'I am Arnaut', often in a very disturbed psychological light. 'Lo ferm voler . . .' (see above) illustrates this, as does

'*En cest sonnet coind'e leri . . .*', which concludes with a picture of a distracted Arnaut who 'swims against the tide', 'seeks to catch the wind in a net', and goes out hunting on the back of a cow, not a horse. But such complexities of style and self-image disappear from canto 26. Though Dante alludes at line 142 to Arnaut's phrase '*Ieu sui Arnaut . . .*', the personality that is here presented, though tense with penitential purpose, has translated desire into an attention wholly focused upon transcendent goodness and a concern, courteous rather than self-obsessed, with Dante's own welfare. Arnaut's language in the *Purgatorio* is correspondingly simple and measured, as if purified of all rhetorical exaggeration or excess.

In its 'fine' – as opposed to its foolish – aspect, courtly love cultivates a highly original notion of ethical balance: through contemplating the perfection of the *donna*, the lover progressively develops his own possible perfections to an ever-higher pitch. His behaviour thus becomes increasingly 'measured'. 'Measure', however, is not the product of some code that is externally imposed or regulated. It is an internal poise born of will and imagination. In this sense, love's service, and the quests to which it might lead, is exactly analogous to the inward search for selfhood that penitence in Purgatory now demands. Arnaut here, freed from madness and distraction, as the last sinner to appear anywhere in the *Commedia*, exemplifies exactly what such poise might look like. (Lust is the last sin to be purified in Purgatory, but also the passion that brings us closest to God.) The writing of poetry likewise offers an analogy for the process of purification. As a 'maker' of verse, Arnaut, in common with Dante after him, would 'file' or 'shape' his verse (the metaphor of the file is commonplace in Provençal poetics) to liberate it from excrescences or distractions.

Speaking a prayer on Dante's behalf, Arnaut, in the last line of canto 26, positively chooses to remain in the fire that 'sharpens', but also directs his attentions, consciously and willingly, as do all the penitents in Purgatory, to the goal on which his own perfections depend. Dante, too, moving closer still to his own true measure in the figure of Beatrice, is cultivating a similar understanding of the self, wholly inward yet wholly dependent upon a being that lies beyond the confines of his own understanding. Poetically, however, canto 26 remains an agitated linguistic construct, responsive to both the negative and positive poles of courtly poetry, which throughout alludes continually to the style and diction of Dante's predecessors in the vernacular as well as classic tradition. The courtesies, for instance, of lines 73–5 – in which Guinizelli recognizes that Dante is travelling to gain a cargo of experience – draws on nautical metaphors that are to be found in Guinizelli's own poetry and in Arnaut's. The metaphor of bird flight in lines 43–5 belongs to a rich vein of ornithological reference which began with the images of larks rising in Occitan poetry and continues in Guinizelli's 'Al cor gentil . . .' These references take a savage turn in Dante's own *Rime Petrose*, where, drawing on Arnaut's example, he is concerned in 'Io son venuto . . .', as here, with bird flight in the winter season. (Compare *Inferno* 5: 46–8; *Purgatorio* 24: 64 and 25: 10–12; also *Paradiso* 18: 73–5 and 21: 34–6.) To the vein of natural observation that underlies these similes Dante, at lines 34–6, adds a reference to the behaviour of ants that draws on Virgil's *Aeneid* 4: 404 and Pliny's *Natural History* 11: 6.

Notes

40–42 For Sodom and Gomorrah as cities of decadence and corruption, see Genesis 18: 16 and 19: 1. For Pasiphae – who had an artificial cow made which she could enter, and so couple with a young bull – see *Inferno* 12: 13 and *Metamorphoses* 8: 738–40; also *Ars Amoris* 1: 290–326 and 2: 21–4.

43–5 The Riphean mountains, not recognized by modern geography, are thought to have been located by classical geographers northwest of the Carpathians, and are taken, for example by Orosius, to have marked the northern boundary of Europe.

67–9 Compare this metaphor with that used to describe Dante's arrival at the height of Paradise (*Paradiso* 31: 31–42).

76–8 From Uguccione da Pisa (d. 1210) Dante may have heard recorded the story told by Suetonius of Julius Caesar's homosexuality, and of how he became the passive partner in a relationship with the king of Bithynia, so that his own troops greeted him with the cry of 'queen!'

82 'Hermaphrodite' here means heterosexual. The story of Hermaphroditus is found in *Metamorphoses* 4: 285–388. Hermaphroditus is the son of Hermes and Aphrodite. He is loved by, but repels the advances of, the nymph Salamcis. She embraces him when he swims in her pool and, though he resists, she is granted her wish to be fused with him, producing a 'half-man'.

94–6 This very condensed and allusive reference recalls the story – which has been described as a 'romance' – told by Statius in the *Thebaid* 5: 499–753. The son of Lycurgus, king of Nemea, is left unattended by his nurse Hypsipyle. (Compare *Purgatorio* 22: 88–9 and commentary on *Purgatorio* 22.) Lycurgus demands that Hypsipyle be slain but she is at this point recognized by two

of Lycurgus's men who prove to be the sons whom she had
deserted twenty years earlier, born to the Argonaut Jason who
earlier had deserted her. (See *Inferno* 18: 88–94.) The sons,
re-united with their mother after long separation, save her from
the threat of death.

118–20   The 'poet from Limoges' is the poet Giraut de Bornelh
(c. 1150–1220), also referred to in *De Vulgari Eloquentia* 2: 5.

139–48   A literal translation of these lines is:

> So pleasing to me is your courteous request that I neither can nor
> will hide myself from you. I am Arnaut, who weeping and singing
> go on my way. With sadness I see my past foolishness and rejoicing
> I see ahead the joy for which I hope. Now I beg you by the power
> that guides you to the summit of the stair, remember my suffering
> when the time is due.

There are many points of comparison and contrast between these
lines and other major episodes of the *Commedia*. Arnaut's closely
resemble that with Francesca da Rimini in *Inferno* 5 (1255–85).
In that episode Dante first revealed the possible deficiencies in
the diction of vernacular love poetry. Now he envisages the
redemption of that tradition. Secondly, the passage recalls
Inferno 26, where Ulysses, like Arnaut, is condemned to the pains
of fire. Ulysses, however, in his search for knowledge, sets out
to break all boundaries. Arnaut restrains himself to stay within
the confines of the penitential flame. Where Ulysses produces
a dangerously exuberant rhetoric, Arnaut's words are notable
for their considerateness and simplicity. Finally, in *Paradiso*
26: 124–38, Dante once more takes up the theme of the mother
tongue in a conversation with Adam about the ways in which
vernacular speech was transformed from the Garden of Eden
onwards.

CANTO 27

Dante passes into the fire that purges the lustful,
where he spends his final night on Mount Purgatory
and dreams of Rachel and Leah.

Commentary

Dante's journey to Beatrice can be viewed not only as an epic but as a quest of the kind described in the romances to which Dante alludes at *Purgatorio* 26: 118. (Compare commentary to *Inferno* 2.) Prose romance – which, before Dante wrote his *Commedia*, had been the principal model of medieval narrative – typically describes the adventures of a chivalric protagonist who sets out, in the service of love or loyalty, to prove his personal merit, sustaining his endeavours over protracted periods of time and also through moments of intense crisis. For Dante, nearing the end of his journey – his entry into the Earthly Paradise, where he will encounter Beatrice – requires him to pass through the penitential flames in which the love poets who have preceded him are purified. His merits – which Virgil finally acknowledges in lines 140–42 – are tested by an ordeal of fire. This ordeal is also a solemn vigil in which Dante is supported – as Virgil advises – by the thought that Beatrice, his immediate goal or grail, stands beyond the limits of the fire. As well as this encouragement, Dante experiences a visionary dream, anticipating the scene that will begin to unfold in canto 28.

The fire in which Dante spends this final night is described as being so fierce that he would have thrown himself into molten glass to refresh himself (49–51). One recalls that, banished from Florence, he was condemned to be burned alive if ever he were arrested. As always, beyond the surface of Dante's fiction lies a field of historical reference and personal experience which distinguishes his writings from the often-fantastical inventions of the romance tradition. At the same time, Dante perceives in the quest motif a profound metaphor for the religious understanding which the *Paradiso* will shortly begin to explore. From now on, his quest, directed towards Beatrice, will also be a quest into the always transcendent 'beyond' of divine existence. This canto, in common with some of the greatest in the *Commedia* (such as *Purgatorio* 9), describes a process of transition. Dante now begins to picture his assimilation into a realm that eludes any purely natural understanding.

This is indicated in the opening sequence of the canto (1–9), which designates the position of the sun as it sinks on the second day, not by astronomical calculation but by a reference to Jerusalem which recalls the passion of Christ in the Crucifixion. Beneath and beyond the patterns of the world, Dante perceives the workings of the love of God who created this world and redeemed it by his sufferings on the Cross. In more extended form, however, the dream that comes to him at **lines 94–108** also points to a new level of thought to which Dante will rise as he enters the Earthly Paradise. Unlike the two previous dreams that he has experienced on Mount Purgatory (in cantos 9 and 19), this dream is, in character, more a vision than a dream, and introduces two women, Leah and Rachel, who foreshadow the two *donne* Matelda and Beatrice – the two main actors in the drama of cantos 28–33.

Leah, seen gathering flowers, speaks at **lines 103–8** of her sister Rachel, who sits all day long in contemplation of herself in her mirror. The primary allusion here is to the account (in Genesis 29–30) of how Jacob visits his uncle Laban and falls in love with his younger daughter, Rachel. Laban demands that Jacob should serve him for seven years, at the end of which time Rachel will be given to him in marriage. However, on the marriage night, Laban substitutes his elder daughter Leah for Rachel, and only allows the marriage of Rachel and Jacob to proceed when Jacob has served a further seven years. Many children are born to Leah, but only two, the especially beloved Joseph and Benjamin, are born to Rachel after a long period of childlessness.

The story is concerned with issues that have been present throughout the *Purgatorio*, with time and how we use it, with labour and its purposes, with the goals that always lie beyond our immediate comprehension. (In these respects, the story is comparable to the love story of Pyramus and Thisbe to which Dante refers at **lines 37–9**.) But Dante must also have in mind here the allegorical use to which the Genesis story was put by scriptural exegetes throughout the Middle Ages. He was probably thinking of Richard of Saint Victor's *Benjamin Minor* (c. 1160) in which Leah represents the active life of practical concern and Rachel the contemplative life of pure intelligence. Thus Richard writes that, after Leah had given birth to her sons, Rachel's desire for children of her own grew stronger:

> As it is Leah's part to love, since she is the affection of the soul, so it is Rachel's part to know, for she is reason. The former gives birth to order and affection; the latter to the reason or the pure intelligence ... And when Judah is born, that is, when desire and love of unseen good things

is rising and growing strong, then Rachel begins to desire children passionately, for she wants to know. Where love is there is vision. We like to look upon him whom we love greatly, and certainly he who can love invisible things will immediately desire to know and see them by intelligence.

Benjamin Minor 13, quoted from the translation by
Clare Kirchberger (1957), p. 91

There is much in Dante that favours the active life, above all his profound commitment to political reform. Yet there is, too, the recognition, which in the *Purgatorio* now begins to come into its own, of contemplation as the path through which divine charity is revealed. The figures here exactly correspond to Matelda who, like Leah, is gathering flowers when Dante first sees her at *Purgatorio* 28: 40–42, and to Beatrice, who will lead Dante forward in contemplation to the realm of Paradise. At no point does Dante disparage work as the expression of human will but, beyond work, there are truths that can only be delivered by the contemplative mind which, in total self-dispossession, looks towards the beautiful and the true.

In its representation of a quest and continuing crisis, as well as in its multiplicity of levels – all now approaching a contemplative synthesis, canto 27 deserves to be placed alongside other cantos (such as *Purgatorio* 9 or *Inferno* 17 – to which Dante alludes at lines 22–3) in which the mark of Dante's narrative is its ability to represent change and transition. Linguistically, too, the canto is distinguished by effects of synaesthesia – as dusk illuminated by violent flames gives way to a night in which the brilliance of star light displays itself through surrounding fire and the first light of a new dawn eventually replaces the conflagration. Particularly notable are the sections that run from line 70 to line 90 and from line 109 to line 114.

Dante's dream of Rachel and Leah, in pointing forward to the *donne* whom Dante encounters in the Earthly Paradise, designates a profound change in the direction of Dante's narrative, which envisages a modulation from a prevailingly masculine to a distinctively feminine ethos. Hitherto, Virgil, as Dante's guide, has sought to instil in him heroic virtues of endurance and sometimes prophetic foresight. Thus, at lines 22–4, he attempts to encourage Dante through the heart of the fire by recalling how he supported Dante during their descent into the deepest pit of Hell on the back of the monstrous Geryon. Geryon, significantly, was one of the beasts that the hero Hercules subdued in the course of his labours on earth. Dante is in Hell faced with a similar labour, which he extends by representing Geryon as the 'filthy image of deceit'

(*Inferno* 17: 7), a force of evil such as those that will take over the world in the days immediately before the Second Coming of Christ. (See commentary to *Inferno* 17.) Yet Virgil's appeal to that memory is not persuasive. It is Beatrice's name alone that inspires in Dante the hope and confidence he needs to proceed through the fire. And it is the many *donne* who appear in the final cantos – some of whom embody the Christian virtues of faith, hope and charity – who now, with Beatrice, direct his progess. The vision into which they lead him, so far from being a vision of apocalyptic evil is a vision of the goodness that human beings were always intended to enjoy.

As will be seen in cantos 30 and 31, this vision of goodness is in many ways stranger and more terrifying than any vision of evil. Nor does it excuse Dante in any way from a further contemplation of apocalyptic disaster. The end to which he is moving is not what he or the unprepared reader are likely to expect. But the final passage of canto 27 hints at where the tensions will arise, simultaneously preparing Dante and also (unintentionally) deluding him on the threshold of this last phase of his purgatorial journey. These words are, in part, a coronation of a sovereign hero, who has now achieved everything that Virgil has taught him. Like Hercules, Dante has proved his moral powers and might be expected now to ascend, like Hercules, directly to the heavens in full possession of his own being, 'free, upright and whole'. Yet his encounter with Beatrice, as described in canto 30, calls any such presumption into question, as Dante, trembling in her presence, is reduced to the passive condition of an inarticulate child. To enjoy the goodness of God requires more than the possession of human goodness. Not surprisingly, Virgil's words betray no sense of the contradictions and the pain ahead. They do, however, speak of pleasure. Virgil, who spoke in *Purgatorio* 17 of the love between creator and creature and prophetically in his *Eclogues* declares that a golden world of pleasure and justice may one day dawn, now as his final demand insists that Dante should take pleasure as his guide (**131**). The one mistake that he can make now is to fail in following the promptings of his own perfected will. But it is through his encounter with the *donne* of the Earthly Paradise that Dante, in preparation for the Celestial Paradise, begins to realize what this might mean. It is a lesson which, if closed to Virgil, can be learned directly from such vernacular love poets as appear in *Purgatorio* 26, or those at least who, in serving the *donna*, have abandoned any attachment to ego and, on their quests, have embraced the pains that intertwine with the ultimate pleasures of love, in bringing the inward image of the lady to fulfilment. (See commentary to canto 26.)

Notes

1–6 If it is sunset in Purgatory, it is sunrise in Jerusalem and therefore midnight over the river Ebro in Spain and noon over the Ganges.

7–9 'Blessed are the pure in heart' is the sixth Beatitude in Matthew 5: 8.

25–7 In Daniel 3: 27, Shadrack, Meshach and Abednego, placed by Nebuchadnezzar in a furnace, remain unharmed. Not a hair on their heads has been touched by fire.

37–9 In *Metamorphoses* 4: 51–166, Pyramus, finding Thisbe's body mauled by a lion, supposes that she is dead and stabs himself. Thisbe, reviving, repeatedly calls his name. But Pyramus only responds when she utters her own name. Pyramus's blood stains with red the hitherto white berries of the mulberry – a detail which led medieval allegorists to speak of Christ's death on the Cross. (Compare *Purgatorio* 33: 67–9.)

58 'Come, ye blessed of my Father' (Matthew 25: 34). In the mosaics of the Baptistery in Florence, these words are depicted in the mouth of an angel at the Last Judgement.

94–9 Cytherea is Venus, who rose from the sea near Cythera in the Peloponnese. In Dante's Italian, the especially complex syntax of these lines delays '*donna*', as the subject of the sentence, in such a way as, firstly, to allow 'lovely and young' to refer, grammatically, either to Venus or the *donna* and then to replace Venus by attention to the *donna*. At line 109, '*antelucani*' in Dante's text – meaning 'before dawn', as does the rare English word 'antelucan' – is one of a number of rare words or neologisms that appear in this canto (others being, at lines 76–84: '*manse*' (tame or 'mild') and '*pranse*' ('fed'), '*pernotta*' ('spend the night').

CANTO 28

*Dante arrives at the Earthly Paradise and encounters
a girl (later identified as Matelda) dancing and
gathering flowers on the far side of a stream. The girl
explains to him how the meteorological conditions of
the Earthly Paradise derive directly from the perfect
workings of the heavenly circles.*

Commentary

Pleasure and perfection are the themes of canto 28. The canto divides
into two main phases. The first (1–84) describes the pleasure of
Dante's first experiences in the Earthly Paradise. Here all his senses
are stimulated and satisfied anew as he and Virgil (at last not having
to climb) wander eagerly in and around the shadowy, scented forest
(1–3). Attention, in the first phase, is concentrated on the figure of a
girl (52–7), dancing and gathering flowers on the further bank of a
stream that marks an apparently impassable division (70–75) between
one side of the Earthly Paradise and the other. In the second phase of
the canto (85–148), the girl discusses the way in which winds and
weathers are regulated in this place. This is the site of Eden – the
garden that God intended humanity to enjoy, undying, to eternity
(91–6). Rising far above any mountain in the northern hemisphere,
the garden is unaffected by the confusions that occur in the lower parts
of the physical world and is governed only by the perfect movements of
the heavenly spheres that God has set in motion. These movements
generate, without impediment, the entirely harmonious and fertile
conditions that prevail here. The Earthly Paradise is traversed by two
rivers. These issue from a single source (121–6; see also canto 33, line
127). However, the waters from that source are produced, not by the
natural cycles of evaporation and precipitation, but directly at the will
of God. The stream which now divides Dante from Matelda is Lethe,
the river of oblivion which appears in classical mythology (and which
he has already mentioned at *Inferno* 14: 136–8). In a form of baptismal
purification, Dante will be drawn through this river at *Purgatorio*
31: 94–105, and be freed from any memory of sin. On the other side
of the garden, the stream takes the name of Eunoe – a word of Dante's
own invention, signifying good remembrance. Dante will pass through
this river in canto 33 and recover the memory of the good deeds he
has performed in his lifetime.

The second phase of canto 28 anticipates the philosophical vision of perfected and transfigured nature that Dante will explore in the *Paradiso*. (Compare *Paradiso* 1 and 13.) It also reflects an appetite for detailed explanation, in quasi-scientific terms, that occurs in all parts of the *Purgatorio*, particularly in Statius's comparable discussion of meteorology. (See *Purgatorio* 21: 40–60.) However, the canto concludes (**139–48**) with neither science fiction nor theology, but with a celebration of myth – which is particularly notable since, as Matelda emphasizes at **line 136**, it involves a celebration of classical antiquity which is, strictly, only a 'footnote' in her discussion of divine creation. The Earthly Paradise is 'perhaps' the place that classical poets dreamed of before the coming of Christ, when they spoke of 'an Age of Gold' and of Parnassus (**140–41**). In the Italian text of **lines 139–41** a significant and very moving sequence of rhymes is constructed to express this: '*poetaro/sognaro*': 'they wrote poetry/they dreamed', translated here with the half-rhyme 'poems/dream'. Poetry and dreaming are, it seems, closely akin, and the dreams of the classical poets are praised here for having kept alive the hopes of justice, peace and fulfilment that are fully realized in the person of Christ.

These lines bring to a climax the concern with Virgil's prophetic writings that began in *Purgatorio* 22: 70–72 with a quotation from his fourth *Eclogue*. They also identify one of the most important strands in the imaginative texture of the *Commedia*. Dante was a syncretist, looking constantly for ways in which classical and Christian texts could be reconciled. He was not, of course, alone in being so. For instance, in the Dominican church of Santa Sabina at Rome (where Aquinas worked on his *Summa Theologiae*) there is still to be seen a ninth-century Paschal candlestick in which the twofold nature of the incarnate Christ – both human and divine – is represented by a column of intertwining spirals which are supported by sphinxes, alluding to the ancient culture of Egypt. Dante in cantos 29 and 30 constructs his own enigmatic image of Christ's double nature in his depiction of the mysterious Gryphon, simultaneously eagle and lion, drawing on Middle Eastern iconographic traditions. Throughout the final cantos of the *Purgatorio*, there is an especially rich fusion (and tension) between recollections of pagan antiquity and the impact of Christian reality. Allusions to ancient legend punctuate canto 28. (See notes below.) The most significant of these, at **lines 49–51**, is to the myth of Proserpina, the daughter of Ceres, who was carried off by Pluto while picking flowers in the apparently perpetual springtime of the vale of Enna. This legend is regularly seen as a myth of the seasonal cycle. But Dante's principal source is *Metamorphoses* 5: 385–408, in which the scene is depicted with Ovid's characteristic eroticism. In Dante's text it is an introduction to his encounter with the complex figure of Matelda (though she is only named as such at *Purgatorio* 33: 119). And with Matelda – delicate as the impression of her is – there appears a wholly new and momentous theme which will lead Dante away from the world of Ovid and (since it is Matelda who draws Dante across the stream of Lethe at *Purgatorio* 31: 91–102) to the final salvation from his sins which awaits him (beyond all merely seasonal change) on the opposite bank of the dividing stream.

Something of Ovid's eroticism does, however, remain in Dante's text. It is appropriate that it should. Pleasure and desire are now – as Virgil has declared – the appropriate guides to Dante's experience. Matelda is characterized by the poise and self-possession of her dance, smiling and laughing (40–69) as no one hitherto has in the course of Dante's journey. At first sight, it might be supposed that this is the Beatrice whom Virgil said Dante would find 'smiling, in all her happiness, on the crest' (*Purgatorio* 6: 46–8). But Beatrice will not appear until canto 30 – and then in a very different guise. A model for the relationship between Matelda and Beatrice is shown to exist, in canto 27, between Leah and Rachel. Beatrice, like Rachel, will open Dante's eyes to ways in which he may contemplate God directly. Matelda, like Leah, serves God's purposes in the active life and is an emblem of the ethical perfection that human beings may enjoy in the perfect exercise of their natural powers. If the Earthly Paradise represents the natural order in its perfect state, Matelda represents the enjoyment that human beings may derive from the full participation in that order, which they acquire by the exercise of their moral and intellectual virtues. In this sense, she is the new Eve, showing what Eve would have enjoyed if she had not been distracted from the path of obedience and justice. In this sense, too, she is an embodiment of all that Virgil would have been if he had been capable of taking 'what pleases you to be your guide' (canto 27, line 131) or if (to put it differently) his own virtues had not been severed from fulfilment by the as-yet unredeemed repercussions of the Fall.

It is for reasons such as this that some critics (including Dante's son, Pietro, in his commentary of about 1340) identify this dancing figure as Matelda, countess of Canossa (1046–1115), a powerful supporter of the Church, in whose courtyard the Emperor Henry IV (1050–1106) was obliged to kneel in the snow and display his allegiance to the pope. The Earthly Paradise is a realm of justice such as Dante, in his political philosophy, regularly supposes might be brought about in temporal circumstances by the ideal emperor. However, once established, the order of justice is consistent with, and prepares for, the revelation of the order of grace, which the Church is commissioned to announce. Debate continues as to the validity (or usefulness) of so precise an identification of Matelda. None the less, this reading is broadly consistent with the allegorical role that she performs in subsequent cantos. Though Beatrice, throughout these cantos, profoundly calls into question the competence of the human intellect in making any approach to the mysteries of divine existence, it is Matelda who stands surety for the enduring value of these virtues, once their relation to God's mystery is properly recognized. Dante must lose himself in the river Lethe. It is Matelda who acts as his baptismal advocate and sponsor, drawing him through the stream while she herself walks on its waves as the transfigured image of perfected humanity. (See *Purgatorio* 31: 91–102.)

Such a reading should not obscure the significance that derives from Matelda's position in the developing narrative, and from the lyric appeal of the verses in which Dante describes her. In narrative terms, her presence in the poem confirms the modulation that occurred at the end of canto 27, where feminine presences begin to displace the male guides on whom Dante has so far been dependent. (Virgil is henceforth silent, while Statius remains a vestigial figure, only intermittently visible.) Matelda is the first of the *donne* – or nymphs, as the poet frequently describes them – who now bring Dante to perfect readiness for Heaven.

In imagining the garden as a pastoral scene, Dante draws not only on classical and Virgilian models but also upon the *pastorelle* of the vernacular tradition. This latter tradition concentrates less upon the perfections of the natural landscape than upon the perfections of the people that inhabit it, and is frequently erotic in its implications. A poet will see a peasant girl or shepherdess, describe her beauty, recognize that she is ready for love and proceed to a (delicately veiled) consummation. An example that Dante would have known is Cavalcanti's '*In un boschetta trova' pastorella . . .*' (quoting lines 3–8 and 26):

> *Cavelli avea biondetti e ricciutelli*
> *e gli occhi pien d'amor, cera rosata;*
> *   con sua verghetta pastorav' agnelli;*
> *discalza, di rugiada era bagnata;*
> *   cantava come fosse 'namorata:*
> *er' adornata – di tutto piacere.*
>
> *. . .*
>
> *che 'l dio d'amore – mi parea vedere.*

(Her sweet hair was blond, with little curls, her eyes full of love, her complexion rosy; with her staff she was pasturing lambs; her bare feet were wet with dew. She was singing as if she were in love. She was adorned with every beauty . . . [She took me by the hand] . . . and there I seemed to see the god of love.)

It is entirely in keeping with the value that Dante places upon the erotic impulse (see commentary to *Purgatorio* 17) that Matelda should exert a comparable influence. Yet Dante's vision is more complex than Cavalcanti's, and brings about a re-adjustment of emphasis comparable to that which emerged in his representation of Arnaut Daniel in *Purgatorio* 26. Above all, Dante recognizes that erotic love can lead (as it does in the final cantos of the *Paradiso*) to literal union with the 'god' of love, in the all-generating harmony of divined charity. But refinement of this love is first of all required. And where, previously, that refinement came in the fire that the lustful accept, it is now secured by the stream that flows between Dante and Matelda. This stream insists upon the distance between them. In that respect, it points to the purifications that in Occitan poetry are secured by '*amor de lonh*'/ 'love from afar'. Such purification leads, if not always to God, then to a courtesy and concern in the lover which finds solace in devotion to the inner image of the *donna*, or else from the conversations that her person calls forth. So here the stream – the waters of which will take away Dante's memory of sin – forbids any possibility of the sexual power play which is evident even in Cavalcanti's poem, whereby the aristocratic lover might violate the peasant girl (willing as she usually seems to be). On the contrary, authority lies entirely with Matelda, as it will with Beatrice, not least in so far as Matelda in the second half of the canto speaks in philosophical terms of precisely those intellectual and scientific themes that, for Cavalcanti, were the proud preserve of the male poet.

Such revisions and transformations are consistent with the linguistic character of canto 28 at large. In his description of natural phenomena Dante far surpasses in sensuality and detail the conventional idiom of Cavalcanti's *pastorelle*. The science (fantastic as it may be) that he brings to bear – through Matelda's mouth – on this natural scene exceeds anything that philosophical poets of his age would have attempted. And so, too, does the rich vein of classical allusion. But into these three strands Dante interweaves a fourth, which is his awareness (as a syncretist) of how all talk of love, perfection or nature is rooted in the Scriptural tradition. In the next cantos Dante will write as if he were a prophet (again taking vernacular poetry to levels that his contemporaries could not emulate). The classical Earthly Paradise will be perceived with increasing clarity as the lost Garden of Eden. In canto 28, however, the constant point of reference is the verse '*Delectasti* . . .', to which Matelda alludes at **line 80**, where (in the Vulgate if less so in the Authorized Version of the Bible) the singer speaks of the all-consuming delight that God offers to those who take pleasure in His creation:

> For thou, Lord, hast made me glad through thy work: I will triumph in the works of thy hand.
>
> Vulgate, Psalms 91: 5–6

Notes

19–21 These pine woods, extending some 30 kilometres along the shore around Ravenna, can be identified from Dante's reference to Chiasso ('*Chiassi*'), the port of Roman and medieval Ravenna, now abandoned save for the basilica of Saint Apollinare. I have translated as Ravenna. Eolo, in the Italian, refers to Aeolus, god of the winds. The scirocco is the warm southerly wind blowing from the coast of Africa.

64–6 Venus was accidentally wounded by Cupid's arrows and consequently fell in love with Adonis. (See *Metamorphoses* 10: 525–739 onwards.)

70–75 Here are two references to the Hellespont (now known as the Dardanelles). Xerxes crossed the Hellespont in 480 BC to launch an attack on Greece, but was defeated at Salamis and put to flight. Leander swam across the narrowest part of the strait between Sestos and Abydos to meet his secret lover Hero, until, risking the winter storms, he drowned. Hero then drowned herself. (See Ovid, *Heroides* 18–19 and Virgil, *Georgics* 3: 258–63.)

103–5 The reference here is to the *Primum Mobile* (see *Paradiso* 27–30), the transparent outer heaven which, while itself unmoving, creates motion, east to west, in all heavens below it and in the sphere of air that surrounds the earth.

130–32 The river Lethe is spoken of by name in classical literature as, for instance, by Virgil at *Aeneid* 6: 748. The word '*Eunoe*' is Dante's own invention, based on the Greek lexis, '*eu-*' signifying good or well and '*-noesis*' signifying knowledge – hence it could be translated as 'happy thinking and remembrance'.

139–41   Parnassus is the hill sacred to Apollo and the Muses near
         Delphi. (Compare *Purgatorio* 31: 139–45 and *Paradiso* 1: 16–
         18.) For the Age of Gold, see the commentary to cantos 21 and 22.

CANTO 29

Led by Matelda from the far side of the stream,
Dante encounters a procession representing the
revelation of divine truth.

Commentary

Canto 29 begins in the shadow of the holy forest. Matelda is spoken
of in courtly terms, as a '*donna innamorata*' – a lady 'deep in love' –
and also, in classical terms, as a wood nymph, dancing forward
through the chequered beams of light and shade (4–6). Then suddenly,
at line 16, another kind of light, accompanied by a rapturously sweet
melody, breaks through the darkness and, far from fading as would
natural light, it grows ever more intense, to the point at which Dante is
disoriented, finding no comparison between this light and any earthly
phenomenon. To describe what he experiences, the poet appeals for
inspiration to the Muses (37–9), in words alluding to *Aeneid* 7: 61.
But this is a supernatural light (which overwhelms Virgil at lines 55–
7), and Dante's narrative now enters new territory – in which it will
remain for the last five cantos of the *cantica*. The detailed attention
that the poet has hitherto paid to the physical terrain or meteorological
conditions of Mount Purgatory now largely disappears, and yields to
the solemn unfolding of a religious and liturgical drama. Dante has
entered the area of prophetic vision, where he can explore the relation-
ship between persons, moving in often-balletic or visionary patterns,
and the divine providence that first established these patterns. As yet,
his poem does not draw directly on the precise argumentation that will
animate the *Paradiso*. The poet's theological *imagination*, however, is
here brilliantly alive.

The burst of light heralds the beginning of a procession reaching its
climax with the arrival of two figures that, each in their own way,
represent the presence and being of Christ. One of these is Beatrice,
Dante's 'God-bearing image' (to use Charles Williams's famous
phrase) who has borne to him throughout his life an understanding of
God's presence in the world. The other draws the triumphal chariot,
symbolic of the true Church, in which Beatrice rides. This is the

Gryphon, the mystic emblem of Christ in his twofold nature, both human and divine. The head and spine of the Gryphon are those of an eagle, as are its wings. These parts of the Gryphon are gold, designating its incorruptible nobility. Its other parts are those of a lion, coloured red and white, to betoken Christ's passionate and vulnerable humanity and his total purity (113–14).

In the climax to canto 31, these two images of Christ are brought into harmony when Dante sees the Gryphon reflected in Beatrice's eyes. In canto 29, however, Dante's concern is with the ways in which, as a preparation for the coming of Christ, God – throughout history and in the traditions of Scripture – has progressively revealed His truth to the world. The Christian Church is the inheritor of this tradition (though often failing in its mission, as cantos 32 and 33 make clear). The allegory in which this vision is expressed over the next five cantos displays, in more concentrated form than any other episode of the *Commedia*, Dante's close and original reading of Scriptural texts and his sensitivity to Christian imagery. Canto 29 serves to establish the repertoire of allusions and images that, in many subtly shifting configurations, will underlie the theological argument that Dante is here beginning to pursue.

Over the whole procession run seven streamers of light in the seven colours of the rainbow, trailing back from seven candlesticks at the head of the column (76–8). The reference here is to Revelation 1: 12–13 and to Isaiah 11: 2, where the prophet speaks of the seven manifestations of the spirit of God. Allegorically, these bands of light are usually taken to represent the seven gifts of God's Holy Spirit, which fall upon human virtue and bring it to perfection. At lines 109–11, the poet imagines very precisely how the central stream flows between the Gryphon's wings, with three streams on either side of each of the wings, so that these eternal gifts are not interrupted but centred and directed by the incarnate presence of Christ. In the narrative, this iridescent banner accentuates and unifies the onward march of successive squadrons.

The vanguard of the procession is formed by twenty-four venerable old men (83–4), who represent the twenty-four books of the Old Testament (on Saint Jerome's reckoning), through which, in anticipation of Christ's coming, God first spoke to the Jewish people. The lilies on their heads are symbols of faith in the Redeemer still to come, and of justice. (Compare *Paradiso* 18: 92–108.) The lily is also the flower associated with the Virgin Mary, whose faith in God is the highest expression of the Jewish tradition and makes the Incarnation possible. The '*Benedicta*' which the elders sing at line 85 is a part of the greeting offered by the Angel Gabriel to Mary at the Annunciation, repeated by Elisabeth, mother of John the Baptist, at Luke 1: 42.

Lines 91–153 represent the arrival of the Christian era. The chariot in which Beatrice rides is drawn by a cruciform pole – which is symbolic of Christ's Cross and will play a significant part in subsequent cantos, particularly at *Purgatorio* 32: 49–60. The wheels of the chariot probably represent (as at *Paradiso* 1: 106–8) the two mendicant orders of friars, the Franciscans and the Dominicans, which Dante regarded as the supreme defenders of the true faith in his own day. At **lines 91–6** Dante alludes to the four-winged creatures that surround the chariot. These are the four evangelists, Matthew, Mark, Luke and John, who expound the meaning of Christ's life on earth. As the poet says, he has in mind here Ezekiel (**100**) and Saint John's Book of Revelation (**106**). These two texts establish the traditional symbolism which sees Saint Mark as a lion, Saint John as an eagle, Saint Luke as an ox and Saint Matthew as a man – all winged, even though Ezekiel and Saint John differ as to the number of their wings. Strangely, Dante does not dwell on the description of the evangelists. It is as if his attention were already drawn to the description at **lines 97–9** of the Gryphon itself as a representation of Christ.

It is an indication of Dante's independence of imagination that, in constructing an image of Christ, he should not have relied upon such ancient devices as the Chi-Rho emblem or the Fish or the Good Shepherd, but trusted to his imagination and developed an exotic construct of his own invention, giving particular prominence to the significance of the eagle in this hybrid. Commentators have, understandably, attempted to define the theological emphasis of this invention. All would agree that the Gryphon is an expression of the twofold nature of Christ. Most would also acknowledge – since the eagle regularly signifies for Dante the authority of Imperial Rome – that, in some way, Dante must also be pursuing here the abiding interest in the theme of justice that inspires his political theory and is reflected consistently in his representation of Virgil from the moment Virgil identifies himself in *Inferno* 1: 67–75. That view is certainly consistent with the syncretic references, at **lines 115–17**, to the military triumphs of Rome, achieved by Scipio and Augustus, where Dante also seems to have in mind certain passages of Ovid's myth of Phaeton. (See notes below.)

For all that, Dante cannot be concerned here simply with the political or secular significance of the Roman empire. As the allegory unfolds in later cantos (especially at canto 32, lines 124–9), despite his prevailing admiration for Rome, he recognizes that the secular empire can itself cause confusion by the misguided favour that it bestows on the Church. In any case, the emphasis in the Gryphon emblem falls upon transcendence and permanence rather than historical conflict. The chariot far exceeds in splendour the chariots of Scipio and Augustus. Its wings disappear into the ether (112). The colour of the eagle anatomy is gold, symbolizing absolute incorruptibility. This is divine justice, or more precisely it is divine justice as expressed through the twofold being of Christ, in relation to human nature.

In this sense, the Gryphon could be interpreted as a cryptic anticipation of the discussion in *Paradiso* 6 and 7 where, in explicitly theological terms, Dante speaks of how Christ atoned for the sins of Adam and restored the relationship between divine and human justice. In the fall of Adam, human beings committed an act of injustice against the divine. (See commentary on *Purgatorio* 32.) Because God is infinite, the offence was infinite, too. And for that reason no finite creature could ever repay the debt it had incurred. But Christ, as God, is infinite. And, in being also human, Christ can repay the debt, as he does in his self-sacrificing acceptance of Crucifixion. Christ is the second Adam. On that account, he suffers justly for the sins of the original Adam. But Christ is also the god of love, and he opens the way for a re-creation of the relationships that originally existed in love between the divine and the human.

In the *Paradiso*, Dante does not hesitate to introduce certain idiosyncratic turns of thought into his theological argument – in particular stressing, as in the prose *De Monarchia*, that Christ's crucifixion took place under the jurisdiction of Rome and that Rome, therefore, can be seen as the legitimate agent of the justice that God pursued against the seed of Adam. Human justice, once reconciled to God through the Atonement, may indeed continue in its divinely appointed task of bringing about a Golden World of justice on earth. In *Purgatorio* 29, however, as in the following cantos, Dante is less concerned with argument than with imagination, and with the possibility of representing the mysterious but urgent reality of Christ in the mind of the believer. In this regard, it is important to remember that, for Dante, the eagle symbolizes not only justice but also divine love and, in particular, the relationship that revelation and contemplation make possible between the human creature and its divine Creator. This is immediately relevant in that Saint John is one of the two most significant sources of reference in the present cantos, and Saint John's emblem is the eagle, as Dante declares at *Paradiso* 26: 52–4, signifying a power to see into the blinding light of God and yet remain unconsumed, as eagles likewise were supposed to be capable of seeing into the sun. Justice, then, is ultimately at one with, and resolves into, love. (See commentaries on *Purgatorio* 9 and *Paradiso* 20.) But this is to be understood supremely and mysteriously through the 'blinding' paradoxes of Christ's incarnation and crucifixion. These are the paradoxes that Christian faith, prepared by the whole history of revelation, must be ready to contemplate.

In that light, it would be misguided to attempt to attach any final meaning to the Gryphon. The very purpose of this enigmatic sign (as of many that follow, particularly in cantos 32 and 33) is that the mind should be drawn to continue the work, and the pleasure, of interpretation which is initiated by revelation (though not always by scholarly commentary). The mystery of Christ which Dante here contemplates does not represent a defeat for the mind, but rather an impulsion to enter into an understanding of love. And since the object of love for any finite creature must be its infinite Creator, the process will be unending, as ever-new meanings emerge from that infinite mystery. (Compare *Purgatorio* 17: 91–3 and commentary on *Purgatorio* 32.)

It is part of the function of the evangelists, who are represented here as winged creatures, to carry forward and accompany the mysteries of Christ's presence on earth. For that reason, it is appropriate that even Matthew, symbolized as a man, should be rendered mysterious by the wings with which he is endowed. But now, at line 121, the procession begins to return to the representation of recognizably human forms. The era depicted is that of the Holy Spirit which, descending to earth after Christ's Resurrection, lives with and strengthens human intentions. The virtues available in this new age are the theological virtues, here represented in the surrealistic but liturgical colours of the three nymphs on the right of the chariot (121–6), where Faith is pure white, Charity is red and Hope is green 'as if her very bones and flesh/were fashioned from the freshest emerald'. On the left of the chariot (130–32) are the moral virtues, Wisdom (bearing a third, all-seeing eye on her brow), Courage, Justice and Temperance. These are the virtues which are acknowledged as necessary if any social order is to flourish, and therefore clothed in Roman purple to associate them with the rectitude that is assured by the rule of Imperial justice.

The figures that follow at lines 133–42 represent the scriptural books that were written in the earliest years of the Church. In the first pair of elders are the Acts of the Apostles, written by the physician Saint Luke and clothed accordingly in the manner of the founder of Greek medicine, Hippocrates. With him is a figure identified by the sword he bears as Saint Paul – since in his letter to the Ephesians 6: 17 he speaks of 'the sword of the Spirit, which is the word of God'. This single figure represents the fourteen Epistles of Saint Paul. The four men with 'humble looks' (142) represent the minor Epistles, written, respectively, by James, Peter, John and Jude. The last figure (143) represents Saint John's Book of Revelation, and is sleeping 'face alert' to signify the mystic rapture of Saint John's vision.

In the course of canto 29, two of Dante's deepest concerns and the relationship between these concerns are formulated in new terms. One of these is his concern with his history; the other is his concern with the status and authority of his own poetic achievements. History – for so long represented in the *Commedia* as a battleground for violent political factions – is now seen as the channel of revelation and redemption. But what place can a vernacular love poet claim for himself among all those who have written as witnesses to God's presence in history? The answer, to Dante, is entirely clear. As he declares through the mouth of Beatrice at canto 32, line 103, his purpose must be to write for the benefit of the world that 'lives all wrong'. The function of the poet, having received the visions that he claims to have had in the Earthly Paradise, is to return to the world, and for its benefit reveal the perspectives of divine truth. (See especially *Purgatorio* 33: 52–7.) He associates himself directly with the seers and prophets of the Old and New Testaments, particularly with Ezekiel and with the Saint John of the Apocalypse, drawing much of his imagery from their visionary writing, as in canto 32. (See notes below.)

In fulfilling this mission, Dante claims to do far more than any of his contemporaries had ever intended, and in the final cantos of the *Purgatorio* he displays his virtuosity and erudition in yet one further genre, that of scriptural exegesis and allegory. Some critics have argued that in this canto Dante challenges, on grounds of direct visionary experience, positions adopted by the prophets themselves. For instance, on the matter of angel wings, Dante numbers them differently from Ezekiel, his primary source, and even asserts that Saint John assents to the view that he himself has taken (105). To count this, however, as some form of literary megalomania is to ignore the principal message of canto 29, which is that prophets and prophetic poets are participants in a communal process of understanding the truth, where all that any single author may say is relative to everything that has been said so far and has still to be said. Saint John, with whom Dante is at one on the question of angel wings, could not have written what he did if he had not known Ezekiel's text.

Dante enacts here the progress of revelation in his own text and, at certain points, claims his legitimate right as inheritor of the tradition to re-read and elaborate upon the texts that he has received. Above all, he brings his unprecedented gifts as a narrative poet to the service of this tradition, orchestrating the pace of the procession and its various groupings. The most significant moment in this sequence, however, is the astonishing interruption which occurs as the procession is halted by a great peal of thunder (152), in an anticipation of the events that are described in cantos 30 and 31.

Notes

1–3   The Latin verse – 'Blessed are those whose sins are [covered] taken away' is a version of the first verse of Psalm 32, a penitential psalm which looks forward, like the procession of revelation depicted here, to the redemptive action of God in history.

37–42 The virgins are the Muses. Helicon is the mountain sacred to Apollo and the Muses. (Compare *Paradiso* 1: 13–27.) Urania is the Muse of geometry and celestial things. (Compare the invocation to Calliope at *Purgatorio* 1: 7–9.)

43–8 These lines refer to the medieval concept of common sensibles (number, size and shape), which are perceived by many of the senses – as contrasted, say, with colour or perfume, which are perceived particularly by the eye or the sense of smell.

76–8 The 'seven streams' are the seven gifts perfected by the seven-fold spirit of God, that is: wisdom, understanding, counsel, fortitude, knowledge, piety, fear of the Lord. See also Isaiah 11: 2. Delia, in classical mythology, is Diana, associated with haloes round the moon.

82–4 For the twenty-four elders, see Apocalypse 4: 1–8.

91–105 Argus was the hundred-eyed monster who guarded Io in *Metamorphoses* 1: 622–723. (Compare *Purgatorio* 32: 64–6.) For his depictions of the four evangelists, Dante draws on the following passages:

> And I looked, and, behold, a whirlwind came out of the north, a great cloud, and a fire infolding itself, and a brightness was about it, and out of the midst thereof as the colour of amber, out of the midst of the fire.
>
> Also out of the midst thereof came the likeness of four living creatures . . . And every one had four faces, and every one had four wings.
>
> Ezekiel 1: 4–6

> And before the throne there was a sea of glass like unto crystal:
> and in the midst of the throne, and round about the throne, were
> four beasts full of eyes before and behind . . . And the four beasts
> had each of them six wings about him.
>
> Revelation 4: 6–8.

115–20 The references are to Scipio, Augustus Caesar and Phaeton.
Scipio Africanus the Younger (185–129 BC) defeated Carthage in
146 BC. Scipio the Elder (235–183 BC) defeated the Carthaginian
Hannibal at Zama in 202 BC. (It is not certain which of these
two Dante is referring to.) Augustus (63 BC – AD 14) was the
first emperor of Rome. For Augustus's triple triumph, see Virgil,
Aeneid 8: 715. For Phaeton, see *Metamorphoses* 2: 107–9 and
Inferno 17: 106–8.

CANTOS 30 AND 31

Dante encounters Beatrice and realizes that Virgil has
disappeared. Beatrice speaks to the angels
surrounding her, explaining why she needs to be
harsh in her treatment of Dante. Turning to Dante,
she elicits a confession from him, after which he is
drawn through Lethe. He then sees the Gryphon
reflected in Beatrice's eyes, and she finally turns her
unveiled eyes upon Dante himself.

Commentary

A distinctive feature of the Christian creed is that divine wisdom is
thought, finally, to be communicated in and through the person of
Christ and not simply by a tradition of teaching or a code of law, or
even by holy writings such as those that are represented symbolically
in the Procession of Revelation. Christ is the *Logos*, or creative word,
of God. This is revealed in the Incarnation and Resurrection, as it will
be at Christ's Second Coming when he appears as judge of the world.
The Eucharist, too, re-enacts the engagement of Christ in bodily form
with his followers. To receive such wisdom, however, demands an act
of faith, an acknowledgement of the human person of Christ. Only
through such an act can one arrive at a full recognition of the *divine*
person and, consequently, begin to participate in the workings of
divine wisdom. Faith in this sense is simple, even childlike. It is a

declaration of loyalty and love. However, the immediate impact of such simplicity may well be surprising or even shocking, for it requires nothing less than the abandonment of all those merely intellectual constructions that the sophisticated mind may have built around itself, and reveals how insufficient human words are when confronted with the paradoxes and transcendent truths that are embodied in the divine word.

It is this act of faith that is now dramatized in cantos 30 and 31 – along with the shock that such an act involves, and the freedom and understanding that follows from it. Here, after the solemn abstraction of cantos 28 and 29, the poet unleashes a storm of primitive emotions, of pity and terror, of conflicting physical sensations, all of which challenge any settled expectations that hitherto Dante as traveller (or his reader) may have conceived. However, the purpose of entering this vortex, as revealed at the end of canto 31, is that Dante should be baptized anew in the river of Lethe and be able to contemplate the Gryphon – representing the twofold nature of Christ – reflected in Beatrice's eyes, thus preparing himself to enter the entirely new dimension of existence that is represented in the *Paradiso*.

Beatrice can usefully be seen as an allegory of the Church, even as a metaphor for the person of Christ. Thus, especially in the adaptation of the opening phrase from the '*Benedictus*' at 30: 19, her appearance is marked by significant references to the Eucharist, which is the principal sacrament of the Church in commemoration of Christ. Yet the emphasis carried by the dramatic immediacy of this episode falls not upon theology or doctrine but upon the inconceivable yet undeniable presence of Beatrice. Thus, at 30: 73, she demands, with an insistence on the simple words 'I am', upon her true being, which now stands revealed once more to Dante as her devoted lover. Beatrice may in part be said to do what a true Church should do, in preparing the believer to engage directly with the truth of existence itself. But she is as much a source of disruption as of comfort. In this respect, too, she acts as a true Church should when it abandons merely institutional edict or formal teaching and proclaims the truths which, as embodied realities, are to be discovered in the lives of particular persons.

Beatrice demands of Dante what Christ demands of the Christian, which is to say a reaffirmation of personal loyalty and, through that, a new realization of what it truly means to exist as a creature reflecting the purposes of God as Creator. Beatrice's physical beauty – to which she draws attention when, at 31: 50, she speaks of the 'beauty and delight' of her limbs – here, as throughout Dante's writing, betokens the physical nature that Christ took on and restored to perfection in the Incarnation. Beatrice also participates in the life that is promised by the Resurrection. Her death was recorded in the *Vita nuova*. Now, the confidence that this was no death at all but a way to new life inspires the whole episode (especially at 30: 127–9). But, above all, in canto 30 and the first phase of canto 31, Beatrice is Dante's judge, as Christ will be at the end of time. Facing Beatrice across the stream – through which he will only pass at 31: 91–105 – Dante is driven to recognize that Beatrice, hitherto his own courtly *donna*, is and has always been the beloved of the God who created her. The judgement that she passes on him is borne in upon him by the realization of how distant he still is from the perfection that God intended him and all human beings to enjoy. This scene of judgement is also a scene of confession in which Dante, as protagonist, may be said to experience, in his own person, the pain that all the penitents he has seen in Purgatory experience, and be brought by that pain to an understanding of his relationship to God. Like Christ, Beatrice works in the core of Dante's being, and brings him to the realization not only of what his specific transgressions have been but also of the fundamental nature of sin. On the account offered here, sin is not merely an offence against the articles of a moral code. It is, rather, a rejection of the happiness and love that the Creator had located at the heart of the human person. Since canto 16, Dante has repeatedly emphasized that the impulse in God's creative act is happiness, and that human desire constantly seeks to recover the initial happiness of creation. Now Beatrice scathingly condemns Dante (30: 74–5) for daring to come in tears to a place where human beings are meant to be happy:

> What right had you to venture to this mount?
> Did you not know that all are happy here?

The Earthly Paradise is an indication of the pleasures that God originally reserved for the human race. (See *Purgatorio* 28: 91–3.) For Dante, Beatrice represents the legitimate object of his desires, and, before her death, Dante had already come to realize this (as recorded in *Vita nuova* 20). But since then, he has deviated from the direction dictated to him by this fundamental and legitimate desire, answering the siren call of lesser goods (31: 45), and inventing for himself reasons and intellectual justifications for the pursuit of such goods. (See commentary on *Purgatorio* 19.) His sin, like all sin, is one of betrayal. (See introduction to *Inferno*, pp. lxxvi–lxxviii.) In betraying Beatrice's memory, he has also betrayed the best that his own desires revealed to him.

At 30: 130–32 (compare 31: 58–60), Beatrice declares that no sooner did she leave this life than Dante sought other consolations. It is clear that, at this point, Dante is not speaking of himself simply as a character in his own poem, but wishes to point beyond the text to events in his own life and intellectual career. There are certainly references in Dante's lyric poems preceding the *Commedia* to 'ladies' other than Beatrice. (See notes to canto 31, below.) These references remain oblique, as they do in cantos 31 and 32. And that obliqueness itself could easily be seen as a sign of shame that leads to a continuing concealment of the 'true' facts. On the other hand, the same indirectness may be regarded as an indication that these deviations were in their intellectual implications far more serious than any merely sexual peccadillo or distraction could ever have been. To this charge Dante is prepared to make a very direct confession. From as early as the *Vita nuova* and *Convivio*, he admitted that, after Beatrice's death, he was drawn towards a certain '*donna gentile*'. But this episode, he insists, represents his attraction, not to some Florentine rival in love of Beatrice, but rather to the excitements of philosophical learning and the comforts and distractions that philosophy could offer in his grief at Beatrice's death. Seen from a theological vantage point, philosophy represents a way of protecting the mind – beneath a veil of rational interests – from the impact of those supra-rational experiences that are realized in Beatrice's life and death.

There can be no doubt of the extreme importance to Dante of philosophical learning in all its forms, scientific, logical and literary. The *Commedia* – even the broadly theological *Paradiso* – could not have been written without it. But now, meeting the resurrected Beatrice in the Earthly Paradise, Dante represents himself as being momentarily deprived of any such self-created shield, and made to acknowledge that even the most elevated examples of human learning depend for their success upon the more radical truths that are communicated by the word of divine revelation. Here Dante represents himself exposed in his own person to what, at first, seems to be the utmost humiliation. This exposure is so radical that, far from speaking coherently to admit any particular accusation, he is bereft of any power to speak or act at all.

There are both theological and literary implications to this collapse. As to theology, Dante here measures his selfhood against Beatrice, and now, being reclaimed by his Creator, he becomes childlike and wholly passive in the grip of conflicting emotions. Contemplating Beatrice's resurrection, his original grief over her death must be converted into grief over his misapprehension of that death and, equally, into the happiness that comes with a true understanding of what her death had led to. Once, he had sought philosophically to control and comprehend such contradictions. Now, the remedy lies in the oblivion that only Beatrice can grant him as he is drawn through the river of Lethe. But this is the oblivion of faith, and it will eventually restore to him, in the waters of Eunoe, an understanding of his own inherent goodness. Correspondingly, in poetic terms, Dante expends the most extreme resources of his art on a depiction of his own humiliation. At the same time, the lyricism and liturgical elevation of these cantos draw on sources that Dante first explored in the *Vita nuova*. The construction, even of a philosophical epic, dissolves at least at the conclusion of the *Purgatorio* into a celebration of Beatrice as the true object of all his most elevated poetry. The last lines of canto 31 anticipate the *Paradiso* but also reformulate the poetry of praise which Dante continually suggests lies at the heart of his poetic purpose. (See commentaries to cantos 23, 24 and 26.)

It is consistent with such considerations that Dante should simultaneously realize that he is now in Beatrice's presence and that Virgil has, unnoticed, disappeared from his side. In a highly developed form, Virgil may be taken to represent all that the '*donna gentile*' represented in the *Convivio* – philosophy, culture, law and morality. Hitherto, Virgil's role in the *Commedia* has been to offer sound guidance to his pupil at moments of turmoil and confusion. Thus the last words that he speaks to Dante, at canto 27, lines 139–42, declare that, having proved his powers by climbing to the Earthly Paradise, Dante stands in complete possession of his own moral being and is sovereign of himself. Such guidance and such assurances have so far been necessary and legitimate. Now, however, in the perspective of faith, as divine love begins to open before him, the very virtues that Virgil has exemplified and applauded have to be viewed as impediments to the surrender that Beatrice demands of Dante. The self-possession that Virgil attributes to Dante may be seen as the last possession that he must abandon. The moral dignity that Virgil recognizes now proves to have value only if it is grounded in the person of God and in the happiness that, as Beatrice makes clear, is the proper condition of the human creature. As Saint Augustine entreats in *Confessions* 10: 50: 'Let me know Thee, O Lord, who knowest me: *Let me know Thee as I am known.*' For Augustine, God knows us better than we know ourselves. The implications of that understanding will be reflected in the many episodes in the sequence where Beatrice claims to know Dante more completely than Dante's conscious mind can tell, or where Dante's progress depends, not, as hitherto, upon heroic effort or intellectual discrimination but upon a descent into unconsciousness, silence, sleep or oblivion. (See *Purgatorio* 32: 61–72 and 85 and 33: 64–6 and 91–6.)

On one view, the art of these cantos is an art in the service of theological understanding which admits that all art must dissolve into the greater wisdom that can only be achieved when divine truths and the truths of persons – be these guilty or happy truths – coincide. At the point where these truths do coincide, the steady sequences that we build for ourselves, in church processions as well as in Virgilian epics, disintegrate into lyrical fragments. On another view, of course, some critics see in this evidence of Dante's flamboyant skill in the manipulation of his fictional text. To them, it will be significant that, while Dante may be said to surrender his being to Beatrice's knowledge of him, he is himself evidently writing the words that he puts in her mouth. The receding perspectives that are opened up by such an observation clearly deserve attention.

Whichever angle of interpretation one chooses to adopt, the full impact of the episode can only be realized if one follows in detail its architecture and linguistic effect, where linguistic coherence and narrative order contend with calculated moments of fracture and diffusion, and where epic, lyric and liturgical registers of verse are constantly shifting in relationship with the evocation of raw emotion and physical response.

In narrative terms, Dante in canto 30 exhibits a sustained control of tempo, in which anticipation becomes suspense and suspense turns to fracture, which is remedied by Beatrice's magisterial monologue till, finally, when Dante passes through the river of oblivion in canto 31, the scene is transformed into one of trancelike relaxation – thus preparing for cantos 32 and 33, where dramatic action is almost wholly suspended, giving way to dreamlike (though sometimes nightmarish) rhythms. In language, the sequence ranges from the most elevated reaches of style to the simplest, and sometimes most violent, depictions of spasmodic body language – of sighs, tears and trembling. Though Virgil disappears from view, Dante's understanding of Latin style does not, nor does his commitment to the principles of syncretism. The opening lines of canto 30 include three phrases in Latin, one quoted almost directly from Virgil's *Aeneid*. Extended similes on an epic model punctuate the episode (30: 58–60, 85–90 and 31: 16–18; 70–72). Dante draws equally on the varied resources of the vernacular tradition, as he does also on the directness of the mother tongue. Throughout, he is acutely aware of the love poetry he wrote in the *Vita nuova* in praise of Beatrice – and also of his relationship to his

poetic predecessors, in particular Guido Cavalcanti. But in writing the
speeches that he attributes to Beatrice he enters unknown linguistic
territory, where lyrical fluency is wholly at one with the syntax and
power of an authoritative moral vision. Finally, in the conclusion
to canto 31, in his description of the Gryphon, Dante produces an
enigmatic, even mystic mode of writing which, arguably, has no paral-
lel even in the *Commedia* itself.

Canto 30 is orchestrated into four major phases. The first (30: 1–48)
describes how the procession of revelation comes to a halt. This is not
a moment of stasis. The long periodic sentences of this description,
elevated in diction and precise in observation, point to a dynamic
interconnection between the eternal and the temporal realms, which
is scanned by suspense at the prospect of still further revelation. The
seven-branched candlestick represents the seven gifts of the Holy Spirit
(see notes to *Purgatorio* 29: 73–5) which bring to perfection, in readi-
ness for eternal life, the seven virtues that human beings are capable of
pursuing in this life – the four cardinal virtues and the three theological
virtues. These seven gifts are viewed, in Dante's metaphor, in terms of
the seven stars of the constellation Ursa Minor which give guidance to
the earthly seafarer (30: 1–7). Thus Dante celebrates the providential
certainties which in both the temporal and eternal spheres lead human-
ity towards its final goal. But beyond this goal there remains a longing
for transcendent consummation.

The cry of '*Veni, sponsa de Libano*!' ('Come with me from Lebanon,
my spouse!'), uttered three times (30: 11–12), is a cry of love and
desire from the biblical Song of Solomon 4: 8 – the great expression
of erotic love which, by Dante's time, had come to be read allegorically
as an account of the loving relationship between God and His creation.
(See commentary on *Paradiso* 15.) Here the cry expresses a yearning
for the mystic marriage that will only come when Christ is reunited
with his Church. But the fulfilment of human nature will occur in a
realm beyond any conception that nature can deliver. Thus the second
simile in this canto (30: 13–16) takes as its reference point the moment
of transformation when, at the Last Judgement, time – both historical
and liturgical – comes to an end and human nature in the Resurrection
becomes complete, as the bodies of all those individuals who have
ever lived rise from the grave.

This moment will be marked by the victory cry of 'Alleluia' – which
Dante registers here with a sonorous elongation of syllables (30: 15).
This is the cry that greets the Resurrection of Christ at Easter. It is
also the acclamation which, in the liturgy of the Mass, immediately

precedes the reading of the Gospel, which is appropriate if Dante is alluding in this episode to the drama of the Mass, in which Christ's continual presence in time is realized anew. And the same explanation may be extended to the second Latin quotation (30: 19). '*Benedictus qui venis!*' ('Blessed is he who comes [in the name of the Lord]') is sung at the end of the '*Sanctus*', in which the congregation on earth joins with the song 'Holy, holy, holy' sung by the angels in Heaven, and in the Mass immediately precedes the transubstantiation of bread and wine into the body and blood of Christ. The '*Benedictus*' is thus another cry of anticipation, in this case directed to the mystery of Christ's continuing presence on earth in the Eucharist. Finally, these expressions of longing and faith are daringly juxtaposed (30: 21) with phrases adapted from Virgil's *Aeneid* 6: 883: '*date manibus lilia plenis* . . .' ('Give me lilies with full hands . . .'), which describe the eager (but frustrated) desire of the spirits in the underworld to celebrate the beauty and goodness of Marcellus (42–23 BC), nephew of the Emperor Augustus, lamenting that he (like Beatrice) died all too young. Placing Virgil's words in this sequence repeats Dante's daring claim for Virgil as in *Purgatorio* 21–2, but it also suggests how far we have travelled from the depths of a Virgilian underworld, the inhabitants of which are all reduced to melancholic shadow, to a realm in which the human person is nourished by the bodily presence of Christ.

At 30: 22–39, the reader's attention is shifted from the workings of providence and revelation to focus directly upon Dante's perception of and involvement in the unfolding scene with the emphatic 'I saw . . .' These lines also call into consideration the whole development of Dante's love poetry from the time of the *Vita nuova*, so that, where in *Purgatorio* 24 and 26 Dante offered a critique of his contemporaries, he now, retrospectively, calls into consideration his own past achievements. Throughout the passage, there are recognizable affinities in diction and rhythmic effect between this and the earlier work, particularly in recording the extreme refinement of visual perception that his love for Beatrice has brought – as, for instance, in '*Vede perfettamente onne salute* . . .' ('He sees perfectly all health and salvation . . .') (*Vita nuova* 26). However, the simile at 30: 22–7, – comparing the advent of Beatrice with the rise of a particular dawn that Dante says he had 'once' experienced, with its particular effects of mist and haze – displays an interest in the precise observation of the physical world and its processes that has developed considerably since he wrote the *Vita nuova*. The sustained, progressive syntax of this passage and its rhetorical sophistication is also characteristic of the style that Dante has developed in writing the *Commedia*. So, too, in the climax of the passage (30: 31–3), picturing Beatrice's dress, Dante alludes to the colours of red, green and white that were associated with her in the *Vita nuova*. Now, in the allegorical setting of the procession, he endows them with emblematic significance as references to faith, hope and charity. Likewise, his tendency to syncretism produces here a fusion of Christian and classical symbolism, in that the olive crown that Beatrice wears associates her with Minerva, the Roman goddess of wisdom and warlike defender of civic order. But then, with its abrupt arrival at the phrase '*donna m'apparve*' ('a lady now appeared to me') (30: 32) – which appears almost *verbatim* in the *Vita nuova* 1 – the passage changes character and begins to revert to the idiom of Dante's earlier style. In particular, the passage at 30: 34–9 recalls those phases of the *Vita nuova* when the poet was still under the influence of Cavalcanti's melancholic understanding of love, and love was, as here, a power that shook the self-possession of the lover to the point of fear and trembling. (See introduction to *Inferno*, pp. xxviii–xxxi.) The rhythms become agitated – under the repeated alliterations of 't' – and the emphasis falls upon the terrifying and apparently destructive impact of love. Then Dante envisages (30: 42) a further regression which would take him back to his boyhood – his '*puerizia*' – when, at the age of nine, he first set eyes on Beatrice.

The climax of this stylistic regression comes at 30: 46–8, when Dante turns, as he has always done before in moments of distress, for mature advice and comfort to Virgil. Now, though, there occurs a stunning *coup de théâtre*, triggered entirely by the words that Dante here places on his own lips. The final words that Dante addresses to Virgil are an exact translation of the words that Virgil himself had put in the mouth of Dido when in the *Aeneid* 4: 23 she recognizes her feelings of love for Aeneas. Virgil's '*agnosco veteris vestigia flammae*' becomes '*conosco i segni de l'antica fiamma*!'/'I recognize the signs of ancient flame!' This allusion may rightly be taken as a final acknowledgement of Virgil's authority, but also of Dante's dependence upon him – both as traveller and as poet – and equally of a new confidence which allows him to embody Virgil's classical sentiments in his own vernacular idiom. Yet, suddenly, Virgil is not there. Nor, within the fiction of the episode, are Dante's words ever actually spoken. They die silently on his lips as, in utter and tearful confusion, he records his sense of overwhelming loss at Virgil's disappearance, and descends from this point into silence.

It is precisely this moment – which Dante has calculated with great narrative skill – that bears in upon the reader the unresolvable contradictions that underlie the whole of the Earthly Paradise episode. On the one hand, Dante owes everything to Virgil as traveller and, scarcely less, as author. On the other hand, the example that Virgil provides is wholly inadequate to – and may even misrepresent – the experience that Dante has now to describe. After all, in quoting Dido's words Dante is comparing himself to a figure for whom love proves to be a force of utter destruction when, deserted by Aeneas, Dido commits suicide. Even as she speaks these words, Dido experiences guilt at the thought that she is betraying her first husband, the long-dead Sichaeus. The love that Dante has to record, however, far from being destructive, is the redemptive love which displays itself in the resurrection of the once-dead Beatrice. If Dante has reason to feel guilty – as he does – then this is because he has diverted his eyes from the true significance of Beatrice's death on earth. Nor is it appropriate to draw comparisons (so central to Dante's procedure throughout the poem) at all between his case and that of any other figure. The love that is expressed in his response to Beatrice needs to be wholly singular – undistracted by comparisons and analogues – if it is to register the utterly singular relationship of love that exists between God and each of His creatures.

It is for this reason that, at 30: 49–55 and 30: 73, names, as a peculiar class of words, become the predominant feature of the text, where Virgil is named four times, where Dante at 30: 55 is named for the only time in the Commedia, and where Beatrice insists through the utterance of her own name that she truly exists, for Dante as for God. Names are marks of identity. Yet to name a human being, and to signify by that name the wholly singular and irreplaceable existence of that being, is almost more than normal words can achieve. It is in any case a difficult and even painful process. In the course of his journey as Dante's guide, Virgil has rarely allowed himself to be named, and only then with extreme embarrassment. (See especially Purgatorio 21: 103–20.) Dante, too, at 30: 62 includes an awkward and apologetic gloss on the 'necessity' which obliges him now to write down his own name. After all, to be identified by name is to be called to account and required to answer to some other who may challenge one's own conceptions of oneself, whether by criticism or by love. This can be painful, as Dante finds, in naming both Virgil and himself. Though Virgil – a noble Roman – seems more interested in matters of public role than of private status, Dante is prepared to speak his name even if (30: 52–4) it entails the loss of Eden or, as he puts it, 'All our primal mother lost'. His tragic sympathy for another human being is teetering on the edge of a second Fall. But this sympathy is immediately wrenched around by Beatrice's utterance of his own baptismal name.

Now his attention must fall not upon human affiliations but upon his relationship with the beings who gave him his identity in the first place – upon Beatrice, who now insists through her name on her own real presence, and beyond Beatrice, on Christ. This is a baptismal naming, such as the Virgil of the *Commedia* could neither conceive nor benefit from. The claim made on Dante will here initiate him into a '*vita nuova*' – a new life in restored relationship with his Creator. But the first effect of this act of naming recalls that, while baptism is a purification from sin, it is also a form of death, in which all claims are renounced except the claim of Christ, and in which an association is established with the suffering, as well as the resurrected God.

In the third sequence of the canto (30: 82–102), the intense concentration on Beatrice and Dante as individuals is replaced by the opening up of a public, indeed theatrical, space as the angels, who have flown around the chariot strewing flowers, respond at 30: 82–4 to the drama they see played out between the two human beings. From this wider audience, there at first comes encouragement as the angels sing verses from Psalm 31: 1–8, which speak of the 'large room' into which God's mercy will liberate the afflicted:

> In thee, O Lord, do I put my trust; let me never be ashamed: deliver me
> in thy righteousness ... Into Thine hand I commit my spirit: thou hast
> redeemed me, O Lord God of truth ... I will be glad and rejoice in thy
> mercy: for thou hast considered my trouble; thou hast known my soul in
> adversities; And hast not shut me up into the hand of the enemy: thou
> hast set my feet in a large room.

The 'large room' here is hope – the theological virtue that will bring Dante through the confusions and shame of the present moment into the spaciousness, inhabited already by the angels, of God's providential presence. (See commentary on *Paradiso* 25.) Significantly, the singing stops before it reaches the verses of the psalm that evoke God's mercy, since that mercy will only be shown once Dante's purgation is complete. But the effect on Dante is cathartic. In his ears, the psalm sounds like an expression of compassion. It is – to him, at least – as if the angels had asked why Beatrice should display so little tenderness.

This instant of cathartic release is registered not by further reference to the scriptures but by a great epic simile (30: 85–90), which again evokes considerations of 'room' – of geographical space and range. In contrast to the spaces of the Earthly Paradise, or those to which the psalm alludes, the point of reference here is winter in Italy, frozen down the length of its Apennine backbone. The purpose, however, of this heroic comparison is to mark the minuscule evidence of new life, which now comes to Dante's spirit as if it were a thaw occurring within the icy body of the snow. In miniature, this passage re-enacts the transition that Dante made from the ice of lower Hell to the fluency of waters throughout *Purgatorio* 1. It likewise recalls that the last of the sins in Hell was the icy-hearted treachery which, in *Inferno* 33: 49, made Ugolino turn himself to stone '[i]nward', and rendered him deaf to any appeal to pity from his dying sons. Dante himself will stand accused by Beatrice of betraying her memory (31: 49–63). But the angelic intervention ensures that he will not respond with the same rigidity that once imprisoned Ugolino in his own self-image. This intervention, calling on the life-giving energy of inarticulate emotion, harks back to a moment in *Vita nuova* 26 when pity also proves to be an indispensable catalyst in Dante's understanding of Beatrice. There, overwhelmed by presentiments of Beatrice's coming death, Dante is joined by a young *donna*, full of pity, and then by other ladies who are no less concerned about the agony that Dante is suffering. They do not, however, cure him of his pain, nor console him, but rather accompany him into the apparently unresolved extremes of his anguish. It is part of his betrayal that in embracing the '*donna gentile*' after Beatrice's death he should seek consolation (be it in love for another or in intellectual devotion to philosophical study) which distracts from the truly cathartic channel of connection.

Yet pity is not the same as sentiment. In *Inferno* 5 Dante showed, through the case of Francesca, how pity can dissolve into self-regard and loosen the grip we have on our best aims and purposes. Pitying Francesca, Dante himself 'falls as bodies fall, for dead' (*Inferno* 5: 142). However, the pity that Beatrice shows to Dante is 'bitter to the taste' (30: 81), intended not to lull but rather to awaken and enliven his awareness of his ultimate goals. Beatrice subsumes and gives new meaning to the '*pietas*' which Virgil in the *Aeneid* constantly attributes to the heroic Aeneas. '*Pietas*', for Aeneas, means that sense of public duty which leads him at all points to consult the best interests of the Roman race. (See notes on *Inferno* 1.) Like Aeneas, Dante is still on a journey which is intended, once he records it in his poem, to bring about a restoration of justice in the contemporary world of fourteenth-century Italy. (See *Purgatorio* 32: 103.) Under Beatrice's guidance, however, it becomes clear that Dante will only complete this task when his whole being – body and soul, mind, emotions and perceptions – has been brought back into harmony with the order of divine creation, acknowledging its utter dependence on the God who first made it.

In the final section of the canto (30: 103–45) Dante, as poet, begins
to offer through Beatrice's words the confession to which, as protagon-
ist, he will give his verbal assent in canto 31. This is not a confession
in any modern (or tabloid journalism) sense of the word, involving
the prurient identification of fascinating failings. Nor, for reasons
that have already been suggested, does this confession involve any
introspective obsession with day-to-day misdemeanours. Confession,
as Dante pictures it here, is a public act concerning the reconciliation
of the individual with the wider community of the Church – from
saints to angels – and the demonstration of the sinner's desire for those
pleasures that can be realized only in the fullness of existence that God
brings about. In this sense, confession is concerned, above all, with a
recovery of the gifts and talents that sin erodes and negates. Beatrice
is now shown to possess herself of the details of Dante's life and to
retell, in overview, the fictional story that Dante has recounted so far
in the *Commedia*. Her emphasis, however, falls not upon the brute
facts of her lover's career, but rather upon the gifts and talents that
were intended in the universal scheme of things to be his and were
borne in upon him by the 'great wheels' of cosmic generation (30: 109–
17; see also *Purgatorio* 28: 91–3). Even after her death, when Dante
began to squander these talents, grace and inspiration were offered to
him, by Beatrice's intercession (30: 133–41), to ensure that he knew
the road he had to take. His sin was perversely to reject all this, until,
by his vision of Hell he was terrified into a new desire to recover all
he had lost. He is now ready to return to his appointed place.

First, though, he needs to speak for himself. He needs to pay the
'tax', as Beatrice puts it – in a surprisingly down-to-earth phrase
(30: 144) which some might translate as 'pick up the tab'. Even this
demand, however, will not require Dante to grovel in the details of
his own shortcomings. Beatrice – and God – already know better than
he does what he is (31: 37–41). His assent is required as a free but
formal token of reconciliation with the court to which he was always
meant to belong. (In a similar way, in *Paradiso* 24 Dante is called
upon to speak of his faith in Christ, not because he has to prove his
understanding, but because his words will celebrate that faith and
strengthen it as much in others as in himself.)

In canto 31 Beatrice turns to Dante, directing the 'sword point' of
her words on him (31: 2) in an attempt to elicit from him a verbal
acknowledgement of sins and wholly eliminate the pride or confidence
in self that led him, as she puts it, to 'flounce' (31: 30) before the
insubstantial attractions of earthly things. In attempting to reply,

Dante's voice at 30: 16–21 breaks beneath the strain like a crossbow shattering. (Compare *Paradiso* 2: 23–4.) Continuing to exert her command over Dante's true being, Beatrice reads his silent assent from the movement of his lips. She then proceeds, at 30: 22–63, to reveal to him the nature and extent of his treachery, concentrating on the mistaken way in which he responded to her death. In the second phase of the canto (31: 49–111), Dante is drawn through the river of Lethe. In the final phase (31: 112–45), Dante sees the Gryphon as a reflection in Beatrice's eyes, and Beatrice then turns her eyes – unveiled, as the angels request (31: 137–8) – to meet his.

In interrogating Dante, Beatrice refers only in very allusive terms to Dante's particular transgressions. Some reasons for this have been discussed above. But the level of abstraction that the poet attributes to Beatrice, especially at 31: 49–63, is also consistent with a recognizably Neoplatonic conception of beauty, desire and love which, in part at least, informs his thinking, here and elsewhere. For the Neoplatonist, beauty, wherever it occurs, is a manifestation of the ultimate unity of design that underlies the created order. In contemplating beauty, our desires are engaged and we begin to perceive, initially in physical objects, a harmony that transcends merely physical phenomena. Entranced by this harmony, mind and spirit are drawn away from present things – from the transient and mutable sphere in which human lives are originally located – to devote themselves in love to an ever-finer perception of the certainties that are displayed in the geometry that sustains the created order. Exactly the reverse has occurred in Dante's case. Loving Beatrice's beauty, Dante should have seen in her death the opportunity to contemplate her position in the divine order with ever greater purity or detachment from physical considerations (31: 49–57). Instead, his attentions have been ever more entangled in the uncertain and untrustworthy flux of earthly existence (31: 58–63).

For all that, canto 31 does not finally recommend that detachment from the human body which Neoplatonic thinking, in emphasizing spiritual contemplation, characteristically pursues. At 31: 85–7 the truth of Beatrice's words possesses Dante as if he has been affected by nettlerash. His whole being, in its psychosomatic unity of body and spirit, is required to answer to the truth she speaks. Dante is called not simply to understand the truth, as if it were a piece of intellectual property, but to enter anew into the divine existence on which his own existence depends. Viewed from a specifically Christian perspective, the body, not the spirit, is the place in which the Incarnation, Passion and Resurrection dramatically enact the living proof of human vulnerability. The death of the body is not a release from physical impediments; it is when the glorification of the human person, at one with its Creator, is finally assured. Dante might have recognized this at Beatrice's death. He is driven to recognize it now in confronting the resurrected Beatrice, and to enact the drama of her death in his own being. The nettlerash he suffers – along with all his unspeaking sighs and far-from-beautiful spasms – is the passion that brings him to see, at 30: 115–26, that the Gryphon, as the transfigured body of Christ, is the ground of his own being, as it is of Beatrice's.

It is therefore appropriate that, interwoven with the abstraction of Beatrice's speech, canto 31 should display, especially at 31: 70–75, a highly specific sense of physical reality. With sarcastic, even comic precision, Beatrice demands that Dante should show himself to be a fully grown man by raising his beard (though Dante is never known to have worn one). Virgil had declared that Dante was mature, 'upright, free and whole' (*Purgatorio* 27: 140). But Beatrice requires more than this. The concern here is not to establish a plateau of achievement but to define a process and condition of growth. Dante has become a child again, and his new maturity involves a capacity to experience, in the form of growing pains, the impact of new life as it continually renews itself within him. At 30: 70–72 Dante expresses this in terms of an epic simile which alludes directly to Virgil's *Aeneid* 4: 196 and evokes considerations of heroic energy and even the male brutality of tyrants. (Iarbas here is the king of the notoriously savage Gaetulians, who once wooed Dido.) All these efforts, however, are exerted by a shame-faced boy (31: 64–6), brought to expend his most Herculean energies in performing the simplest of physical actions.

The result is that Dante is now ready to lose himself in Lethe, surrendering to the *donne*, particularly to Matelda, who now drags him through the baptismal stream. A fissure of oblivion enters the psyche which, at one point, seemed to enjoy a Herculean self-possession. Cantos 32 and 33 examine further the meaning of this new passivity. This is not, however, to say that the moral integrity which Dante has learned from Virgil ceases to be significant. Matelda supervises Dante's immersion in Lethe, and she remains, as from the first, a *figura* for the virtues that Virgil once exemplified. Moreover, on leaving the stream, Dante is initially delivered into the hands of the four nymphs who represent the four cardinal virtues of wisdom, courage, justice and temperance (which, as 31: 106 recalls, were also represented in *Purgatorio* 1: 22–4 as the four stars that shine in the skies above the mountain). These nymphs, however, now lead Dante to their companions who represent the three theological virtues. Thus the emphasis falls on the way in which all the virtues that human beings practise are brought to their consummation through grace, when they are seen as the gifts of the Holy Spirit. It is here that pleasure in the gift of moral virtue, as a way to participate in the gift of existence, begins to display itself.

A canto which has been devoted to the urgency and pressure of Beatrice's words – and Dante's corresponding inarticulacy – concludes with the free play of visual images and evocations of light reflected from eye to eye. At 30: 76, Dante's eyes, unable to meet Beatrice's, glance down, only for him to see himself reflected in the stream. He is, at this point, as incapable of tolerating the image of his own self as he is of contemplating Beatrice's perfection. But in the 'death' of baptism, self is now forgotten, or rather it is rediscovered beyond the confines of ego in the reflection of the Gryphon in Beatrice's eyes, where reciprocation replaces self-affirmation. And this moment – since Dante is contemplating the eternal foundation of selfhood in the person of Christ – is a beginning rather than an end. The image he sees is not static, but constantly both still and moving (31: 121–3). Dante has already spoken of how the shifting things of this world can distract the eye. In canto 32, lines 148–60 he will offer a parody of the present episode, when he describes how the Whore of Babylon casts cupidinous eyes on him. The image of the Gryphon, however, is wholly different. In its simultaneous stillness and motion it draws the onlooker ever deeper into the creative mystery of Christ's being, which, beyond logical comprehension, is both human and divine.

Stylistically, the effect that Dante is attempting to create here might be compared to the effect of such optical illusions as Rubin's vase:

Here, at one moment, one can see a vase; at another, two identical faces gazing each at the other. Yet it is not possible to see the two images together at the same time, and the gaze is at every moment driven on to further inspection. So it is with the human and divine natures as they are embodied in the Gryphon. And where words along with logic fail, the visual image continues to intrigue. (Compare the artistic illusions of *Purgatorio* 10: 58–63, and the final vision of God in *Paradiso* 33: 127–38.)

The silence that, hitherto, has signified the agony that Dante is made to suffer now becomes the silence of admiration in front of the higher understanding that only images can deliver. So, too, where Beatrice began by turning the 'sword point' of her words on Dante, now finally, at 31: 136–8, she unveils her lips and eyes, as the angels ask her to do, and looks directly at him. Now, at 31: 139–45, the linguistic character of the canto changes completely from the mode of tense accusation to one of lexical play, rhythmic exuberance and pure aesthetic pleasure. The reader is drawn, at 31: 124–6, to witness how far beyond the reach of words Dante's experience is, even for those (31: 139–41) who have studied long and hard at the school of the Muses on Mount Parnassus. But the images that Dante uses in admitting this insufficiency produce their own indefinable dapple of visual enjoyment: those who have grown 'pale' on Parnassus – the most inspired of poets – cannot tolerate or encompass a *light* that paradoxically casts a *shadowy adumbration* of Heaven into the forest of the Earthly Paradise. This visual play is accompanied by phonetic pleasures as Dante inconguously rhymes '*etterna*' ('eternal') with '*cisterna*' (literally, 'cistern' or 'well') and, at 31: 130–32, '*tribo*' ('tribe') with '*caribo*', signifying a dance to words. (*Caribo* might be translated as 'carol', but derives from the Occitan '*garip*', and so, for the sake of comparable lexical density, is here translated with a French term for a formal dance.) The '*cisterna*' which was once in shadow is now illuminated by a light that comes, not from the sun but from the eyes of persons alone. (Compare Dante's use of '*ombra*' ('shadow') in *Paradiso* 1: 22–4.) Above all, attention is drawn by the word play of 31: 136 to the notion of grace. The reverse side of self-abandonment is entry into a realm where grace – as the entirely free and unconstrained action of God – is the element in which the human being lives, entirely regardless of merit. The food of grace is the food which satisfies and makes us ask for more (31: 127–9). The aesthetic pleasure of this conclusion is an analogy for the enjoyment of such existence.

Notes to Canto 30

16   '[A]t the voice of the great elder.' This phrase was devised by
      Dante.

61–3 In *Convivio* 1: 2, 13–14, Dante argues that there are only two
      occasions on which an author may legitimately name himself in
      his own writings. One is when he seeks to clear his reputation of
      blame (Boethius did this in his *Consolation of Philosophy*). The
      other is when, like Saint Augustine in his *Confessions*, he may
      offer an improving example to others. Both reasons apply in the
      present case. Granted the privilege of returning to Eden – the
      original homeland of humanity – Dante implicitly demonstrates
      the injustice of his exile from Florence. On the other hand, in
      allowing Beatrice to lay bare his failings, he makes an example
      of his own transgressions.

Notes to Canto 31

58–60 The '*pargoletta*', translated here as 'girl', may be associated
      with the 'stony lady' of Dante's *Rime Petrose*. Beatrice herself
      has now assumed some of the characteristics of this daunting
      and resistant figure. Of the '*pargoletta*' Dante writes else-
      where:

> *Chi guarderà già mai sanza paura*
> *ne li occhi d'esta bella pargoletta,*
> *che m'hanno concio sì, che non s'aspetta*
> *per me se non la morte, che m'è dura?*

(Who will look into this lovely girl's eyes that have so affected me
that all I can do is await death, which is so harsh to me?)

'*Chi guarderà già . . .*' lines 1–4

In the *Vita nuova* 4–12, Dante adopts the lover's device of a
series of 'screen ladies', writing poems intended for Beatrice to
other *donne*, ostensibly to protect Beatrice's reputation. Sus-
picious as modern eyes may be of this tactic, it evolves into one
of the most important features of Dante's narrative technique and
theological interest. We approach the truth only on a journey,
through a series of veils, each of which is significant, each of
which has to be put aside as a clearer manifestation of truth
emerges. Leah in Dante's dream at *Purgatorio* 27: 94–108 antici-

pates Matelda, Matelda anticipates Beatrice, who herself antici-
pates the Virgin Mary, who is the supreme instance of a veil,
embodying Christ but also pointing beyond to his transcendent
reality. (See also commentaries on *Paradiso* 23 and 30–33.)

88–90 These lines directly echo *Inferno* 5: 142. Having earlier empha-
sized that love is the way to death unless it involves conscious
and intelligent responsibility, Dante now recognizes that it can
also be expressed in surrender. God's love requires no less than
this. (See *Paradiso* 33: 76–102, where there are also echoes of
Inferno 5.) Dante's passivity in his response to Beatrice antici-
pates this final surrender.

121–3 There are similarities in imaginative character between the
Gryphon and Geryon (mentioned at *Purgatorio* 27: 23), on
whose back Dante descends into the pit of Hell. (See commentary
on *Inferno* 17.) Where Geryon as a twofold beast is the 'filthy
image of deceit' and anticipates all the falsehood that will flood
into the world in the days before the Second Coming, the Gry-
phon represents the unimaginable truth which the Second
Coming will bring.

130–32 For the use of '*en loure*' as a translation of Dante's '*caribo*',
see commentary above. A '*loure*' is a French courtly dance.

CANTOS 32 AND 33

Beatrice prepares Dante to carry his vision back to
the earth. Dante is washed in the stream of Eunoe.

Commentary

At 33: 10–12, Beatrice speaks to the *donne* that surround her in the
words that Christ addresses to his disciples in John 16: 16:

> A little while, and ye shall not see me: and again, a little while, and ye
> shall see me because I go to the Father.

These words – repeated three times in the Gospel, as if they were some
sort of riddle or charm – are deliberately enigmatic. Jesus knows, it
seems, that his followers will not understand them. They are uttered,
though, at the climax of His time on earth, and immediately precede
the events through which, going 'to the Father', Christ will redeem
human beings in the Crucifixion and Resurrection and make possible

the coming of the Holy Spirit at Pentecost. In this developing context, the Gospel defines the way in which all Christians are to live their temporal lives, knowing always that their existence depends upon a source beyond their immediate comprehension. The truths that life depends upon are not seen, since they are with the Father in the creative mystery of the Trinity. Yet these truths are not merely transcendent abstractions. They are present and always visible to the eyes of Faith, Hope and Charity, as they are, too, in the Eucharist, always evolving towards the point at which, with the resurrection of the dead, Christ will come once more in judgement. Christian time, on this understanding, is a time of attentive waiting and evolution. Certain only that absolute reality is utterly beyond our comprehension, the human mind looks intently at the phenomena of this world expecting that, through the perceptible gaps in its logic, new enigmas with new implications will continue to reveal themselves. There is thus 'a tension in Christian understanding,' (to quote Rowan Williams) 'between the familiar and the strange . . . "Theologies" [or schemes of systematic interpretation] . . . only do their job . . . by their capacity to point back towards the disorienting' (*Resurrection* (1982), p. 112).

Cantos 32 and 33 are, throughout, as enigmatic as the Gospel words that Beatrice recalls. They are also an appropriate supplement to Dante's vision of the mystic Gryphon. The visions that these last two cantos of the *Purgatorio* register seem to invite close allegorical interpretation, and such a reading can certainly yield interesting theological meaning. However, there is much in the narrative, especially of canto 32 (which is the longest canto in the *Commedia*), that seems designed to be disorienting – for the reader as well as for Dante as a character in his own story. The cathartic concentration of pity, terror and, finally, joy that governed cantos 30 and 31 here dissolves into a play of images, impressions and sensations to which no easily recognizable emotion can be ascribed. Like the spirits in the Ante-Purgatory, Dante shows himself to be in a state of waiting. So, at 32: 100–102, Beatrice declares that he is to be here only temporarily, a 'woodsman' far from the centres of civilization, for a brief but indeterminate period. Yet, unlike the spirits in the Ante-Purgatory, Dante receives no indication of what he is waiting for. The prospect of Paradise is rarely mentioned. More, in fact, is said about the mission that Dante as a poet must fulfil when he returns to earth. The episode designates a gap in the sequence of Dante's journey and of his narrative, a hiatus between time and eternity. All connection with past experience has been severed, since, in passing through Lethe, the connections and associations that memory contains have been erased, as though it were a sin even to presume to construct a self out of one's memories. And Dante will only pass through Eunoe – which restores to him the remembrance of the good he has done in his life – at the very conclusion of the episode (33: 127–35).

At the outset, the Earthly Paradise was represented as a place in which all lost time was recovered. It is seen now as a place of oblivion, as when, at 32: 64–9, Dante is gripped by sudden and inexplicable sleep. It is also a place of heightened perception. In his sleep Dante does not dream (as he did in *Purgatorio* 9, 19 and 27). It is when he wakes that the dream comes upon him, the more vividly because there is no consistent logic that he can project upon the scene, nor any single point of view that he is able to adopt in witnessing it. In the two preceding cantos, he has been berated for failing to keep his eyes fixed firmly on Beatrice, in the Earthly Paradise as in the earthly life. Now, at 32: 7–9, he is forbidden to look at her 'too fixedly', and is asked to turn his eyes to the other 'deities' – or God-bearing images – that inhabit the garden. Dante, as traveller, is not endowed with any power to make sense of what he sees. As Beatrice constantly reminds him, his mind is necessarily dazzled by what he experiences (33: 73–5). He has always been too petrified by its own confusions to appreciate the vivacity of the present display (33: 67–9).

In terms of visual style, the opening sections of these two cantos, especially canto 32, might be compared to the formal and hieratic representations of processions that appear in some of the Byzantine mosaics that Dante would have been familiar with in the churches of Ravenna, where figures are suspended against a background of illuminated gold, as if to announce an eternal rather than a temporal triumph. Or – particularly in the later passages of canto 32 – one may accurately describe this as a masque, or very elaborate form of religious theatre. (In *Paradiso* 30: 91–3, Dante employs the simile of masqueraders when speaking of the final revelation of God's presence.) This masque shows, in dramatized form, the very opposite of all the procession has so far signified, representing, often in a parodic way, the tribulations to which the Church militant has been subject in the course of its history. But these disasters are viewed now by an audience consisting of the Church triumphant, as it will be in Heaven. In the perspective of eternity, such temporal tragedies can be approached dispassionately, or even as a light-hearted entertainment in which (as in a horror film) fright is itself a component of pleasure. Many of the issues that are raised in this section of the canto concern events in ecclesiastical and political history that, in preceding parts of the *Commedia*, have been the subjects of explicit and precisely focused attacks

– as, for instance, in the assault on the corruptions of particular popes in *Inferno* 19. These attacks will resume in the *Paradiso* – very violently in *Paradiso* 27 and 29. But here, in place of open polemic, Dante now creates a phantasmagoria of often grotesque, sometimes comic metamorphoses in which there does not seem to be any urgent need to fix upon a specific target or to speak of it with any precision.

A related aspect of the sequence is Dante's continuing reflection on his own poetic mission. Most notably, at 32: 103–5, Beatrice speaks of how, in contemplating the present vision, Dante should prepare himself to return to the temporal world which 'lives all wrong', and speak of what he has seen for the moral benefit of his fellow men. The passage may be compared with *Paradiso* 17: 124–42, in which Dante's ancestor, the crusader Cacciaguida, prepares his descendant for the crusading mission that he will pursue on earth, and urges Dante to name those who corrupt the world and adopt a style so direct that he will make the guilty scratch at the itch of their consciences. Such colloquial directness, however, has no part in the present episode. On the contrary, the words are somehow to be held in suspension, short of being written down, as images in his mind, as inarticulate and yet sustaining as a pilgrim's staff (33: 78). Beatrice acknowledges that the images Dante is now seeing are not yet written, nor do they need to be. This is disconcerting, since of course it leads us to ask what exactly it is that Dante's text here means to offer to the reader. An explanation follows. What the reader is witnessing is not the final form in which his thoughts will be cast when he re-enters the public arena; it is a glimpse of the private world of his imagination. The images we look in upon, says Beatrice, are there to enrich Dante's mind and to support him when he resumes his earthly mission. As a pilgrim to the Holy Land brings back a staff wreathed with palm fronds – recalling Christ's triumphant entry into Jerusalem in the week which ended with his crucifixion – the present experiences will remain (subconsciously, it seems) in Dante's mind as he beats out the homeward track of his metrical narrative. (In a similar way, on the last page of the *Vita nuova* Dante declares that he has had a vision of which he will say nothing at all until he is competent to deliver its full significance to the world.)

In earlier cantos of the *Commedia*, Dante's poetic self-awareness led him to locate himself very precisely in the continuing development of his cultural tradition, celebrating the names of his influential predecessors (*Inferno* 4) or touching the itch of competitors such as Guittone d'Arezzo and Guido Guinizelli (*Purgatorio* 24 and 26). Now he associates himself with the prophets, in particular with the apocalyptic writings of Ezekiel and Saint John. Cantos 32 and 33 are underpinned by constant allusion to the Scriptures. But even in this there is a playful element. Dante at no point hesitates to adapt or ornament the original text – as when, in quoting Christ's words to his disciples at 33: 10–12, he introduces an attribution which reminds us that these words are now being spoken by Beatrice to her 'most beloved sisters'. This could be read as an exhilarating presumption on Dante's part. It could also be seen as evidence of a mind so well stored and familiar with the Scriptures that it can legitimately enjoy the process of interpretation and elaboration. On that view, it is appropriate that Dante at the very conclusion of 33: 136–41, should speak of how willingly he would continue to write in the manner of this episode, as though it were a carnival of the imagination. However, the constraints of his mission and the practicalities of writing deny him that indulgence. Nothing that he subsequently writes in the *Paradiso* will resemble this sequence.

Canto 32 divides into four movements. The first (32: 1–30) describes the changed direction of the procession as it turns to march towards the rising sun. The second (32: 31–60) evokes the mystery of the Fall and the Atonement, as the parade contemplates the tree where Adam committed the first of sins. The third movement (32: 61–85) speaks of how sleep overcomes Dante – of a *lacuna* in which his powers as a poet desert him, and of when, on waking, he finds that Beatrice has momentarily left him. The fourth movement (32: 86–160) describes the enactment of a masque showing the seven afflictions of the Church, the early persecutions it suffered and its subsequent corruption in the hands of contemporary popes.

Though the similes in the opening phase of the canto are drawn from a precise observation of military manoeuvres, their effect is hypnotic rather than martial. Attention focuses on the wheeling of the march and the rotation of the chariot's wheels – while the wings of the Gryphon remain preternaturally still (32: 27). Topographical space and sequential time disappear. This is an empty arena, widowed of its original inhabitants, Adam and Eve. But, temporarily, this arena is marked out by a choreography in which space is delimited by the kinetic grace of human movements and time is told by reference to the forward pace of mysterious but firm intentions. There is much in this play of dynamic pattern that anticipates the *Paradiso*.

The point to which the procession circles is the archetypal tree of the knowledge of good and evil which – although beyond history – is the origin of the history that human beings experience in their fallen state. This tree stands stripped of all its foliage (32: 37–9). At the Fall, the knowledge that Adam and Eve enjoyed in the garden, which derived from the pleasure of their direct relationship with God, was replaced by knowledge of their own devising, intended to satisfy their own expectations and ambitions. With the exchange of one form of knowledge for another, there began a long decline into cupidity and the proliferation of all those mistaken or ill-founded purposes and goals which Dante analyses in the first two *cantiche* of the *Commedia*. (See, in particular, *Inferno* 26 and *Purgatorio* 19: 1–24.) Against this sequential decline, however, divine providence – here depicted in the procession itself – sets out to reveal itself in and beyond history and to lead humanity, not only back to the garden from which it was first expelled, but further than it otherwise would have progressed, into the presence of God in Heaven itself. Christ – here represented as the Gryphon – makes possible this reconciliation. So, at 32: 49–60, the effects of Christ's Atonement for Adam's sin, in the Crucifixion, are pictured, when the cruciform pole by which the chariot is drawn is attached to the leafless tree, which at once bursts into new life. (Legend has it that the wood of the Cross derived from the tree of knowledge.)

A notable feature of this second phase of the canto is the dreamlike detachment with which Dante views the disastrous history of the Fall and the tragic solution enacted by a crucified God. The catastrophe of the Fall attracts no violent judgement against Adam or Eve, both of whom, by now, have been elevated to Paradise. (See *Paradiso* 26: 82–142 and 32: 4–6.) At 32: 37 records a gently rising murmur enfolds the name 'Adam' in a sequence of 'm's very close (as the letter 'm' so often is for Dante) to the mode of infantile speech. (See commentaries on *Purgatorio* 22 and *Paradiso* 33.) The tree – both familiar and strange – is an exotic specimen, stupendous in its height as though it were growing in a region of India (32: 40–42), far beyond Dante's normal range of experience. The Gryphon, too, is a fabulous beast, a hybrid of two predatory animals that suffers from no physical appetite at all (32: 43–5). Finally, when life surges back into the tree (32: 52–60) the flowering is visionary rather than organic. Dante's complex sentence, evolving in the Italian over three *terzine*, follows the process of natural growth with the same accuracy and precision of observation that is to be found, for example, in the description of dawn at the opening of *Purgatorio* 30. But the flowers that are produced are symbolic in their coloration. Their scarcely perceptible mingling of rose red and black-ish violet produces a dark crimson hue. Red is the colour of charity, and violet purple is the colour of Imperial justice. Together, these produce the dark crimson which is associated with the blood of Christ's passion, in which just retribution for Adam's sin is combined with the absolute charity of God as Creator.

So far, in its portrayal of purposeful marches and fertile growth, canto 32 has concerned itself with sequence, connections and the re-establishment of continuity. Now, in its third phase (32: 61–85), the text contemplates an interruption in the narrative. Dante does not understand the hymn that is sung as the tree comes to life, and, unable to bear the sweetness of the song, he falls asleep. The reader, too, is here drawn away from the immediate action by two cryptic and highly allusive similes – one from classical mythology, the other from Scripture – into a digression apparently unconnected to the preceding narrative.

The first of these allusions involves a story told in *Metamorphoses* 1: 622–723, to which Dante has already made an equally oblique reference, at *Purgatorio* 29: 95–6. Argus – who has a hundred eyes all round his head and is described by Ovid as 'star-eyed' – has been commissioned to guard Io, the victim of Jupiter's lust, whom Juno, out of jealousy, has transformed into a cow. Jupiter, however, sends Mercury to rescue her. He decapitates Argus, having charmed him into sleep and then told him the tale of Syrinx (32: 65), who herself had been transformed, when fleeing from the danger of rape, into the shape of pan pipes. The Ovidian tale of erotic violence and naked power is transformed into a description of Dante's present powerlessness. And where, earlier, the alliterated 'm's, surrounding Adam's name, produced an effect of chant or charm, the patterning here of 's's leads to the Italian subjunctive '*potessi*' ('were I able', here translated as 'if I could') (32: 64) – where the mood of the verb indicates an unrealized, or virtual condition. If Dante *could* describe the way in which sleep overcame Argus's innumerable eyes, then he *might* describe the sleep that came over him. But he cannot. Only someone who could 'feign sleep well' could rise to that. Yet is there such a person? Does not sleep eclipse the object of description and equally the power to describe? The interruption in the narrative is flooded by these ever-receding, ever more teasing questions.

Dante's account of his awakening is extended over twelve lines (32: 70–84) with references to the moment of waking bracketing the intervening verses. It is as if this split second of returning consciousness had been penetrated and divided by consciousness deriving from a different dimension, and as if the brightness deriving from that dimension might never end. Subtextually, however, there are significant connections to be drawn here which did not arise in Dante's earlier allusion to Ovid's *Metamorphoses*. The following lines (32: 73–81) are traversed by references to Scripture which, in particular, link the sequence to Christ's '*Modicum et non videbitis me . . .*', quoted at

33: 10–12. The principle point of reference is to the Transfiguration – as recorded in Luke 9: 28–36, Matthew 17 and Mark 9: 1–8. Saint John was himself present at the Transfiguration, and is thought to be alluding to this event when, in his Gospel, at 1: 14, he speaks of how 'we beheld the glory, the glory as of the only begotten of the Father'. Luke records the episode as follows:

> . . . [Jesus] took Peter and John and James, and went up a mountain to pray.
>
> And as he prayed, the fashion of his countenance was altered, and his raiment was white and glistering.
>
> And, behold, there talked with him two men, which were Moses and Elias:
>
> Who appeared in glory, and spake of his decease which he should accomplish at Jerusalem.
>
> But Peter and they that were with him were heavy with sleep: and when they were awake, they saw his glory, and the two men that stood with him.
>
> And it came to pass, as they departed from him, Peter said unto Jesus, Master, it is good for us to be here: and let us make three tabernacles; one for thee, and one for Moses, and one for Elias: not knowing what he said.

In this moment, which can be taken to mark the culmination of Jesus's public ministry, the unique relation of Jesus to God's glory is re-established, as also is his relation to the prophetic tradition, here exemplified by the greatest of the prophets, Moses and Elijah. The epiphanic strangeness of the moment confuses the disciples. 'Not knowing what they said', according to Luke, all they can do is to offer familiar things – such as building shelters for the three prophets to rest in. Readers of Dante's text may not, at first, be much clearer about what they should make of this episode. But Dante himself draws the passage into interpretive relationship with three other scriptural texts that point to the heart of the Christian mystery. One instance is the allusion to the raising of Lazarus at 32: 77–8 where Christ's word is seen to be capable of raising the dead (from their 'greater sleep') in anticipation of his own Resurrection. (See John 11: 43–4.) A second, at 32: 74, is to the Song of Solomon 2: 3, where the bridegroom is described as 'the apple tree among the trees of the woods, so is my beloved among the sons', which is taken as an allegorical reference to the love that will be consummated between Christ and his chosen people. The third allusion, at 32: 73–5, is to Revelation 19: 9: 'Blessed are they which are called unto the marriage supper of the Lamb.'

Pointing beyond the sphere of time – and beyond both Dante's text and Ovid's accounts of metamorphoses – the truth of the Transfiguration will be realized when, at Judgement Day, all humanity enters the light of the divine presence.

The transfigured Christ is the more vividly present to his disciples by *not* being present to them in any day-to-day sense. The same may be said of Beatrice, who, as Dante returns fully to consciousness at 32: 85, has left the space in which she had originally been seen: 'Where's Beatrice?' (Compare *Paradiso* 31: 58–66.) This sudden estrangement leads Dante to rediscover her with intensified concentration (listening only partially at 32: 86–93 as Matelda repeats the injunction, heard in the opening lines of the canto, that Dante should turn his gaze to other objects). Such attention is now made necessary by the long sequence which stretches to the end of the canto. Witnessing the degradations to which the Church has been subject throughout its history, Beatrice – in terms of allegory – offers a constant image of all that the Church should, properly, have sought to defend and celebrate.

The drama of the Masque goes through seven acts, in which Dante continues to cite and modify Scriptural references, particularly to the writings of Ezekiel and Saint John. At each point he is especially interested in the often disastrous relationship between Church and State.

The first of these acts (32: 112–17) refers to the persecutions that the early Church suffered under Nero (AD 37–68) and Diocletian (AD 243–316). This is followed, at 32: 118–23, by a reference to the early heresies – principally perhaps Gnosticism – by which the primitive Church was afflicted. The figure of false prophecy as a vixen (here driven away by Beatrice in the role of embodied truth) draws on Ezekiel 13: 4 and the Song of Solomon 2: 15. The third phase (32: 124–9) pictures the moment at which the Church received from the Emperor Constantine (AD 272–337) the very equivocal gift of power and wealth, which Dante constantly sees as the source of an ill-judged mixing of secular and spiritual power. (See, especially, *Inferno* 19.) The chariot of the Church thus becomes confused with the 'feathers' of the Imperial eagle. The voice from Heaven grieving over the Church may be that of Saint Peter, as recorded in the apocryphal Acts of Saint Peter. (Compare the violent diatribe that Dante gives to Saint Peter in *Paradiso* 27.) The fourth assault (32: 130–35) on the Church probably refers to the sudden rise of Islam in the seventh century, and is connected to the second attack, in so far as Mohammed was thought to be a heretic and schismatic (see *Inferno* 28) – hence the emphasis upon

the effects of splintering. The fifth phase of disaster is alluded to at
32: 136–41, which probably refer to further grants of land and prop-
erty by well-intentioned precursors of the medieval Holy Roman
Empire: Pepin the younger (714–68) and Charlemagne (742–814), in
755 and 775. The further confusion of Church and State brought
about by Pepin and Charlemagne prepares for the corruption that
Dante vividly perceives in the Church of his own day. In general but
graphic terms, the lines at 32: 142–7 imagine the grotesque transfor-
mation of the Church, as bride of Christ, into a deformed, seven-
headed monstrosity. Dante here follows Revelation 13: 1 very closely:
'And I stood upon the sand of the sea, and saw a beast rise up out of
the sea, having seven heads and ten horns . . .', but at every stage in
the transformation, the poet has in mind specific ways in which the
sacraments and commandments of Christ are parodied by the Church
which should be their protector.

The seventh and final transformation occurs at 32: 148–60. Here
the Whore of Babylon (drawn from Revelation 17: 1) – the Church as
the now-corrupted bride of Christ – is seen in dalliance with the kings
of France, who in the fourteenth century came to exert a particularly
strong ('giant') influence over papal policy. The seductive talk between
the whore and the giant may represent the diplomatic negotiations
between Pope Boniface VIII (c. 1235–1303) and Charles de Valois
(1270–1325) which led to the invasion of Italy in 1301. The beating
of the whore might refer to the humiliating treatment meted out to
Boniface by the French. (Compare *Purgatorio* 20.) The removal of the
chariot to the wood probably refers to the removal of the papal seat
to Avignon in 1309 – from where it only returned in 1378.

No reliable explanation can be offered for 32: 154–6, where the
whore casts her lascivious eye on Dante – though Dante is always
aware of the malign effect that French interference has on the Floren-
tine politics of his day. (See introduction to *Inferno*, pp. xvii–xix.)
There is, however, significance in the grotesque comedy of this episode.
Eyes and eyesight, cupidity and contemplation have been an issue
throughout the last two cantos. Dante is now distant from all danger of
sin, having passed through Lethe. It is an expression of contemplative
confidence that he should be able to imagine, in the wandering eyes
of the whore, a parodic reversal of that constantly shifting, but always
steady image of Christ that he saw at the end of canto 31 reflected in
Beatrice's eyes.

Canto 33 is mainly concerned with a conversation between Beatrice
and Dante (33: 19–102) which reflects upon the masque of the pre-

vious canto and prepares Dante for his immersion in Eunoe (33: 127–35). This long and intimate conversation is introduced by two solemn quotations in Latin, (33: 1 and 33: 10–12).

The first of these is the opening of Psalm 79:

> O God, the heathen are come into thine inheritance; thy holy temple have they defiled; they have laid Jerusalem on heaps.
> The dead bodies of thy servants have they given to be meat unto the fowls of heaven, the flesh of thy saints unto the beasts of the earth.

This psalm refers to the destruction of the temple in Jerusalem by Nebuchadnezzar (605–562 BC) in 587 BC, and contemplates the total defeat of God's chosen people. Yet, in the perspective of the New Testament, and particularly of the Book of Revelation, the absolute victory of evil is viewed as the direct preparation for the Second Coming of Christ in judgement. (Compare *Inferno* 18–30 and commentary to *Inferno* 17.) In that sense, the psalm is rightly to be read in conjunction with the words of Christ as recorded at John 16: 16–19. As has been said above, these words define the ways in which Christians, in a time of waiting, are bound to perceive the truth through a veil of ungraspable ambiguities. These same words, in anticipating the Passion and Resurrection of Christ, speak of how utter hopelessness – waiting without hope – is the very condition of faith through which true hope will be renewed.

Beatrice hears the psalm sung, and her complexion changes as if she were the Virgin Mary at the foot of the Cross (33: 4–6). But then she is transfigured by the passionate red that signifies charity (33: 7–9). These are the poles that generate Christian existence – desperate hope and all-consuming charity – and an oscillation between these two poles traverses the whole of the exchange that now follows.

There is a considerable degree of familiarity between the Dante and Beatrice in canto 33. Abandoning the authoritative posture of cantos 30 and 31, Beatrice, at 33: 19, calls to Dante take a place by her side, as she walks along, with a recognizably realistic gesture. There is also a certain comic realism – where in earlier cantos there was agony – as Dante, failing to speak clearly once again, 'can't get living voice behind [his] teeth' (33: 25–8). Of course, Beatrice continues to chide him. So, at 33: 94–9, she insists that, if Dante, having now passed through Lethe, cannot remember ever having betrayed her, then this lapse of memory is itself evidence that he has betrayed her. The present gap must once have been filled with that knowledge. There is a serious point here, in that Beatrice is shown, as before, to know Dante better than he knows himself. But the moment is also (in a proto-Freudian way) playfully perverse, acknowledging its own playfulness. As she speaks, Beatrice is smiling (33: 95). This smile will continue to punctuate and illuminate all the conversations between Dante and Beatrice that follow in the *Paradiso*.

For all that, the conversation is as strange as it is familiar. Beatrice's purpose is to ensure that Dante, in preparation for the composition of the *Commedia*, has a clear grasp of what has been shown to him in the previous cantos. None the less, there is an evident reluctance on Beatrice's (or Dante's) part to offer the clear paraphrase that, subsequently, many commentators have sought to deliver. Constant reference is made to Dante's continuing obtuseness. But Beatrice's words seem designed as much to obfuscate, or to wrap up meaning in allusive reference, as to clarify. At 33: 47–8, words are said to 'blunt' the intellect, while 33: 100–102 allude to a time – which has not yet arrived – when they will be 'naked' and wholly comprehensible.

One reason for such wilful obscurity is suggested by 33: 85–7, where Beatrice continues her attack on the pretensions of mere intellect: no philosophical school will ever fully understand what these meanings are. At the same time, her words recall the way in which Christ himself spoke of his own enigmatic parables in John 16: 25: 'These things have I spoken unto you in proverbs: but the time cometh, when I shall no more speak unto you in proverbs, but I shall shew you plainly of the Father.' But, when that time does come, the medium in which truth is expounded will not be a linguistic medium at all, but a direct engagement in God's unfolding activity in the Passion and the Resurrection. Thus, at 33: 46–51, the text delves back into the pre-Christian history of enigmas and oracles, and traces the disasters that flowed from any attempt to solve the riddle of the Sphinx. Such disasters will always befall those who, as descendants of Adam, pride themselves on their possession of knowledge. But 'real events will soon prove Naiades' (33: 49) – and these events will be the actions, suffering and deeds that manifest the unfolding of the providential drama. Beatrice insists that this caution, too, be carried back to the world along with any clear recommendation for moral improvement. (Compare *Vita nuova* 12: 3 and *Paradiso* 17: 31–6.)

If theologies should disorient, then, point by point, Beatrice's speech at 33: 31–66 continues to do that, as she prophesies an end to the evils that were witnessed in the Masque of the Church. Her first target, at 33: 34–9 is (probably) the unholy alliance between the Church and the kings of France, which lead eventually to the transferral of the papal throne to Avignon – the 'vessel that the serpent broke' being the

Church. Dante's phrasing here recalls the Book of Revelation 17: 8: 'The beast that thou sawest was, and is not; and shall ascend out of the bottomless pit, and go into perdition.' Where Christ will not for a little while be seen and then will be seen again (33: 10–13), the beast of ecclesiastical corruption will be consigned eternally to Hell when salvation comes. The time of salvation is close at hand – but is designated, at 33: 36 by a ghoulish reference to medieval notions of sanctuary. (See note below.) The agent of salvation may be Christ in judgement. But since, for Dante, the Emperor is the representative of Christ's justice on earth, at 33: 37–8, he speaks of the Saviour as heir to the Imperial eagle. The eagle left its 'feathers on the cart' when Constantine ill-advisedly endowed the Church with temporal power (see commentary on 32: 124–9), making it into a 'monster' and laying it open, eventually, to the corrupting ambitions of France. The promised saviour who will destroy both the corruption of the Church and the pretensions of the French is referred to in an impenetrable piece of numerological symbolism, 'FIVE HUNDRED TEN AND FIVE' (33: 43). From the point at which (in *Inferno* 1: 100–105) Dante first referred to the saviour of the world as the '*veltro*' or 'hunting hound', all such references have been deliberately cryptic, and commentators have expended great ingenuity on attempting to solve what Dante has, in all likelihood, been at pains to make insoluble. Most agree that the reference is to an Imperial authority. Others, however, reverse the Latin numerals DXV to yield VXD, and see in this a liturgical acronym for the words that, in the Mass, immediately precede the Canon – '*Vero dignum et iustum*' – 'It is truly fitting and just'. As with the visual image of the Gryphon, these enigmatic words produce an animated, if uncertain response.

So does the reference to the tree at 33: 55–72, particularly in consideration of line 72, which speaks of the tree as the emblem of God's power to control and prohibit. Here, however, it seems clear that Dante wishes to emphasize that the assault upon the tree by Adam and Eve is essentially an act of injustice, which offended against the just and good order which are essential for the harmony of life in the universe at large. The love that God shows in creating the world expresses itself in the justice that underlies that world. Merely by intending to climb the unclimbable tree, Adam and Eve set their minds against that order and offend justice. They also offend – or blaspheme – against love, the more so since God's love is infinitely transcendent and cannot be comprehended by a finite creature, except in the appropriate and just measure that befits the nature of finite creatures. To preserve justice is itself an act of worship, worth performing entirely for its own sake. In the reference at 33: 57 to subsequent robberies committed against the tree, there is again no consensus as to any specific target. It is possible that Dante is referring once again to the transference of papal power to Avignon and the possibilities that this opened up of schism in the Church.

These knotty prophecies are replaced in the final phase of the canto (33: 103–45) by a luminous return to description and narrative. As in the conclusion to canto 32, imagery of light and shade here produces a particularly delicate design, especially at 33: 103–9. Dante now approaches Eunoe, which rises from the same source as Lethe but branches off in a different direction, as if the two streams were friends parting unwillingly. The reference to the Tigris and Euphrates at 33: 112–14 recalls that these rivers were thought to be two of the four rivers of Eden (Genesis 2: 10–14) – the other two being Gihon and Pison, identified by Saint Augustine as, respectively, the Nile and the Ganges. Interpretative solemnity, however, dissolves now into something approaching banter and byplay. At 33: 118, Beatrice seems to accuse a somewhat ruffled Matelda of an oversight in teaching Dante his lesson in paradisal geography since he apparently cannot remember what Eunoe is. As usual, the fault turns out to be Dante's. Yet his immersion in Eunoe (along with that of the long-forgotten Statius (33: 135)) is rapid and unmomentous. Nor is any account given of the good deeds and good thinking of which Dante is assured by this further baptism. This is appropriate. Good deeds are to be viewed not as personal attributes but as gifts from God.

The final lines of the *cantica* may usefully be contrasted with the opening lines of the *Paradiso*. Where the third *cantica* begins with an unprecedented solemnity of rhythm and balanced phrase, the *Purgatorio* ends – much as it began – with fluent and fluctuating verses impelled by alliteration and an almost naive repetition of the word *'novelle'* or 'new', or its cognates. 'Newness' has been the recurrent motif of a *cantica* concerned with regeneration.

Notes to Canto 32

13–15 The terminology here is technical and Aristotelian. A 'sensible' is any object offered to the senses and perceptible by them. The sense involved is, in this case, sight.

70–72 Dante's Italian text – *'squarciò'* ('tore apart') – directly recalls the phrasing of *Inferno* 33: 27 where the traitor Ugolino dreams, in the Tower of Hunger, of his coming fate, which is to die of starvation along with his innocent children. That dream is said to have torn 'wide the veil' of Ugolino's future. Dante rarely repeats himself. However, at two other salient points in the present sequence, phrases from the *Inferno* recur. As above, at *Purgatorio* 31:89, Dante speaks of how he falls, recalling the trauma he experienced at the end of *Inferno* 5. At lines 122–3 '*ossa sanza polpe*' ('fleshless bones') recalls the phrase he had put into Guido da Montefeltro's mouth at *Inferno* 27: 73 ('such pulp and bone'). In each of these three cases, the graphic violence of the earlier phrasing dissolves into the visionary distance of the present episode, free of judgemental or dramatic implications.

97–9   The Aquilonian are northern winds and the Austral are southern.

109–11 In the fourteenth century, lightning was thought to be vapour that ignited by friction in a cloud and exploded from the cloud towards the earth. (Compare *Purgatorio* 5: 37; 21: 49–53; 28: 97–9.)

Notes to Canto 33

34–6   This very obscure line seems to refer to a feudal convention, according to medieval commentators, whereby a murderer, if he succeeded in eating a sop of bread for three days in succession while seated on the grave of his victim, would escape revenge. In a sequence where gaps in time are a constant theme, this grave-yard gap is invoked to indicate that God's revenge will come with no delay.

46–51 Themis, mother of Prometheus, is enraged by the success of the Naiads in solving the riddle of the Sphinx which she could not solve and causes their territories to be devastated, as Ovid tells in *Metamorphoses* 7: 749–65. In fact, Dante has misread Ovid's text, which refers properly to 'Laiades' not 'Naiades'. The passage refers to Oedipus as the son of Laius. There is some irony in this scholarly lapse, considering that Dante is concerned throughout this passage with the ways in which lapses in rational sequence are necessary if the truths of revelation are to be appreciated. Saint Augustine, for instance, in his work on Christian teaching takes pleasure in interpretation, or even mis-reading, for its own sake. Comparing a description of twelve lambs crossing a stream to the twelve disciples of Christ, he declares that he knows the apostles are not lambs but still enjoys thinking of them in those terms. It is also relevant throughout cantos 32 and 33 to remember that the early Christian scholar

Origen (185–c. 254) in the third century held that allegory was
as likely to be significant in its obscurities and resistance to
comprehension as in what it openly declared.

67–9 The Tuscan river Elsa is rich in calcium carbonate, which coats
objects that are dipped in it with a mineral crust. In *Metamor-
phoses* 4: 162–66, the blood of the dying lover Pyramus stains the
white fruit of the mulberry tree dark red. (Compare *Purgatorio*
27: 37–9.)

PENGUIN CLASSICS

PARADISO
DANTE

'And so my mind, held high above itself,
looked on intent and still, in wondering awe'

Leaving Hell and Mount Purgatory far behind, Dante in the *Paradiso* ascends to heaven and crosses the planetary spheres that circle round the Earth, now guided by his beloved Beatrice. Here Dante encounters spirits, from Thomas Aquinas to Saint Peter, who engage him in passionate conversation about history, politics and Christian doctrine. Ascending finally to a sphere beyond space and time, Dante miraculously sees the faces of human beings with greater clarity than ever before and prepares to contemplate the face of God. The *Paradiso* is an account of the order, harmony and beauty of the universe in which Dante offers a deeply personal and unfailingly inventive exploration of divine truth and human goodness.

Robin Kirkpatrick's new translation captures the sublime imaginative power of the final sequence of the *Commedia* and the vigour of the original Italian, which is printed on facing pages. This edition includes an introduction, a map of Dante's Italy and a plan of Paradise. Commentaries on each canto explain the work's ethical, theological and political subtexts.

Translated and edited with an introduction, commentary and notes by Robin Kirkpatrick

---

PENGUIN CLASSICS

LA VITA NUOVA (POEMS OF YOUTH)   DANTE

'When she a little smiles, her aspect then
No tongue can tell, no memory can hold'

Dante's sequence of poems tells the story of his passion for Beatrice, the beautiful sister of one of his closest friends, transformed through his writing into the symbol of a love that was both spiritual and romantic. *La Vita Nuova* begins with the moment Dante first glimpses Beatrice in her childhood, follows him through unrequited passion and ends with his profound grief over the loss of his love. Interspersing exquisite verse with Dante's own commentary analysing the structure and origins of each poem, *La Vita Nuova* offers a unique insight into the poet's art and skill. And, by introducing personal experience into the strict formalism of Medieval love poetry, it marked a turning point in European literature.

Barbara Reynolds's translation is remarkable for its lucidity and faithfulness to the original. In her new introduction she examines the ways in which Dante broke with poetic conventions of his day and analyses his early poetry within the context of his life. This edition also contains notes, a chronology and an index.

Translated with a new introduction by Barbara Reynolds

PENGUIN CLASSICS

THE DECAMERON   GIOVANNI BOCCACCIO

'Ever since the world began, men have been subject to various tricks
of Fortune'

In the summer of 1348, as the Black Death ravages their city, ten young
Florentines take refuge in the countryside. They amuse themselves by each
telling a story a day for the ten days they are destined to remain there –
a hundred stories of love, adventure and surprising twists of fate. Less
preoccupied with abstract concepts of morality or religion than earthly
values, the tales range from the bawdy Peronella hiding her lover in a tub
to Ser Cepperallo, who, despite his unholy effrontery, becomes a Saint.
The result is a towering monument of European literature and a
masterpiece of imaginative narrative.

This is the second edition of G. H. McWilliam's acclaimed translation of
The Decameron. In his introduction Professor McWilliam illuminates the
worlds of Boccaccio and of his storytellers, showing Boccaccio as a master
of vivid and exciting prose fiction.

Translated with a new introduction and notes by G. H. McWilliam

PENGUIN CLASSICS

THE BOOK OF THE COURTIER
BALDESAR CASTIGLIONE

'The courtier has to imbue with grace his movements, his gestures, his way of doing things and in short, his every action'

In *The Book of the Courtier* (1528), Baldesar Castiglione, a diplomat and Papal Nuncio to Rome, sets out to define the essential virtues for those at Court. In a lively series of imaginary conversations between the real-life courtiers to the Duke of Urbino, his speakers discuss qualities of noble behaviour – chiefly discretion, decorum, nonchalance and gracefulness – as well as wider questions such as the duties of a good government and the true nature of love. Castiglione's narrative power and psychological perception make this guide both an entertaining comedy of manners and a revealing window onto the ideals and preoccupations of the Italian Renaissance at the moment of its greatest splendour.

George Bull's elegant translation captures the variety of tone in Castiglione's speakers, from comic interjections to elevated rhetoric. This edition includes an introduction examining Castiglione's career in the courts of Urbino and Mantua, a list of the historical characters he portrays and further reading.

Translated and with an introduction by George Bull

PENGUIN CLASSICS

THE ALEXIAD OF ANNA COMNENA

'The shining light of the world, the great Alexius'

Anna Comnena (1083–1153) wrote *The Alexiad* as an account of the reign of her father, the Byzantine Emperor Alexius I. It is also an important source of information on the Byzantine war with the Normans, and on the First Crusade in which Alexius participated. While the Byzantines were allied to the Crusaders, they were nonetheless critical of their behaviour and Anna's book offers a startlingly different perspective to that of Western historians. Her character sketches are shrewd and forthright – from the Norman invader Robert Guiscard ('nourished by manifold evil') and his son Bohemond ('like a streaking thunderbolt') to Pope Gregory VII ('unworthy of a high priest'). *The Alexiad* is a vivid and dramatic narrative, which reveals as much about the character of its intelligent and dynamic author as it does about the fascinating period through which she lived.

E. R. A. Sewter's translation captures all the strength and immediacy of the original and is complimented by an introduction, which examines Anna's life and times. This edition also includes maps, appendices, genealogical tables, a bibliography, and indexes of events and names.

Translated with an introduction by E. R. A. Sewter

PENGUIN CLASSICS

CITY OF GOD   ST AUGUSTINE

'The Heavenly City outshines Rome, beyond comparison. There, instead of victory, is truth; instead of rank, holiness'

St Augustine, Bishop of Hippo, was one of the central figures in the history of Christianity, and *City of God* is one of his greatest theological works. Written as an eloquent defence of the faith at a time when the Roman Empire was on the brink of collapse, it examines the ancient pagan religions of Rome, the arguments of the Greek philosophers and the revelations of the Bible. Pointing the way forward to a citizenship that transcends the best political experiences of the world and offers citizenship that will last for eternity, *City of God* is one of the most influential documents in the development of Christianity.

This edition contains a new introduction that examines the text in the light of contemporary Greek and Roman thought and political change. It demonstrates the religious and literary influences on St Augustine and his significance as a Christian thinker. There is also a chronology and bibliography.

Translated with notes by Henry Bettenson with an introduction by Gill Evans

PENGUIN CLASSICS

WAR AND PEACE
LEO TOLSTOY

'Yes! It's all vanity, it's all an illusion, everything except that infinite sky'

At a glittering society party in St Petersburg in 1805, conversations are dominated by the prospect of war. Terror swiftly engulfs the country as Napoleon's army marches on Russia, and the lives of three young people are changed forever. The stories of quixotic Pierre, cynical Andrey and impetuous Natasha interweave with a huge cast, from aristocrats and peasants, to soldiers and Napoleon himself. In *War and Peace* (1863–9), Tolstoy entwines grand themes – conflict and love, birth and death, free will and fate – with unforgettable scenes of nineteenth-century Russia, to create a magnificent epic of human life in all its imperfection and grandeur.

Anthony Briggs's superb translation combines stirring, accessible prose with fidelity to Tolstoy's original, while Orlando Figes's afterword discusses the novel's vast scope and depiction of Russian identity. This edition also includes appendices, notes, a list of prominent characters and maps.

'A book that you don't just read, you live' Simon Schama

'A masterpiece … This new translation is excellent' Antony Beevor

Translated with an introduction and notes by Anthony Briggs
With an afterword by Orlando Figes

PENGUIN CLASSICS

THE REPUBLIC
PLATO

'We are concerned with the most important of issues, the choice between a good and an evil life'

Plato's *Republic* is widely acknowledged as the cornerstone of Western philosophy. Presented in the form of a dialogue between Socrates and three different interlocutors, it is an inquiry into the notion of a perfect community and the ideal individual within it. During the conversation other questions are raised: what is goodness; what is reality; what is knowledge? *The Republic* also addresses the purpose of education and the roles of both women and men as 'guardians' of the people. With remarkable lucidity and deft use of allegory, Plato arrives at a depiction of a state bound by harmony and ruled by 'philosopher kings'.

Desmond Lee's translation of *The Republic* has come to be regarded as a classic in its own right. The new introduction by Melissa Lane discusses Plato's aims in writing *The Republic*, its major arguments and perspective on politics in ancient Greece, and its significance through the ages and today.

Translated with an introduction by Desmond Lee

THE STORY OF PENGUIN CLASSICS

Before 1946 ... 'Classics' are mainly the domain of academics and students; readable editions for everyone else are almost unheard of. This all changes when a little-known classicist, E. V. Rieu, presents Penguin founder Allen Lane with the translation of Homer's *Odyssey* that he has been working on in his spare time.

1946 Penguin Classics debuts with *The Odyssey*, which promptly sells three million copies. Suddenly, classics are no longer for the privileged few.

1950s Rieu, now series editor, turns to professional writers for the best modern, readable translations, including Dorothy L. Sayers's *Inferno* and Robert Graves's unexpurgated *Twelve Caesars*.

1960s The Classics are given the distinctive black covers that have remained a constant throughout the life of the series. Rieu retires in 1964, hailing the Penguin Classics list as 'the greatest educative force of the twentieth century.'

1970s A new generation of translators swells the Penguin Classics ranks, introducing readers of English to classics of world literature from more than twenty languages. The list grows to encompass more history, philosophy, science, religion and politics.

1980s The Penguin American Library launches with titles such as *Uncle Tom's Cabin*, and joins forces with Penguin Classics to provide the most comprehensive library of world literature available from any paperback publisher.

1990s The launch of Penguin Audiobooks brings the classics to a listening audience for the first time, and in 1999 the worldwide launch of the Penguin Classics website extends their reach to the global online community.

The 21st Century Penguin Classics are completely redesigned for the first time in nearly twenty years. This world-famous series now consists of more than 1300 titles, making the widest range of the best books ever written available to millions – and constantly redefining what makes a 'classic'.

The Odyssey continues ...

The best books ever written

PENGUIN (P) CLASSICS

SINCE 1946